THIRD EDITION

TEACHING LANGUAGE AND LITERACY

Preschool through the Elementary Grades

JAMES CHRISTIE
Arizona State University

BILLIE JEAN ENZ
Arizona State University

CAROL VUKELICH
University of Delaware

PEARSON

Boston ▪ New York ▪ San Francisco ▪ Mexico City
Montreal ▪ Toronto ▪ London ▪ Madrid ▪ Munich ▪ Paris
Hong Kong ▪ Singapore ▪ Tokyo ▪ Cape Town ▪ Sydney

KH

Executive Editor: *Aurora Martínez Ramos*
Editorial Assistant: *Lynda Giles*
Executive Marketing Manager: *Krista Clark*
Production Editor: *Gregory Erb*
Editorial Production Service: *Nesbitt Graphics, Inc.*
Composition Buyer: *Linda Cox*
Manufacturing Buyer: *Megan Cochran*
Electronic Composition: *Nesbitt Graphics, Inc.*
Cover Administrator: *Kristina Mose-Libon*

For related title and support materials, visit our online catalog
at www.ablongman.com.

Between the time Web site information is gathered and then published, it is not unusual
for some sites to have closed. Also, the transcription of URLs can result in typographical
errors. The publisher would appreciate notification when these errors occur so that they
may be corrected in subsequent editions.

Library of Congress Cataloging-in-Publication Data

Christie, James F.
    Teaching language and literacy: preschool through the elementary grades / James
    Christie, Billie Jean Enz, Carol Vukelich.—3rd ed.
        p.   c.m.
    Includes bibliographical references and index.
    ISBN 0-205-50175-3 (alk. paper)
    1. Language arts (Elementary)—Case studies.   2. Language arts (Preschool)—Case
    studies.   3. Curriculum planning.   4. Portfolios in education.   5. Education—Parent
    participation.   I. Vukelich, Carol.   II. Enz, Billie.   III. Title.

LB1576.C5564 2006
372.6—dc22

                                                    2006045396

Printed in the United States of America

10 9 8 7 6 5 4 3   RRD-VA   10   09   08   07

7/29/08

CONTENTS

CHAPTER FOUR
Building a Foundation for Literacy Learning   113

CHAPTER FIVE

Teaching Early Reading and Writing 166

CHAPTER EIGHT
Teaching Writing the Workshop Way   268

CHAPTER ELEVEN

Parents As Partners in Literacy Education   398

PREFACE

Teaching Language and Literacy: Preschool through the Elementary Grades is about teaching the language arts, about facilitating children's reading, writing, speaking, and listening development in pre-kindergarten through the upper elementary grades. The language arts are essential to everyday life and central to all learning; through reading, listening, writing, and talking, children come to understand the world. To be a successful teacher of language and literacy, you need to understand how children's language and literacy develop and how to help children become fluent, flexible, effective users of oral and written language.

THEMES

Children are at the center of all good language and literacy teaching. This principle underlies the three themes that run throughout this book: a perspective on teaching and learning that blends constructivism and science-based instruction, respect for diversity, and instruction-based assessment.

This book describes how children acquire language and literacy knowledge in many different contexts and how teachers can promote the development of oral and written language effectively. It also describes numerous science-based instructional practices teachers can use to enhance children's language and literacy knowledge. We believe that children construct their own knowledge about oral and written language by engaging in integrated, meaningful, and functional activities with other people. Children do not first "study" speaking, then listening, then reading, then writing. They learn by engaging in activities in which language and literacy are embedded. We also believe, however, that literacy skills can be increased via direct, systematic instruction. This instruction can often take the form of games and other engaging activities, but it also contains the elements of direct instruction: explanations, teacher modeling, guided practice, and independent practice. We begin with a discussion of the recent key national policies and initiatives that have affected the teaching of reading at the preschool and elementary levels. We begin with this description of the national landscape because of the significant effect recent policies and initiatives have had on the literacy field. Then, we describe the beliefs and the research base of the diverging views on the teaching of reading. We end with a set of principles that guide our view of the effective teaching of literacy in preschool and elementary classrooms.

We maintain that children build knowledge by combining new information with what they already know. Thus, children's personal experiences, both at home and at school, are important factors in learning. In our diverse society, children come to school with vastly different backgrounds, both in terms of life experiences and language. This diversity needs to be taken into account when designing instructional activities for children and in evaluating children's responses to these activities. Illustrations of how teachers can work effectively with diverse learners can be found throughout this book. In many Special Features throughout this book, colleagues have described how to use science-based instructional strategies to meet all children's needs. Special emphasis is given to linguistic diversity. In a series of special features, Sarah Hudelson and Irene Serna describe how teachers can help second-language learners become bilingual and biliterate.

Every child comes to school with a wealth of information about how written and spoken language works in the real world. To build on that student's knowledge through appropriate classroom activities, teachers must discover what each student already knows. Because we recognize that assessment—understanding what children know and have learned—cannot be separated from good teaching, instructionally linked assessment is our third major theme. We introduce two principles of instruction-based assessment in Chapter 1. Many subsequent chapters contain information on strategies that teachers can use to understand children's language and literacy knowledge in the context of specific learning/teaching events. In addition, Chapter 10 describes how to meld the chapter-by-chapter assessment strategies into a coherent assessment program centered around portfolios. Yet we know that ongoing assessment (gathering information in the context of specific learning and teaching events) is not the only assessment strategy teachers use today to discover what children know and can do. In addition, teachers use on-demand assessment, particularly to discover what children have learned. Both kinds of assessment provide guide teachers in meeting children's learning needs.

ORGANIZATION

We begin with the foundation of language and literacy learning. Chapter 1 describes the constructivist/emergent literacy and scientifically based reading research perspectives on children's language and literacy learning. Because we believe that both approaches to language and literacy learning have much to offer, we advocate for instruction that blends the two perspectives. By combining the two perspectives, we have created a set of basic principles of effective literacy instruction. We believe that these principles should guide how children are taught spoken and written language in preschool through elementary classrooms. These principles run throughout the book and underlie all the teaching strategies that we recommend in subsequent chapters.

Chapters 2 and 3 focus on children's oral language development. Chapter 2 describes the phenomenal development of oral language that occurs in a child's home between birth and age eight. Chapter 3 explains what parents and teachers can do to facilitate children's oral language learning by providing opportunities for reciprocal conversation and discussion, activity-centered language (e.g., dramatic play, cooperative learning), and language-centered activities (e.g., sharing, movie and book reviews).

Chapters 4 and 5 focus on strategies for teaching language and literacy at the preschool and kindergarten level. Chapter 4 details what young children learn about reading and writing at home and in preschool and kindergarten. We explain how both forms of language—oral and written—are acquired in much the same way. Children learn by using language in connection with meaningful activities. We discuss the core components of a blended curriculum that form the foundation of developmentally appropriate preschool and kindergarten language arts programs: functional literacy activities, sharing literature, literacy play, and the language experience approach (also known as shared writing). We build on these components in Chapter 5, where we describe three other key components of a blended early literacy program: writing instruction, reading instruction, and assessment. That chapter begins with a description of developmentally appropriate strategies for teaching "core" early reading skills (phonological awareness, alphabet knowledge, print awareness, word recognition, and phonics).

Chapters 6 through 9 focus on elementary-grade reading and writing instruction. Chapter 6 discusses the five key psychological components (i.e., rate and fluency, phonemic awareness, phonics, comprehension, and vocabulary) of the process that are the key objectives of primary- and middle-grade reading instruction. Although this chapter's author, Mary Roe, discusses each component separately for clarity, she stresses that four of them (fluency, phonemic awareness, phonics, and vocabulary) of reading coalesce and that the result is comprehension. Following this discussion, our colleagues begin the description of how primary-grade teachers use their knowledge about the reading process to develop a reading program for the students in their classroom. The chapter continues what Roe began with rich descriptions of how elementary-grade teachers help their students learn to construct a personal understanding of text and how they teach specific decoding and comprehension skills within a blended approach to teaching reading. One of these descriptions is provided by our colleague Sara McCraw, who takes us into two first-grade classrooms to learn how three teachers use their knowledge of high-quality reading programs for their young students. We also provide a second description of a sixth-grade teachers' reading program. Finally, our colleague Deanne McCredie describes how, through the study of immigration, her third-graders used their language and literacy knowledge while at the same time learning content. Chapter 8 describes the writing workshop and explains why it is an ideal strategy for helping elementary-grade students become proficient writers. In Chapter 9, we explain how instruction in mechanical skills—handwriting, spelling, capitalization and punctuation, and grammar—can be embedded within the writing workshop.

Chapters 10 and 11 cover important aspects of reading instruction that apply to all levels, pre-K through the elementary and middle grades. Chapter 10 focuses on assessment. We explain how to create portfolios and use them to assess children's language and literacy learning. Portfolios are an effective means for organizing, sharing, and evaluating the information gained using the various assessment procedures described in other chapters of this book. Because states are making increased use of on-demand, standardized tests, we also discuss this kind of assessment. Finally, Chapter 11 discusses the importance of home–school collaboration and describes strategies for promoting parental involvement in language arts education.

KEY FEATURES

To give concrete illustrations of language and literacy learning, this book contains several **Special Features.** Interspersed throughout the book, they provide in-depth information about topics relating to language and literacy learning and to teaching the language arts. Most notable are the series of features by Sarah Hudelson and Irene Serna that provide information about how teachers can adjust instruction to meets the needs of second-language and bilingual learners. Other experts, like Sara McCraw and Deanne McCredie, take readers into classrooms to experience groups of children's language and literacy learning.

The book also contains a number of **Trade Secrets** in which veteran teachers describe how they provide students with effective language arts instruction. These Trade Secrets illustrate how teaching strategies can be applied in specific situations and reveal how teachers deal with practical problems that arise in the course of daily life in the classroom.

A third feature is the **broad scope** of this book, covering language arts instruction from preschool through the upper elementary grades. This coverage makes the book suitable both for elementary (K–8) and early childhood (preschool–grade 2/3) language arts methods courses.

CHANGES IN THE THIRD EDITION

The most important change in this third edition involves a shift toward a strong emphasis on scientifically based reading research (SBRR) throughout, blending SBRR with other perspectives to create a "value-added" approach to language and literacy teaching and learning. This blended approach t includes both authentic, activity-linked learning experiences and developmentally appropriate teaching. Other changes include strong coverage of the national literacy policies and initiatives; attention to explicit instruction of literacy skills at the early childhood level in the key early reading areas (oral language comprehension, vocabulary, phonological awareness, print awareness, and alphabet knowledge); and an increased emphasis on the explicit teaching of phonics, word meaning, and comprehension and writing mechanics in the elementary grades. We have also broadened the instructional scope of this text, strengthening the descriptions of teaching in the upper elementary grades, and have included examples and teaching strategies that deal with older students.

We have continued and enhanced the use of a number of pedagogical features designed to make this book easier for students to read and comprehend. All chapters begin with a introductory vignette that illustrates a major concept being presented in that chapter. The vignette is then "debriefed" in a manner that helps the reader begin to develop an interest in the topic. In addition, as part of the introduction, each chapter asks a series of *Think About* questions that enable readers to connect new material in the book with past personnel experiences and prior knowledge. The beginning of each chapter also includes *Definitions* of key terms and a series of *Focus Questions* to alert the reader to the key concepts of that chapter. The *Summary* at the end of each chapter contains answers to each Focus Question, providing a review of the key concepts in each chapter and giving readers an opportunity to self-check their comprehension. In addition, *Linking Knowledge to Practice* activities at the end of each chapter allow students to connect the theories and practices discussed in the book to practices they are observing or experiencing in real preschool, kindergarten, and elementary classrooms.

ACKNOWLEDGMENTS

Many outstanding educators helped us write this book. Our very special thanks go to Mary Roe for her significant contribution to this book on the new theory and research on the reading process and to Sarah Hudelson and Irene Serna for their special features on second-language and bilingual learners. Like us, they sat before their computers for many days. From Sarah and Irene, we learned how our ideas about teaching the language arts are appropriate for use with children whose primary language is a language other than English. From Mary, we learned how to use the new research on the reading process to develop high-quality reading programs for elementary students. We also extend a special thanks to Sara McCraw and Deanne McCredie for helping us hear teachers' and children's voices during rich language and literacy times in real classrooms. From them, we learned how the ideas on the reading process Mary presented come alive in elementary classrooms. Several of our colleagues added their special insights to this book, and we thank them. Sandra Twardosz helped us understand brain development and the effect of life experiences on the structure and function of the brain. Karen Burstein and Tanis Bryan helped us better understand the special needs of exceptional children. Bonnie Albertson shared a rich description of a state's creation of its standardized assessment instrument. Barbara Gaal Lutz helped us better understand the writing of English language learners. Patricia Scott taught us about new technology to enhance classroom writing programs. We thank each of them for their important contributions to this book.

Many classroom teachers shared their secrets, showing how theory and research link with quality classroom practice. We are grateful to Chris Boyd, Karen Eustace, Annapurna Ganesh, Michelle Gerry, Cory Hansen, Phoebe Bell Ingraham, and Carolyn Lara from Arizona; and Deirdra Aikens, Margaret Dillner, Dawn Downs, Ginny Emerson, Christine Evans, Maryanne Lamont, Jayne Ragains, and Jackie Shockley from Delaware for their description of exemplary teaching practices. From these teachers, and others like them, we have seen how exciting language and literacy learning can be when teachers and children are engaged in purposeful language arts activities. From them, and their students, we have learned much.

Several of our colleagues played roles in the construction of this book through their willingness to engage us in many conversations about children's language and literacy learning. Never unwilling to hear our ideas and to share their own, colleagues Kathy Roskos, John Carroll University; Laura Justice, University of Virginia; Lesley Mandel Morrow, Rutgers University; Bonnie Albertson, Martha Buell, Peggy Dillner, Myae Han, Deanne McCredie, and Laurie Palmer, University of Delaware; Doreen Bardsley, Cory Hansen, Lyn Searfoss, Jill Stamm, Elaine Surbeck, and Chari Woodward, Arizona State University; Sandy Stone, Northern Arizona University; Cookie Bolig, Delaware Department of Education; and Rebecca Haynes,

Jill Stewart, and Patricia McKee, U.S. Department of Education, have greatly helped us frame our arguments.

Graduate students Gaysha Beard, Christine Evans, Martha Ford, Sara McCraw, and Julia Park of the University of Delaware have been helpful in contributing features, locating references, cross checking the reference list, constructing the index, and so forth. Doctoral students from Arizona State University Kevin Thresher, Melanie Latimer, Debbie Pischke, Meral Ergisi and Allison Mullady have offered advice and feedback throughout this revision process. An-Chi Lin provided valuable assistance with the table of contents, and Na Liu, Byeong-Keun You, and Julia Parks provided help with the subject index. Likewise, program coordinator Monique Davis has given considerable time to final editing.

The students we have nurtured and taught, both young children and college students, have also influenced the development of our ideas. Their questions, their talk, their play, their responses, their enthusiasm—each one of them has taught us about the importance of the language arts in our lives. Their positive response to our ideas fueled our eagerness to share those ideas more broadly. What better honor than to learn that a "black market" of photocopies of the early drafts of the chapters of this book had developed on our campuses.

Finally, our families have helped us write this book. Our grandchildren and grand nieces and nephews have provided wonderful examples of their use and enjoyment of oral and written language. The story of their journey to being competent language users brings life to the research and theory discussed in our book. Mary Christie, Don (Skip) Enz, and Ron Vukelich gave us time to write but also pulled us from our computers to experience antique shows, museums, trips, home repairs—life. And then, of course, there is our extended family—our parents, David and Dorothy Palm, Art and Emma Larson, Bill and Jeannine Fullerton, John and Florence Christie—who provided our early reading, writing, speaking, and listening experiences and helped us know firsthand the joys of learning and teaching the language arts.

Jim Christie
Billie Enz
Carol Vukelich

CHAPTER 1

FOUNDATIONS OF LANGUAGE AND LITERACY

In recent years, the field of literacy has been thrust into the spotlight. A flurry of new studies, consensus reports, and national literacy policies have had a significant effect on literacy instruction in the United States. Being in the spotlight is, as Margery Cuyler (1991) reported in her delightful children's book *That's Good! That's Bad!*, good and bad. What's good is that additional financial resources have been funneled into the literacy field. The resulting research has enriched our knowledge about literacy and the teaching of reading. This research, detailed throughout this book, has identified (1) the key language and early literacy skills preschool children need to know and be able to do if they are to become successful readers, (2) effective instructional strategies that teachers of young children need to use to support their young learners' language and literacy development, (3) five key elements crucial to elementary children's reading success, and (4) methods and approaches for teaching the key elements to elementary children. Funded initiatives, in the form of national policies and programs described later in this chapter, provided incentives for educators to begin to use the new research-based strategies to teach children the key skills.

The bad news is that while the new resources, research findings, and initiatives provide rich resources to improve early and later literacy instruction, they also present educators with some daunting challenges. Preschool teachers are experiencing mounting pressure to increase children's literacy development, raising concerns that drill-and-practice, workbooks, basal readers, and other types of "developmentally inappropriate" instruction will find their way into the preschool. Many educators are concerned that elementary school practices will be pushed down to the preschool level. Preschool teachers also worry that academic instruction (i.e., a teacher standing before a group of young children and delivering content) will replace the preschool staples of children learning through play and adults reading stories to children purely for the enjoyment of the literature. Elementary school teachers worry that reading instruction will become one-dimensional, as opposed to a comprehensive literacy program, and that all children will be subjected to instruction that might be valuable for a select group of students only. For example, phonics, an identified key element to helping children become good readers, might become the instructional approach to teaching reading, with all children experiencing a systematic phonics program (even those who have already mastered phonics). Elementary teachers worry that they no longer will be free to make decisions about the when, why, how, and to whom they provide instruction in the key elements of reading; all children will receive the same instruction in the same dosage.

This book draws on current research and best practices, blending the previously held theory and research-based instructional practices that have proved successful in supporting children's reading, writing, and speaking development with the new scientifically based reading research. Our goal is to provide teachers with the foundations—the core content and the best-practice teaching strategies—needed to provide high-quality reading, writing, and speaking programs for children from preschool through elementary school. While the field wants to divide reading instruction into "camps"—at the preschool level, emergent literacy versus scientifically based reading research instruction, and at the elementary level, reading workshop instruction versus scientifically based reading instruction—we believe that the two views need to be merged to provide an effective reading, writing, and speaking program for all children.

We begin this book with a brief overview of the recent key U.S. policies and initiatives that have affected the teaching of reading at the preschool and elementary levels. Because of the significant effect these policies and initiatives have had on the literacy field, we start with this description of the national landscape. Then, we describe the beliefs and the research base of the diverging views on the teaching of reading. We end with a set of principles that guide our view of the effective teaching of literacy in preschool and elementary classrooms.

BEFORE READING THIS CHAPTER, THINK ABOUT . . .

- Your beliefs about how young children first learn to read and write. At what age do children begin to learn about literacy? Is knowledge about reading and writing transmitted from adults to young children, or do children construct this knowledge on their own?

- Your beliefs about effective language and literacy instruction. How can teachers best help young children become skilled speakers, listeners, readers, and writers?

- Your memories about how you learned to talk, read, and write. Do you recall, for example, reading cereal labels at an early age? Do you recall writing messages to loved ones?

- Your memories about how you were taught to read and write in elementary school. Do you recall being explicitly taught how to sound out words? Do you recall reading aloud? Do you recall "popcorn" reading, when your teacher randomly called on you and your classmates to read? Do you remember engaging in silent reading? Do you remember being taught how to be aware of your understanding of the passages you were reading?

FOCUS QUESTIONS

■ How have U.S. literacy polices and initiatives affected preschool and elementary reading instruction?

■ How did the standards movement change literacy instructional practices and the assessment of children?

■ How is the emergent literacy perspective different from the scientifically based reading research perspective on young children's early literacy learning?

■ What principles should guide teachers when teaching language and literacy?

■ ■ ■ ■ ■

BOX 1.1
DEFINITION OF TERMS

annual yearly progress (AYP): Using 2001–2 achievement data, U.S. states were required to set expectations for growth in student achievement that is continuous and substantial (shows increases each year) such that all students (100 percent) will be judged proficient in reading and math no later than the 2013–14 academic year. (See www.ed.gov/policy/elsec/guid/secletter/020724.html.)

benchmarks: Expected or anticipated skills or understandings at various developmental levels (e.g., by third grade, students will know and be able to . . .).

comprehension: A complex cognitive process; an active process that requires an intentional and thoughtful interaction between the reader and the text.

content standards: Define the knowledge and skills that students must attain in each content area (e.g., English language arts, mathematics, science).

fluency: Reading out loud with speed, accuracy, and proper expression.

grade level expectations: What students are expected to demonstrate that they know and can do at each grade level.

performance standards: What students are expected to demonstrate that they know and can do.

phonemic awareness: Phonemes are the smallest units of sound in a language. English consists of approximately forty-one phonemes. Phonemic awareness refers to the ability to focus on and manipulate these phonemes in spoken words. (Official definition is from http://www.nationalreadingpanel.org/faq/faq.htm#7.)

phonics instruction: A way of teaching reading that stresses learning how letters correspond to sounds and how to use this knowledge in reading and spelling. (Official definition is from http://www.nationalreadingpanel.org/faq/faq.htm#9.)

NATIONAL LITERACY POLICIES AND INITIATIVES

National literacy policy changed dramatically at the beginning of the twenty-first century. At the pre-kindergarten (pre-K) and primary-grade levels, these policies placed early literacy directly on center stage. At the pre-K level, the growing body of research indicating that early exposure to oral language and literacy skills (skills such as phonological awareness and alphabet knowledge) put children at an advantage for later reading achievement pushed policy makers to institute new initiatives that changed instructional practices in early childhood programs. These new pre-K policies grew out of movements begun in the 1980s. The publication of the scientifically based findings of the National Reading Panel suggesting that all students need explicit instruction in phonics, fluency, comprehension, phonemic awareness, and vocabulary development and the resulting national legislation mandating instruction in these key areas in federally funded programs dramatically changed reading instruction. In this section, we provide a brief history of the genesis of several significant national literacy policies. Figure 1.1 summarizes some significant national educational events affecting literacy.

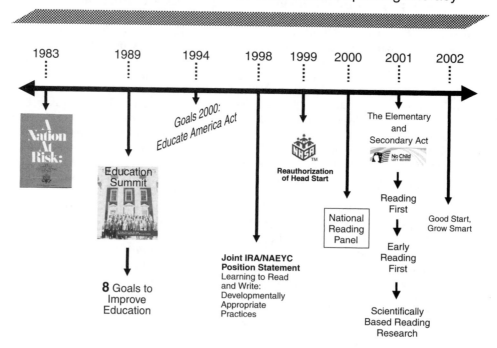

Significant National Educational Events Impacting Literacy

FIGURE 1.1

The Standards Movement

In 1983, the National Commission on Excellence in Education prepared a report titled *A Nation at Risk*. The commissioners warned that a "rising tide of mediocrity" in our schools threatened our future as a nation. Action was needed. The solution recommended by the commissioners was the creation of standards. High and rigorous standards, the commissioners believed, would restore the nation's place in the world.

Standards? What are they? Standards define the knowledge and skills that students—all students—must attain. They clarify and raise expectations. Because they identify what all students must know and be able to do, they define what is to be taught and what kind of student performance is expected.

Following the publication of *A Nation at Risk*, a few states and some national professional organizations (such as the National Council of Teachers of Mathematics) began to develop standards in the core content areas (English language arts, mathematics, science, social studies). Two subsequent events pushed states into high gear. The first was the 1989 meeting in Charlottesville, Virginia, of the nation's governors. A significant outcome of this education summit was a list of eight goals aimed at improving education. Goals 3 and 8 are particularly relevant to our interests. Goal 3 reads, "By the year 2000, American students will leave grades 4, 8, and 12 having demonstrated competency in challenging subject matter including English, mathematics, science, history, and geography." Goal 8 reads, "By the year 2000, all children will start school ready to learn." Collectively, these eight goals (known as Goals 2000 because of the date by which they were to be achieved) provided a set of directions for improving public education.

The second event that nudged states' standards-writing efforts forward was the passage of the Educate America Act (Goals 2000, Title III, Educate America Act, 1994). This legislation provided federal funding to states to support their writing of standards. To receive these federal funds states had to (1) develop reliable state assessments at three grade spans; (2) align local curricula to state standards and assessments; and (3) educate teachers and the general public about the standards.

These funds allowed many states to support the work of committees of teachers, administrators, parents, and other key stakeholders (business leaders, school board members, legislators, and other community leaders) to draft academic content standards with grade-level benchmarks (what students must demonstrate they know and can do by a particular grade).

By the mid- to late 1990s, the standards were developed, and states' attention turned toward the three conditions noted above. State departments of education held meetings to introduce the public and educators to the standards and the grade-level benchmarks. Groups of educators began the work of aligning their curricula to their state's standards. Did the chosen reading series provide the district's students with the opportunity to learn the content by the designated time? If not, new series would need to be ordered or adjustments made to when the content would be delivered. Finally, state departments of education began to select or design standardized assessments (tests) linked to their standards. Were students achieving the standards? The massive effort of implementing K–12 standards-based education reform was under way. By 2004, all but one state (Iowa) had adopted K–12 standards. (See Table 1.1 for an example of one state's English language arts standards.) As 2006 began, states were beginning to make revisions to their earlier-developed K–12 standards, revisions aimed at ensuring consistency with the new knowledge about each of the content areas.

No Child Left Behind Act

The passage of the No Child Left Behind (NCLB) Act in 2001 dramatically increased the importance of the standards-based reform efforts. Before, to obtain some federal education funds (like Title I funds to improve the quality of education in high-poverty schools and/or give extra help to struggling students), the federal government required states to have standards. With the passage of NCLB, the federal government began requiring states to hold schools and students, *all* students, accountable for meeting the state's content standards. NCLB requires states to assess grades 3–8 students' success annually in meeting state standards in reading, mathematics, and science. It also requires states to design and then implement an accountability system that holds students and the education system (schools and districts) responsible for all students' achievement in the specified content areas. Further, every state's accountability system must ensure that all groups of students reach proficiency. That is, the assessment results must be broken out by poverty (family socioeconomic status), race, ethnicity, disability, and limited English proficiency. Student performance within each group must show improvement; no group can be left behind. The law requires that not later than twelve years after the end of the 2001–2 school year, all students in each group must meet or exceed the state's proficiency level of academic achievement on the state assessments. School districts and schools that fail to make adequate annual progress toward the statewide proficiency goals are required to design plans to improve their students' performance. Should these plans fail to produce the desired results, the school districts and schools are subject to corrective action and restructuring measures aimed at getting them back on course so that all their students meet the state standards in reading and mathematics (and eventually science). (For details on the No Child Left Behind Act, see www.ed.gov/nclb/overview/intro/index.html.)

Reading First. Reading First is a component of the No Child Left Behind Act. This program calls for high-quality, evidence-based reading programs in the nation's poorest schools in kindergarten through grade 3. Reading First provides funding to help states and local school districts serving low-income children eliminate reading deficits by establishing high-quality, comprehensive reading instruction, instruction built on the scientific research described in the National Reading Panel (2000) report (see below). States receive Reading First funds and then award subgrants to eligible school districts through a competitive process. School districts receiving Reading First funds are required to provide their teachers with professional

TABLE 1.1 **Delaware's English Language-Arts Content Standards and the Performance Indicators for the end of K–5**

English Language Arts Content Standards

Standard One: Students will use written and oral English appropriate for various purposes and audiences.

Standard Two: Students will construct, examine, and extend the meaning of literary, informative, and technical texts through listening, reading, and viewing.

Standard Three: Students will access, organize, and evaluate information gained through listening, reading, and viewing.

Standard Four: Students will use literary knowledge gained through print and visual media to connect self to society and culture.

(Indicators of required performance for each standard at four grade clusters—K-3, 4-5, 6-8, and 9-10—are provided. One such set of indicators for K-5 students for one standard, Standard One, is detailed below.)

Performance Indicator for the End of K–Grade 5

Writers will produce texts that exhibit the following textual features, all of which are consistent with the genre and purpose of the writing:

Development: The topic, theme, stand/perspective, argument, or character is fully developed.

Organization: The text exhibits a discernible progression of ideas.

Style: The writer demonstrates a quality of imagination, individuality, and a distinctive voice.

Word Choice: The words are precise, vivid, and economical.

Sentence Formation: Sentences are completed and varied in length and structure.

Conventions: Appropriate grammar, mechanics, spelling, and usage enhance the meaning and readability of the text.

Writers will produce examples that illustrate the following discourse classifications:

1. **Expressive** (author-oriented) texts, both personal and literary, that
   a. reveal self-discovery and reflection;
   b. demonstrate experimentation with techniques, which could include dialogue;
   c. demonstrate experimentation with appropriate modes, which include narration and description;
   d. demonstrate experimentation with rhetorical form.
2. **Informative** (subject-oriented) texts that
   a. begin to address audience;
   b. exhibit appropriate modes, which could include description, narration, classification, simple process analysis, simple definitions;
   c. conform to the appropriate formats, which include letters, summaries, messages, and reports;
   d. contain information from primary and secondary sources, avoiding plagiarism.
3. **Argumentative and persuasive** (audience-oriented) texts that
   a. address the needs of the audience;
   b. communicate a clear-cut position on an issue;
   c. support the position with relevant information, which could include personal and expert opinions and examples;
   d. exhibit evidence of reasoning.

Speakers demonstrate oral-language proficiency in formal and informal speech situations, such as conversations, interviews, collaborative group work, oral presentations, public speaking, and debate. Speakers are able to

1. **Formulate** a message, including all essential information.
2. Organize a message appropriately for the speech situation.
3. **Deliver** a message,
   a. beginning to control volume, tone, speed, and enunciation appropriately for the situational context;
   b. using facial expression to reinforce the message;
   c. maintaining focus;
   d. creating the impression of being secure and comfortable, and in command of the situation;
   e. incorporating audiovisual aids when appropriate.
4. **Respond** to feedback, adjusting volume and speed, and answering questions.

Source: Delaware Department of Education

development on scientifically based reading programs and instructional strategies; to implement the selected reading program with fidelity; and to assess the children's reading achievement through ongoing, valid and reliable screening, diagnostics, and classroom-based assessments. Specifically, teachers must be provided with professional development in the essential reading skills (phonemic awareness, phonics, fluency, vocabulary, and comprehension), and children must be offered explicit instruction in each of the skills identified by the National Reading Panel as key to children's reading achievement. (These key skills are discussed later in this book.)

Through requiring schools to use "what works," the federal government hoped to improve student achievement and ensure that all children learn to read well by the end of third grade.

Good Start, Grow Smart.   No Child Left Behind also drew attention to the need to prepare children before they started school. Supported by the burgeoning body of research on the importance of the early years in young children's later achievement, some of which is discussed in this book, and the findings that some children enter school with deficits that put them at risk for long-term academic achievement, the George W. Bush administration developed a plan to strengthen early learning to equip young children with the skills they need to start school ready to learn. This initiative, known as Good Start, Grow Smart (2002), addressed three major areas:

■ **Strengthening Head Start:** Congress's 1999 reauthorization of Head Start mandated a set of learning goals for children enrolled in Head Start, goals such as "develop phonemic, print, and numeracy awareness, recognize a word as a unit of print, and identify at least 10 letters of the alphabet" (*Good Start, Grow Smart*, 2002, p. 8). From the administration's perspective, the goals had not been fully or effectively implemented by 2002. Hence, the administration directed the Department of Health and Human Services (HHS) to develop an accountability system for Head Start to ensure that every Head Start center assesses each child's early literacy, language, and numeracy skills at the beginning, middle, and end of each year and that every center analyzes the data to judge the progress of the children toward the stated learning goals.

■ **Partnering with states to improve early childhood education:** The Bush administration asked states to engage in three activities aimed at defining quality criteria for early childhood education. The first activity was to develop voluntary guidelines (standards) in prereading and language that aligned with their K–12 standards for children ages three through five. By the beginning of 2004, thirty-four states had developed early reading standards. (See Figure 1.2 for one state's language and early reading standards.) The second was to develop a plan for offering education and training activities to child care and preschool teachers and administrators. The third activity was to design a plan for coordinating at least four early childhood programs funded with federal and/or state dollars. Ultimately, the administration's goal was for states to take steps that would help prepare children before they entered kindergarten to be ready to learn.

ORAL EXPRESSION

The child will develop listening and speaking skills by communicating experiences and ideas through oral expression.

- Listen with increasing attention to spoken language, conversations, and stories read aloud.
- Correctly identify characters, objects, and actions in a picture book as well as stories read aloud, and begin to comment about each.
- Make predictions about what might happen in a story.
- Use two words to ask and answer questions to include actions.
- Use appropriate language for a variety of purposes (e.g., ask questions, express needs, get information).
- Engage in turn-taking exchanges and rules of polite conversation with adults and peers.
- Listen attentively to stories in a whole-class setting.

VOCABULARY

The child will develop an understanding of words and word meanings through the use of appropriate vocabulary.

- Use single words to label objects.
- Listen with increasing understanding to conversations and directions.
- Follow simple, one-step oral directions.
- Engage in turn-taking exchanges with adults and peers.
- Use new vocabulary with increasing frequency to express and describe feelings and ideas.

PHONOLOGICAL AWARENESS

The child will manipulate the various units of sounds in words.

- Successfully detect beginning sounds in words.
- Listen to two one-syllable words and blend together to form the compound word (e.g., *Rain, bow* is *rainbow*).
- Identify words that rhyme; generate simple rhymes.
- Listen to a sequence of separate sounds in words with three phonemes and correctly blend the sounds to form the whole word (e.g., cat = /k/ /a/ /t/).

FIGURE 1.2   Virginia's Literacy Foundation   *(continued)*

LETTER KNOWLEDGE AND EARLY WORD RECOGNITION

The child will demonstrate basic knowledge of the alphabetic principle.

- Correctly identify ten to eighteen alphabet (uppercase) letters by name in random order.
- Select a letter to represent a sound (eight to ten letters).
- Correctly provide the most common sound for fifty-eight letters.
- Read simple or familiar high-frequency words, including his or her name.
- Notice letters around him or her in familiar, everyday life, and ask how to spell words, names, or titles.

PRINT AND BOOK AWARENESS

The child will demonstrate knowledge of print concepts.

- Identify the front of a book.
- Identify the location of the title of a book.
- Identify where reading begins on a page (first word or group of words).
- Demonstrate directionality of reading left to right on page.
- Identify part of the book that "tells the story" (print as opposed to pictures).
- Turn pages one at a time from the front to the back of a book.

WRITTEN EXPRESSION

The child will write using a variety of materials.

- Copy letters using various materials.
- Print first name independently.
- Print five to eight letters with a pencil using appropriate grip.
- Copy simple words (three to five letters).
- Use inventive spellings to convey messages or tell stories.

FIGURE 1.2   (continued)

- **Providing information to teachers, caregivers, and parents:** To assist states in writing their voluntary guidelines and to close the gap between research and current practices in early childhood education, the Department of Education offered Early Childhood Academies across the country. These academies overviewed the recent prereading and language research and described research-based teaching techniques.

In addition, HHS was directed to implement a national training program, called Project STEP, to show Head Start teachers early literacy teaching techniques.

If Head Start children were to be able to demonstrate the identified early literacy and language skills, then their Head Start teachers would need training in research-based strategies so that they could provide Head Start children with high-quality instruction.

Further, the administration provided funding to identify effective prereading and language curricula and teaching strategies. Preschool Curriculum Evaluation Research (PCER) researchers rigorously evaluated the impact of preschool curricula on children's prereading and language learning. During Year 1, the children participated in a preschool program that used a particular language and early reading curriculum, and their progress in achieving important language and early reading skills was measured. These children were followed into kindergarten and first grade in an effort to understand the long-term effects of the preschool curriculum on the children's reading achievement. As of this writing, the government has not issued this project's report. Readers are encouraged to monitor the PCER Web site for this information (http://pcer.rti.org).

Finally, the administration prepared several publications (called "guidebooks") for parents, families, and early childhood educators and caregivers. Each booklet (*A Child Becomes a Reader: Birth through Preschool* and *A Child Becomes a Reader: Kindergarten through Grade 3*) summarizes the scientific research and provides descriptions of activities that parents can do with their children to "start them down the road to becoming readers from the day they are born" (Armbruster, Lehr, & Osborn, 2003, p. 2). Readers can order these free booklets from the National Institute for Literacy (1-800-228-8813). The free guidebook for early childhood educators (*Teaching Our Youngest*) can be ordered online at www.ed.gov/pubs/edpubs.html.

Early Reading First.   Funded in NCLB and as a part of the administration's Good Start, Grow Smart initiative, Early Reading First is a competitive grant program. It provides funding to local educational agencies and to public and private organizations serving low-income preschool children. The program was created to address the growing concern that many of the nation's children begin kindergarten without the necessary foundation to benefit fully from formal school instruction. Therefore, the intent of the program is to transform existing preschool programs into centers of excellence that prepare young children to enter kindergarten ready to learn and that serve as models for other preschool programs to emulate. The program's goals include (1) to enhance preschool children's language, cognitive, and early reading development, particularly low-income children's, by using scientifically based teaching strategies; (2) to demonstrate language and literacy activities based on scientifically based reading research that support young children's oral language, phonological awareness, print awareness, and alphabet knowledge; (3) to use screening assessments to identify effectively preschool-age children who may be at risk for reading failure; and (4) to create high-quality language and print-rich environments. To achieve these goals, funded programs must provide teachers with high-quality professional development experiences to build their knowledge of scientifically based language and early reading research and instructional teaching practices.

USING SCIENTIFICALLY BASED READING RESEARCH TO MAKE CURRICULAR AND INSTRUCTIONAL DECISIONS

Intertwined with the standards-based educational reform agenda described above is the recent requirement that federally funded programs, such as Early Reading First and Reading First, use curricula, programs, and instructional methods that have been "proven" to be effective. The official definition of what is acceptable as proof of effectiveness first appeared in federal legislation in 1999 in the Reading Excellence Act (see www.ed.gov/inits/FY99/REAguidance/sectionB.html). This statute defined acceptable research as "scientifically based reading research." As defined, this research applies "rigorous, systematic, and objective procedures to obtain valid knowledge relevant to reading development, reading instruction, and reading difficulties." The term *scientifically based research* was specifically defined in the No Child Left Behind Act. This legislation identified several features that must be present to meet the criteria of scientifically based research (Box 1.2).

This new policy has generated considerable debate. Some researchers are pleased with the focus on the kind of research supported by NCLB. Other

■ ■ ■ ■ ■

BOX 1.2

No Child Left Behind Act defines "scientifically based research" as detailed below.

Scientifically based research includes research that

(i) employs systematic, empirical methods that draw on observations or experiment;

(ii) involves rigorous data analyses that are adequate to test the stated hypotheses and justify the general conclusions drawn;

(iii) relies on measurements or observational methods that provide reliable and valid data across evaluators and observers, across multiple measurements and observations, and actual studies by the same or different investigators;

(iv) is evaluated using experimental or quasi-experimental designs in which individuals, entities, programs, or activities are assigned to different conditions with appropriate controls to evaluate the effects of the condition of interest, with a preference for random-assignment experiments, or other designs to the extent that those designs contain within-condition or across-condition controls;

(v) ensures that experimental studies are presented in sufficient detail and clarity to allow for replication, or, at a minimum, offer the opportunity to build systematically on their findings; and

(vi) has been accepted by a peer-reviewed journal or approved by a panel of independent experts through a comparably rigorous, objective, and scientific review.

Source: *No Child Left Behind Act of 2001*, pp. 126–127.

researchers have expressed concern about the implications of the legislation on research in education. Will only one kind of research (experiments, meta-analyses, and randomized trials) be judged as acceptable educational research?

In fact, the NCLB legislation *requires* teachers and administrators to answer affirmatively two key questions before the reading program or approach is approved for use in federally funded programs, including Reading First. Reid Lyon and Vinta Chhabra (2004, p. 13) identify these two questions:

1. Does the program comprehensively cover each of the evidence-based skills, specifically those identified by the National Reading Panel (see below), that students need to read proficiently?

2. Has the program or approach been proven scientifically to work with students like mine? In other words, does the research on the program or approach, and the instructional strategies it uses, meet the criteria listed in Box 1.2? Does the research show that the program or approach positively affected the participating students' reading performance?

Scientifically based reading research has had a significant impact on educators' thinking about how children become successful readers, writers, and speakers.

The National Reading Panel

To understand which approaches to teaching children to read are supported by scientifically based reading research, Congress directed that the National Reading Panel (NRP) be formed to assess the status of research-based knowledge about reading. Using the definition of scientifically based reading research presented in Box 1.2, the panel reviewed articles published in peer-reviewed journals on the following topics: alphabetics (phonemic awareness instruction and phonics instruction), fluency, comprehension (vocabulary instruction, text comprehension instruction, teacher preparation and comprehension strategies instruction), teacher education and reading instruction, and computer technology and reading instruction. The panel suggests that it missed reporting on some areas that likely are important to children's reading achievement (e.g., writing development, self-regulation, motivation) because of the lack of an adequate number of investigations that met the criteria of scientifically based reading research. The panel reported the following conclusions relative to the five key elements it identified as crucial to children's reading success (NRP, 2000).

■ **Phonemic awareness:** Teaching children to manipulate the sounds in language (phonemes) helps them learn to read. In fact, phonemic awareness training improves students' phonemic awareness, spelling, and reading, with the effects on reading lasting well beyond the end of the training.

■ **Phonics:** Systematic phonics instruction leads to significant positive benefits for students in kindergarten through sixth grade and for children with difficulty learning to read. It enhances children's success in learning to decode, spell, and comprehend text.

■ **Vocabulary:** Vocabulary development has long been considered important for reading comprehension. The panel concluded that vocabulary should be taught both directly and indirectly. Repetition and seeing vocabulary words several times are important.

■ **Comprehension:** Text comprehension is improved when teachers use a combination of reading comprehension techniques such as question answering, question generation, and summarization. When students are able to use these techniques successfully, they perform better in recall, answering questions, generating questions, and summarizing texts.

■ **Fluency:** Guided repeated oral reading has a significant and positive impact on word recognition, reading fluency, and comprehension for students of all ages.

A CONTINUUM OF INSTRUCTIONAL APPROACHES

The field of elementary-grade reading instruction has witnessed a century-old debate between the proponents of two very different views of how to teach reading. On one side are the supporters of meaning-based approaches that stress comprehension, connected reading, good literature, and the integration of reading and writing. These approaches assume that if children engage in lots of meaningful reading and writing activities with support from teachers and peers, they will acquire literacy. The terms *literature based* and *whole language* are sometimes used to describe this perspective. On the other side are proponents of a skill-based view who emphasize direct instruction on skills such as phonics, alphabet recognition, and fluency that enable children to decode written texts. The assumption is that once children are taught to recognize written words fluently, they will comprehend the texts that they read. The end point for both approaches is the same: fluent reading with good comprehension. This debate, however, has often been harsh, politicized, and polarized, leading some to use the term *reading wars* to characterize the discourse between the two groups (Joyce, 1999).

Emergent Literacy Approach

During the 1990s, the field of pre-K reading had largely escaped the bitter debate that was raging at the elementary level. Emergent literacy was the predominant view of early reading and writing, and most conceptions of best practice stemmed from this meaning-centered perspective. According to this view, children begin learning about reading and writing at a very early age by observing and interacting with adults and other children as they use literacy in everyday life activities. For example, young children observe the print on cereal boxes to select their favorite brands, watch as their parents write notes and read the newspaper, and participate in special literacy-focused routines such as storybook reading with a parent or older sibling. On the basis of these observations and activities, children construct their own concepts about the functions and structure of print and then try them out by engaging in emergent forms of reading and writing, which often are far removed from the conventional forms used by adults. Based on how others respond to their early attempts, children make modifications and construct more sophisticated systems of reading and writing. For example, early attempts at writing often shift from scribbles, to random streams of letters (SKPVSSPK), and to increasingly elaborate systems of invented spelling such as *JLE* for *jelly* (Sulzby, 1990). Eventually, with many meaningful opportunities to engage in meaningful literacy activities, much interaction with adults and peers, and some incidental instruction, children become conventional readers and writers.

Proponents of emergent literacy believed that if provided with the right kind of environments, experiences, and social interactions, most children require very little, formal instruction to learn to read and write. Early-childhood language arts programs based on the emergent literacy perspective feature the following components:

- Print-rich classroom settings that contain large numbers of good children's books, displays of conventional print (e.g., alphabet friezes, charts written by teachers), functional print (helper charts, daily schedules, labels), student writing, and play-related print (empty cereal boxes in the home center)
- Frequent storybook reading by the teacher with lots of student interaction
- Shared reading of big books coupled with embedded instruction on concepts about print (e.g., book concepts such as *author* and *title* and the left-to-right sequence of written language)
- Shared writing experiences in which the teacher writes down oral stories dictated by children
- Projects and/or thematic units that link language, reading, and writing activities
- Opportunities for children to engage in meaningful reading and writing during "center time" activities, and a family literacy component

Emergent literacy proponents contend that these types of emergent literacy experiences build on what children have already learned about written language, provide a smooth transition between home and school, and help ensure initial success with learning to read and write. The teacher's role is to provide the materials, experiences, and interactions that enable children to learn to read and write. Direct instruction on skills such alphabet recognition and letter–sound relationships is only used with children who fail to learn these skills through meaningful interactions with print. This approach is described in detail in Chapter 4.

Scientifically Based Reading Research Approach

During the late 1990s, the standards movement and other national literacy policies and initiatives described at the beginning of this chapter began to have an impact on the field of early literacy. By 2002, initiatives such Good Start, Grow Smart and the Early Reading First grant program pushed a skills-based approach to early literacy instruction, often referred to as scientifically based reading research (SBRR), into prominence. Perhaps the most valuable contribution of the SBRR movement has been the identification the "core" knowledge and skills that young children must have to become successful readers (Snow, Burns, & Griffin, 1998). Longitudinal studies have shown that preschool-age children's *oral language* (expressive and receptive language, including vocabulary development), *phonological awareness,* and *alphabet knowledge* are predictive of reading achievement in the elementary grades. *Print awareness,* which includes concepts of print (e.g., left-to-right, top-to-bottom sequence), book concepts (author, title), and sight word recognition, has also been found to be positively correlated with reading ability in the primary grades.

SBRR investigators have also focused on identifying effective strategies for teaching this core literacy content to young children. One of the most consistent research findings is that core early literacy skills can be increased via *direct, systematic instruction.* This instruction can often take the form of games and other engaging activities, but it also contains the elements of direct instruction: explanations, teacher modeling, guided practice, and independent practice.

Scientifically based reading research instruction occurs during large and small group settings. Large group instruction occurs during "circle time" when the entire class sits on the floor near the teacher; it may include the following:

■ Songs, such as "Down by the Bay," coupled with instruction on rhyme production ("Did you ever see a whale with a polka-dot . . . (tail), Down by the bay.") [SBRR skill: phonological awareness.]

■ Storybook reading, coupled with instruction on vocabulary (after reading "Did you see llamas eating their pajamas, Down by the bay," the teacher asks, "Does anyone know what a llama is?"). [SBRR skill: oral language.]

■ Alphabet charts with a poem for each letter that contains many examples of the "target" letter. For example, after reading a poem for the letter *P* (Patty Panda likes to draw, holds a pencil in her paw . . ."), the teacher asks children to come up and point to the words that contain *P* and say the letter name. [SBRR skill: alphabet knowledge.]

■ Every pupil response activity in which all children have a chance to respond at the same time. For example, the teacher might say a series of words, some of which begin with the /p/ sound and some that do not. Children hold their thumbs up if a word starts with the sound of *p.* [SBRR skill: phonological awareness.]

Instruction can also be conducted in small groups. The advantage is that if an activity requires that one child respond at a time, all children get multiple opportunities to participate. For example, using a pocket chart, a teacher could give a small group of children each a high-frequency word flash card (my, the, is, big, fast) or a rebus picture card (truck, cat, girl, house). After reviewing the words on the cards, the teacher would help the children build sentences by saying words and having the children bring up their cards and place them in the chart ("My cat is big"; "The truck is fast"; "My house is big"). [SBRR skill: print awareness.]

Children also need opportunities to practice and consolidate what has been taught in large and small group settings. This chance usually occurs during an "activity" time during which children work individually or in small groups in learning centers. It requires that the teacher link the center activities to the skills being taught in the curriculum.

Blended Instruction: A "Value-Added" Approach

Both the emergent literacy and SBRR approaches to early literacy instruction have their advantages. Emergent literacy programs provide opportunities for children to learn about literacy on their own and with help from the teacher and peers. Learning can occur at the appropriate pace for each child and can build on what he or she already knows. This approach provides children with rich opportunities to acquire oral language and move through the developmental progressions in emergent reading and writing. The downside is that not all children are ready or able to take full advantage of these learning opportunities. Some children have a tendency to "fall through the cracks" in emergent literacy programs and make very little progress. Such children need to be directly taught vocabulary, phonological awareness, alphabet, and concepts of print before they can fully profit from the learning experiences in an emergent literacy program.

We advocate instruction that blends together the key components of both approaches (Figure 1.3). This approach features the print-rich classrooms, storybook reading, shared writing, projects/units, and meaningful center-based literacy activities advocated by proponents of emergent literacy, coupled with direct instruction and practice on core language and literacy skills featured in the SBRR approach. Blended instruction is therefore a "value-added" approach to

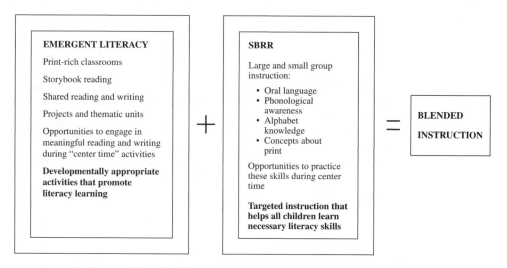

FIGURE 1.3   Blended Instruction

early literacy instruction, combining the best aspects of the emergent literacy and SBRR perspectives.

Fortunately, we are not alone in this view. Most, if not all, of the comprehensive pre-K early literacy curricula developed since 2002 are blended programs. All have been strongly influenced by the SBRR perspective and use the term *science-based instruction* in their promotional literature. These new programs place heavy emphasis on the "big four" science-based skills: oral language, phonological awareness, alphabet knowledge, and print awareness. Direct instruction on these skills in large and small group settings is also now a standard feature, although the nature and intensity of this instruction varies from program to program. These programs also include the main components recommended by emergent literacy: frequent storybook reading, print-rich classroom environments, and center activities that involve reading and writing. Box 1.3 describes the blended program that is being used in an Early Reading First grant project in Arizona.

Of course, how teachers implement a curriculum has a big influence on how appropriate and effective the curriculum will be for specific groups of children. Susan Neuman and Kathy Roskos (2005b) give an example of an observation they made in a preschool that used a commercially published early literacy curriculum fitting our definition of a "blended" program. The classroom did have a print-rich environment, but the instruction that Neuman and Roskos observed was not developmentally appropriate for the three-and-a-half and four-year-old children-participating in the lesson. Here is a vignette that describes the lesson (Neuman & Roskos, 2005b, p. 22):

> The local school administrator recommends an exemplary school for us to visit. We watch a day unfold in a room filled with print. The walls are adorned with words; pocket charts, alphabet letters, numbers, signs, and environmental print claim every available space. A big book stands ready in the circle area, accompanied by a pointer for tracking print. The children sit "station style," with "quiet hands and feet," in their designated space in the circle and sing "Stop, Look, and Listen" along with their teacher. The day is about to begin.
>
> Taking flash cards in hand, the teacher begins, "Good morning, Charley. Do you know the first two letters of your name?" Charley moves tentatively to the board and slowly writes *C* and *H*. Moving to the next child, then the next, the teacher follows a similar routine. Some fourteen children later, she reviews many of the letters, asking children to spell the names of the helpers of the week. The days of the week are next, and children repeat them in chorus. They compare the letters in Monday with the letters in Tuesday, then Tuesday with Wednesday, and Tuesday with Thursday. What follows is the Counting Calendar and "My, oh my, it's the thirtieth of the month," and so the children count each day up to thirty. Finally, with an "I like how you're listening" some forty-five minutes later, circle time is about to end. Even so, the transition allows for one last teachable moment focusing on the *t-t-t* in *teacher,* the *m-m-m* in *Ms.,* and the j-j-j in *jingle.*

This vignette shows that it is possible to take a blended curriculum and skew it one way or the other, resulting in too little or too much instruction. There is nothing inherently wrong with the activities themselves: writing the letters in children's

■ ■ ■ ■ ■

BOX 1.3

THE ARIZONA CENTERS FOR EXCELLENCE IN EARLY EDUCATION PROJECT

The Arizona Centers for Excellence in Early Education (ACE[3]) is an Early Reading First project that serves children in twenty-four Head Start and state-funded preschools in San Luis and Somerton, Arizona. A vast majority of these children are learning English as second language. Like all Early Reading First projects, the primary goal of ACE[3] is to promote preschoolers' readiness for kindergarten by teaching them "science-based" early reading skills: oral language, phonological awareness, alphabet knowledge, and concepts of print.

The program uses a commercially published curriculum, *Doors to Discovery* (Wright Group/McGraw-Hill, 2002), which is a good example of a blended early literacy program. The *Doors* program is organized into one-month "explorations" or units that focus on topics that appeal to young children, such as transportation, nature, food, and school. The *Doors* curriculum consists of three interrelated components:

■ **Large group time:** Song and Rhyme posters are used as a warm-up and to teach phonological awareness (e.g., rhyme recognition). They are followed by shared reading of big books in which the teacher encourages children to read along and engage in book-related talk. Three shared reading books are used in each unit: a narrative storybook, an informational book, and a concept book. When stories are initially introduced, the teacher does a "picture walk" to introduce key concepts and vocabulary. Instruction on concepts of print, phonological awareness, and alphabet knowledge are incorporated into the shared reading sessions.

■ **Discovery centers:** During a sixty-minute period, children engage in self-selected activities in a variety of learning centers, including dramatic play, art, blocks, writing, mathematics,

and science. Many of these activities are linked to the theme and to the stories that are read during shared reading. The teacher manual contains lists of theme-related Wonderful Words that the teachers use with the children while they are engaging in center activities. Discovery centers are stocked with theme-related literacy props and materials, providing children with a print-rich environment. For example, during the unit on transportation, the dramatic play center is turned into a gasoline station. Props include a gas station sign (e.g., "Chevron") and a cardboard gas pump with a label ("gas") and numerals to represent the gallons and cost of gas that is pumped.

■ **Small group time:** During the second ten-minute segment of discovery center time, the teacher meets with small groups of students and conducts a vocabulary lesson using an Interactive Book, a wordless big book that contains illustrations related to the unit theme. For example, *Our Big Book of Driving*, which is used in the unit on transportation, contains pictures of different types of vehicles (bus, ambulance, motorcycle), parts of a car (door, tire, speedometer), and a scene of a busy intersection. Children are encouraged to discuss the pictures (initially in Spanish and then in English).

Once a week, during the third ten-minute segment of discovery center time, the teacher also teaches a small group lesson using Our Big Scrapbook, a blank big book. In a variation of the Language Experience Approach or shared writing, the teacher writes down children's oral language while the children watch. The subject of the children's dictation is usually photographs of children's play activities or their artwork. For example, children may draw pictures of the type of vehicle their parents drive. Each child then dictates a sentence

(continued)

■ ■ ■ ■ ■

BOX 1.3   CONTINUED

("My mom drives a blue van"), which the teacher writes below the picture. The children's contributions are then pasted or taped to the blank pages of the scrapbook. Completed scrapbooks are placed in the classroom library center for children to read during the center time.

A positive feature of this program is the way in which the different components and activities are linked together around the current theme. The following vignette occurred during a unit on building and construction:

> During large group circle time, the teacher and children sang a song that had to do with building a tree house. The teacher paused to point out the words that rhymed in the story and then encouraged the children to come up with other words that ended with the same rhyming sound. She also focused on several tool-related vocabulary terms: hammer and nail. Next, the teacher did a shared reading lesson with a big book about building a doghouse. Before reading the book with the children, she did a "picture walk," engaging the children in a discussion about objects in the photos in this informational book. The teacher focused children's attention

on several tool vocabulary terms: hammer, nail, saw, measuring tape, and safety goggles. Then the teacher read the book and encouraged the children to read along. Some were able to do so because of the simple text and picture clues. During center time, several children chose to play in a dramatic play center that was set up as a house construction site. There was a "house" made out of large cardboard boxes as well as toy tools (hammers, saw, measuring tape, level), safety goggles, hard hats, some golf tees that were used as make-believe nails, and several signs ("Hard Hat Area," "Danger," "Construction Site"). Two girls and a boy spent thirty minutes in the center, using the toy tools to measure, plan, and build the house. During this play, they used the target vocabulary repeatedly and also explored the uses of the tools. For example, when the boy attempted to use the toy saw without first putting on his safety goggles, one of the girls reminded him to put on the goggles. The dramatic play center was used as a means to provide children with an opportunity to practice and consolidate the vocabulary and concepts that were being taught in the instructional part of the curriculum.

names, spelling the names of classroom helpers, reciting the days of the week, comparing the letters in the days of the week, counting, and sounding out the initial sounds in words. In fact, with a few modifications, each of these activities could have been a very effective lesson. The problem is that the lesson contained all these activities, making it much too long for three- and four-year-olds. These instructional activities could have been shortened (e.g., writing the beginning letters in several children's names, but not all fourteen) and spread across several days.

For guidance in appropriate instructional early literacy practices, Neuman and Roskos send preschool teachers to *Learning to Read and Write: Developmentally Appropriate Practices,* the 1998 joint position statement published by the International Reading Association and the National Association for the Education of Young Children. To prepare this statement (a task spearheaded by Susan Neuman, Sue Bredekamp, and Carol Copple), representatives of the two organizations engaged in a "thorough review of the research" to define a set of principles to guide teaching practices and public policy (p. 4). Neuman and Roskos (p. 23) summarize these principles:

> The research-based statement stresses that for children to become skilled readers, they need to develop a rich language and conceptual knowledge base, a broad and deep vocabulary and verbal reasoning abilities to understand messages conveyed through print. . . . it recognizes that children also must develop code-related skills: an understanding that spoken words are composed of small elements of speech (phonological awareness), the idea that letters represent these sounds (the alphabetic principle), and the knowledge that there are systematic correspondences between sounds and spellings. But . . . *meaning*, not sounds or letters, drives children's earliest experiences with print. . . . Although specific skills like alphabet knowledge are important to literacy development, children must acquire these skills . . . [through] meaningful experiences.

Note a level of consistency between these skills and at least some of those identified as key language and early literacy skills in the position statement with those identified by SBRR research. The difference, then, is not in the key skills as much as in instructional strategies some preschool educators elect to use to teach these skills. Neuman and Roskos's view is that pre-kindergarten teachers should use "content- and language-rich instruction" that includes "time, materials, and resources that . . . build language and conceptual knowledge; a supportive learning environment . . . ; . . . different group sizes (large, small, individual) . . . to meet the needs of individual children; and opportunities for sustained and in-depth learning, including play"(p. 26). To this list of suggestions could be added the position statement's perspective (p. 6): "But the ability to read and write does not develop naturally, without careful planning and instruction."

The challenge, then, for early childhood educators is to carefully plan and teach the key elements through meaningful experiences. Our goal is to provide teachers with research-based information on how to combine the emergent literacy and the scientifically based reading research perspective to create a blended, effective early literacy program, one with meaningful experiences and with direct, developmentally appropriate instruction in the key early literacy areas.

A BLENDED LITERACY INSTRUCTIONAL PROGRAM

We believe that to provide preschool through elementary school children with a high-quality, effective reading, writing, and speaking program, the two perspectives need to be interwoven and that both views make significant contributions to such a program. Children need meaningful interactions with print in print-rich environments and in books. They need social interactions with their peers and their teachers in literacy events. They need many opportunities to engage in meaningful reading, writing, and speaking events. In addition, they need explicit instruction in reading, writing, and speaking skills.

By combining the two perspectives, we have created a set of basic principles of effective literacy instruction. These principles should guide how children are taught spoken and written language in preschool through elementary classrooms.

Effective Teachers Provide Children with a Print-Rich Classroom Environment

High-quality literacy programs require a literacy-rich environment with many materials to support children's learning. As Neuman and Roskos (1993, pp. 20–21) explain, a print-rich classroom can help children learn about language and literacy:

> The quality of the physical environment is a powerful factor in language learning. The objects and opportunities it provides are the stuff out of which basic concepts are spun. What is available to label and to talk about, how accessible it is to touch and explore, and how it is organized influence both spoken and written language development.

Rich physical environments do not just happen; the creation of a classroom environment that supports children's learning, teachers' teaching, and the curriculum requires forethought. Some characteristics of this type of classroom environment include a well-stocked library corner and writing center; lots of functional print; theme-related literacy props in play areas; and displays of children's writing. This type of environment offers children opportunities to talk, listen, read, and write to one another for real-life purposes.

Effective Teachers Demonstrate, Model, and Scaffold Instruction

Because children will try to do what others do, demonstrating and modeling literacy events will lead to children imitating these events. When a teacher reads books to young children, children independently pick up the books and say words in ways that would lead a listener to think they are reading. The children sound as though they are reading words, yet their eyes are focused on the illustrations. When children see parents and teachers using print for various purposes—writing shopping lists, looking up information in a book, and writing notes—they begin to learn about the practical uses of language and to understand why reading and writing are activities worth doing.

Deborah Rowe (1994) provides an example of a preschool teacher's demonstration of the use of exclamation points. The teacher is sitting in the writing center with a small group of children. She writes a get-well card to a sick colleague. She writes: "Dear Carol, We hope you get well SOON!!!" She explains, "exclamation mark, exclamation mark, exclamation mark. Because I want her to get well *soon*." Moments later, Kira and Hana talk about exclamation marks.

Kira: And this is [pause] extamotion [sic] point. How come?

Hana: Put three cause it's big letters.

Still later, Hana and Kira include exclamation marks in their writing. Kira writes the letters *COI* over and over inside one band of a rainbow and exclamation marks inside another band, and Hana writes her name and fills the bottom of the page with upside-down exclamation marks (Rowe, 1994, pp. 168–169). This preschool teacher probably did not set out to teach her young students about exclamation points. In the act of writing and talking about her writing, she demonstrated to curious, observant preschool apprentices the purpose of using an exclamation mark. Notice how she showed her student "observers" what is done during reading and writing. She acted as a writer, not as a teacher of reading and writing. In this way, she shared with the children how a reader or a writer thinks as well as acts.

Effective Teachers Explicitly Teach Children Skills That Research Supports as Key Elements of Reading, Writing, and Speaking

Scientifically based reading research has identified key skills of early and later reading. This literature tells us that early language and literacy instruction should focus on the core content: the knowledge, skills, and dispositions that are predictive of later reading success (i.e., oral language, phonological awareness, alphabet knowledge, concepts of print). This literature tells us that later reading instruction should focus on those key elements crucial to children's success as readers (i.e., phonemic awareness, phonics, vocabulary development, comprehension, fluency). Writing research and theory has identified the elements of quality expressive, informative, and persuasive texts (e.g., organization, development). There is a rich body of language development research to help teachers understand the key features of language (e.g., phonology, syntax, semantics, pragmatics). In each area, a rich literature identifies research-based instructional strategies for teaching children these skills, elements, and features. Many of these instructional strategies call for teachers to explicitly teach children: large groups of children, small groups of children, and individuals. In all instances, the strategies used should be appropriate for the age of the children.

Effective Teachers Read to Children Daily and Encourage Them to Read Books on Their Own

Living in a print-rich world provides children with many opportunities to read *contextualized* print. That is, children form hypotheses about what words say because of the context in which the words are embedded. As described in other sections of this chapter, children learn to read cereal boxes, stop signs, and the McDonald's sign early in life. While making such connections with print is important, young children also need multiple experiences with decontextualized print. Neuman and Roskos (1993, p. 36) explain the meaning of decontextualized print:

> Essentially, . . . unlike contextualized print experiences, written language has meaning apart from the particular situation or context of its use. The meaning of decontextualized print is derived from the language itself and from the conventions of the literary genre. Over time, [children] develop a frame, or sense of story, a mental model of basic elements of a story.

Reading stories to children is one of the best ways to familiarize them with decontextualized print. Effective teachers plan numerous opportunities for story-book reading experiences. These teachers read aloud daily to individual children, small groups of children, and the whole class. Sometimes the books are regular-size books, like the ones obtained from the public or school library. Other times, the books are big books, enlarged (about twenty-four- to twenty-six-inch) versions of regular-size books.

Hearing stories read aloud, however, is not enough for children of any age. Studies have shown the importance of talking about the books read (Heath, 1983; Yaden, Smolken, & Conlon, 1989). Many teachers begin their read-alouds by engaging children in a discussion related to the story they are about to read. A teacher might read the title and ask the children what they think the story might be about or ask a question related to the book's content. While reading, the teacher might invite the children to make comments, to share reactions, or to ask questions. The teacher might invite the children to turn to their reading partner to discuss a section of the book just read. After reading, the teacher will likely engage the children in a discussion aimed at extending their understanding of the story. This framework for read-alouds has been called a "grand conversation" (Clay, 1991). Such conversations help children understand how to process the decontextualized text found in books both in terms of the story's structure and by making connections between the text and their experiences.

It is also important to provide opportunities for children to read books to themselves and to one another. Through such occasions, children have the opportunity to practice what they have learned during the interactive storybook readings and to refine the strategies needed to construct meaning from texts. To learn to enjoy making meaning from written texts, each person must do the work, the thinking, independently. Children learn to read by reading.

Effective Teachers Provide Opportunities for Children to Collaborate and Help Each Other Learn about Language and Literacy

Of course, teachers are not the only people in the classroom environment who offer demonstrations of literacy. "Knowledgeable teachers understand that the social, collaborative nature of learning to read and respond to books goes beyond the relationship between adult and child, teacher and student, and includes peers" (Galda, Cullinan, & Strickland, 1993). This statement about learning to read is equally applicable to learning to write. Creating a "community of literacy learners" is often suggested in the professional literature. Children select books to "read" because their peers have selected the book. Children talk to each other about books they are reading or have had read to them. Children turn to each other for information and help in decoding or spelling words. "How do you spell *morning*?" "What's this word say?"

When teachers know that learning is a social act and that readers, writers, and speakers develop new understandings as a result of the rich exchange of ideas in collaborative learning contexts, they intentionally create new kinds of classroom participation opportunities for their students. For example, these teachers provide their students with opportunities to engage in discussion groups about books, to form literacy clubs, or to work in small groups to investigate specific topics within a content area.

Such collaborative learning opportunities will not "just happen." Teachers must create an environment in which children can demonstrate for, or coach, each other. Several researchers have documented what happens when teachers create such opportunities. For example, researchers (e.g., Christie & Stone, 1999; Vukelich, 1993) have studied how play in literacy-enriched play settings provides children with opportunities to teach each other. Carol Vukelich (1993), for example, studied how children teach each other about the functions, features, and meaning of print in play. The following peer-to-peer interaction illustrates how one child coaches another child about how to spell his name.

> Jessie is the forest ranger. She is seated at the entrance to the campsite, directing potential campers to get a sticker from her before entering the campground, and *then* she'll tell them which tent they can use.

Jessie: Ronald, how do you spell your name?

Ronald: *R.* [Jessie writes *r.*] No, it's the big kind.

[Ronald forms the letter with his finger on the table. Jessie writes *R.*] Good!

Jessie: What else?

[Jessie writes as Ronald dictates each letter of his name, looking up at him after each one. When finished, she gives Ronald the sticker with his name on it.] (p. 390)

This example was from a kindergarten classroom. Similar rich examples of teachers and children learning together in literacy-enriched environments are reported in the literature about elementary children's literacy development, particularly relative to the teaching of writing. As children write and share their texts with their peers and teachers, they come to understand the needs of their audience in addition to gathering specific feedback on the quality of their writing (e.g., "Does my beginning make you want to read more?"). As the following example illustrates, seven-year-old Kristi had learned much by sharing her writing with her peers.

Kristi is about to begin a new story. She sits, staring at her paper and twiddling her pencil. Suddenly she grabs a piece of scrap paper, leaps up, and approaches her friend Shannon.

Kristi: What do you want to know about my burned hand?

Shannon: How did you do it?

Kristi moves on, approaching Charlie.

Kristi: What do you want to know about my burned hand? Shannon wants to know how I did it.

Charlie: What did you do after you burned it?

And so Kristi proceeded, one by one, asking several of her peers what they would like to know about her burned hand. When her teacher questioned her use of this strategy, Kristi responded, "I might as well find out what they want to know before I begin my piece, rather than after!" Clearly, Kristi had developed a sense of writing for others, not just herself.

When teachers value children's contributions and celebrate what they know, children see the strengths in each other. Within such a supportive climate, children practice what they know and take the risks necessary for learning to occur. This kind of environment encourages children to learn from themselves, from each other, and from the teacher.

Effective Teachers Provide Opportunities for Children to Use Language and Literacy for Real Purposes and Audiences

Most research on learning supports the proposition that knowing the reason for a learning situation and seeing a purpose in a task help children learn. Through their lives outside the classroom, children have experienced a wide variety of purposes for writing to various audiences. If children are allowed to experiment with paper and pencils and to write on topics of their choice, these purposes will begin to show up in their early attempts at writing. They will jot down lists of things they need to do, make signs for their doors warning intruders to stay out, and write letters to the editor to complain about injustices.

Similarly, children have experienced many opportunities to read for real purposes. They have shopped in grocery and toy stores, and sometimes they have screamed when their parent refused to purchase the cereal or toy whose label they read and wanted. They have told the car driver who slowed but didn't come to a full stop at the stop sign to STOP! They have read the address on an envelope collected at the mailbox and said, "You won't like this one. It's a bill!"

Notice how many of these reading and writing opportunities are literacy events woven into daily life. The event defines the purpose of the literacy activity. When children read and write for real people, for real purposes, and in ways that are linked with their lives outside of school, they are more likely to be motivated, and motivation is believed to result in learning that is deep and internalized (Gambrell & Mazzoni, 1999). Furthermore, through such meaningful literacy events, school and community are bridged. Just outside the walls of every school are a number of real problems awaiting study. Reading and writing for real purposes abound.

Effective Teachers Support Children's Experimentations with Print

As we blend the two perspectives, it is important that teachers allow children a "risk-free" environment in which they practice and integrate new skills they are learning with what they already know. Years ago, young children were not considered to be writing until they were writing conventionally, that is, correctly forming the letters and spelling the words. They were not considered to be reading until they could correctly recognize numerous printed words. In the 1970s, Marie Clay (1975) and Charles Read (1971) helped us understand emergent forms of writing and reading. We learned that children construct, test, and perfect hypotheses about written language. Their research led Elizabeth Sulzby and her colleagues (Sulzby, 1985a, 1985b; Sulzby, Barnhart, & Hieshima, 1989) to create developmental sequences that children pass through on their way to becoming conventional readers and writers.

While excellent teachers continue to model correct forms of writing during guided writing and to support and scaffold children's reading and writing efforts, excellent teachers realize that children continue to develop and evolve to more conventional forms of reading and writing through practice and time. Teachers' support for the construction of knowledge through experimentation and risk taking does not end when children's print understandings more closely resemble that of adults. When children reach this stage in their literacy development, teachers support their efforts to search for and construct new meanings in reading and through writing. They encourage them to test the word: Does it make sense in this sentence? They work to make children strategic readers, readers who dare to employ different strategies with different texts read for different purposes. These teachers and their children view reading and writing as meaning making or producing events.

Effective Teachers Use Multiple Forms of Assessment to Find Out What Children Know and Can Do

Is the child's development following the expected stages? Is the child acquiring the core-content early literacy skills or the crucial-element early elementary skills? Today, teachers use standardized and curriculum-based measures and other ongoing measures to assess children's progress in acquiring the crucial elements or core content skills.

Not so long ago, the literacy field recommended against the use of standardized tests, particularly with young children and particularly paper and pencil group-administered tests. For example, the 1998 joint International Reading Association and National Association for the Education of Young Children joint statement had the following to say about testing young children:

> **Accurate assessment** of children's knowledge, skills, and dispositions in reading and writing will help teachers better match instruction with how and what children are learning. However, early reading and writing cannot simply be measured as a set of narrowly defined skills on standardized tests. These measures often are not reliable or valid indicators of what children can do in typical practice, nor are they sensitive to language variations, culture, or experiences of young children. Rather, a sound assessment should be anchored in real-life writing and reading tasks and continuously chronicle a wide range of children's literacy activities in different situations. Good assessment is essential to help teachers tailor appropriate

instruction to young children and to know when and how much intensive instruction on any particular skill or strategy might be needed. (p. 38)

This joint statement advised teachers of young children to use multiple indicators to assess and monitor children's development and learning. We concur.

Now, however, the field also acknowledges that standardized assessments—such as the *Peabody Picture Vocabulary Test* (Dunn & Dunn, 1997), the *Individual Growth and Developmental Indicator* (IGDI) (Early Childhood Research Institute on Measuring Growth and Development, 2000), and the *Phonological Awareness Literacy Screening* (Invernizzi, Meier, Swank, & Juel, 1999)—can provide teachers with valuable information. Repeated use of the same instruments allows teachers to chronicle children's development over time. Neither standardized nor informal, ongoing assessment should be used alone, however. When multiple sources of data are used, the likelihood of an accurate understanding of children's literacy knowledge and learning is increased (IRA/NCTE, 1994).

Teachers must use both kinds of assessment to improve their instruction. Teachers must gather information, analyze the information, and use what they learn to inform their instruction. In fact, that is a key purpose of assessment. The model Assess-Plan-Teach-Assess must be central to teachers' classroom assessment procedures.

Effective Teachers Respect and Make Accommodations for Children's Developmental, Cultural, and Linguistic Diversity

Children arrive in the classroom with different individual language and literacy needs. Our challenge is to offer good fits between each child's strengths and needs and what we try to give the child. The instruction we provide needs to dovetail with where children are developmentally and with their language and culture.

Some children will come to school having learned how to talk in ways that are consistent with their teachers' expectations; other children will not. "We come to every situation with stories: patterns and sequences of events which are built into us. Our learning happens within the experience of what important others did" (Bateson, 1979, p. 13). In other words, the ways in which we make meaning and use words are dependent on the practices shared by the members of our community: the words chosen; the sentence structures used; the decision to talk after, or over, another's comment; and so on. As Allan Luke and Joan Kale (1997, p. 13) point out, "Different cultures make meaning in different ways, with different patterns of exchange and interaction, text conventions and beliefs about reading and writing." Given our increasingly diverse communities composed of many different cultures, teachers are more challenged than ever before to understand what this diversity means for their teaching and for their children's learning. Children cannot be asked to leave their family and cultural backgrounds at the classroom door and enter into a "hybrid culture" (Au & Kawakami, 1991). Teachers must teach in ways that allow their children to work to their strengths.

Children's strengths are often linked to their cultural backgrounds.

Only since the 1980s have researchers investigated early literacy learning in nonmainstream homes and communities. In one pioneering study, Shirley Brice Heath (1983) described how children growing up in one working-class community learn that reading is sitting still and sounding out words, following the rules, whereas children in another working-class community learn that being able to tell a story well orally is more important than being able to read written texts. These conceptions of literacy were quite different from those found in children from middle-class families. The important question is, should these types of cultural differences be viewed as deficits that must be "fixed" for children to succeed in school, or should these differences be viewed as positive characteristics that teachers can take advantage of when helping children learn language and literacy?

Will children with different experiences meet teachers who have engaged in the study of the children's communities' ways with words and texts? Will their teachers provide scaffolded language activities and instruction that will enable these children to be successful in their efforts to learn mainstream English? Will they meet teachers who have redesigned reading lessons so the lessons better fit the speech events the children are accustomed to at home and in their community (Au & Jordan, 1981)? Will their teachers understand and value the patterns of teaching and learning evidenced in their homes and build on these patterns so that these children are drawn into the school world (Tharp & Gallimore, 1988)? Will their teachers understand that these children might be quiet in school because their parents have taught them to show respect by being quiet and deferential (Volk, 1997)?

Throughout this book, we give pointers on providing culturally sensitive language and literacy instruction.

A significant and growing group of diverse learners are second-language learners. The population of children who speak English as a second language was estimated at 3.5 million in the year 2000 and is projected to grow to 6 million by 2020 (Faltis, 2001). Of this group, those children who speak little or no English are referred to as limited English proficient. Other children are bilingual and can speak both English and their native language with varying degrees of proficiency. These children's native language might be Spanish, Portuguese, Japanese, or some other world language. When they come to school, young second-language learners are typically competent users of their native language, and this competence is a strength to be exploited by sensitive teachers.

We have included several Special Feature sections in subsequent chapters of this book that focus on second-language and bilingual learners' literacy development. From these features, readers will learn which strategies presented in this book are appropriate for use with children whose primary language is a language other than mainstream English and which strategies need to be adapted to meet the needs of these children.

Effective Teachers Recognize the Importance of Reflecting on Their Instructional Decisions

The importance of "learning by doing," standing back from each teaching/learning event to learn from one's teaching, is not new. John Dewey (1938) is usually credited with proposing the importance of this activity and Donald Schon (1983) with reintroducing the idea into the educational literature. To reflect is to take an active role in studying one's own instructional decisions to enhance one's knowledge and make informed decisions. Not all such reflections will be on past actions (retrospective); some might be on the potential outcomes of future actions (anticipatory), and others will be "in action" while teaching (contemporaneous) (van Manen, 1995). To reflect is to put a new lens on one's teaching: to consider and reconsider the procedures for technical accuracy (e.g., the procedural steps to follow while conducting a guided reading lesson), the reasons for instructional actions and outcomes, and the underlying assumptions of actions that impact social justice (e.g., curriculum mandates that affect teacher decision making or inequities that inhibit student learning).

Being a reflective practitioner is important for literacy teachers who seek to provide learning experiences that meet each child's instructional needs. As the decision makers, these teachers determine which literacy skills or components to teach and when to move their community of learners toward the desired instructional goals, adjusting the when and how to meet each learner's needs. Reflection is central to making these critical decisions.

We have challenged ourselves to provide readers with information on what is known about ways to meet all children's needs.

SUMMARY

In this chapter, we briefly explained the significant impact of recent national literacy policies on the literacy field and compared the constructivist approaches to literacy learning (emergent literacy and reading workshop) with the new scientifically-based reading research approach to literacy learning. We believe that the best literacy practices use strategies from both approaches. We firmly believe that teachers must use evidence (from research and from their students' performance) to guide their teaching.

In subsequent chapters, we provide many explanations of how to implement teaching strategies aimed at promoting different aspects of language and literacy development. In addition, the themes of respect for student diversity and instruction linked to assessment appear throughout the book. When appropriate, Special Features about the special needs of second-language learners are included. Further, a section titled Assessment: Discovering What Children Know and Can Do, is included in several chapters.

To summarize the key points from this chapter, we return to the focus questions at the beginning:

- *How have U.S. literacy policies and initiatives affected preschool and elementary reading instruction?*

Beginning with the 1983 (*A Nation at Risk*) suggestion that students be held to high and rigorous standards to the passage of the No Child Left Behind Act in 2001 requiring schools and school districts to hold *all* students responsible for demonstrating that they know the content of the standards, recent national policies have had a significant impact on literacy instruction in the United States. Two literacy programs were funded by the No Child Left Behind Act (Reading First, the program that provides funding to help states and local school districts serving low-income children eliminate reading deficits by establishing high-quality, comprehensive reading instruction built on the scientific research; and Early Reading First, the program that aims to transform existing preschool programs into centers of excellence that prepare young children to enter kindergarten ready to learn and that serve as models for other preschool programs). To obtain these funds, agencies must demonstrate that they will use reading programs and instructional strategies that are consistent with scientifically based reading research and that they will provide teachers with extensive professional development on these programs and strategies. The *required* use of "scientifically based reading research," research meeting a set of specific criteria, has received mixed response from the literacy field.

Recent national initiatives and legislation have drawn attention to the need to prepare children before they started school. From the reauthorization of Head Start, to the writing of pre-kindergarten literacy standards, to funded research and preschool-teacher professional development programs, to President George W. Bush's Good Start, Grow Smart initiative, the nation now realizes the importance of children's early years to their later academic success, particularly their reading achievement.

- *How did the standards movement change literacy instructional practices and the assessment of children?*

The No Child Left Behind (NCLB) Act requires states and school districts to hold all students, grades 3 through 8, responsible for demonstrating that they know the content of their state's English language arts standards. Specifically, NCLB requires states to assess students' success annually in meeting state standards in reading, mathematics, and, soon, science. To ensure that *all* students demonstrate progress toward proficiency in "meeting the standards," each state was required to design an accountability system. All students must meet or exceed the state's standards no later than twelve years after the end of the 2001–2 school year. Clearly, if students are to "know" the standards, then the curriculum must be aligned with the standards. Teachers must ensure that their students have the opportunity to learn the content specified by the standards.

- *How is the emergent literacy perspective different from the scientifically based reading research perspective on young children's early literacy learning?*

The emergent literacy perspective suggests that children learn about language and literacy by observing, exploring, and interacting with others. Children assume the role of apprentice: mimicking, absorbing, and adapting the words and literacy activities used by more knowledgeable others. As they engage in social interactions, children integrate new experiences with prior knowledge, constructing and testing hypotheses to make meaning.

The scientifically based reading research perspective argues that children need to be explicitly taught those skills that the research literature has identified as predictive of later reading success. To date, twelve variables have been identified as predictive of later reading success: *alphabet knowledge,* print knowledge, *oral language/vocabulary,* environmental print, invented spelling, listening comprehension, phonemic awareness, *phonological short-term memory,* rapid naming, *phonemic awareness,* visual memory, and *visual perceptual* skills (italics indicate those skills evidencing the highest correlation with school-age decoding).

A key difference between the two perspectives, then, is the early literacy practices recommended as appropriate: explicit instruction versus allowing the children to acquire the skills of literacy through multiple interactions with print and more-knowledgeable others. Unfortunately, to date there are few research-based suggestions on early literacy instructional strategies and programs. What do appropriate instructional strategies look and sound like? Teachers of young children must ensure that inappropriate strategies do not creep into their teaching practices as they shift to teaching the skills identified as central to children's success as readers.

■ *What principles should guide teachers when teaching language and literacy?*

Effective teachers

- Provide children with a print-rich classroom environment
- Demonstrate, model, and scaffold instruction
- Explicitly teach children skills that research supports as key elements of reading, writing, and speaking
- Read to children daily and encourage them to read books on their own
- Provide opportunities for children to collaborate and help one another learn about language and literacy
- Provide opportunities for children to use language and literacy for real purposes and audiences
- Support children's experimentations with print
- Use multiple forms of assessment to find out what children know and can do
- Respect and make accommodations for children's developmental, cultural, and linguistic diversity
- Recognize the importance of reflecting on their instructional decisions

LINKING KNOWLEDGE TO PRACTICE

1. Access your state's Department of Education Web site and bookmark your state's English language arts standards and grade-level benchmarks. Don't forget to look for the pre-K standards also. Compare what your state expects third-graders to know with what a neighboring state expects third-graders to know.

2. Access the U.S. Department of Education Web site. List three things you learned about Reading First and Early Reading First that surprised you. Which schools in your area are Reading First schools? Are there any Early Reading First funded programs in your area?

3. Observe a teacher in a nearby classroom. How does this teacher's language and literacy instruction match up with the teaching principles described in this chapter?

CHAPTER 2

ORAL LANGUAGE DEVELOPMENT

Perched in the shopping cart, nine-month-old Dawn babbles away to her mother. As they approach the checkout register, the clerk greets her mother. Dawn smiles. She loudly says "Hi!" and waves her hand. The startled clerk smiles at Dawn and begins to talk to her. Dawn, obviously pleased with this attention, now babbles back to the clerk.

As this scenario reveals, the power of language is evident to even its youngest users. Dawn demonstrates that she knows how to use language to express—and realize—her desire to become a significant, communicating member in her world. By age eighteen months, Dawn will have a vocabulary of dozens of words, and she will begin speaking in rule-governed, two-word sentences. By age thirty-six months, her vocabulary will number in the hundreds of words, and she will be using fully formed, five- and six-word sentences.

Children's oral language development is remarkable. Lindfors (1987, p. 90) outlines the typical accomplishments of young language learners:

> Virtually every child, without special training, exposed to surface structures of language in many interaction contexts, builds for himself—in a short period of time and at an early stage in his cognitive development—a deep-level, abstract, and highly complex system of linguistic structure.

How does Dawn—and every other human child, for that matter—learn to communicate? How does this development occur so rapidly and without any seeming effort on the part of children or their parents? This question has fascinated scholars and parents for hundreds of years and is the subject of this chapter.

BEFORE READING THIS CHAPTER, THINK ABOUT . . .

- Your first words. What were they? Although you probably do not recall uttering those words, maybe your parents or older siblings recollect your having spoken to them.

■ How children acquire language. Is language development primarily a matter of genetics (an inborn ability to learn languages), the types of experiences and support children receive from their parents and other people, or a combination of these factors?

■ The age at which children begin to express their thoughts orally. Why do some children develop language early, whereas others experience language delays?

■ Being in an environment with foreign speakers. Have you ever been in a situation in which everyone around you used a language you don't know? How did you feel? How did you communicate with these speakers?

FOCUS QUESTIONS

■ What are the major views on how children's language develops? Which aspects of language development does each view adequately explain?

■ What are the major components of language?

■ How does the structure of an infant's brain develop? How does this structural development affect language acquisition?

■ What factors affect children's rate of language acquisition?

■ How does children's acquisition of a second language compare with their first language acquisition?

■ What should adults do to make it easier for children to learn English as a second language?

LANGUAGE ACQUISITION THEORIES

Language has been called the symbolization of thought. It is a learned system of sounds and rules that enables humans to communicate ideas and express wants and needs. Reading, writing, nonverbal gestures (called signs), and speaking are all forms of language. Language falls into two main divisions: receptive language (understanding what is said, written, or signed) and expressive language (speaking, writing, or signing). There are four views on how children learn language—behaviorism, linguistic nativism, social interactionism, and the neurobiological perspective—and we present a brief description of each in this chapter. Our experiences as parents, teachers, and researchers lead us to believe that the social-interactionism perspective most realistically accounts for similarities and differences in young children's language development. Therefore, we present a more detailed description of what is currently known about children's language acquisition from this perspective. We also acknowledge, however, the importance of the growing body of neurobiological information provided by neuroscientists to help us understand the biology of language acquisition. Together, the social-interactionist and the neurobiological perspectives

██ ██ ██ ██ ██

BOX 2.1

DEFINITION OF TERMS

behaviorist perspective: the view that language acquisition is a result of imitation and reinforcement.

cerebral cortex: the largest part of the brain, composed of two hemispheres that are responsible for higher brain functions, including thought and language.

experience-dependent development: development that refers to the way experience is incorporated into brain structure and function throughout life.

experience-expectant development: development that is associated with sensitive periods, times when the brain is more responsive to a certain type of experience than it will be later.

morphemes: the smallest units of meaning in oral language. The word *cats* contains two morphemes: *cat* (name of a type of animal) and *s* (plural).

myelineation: a process in which the neurons of the brain become coated with a white substance known as myelin, which facilitates the transmission of sensory information and promotes learning.

nativist perspective: the view that language development is a result of an inborn capacity to learn language.

neurobiological perspective: the view that language acquisition can be explained by studying the structural development of the brain.

neurons: the impulse-conducting cells that make up the brain.

otitis media: an inflammation of the inner part of the ear that can retard language acquisition.

phoneme: the smallest unit of sound in a language. There are forty-four phonemes in English.

pragmatics: rules that affect how language is used in different social contexts.

semantics: the part of language that assigns meaning to words and sentences.

social-interactionist perspective: the view that language development is a result of both genetics and adult support.

synapses: connections between the neurons of the brain.

syntax: rules for arranging words into sentences.

---

provide important insights for teachers and future teachers on how children acquire language. In Figure 2.1, we summarize these four views of language acquisition.

Behaviorist Perspective

The behaviorist view suggests that nurture—the way a child is taught or molded by parents and the environment—plays a dominant role in children's language development. Through the first half of the twentieth century, this view was the prevalent one. Researchers and teachers believed that all learning (language included) is the result of two basic processes: classical and operant conditioning (Skinner, 1957). Behaviorists attribute receptive language to associations that result from classical conditioning. For example, every time the baby is offered a bottle, the mother names the object when she says, "Here's the bottle." After numerous repetitions with the adult presenting the action/object and phrase, the baby learns that the clear cylinder filled with food is called a bottle.

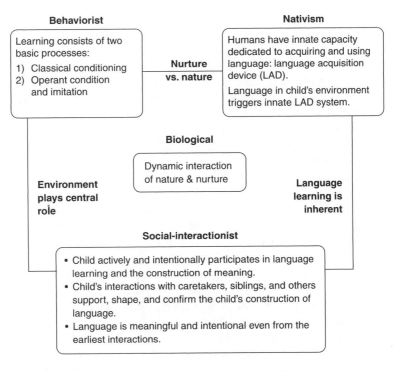

FIGURE 2.1   Theoretical Perspectives on Language Acquisition

Behaviorists suggest that through operant conditioning, infants gradually learn expressive language by being rewarded for imitating the sounds and speech they hear. For instance, a baby spontaneously babbles and accidentally says or repeats the sound "mama." The mother responds joyfully, hugging and kissing the baby, saying "Yes, Mama!" The baby, given this reward, is reinforced and attempts to repeat the behavior. Once the behavior is repeated and rewarded often enough, the child connects the word sound to the object or event.

Nativist Perspective

The nativist view of learning and development, with its emphasis on nature, is at the opposite end of the continuum from the behaviorist perspective. According to the nativist view, a person's behavior and capabilities are largely predetermined. Nativists believe that every child has an inborn capacity to learn language. If these theorists were using computer terminology, they would say that humans are hardwired for language. Noam Chomsky (1965) called this innate capacity a language acquisition device (LAD). Nativists posit that the LAD allows children to interpret phoneme patterns, word meanings, and the rules that govern language. For example, when children first begin to use past tenses, they often overgeneralize certain words, such as *goed* for *went*, or *thinked* for *thought*. Because *goed* and *thinked* are not words that children would hear adults say, these examples illustrate that children are using some type of internal rule system, not simple imitation, to govern their acquisition of language.

Nativists also believe that this innate language structure facilitates the child's own attempts to communicate, much the same way as the computer's wiring facilitates the use of a number of software programs. Nativists believe that language learning differs from all other human learning in that a child learns to communicate even without support from parents or caregivers. They view the environment's role in language acquisition as largely a function of activating the innate, physiologically based system. Environment, these theorists believe, is not the major force shaping a child's language development.

Social-Interactionist Perspective

Social interactionists do not come down on either side of the nature versus nurture debate; rather, they acknowledge the influence of genetics and parental teaching. They share with behaviorists the belief that environment plays a central role in children's language development. Likewise, along with nativists, they believe that children possess an innate predisposition to learn language. In addition, social interactionists stress the child's own intentional participation in language learning and the construction of meaning.

Lev Vygotsky's theory (1978) forms the foundation of the social-interactionist view of language development. Vygotsky believed that language develops in the context of social interaction and language use. As children experience the wide variety of functions and forms of language, they internalize the way their society uses language to represent meaning. Social experiences shape the language the child internalizes. At the same time, the child is making an internal effort to assign meanings to experience and to communicate with the outside world. These efforts are simultaneous. Two forces, within and without the child, work together to propel language learning.

The social interactionist's point of view emphasizes the importance of the infant's verbal negotiations or "verbal bouts" (Golinkoff, 1983; Golinkoff & Hirsh-Pasek, 1999) with caregivers. These negotiations occur partly because mothers or other caretakers treat children's attempts at speech as meaningful and intentional (Piper, 1993). An example is shown by eleven-month-old Dawn, standing by the garage door. Dawn is patting the door.

> **DAWN:**   Bice!
>
> **MOM:**   Do you want ice?
>
> **DAWN:**   [shaking her head] Biiisse.
>
> **MOM:**   [opening the garage door] Bise?
>
> **DAWN:**   [pointing at the bike] Bise.
>
> **MOM:**   You want to go for a bike ride?
>
> **DAWN:**   [raising her arms, nodding her head vigorously] Bice!

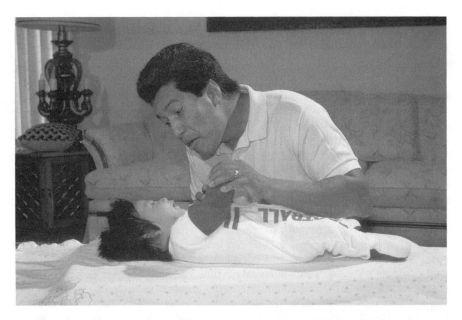

The social-interactionist perspective highlights the importance of infants' verbal "bouts" with caregivers

As Dawn's mother (and most mothers) begins to make sense of her child's speech, she also begins to understand her child's meaning or intent. Vygotsky (1962) described this type of adult support, or scaffolding, as facilitating the child's language growth within the zone of proximal development, the distance between a child's current level of development and the level at which the child can function with adult assistance. In the preceding example, the mother's questions enable Dawn to communicate successfully using a one-word sentence, something she could not have done on her own. Parents also support children's efforts to learn language by focusing the child's attention on objects in the immediate environment and labeling each object and its action.

A Biological Perspective

The psychologists, linguists, and anthropologists who developed the three preceding perspectives of language acquisition had to infer the origins of language and brain activity from careful, long-term observations of external behavior. Since the 1980s, technological innovations have enabled neuroscientists to study the brain at a cellular level. Brain-imaging techniques are noninvasive procedures that allow researchers to graphically record and simultaneously display three-dimensional, color-enhanced images of a living brain as it processes information (Sochurek, 1987).

Experience and the Developing Brain

BY SANDRA TWARDOSZ

Some concepts describe how life experiences affect the structure and function of the brain, not only during infancy and childhood, but throughout the brain's life span. Recall that the brain is not finished at birth and that children's experiences—their interactions with family and the environment—play a major role in the brain's further development. That is part of what we mean when we say that the brain is plastic: it can be changed by experience. Not all brain development, however, is guided by experience. Much of what occurs before birth, for example, is genetically regulated and protected from minor variations in the environment; it is organized ahead of experience (Black, 2003; Marcus, 2003). Nerve cells (neurons) are born, migrate to precise locations, such as the frontal cortex or cerebellum, and take on their appropriate functions. These complex processes are guided primarily by gene expression; in other words, the genes provide an explicit blueprint of instruction for the construction of the brain. The result is that the infant enters the world with an unfinished brain but one that is human, individually unique, and set up to use experience to develop throughout life (Marcus, 2003).

Although billions of neurons have been produced and have migrated to specific locations during prenatal development, most of the connections or synapses among the neurons develop after birth. Neuroscientists who study the way the brains of animals and humans change across the life span believe that experience plays a role in the development of those connections in at least two major ways: through experience-expectant development and through experience-dependent development. Experience-expectant development is associated with sensitive periods, times when the brain is more responsive to a certain type of experience than it will be later; experience-dependent develop-

ment refers to the way experience is incorporated into brain structure and function throughout life (Greenough, Black, & Wallace, 1987; Bruer & Greenough, 2001).

Experience-expectant development occurs when the brain produces an overabundance of synapses at specific times in preparation for the stimulation that children will almost certainly have simply because they are human beings growing up in typical human environments. For example, almost all children are exposed to touch, sights, sounds, language, and parental care; the brain anticipates those experiences by producing an overabundance of connections and allowing experience to shape and prune them. Seeing patterned light or hearing the sounds of language help select and organize the connections that will survive in the brain; those that are not selected by experience die, an essential part of the process that allows the brain to function normally and efficiently (Greenough & Black, 1999).

The overproduction and pruning of synapses does not occur simultaneously in all areas of the brain. For example, these processes occur in the visual and auditory areas of the cerebral cortex before they occur in areas devoted to language. The pruning of synapses in areas of the prefrontal cortex that control higher cognitive functions and self-regulation is not finished until midadolescence (Huttenlocher, 1999; Thompson & Nelson, 2001). Thus, different parts of the brain will be most responsive to experience at different times, and the earlier development of some areas may provide the basis for the development of others (Greenough & Black, 1999).

Periods of overproduction and pruning of connections mark the times when the brain is particularly sensitive to certain types of experience; if that experience is not available or if sensory organs are not functioning properly, then normal development may not occur even if the experience is available later. The child's developing visual system, for example, requires that both eyes send clear images to the brain and be pointed in the same direction for visual acuity and binocular vision to develop. The reason is because the visual cortex "expects" this type of information about the world so as to organize and prune the connections that have been produced in anticipation of this experience. Infants born with cataracts that cloud their vision or whose eyes are misaligned must have these conditions corrected very early in infancy if normal development of the visual cortex, and thus normal vision, is to occur (Tychsen, 2001).

Some aspects of language development also appear to operate in an experience-expectant manner. For example, before the age of twelve months, infants can discriminate among the phonetic units of all human languages; by the time they are one year old, however, they have lost that ability and resemble adults in being able to discriminate only among the sounds of the languages they have been hearing. As a result of being exposed to those specific sounds, the brain may have altered its structure, and this new structure interferes with learning the phonetic distinctions of a second language (Kuhl, 1999). Similarly, children who have been deprived of the opportunity to develop attachments with caregivers during infancy sometimes face difficulties with subsequent social development. The brain may be particularly responsive during infancy to the "expected" experiences provided to infants as they are protected and nurtured (Thompson, 2001). Experience-expectant development predominates during infancy and early childhood, and it even extends into adolescence. It is not the only way in which experience shapes the brain, however. There is another mechanism that begins at birth and continues throughout life in which experience exerts its effect on brain connections in a different way.

Experience-dependent development occurs when new synapses are formed or existing synapses are modified in response to the experiences of the individual. Connections are produced when they are needed rather than being produced in advance, and these new or modified synapses are then available to help with future learning. The ability to change in response to experience is a type of plasticity that the brain retains throughout life and that allows individuals to store information that is unique to them as a member of a specific culture, community, and family. These unique experiences are acquired through exploration of the environment, play, social interaction, or specific teaching (Greenough, Black, & Wallace, 1987; Bruer & Greenough, 2001; Black, 2003).

As the individual matures beyond infancy, more brain development is likely to be experience dependent (e.g., Black, 2003), and this concept is probably more relevant for describing how children acquire vocabulary and literacy skills and how teachers learn new strategies for teaching them. Some evidence exists that the mature brain does respond in this way to experience. For example, Bob Jacobs, Mathew Schall, and Arnold Scheibel (1993) found that there was greater dendritic branching in Wernicke's area (a part of the brain involved with processing language) in the brains of adults with higher levels of education.

The concepts of experience-expectant and experience-dependent development can help us think about how experience may be affecting the brain as we observe, interact with, and teach children, and as we struggle with and enjoy learning as adults. We must also be cautious with this information. Despite the enormous advances that have been made in recent years, the study of the brain, particularly the human brain, is in its infancy. Thus, information from developmental neuroscience must be viewed as a supplement to the understanding we have about teaching and learning from other disciplines such as developmental psychology and education.

These data provide researchers with a better way to understand the organization and functional operations of the brain.

According to this new perspective, the capacity to learn language begins with brain cells called neurons. Neurons emerge during the early phases of fetal development, growing at the fantastic rate of 250,000 per minute (Edelman, 1995). As neurons multiply, they follow a complex genetic blueprint that causes the brain to develop distinct but interdependent systems: brain stem and limbic system, cerebellum and cerebral cortex (MacLean, 1990).

New brain-imaging technology has allowed scientists to locate specific areas in the brain that are dedicated to hearing, speaking, and interpreting language. Thus, the nativist linguistic theory of language acquisition is, in part, correct: the human brain has dedicated structures for language, and infant brains are born capable of speaking any of the more than three thousand human languages (Kuhl, 1993). Infants, however, are not disposed to speak any particular language, nor are they born language proficient. The language a child learns is dependent on the language the child hears spoken in the home (Sylwester, 1995).

In fact, the recent discoveries in neurobiology support elements of the nativist, behaviorist, and social-interactionist views of language development. These biological findings reveal that language learning is a reciprocal dialogue between genetics (nature) and environment (nurture). Clearly, infants are born with key brain areas genetically dedicated to language functions. Yet for children to learn the language of their culture, it is necessary that they have consistent, frequent opportunities to interact with a persistent caregiver who models the language with the child. Likewise, neuroscientists agree that a child's language capacity is dependent on the quality of language input (see Special Feature 2.1). Parents and caregivers who consistently engage in conversation with their infants actually help their children develop neural networks that lead to language fluency and proficiency (Healy, 1994, 1997; Kotulak, 1997; Sprenger, 1999; Oates & Grayson, 2004).

LINGUISTIC VOCABULARY LESSON

Linguistics is the study of language. To understand the complexities of linguistic acquisition better, we provide a brief discussion of the components of linguistic structure, of phonology, morphology, syntax, semantics, and pragmatics.

Phonology

The sound system of a particular language is its phonology, and the distinctive units of sound in a language are its phonemes. Individual phonemes are described according to how speakers modify the airstream they exhale to produce the particular sounds. In the English language, the number of phonemes ranges between 41 and 45; this variation depends on regional dialect.

Phonological development begins when sounds of speech activate neural networks in the infant's brain. This process begins during the last two months of prenatal development as babies are able to hear intonation patterns from their mother's voice (Shore, 1997).

In the search for the origins of language development, scientists around the world are discovering that early speech recognition actually begins in the womb, where the rhythms of the mother's voice and native language are communicated to the child—at approximately six months in utero—through the reverberations of bones of her body and the fluid in the womb (Jusczyk, 1997). After birth, face-to-face verbal interactions with caregivers allow babies to hear sounds of their native language(s) clearly and to observe how the mouth and tongue work to create these unique sounds. Simultaneously, as babies babble, they gain motor control of their vocal and breathing apparatus. Interactions with caregivers allow babies an opportunity to listen, observe, and attempt to mimic sounds they hear and the mouth and tongue movements they see. Through this process, babies begin to specialize in the sounds of their native language(s). The developmental window of opportunity (sometimes called the critical period) for mastering sound discrimination occurs within the first six months of an infant's life. By this time, babies' brains are already pruning out sensitivity to sounds that are not heard in their environment (Kuhl, 1993). This pruning is so efficient that children actually lose the ability to hear phonemes that are not used in their mother tongue. Children who consistently hear more than one language during this time may become native bi- or trilingual because they retain the ability to hear the subtle and discrete sounds.

Another important aspect of the English phonology is its prosody, or the stress and intonation patterns of the language. Stress refers to the force with which phonemes are articulated. Where the stress is placed may distinguish otherwise identical words (RECord [noun] versus reCORD [verb]). Intonation, on the other hand, refers to the pattern of stress and of rising and falling pitch that occurs within a sentence. These changes in intonation may shift the meaning of otherwise identical sentences:

IS she coming? (Is she or is she not coming?)
Is SHE coming? (Her, not anyone else)
Is she COMING? (Hurry up; it's about time)

Babies as young as four and five months old begin to experiment with the pitch, tone, and volume of the sounds they make and often produce sounds that mimic the tonal and stress qualities of their parents' speech.

Morphology

As babies' phonological development progresses, the infants begin to make morphemes. Morphemes are the smallest units of meaning in oral language. Although it used to be thought that children did not make word meaning to sound connect until around their first birthday, through the science of infant language acquisition we have learned a great deal more about how infants and toddlers develop language. For instance, scientists (Tincoff & Jusczyk, 1999) now report that the sounds that give parents such a thrill—*Mama, Dada*—actually mark the very beginning of human word comprehension. It is now believed that the origins of language—linking sound patterns with specific meanings—stem from discrete associations infants make, beginning with socially significant people, such as their parents, at six months of age. Real words are mixed with wordlike sounds (echolalia). As real words emerge, they can be categorized into the following:

> *Lexical:* individual meaning carrying words, such as *cat, baby*
>
> *Bound:* units of sound that hold meaning (like *re, un*) but that must be attached to other morphemes (*reorder, unbend*)
>
> *Derivational and inflectional:* usually suffixes that change the class of the word (i.e., noun to adjective: *dust* to *dusty;* verb to noun: *teaches* to *teacher*)
>
> *Compound:* two lexical morphemes that together may form a unique meaning, such as *football* or *cowboy*
>
> *Idiom:* an expression whose meaning cannot be derived from its individual parts (i.e., *Put your foot in your mouth* carries a very different meaning from the visual image it conjures)

Syntax

Syntax refers to how morphemes, or words, are combined to form sentences or units of thought. In English, there are two different types of order: linear and hierarchical structure. Linear structure refers to the object-verb arrangement. For example, *Building falls on man* means something very different than *Man falls on building.* Hierarchical structure refers to how words are grouped together within a sentence to reveal the speaker's intent. Different languages, however, have unique and inherent rules that govern syntax. A speaker of English might say: *The long, sleek, black cat chased the frightened tiny, gray mouse.* A language with syntactical rules that differ from English could state it this way: *Chasing the gray mouse, tiny and frightened, was the cat, long, sleek, and black.*

Shortly after their first birthdays, most children are able to convey their intentions with single words. Have you ever heard a young child use the powerful words *no* and *mine?* More complex, rule-driven communication usually emerges between the ages of two and three, when children are able to construct sentences of two or more words.

Although children have prewired capacity for language rules (such as past tense), adult scaffolding or support plays a significant role in extending and expanding a child's language development. For instance, when Joe says *deenk,* his day care teacher can extend and clarify Joe's intentions: *Joe, do you want to drink milk or juice?* If Joe says *I drinked all the milk,* his teacher might tactfully expand his statement. *Yes, Joe, you drank all your milk.* This type of subtle modeling is usually the most appropriate way to support children as they learn the conventional forms and complexities of their language. Yet even when adults expand a child's speech, the child's own internal rule-governing system may resist modification until the child is developmentally ready to make the change. The following interaction between a four-year-old and an interested adult illustrates this phenomenon (Gleason, 1967):

CHILD: My teacher holded the baby rabbits and we patted them.

ADULT: Did you say your teacher held the baby rabbit?

CHILD: Yes.

ADULT: What did you say that she did?

CHILD: She holded the baby rabbits and we patted them.

ADULT: Did you say she held them tightly?

CHILD: No. She holded them loose.

Semantics

"How would you differentiate among the following words that a blender manufacturer has printed under the row of buttons: stir, beat, puree, cream, chop, whip, crumb, mix, mince, grate, crush, blend, shred, grind, frappe, liquify?" (Lindfors, 1987; p. 47). Semantics deals with the subtle shades of meaning that language can convey. Variations in language meanings generally reflect the values and concerns of the culture. For instance, dozens of Arabic words may be dedicated to describing the camel's range of moods and behaviors. The Polynesian language has many words that define variations in the wind; likewise, Inuit languages include many words for snow.

Knowledge of word meaning is stored throughout the brain in a vast biological forest of interconnected neurons, dendrites, and synapses. Beyond culture, children's ongoing personal experience allows them to connect words and meaning. Because words are symbolic labels for objects, events, actions, and feelings, a child may initially call all four-legged animals *kittie*. After several firsthand encounters with kitties (with the support of adults who can help label and describe the event), however, a child will likely develop the concepts and vocabulary to discriminate kitties from doggies, kittens from cats, and, eventually, Persian cats from Siamese cats.

Pragmatics

Sitting in his bouncer, two-month-old Marcus studies his mother's face as she talks to him. In a high-pitched voice, she exaggerates her words in a singsong manner: *Lookeee at Mommeeee. I see baabee Marceee looking at Mommeee.* Baby Marcus appears to mimic her mouth movements and responds to her conversations with smiles, wiggles, and very loud coos. After Marcus quiets, his mother knowingly responds to her baby's comments, *Yes, you're right, Mommeee does love her Marceee-Boy.*

When parent and child engage in singsong conversation of "parentese" and baby vocalizations, the basic conventions of turn taking are learned, but rarely does the teacher or student realize that a lesson was being taught. Pragmatics deals with the conventions of becoming a competent language user. One convention, for

FIGURE 2.2   **Language Is More Than Words**

instance, include rules on how to engage successfully in conversation with others, such as how to initiate and sustain conversation, how to take turns, when and how to interrupt, how to use cues for indicating subject interest, and how to change subjects tactfully.

Pragmatics also refers to the uses of language (spoken and body) to communicate one's intent in real life. The message of a speaker's actual words may be heightened or may even convey the opposite meaning, depending on the manner in which the words are delivered. This delivery may include inflection, facial expressions, or body gestures. Take, for example, the statement *I'm having such a great time* (Figure 2.2). Imagine that the person saying this phrase is smiling easily and widely, with eyes making direct contact with the person with whom she is sharing her time. Now, picture the person saying *I'm having such a great time* while sneering and rolling her eyes. Although the words are identical, the intent of the two speakers is obviously completely different. Further, pragmatics deals with an increasing conscious awareness of being able to accomplish goals through the use of language.

As children mature, they are able to use social registers, or the ability to adapt their speech and mannerisms to accommodate different social situations. This level of communicative competence can be observed in children as young as five as they engage in pretend play. During dramatic play children may easily switch roles—baby to parent, student to teacher, customer to waiter—by using the vocabulary, mannerisms, and attitudes that convey the role they wish to play.

In reviewing these linguistic structures—phonology, morphology, syntax, semantic, and pragmatics—it seems amazing that children acquire these components naturally. Parents rarely teach these intricate conventions directly. Instead, children acquire these intricate communication skills by listening, imitating, practicing, observing, and interacting with supportive caregivers and peers.

OBSERVING THE DEVELOPMENT OF CHILDREN'S LANGUAGE

"One of the most remarkable cognitive achievements of early childhood is the acquisition of language" (Black, Puckett, & Bell, 1992, p. 179). By the time they enter school, most children have mastered the basic structures of language and are fairly accomplished communicators. Although individual variations do occur, this rapid acquisition of language tends to follow a predictable sequence.

This progression will be illustrated by following Dawn from infancy through second grade. Dawn is the child of educational researchers. Her development is like that of almost every other normal child throughout the world except that it was documented by her researcher-parents. Dawn's parents used a simple calendar-notation procedure to collect information about their children's language development. When Dawn's parents reviewed the date book/calendar each morning, new words were recorded. Thus, it became quite easy to document Dawn's growth over time. When these busy parents had a reflective moment, they recorded their recollections (vignettes) of an event and dated it. Often, at family celebrations, a video camera was used to record the events of Dawn's use of language in great detail. Occasionally, videotapes also documented story times. By using the calendar vignettes and the videotapes, Dawn's parents were able to marvel at her growth and development.

In Dawn's seven-year case study, we observe her language acquisition from a social-interactionist perspective and a neurobiological view. By intertwining the two views we can easily see how Dawn's language development is a dynamic interaction of her intentions, the physical coordination of her mouth and tongue, her neural development, and the support of her family members. This complex dance of nurture and nature reveals that Dawn's skills do not automatically develop at a certain point in brain maturation, but, by the same token, without a particular level of neural growth, Dawn would not be able to accomplish her goals.

Birth to One Month

During the first month of Dawn's life, most of her oral communication consisted of crying, crying, crying. The greatest challenge her parents faced was interpreting the subtle variations in her cries. It took about three weeks for them to understand that Dawn's intense, high-pitched cry meant that she was hungry. Dawn's short, throaty, almost shouting cries indicated that a change of diaper was necessary, and the whining, fussy cry, which occurred daily at about dinner time, meant she was tired.

At birth, the human brain is remarkably unfinished. Most of the one hundred billion neurons, or brain cells, are not yet connected. In fact, only two regions of the brain are fully functional at birth: the brain stem, which controls respiration, reflexes, and heartbeat; and the cerebellum, which controls the newborn's balance and muscle tone. Likewise, infants' sensory skills are rudimentary; for instance, newborns can only see objects within twelve to eighteen inches of their faces. Nonetheless, newborns are able to distinguish between faces, and other objects and they recognize the sound of their parents' voices. In fact, infants as young as one day old can recognize and show a preference for their native tongue (Juscyzk, Luce, & Charles-Luce, 1999).

Two to Three Months

During the second and third months after her birth, Dawn began to respond to her parents' voices. When spoken to, Dawn turned her head, focused her eyes on her mother or father, and appeared to listen and watch intensely. Her parents and grandparents also instinctively began using an exaggerated speech pattern called *parentese* (often called *baby talk*). Until recently, parents were cautioned against using baby talk or parentese with their infants because it was believed to foster immature forms of speech. Recent studies (Cowley, 1997; Field, Woodson, Greenberg, & Cohen, 1982; Healy, 1994; Shore, 1997), however, have demonstrated that this slowed-down, high-pitched, exaggerated, repetitive speech actually seems to facilitate a child's language development for two reasons:

■ The rate and pitch of parentese perfectly matches the infants' auditory processing speed. As babies mature, their brains eventually reach normal speech rates.

■ Parentese allows babies many opportunities to see and hear how sounds are made and, thus, to learn how to control their own vocal apparatus. As babies carefully observe parents, siblings, and other caregivers, they often mimic the tongue and mouth movements they see.

During the first three months of life, the number of neural synapses, or connections, increases twenty times to more than one thousand trillion. These neural connections are developed through daily verbal and physical interactions that the infant shares with parents, siblings, and other caregivers. Daily routines such as feeding and bathing reinforce and strengthen particular synapses, whereas neural networks that are not stimulated will eventually wither away in a process called neural pruning.

Four to Six Months

During conversations with her parents, Dawn would often move her mouth, lips, and eyes, mimicking the facial movements of her parents. At the beginning of the fourth month, Dawn discovered her own voice. She delighted in the range of sounds she could make and sometimes chuckled at herself. At this point, Dawn (and most normally developing infants) could make almost all the vowel and consonant sounds. She cooed and gurgled endlessly, joyfully experimenting with phonemic variations, pitch, and volume. When spoken to, she often began her own stream of conversation, called "sound play," which would parallel the adult speaker. At six months, Dawn was becoming an expert at imitating tone and inflection. For example, when her mother yelled at the cat for scratching the furniture, Dawn used her own vocal skills to yell at the poor animal, too.

The cerebral cortex, the part of the brain that is responsible for thinking and problem solving, represents 70 percent of the brain and is divided into two hemispheres. Each hemisphere has four lobes: the parietal, occipital, temporal, and frontal. Each lobe has numerous folds, which mature at different rates as the chemicals that foster brain development are released in waves. This sequential development explains, in part, why there are optimum times for physical and cognitive development. For instance, when a baby is three or four months old, neural connections within the parietal lobe (object recognition and eye–hand coordination), the temporal lobe (hearing and language), and the visual cortex have begun to strengthen and fine-tune. This development allows babies' eyes to focus on objects that are more than two feet away from their faces. This new ability allows them to recognize themselves in a mirror and begin to discern visually who's who. At this same time, babies begin to mimic the tongue and mouth movements they see. They also experiment with the range of new sounds they can make. These trills and coos are also bids for attention, as most babies have begun to make simple cause-and-effect associations, such as crying equals Momma's attention.

Six to Nine Months

During her sixth month, Dawn's muscle strength, balance, and coordination allowed her to have greater independent control over her environment as she mastered the fine art of crawling and stumble-walking around furniture. These physical accomplishments stimulated further cognitive development because she now had the ability to explore the world under her own power.

At seven months, Dawn's babbling increased dramatically. The sounds she produced now, however, began to sound like words, which she would repeat over and over. This type of vocalizing is called *echolalia*. Although "MmmaaaMmmaaa" and "Dddaaaddaaa" sounded like "Mama" and "DaDa," they were still not words with a cognitive connection or meaning.

In her eighth month, Dawn's babbling began to exhibit conversation-like tones and behaviors. This pattern of speech is called *vocables*. Although there were still no real words in her babble, Dawn's vocalizations were beginning to take on some of the conventions of adult conversation, such as turn taking, eye contact, and recognizable gestures. These forms of prelanguage are playlike in nature, being done for their own sake rather than as a deliberate use of language to communicate a need or accomplish a goal.

At approximately nine months, Dawn first used real, goal-oriented language. As her father came home from work, she crawled to him shouting in an excited voice, "Dada, Dada," and held her arms up to him. Dawn's accurate labeling of her father and her use of body language that expressed desire to be picked up were deliberate actions that revealed that Dawn was using language to accomplish her objectives.

As a child matures, the actual number of neurons remains relatively stable. The human brain, however, triples its birth weight within the first three years of a child's life. This change is caused as neurons are stimulated and synapse connections increase and the message-receiving dendrite branches grow larger and heavier. In addition, the long axons over which sensory messages travel gradually develop a protective coating of a white, fatty substance called myelin. Myelin insulates the axons and makes the transmission of sensory information more efficient. Myelineation occurs at different times in different parts of the brain and seems to coincide with the emergence of various physical skills and cognitive abilities. For instance, the neuromuscular development during the first months of life is dramatic. Within the first six months, helpless infants develop the muscle tone and coordination that allow them to turn over at will. Babies develop a sense of balance and better eye–hand coordination as neural connections in the cerebellum and parietal lobe strength, which allows most six-month-old babies to sit upright, with adult support, and successfully grasp objects within their reach. The ability to hold and inspect interesting items gives babies a lot to "talk" about.

Between six and seven months, the brain has already created permanent neural networks that recognize the sounds of a child's native language(s) or dialect. Next, babies begin to distinguish syllables, which soon enables them to detect word boundaries. Prior to this, the phrase, "doyouwantyourbottle?" was a pleasant tune, but it was not explicit communication. After auditory boundaries become apparent, babies will hear distinct words: "Do / you / want / your / BOTTLE?" As sounds become words that are frequently used in context to label a specific object, the acquisition of word meaning begins. At this stage of development, babies usually recognize and have cognitive meaning for words such as bottle, momma, and daddy. Their receptive or listening vocabulary grows rapidly, although it will take a few more months before their expressive or oral language catches up.

From about the eighth to the ninth month, the hippocampus becomes fully functional. Located in the center of the brain, the hippocampus is part of the limbic system. it helps index and file memories, and, as the hippocampus matures, babies are able to form memories. For instance, at this age, babies can now remember that when they push the button on the busy box it will squeak. At this point, babies' ability to determine cause-and-effect and remember words greatly increases.

Nine to Twelve Months

Between age nine months and her first birthday, Dawn's expressive (speaking) and receptive (listening and comprehending) vocabulary grew rapidly. She could understand and comply with dozens of simple requests, such as "Bring Mommy your shoes" or the favorite label-the-body game, "Where is Daddy's nose?" In addition, Dawn's command of nonverbal gestures and facial expressions were expanding from waving "bye-bye" to scowling and saying "no-no" when taking her medicine. In addition, holophrastic words began to emerge, in which one word carried the semantic burden for a whole sentence or phrase. For example, "keeths," while holding her plastic keys, purse, and sunglasses meant "I want to go for a ride," and "iith" meant "I want some ice." Dawn also used overgeneralized speech in which each word embraced many meanings. For instance, *doll* referred not only to her favorite baby doll but to everything in her toy box, and *jooth* stood for any type of liquid she drank.

At the end of the first year, the prefrontal cortex, the seat of forethought and logic, forms synapses at a rapid rate. In fact, by age one, the full cortex consumes twice as much energy as an adult brain. This incredible pace continues during the child's first decade of life. The increased cognitive capacity and physical dexterity stimulate curiosity and exploration and a deep desire to understand how things work. Neural readiness, in combination with countless hours of sound play and verbal exchanges with loving caregivers, allows most children to begin speaking their first words.

Twelve to Eighteen Months

After her first birthday, Dawn's vocabulary expanded quickly. Most of her words identified or labeled the people, pets, and objects that were familiar and meaningful to her. Eve Clark's research (1983) suggests that young children between one and six will learn and remember approximately nine new words a day. This ability to relate new words to preexisting internalized concepts, and then remember and use them after only one exposure, is called *fast mapping* (Carey, 1979).

Because chronological age is not a reliable indicator of language progression, linguists typically describe language development by noting the number of words used in a sentence, called mean length of utterance. At this point, Dawn was beginning to use two-word sentences such as "Kitty juuth." Linguists call these two- and three-word sentences "telegraphic speech" because they contain only the most necessary of words to convey meaning. These first sentences, however, may have many interpretations; for instance, Dawn's sentence "Kitty juuth" might mean "The kitty wants some milk" or "The kitty drank the milk" or even "The kitty stuck her head in my cup and drank my milk." Obviously the context in which the sentence was spoken helped her parents better understand the intent or meaning of her communication.

By eighteen months, neural synapses have increased and strengthened and are beginning to transmit information quite efficiently; hence, most toddlers begin to experience a language "explosion." Brain-imaging technology clearly reveals that the full cortex is involved in processing language. During this time, children are able to learn as many as twelve words a day. Linguists call this phonenomenon fast mapping.

Eighteen to Twenty-four Months

Around age eighteen months to two years, as Dawn began using sentences more frequently, the use of syntax became apparent. "No shoes" with a shoulder shrug meant that she couldn't find her shoes, but "Shoes, no!" said with a shaking head, meant that Dawn did not want to put on her shoes.

At two years of age, most children have fully wired brains and nimble fingers and are sturdy on their feet. Although they are generally aware of cause and effect, they are still unable to foresee potential problems. In other words, children's physical abilities may exceed their common sense. By this time, most children are able to use language to communicate their needs and accomplish their goals. Increased neural activity, plus verbal expression and physical skill, also gives rise to greater independence. At this time, parents may hear the word "No!" quite often.

Biologically, the brain is fully functional by this time. The remainder of a child's language development relies on the experiences and opportunities the child has to hear and use language with more experienced language users.

Twenty-four to Thirty-six Months

Although Dawn's vocabulary grew, her phonemic competence did not always reflect adult standards. Many of her words were clearly pronounced (*kitty, baby*), whereas others were interesting phonemic attempts or approximations (*bise* for *bike, Papa* for *Grandpa, bawble* for *bottle*); others were her own construction (*NaNe* for *Grandma*). At this age, most children are unable to articulate perfectly the sounds of adult speech. Rather, they simplify the adult sounds to ones they can produce. Sometimes they pronounce the initial sound or syllable of a word (*whee* for *wheel*), and at other times they pronounce only the final sound or syllable (*ees* for *cheese*). Another common feature is temporary regression, meaning that they may pronounce a word or phrase quite clearly and then later produce a shortened, less mature version. This phase, too, is a normal language developmental phase for all children. Thus, it is important that parents accept their child's language and not become overly concerned with correcting their pronunciation.

Likewise, children's early attempts to use sentences need thoughtful support, not critical correction. Parents can best support their child's attempts to communicate through extensions and expansions. Extensions include responses that incorporate the essence of a child's sentence but transform it into a well-formed sentence. For example, when Dawn said, "ree stor-ee," her father responded, "Do you want me to read the storybook to you?" When parents and caregivers use extensions, they model appropriate grammar and fluent speech and actually help extend a child's vocabulary.

When parents use expansions, they gently reshape the child's efforts to reflect grammatically appropriate content. For example, when Dawn said, "We goed to Diseelan," instead of correcting her ("We don't say *goed* we say *went*") her mother expanded Dawn's language by initially confirming the intent of Dawn's statement while modeling the correct form: "Yes, we went to Disneyland."

The adaptations parents make when talking to young children—such as slowing the rate of speech, using age-appropriate vocabulary, questioning and clarifying the child's statements, and extensions and expansions—occur in all cultures. These early interactions with children and the gradual and building support is called parentese or, more gender-specifically, motherese and fatherese. When parents use this form of support, they are actually helping their children gain communicative competence and confidence (White, 1985). Between the ages of two and three, Dawn's language had developed to the point at which she could express her needs and describe her world to others quite well. In addition to using pronouns, she also began to produce grammatical inflections: -*ing*, plurals, the past tense, and the possessive.

STATEMENT	AGE*
"I lub you, Mama."	2.0
"Boot's crywing."	2.1
"Dawn's baby dawl."	2.2
"My books."	2.4
"Grover droppted the radio."	2.6
"Cookie monster shutted the door."	2.8
"She's not nice to me."	2.9
"Daddy's face got stickers, they scratch."	3.0

*Age given in years and months.

Dawn also loved finger plays such as the "Itsy, Bitsy Spider" and "Grandma's Glasses," poems such as "This Little Pig," and songs such as "Jingle Bells," "Yankee Doodle," and the "Alphabet Song." She was also beginning to count and echo-read with her parents when they read her favorite stories. For instance, when her parents read "Three Little Pigs" to her, Dawn would "huff and puff and blow your house down" as many times as they would read the story.

Three to Four Years

Dawn had become a proficient language user. She could make requests, "Please, may I have some more cake?" and demands, "I need this, now!" depending on her mood and motivation. She could seek assistance, "Can you tell me where the toys are?" and demonstrate concern, "What's the matter, Mama?" She sought information about her world, "Why is the moon round one time and just a grin sometimes?" She could carry on detailed conversations just as she did in the grocery store at 4.0 (four years and no months):

MOM: Dawn, what juice did you want?

DAWN: Orange juice. but not the kind that has the little chewy stuff in it.

MOM: That is called pulp.

DAWN: Pulp—ick! I don't like it because it tasted badly.

MOM: Well, do you remember what kind has the pulp?

DAWN: You know, it comes in the orange can and has the picture of the bunny on it.

MOM: Well, there are several kinds in orange cans.

DAWN: Mom, I know that, cause orange juice is orange. But this one I don't like, at all, has a bunny on it.

MOM: Can you remember the name?

DAWN: Yeah, the writing words have a-b-c-o.

MOM: Oh, I know, the store's brand, abco.

DAWN: Yes, here it is. Now don't buy it!!

Four to Five Years

Dawn began to engage in dramatic play, using her knowledge of common events in familiar settings such as the grocery store and the doctor's office to act out life scripts with other children. These dramas allowed Dawn and her peers the opportunity to use their language in many functional and imaginative ways. Her favorite script was the restaurant; she always enjoyed being the waitress, describing the daily special to her customers, and then pretending to write their orders.

Jim Johnson, Jim Christie, and Thomas Yawkey (1999) suggest that during dramatic play, two types of communication can occur. First, *pretend communication* takes place when the child assumes a role and talks, in character, to other characters in the drama. The second type, *metacommunication,* occurs when the children stop the ongoing dramatic-play script and discuss the plot or character actions. The following is an example of metacommunication between Dawn and her friend Jennifer at five-and-a-half years:

DAWN: Pretend you ordered pizza and I have to make it, okay?

JENNIFER: Okay, but it should be cheese pizza, 'cause I like it best.

DAWN: Okay, I can use yellow strings [yarn] for the cheese.

JENNIFER: Waitress, I want yellow cheese pizza, in a hurry. I'm hungry.

Six to Eight Years

Almost all six- to eight-year-old children have extremely elaborate vocabularies, with estimates ranging between twenty-five hundred and eight thousand words (Gleason, 1967). During these years, Dawn's expressive and receptive vocabulary continued to grow as she interacted with teachers, classmates, and family. There are, however, differences between home and school language. Classroom language may be more formalized because children respond to specific, fact-oriented, teacher-directed questions. To illustrate this point, the following dramatic-play scenario took place in Dawn's bedroom, where she had established a pretend school consisting of a teacher's desk, student's table, chalkboard, reading books, paper, pencils, and markers. Dawn (age 6.6 years), wearing high heels, a long, dark dress and jacket, and an old pair of glasses, had assumed the role of teacher, while two classmates, Amy and Jennifer, took the roles of students.

> **DAWN:** [standing very straight and holding the chalk] What is the first thing we write on the page? Class, together, one, two, three.
>
> **CLASS:** [in unison] Our name.
>
> **DAWN:** What goes on the paper next? Class, together, one, two, three.
>
> **CLASS:** [in unison] The date.
>
> **DAWN:** Good thinking, students. You may begin your assignment.

During this play episode, it became clear that Dawn had carefully observed her teacher's dress, mannerisms, voice inflection, and tone. Dawn's portrayal of her teacher also demonstrated how easily children may adapt their speech pattern to effectively role-play adult characters or to interact with adults or other children in many different contexts. Children appear to modify their communication style intuitively by assessing multiple social factors such as the age, gender, and status of the person with whom they are interacting and the context in which the conversation is taking place. The combination of these variables will significantly influence what children say and how they say it. In other words, Dawn might behave and communicate quite freely with peers her own age, yet she might act much more formally and maturely around the teenage babysitter. This ability is sometimes called *language register.*

Although classroom conversation may be more structured, playground conversations with peers are generally more colorful and imaginative, as children integrate information from television, movies, books, and comics. The following scenario with Dawn at age 7.0 years provides an illustration.

> **DAWN:** Jason, Jason, *Jason!!!!*
>
> **JASON:** What?
>
> **DAWN:** I'm going to be Princess Leia from *Star Wars* for Halloween.
>
> **JASON:** Well, you maybe can be her, but you can't have the "force" with you.
>
> **DAWN:** I can too.
>
> **JASON:** Nu-uh.
>
> **DAWN:** Yes, sir.
>
> **JASON:** You can't 'cause only boys can have the force, like Luke Skywalker and Yoda.

>   **DAWN:**   Well, Princess Leia can shoot zappers and boss Han Solo.
>
>   **JASON:**   Maybe so, but she'll never be a boy!

Dawn's language development, although completely normal, is also a human miracle. Language plays a central role in learning, and the success of children in school depends to a very large degree on their ability to speak and listen. Dawn's case study also confirms the critical role of social interaction in language development. In recognition of this importance, the following section provides more information about how parents and caregivers can support a child's language acquisition.

WHAT IS NORMAL LANGUAGE DEVELOPMENT?

Even though the process of learning to talk follows a predictable sequence, the age at which children say their first word may vary widely from one child to another. Developmental guidelines provide descriptions of specific behaviors and delineate the age at which most children demonstrate this physical or cognitive skill. This type of information helps parents and physicians anticipate normal physical and cognitive growth. Physical maturation is easy to observe, but cognitive development is less obvious. Fortunately, children's language development provides one indication that their cognitive abilities are developing normally. Table 2.1 presents the average ages for language acquisition and reviews Dawn's development from birth to age two. In comparing their progress, it is clear that both children followed the same sequence of language acquisition, but at different rates. Although the age they displayed specific skills differed, their language abilities matured within the age range offered for normal language development. Most children demonstrate language skills well within the normal age range, but some do not. If a child's language is delayed more than two months past the upper age limits, caregivers should seek medical guidance, as delays may indicate problems (Copeland & Gleason, 1993; Oates & Grayson, 2004). Early identification of problems leads to appropriate intervention.

Although helpful, developmental guidelines are not perfect. To determine norms, data must be collected on specific populations. In most cases, these data were collected on middle-income Caucasian children born in modern industrial-technological societies. Because this sample does not represent the world's population, the upper and lower age limits of these "universal" norms must be interpreted carefully.

FACTORS CONTRIBUTING TO VARIATION IN RATE OF LANGUAGE ACQUISITION

Because the critical period for language development occurs within the first thirty-six months of a child's life, significant language delay may indicate specific medical or cognitive problems. Beyond medical problems, several factors could modify

TABLE 2.1   Language Development Chart

AGE IN MONTHS	TYPICAL LANGUAGE DEVELOPMENT
0–3	Majority of communication consists of crying because larynx has not yet descended. Turns head to the direction of the families voices. Is startled by loud or surprising sounds.
3–6	Begins to make cooing sounds to solicit attention from caregivers. Makes "raspberry" sounds. Begins to play with voice. Carefully observes caregiver's face when being spoken to, often tries to shape mouth in a similar manner.
6	Vocalization with intonation. Responds to his or her name. Responds to human voices without visual cues by turning his or her head and eyes. Responds appropriately to friendly and angry tones.
12	Uses one or more words with meaning (may be a fragment of a word). Understands simple instructions, especially if vocal or physical cues are given. Practices inflection. Is aware of the social value of speech.
18	Has a vocabulary of approximately five to twenty words. Vocabulary is made up chiefly of nouns. Some echolalia (repeating a word or phrase over and over). Much jargon with emotional content. Is able to follow simple commands.
24	Can name a number of objects common to his or her surroundings. Is able to use at least two prepositions such as *in, on, under.* Combines words into a short sentence, largely noun–verb combinations. Approximately two-thirds of what child says should be understandable. Vocabulary of approximately 150 to 300 words. Rhythm and fluency often poor; volume and pitch of voice not yet controlled well. Can use pronouns such as *I, me, you.* *My* and *mine* are beginning to emerge. Responds to such commands as "Show me your eyes (nose, mouth, hair)."
36	Is using some plurals and past tenses: "We played a lot." Handles three word sentences easily: "I want candy." Has approximately 900 to 1000 words in vocabulary. About 90 percent of what child says should be understandable. Verbs, such as "let's go, let's run, let's climb, and let's play," begin to predominate. Understands most simple questions dealing with his environment and activities. Relates his or her experiences so that they can be followed with reason. Is able to reason out such questions as "What do you do when you are hungry?" Should be able to give his or her sex, name, and age.
48	Knows names of familiar animals. Names common objects in picture books or magazines. Knows one or more colors and common shapes.

(continued)

TABLE 2.1   Continued

AGE IN MONTHS	TYPICAL LANGUAGE DEVELOPMENT
	Can repeat four digits when they are given slowly.
	Can usually repeat words of four syllables.
	Demonstrates understanding of *over* and *under*.
	Often engages in make-believe.
	Extensive verbalization as he or she carries out activities.
	Understands such concepts as *longer* and *larger* when a contrast is presented.
	Much repetition of words, phrases, syllables, and even sounds.
60	Can use many descriptive words, both adjectives and adverbs, spontaneously.-
	Knows common opposites: *big–little, hard–soft, heavy–light*.
	Speech should be completely intelligible, despite articulation problems.
	Should be able to define common objects in terms of use (hat, shoe, chair).
	Should be able to follow three commands given without interruptions.
	Can use simple time concepts: morning, night, tomorrow, yesterday, today.
	Speech on the whole should be grammatically correct.
72	Speech should be completely intelligible and socially useful.
	Should be able to tell a rather connected story about a picture, seeing relationships between objects and happenings.
	Can recall a story or a favorite video.
	Should be able to repeat sentences as long as nine words.
	Can describe favorite pastimes, meals, books, and friends.
	Should be using fairly long sentences and should use some compound and some complex sentences.

the rate of normal language production. We review these factors in the following discussion.

Gender Differences

Are there differences in the rate and ways that boys and girls develop language fluency and proficiency? This question reflects another facet of the ongoing nature versus nurture debate. Observational research consistently reveals that a majority of girls talk earlier and talk more than the majority of boys. It is also true that the majority of late talkers are young boys (Healy, 1997; Kalb & Namuth, 1997). Yet it is difficult to determine whether differences in the rate of language acquisition are biological or whether biological differences are exaggerated by social influences. There is evidence for both views. For example, neural-biological research offers graphic images that illustrate how men's and women's brains process language somewhat differently (Corballis, 1991; Moir & Jessel, 1991). Although this research appears to support nature as the dominant factor in language differences, it is also important to consider how powerful a role nurture plays. Experimental research consistently documents differential treatment of infants based on gender. In other words, men and women tend to cuddle, coo at, and engage in lengthy face-to-face conversations with baby girls. Yet, with baby boys, adults are likely to exhibit "jiggling and bouncing" behaviors but are not as likely to engage in sustained face-to-face verbal interactions. Perhaps girls talk earlier and talk more because they receive more language stimulation (Huttenlocher, 1991).

Socioeconomic Level

Numerous studies have documented the differences in the rate of language acquisition and the level of language proficiency between low- and middle-socioeconomic families (Hart & Risley, 1995; Morisset, 1995; Walker, Greenwood, Hart, & Carta, 1994). These studies found that children, especially boys, from low-income homes were usually somewhat slower to use expressive language than children from middle-income homes. These findings likely reflect social-class differences both in language use in general and in parent–child interaction patterns. For example, Betty Hart and Todd Risley (1995) estimate that, by age four, children from professional families have had a cumulative total of fifty million words addressed to them, whereas as children from welfare families have been exposed to only thirteen million words. The children from professional families have had more than three times the linguistic input than welfare families' children, which gives them a tremendous advantage in language acquisition.

Results of long-term observations of middle-income and lower-income families concluded that all mothers spent a great deal of time nurturing their infants (e.g., touching, hugging, kissing, and holding), but that there were differences in the way mothers verbally interacted with their children. Middle-income mothers spent a great deal more time initiating verbal interactions and usually responded to and praised their infants' vocal efforts. Middle-income mothers were also more likely to imitate their infants' vocalizations. These verbal interactions stimulate neural-synapse networks that foster expressive and receptive language. It is still unclear why lower-income mothers do not engage their children in verbal interactions at the same level as middle-income mothers. The authors of these studies speculate that this finding may be a reflection of social-class differences in language use in general.

Cultural Influences

The rate of language acquisition may be somewhat different for children of different cultures. Because spoken language is a reflection of the culture from which it emerges, it is necessary to consider the needs verbal language serves in the culture. Communication may be accomplished in other meaningful ways (Bhavnagri & Gonzalez-Mena, 1997). Janet Gonzalez-Mena (1997, p. 70) offers this example:

The emphasizing or de-emphasizing of the verbal starts from the beginning with the way babies are treated. Babies carried around much of the time get good at sending messages nonverbally, through changing body positions or tensing up or relaxing muscles. They are encouraged to communicate this way when their caregivers pick up the messages they send. They do not need to depend on words at an early age. Babies who are physically apart from their caregivers learn the benefits of verbal communication. If the babies are on the floor in the infant playpen or in the other room at home, they need to learn to use their voices to get attention. Changing position or tensing muscles goes unperceived by the distant adult.

Likewise, some cultures do not view babies' vocal attempts as meaningful communication. Shirley Brice Heath (1983) describes a community in which infants' early vocalizations are virtually ignored and adults do not generally address much of their talk directly to infants. Many cultures emphasize receptive language, and children listen as adults speak.

Medical Concerns

Beyond gender, socioeconomic, and culture differences, other reasons children's language may be delayed include temporary medical problems or congenital complications, including hearing loss. Estimates of hearing impairments vary considerably, with one widely accepted figure of 5 percent representing the portion of school-aged children with hearing levels outside the normal range. Detection and diagnosis of hearing impairment have become very sophisticated. It is possible to detect the presence of hearing loss and evaluate it severity in a newborn child. There are four types of hearing loss:

- Conductive hearing losses are caused by diseases or obstructions in the outer or middle ear and can usually be helped with a hearing aid.
- Sensorineural losses result from damage to the sensory hair cells of the inner ear or the nerves that supply it and may not respond to the use of a hearing aid.
- Mixed hearing losses are those in which the problem occurs both in the outer or middle ear and in the inner ear.
- A central hearing loss results from damage to the nerves or brain.

In Special Feature 2.2, we provide an example of one the most common childhood problems, otitis media, that, when left unattended, could cause significant language delays, speech distortion, and, ultimately, difficulty in learning to read and write.

Language Disorders

For most children, learning to communicate is a natural, predictable developmental progression. Unfortunately, some children have congenital language disorders that impair their ability to learn language or use it effectively. The origin of these disorders may be physical or neurological. Examples of physical problems include

SPECIAL FEATURE 2.2
She Just Stopped Talking

On her first birthday, Tiffany mimic-sang "Hap Birffaay meee" over and over. She said "Sank oo" when she received her birthday gifts and "Bye, seeoo" when her guests left. Later that summer, after a bad bout with an ear infection, Tiffany's mother noticed that Tiffany was turning up the volume on the television when she watched *Sesame Street*. A few days later, after several restless nights, Tiffany became very fussy and irritable and began tugging on her ear. Her parents again took her to the doctor, who diagnosed another ear infection. After a ten-day treatment of antibiotics, Tiffany appeared to be fine, except that she seemed to talk less and less.

About a month later, the situation worsened. Tiffany would not respond to her mother's speech unless she was looking directly at her mother. At that point Tiffany had, for the most part, stopped talking.

Tiffany's story is all too common. She was suffering from otitis media, an inflammation of the middle part of the ear. The symptoms of otitis media usually appear during or after a cold or respiratory infection. Because fluid can collect in the middle ear (behind the eardrum) without causing pain, children with otitis media may not complain. in the following list of possible symptoms, any one symptom could indicate that a child has otitis media:

- Earaches or draining of the ears
- Fever
- Changes in sleeping or eating habits
- Irritability
- Rubbing or pulling at the ears
- Cessation of babbling and singing
- Turning up the television or radio volume much louder than usual
- Frequently need to have directions and information repeated
- Unclear speech

- Use of gestures rather than speech
- Delayed speech and language development

From twelve months through four years of age, language development is at its peak. Even a temporary hearing loss during this time interferes with speech articulation and language learning. Otitis media causes temporary loss of hearing when the fluid pushes against the eardrum. The pressure prevents the eardrum from vibrating, so sound waves cannot move to the inner ear and the child's hearing is greatly distorted or muffled. Consequently, final consonant sounds and word endings are often unheard, and words blend into one another. Because one of the main reasons people talk is to communicate, a child who cannot understand what is said becomes frustrated and easily distracted. This type of hearing loss may continue for up to six weeks after the ear infection has healed.

Although hearing loss caused by otitis media is described as "mild and fluctuating," it is a major cause of speech distortion and language delay in the preschool years. If left untreated, young children with recurrent and persistent otitis media may develop permanent hearing loss, speech distortions, language delays, and problems with focusing attention.

When Tiffany's parents realized that she had stopped speaking, their pediatrician referred them to an otolaryngologist (ear, nose, and throat specialist). The doctor was pleased that Tiffany's parents had written down new words Tiffany had used on the family calendar. As the doctor reviewed the calendar, it became apparent that Tiffany's normal language development had virtually stopped. He did not seem surprised when her parents mentioned that she had also stopped babbling and singing and that she no longer danced when music was played. Because Tiffany's pediatrician had already tried three

(continued on next page)

months of antibiotics to control the infection with no success, the specialist suggested surgically placing bilateral vent tubes in the eardrum to drain the fluid from the middle ear. When the fluid is drained, the eardrum can then vibrate freely once again and normal hearing may be restored.

After a brief operation (approximately thirty minutes), eighteen-month-old Tiffany began to speak once again. Although her hearing was restored, the doctor suggested that Tiffany and her parents visit a speech therapist to help her fully regain her language.

Within a year, Tiffany's development was progressing normally, and by age three, the surgically implanted tubes naturally fell out of her eardrums. Since that time, Tiffany has not had a recurrence of otitis media.

malformation of the structures in the inner ear and a poorly formed palate. Neurological problems include dysfunction in the brain's ability to perceive or interpret the sounds of language.

Although the symptoms of various language disorders may appear to be similar, effective treatment may differ significantly, depending on the cause of the problem. For example, articulation problems caused by a physical malformation of the palate might require reconstructive surgery, whereas articulation problems caused by hearing impairment might require a combination of auditory amplification and speech therapy. Two of the most common symptoms of congenital language disorders are disfluency and pronunciation.

Disfluency. Children with fluency disorders have difficulty speaking rapidly and continuously. They may speak with an abnormal rate, such as too fast or too slow; in either case, their speech is often incomprehensible and unclearly articulated. The rhythm of their speech may also be severely affected. Stuttering is the most common form of this disorder. Many children may have temporary fluency disruptions or stuttering problems as they are learning to express themselves in sentences. Children who are making a transition to a second language may also experience brief stuttering episodes. It is important for parents or teachers to be patient and supportive because it may take time to distinguish normal developmental or temporary lapses in fluency from a true pathology. Stuttering may have multiple origins and may vary from child to child. Regardless of cause, recently developed treatment protocols have been effective in helping stutterers.

Pronunciation. Articulation disorders make up a wide range of problems and may have an equally broad array of causes. Minor misarticulations in the preschool years are usually developmental and will generally improve as the child matures. Occasionally, as children lose their baby teeth, they may experience temporary challenges in articulation (see Special Feature 2.3). Articulation problems that seriously impede a child's ability to communicate needs and intentions,

SPECIAL FEATURE 2.3
Temporary Articulation Problems

Three-year-old Annie points to a picture of an elephant and says, Yes, that's a ella-pant.

Two-year-old Briar sees her favorite television show and shouts, *It's da Giggles!* (Wiggles)

Two-and-a-half-year-old Robbie asks his grandma, *Gigi, can I have some tandy?* (Candy)

Parents both delight in and worry about these darling mispronunciations, which are a normal part of the language development process.

Mispronunciations are usually caused by a combination of children mishearing sounds and misarticulation of new words. Most of these mispronunciations self-correct with maturation. The following list provides speech-language pathologists terms for specific mispronunciations, examples of the articulation error, and the typical age these mispronunciations disappear.

Speech Pathologists' Term	Example	Age of Maturation*
Context-sensitive voicing	cup = gup	3.0
Final devoicing	bed = bet	3.0
Final consonant deletion	boat = bow	3.3
Velar fronting	car = tar	3.6
Consonant harmony	kittycat = tittytat	3.9
Weak syllable deletion	elephant = effant	4.0
Cluster reduction	spoon = boon	4.0
Gliding of liquids	leg = weg	5.0

* Ages given in years and months.

Some children may simply show delayed language development, which may mean that a child is gaining control over speaking mechanisms at a slower rate than same-age peers or has had limited opportunity to hear speech or to interact with others. Children who are learning a second language may also appear to have articulation difficulties when they attempt to use their second language. As explained in Special Feature 2.4, anyone learning a new phonemic system will experience some difficulty in expressing new sound combinations. "Bilingual children should be assessed in their native language and referred for therapy only if an articulation disorder is present in that language" (Piper, 1993, p. 193). Caregivers and teachers should not confuse the normal course of second-language acquisition with speech disorders.

however, must be diagnosed. Causes of such problems may include malformation of the mouth, tongue, or palate; partial loss of hearing due to a disorder in the inner ear; serious brain trauma; or a temporary hearing loss due to an ear infection (Copeland & Gleason, 1993).

Young Children's Second-Language Development

BY SARAH HUDELSON AND IRENE SERNA

Have you ever been in a situation in which everyone around you is using a language that you do not know? How did you feel when the language around you sounded like gibberish? How did you respond? Were there some strategies that you used to cope? Think about yourself in this kind of situation as you read about young children learning a second language.

In this chapter, you have learned about how children acquire their native language. Dawn's language acquisition is typical for a child brought up in a monolingual home, that is, a home in which one language is spoken. A growing number of children in the United States, however, are raised in homes in which two languages are used regularly and in which two languages are addressed to young children. Children raised in such bilingual environments have not one but two native languages, what Swain (1972) refers to as bilingualism as a native language.

Years ago, there was concern that young children would be cognitively damaged by such early exposure to two languages, that there would be considerable confusion on the child's part, and that normal language development would be delayed (Hakuta, 1986). Recent investigations, however, have made it clear that these assumptions are not true. Ample evidence now supports that young children raised from birth with two languages develop language at rates comparable to monolingual children. They begin to use single words and multilingual word combinations at the same time as monolingual children. Young bilingual children develop separate language systems and use them appropriately (Hakuta, 1986). Depending on the frequency of use, one language may develop more fully than the other. It is also common for young bilingual speakers to borrow words from one language and use them in speaking the other language so

as to communicate their intentions. Fluency in two languages, however, is a common occurrence among young children (see Goodz, 1994, for a review of research on preschool bilingualism). It is certainly possible that some of the young children in a prekindergarten or primary grade classroom will be bilingual in English and another language.

It is even more probable, however, that a classroom will contain some children whose native language is other than English: Spanish, French, Russian, Polish, Croatian, Arabic, Vietnamese, Chinese, Khmer, Japanese, Urdu, Navajo, Hopi, Apache, to name a few. Millions of young children in the United States are being raised in households in which a language other than English is spoken (Waggoner, 1992). Cultural and linguistic diversity is increasing in U.S. schools. Like monolingual English speakers, non-English-speaking children have learned their native languages by living in and being socialized into particular speech communities. Non-English-speaking children come to school having acquired the structural systems (phonological, syntactic, morphological, semantic) of one language as well as the pragmatics of what is appropriate language use—in terms of social and cultural norms—of their native language speech community. Thus, these learners bring to school understandings of what language is, what language can do, what language is for, and how to use language appropriately in their own communities (Lindfors, 1987).

Often, appropriate ways of using language in these diverse communities are significantly different from the ways of mainstream English-speaking children. For example, Concha Delgado-Gaitan and Henry Trueba (1991), studying the language socialization of Mexican immigrant children in one California town, discovered that young children were socialized to talk with their siblings and other children, yet to be quiet around adults.

When young speakers of languages other than English enter school, they may be fortunate enough to be placed in bilingual classrooms, where children and adults make use of the native language for learning and where the English language and academic instruction through English are introduced gradually. Alternatively, they may find themselves in settings in which English is the basic language of the class and of instruction. In either case, children find themselves in the position of acquiring English as a second or additional language (ESL). Such children must develop new ways of expressing themselves, new ways of talking about their experiences, new ways of asking questions, and new ways of using language to help them learn. They must also learn to behave appropriately in settings, including school, in which the new language is used. This hard work makes them strive both to understand the language around them and to use that language for themselves and with others (Lindfors, 1987; Tabors & Snow, 1994).

The perspective on child second-language acquisition that most researchers and educators take is similar to the social-interactionist perspective articulated in this chapter. That is, in learning a new language, children engage in the creative construction of the rules of the new language, and this creative construction occurs within the context of multiple social interactions as children use the new language with others (Allen, 1991). The discussion that follows summarizes some essential points about children's ESL acquisition. Most of the understandings presented have been formulated through careful observation of children and teachers in prekindergarten and primary grade settings.

Creative construction means that the ESL learner is not simply an empty jar into which the new language is poured. Rather, the learner is an active participant in the development of abilities in the new language. Learners use language from the environment and from specific others to make predictions about how English works, and then they try these predictions in the form of English utterances. Sometimes learners predict that the second language works like the first one, and sounds, lexical items and morphosyntactic patterns from the native language may influence English. Always, creative construction involves making mistakes, but mistakes need to be seen as the learner's attempt to make sense of the new language, to figure out how that language is put together (Allen, 1991).

Nora, a first-grade Spanish-speaking child whose acquisition of English was studied by respected researcher Lily Wong Fillmore (1976), provides a good demonstration of the child as creative constructor. Early in first grade, Nora memorized such phrases as "Do you wanna play?" and used them to initiate contact with English-speaking children. Soon she began to use the phrase "How do you do dese?" as a general formula to ask for information and help. After a while she added elements to the formula so that she could ask such questions as "How do you do dese little tortillas?" and "How do you do dese in English?" Gradually, she was able to vary the sentence after the word you to produce "How do you like to be cookie cutter?" "How do you make the flower?" and "How do you gonna make these?" She was also able to use *did* as in "How did you lost it?" Later still, she was able to use *how* in sentences very different from the original formula, as in "Because when I call him, how I put the number?" (pp. 246–247). These efforts illustrate how Nora, over time, constructed and reconstructed her English to convey her meanings and accomplish her purposes.

Patton Tabors and Catherine Snow (1994) have documented a general sequence in young children's ESL acquisition that appears to be fairly common. When young learners first encounter the new language, many will continue to use their native language when speaking to English speakers. This behavior is often followed by a period when they do not talk at all but instead attempt to communicate nonverbally through gestures, mimes, and cries or whimpers to attract attention. Young ESL learners also have been observed to engage in spectating (paying

(continued on next page)

close attention to the actions and utterances of English speakers so that they can connect words to activities) and rehearsing (practicing the new language to, by, and for themselves, repeating words, phrases, and sounds in English at a very low volume). Following the nonverbal period, children begin to use formulaic expressions in English (e.g., "What's that?" "Wanna play?" "I want that." "I don't know." "Gimme!"), which may get them into the action with other children. From formulas, as Nora demonstrated, children gradually begin productive language use, moving beyond memorized utterances and formulaic expressions to creative construction. Although this sequence has been described as if it were discrete and unidirectional, it is not necessarily true for all learners.

There are tremendous individual differences in children's second-language learning. Learners differ in the rate at which they learn the second language. They differ in their willingness to learn English and in their avoidance or nonavoidance of the new language. They differ in the language-learning strategies they use. They differ in whether their stance is more participator or observer. The least successful English learners seem to be those who avoid contact with English speakers and who do not engage with what is going on around them in English (Fillmore, 1976; Saville-Troike, 1988). Some research has suggested that the best ESL learners are those children who are most eager to interact with English speakers, who are most willing to participate and use whatever English they have at a particular point in time, who are risk takers and are not afraid to make mistakes, and who identify with English speakers (Fillmore, 1976; Strong, 1983). Researchers, however, also have discovered that quiet children who pay close attention to what is going on around them (the careful observer stance) may also be quite effective language learners (Fillmore, 1983; Flanigan, 1988). Thus, not all young children learn a second language in exactly the same way.

What is crucial to children's successful second-language acquisition is the learner's choosing to work at communicating with people who speak the new language. Young ESL learners find themselves in environments where English is used, but they must choose to work at learning the new language; they must want to interact with others in English if acquisition is to occur. Interaction is critical in two ways: (1) it gives learners opportunities to try the new language to see if they can make themselves understood; and (2) fluent English speakers respond to the learner's efforts, providing both additional language input and a gauge on how well the learner is communicating. This language give and take is critical to continued learning (Ellis, 1985; Tabors & Snow, 1994).

In the ESL, setting both adults and other children may act as language teachers for children. Adults tend to modify or adapt their ways of speaking to what they think the ESL learner will understand and respond to. Studies of primary teachers working with ESL learners have reached the following conclusions: As with "baby talk" in native language settings, effective teachers tend to speak slowly, using clear enunciation, somewhat simplified sentences, and exaggerated intonation. They often use repetitions or restatements of sentences. They also contextualize their speech by using objects and physical gestures so that learners may use nonlinguistic cues to figure out what has been said. Finally, adults make concerted efforts both to encourage the ESL child to talk and to understand what the learner is saying. In their efforts to understand children, adults frequently expand children's incomplete sentences or extend what they have said (Enright, 1986; Fillmore, 1982, 1983). Through all these provisions of "comprehensible input" (Krashen, 1982), adults are responsive persons with whom to try the new language.

Fluent English-speaking children are also important language models and teachers for their ESL counterparts. During interactions, English-speaking children may assist their non-English-speaking peers by gesturing, correcting, giving feedback, engaging in language play, and encouraging the second-language learner to talk (Ventriglia, 1982). Children, however, do not make the consistently concerted efforts that adults do to be understood by and to understand

ESL learners unless they have been coached to do so (see Tabors & Snow, 1994). They may tire of the teacher role and move away from it more quickly than an adult would. In addition, children do not tend to focus as exclusively on understanding the ESL child as adults do; what is often most important is carrying out whatever activity they happen to be engaged in (Fillmore, 1976; Peck, 1978). Given that children often (but not always) are more interested in interacting with other children than they are with adults, however, other children provide strong incentives for ESL children to use their developing English and to make themselves understood. The desire to communicate is at the heart of young children's second-language learning.

Earlier we distinguished bilingual from ESL classrooms. Despite research evidence that speaks to the efficacy of teaching children through their native language, a major issue with regard to non-English-speaking learners has been the role that languages other than English play in children's learning. The commonsense belief that the most efficient way to encourage English language proficiency is to use only English is still adhered to by numbers of early childhood educators (see Fillmore, 1991). Thus, numbers of Head Start and kindergarten programs have embraced the idea of an early school introduction of, and sometimes school immersion in, English, with the understanding that parents will continue to use their native languages at home so that young children continue to develop linguistic abilities and communicative competence in their home tongues while acquiring English (Tabors & Snow, 1994). Theoretically, this situation should result in young children becoming bilingual, but using their two languages in different settings.

Unfortunately, the reality is that early introduction to English in school has often meant that non-English-speaking children refuse to communicate in their native languages and try to use English exclusively. In a study of the home language practices of more than three hundred immigrant preschoolers, Lilly Wong Fillmore discovered that these young learners, whether they were enrolled in bilingual or English-only classrooms, were particularly vulnerable to language loss. The longer they stayed in school, the more they relied on English for communication, even at home. This jeopardized non-English-speaking parents' abilities to interact verbally with their children and socialize them.

Fillmore raises the issue of whether English-language acquisition has to come at the expense of other languages. Her data point out the potentially devastating consequences of children's refusal to speak their native languages. Parents anguish over how to communicate with their children, how to pass on family and community histories, how to transmit cultural expectations, how to discipline them, and so on if they are unable to communicate with them. We believe that not only early childhood educators but all educators, whether bilingual or not, must wrestle with the reality of how to respect and value children's home languages and cultures.

In many important ways, second-language acquisition in young children is quite similar to first-language acquisition. This general statement means that adults working with second-language learners need to focus both on making themselves understood by children and on understanding children and encouraging them to use their new language. Adults need to focus on the learners' communicative intentions, not on the conventionality of their utterances. Adults also need to be sensitive to individual differences in children's rates of second-language learning and accepting of these differences. Children should be encouraged but not forced to use the new language, and children should not be belittled for hesitancy in trying out English. Adults need to recognize that children are learning English even if they are not responding verbally. Adults need to encourage other children who are native speakers of English to have patience with ESL learners and to assist them in their learning. Finally, adults should value the native languages that children bring to school with them and encourage them to continue to use their native languages.

SUMMARY

Children's acquisition of oral language is truly remarkable. By the time children enter kindergarten, most have mastered the basic structures and components of their native language, all without much stress or effort. How did the information contained in this chapter compare with what you were able to discover about your own first words and early language learning? Which of the four perspectives described in this chapter comes closest to your view about children's language development?

To summarize the key points about oral language development, we return to the guiding questions at the beginning of this chapter:

- *What are the major views on how children's language develops? Which aspects of language development does each view adequately explain?*

Four competing perspectives have been used to explain how children acquire language. The behaviorist perspective emphasizes the important role of reinforcement in helping children learn the sounds, words, and rules of language. This view handily explains the imitative aspects of initial language learning. Nativists stress the importance of children's inborn capacity to learn language and suggest that a portion of the brain is dedicated to language learning. Nativist theory explains how children "invent" their own two- and three-word grammars and overgeneralize rules for past tense ("He goed to the store") and plural ("I saw two mouses today!"). The social-interactionist perspective emphasizes the importance of both environmental factors and children's innate predisposition to make sense of language and use it for practical purposes. According to this view, children learn about language by using it in social situations. The social-interactionist view highlights the role of parental support in language acquisition. Finally, new technology has allowed scientists to observe how the brain perceives, interprets, and expresses language. These developments have lead to a new perspective of children's language learning, the neurobiological view, which complements the three earlier views on language development. This perspective explains how the structural development of the brain is related to language acquisition. It helps explain why children's experiences during infancy have such a crucial effect on later language learning.

- *What are the major components of language?*

The major components of language are (1) phonology, he sounds that make up a language; (2) morphology, the meaning bearing units of language, including words and affixes; (3) syntax, the rules for ordering words into sentences; (4) semantics, the shades of meaning that words convey; and (5) pragmatics, the social rules that enable language to accomplish real-life purposes.

■ *How does the structure of an infant's brain develop? How does this structural development affect language acquisition?*

At birth, the human brain is remarkably unfinished. Most of the one hundred billion neurons or brain cells are not yet connected. During the first month of life, the number of neural synapses or connections increases twenty times to more than one thousand trillion. As a child matures, the actual number of neurons remains stable; the number of synapse connections increases, however, and the message-receiving dendrite branches grow larger and heavier. At age one, the full cortex consumes twice as much energy as an adult brain. This neural readiness, in combination with countless hours of sound play and verbal exchanges with loving caregivers, allows most children to begin speaking their first words at this age.

By eighteen months of age, children's neural synapses have increased and strengthened and are beginning to transmit information efficiently. Hence, most toddlers begin to experience a language explosion, particularly in the areas of vocabulary and syntax. During this time, children are able to learn as many as twelve words a day. Thus, the neurobiological perspective reveals how the rapid development of the brain during the first few years of life makes it possible for children to acquire language so quickly and efficiently. This perspective also explains why the first thirty-six months are a critical period for language development.

■ *What factors affect children's rate of language acquisition?*

Although language development follows a predictable sequence, the rate at which children acquire language varies tremendously. Gender, socioeconomic level, and cultural influences can all affect the rate of language acquisition. A child's language learning can also be impeded by illnesses, such as otitis media, and by a variety of congenital problems of a physical or neurological nature. Parents and caregivers are cautioned to seek a medical diagnosis if language development is significantly delayed; early identification and treatment can often avoid irreparable disruption of the language acquisition process.

■ *How does children's acquisition of a second language compare with their first language acquisition? What should adults do to make it easier for children to learn English as a second language?*

In many ways, second-language acquisition in young children is similar to their acquisition of their first language. In learning a new language, children engage in the creative construction of the rules of the new language, and this creative construction occurs within the context of multiple social interactions as children use the new language with others.

Adults working with second-language learners need to focus both on making themselves understood by children and encouraging these children to use their new language. Adults need to focus on the learners' communicative intentions, not on the conventionality of their utterances. Children should be encouraged but not forced to use the new language, and children should not be belittled for hesitancy in trying it. Adults need to recognize that children are learning English even if they are not responding verbally. Adults need to encourage other children who are native speakers of English to have patience with ESL learners and to assist them in their learning. Finally, adults should value the native languages that children bring to school with them and encourage them to continue to use their native languages.

LINKING KNOWLEDGE TO PRACTICE

1. Interview two parents and two early childhood teachers regarding how they believe children learn language. Consider which theory of language acquisition best matches each interviewee's beliefs.

2. Interview a school nurse or health care aide about the number of children she or he sees who are affected by illnesses and congenital problems. From the health care worker's perspective, what effect do these medical problems have on children? How often should children be screened for auditory acuity? If a family has limited financial recourses, what agencies can provide medical services?

3. Observe a second-language learner in a preschool or day care setting. Does the second-language learner comprehend some of the talk that is going on in the classroom? How does the child communicate with other children? How does the teacher support the child's second-language acquisition? Are other children helping? Does the second-language learner have any opportunities to use his or her native language?

CHAPTER 3

FACILITATING EARLY LANGUAGE LEARNING

Four-year-old Evan, from Arizona, was visiting his grandmother in Vermont during the Christmas holiday. Upon opening the drapes one morning, he viewed snow-covered trees and fields. Evan gasped, "Grammie, who spilled all the sugar?" His grandmother responded, "Evan, that's very clever. It sure looks like sugar. Actually, it's snow."

Clearly, Evan's unfamiliarity with snow didn't prevent him from drawing a clever comparison. His grandmother responded by first showing appreciation for Evan's deduction and then providing the correct word, *snow*. Evan had a great opportunity to learn about the qualities of snow through conversations with his parents, grandparents, and older sister as they played together outside. During these adventures, they offered appropriate words for and information about all the new sights, sounds, tastes, smells, and feelings. By the end of the week, Evan knew the difference between wet snow and powder snow. He made snow angels, helped build a snowman and snow fort, engaged in a snowball war, and had an exhilarating ride on a sled. The new experiences he shared with older and more snow-experienced language users allowed Evan to build new vocabulary and cognitive understandings.

Chapter 2 discussed how infants and toddlers learn their native language through complex social interactions with parents, siblings, and other caregivers. These individuals are essentially a child's first and most important teachers. Throughout the preschool years, the family plays a significant role in helping children become accomplished language users. In this chapter, we examine the talk that goes on in homes and describe ways parents can support and enrich language development. We also discuss the many ways teachers can create learning environments that invite the types of rich oral interactions that promote language acquisition and enhance learning in all areas of the curriculum.

BEFORE READING THIS CHAPTER, THINK ABOUT . . .

■ Your home language environment when you were a child. Did you engage in lengthy conversations with your parents and siblings? Did you have an appreciative audience when you told stories about your own experiences? Did your family discuss the TV shows, videos, and DVDs that you watched?

■ The conversations that took place in your classroom when you were in school. Were they mainly teacher-centered exchanges in which you and your classmates responded to questions asked by the teacher, or did you have the opportunity to engage in two-way conversations with the teacher and other students?

■ Sharing or show-and-tell. What did you like about this activity? What, if anything, did you not like about it?

■ The make-believe play you engaged in when you were a child. What were some of the favorite roles and themes that you acted out during this play?

■ How did you feel when you gave an oral presentation in class. Did you feel embarrassed or confident?

FOCUS QUESTIONS

■ How can parents best facilitate their children's oral language development?

■ What is the initiation, response, evaluation (IRE) pattern of class talk? What problems are associated with this type of discourse? How can teachers provide students with more stimulating conversations in the classroom?

■ How do group activities, learning centers, and dramatic play promote oral language acquisition?

■ What can teachers do to promote language-rich dramatic play?

■ How can sharing or show-and-tell be turned into a valuable oral language activity?

■ How can teachers effectively assess students' oral language development?

■ What can teachers do to optimize oral language experiences for bilingual and second-language learners?

HOME TALK: A NATURAL CONTEXT FOR LEARNING AND USING LANGUAGE

Evan's family helped him understand and label his new experience with snow. Their language support was natural and was guided by Evan's constant questions: "Why doesn't this snow make a snowball? Why can't I make an angel on this snow?" Evan's learning while he played was nothing new or extraordinary; he has received language support from his parents and sibling from the moment he was born. His parents and older sister intuitively supported his attempts to communicate. When Evan was an infant, his parents, like most parents, naturally used parentese. That is, they talked to him in higher pitched tones, at slower rate of speech, and with exaggerated pronunciation and lots of repetition of phrases. Parentese

■ ■ ■ ■ ■ ■

BOX 3.1

DEFINITION OF TERMS

active listening: the listener combines the information provided by the speaker with his or her own prior knowledge to construct personal meaning.

anecdotal record: a brief note describing a child's behavior.

checklist: a observation tool that specifies which behaviors to look for and provides a convenient system of noting when these behaviors are observed.

dramatic play: an advanced form of play in which children take on roles and act out make-believe stories and situations.

initiation, response, evaluation (IRE): a pattern of classroom talk in which the teacher asks a question, a student answers, and the teacher either accepts or rejects that answer and then goes on to ask another question.

metalinguistic awareness: the ability to attend to language forms in and of themselves. For example, a child may notice that two words rhyme with each other.

metaplay language: comments about play itself ("I'll be the mommy, and you be the baby").

personal narrative: a story told in the first person about a personal experience.

pretend language: comments that are appropriate for the roles that children have taken in dramatic play. For example, a child pretending to be a baby might say "Waah! Waah!"

rubric: a scoring tool with a list of criteria that describe the characteristics of children's performance at various proficiency levels.

scaffolding: temporary assistance that parents and teachers give to children to enable them to do things the children cannot do on their own.

---

helped Evan hear the sounds and words of his native language. Between the age of eighteen months and three years, as Evan's communicative competence grew, his family intuitively adjusted their verbal responses so that he could easily learn new vocabulary and grammatical structures.

In fact, the most important component of learning language is actually engaging children, even infants, in conversational bouts. In Chapter 2 we discussed how families provide the rich social context necessary for children's language development. The thousands of hours of parent–child interactions from the moment of birth through the preschool years provide the foundation for language. As children acquire language, they are able to share with others what they feel, think, believe, and want. Although most children begin to use their expressive vocabulary in the second year of life, research has long documented that children differ in their ability to learn and use new words (Smith & Dickinson, 1994). In an effort to understand what accounts for these differences, researchers Betty Hart and Todd Risley (1995) documented parent and child interactions during the first three years of children's lives. The research team observed forty-two families from different socioeconomic and ethnic backgrounds one hour each month for two-and-a-half years. Their data revealed vast differences in the amount of language spoken to children. Children from homes that received welfare assistance heard an average of 616 words an hour; children from working-class families heard 1,251 words an hour; and children from professional homes heard 2,153 words per hour. If one thinks of words as dollars, the children from these different socioeconomic homes would have significantly disparate bank accounts. Further, this long-term study revealed that early language differences had a lasting effect on children's subsequent language accomplishments both at age three and at age nine. In other words, talk between adults and children early in life makes a significant difference. To look at an example of how this language difference begins to multiple, observe the following language of three parents when interacting with their babies when preparing to eat a meal.

- **Mom 1:** *Okay, Crystal, let's eat.*
- **Mom 2:** *Okay, Paulie, it's time to eat our lunch. Let's see what we are having? Yes, let's have carrots.*
- **Mom 3:** *Okay, Teryl, it's lunchtime. Are you hungry? Mommy is so hungry! Let's see what we have in the refrigerator today. What is this? It's orange. Could it be peaches? Could it be apricots? Let's see! See the picture on the jar? That's right, it's carrots.*

Talk between adults and young children makes a significant difference to language development, but it is equally important for older children to have consistent opportunities in their homes to express their views on current events, offer their opinions about movies and television programming, and recount the daily details of their school lives.

In Special Feature 3.1, we describe the types of verbal scaffolding Evan's family and most adults automatically use to support children's language development. This type of scaffolding is a prime example of Lev Vygotsky's (1978) zone of proximal development in which adults help children engage in activities that children could not do on their own. Through ongoing interactions with his parents, sister, and other caregivers, Evan (and most children) quickly learn basic conversation skills (Danst, Lowe, & Bartholomew, 1990; Manning-Kratcoski & Bobkoff-Katz, 1998; Norris & Hoffman, 1990). By age three, Evan, like most children, had learned to take turns, back channel (use fillers such as "uh-huh" to keep conversations going), be polite, and make appropriate responses (Menyuk, 1988). He knew how to engage in conversations with adults and his peers.

Encouraging Personal Narratives

Evan's family played a vital role in helping him interpret, label, and recall his new experiences with snow. Back in Arizona, Evan had many stories to tell his teacher and playmates at preschool. For the next several months, each time he spoke with his grandparents, he relived his snow-day tales. The stories, or personal narratives, that Evan told helped him make sense of this new experience, broadened his vocabulary, and reinforced his expressive language skills. Likewise, each time

SPECIAL FEATURE 3.1

Caregivers' Strategies for Supporting Children's Language Development

In almost all cases, caregivers intuitively scaffold children's language development. These communication strategies have been observed across all cultures.

Expansions: Adult recasts the child's efforts to reflect appropriate grammar. When adults use expansions, they help introduce and build new vocabulary.

> **Child:** Kitty eat.
> **Adult:** Yes, the kitty is eating.

Extension: Adult restates the child's telegraphic speech into a complete thought and may add new information in response to the child's comments.

> **Child:** Kitty eat.
> **Adult:** Kitty is eating his food.
> **Child:** Kitty eat.
> **Adult:** The kitty is hungry.

Repetitions: Adult facilitates the development of new sentence structure by repeating all or part of the child's comment.

> **Child:** Kitty eat.
> **Adult:** Time for kitty to eat. Time for kitty to eat.

Parallel talk: Adult describes the child's actions. Parallel talk is an effective way to model new vocabulary and grammatical structure.

> **Child:** Kitty eat.
> **Adult:** Jimmy is watching the kitty eat.

Self-talk: Adult describes his or her actions. Like parallel talk, self-talk effectively models new vocabulary and grammatical structures.

> **Adult:** I'm feeding the kitty.

Vertical structuring: Adult uses questions to encourage the child to produce longer or more complex sentences.

> **Child:** Kitty eat.
> **Adult:** What is the kitty eating?
> **Child:** Kitty eat cat food.

Fill-in: Adult structures the conversation so that the child must provide a word or phrase to complete the statement.

> **Adult:** The kitty is eating because she is—
> **Child:** Hungry.

Adapted from A. Manning-Kratcoski & M. Bobkoff-Katz (1998). Conversing with young language learners in the classroom. *Young Children,* 53(3): 30–33.

Evan told the story about how the snowball he threw at his sister knocked off the snowman's nose and made his dad laugh, he deepened his memory of the event.

Children's personal narratives are a window into their thinking. Their language also reveals how they use current knowledge to interpret new experiences. Evan's first interpretation of a snowy field was to relate it to a recent incident with a broken sugar bowl. These verbal expressions of new mental constructions can be both fascinating and humorous. Likewise, children's personal narratives offer insight into their language development and overall intellectual, social, and emotional growth (Dodici, Draper, & Peterson, 2003).

Although children instinctively know how to put experiences, feelings, and ideas into story form, parents and caregivers can encourage their children's language development by offering many storytelling opportunities and attentively listening while children share their accounts of events (Canizares, 1997). And even though nothing can replace quiet and private time to listen to children, many working parents report that they use the time in the car, bus, or subway going to and from day care and/or errands to listen carefully to their children.

Children often share what they know or have learned in story form. They do so because the human brain functions narratively; for most of us it is much easier to understand and remember concepts when we are given information in story form rather than as a collection of facts. Because the human brain retains information more efficiently in story form, parents can explain new information using stories. For example, when five-year-old Tiffany wanted to know how to tie her shoelaces, her daddy told her the following story:

> Once upon a time, there were two silly snakes [the shoelaces] who decided to wrestle. They twisted around each other and tied themselves together very tightly [first tie]. The snakes became scared and tried to curl away from each other [the loops]. But the snakes tripped and fell over each other and tied themselves in a knot.

Reading Storybooks

Research reveals a connection between the amount of time adults spend reading storybooks to children and the level of children's oral language development. The stories, pictures, and accompanying adult-to-child interactions facilitate language use and increase expressive and receptive vocabulary. Children are able to learn new vocabulary during storybook time as they point to pictures they see in the book and when an attentive adult labels the picture or illustration. This interaction, called joint visual gaze, is the basis of a great deal of vocabulary development (Corkum & Moore, 1998). Further, children who have been read to frequently are better able to retell stories than children who have had few opportunities to engage in story time (Auerbach, 1995; Barrentine, 1996; Durkin, 1966). Caregivers may also encourage discussion and comprehension by asking open-ended questions about the story. Children often relate to the characters and story lines, and, when encouraged, they reveal interesting views. The following conversation occurred when Dominique was four years old, after a reading of *Goldilocks and the Three Bears:*

> **MOM:** What part of the story did you like the best?
>
> **DOMINIQUE:** When Goldilocks kept messing up baby bear's stuff.
>
> **MOM:** Who did you like best in the story?
>
> **DOMINIQUE:** Baby bear.

MOM: Why?

DOMINIQUE: 'Cause baby bear is like me. All his stuff is wrecked up by Goldilocks, like Sheritta [her 18-month-old sister] messes up mine.

Notice that Dominique's mother asked open-ended opinion questions and accepted her child's responses. This type of question encourages oral responses and children's personal interpretation of the story. Adults should refrain from asking interrogation or detail questions, such as "What did Goldilocks say when she tasted the second bowl of porridge?" Detail questions tend to make story time avoidable, not enjoyable.

As children snuggle in a parent's lap or beside their parent in a chair or bed, story time creates a comforting, private time to talk together. In addition to providing wonderful language opportunities, story time also establishes a foundation for children to become successful readers.

In today's culturally, linguistically, and socioeconomically diverse society, teachers may find that some of their students' parents may not have the ability to read to their children or the financial means to purchase storybooks. Even more parents are unsure how to engage their children in story time successfully. Special Feature 3.2 offers several suggestions for parents. In addition, teachers may need to help parents by acting as a resource. In Chapter 11, readers will discover a number of concrete suggestions for ways in which teachers can help parents support their children's language and literacy growth.

Television as a Language Tool

Deeply engrossed in a video about birds, three-year-old Annie cheers when a duck slowly hatches from its egg. She watches this video several times, frequently asking questions about "How did the duck get into the egg?"

In the middle of the night, several evenings later, Annie's father awakens to noises coming from the family room. As he walks into the living room, he realizes that Annie has begun to play the bird video. He also observes that her hands are full of eggshells and yolks. She asks, "Daddy, where's the baby duck?"

As you can see, Annie's interest in ducks, eggs, and the mysteries of hatching were clearly sparked by her observation of a science video. Children today have a wide range of electronic media to watch and interact with. Television, the oldest medium, is still the most influential and easily accessible, and opens the door for cable programming, videos, and DVDs. Parents have the choice to view television as a hazard to their child's intellectual development, or they can explore its potential as an inexpensive tool that can broaden their child's curiosity and vocabulary (Foley & Enz, 2004).

Television has been a major influence in family life in almost all U.S. households since the 1950s. More recently, the availability of video/DVD rentals and inexpensive video/DVD players, video/DVD movies, and video/DVD storybooks, cartoons, and games have added yet another dimension to television

SPECIAL FEATURE 3.2
Language Development via Storybook Reading

In recent years, studies have revealed that home literacy experiences, or the lack of them, profoundly influence children's later literacy development and language development. Storybook reading, however, is not an instinct. Knowing how to interact with children and storybooks takes time and practice. One simple approach that significantly increases a child's involvement in the story-time experience is called dialogic reading. It involves parents asking questions about the stories as they read, such as asking children to describe what they are seeing on the page. In addition, parents are also encouraged to add information.

The following scene illustrates the dialogic reading approach. Dad is reading Jane Manning's *Who Stole the Cookies from the Cookie Jar?* (Harper Festival, 2001) to three-year-old Jasper. Before Dad begins the story, he asks Jasper about the cover illustration.

> **Dad:** Jasper, who is on the cover?
> **Jasper:** Doggie, kitty, piggy, rabbit, and mouse.
> **Dad:** Look, Jasper. Do you see that the book is shaped like our cookie jar?
> **Jasper:** Daddy, see the cookies, they are chocolate chip!
> **Dad:** Your favorite. Jasper, the title of this book is *Who Stole the Cookies from the Cookie Jar?* Who do you think stole the cookies?
> **Jasper:** I think Piggy or Cookie Monster.

The reading and conversation about this twelve-page storybook lasted more than a half hour, with Jasper deeply engaged with describing the richly detailed illustrations and guessing who had stolen the cookies.

In addition to dialogic reading, parents can use other simple and enjoyable strategies to help their children get the most from story time:

- Read the same books again and again. Children learn new things each time they hear story and look at the pictures.
- Ask children to find and label objects to keep them involved in the story.
- Ask open-ended questions. Asking questions such as "What do you think will happen next?" or "What was your favorite part of the story?" encourages children to share their feelings and opinions. Figure 3.1 provides several examples of open-ended questions.
- Expand children's answers. Adding to your child's responses encourages them to interact with you and keeps them involved.
- Read with enthusiasm. Taking on the voices of the three little pigs and the wolf is fun and exciting and brings the story to life.

watching. It is estimated that 99 percent of U.S. homes had at least one television set (Hancox, Milne, Poulton 2005). In addition, the television is usually in the part of the home where most family interactions occur. Research reveals that the average child between two and five years of age will spend twenty-seven hours a week viewing television programming (Miller, 1997). Because anything that occupies children for so many hours a week deserves careful consideration, what are some

FIGURE 3.1   Closed- and Open-Ended Questions

Closed-ended questions usually only require a single word answer—"yes" or "no"—or require the "right answer." Open-ended questions, on the other hand, have no right or wrong answers, and they encourage students to talk more and to use richer language.

This set of example questions for early primary-grade children refers to Maurice Sendak's *Where the Wild Things Are.*

Closed-Ended Questions	Open-Ended Questions
Did you like Max?	What did you think about Max?
Why did Max get in trouble?	How did you feel when Max's mother sent him to bed?
Were the wild things monsters?	Tell me about the wild things. What did they look like?
What did Max do to the wild things?	Why did Max stare at the wild things? How would you tame wild things?
Did you like the story?	What part of the story did you like best?

This set of questions for middle school students refers to J. K. Rowling's *Harry Potter and the Sorcerer's Stone.*

Closed-Ended Questions	Open-Ended Questions
Do you like the Dursleys?	How would you describe the Dursleys?
Is Hagrid a giant?	How do you think the Dursleys felt when Hagrid arrived?
Did Mr. Dursley let Harry read the letter from Hogwarts?	Why didn't Mr. Dursley want Harry to read the letter from Hogwarts?
How many wands did Harry try?	What do you think it means when the wand seller said, "The wand chooses the wizard?"
What did Harry get at Gringotts?	Hagrid got something secret at Gringotts. What do you think it was?

Remember to ask questions before, during, and after the story as that helps maintain child involvement.

the key elements a parent needs to consider when determining how to use this powerful medium?

Time.   Research regarding the amount of time young children watch television and the effect of viewing on later academic success is inconclusive, although the data clearly suggest that watching for many hours per day or week has a negative effect on children's academic performance. Susan Neuman (1988) suggests that more than four hours of TV viewing a day has a negative effect on children's reading achievement. Likewise, Angela Clarke and Beth Kurtz-Costes's (1997) study of low-socioeconomic African American preschool children shows that children who watched the most television (between thirty and fifty-five hours per week) exhibited poorer academic skills than their peers who watched fewer than twenty-five hours per week. On the other hand, moderate amounts of TV viewing may be beneficial. A landmark report by the Center for the Study of Reading, "Becoming a Nation of Readers," suggests that there is actually a positive link between watching up to ten hours of television a week and reading achievement (Rice, Huston, Truglio, & Wright, 1990). Clarke and Kurtz-Costes (1997) suggest that the variation in researchers' findings may be due in part to the home climate. They suggest that *who* watches television with young children and *how* television is watched may have a greater effect on children's learning than simply the *amount* of TV viewing.

Choosing Programming for Children.   Selecting appropriate children's programming has become more challenging in recent years. In addition to regular public access, cable and satellite service may offer hundreds of options to choose from each hour of the day. And even though there are a number of proven classics—such as *Sesame Street, Reading Rainbow,* and *Mister Rogers*—children's programs change from year to year. One way parents can determine the quality of children's programming is through considering children's needs (Levin & Carlsson-Paige, 1994) created a list of children's developmental needs and suggested program criteria to accommodate these concerns. Of course, parents need to watch programs with their children.

Active Viewing.   Children are extremely impressionable, and television's visual imagery is a powerful force in their lives. Therefore, it is important for parents to help guide and mediate the viewing process. Susan Miller (1997) suggests the following ways parents and caregivers may interact with children as they view television:

- *Watch television together.* Help children interpret what is seen on the screen.
- *Talk about the programs.* Conversations initiated by television programming offer opportunities to discuss a wide variety of issues.
- *Observe children's reactions.* Ask children to label or describe their feelings.
- *Foster critical thinking.* Ask children what they think about a program. Would they have handled the problem differently? Did they agree with the character's actions?
- *Extend viewing activities.* Children are often motivated to learn more about a topic or activity once television has sparked their interests. For instance, Annie's interest in the hatching sequence in the video inspires her to find her *Egg Becomes Chick* book. She poured over this early science text that features actual photographs of the development of a chick inside the egg. A trip to the zoo in early spring also provided her with the opportunity to see more chicks being hatched in a large incubator.

In short, although the television can be a powerful tool in children's learning, careful consideration of how much, what, and how children view TV programs is needed.

SCHOOL TALK: A STRUCTURED CONTEXT FOR LEARNING AND USING LANGUAGE

By the time most children enter preschool, they are capable of conversing with both adults and their peers. Language learning, however, is far from complete. Research has revealed that the semantic, syntactic, and pragmatic aspects of oral language continue to develop throughout the elementary school years (Chomsky, 1969; Karmiloff-Smith, 1979; Menyuk, 1988). Teachers therefore have the responsibility to promote language learning by engaging in conversations with students and by encouraging children to converse with each other (Roser, 1998). In fact, national teaching standards require elementary educators to be able to apply their knowledge of linguistics (morphemes, syntax, grammar, etc.) and theories of language learning. More specifically, teachers in the elementary grades are expected to use teaching strategies that:

- Build on students' experiences and current oral language skill
- Enhance students' listening skills
- Support students who are learning English as a second language and those who speak with dialects

In addition, teachers should be able to assess students' ability to accomplish their goals using language and use language assessment information to plan and modify future instruction.

Teacher Discourse

Every school day offers dozens of possibilities for verbal interactions (Smith & Dickinson, 1994). Unfortunately, research indicates that these opportunities are often overlooked in traditional transmission-oriented classrooms. Studies have shown that in many classrooms the teacher dominates the language environment, which does little to promote the children's oral language growth (Cazden, 1988; Howard, Shaughnessy, Sanger, & Hux, 1998; Wells, 1986). For example, in some classrooms:

- Teachers spend most of the time talking *to* rather than talking *with* children.
- Teachers dominate discussions by controlling how a topic is developed and who gets to talk.
- Children spend most of their time listening to teachers.
- When children do talk, it is usually to give a response to a question posed by the teacher.
- Teachers tend to ask testlike, closed-ended questions that have one correct answer (that the teacher already knows).

The typical pattern of classroom discourse is characterized by teacher initiation, student response, and teacher evaluation. In the IRE pattern, the teacher asks a question, a student answers, and the teacher either accepts or rejects that answer and goes on to ask another question (Galda, Cullinan, & Strickland, 1993). For example, before the following discussion, the kindergarten children had listened to *The Three Little Pigs*.

TEACHER: What material did the pigs use to build their first house?

BOBBIE: They used sticks.

TEACHER: Yes. That is correct, the pigs used sticks for the first house. What did the pigs use to build the third house?

MANUEL: They used cement.

TEACHER: No. Who remembers what the book says? Jon?

JON: Bricks.

TEACHER: Yes. The pigs used bricks.

Notice how the teacher's questions are not real questions; rather, they test whether these young students recalled specific details of the story. Notice also that these children have no opportunity to construct their own meaning of the story by combining text information with their prior knowledge. For example, Manuel's answer, *cement,* suggests that Manuel was making inferences based on prior experience. The teacher's negative response to Manuel's comment probably communicates to him that it is incorrect to make inferences when reading. This response sends a message to students that one should recall exactly what is said in the text. Finally, notice that there is absolutely no interaction from student to student. The turn-taking pattern is teacher–student–teacher–student.

These types of IRE interactions are sometimes appropriate because teachers do need to get specific points across to students (Dyson & Genishi, 1984). Problems ensue, however, if this is the only type of talk that is taking place in the classroom. IRE discussions do not provide the type of language input and feedback that "advance children's knowledge of language structure and use" (Menyuk, 1988, p. 105). In addition, these teacher-dominated exchanges do not allow students to negotiate and build meaning through dialogue (Hansen, 1998).

What can early childhood teachers do to provide children with more stimulating experiences with language? We offer three recommendations:

1. Engage students in reciprocal discussions and conversations.
2. Provide ample opportunities for activity-centered language that invite (and, at times, require) students to use language to get things done.
3. Provide language-centered activities that focus students' attention on specific aspects of language.

In the sections that follow, we present guidelines for implementing each of these recommendations.

Reciprocal Discussions and Conversations

Teachers' verbal interaction styles set the general tone for classroom language environments. The worst-case scenario occurs when a teacher insists on absolute silence except during teacher-led initiation, response, evaluation discussions. Such environments definitely limit continued oral language development. Other teachers provide ideal language environments by engaging students in genuine conversations, conducting stimulating reciprocal discussions, and allowing children to converse with each other at a moderate volume during classroom learning activities, using "inside voices" (soft voices that do not disrupt classroom learning).

Teachers have many opportunities to talk with students throughout the school day, ranging from one-to-one conversations to whole-group discussions. Following is an example of an effective conversation between Ms. E., a preschool teacher, and Roberto, age four:

> **ROBERTO:**   See my new backpack, Teacher?
>
> **MS. E.:**   What a neat backpack, Roberto. Show it to me.
>
> **ROBERTO:**   It has six zippers. See? The pouches hold different stuff. Isn't it neat?
>
> **MS. E.:**   I like the different-size pouches. Look, this one is just right for a water bottle.
>
> **ROBERTO:**   Yeah. The arm straps are great too. See, I can make 'em longer.
>
> **MS. E.:**   Yes [nods and smiles]. It fits your arms perfectly. Where did you get this nifty backpack?
>
> **ROBERTO:**   We got it at the mall.
>
> **MS. E.:**   What store in the mall?
>
> **ROBERTO:**   The one that has all the camping stuff.
>
> **MS. E.:**   The Camping Plus store?
>
> **ROBERTO:**   Yeah. That's the one.

Notice how Ms. E. allowed Roberto to take the lead by listening carefully to what he said and by responding to his previous statements. She let him do most of talking, using back channeling (nodding and smiling) to keep the conversation going. Ms. E. asked only three questions, and they were genuine: she wanted to know where Roberto purchased the backpack.

Reciprocal conversations are not restricted to one-to-one situations. Teachers can also engage children in genuine discussions pertaining to ongoing instructional activities. Cory Hansen (1998) gives an example of group discussion of George MacDonald's 1872 classic, *The Princess and the Goblin* (Puffin Books). The chapter book is being discussed by a group of kindergarten students in Chris Boyd's classroom.

Previously in the story, the grandmother had given the princess a gift of a glowing ring from which a thread would lead her to comfort if she were frightened.

The princess assumed it would lead her to her grandmother, but one night it led her deep into a cave and stopped at a heap of stones. The chapter ("Irene's Clue") ends with the princess bursting into tears at the foot of the rocks. Curdie, the fearless miner's son, was missing.

> **JOSEPH:**   I think that Curdie's on the other side of the rocks.
>
> **MRS. B.:**   Where'd you get the clue for that?
>
> **ANNA:**   Because the strings led her to the mountain. That means it was close to Curdie because Curdie lived by the mountain.
>
> **KIM:**   Maybe Curdie's on the other side of the stones!
>
> **JAMAL:**   I think her grandmother was a goblin since she could have went through the rocks.
>
> **JORDAN:**   I know. Maybe—when she was falling asleep on the other side—but how could the goblins be that fast?
>
> **ANNA:**   Because they're magic.
>
> **RICHARD:**   I know how Curdie got to the other side.
>
> **CHORUS:**   Children begin to talk in small groups simultaneously.
>
> **JOSEPH:**   Maybe Curdie's in the heap of stones.
>
> **MRS. B.:**   What makes you say that?
>
> **JOSEPH:**   Because in the last chapter—"Curdie's Clue"—it said they piled the rock—a big stone in the mouth of the cave.
>
> **KIM:**   The grandmother said the ring always led to the grandmother's bedroom so she . . .
>
> **ANNA:**   No it didn't. It said, "This will take me to you—wherever it takes you, you go." And the grandmother said, "Wherever it takes you, you will go."
>
> **MRS. B.:**   Can you think of any reason why the princess should go to the cave?
>
> **JOSEPH:**   Because it said, "You must not doubt the string."
>
> **ADAM:**   The grandmother said the thread would lead to her but it ended up leading her to Curdie.
>
> **ALONDRA:**   I think the grandmother knows about Curdie.
>
> **KIM:**   It's because her grandmother wanted her to save Curdie!
>
> **ANNA:**   That was the clue.
>
> **JAMAL:**   To get Curdie out cuz she know about him.
>
> **JOSEPH:**   Yeah. (Hansen, 1998, pp. 172–173)

Here, Mrs. B. let the students take the lead by listening closely to what they said and responding to their comments. Her questions were genuine (she did not know what the children's responses would be) and were open-ended in nature ("What makes you say that?"). By welcoming the children's viewpoints, she encouraged them to bring their personal interpretations to the story. Also notice that the children talked to each other; they engaged in real conversations. The teacher facilitated this child–child turn-taking pattern by encouraging the students to respond to other's ideas.

Ms. E.'s and Mrs. B.'s effective use of reciprocal questions allowed students to engage in authentic discussion with the teacher and each other. Obviously, the way a teacher interacts with children influences the way children communicate. Therefore, it is important for teachers to reflect on the quality of their conversations and discussions with students of all ages.

As teachers work with the students in their classrooms it is important to remember that many children do not speak academic or "standard" English. Teachers must be sensitive and respectful to the wide range of dialects they hear, always remembering that the language of the child's home must be valued even as teachers help children learn a more academic vocabulary. Special Feature 3.3 offers some guidance for teachers in understanding and supporting language variation.

Contexts for Encouraging Language for Children

What students say and do is greatly influenced by where they are and what is around them. For example, as Evan played in the snow, he learned snow-related vocabulary with his family. Teachers must create dynamic learning environments that are contexts for language development. In other words, the curriculum must give children something to talk about. In the following section, we describe how teachers might use group activities, learning centers, and dramatic play to expand students' learning and opportunities to use language.

Group Activities.   Teachers can support language by involving children with group activities that encourage, and at times necessitate, verbal interaction. What sort of activities would require children to talk? As Celia Genishi (1987) points out, "Almost every object or activity presents an opportunity for talk when teachers allow it to" (p. 99). Likewise, researchers Susan Burns, Peg Griffin, and Catherine Snow suggest that "sociodramatic play activities give children a chance to develop language and literacy skills, a deeper understanding of narrative, and their own personal responses to stories," (1999, p. 72). In the following vignette, we provide an illustration of a whole-group activity that required a rather large group of multilingual, four-year-old children to reveal and assert needs and wants and connect with themselves and others.

The young students have been learning about manners and balanced meals. As part of a culminating activity, the entire room has been transformed into a restaurant. Twelve little tables are draped with tablecloths, and on each table sits a vase of flowers. Today, the teachers are waitresses, and a few parents

Understanding and Supporting Language Variation

Welcome to my home. Please, do come in.
Hey yaw'l. Jes come rite-on in ta mah
*   plaaace.*
Dude, catch the pad. Wanna crash?

As you read the sentences above, did you begin to form mental images about the speakers? Did you make predictions about their ages, places of origins, and social status? If you did, then you are not alone; the study of dialects offers a fascinating look at how the language we use is linked to our social identity. Likewise, the study of dialects often provides the most vivid illustration of how language changes over time (Hazen, 2001).

Many people believe that there is only one correct form of English, what is often called Standard English. According to this view, the phrase *My sister is not home* will always be preferred to the phrase *My sister ain't home*. Linguists, however, suggest that what is appropriate language depends on the situation. In many contexts, *My sister ain't home* is more acceptable. This wording, called Rhetorically Correct English, suggests that what is "correct" varies and is governed by the speaker's intention, the audience, and the context (Crystal, 1995; Demo, 2000).

Unfortunately, dialect discrimination is widely tolerated in the United States. Many people believe that there is only one kind of appropriate English that all children should learn and that all teachers should be required to teach. Today, however, even this long-held view is being challenged. In the mid-1990s, the Oakland, California, school board proposed that Ebonics be accepted as a school language. The outcry against this idea was national: the frequent response was the only Standard English should be taught in schools. When educator-linguist Lisa Delpit (1997) was asked if she was for or against Ebonics her answer was complex:

My answer must be neither. I can be neither for Ebonics nor against Ebonics any more than I can be for or against air. It exists. It is the language spoken by many of our African-American children. It is the language they heard as their mothers nursed them and changed their diapers and played peek-a-boo with them. It is the language through which they first encountered love, nurturance and joy. On the other hand, most teachers of those African-American children who have been least well-served by the educational system believe that their students' chances will be further hampered if they do not learn Standard English. In the stratified society in which we live, they are absolutely correct. (p. 6)

As Delpit suggests, no matter how accepting teachers may be of a child's home language in the classroom, a child's dialect may serve as a source of discrimination as he or she matures. So what is the role of the teacher? According to Lily Wong Fillmore and Catherine Snow (2000, p. 20): "Teachers must provide children the support needed to master the English required for academic development and for jobs when they have completed school. However, this process does not work when the language spoken by the children—the language of their families and primary communities—is disrespected in school."

In summary, teachers need to teach children the dialect of school and work. To accomplish this goal, teachers need to provide the same type of scaffolding parents used when children were first learning to talk (Manning-Kratcoski & Bobkoff-Katz, 1998). Teachers must extend and expand children's language in a respectful manner, for example, as a simple expansion:

CHILD: That ain't right.
TEACHER: I agree, this isn't right.

Notice how the teacher recasts the child's effort in Standard English. Notice also that the teacher does not emphasize the correct form, but uses it naturally. When adults use expansions, they introduce and help children build new vocabulary.

have volunteered to cook real food. The children must choose between the Panda Café (spaghetti, meatballs, garlic toast, juice or milk) or the Café Mexico (burrito, chips, salsa, juice or milk). Each café has a menu with words and pictures. The children must select the specific items they wish to eat and give their orders to the waitress. The waitress takes the children's orders on an order form and gives the order form to the cooks. The cooks fill the orders exactly as the children request. Then, the waitress returns with the food and the order form and asks the children to review the order.

TEACHER: What café would you like, sir?

ROBERTO: [Points to menu.]

TEACHER: Which café? You must tell me.

ROBERTO: The Café Mexico.

TEACHER: Right this way, sir. Here is your menu. Take a moment to decide what you want to eat. I'll be right back to take your order.

ROBERTO: [Looks over the menu and shares his choices with his friend by pointing to the items he wants.]

TEACHER: OK, sir. What would you like?

ROBERTO: [Points to the items on the menu.]

TEACHER: Please, sir. You will have to tell me.

ROBERTO: [Hesitates for a few seconds.] I want the burrito and chips and juice.

TEACHER: Do you want salsa? [She leans over so he can see her mark the items on the order form.]

ROBERTO: No. [Firmly.]

Notice how the teachers organized this activity so that the children had to verbally express their needs multiple times throughout the restaurant adventure. In addition, the children had many opportunities to see how print is used in real life. Teachers, however, are not the only valuable source of language input. Children can also gain valuable oral language practice from talking with peers who are not as skilled as adults in initiating and maintaining conversations. To encourage peer-to-peer interactions, these teachers also created a miniature version of the restaurant in a dramatic play learning center. In this center, Roberto and his classmates will be able to play restaurant together for a few weeks.

As teachers of children observe their students in a variety of learning situations that require the children to use their language skills, they will often notice some who are having difficulty with the production of speech. Good teachers know that children with speech challenges and language delays should receive specialized support. Trade Secret 3.1 provides a brief overview of the most common speech challenges children display.

TRADE SECRET 3.1
Supporting Children Who Experience Language Delay or Speech Challenges

BY KATHY EUSTACE

I teach in an inclusion preschool of four-year-olds. Each year, nearly half my students exhibit some type of speech production challenge. As their teacher, I see one of my roles as being a language facilitator for *all* my students. Whether the child is classified as typically developing or exhibits a speech production disorder or presents evidence of language delay, each is merely at a specific stage of development. My job is the same for all students: to assess their current level of ability, support mastery at this stage, and then help them learn the skills necessary to move on to the next stage. The most common challenges I see when I work with children include articulation disorders, fluency disorders, and language delay.

Articulation disorders account for the majority of all speech production difficulties in young children. They generally involve the mispronunciations of the *s, r, l, th,* and *sh* sounds. The child will do one of the following:

- Omit the sound completely (e.g., *alt* for *salt*)
- Substitute one sound for another consistently (e.g., *wabbit* for *rabbit*)
- Distort or not produce the sounds precisely (e.g., *Eidabeth* for *Elizabeth*)

Nearly all children experience some level of misarticulation while they are learning to speak, and most children correct through normal development. Speech therapy is usually only necessary if the misarticulations prohibit others from understanding the child's verbal communication or if the problem persists and becomes embarrassing for the child.

Fluency disorders occur when the normal rate of speech "flow" is atypical. Stuttering is one form of fluency disorder. Stuttering occurs when repetitions of sounds interrupt the child's flow of speech, such as *ppppp please.* Cluttering is

another form of disfluency. Cluttering involves excessively fast speech in which word boundaries are often obscured or garbled, such as *Idonwnnagotoleep* for *I don't want to go to sleep.* Once again, nearly all children occasionally stutter and/or clutter when they are excited or tired. Disfluency disorders are not considered problematic unless they are constant and prevent a child from communicating his or her intentions.

Language delay is diagnosed when children have difficulty understanding a communicated message or expressing their thoughts verbally as contrasted to a developmental standard. For example, a two-year-old who responds in one- or two-word sentences is developmentally normal, but a four-year-old who only responds in one- or two-word sentences would be classified as language delayed.

Language delays may be exhibited as a primary condition caused by temporary health concerns such as colds or ear infections. Other more serious causes of language delay include language-impoverished home environments and damage to the areas of the brain that process language. Language delays also occur as secondary symptoms to other physical conditions such as mental retardation, autism, cleft plate, or cerebral palsy.

Although there are many reasons children many not acquire the typical language skills expected for their age, the cause is less important than the treatment. For example, a child may exhibit language delays due to mental retardation or a child with normal intelligence may not have acquired normal language due to temporary hearing loss or an environment that was not verbally interactive. Regardless of the circumstance, because the instructional goal is to increase the production of verbal communication, the treatment is nearly identical.

When I plan activities for my inclusive class, I plan language opportunities that would be appropriate for a range of abilities, from the typically

---

TRADE SECRET 3.1 (continued)

developing child to the children who exhibit speech production challenges to language delays. I also facilitate student participation based on the ability level of each child, always keeping the child's individual goals in mind. These open-ended activities are designed to elicit responses at all four levels. The following examples are based on a discussion I had with my class after we had read *Little Cloud* by Eric Carlile (Scholastic, 1996).

Level 1 involves an indication that the child has a receptive understanding of a new concept, in this case, clouds. At this level, I merely ask the child to demonstrate his or her understanding of the new concept by pointing to a visual representation of the concept. *Where are the clouds in this picture, Jamie?*

Level 2 asks a child to use a one-word response to communicate. This one word may

help me gauge a child's receptive understanding or a linguistic concept, or it may include a targeted speech sound that is typically mispronounced by this child. For example, *On this page what did little cloud turn into? Gustavo? Yes, that is right. RRRRabbit.*

Level 3 involves a multiword response from a child whose goal it is to increase his or her mean length of utterance or who is working on syntax. *Can you tell me three or four things that Little Cloud changes into? Sarafina?*

Level 4 involves helping children make inferences or comparisons. This level of response gives children an opportunity to elaborate their thoughts and work on the aspect of their language that is in question. *How are sheep and clouds alike? Who helped Little Cloud make the rain?*

Learning Centers.   Because children's learning and language is greatly influenced by their environment, good teachers guide children's language development through the deliberate structuring of the classroom environment. For example, the teachers in the previous vignette created a restaurant to encourage talk about food, ordering meals, taking orders, cooking meals, and the like. Later, as the children interacted together in the restaurant dramatic play center, they continued to help each other build and reinforce their knowledge of restaurants. In learning center classrooms, the teacher's role is to set up the environment, observe as children interact with the materials, supply help and guidance when needed, and engage in conversations with the children around the materials and the children's use in their learning. A good deal of the teacher's effort is expended on the setting-up or preparation phase. Centers are created when the teacher carves the classroom space into defined areas. Readers seeking more information on establishing centers will find *The Creative Curriculum for Early Childhood Education* (Dodge & Colker, 1992) a useful resource. This book presents detailed, easy-to-follow instructions for setting up popular interest areas (centers). It also contains practical tips on schedules, routines, and other aspects of classroom management, plus good suggestions for encouraging parental involvement.

Dramatic Play.   Another context for activity-centered language is dramatic play. Dramatic play occurs when children take on roles and use make-believe transformations to act out situations and play episodes. For example, several children might adopt the roles of family members and pretend to prepare dinner, or they may become superheroes who are engaged in fantastic adventures. This type of play—also called sociodramatic, make-believe, pretend, or imaginative play—reaches its peak between the ages of four and seven.

Although to some dramatic play appears simple and frivolous at first glance, close inspection reveals that it is quite complex and places heavy linguistic demands on children (Burns, Griffin, & Snow, 1999; Fessler, 1998). In fact, Jerome Bruner (1983, p. 65) reported that "the most complicated grammatical and pragmatic forms of language appear first in play activity." When children work together to act out stories, they face formidable language challenges. They not only need to use language to act out their dramas, but they must also use language to organize the play and keep it going. Before starting, they must recruit other players, assign roles, decide on the make-believe identities of objects (e.g., that a block of wood will be used as if it were a telephone), and plan the story line. Once started, language must be used to act out the story, keep the dramatization heading in the right direction (e.g., be sure that everyone is doing things appropriate to their role), and reenergize the play if it is becoming repetitive and boring.

To accomplish these tasks, children must use two different types of language: (1) pretend language that is appropriate for their roles and (2) metaplay language about the play itself. Children switch between their pretend roles and their real identities when making these two types of comments. This linguistic complexity is illustrated in the following example.

Three preschoolers are enacting a domestic scene in their classroom's housekeeping corner. John has taken the role of the father; Wendy is the mother; and George, the youngest of the three, has reluctantly agreed to be the baby.

WENDY: Baby looks hungry. Let's cook him some food. [Pretend.]

JOHN: Okay. [Pretend.]

WENDY: [Addressing George.] Cry and say that you're hungry. [Metalanguage.]

GEORGE: But I'm not hungry. [Metalanguage.]

WENDY: Pretend that you are! [Metalanguage.]

GEORGE: [Using a babyish voice.] I'm hungry. [Pretend.]

WENDY: [Addressing John.] Father, what should we have for dinner? [Pretend.]

JOHN: How about eggs? [Pretend.]

WENDY: I'll go get some eggs from the 'frigerator. [She goes to a wall shelf and takes several cube-shaped blocks.] [Pretend.]

GEORGE: Aah! I'm hungry! [Pretend.]

WENDY: [Pretending to scold George.] Be quiet! [She puts the blocks in a toy pan and places the pan on the toy stove.] The eggs are cooking. Father, you'd better set the table.

JOHN: Okay. [Pretend.]

GEORGE: Let me help, Daddy. [Pretend.]

JOHN: No! Babies don't set tables! You're just supposed to sit there and cry. [Metalanguage.] (Johnson, Christie, & Yawkey, 1999, p. 1)

In this example, Wendy is in her role as mother when she makes her initial comment about the baby. She reverts to real-life identity when she tells George what to say next and to pretend to be hungry. Then she shifts back to the role of mother when she asks father what he wants for dinner.

To take full advantage of dramatic play's potential as a medium for language development, attention needs to be given to three factors: (1) the settings in which play occurs, (2) the amount of time allocated for play activities, and (3) the type of teacher involvement in play episodes.

Play Settings. It is important to remember that children play best at what they already know. Therefore, dramatic play settings need to be familiar to children and consistent with their culture (Neuman, 1995). For example, the domestic play themes, such as parents caring for a baby or a family eating a meal, are very popular with

Dramatic play is an ideal medium for promoting oral language development

young children because these are the roles and activities with which they are most familiar. For this reason, we recommend that preschool and kindergarten classrooms contain a housekeeping dramatic play center equipped with props that remind children of their own homes. Not only do such centers encourage dramatic play, but they also provide a context in which children can display the types of literacy activities they have observed at home.

The range of children's play themes and related literacy activities can be greatly expanded by the addition of a theme center to the classroom. These centers have props and furniture that suggest specific settings that are familiar to children, such as a veterinarian's office, restaurant, bank, post office, ice cream parlor, fast-food restaurant, and grocery store. (Table 4.1 contains lists of literacy materials that can be used in a variety of theme centers.) For example, a veterinarian's office might be divided into two areas: a waiting room with a table for a receptionist and chairs for patients and an examination room with another table, chairs, and a variety of medical props (doctor's kit, scales, etc.). Stuffed animals can be provided as patients. Theme-related literacy materials—appointment book, patient folders, prescription forms, wall signs, and so on—should also be included to encourage children to reenact the literacy activities they have observed in these settings. Children will use their knowledge of visits to the doctor to engage in play with their peers. The following scenario illustrates how three preschoolers verbalize their knowledge of what occurs at the animal hospital.

> **SERGIO:** [The vet is looking at the clipboard.] It says here that Ruffy is sick with worms.
>
> **MARIE:** [Owner of a toy kitty named Ruffy.] Yep, uh huh. I think she ate bad worms.
>
> **SERGIO:** That means we gotta operate and give Ruffy big horse pills for those worms.
>
> **JOY:** [The nurse.] Okay, sign here. [Hands Marie a big stack of papers.] Sign 'em all. Then we'll operate. But you gotta stay out in the people room. You could faint if you stay in here.

Chari Woodard (1984), a teacher who has had considerable success with theme centers in her university's laboratory preschool, recommends that one theme center be introduced at a time and left for several weeks. Then the center can be transformed into another theme. She also advises locating these centers near the permanent housekeeping center so that children can integrate the theme center activities with their domestic play. Children acting as parents for dolls, pets, or peers in the housekeeping area might, for example, take a sick baby to the doctor theme center for an examination. Or, children might weld or examine cars in the classroom garage (Hall & Robinson, 1995). Woodard found that children, particularly boys, began engaging in more dramatic play when the theme centers were introduced.

Time.   Dramatic play requires providing a considerable amount of time for children to plan and initiate. If play periods are short, then children have to stop their dramatizations right after they have started. When that happens frequently, children tend to switch to less advanced forms of play, such as functional (motor) play or simple construction activity, which can be completed in brief sessions.

Research has shown that preschoolers are much more likely to engage in rich, sustained dramatic play during thirty-minute play periods than during shorter fifteen-minute sessions (Christie, Johnsen, & Peckover, 1988). Our experience indicates that even longer periods are needed. For example, Billie Enz and Jim Christie (1997) spent a semester observing a preschool classroom that had forty-minute play periods. Very often, the four-year-olds had just finished preparing for a dramatization when it was time to clean up. Fortunately, the teachers were flexible and often let the children have an extra ten to fifteen minutes to act out their dramas. We recommend that center time last for at least sixty minutes whenever possible.

Teacher Involvement.   For many years, it was believed that teachers should just set the stage and not get directly involved in children's play activities. This hands-off stance toward play has been seriously challenged by a growing body of research that suggests that classroom play can be enriched through teacher participation. Teacher involvement has been found to assist nonplayers to begin to engage in dramatic play, to help more proficient players enrich and extend their dramatizations, and to encourage children to incorporate literacy into their play episodes (Enz & Christie, 1997; Roskos & Neuman, 1993).Teachers, however, need to use caution because overzealous or inappropriate forms of involvement can interfere with ongoing play and can sometimes cause children to quit playing altogether (Enz & Christie, 1997).

The simplest and least intrusive type of teacher involvement in play is observation. By watching children as they play, teachers demonstrate that they are interested in the children's play and that play is a valuable, worthwhile activity. Observation alone can lead to more sustained play. Jerome Bruner (1980) reported that preschoolers' play episodes lasted roughly twice as long when a teacher was nearby and observing than when children played completely on their own. In addition, the children were more likely to move toward more elaborate forms of play when an adult was looking on.

Observation can also provide clues about when more direct forms of teacher involvement in play are appropriate. A teacher may find that, despite conducive play settings, some children rarely engage in dramatic play. Or, the teacher may notice that there is an opportunity to extend or enrich an ongoing play episode, perhaps by introducing some new element or problem for children to solve (Hall, 1999). Both situations call for active teacher involvement.

Chapter 4 describes three roles that are ideal for initiating and extending dramatic play: the stage manager role, in which the teacher supplies props and offers ideas to enrich play; the coplayer role, in which the teacher actually takes on a role and joins in the children's play; and the play leader who stimulates play by introducing, in a role, some type of problem to be resolved. (For more information about these roles and other roles that teachers can adopt during play, see Jones and Reynolds, 1992.)

In addition to promoting language acquisition, dramatic play encourages children to help each other learn academic skills and content (Hansen, 1998; Christie & Stone, 1999), make friends, and develop important social skills (Garvey, 1977). Peer-to-peer interaction is particularly important for the growing numbers of students who are learning English as a second language and need help with more basic aspects of oral language (Fessler, 1998). For these reasons, dramatic play centers need to be a prominent feature in early childhood classrooms.

Language-Centered Activities for Children

Beyond creating contexts that encourage language and facilitate verbal interactions, teachers can also provide activities that focus specifically on language. Read-alouds, sharing, storytelling, and language play all fall into this category. (Teacher read-alouds is the subject of an entire section in Chapter 4.) Storybook reading can be an ideal context for promoting attentive listening and oral discussion skills. We discuss the remaining four language-centered activities below.

Sharing.   Sharing, or show-and-tell, is a strategy designed to promote students' speaking and listening abilities. Traditionally, sharing has been a whole-class activity in which one child after another gets up, takes center stage, and talks about something of her or his own choosing, often some object brought from home (Gallas, 1992). Children in the audience are expected to listen quietly and not participate.

In this traditional format, sharing is not a very productive language experience for the child who is speaking or for those who are listening. The large group size can intimidate the speaker and reduce participation because only a small percentage of students get to share on a given day. If many students share, it becomes a very drawn-out, boring affair. The lack of participation on the part of the audience leads to poor listening behavior. Listening is an active, constructive process in which listeners combine information provided by a speaker with their own prior knowledge to build personal meaning. Mary Jalongo (1995) relates a teacher's definition of listening that captures the essences of active listening: "It is hearing and making and shaping what you heard—along with your own ideas—into usable pieces of knowledge" (p. 14). The passive role of the audience in traditional sharing works against this process.

With two modifications, sharing can be transformed into a very worthwhile language activity. First, group size should be "small enough to reduce shyness, encourage interaction, permit listeners to examine the object, and afford everyone a long enough turn without tiring the group" (Moffett & Wagner, 1983, p. 84). Groups of three to six students are ideal for this purpose. Second, listeners should be encouraged to participate by asking questions of the child who is sharing. "Let the sharer/teller begin as she will. When she has said all that initially occurs to her, encourage the audience by solicitation and example to ask natural questions" (Moffett and Wagner, 1983, p. 84). The teacher's role is to model questioning that encourages elaboration and clarification ("When did you get?" "What happened next?" "What's that for?"). After asking one or two questions, teachers should pause and encourage the audience to participate. Prompts such as "Does anyone have questions for Suzy?" may sometimes be needed to get the process started. Once children realize that it is acceptable for them to participate, prompting will no longer be necessary.

This peer questioning stimulates active listening by giving the audience a reason to listen to the child who is sharing. Children know that to ask relevant questions they are going to have to listen very carefully to what the sharer has to say. The child who is sharing benefits as well. Children can be encouraged to elaborate their brief utterances or organize their content more effectively and to state it more clearly (Moffett & Wagner, 1983).

Teachers can add variety to sharing by occasionally giving it a special focus. For instance, they can ask students to bring in an item that:

1. Has a good story behind it, which encourages narrative discourse
2. They made or grew, which facilitates explanation or description
3. Works in a funny or interesting way, which fosters expositive communication

Storytelling. Telling stories to children is also very worthwhile. The direct connection between the teller and audience promotes enjoyment and active listening. Marie Clay (1989) describes some of the values of storytelling:

> Storytelling is more direct than story reading. Facial expressions, gestures, intonations, the length of pauses, and the interactions with the children's responses create a more direct contact with the audience, dramatic in effect. The meaning can be closer to the children's own experiences because the teller can change the words, add a little explanation, or translate loosely into a local experience. (p. 24)

The first stories that children tell usually involve real-life experiences: they relate something that has happened to them. Sharing can be an ideal context to allow children to tell these types of stories in the classroom. Small-group, interactive sharing provides feedback that enables children to tell clearer, better-organized stories about personal experiences (Canizares, 1997).

Some children need assistance in broadening the range of their storytelling to imaginative, fictional stories. The following suggestions can help with this task.

■ Open up the sharing period to include fantasy stories. Once teachers begin permitting their children to tell "fictitional" stories, the children may begin sharing imaginative, creative stories that feature language that is much richer than that used in their show-and-tell sharing (Gallas, 1992).

■ Encourage children to retell the stories contained in their favorite storybooks. Books remove the burden of creating an original story to tell. Story retelling has other benefits for children, including enhanced oral fluency and expression and improved story comprehension (Morrow, 1985).

■ Have children make up words for the stories in wordless picture books, such as *Pancakes for Breakfast* by Tomie dePaola (Harcourt, Brace, Jovanovich, 1978). Here again, the book is providing the content for the child's story.

■ Link storytelling with play and writing. Vivian Paley (1990) has developed a strategy in which children come to a story table and dictate a story that the teacher writes down. During this dictation, the teacher asks the children to clarify any parts of the story that are unclear or difficult to understand. The teacher reads the story plays to the class. Finally, children serve as directors and invite classmates to join in acting out their stories. Children enjoy watching their stories dramatized, motivating them to create additional imaginative stories.

Language Play.   In addition to using language in their dramatic play, children also play with language. This intentional "messing around" with language begins as soon as children have passed through the babbling stage and have begun to make words (Garvey, 1977). This play involves the phonological, syntactic, and semantic aspects of language. By age two, language play becomes quite sophisticated. Ruth Weir (1962) placed a tape recorder in her two-and-a-half-year-old son Anthony's crib and turned it on after he had been placed in his crib for the evening. During this presleep time, Anthony engaged in an extensive amount of systematic language play. He experimented with speech sounds ("Babette Back here Wet"), substituted words of the same grammatical category ("What color. What color blanket. What color mop. What color glass"), and replaced nouns with appropriate pronouns ("Take the monkey. Take it." and "Stop it. Stop the ball. Stop it"). These monologues constituted play because language was being manipulated for its own sake rather than being used to communicate.

Young children also make attempts at humor, playing with semantic aspects of language. Kornei Chukovsky (1976) explains that "hardly has the child comprehended with certainty which objects go together and which do not, when he begins to listen happily to verses of absurdity" (p. 601). This play, in turn, leads children to make up their own nonsense. Chukovsky uses his two-year-old daughter as an example. Shortly after she had learned that dogs say "bow wow" and cats say "miaow," she approached him and said, "Daddy, 'oggie—miaow!" and laughed. It was his daughter's first joke!

Children gain valuable practice while engaging in these types of language play. They also begin to acquire metalinguistic awareness, the ability to attend to language forms as objects in and of themselves. Courtney Cazden (1976) explains that when language is used for its normal function—to communicate meaning—language forms become transparent. We "hear through them" to get the intended message (p. 603). When children play with language, the situation is reversed. The focus is on the language, on the grammatical rules and semantic relationships they are manipulating.

The type of language play children engage in is also age related (Geller, 1982). At age three, children like to repeat traditional rhymes ("Mary had a little lamb"). They eventually begin to make up their own nonsense rhymes, playing with sound patterns ("Shama sheema / Mash day n' pash day"). By ages five and six, children delight in verbal nonsense ("I saw Superman flying out there!") and chanting games ("Cinderella, dressed in yellow / Went upstairs to kiss her fellow / How many kisses did she get? / 1, 2, 3, 4, 5"), which are forms themselves rather than meaning. Children become aware of the sounds (Teddy bear, Teddy bear, turn around, Teddy bear, Teddy bear, touch the ground).

The obvious educational implication is that language play should be encouraged and supported at school (Cazden, 1976). Judith Schwartz (1983) recommends that teachers try three things to stimulate their students to play with language:

1. Teachers should create a climate that allows play to flourish, a classroom atmosphere in which "children and teacher laugh easily and often."
2. Teachers should serve as a model by sharing humorous anecdotes, word play, folk literature, jokes, and stories with children and by using gentle humor in interpersonal relationships with children.
3. Teachers should value each child's contributions by allowing many opportunities for sharing oral and written language play.

Songs and Finger Plays.   Sitting on the floor with a small group of preschoolers, Ms. K. begins:

Where is Thumbkin?
Where is Thumbkin?
Here I am! Here I am!
How are you today, sir?
Very well, I thank you.
Run away, Run away.

The three- and four-year-old children quickly join in and immediately start the finger movements that accompany this familiar song. Very young children love to sing. The human fondness for a catchy tune and a snappy, clever rhyme begins early. Beginning in infancy and continuing on throughout their childhood, children experiment with their voices and the sounds that they can make. In Special Feature 3.4, we describe children's musical development from infancy through kindergarten. Singing encourages risk-free language play, especially for children who are learning a second language (Freeman & Freeman, 1994b; Jackman, 1997). Singing songs in a new language allows children to make safe mistakes as they experiment with the new phonemic system, in a similar way as toddlers may begin to sing jingles they hear on the television long before they can actually speak in full sentences. As noted in a report by Catherine Snow and her colleagues (1998), singing songs is an important literacy activity.

SPECIAL FEATURE 3.4

Musical Development from Infancy through Kindergarten

■ **Birth to nine months**

Begins to listen attentively to musical sounds; is calmed by human voices. Starts vocalization, appearing to imitate what he or she hears.

■ **Nine months to two years**

Begins to respond to music with clear repetitive movements. Interested in every kind of sound; begins to discriminate among sounds and may begin to approximate pitches. Most attracted to music that is strongly rhythmic.

■ **Two to three years**

Creates spontaneous songs; sings parts of familiar songs; recognizes instruments and responds more

enthusiastically to certain songs. Strong physical response to music.

■ **Three to four years**

Continues to gain voice control; likes songs that play with language; enjoys making music with a group as well as alone. Concepts such as high, low, loud, and soft are beginning to be formed. Likes physical activity with music.

■ **Four to six years**

Sings complete songs from memory; is gaining pitch control and rhythmic accuracy. Loves language play and rhyming words. Attention span increases for listening to tapes and compact discs.

Adapted from M. Collins (1997), Children and music. In B. Farber (Ed.), *The parents' and teachers' guide to helping young children learn.* Cutchogue, NY: Preschool Publication.

Therefore, teachers of young children would be wise to build in singing as part of their language arts curriculum (Collins, 1997). In particular, children enjoy songs that offer repetition and chorus, such as "Polly Put the Kettle On," "Mary Had a Little Lamb," and "Here We Go Round the Mulberry Bush"; provide repeated words or phrases that can be treated like an echo, such as "Miss Mary Mack" and "She'll Be Comin' Round the Mountain"; require sound effects or animal noises, such as "If You're Happy and You Know It" and "Old MacDonald Had a Farm"; tell a story, such as "Hush, Little Baby," "Humpty Dumpty," and "Little Bo Peep"; and ask questions, such as "Where Is Thumbkin?" and "Do You Know the Muffin Man?" In addition to singing, many songs or poems include finger plays. Do you recall the "Itsy-Bitsy Spider" and how your fingers became the spider that climbed up the waterspout? Children's minds are fully engaged when they act out the words of a song or poem with their fingers (Collins, 1997).

Many preschool and kindergarten teachers write the songs the children love to sing on chart paper or purchase the big book format of these beloved songs. As the children sing, the teacher uses a pointer to underline each word. The follow-the-bouncing-ball approach to teaching reading is quite effective with some children (Segal & Adcock, 1986). Singing is a wonderful way for children to play with and enjoy language.

Children who are learning a second language need many opportunities to practice their new language in a safe classroom environment. Special Feature 3.5 offers classroom teachers suggestions on how to encourage language learning in their classrooms.

SPECIAL FEATURE 3.5
Optimizing Oral-Language Learning Experiences for Bilingual and Second-Language Learners

BY SARAH HUDELSON AND IRENE ALICIA SERNA

In Chapter 2, several general points were made about young children's second-language acquisition. Second-language development was discussed from the perspective of creative construction, suggesting that learners, at their individual rates and using their individual styles, engage in figuring out how their new language works, much as they had to figure out how their native language works. The focus was on the social-interactionist perspective on language acquisition, noting that children learn a second language as they interact with others (adults and other children) in that language. Thus, teachers and English-speaking children in classrooms are all language teachers. Also, as noted earlier, there is evidence that teachers of second-language learners use language in ways that are similar to the talk parents use with their young children. This observation suggests that the attributes of parental talk discussed at the beginning of this chapter would also apply to adults working with second-language learners. With this general perspective in mind, the specific recommendations for promoting oral language articulated are discussed as they relate to educators who work in bilingual and second-language settings.

■ The Use of Reciprocal Discussions and Conversations with Bilingual and Second-Language Learners

Environments that promote genuine conversations and discussions—both among children themselves and between children and adults—are critical to the language growth of bilingual and second-language learners. Teachers' understandings and attitudes are central to the establishment of these linguistic contexts. In bilingual education settings, in which the philosophy is to use both the children's native language and English as vehicles for learning, teachers provide nonnative-English-speaking children with opportunities to extend both native and English language ability by using both languages in academic settings. As they provide these opportunities, bilingual teachers must decide how to allocate the use of the two languages in the classroom. Such allocation often depends on program design and goals and on the language abilities of specific teachers and children (Lessow-Hurley, 1990).

Bilingual teachers may use one language for certain content or activities (such as language arts and mathematics) and the other language for other content and activities (such as science and art). Instead, one language may be used for part of the day and the other language for the rest of the time. Alternatively, the teacher and the children may use both languages freely, alternating between them in the ways that bilingual people often do (Jacobson & Faltis, 1990). In some settings, more of the native language is used in conversations and discussions when children are less comfortable in English. As the children gradually become more fluent in English, more time is spent in English. In other settings, teaming occurs, with one teacher using only a language other than English for instruction and the other educator using only English. Across these settings, the messages that teachers send to children is that of valuing and using both languages and that it is possible to learn English without sacrificing their home language. In many classrooms, teachers also encourage English speakers to try to learn some of the non-English language, just as they encourage non-English speakers to use English (Reyes, Laliberty, & Orbansky, 1993; Turner, 1994).

Many elementary school teachers, however, are not bilingual and will therefore use only English in their teaching, even though several of their students may use languages other than English. In these settings, it is necessary for teachers to make adjustments in their ways of talking and presenting content so that children who are still learning English will participate more fully. These adjustments are also the case for bilingual teachers when they are working in

(continued on next page)

the learners' second language. Teachers need to make adjustments in the following ways:

■ Teachers need to provide contextual, extralinguistic support for their spoken language in the form of gestures, acting out, facial expressions, and use of visual aids (e.g., objects, pictures, diagrams, or films), so that visual information makes clear what is being said. Early in their language acquisition, second-language learners need more than the spoken language to understand what is going on in the classroom (Enright, 1986; Freeman & Freeman, 1994b). Their reliance on extralinguistic cues and modified input diminishes over time as they learn more English (Willett, 1995).

■ Teachers need to organize class environments that are rich with materials and that provide opportunities for collaborative, hands-on experiences (Enright, 1986; Enright & McCloskey, 1988).

■ Teachers need to adjust their own speech when speaking with and responding to second-language learners, focusing on the here and now, slowing their delivery, simplifying their syntax and repeating and rephrasing, attending carefully to children's understandings or confusion, focusing on the child's meaning over correctness, and extending and expanding the second-language learner's language (Enright, 1986; Freeman & Freeman, 1994b; Lindfors, 1987).

■ Teachers need to structure opportunities for second-language learners to experiment with English and need to encourage learners to do so (Ernst, 1994). Early on, second-language learners may do better in situations in which teachers are involved directly. As these children become more fluent, they need to interact with their peers in English and use the new language for academic content (Willett, 1995).

■ Teachers need to acknowledge that mistakes are a natural and necessary part of language learning and set up environments that encour-

age risk taking and allow mistakes (Freeman & Freeman, 1994b).

■ Teachers need to provide learners with feedback on their efforts within the context of their engagement with content. The focus needs to be on the learners' ability to communicate, not simply on the accuracy of grammatical forms (Freeman & Freeman, 1994b).

■ Teachers need to allow children to use languages other than English as a way to negotiate content before expressing their understandings in English (Freeman & Freeman, 1994b; TESOL, 1996).

■ Teachers may need to sensitize native or fluent English-speaking children to the struggles of children who are working both to learn English and to use English to learn. It may be done, for example, through using a language other than English to teach a lesson or through reading a story to English-speaking children and then discussing how the children felt, what problems they had in understanding, and how they could help others in similar situations (Rudnick, 1995).

Keeping these factors in mind should mean that children who are learning English as a second language have more opportunities to participate in classroom activities, conversations, and discussions.

■ The Use of Contexts for Activity-Centered Language with Bilingual and Second-Language Learners

Children, including English-language learners, learn a lot of language from each other and often prefer to interact with peers instead of with adults. English learners will learn the new language most naturally when they need to use it to engage with others, at least with some others who are more proficient in English than they are (TESOL, 1997). In a school setting, such engagement logically springs from interesting and meaningful content that children examine in collaboration with others in thematic units, in centers, and in paired and group projects. One challenge many teachers face is how to structure activities to promote collaboration, including verbal interactions. An added challenge is how to structure groups to maximize the participation of children who are learning English.

As they form groups, teachers whose classes include second-language learners need to give serious consideration to the linguistic abilities of children. At times, children organize their own groups. There is evidence that ESL learners who choose to work with others still learning the language can be successful at negotiating content and using English to learn, especially if the learners come from different native language backgrounds and are in the numerical minority in a classroom (Willett, 1995). At other times, however, teachers may assign children to work or play with others. At these times, particularly if they have an agenda of language development along with academic learning, teachers may group heterogeneously in terms of language ability, making sure that groups contain more- and less-able users of English. In this way, the less proficient speakers learn from those with more proficiency. Factors other than language proficiency, however, may also need to be taken into account when organizing groups. Jerri Willett, for example, has reported that a teacher grouped two English speakers with a Spanish speaker, thinking that the English speakers would work with the other child and thus facilitate his English development (1995). The two English speakers were girls, though, and they resisted collaborating with the Spanish-speaking boy, refusing to interact with him. Collaboration became a reality only when this young child worked (and played) with other boys.

In settings in which many of the learners come from one home language (e.g., Spanish), groups may be formed that include at least one native English speaker, one child who is bilingual, and one child who speaks Spanish fluently but is not yet fluent in English. In these groupings, the bilingual learner often acts as a language broker, assisting the other children in communicating with each other (Fournier, Lansdowne, Pastenes, Steen, & Hudelson, 1992). This method assumes that children are free to use languages other than English in the classroom, even if children ultimately share their work in English.

■ **The Use of Language-Centered Activities with Bilingual and Second-Language Learners**

In bilingual and second-language classrooms, many activities that teachers organize focus specifically on language. This section discusses the language-centered practices of read-aloud experiences, sharing, storytelling, and language play, all of which need to be considered for bilingual and ESL learners. Each language-centered practice is discussed in turn.

Read-Aloud Experiences. Reading aloud is a central component of instruction, not a frill. It is central to both first- and second-language development. Reading aloud should be done in children's home languages as well as in English, even if there is not a formal bilingual program in place. In some Spanish–English bilingual classrooms, teachers group children by language for one read-aloud experience daily so that the Spanish-dominant children listen and respond to Spanish-language literature and the English-dominant children do the same in English. At other times, the children are mixed, and both languages are used to negotiate story content.

Read-aloud experiences need to be chosen carefully. Ms. Espinosa and Ms. Moore chose some books, particularly those read early in the children's second-language development, on the basis of predictability to ensure that the children would understand the stories. Other books should be chosen for the quality of the story, the potential for discussion by children and teacher, and cultural relevance and authenticity (Espinosa & Fournier, 1995; Hudelson, Fournier, Espinosa, & Bachman, 1994). It is important to choose some books that reflect the experiences of the children (Barrera, Ligouri, & Salas, 1992).

(continued on next page)

Sharing. Sharing is a practice employed by many teachers because it gives children an opportunity to talk about aspects of their own lives and encourages them to listen to each other. There is evidence that successful participation in such classroom activities is important for ESL learners' linguistic development and for their ability to negotiate in mainstream classrooms (Ernst, 1994). Children who are just learning English, however, may be much less confident in using the new language than their English-speaking peers. They may speak more slowly, with more hesitations. They may not articulate as native speakers do. Their verbalizations may be incomplete or unconventional syntactically. Therefore, it may be more difficult for them to share their experiences and get and maintain the attention of their peers. Given these realities, teachers may need to take an active role in facilitating the participation of ESL children. This role may include negotiating with others opportunities for ESL learners to talk, assisting children in articulating what they want to contribute, and sensitizing other children to their struggles to express themselves (Ernst, 1994; Rudnick, 1995).

Storytelling. Many bilingual and second-language learners come from cultures in which oral stories abound and storytelling traditions are strong (Au, 1993). Therefore, storytelling should occupy a prominent place in classrooms that are populated by numbers of culturally and linguistically diverse students. When teachers are telling stories, they need to incorporate stories that reflect the heritages of the children with whom they work (see, for example, Bishop, 1994; Bosma, 1994; Harris, 1992; and Miller-Lachman, 1995, for animal stories, fables, folktales, legends, and myths that might be used). Children need to be encouraged to tell stories from their cultural backgrounds. Parents may also be invited to classrooms to participate in storytelling. Storytelling opens up multiple possibilities for understanding diverse world views.

Language Play. Across cultures, children engage in language play (Lindfors, 1987). An oral tradition of many cultures is the sharing of rhymes, songs, riddles, games, tongue twisters, jokes, and so on across generations and among children. Teachers should make deliberate plans to use these forms, both to foster appreciation for other languages and cultures and to provide children with opportunities to manipulate the sounds of familiar and new languages. For example, teachers can make written records of these rhymes, songs, and finger plays in Spanish and English and can use them repeatedly in daily routines such as opening exercises, transitions between activities, introduction to read-aloud time, and school closing. Because children usually chant these forms in chorus, practice with the sounds of the new language takes place in a risk-free environment.

Many collections of such traditional lore in Spanish are readily available in the United States (e.g., Bravo-Villasante, 1980; Delacre, 1989; Jaramillo, 1994; Schon, 1994). Shen's Books and Supplies (8221 South First Avenue, Arcadia, CA 91006; www.shens.com) has collections of traditional poetry available in Japanese, Chinese, Korean, and Vietnamese, as well as in English translations. In languages in which material is not available commercially, teachers might invite parents to share traditional forms. The use of material from the oral tradition is strongly recommended.

CONTEXTS FOR ENCOURAGING LANGUAGE FOR OLDER CHILDREN

Just like teachers of younger children, the teachers of older students also need to provide specific contexts for helping their students interact verbally. Older students need opportunities to learn how to share their views in an organized manner, listen thoughtfully to others, and use language for the sheer enjoyment of communicating. We present three language-centered activities for older students.

Cooperative Learning Groups

Cooperative learning groups are an instructional context that provide the social structure for students to work together in small groups to accomplish a common goal (Calderon & Slavin, 1999). Such groups are an ideal context for language development. Students in a cooperative learning group are more motivated to speak because they (1) need to communicate to accomplish the common goal, (2) are taught to praise and encourage each other, and (3) are made interdependent so that they need to know what the others know. Because of these factors, cooperative learning provides a supportive, motivating context for speech to emerge. Cooperative learning groups allow for multiple opportunities for listening and speaking. The talk between students has multiple characteristics:

■ It is frequent. The single greatest advantage of cooperative learning over traditional classroom organization for the acquisition of language is the amount of talking students do within the group.

■ It is redundant. Students gain fluency if they have the opportunity to speak repeatedly on the same topic. Many cooperative learning structures, such as Pair Share, in which children discuss recent personal events with a partner, are explicitly designed to provide redundancy of talking opportunities. Even informal, cooperative learning discussion provides redundancy as students discuss a topic with each of their teammates. There is not enough time in the traditional classroom to call on each student to talk about a topic more than once.

■ It is developmentally appropriate. Speech to a whole class is often formal and less contextualized than speech within a cooperative group. It is easy to share an idea with a friendly peer; it is hard to answer a question or speak on an assigned topic before the whole class. Students within a small group have more opportunities to enter conversation at the level appropriate to their own development.

■ It is rich in feedback. Students talk to each other, providing immediate feedback and correction opportunities. Feedback and correction in the process of communication ("Give me that," "Sure, you take the ruler," etc.) lead to easy acquisition of vocabulary and language forms, whereas formal correction opportunities ("What is that?" "It is a ruler," etc.) lead to self-consciousness and anxiety, which inhibit, rather than facilitate, language acquisition.

The nature of cooperative learning activities also facilitates second-language learning because students speak in real time, about real events and objects, to accomplish real goals. They talk over things they are making and therefore negotiate meaning (Ovando & Collier, 1998).

Dramatic Simulations

Another language-centered activity ideally suited for older children is dramatic simulation or role-play. Like dramatic play for younger children, simulations allow students to try on different personas, create scripts, engage in metaplay language, and enjoy oral presentation (Brice-Heath, 1993). Trade Secret 3.2 by multiage teacher Carolyn Lara shows how she uses dramatic simulations to encourage language.

Movie, Video, Book, and Music Reviews

Another interesting way teachers can provide time for older students to share their thoughts and opinions orally is through the use of movie, video, book, and music reviews. The following scenario provides an example of how fifth- and sixth-grade students in Mr. Falconer's multiage classroom have arts in review time. For a half hour after lunch on Mondays, Mr. Falconer asks his students to break into small groups of three to four students to share their views of recent movies, videos, books, and music. The students are reminded to discuss only G or PG-13 movies (school policies restrict students and teachers from discussing R-rated movies in class).

> **MALCOLM:**   I watched *Shrek* this weekend. I saw it when it first came out but I missed some of the funny stuff the first time, like when the Gingerbread Man said "Eat Me" to the bad guy. The video also added a special feature where the characters sang and danced. That was excellent!
>
> **BRITTANY:**   I saw the movie but not the video. Did you know they [the filmmakers] are making fun of the guy that runs Disney? I wonder what he felt like when he saw how short they made that Lord Farquaad guy? Is he really that short?
>
> **JESSIE:**   I don't think he is that short, but I liked the fact that when the spell was broken that Pincess Fiona was still an ogre. It was a surprise 'cause I thought it was going to end like *Beauty and the Beast.*
>
> **BRITTANY:**   I know what you mean. It was surprising, but I thought, if she turned into a beautiful princess, how could they have a happy ending?
>
> **JESSIE:**   I think that they don't have to be the same physically to be happy—you know, both beautiful like *Beauty and the Beast* or both ogres, like Shrek. I would have liked it if they are different. How would it have been if she were an ogre and Shrek became a handsome prince?

In other parts of the room, students were talking about *Harry Potter, Lord of the Rings,* and a TV special, *Walking with Prehistoric Beasts.*

TRADE SECRET 3.2

How My Fourth- to Fifth-Grade Multiage Class Becomes TV Journalists: Using Dramatic Simulations to Encourage Language, Reading, and Cooperating

BY CAROLYN LARA

As a teacher of a combined fourth- and fifth-grade multiage class, I have a number of objectives that include oral presentation and language skills. Some of the academic goals for my elementary students include being able to

- Retell stories
- Express themselves in small group settings
- Express themselves in large group settings
- Use their language skills work cooperatively in small groups

One way I help my students learn presentation skills is through dramatic simulations. I use this approach because I have found that older children often express themselves more freely and are less self-conscious when they role-play. I have also observed that my students use more mature vocabulary when they play adult roles.

To begin this process, I schedule the first field trip of the year to a local TV station. The students observe the midday news being televised and have an opportunity to talk to the anchors, field reporters, and news producer. For the next few days, the class watches videos of the midday news show. As a class, we analyze the news, talk about story length (typically one to two minutes), and discuss how the newscasters summarize the "who, what, when, where, and why" of each story. We also talk about how newscasters use graphics to illustrate their stories.

During our reading time, we also study the characteristics of print media: the newspaper, news magazines, our weekly readers, and so on. We examine stories for the main ideas andsupporting details, and we also look at how news reporters can tell a story from multiple points of view. We practice by reading two versions of the "Three Little Pigs": the traditional story, told from the pig's view, and *The True Story of the*

Three Little Pigs (by Jon Scieszka), told from the wolf's perspective.

After the basics of newscasting have been explored, we begin to do our own weekly news show. We usually do newscasts on Friday mornings. I begin by randomly assigning students to five news beats (I pull their name cards from a bowl). One group takes world and national news, another group takes state and local news, a third group handles entertainment and the arts, a fourth takes sports, and the fifth handles the weather. After the students receive their group assignment, they individually review their section of the newspaper (each student receives a copy of the local newspaper). After ten minutes, I ask the groups to convene and to decide which stories they want to report about "on air." I serve as the news producer, and each group must receive story approval from me (which prevents stories that could be considered too controversial for fourth- and fifth-graders from being "aired"). Each news-beat group may only report three two-minute stories. After the news-beat groups decide which stories they want to report, they have another fifteen to twenty minutes to figure out how to summarize and present the information. During this process, they have to determine the facts, write their script, and figure out the type of reporting style they wish to use: the news anchor reader approach, the "in-the-field" reporter, live on-camera eyewitness interviews, or a combination of approaches. They also must decide on graphics or props. The students are free to use any art materials they need. Among their favorite graphics are transparencies and overhead pens as students find it enjoyable to project the graphic on the screen.

Next the broadcast begins. I am the video camera operator, but I also draw two student's names to be coproducers. The coproducers watch the time and cue the group and the camera

(continued on next page)

TRADE SECRET 3.2 (continued)

when to start and stop. The following is an example of a weather script the students wrote.

Celina: [wearing five or six coats.] Today it is cold in Phoenix, just 45 degrees. Let's ask the average person on the street what they think of our record-breaking temperatures. What do you think, average person? Is it cold?

Marcus: Hey, lady, I'm from Michigan, and this feels like summer to me [he has put on sunglasses to make his point and he is pretending to put on sunblock]. I'm just afraid I'm going to get a burn.

Celina: Well, let's find an Arizona native and see what he or she thinks. You over there, yes, you. What do you think?

Regina: [wearing an sign that says Arizona native] It is so cold! Did you know that this is the coldest it has been on this day since 1943? The cold weather is being caused by a low front coming from the Gulf of Mexico.

George: [wearing a sign that says farmer] Yes, and the farmers in the area are worried about their citrus crops. If it gets too much colder, we could lose a lot of grapefruits and oranges.

During this process, the students have a wonderful time figuring out how to share their stories and keep the "viewing audience" watching. Many students who are too shy to raise their hands during classroom discussion often blossom in during newscast days. In addition to being a wonderful opportunity for oral expression, this project helps students with reading comprehension and learning how to work together in small groups.

Due to the oftentimes sensitive and violent nature of the news, many districts now require the news broadcast to be videotaped and prescreened by the teacher prior to the students' viewing it. Prescreening gives the teacher an opportunity to edit out any material that might cause concern to the local community. It also gives the teacher an opportunity to observe and highlight specific newscasting techniques that might be of interest to the students.

During these sessions, Mr. Falconer drops into the groups to listen and share his views as a member of the discussion. He gives the small groups about fifteen minutes to talk. At the end, he asks if any group would like to share opinions with the whole group. Several of the groups talk about their discussions, and other individuals in the class offer additional comments. Mr. Falconer has noticed that since he began using this strategy to encourage oral discussion with older students, they are more willing to discuss their views during Readers' Workshop and Writing Workshop.

ASSESSMENT: FINDING OUT WHAT CHILDREN KNOW AND CAN DO

By the time most children are preschoolers, their oral language is quite rich and complex. This complexity makes assessment difficult. The only way to truly capture the full richness of children's language is to tape-record their conversations and then make a verbatim transcription of what is said, along with a detailed description of the context in which the language occurred. The transcript can then be analyzed to determine the mean length of sentences used, which forms of language the child used, the pragmatic rules followed, and so forth (see Genishi & Dyson, 1984). Unfortunately, such endeavors are very time consuming and are not practical in most teaching situations.

A number of more practical options are available for assessing children's oral language abilities. To illustrate these options, we use an incident observed in a university preschool. Julie is a four-year-old Korean girl who has been in the United States for about eight months. She participates in classroom activities, especially dramatic play, but rarely speaks either in Korean (she is the only child from Korea in the class) or in English. Chari, Julia's teacher, is playing with several other children at the time of the incident. Chari takes on the role of a customer and asks to use the toy phone in a post office theme center. She picks up the phone and makes a pretend phone call to Buddy, whose behavior is becoming very raucous. Chari says, "Ring, ring, ring. Buddy, there's a package waiting here for you in the post office." This "phone call" is successful in redirecting Buddy away from the rough-and-tumble play that he had been engaging in.

Julia is playing by herself in the housekeeping center, pretending to be a parent taking care of a baby (a doll). Julia overhears Chari's pretend phone call to Buddy, but she continues with her solitary play. A few minutes later, Julia picks up a toy phone in the housekeeping center, and says: "Ring, ring. Miss Chari, will you come over to my house?" It is Julia's first complete sentence used in the classroom.

Chari has several options for recalling Julia's language breakthrough. She might use a checklist. Figure 3.2 is a checklist used in a multilingual classroom. Such checklists are easy to use and require little time. This checklist can be easily modified to fit other situations (for example, for a monolingual classroom, the language columns could be eliminated) or to focus on other aspects of language (grammatical forms could replace Halliday's functional uses of language). Such instruments provide a broad view of the language that children use in the classroom. Much of the richness of the children's actual language, however, is lost.

Chari might use an anecdotal record. Anecdotal records are even less structured than an observation recording form (Figure 3.3). Here, the teacher writes a brief description of the language incident on a piece of paper, index card, or Post-it note. Later, Chari can file these anecdotes in individual folders for each of her students. This unstructured format allows Chari to make a detailed description of Julia's language exchange with her. Of course, anecdotal records require more time and effort on the part of the teacher than do the two previous methods.

As suggested earlier, teachers may elect to make audio or video recordings of children's language activity. Genishi and Dyson (1984) have developed guidelines for making audio recordings, which are adapted to include video recordings.

Child's Name	Language			Partner(s)			Location								Function						
	English	Spanish	Other	Child	Several Children	Adult	Library	Writing	Listening	Housekeeping	Theme (play)	Blocks	Math/Sci	Art	Instrumental	Regulatory	Interaction	Personal	Heuristic	Imaginative	Informative
Julia	✓									✓										✓	

FIGURE 3.2 Oral Language Checklist

1. Select an activity setting that encourages language interaction. (Dramatic play areas are a good place to start.)

2. If you are using a tape recorder, place it in the target setting and turn it on, checking first to make sure that the equipment is working. If using a video camcorder, place the camera on a tripod and adjust the zoom lens so that it covers the main area where children will be interacting. Turn the camera on, and check it occasionally to make sure that the camera angle is capturing the significant action.

3. Do a trial recording to make sure that the equipment is working correctly and that the children's language is being clearly recorded. This trial will also help desensitize the children to the equipment.

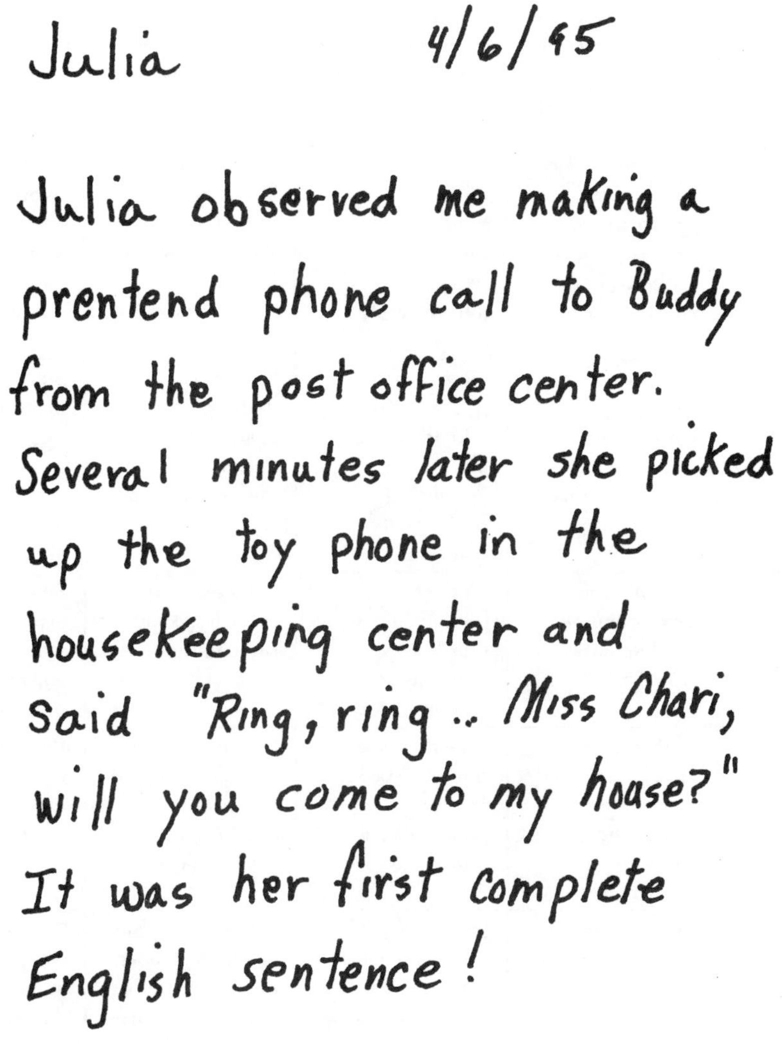

Julia   4/6/95

Julia observed me making a prentend phone call to Buddy from the post office center. Several minutes later she picked up the toy phone in the housekeeping center and said "Ring, ring .. Miss Chari, will you come to my house?" It was her first complete English sentence!

FIGURE 3.3   Anecdotal Record

4. Listen to or view the recordings as soon as possible so that your memory can help fill in the gaps in unintelligible parts of the recordings.

An effective way to analyze the data contained in audio and video recordings is to use a rubric to judge the quality of individual's oral language behavior. A rubric is a set of criteria that describe student performance in terms of proficiency levels (O'Neil, 1994). Figure 3.4 offers an example of a rubric that can be used to assess older children's oral presentations and guide their efforts to develop more effective presentations.

FIGURE 3.4   A Rubric to Assess Oral Presentations

Evaluating Student Presentations

	1	2	3	4	Total
Organization	Audience cannot understand presentation because there is no sequence of information.	Audience has difficulty following presentation because student jumps around.	Student presents information in logical sequence that audience can follow.	Student presents information in logical, interesting sequence that audience can follow.	
Subject Knowledge	Student does not have grasp of information; student cannot answer questions about subject.	Student is uncomfortable with information and is able to answer only rudimentary questions.	Student is at ease with expected answers to all questions, but fails to elaborate.	Student demonstrates full knowledge by answering all class questions with explanations and elaboration.	
Graphics	Student uses superfluous graphics or no graphics.	Student occasionally uses graphics that don't support text and presentation.	Student's graphics relate to text and presentation.	Student's graphics explain and reinforce screen text and presentation.	
Mechanics	Student's presentation has four or more grammatical errors.	Presentation has three misspellings and/or grammatical errors.	Presentation has no more than two misspellings and/or grammatical errors.	Presentation has no misspellings or grammatical errors.	
Eye Contact	Student reads all of report with no eye contact.	Student occasionally uses eye contact, but still reads most of the report.	Student maintains eye contact most of the time but frequently returns to notes.	Student maintains eye contact with audience, seldom returning to notes.	
Elocution	Student mumbles, incorrectly pronounces terms, and speaks too quietly for students in the back of class to hear.	Student's voice is low. Student incorrectly pronounces terms. Audience members have difficulty hearing presentation.	Student's voice is clear. Student pronounces most words correctly. Most audience members can hear presentation.	Student uses a clear voice and correct, precise pronunciation of terms so that all audience members can hear presentation.	

Adapted from a rubric developed by Information Technology Evaluation Services, NC Department of Public Instruction.

SUMMARY

This chapter began with a review of the many ways parents can support their child's language development within the home. The remainder of the chapter described ways that teachers can provide young children with stimulating oral language experiences that promote active listening and more precise, sophisticated speech. How did your own experiences at home and at school compare with those described in this chapter? Did you recall other types of beneficial oral language activities that were not covered?

To summarize the key points about facilitating oral language learning, we return to the guiding questions at the beginning of this chapter:

- *How can parents best facilitate their children's oral language development?*

Parents can promote their children's oral language by scaffolding their children's language, encouraging them to tell personal narratives about their experiences, reading stories to them on a regular basis, monitoring their TV viewing, and encouraging active viewing.

- *What is the initiation, response, evaluation (IRE) pattern of class talk? What problems are associated with this type of discourse? How can teachers provide students with more stimulating conversations in the classroom?*

The IRE pattern of discourse occurs when the teacher asks a question, a student answers, and the teacher either accepts or rejects that answer and goes on to ask another question. These types of question-and-answer exchanges do not provide the type of language input and feedback needed to advance children's language skills. Teachers can provide richer oral language experiences for children by engaging them in reciprocal conversations and discussions: listening closely and responding to their comments; asking genuine, open-ended questions; welcoming the interjection of personal experiences; and encouraging child–child turn-taking interactions.

- *How do group activities, learning centers, and dramatic play promote oral language acquisition?*

These types of activities create language content (i.e., give children something to talk about). In addition, children must use language to participate successfully in these types of activity.

- *What can teachers do to promote language-rich dramatic play?*

Teachers can promote language-rich play by providing (1) settings equipped with theme-related, culturally relevant props; (2) scheduling lengthy play periods; and (3) being actively involved in children's play activities.

■ *How can sharing or show-and-tell be turned into a valuable oral language activity?*

Traditional sharing involves having one child speak to the entire class. This activity can be transformed into a valuable oral language activity by limiting group size and encouraging children in the audience to participate actively by ask questions and making comments.

■ *How can teachers effectively assess students' oral language development?*

Teachers should observe children interacting during regular classroom activities and use checklists, observation sheets, and/or anecdotal records to document significant milestones in their oral language acquisition.

■ *What can teachers do to optimize oral language experiences for bilingual and second-language learners?*

The same strategies recommended for native English speakers are also appropriate for use with bilingual and second-language learners. The major adaptations that are needed are (1) exposing children to books and other print in child's native language and (2) allowing children lots of opportunity to speak, listen, read, and write in their native language.

LINKING KNOWLEDGE TO PRACTICE

1. Visit an early childhood classroom and observe children interacting in a dramatic play center. Notice the theme that the children are acting out and the roles that they are playing. Record examples of both metaplay language and pretend language.

2. Observe students engaging in a sharing (show-and-tell) activity. Describe the teacher's role and the students' behavior (both the speaker and the audience). Did this sharing time involve most of the students in active listening?

3. Make an observation recording form similar to the one in Figure 3.3. Visit an early childhood classroom and observe a small group of children interacting at a learning center. Use the observation recording form to record several significant utterances from each child. What do these behaviors indicate about each child's language development?

CHAPTER 4

BUILDING A FOUNDATION FOR LITERACY LEARNING

As Isaac enters his kindergarten classroom, he and his classmates collect laminated helper necklaces from their name pockets on the attendance chart. Each necklace has a tag listing a classroom task. Isaac "reads" his tag: Errand Runner. He checks the nearby Helper Board, where all the duties for each task have been described in both words and pictures. Today he will run errands for his teacher, such as taking the attendance count to the center's office. Yesterday, Isaac was Pencil Sharpener, which involved gathering and sharpening pencils. He hopes to be Pet Feeder tomorrow.

According to the emergent literacy view, the literacy learning process shares much in common with oral language development process. Literacy acquisition, like oral language development, begins early. For many children, literacy development begins in infancy when caregivers read storybooks to children and when children begin to notice print in the environment. Literacy learning is an active, constructive process. By observing print and having stories read to them, young children discover patterns and create their own early versions of reading and writing that initially have little resemblance to conventional forms: the story they "read" may be quite different from the one in the book, and their writing may look like drawing or scribbles. As children have opportunities to use these early forms of literacy in meaningful social situations and as they interact with adults who draw their attention to the features and functions of print, their constructions become increasingly similar to conventional reading and writing.

Home literacy experiences help children develop an awareness of the forms and functions of print. Therefore, developmentally appropriate early childhood programs feature literacy activities that mirror the types of literacy experiences found in enriched home environments, such as print-rich settings, storybook reading, demonstrations of various forms of literacy, and many opportunities for children to engage in meaningful reading and writing activities. Such experiences build on what children have already learned about written language, provide a smooth transition between home and school, and help ensure initial success with language arts instruction.

In the sections that follow, we discuss four strategies that form the foundation of developmentally appropriate preschool and kindergarten language arts programs: functional literacy activities, sharing literature, literacy play, and the language experience approach (also known as shared writing). These strategies are particularly valuable because they provide a broad spectrum of learning opportunities appropriate for children at different ages and with different prior experience with print. When used with large groups of children, opportunities exist for *all* children to gain valuable knowledge about literacy.

BEFORE READING THIS CHAPTER, THINK ABOUT . . .

- How you used print as a child. Did you write notes to your family? Did you pretend to write checks? Send a letter to Santa? Write a thank-you card to Grandma?

- Advertising logos you remember from your childhood. Could you spot a McDonald's a mile away? Did your favorite toy or snack food have a special logo or trademark?

- The favorite books from your childhood. Did you have one or two favorite books that you liked to have your parents, siblings, or other adults read to you? Did you have a favorite book that you liked to read on your own?

- How you played house as a child. Did you have real cereal boxes and egg cartons for your pretend kitchen? Did an interested adult join in your pretend play?

FOCUS QUESTIONS

- What are functional literacy activities, and how can teachers use these activities in a preschool or kindergarten classroom?

- How can teachers set up a well-designed library center?

- What are the characteristics of effective adult storybook reading?

- How can dramatic play centers be used to encourage young children's literacy development?

- How do the language experience approach (or shared writing) and interactive writing increase a child's understanding of print and facilitate reading development?

HOME LITERACY EXPERIENCES

Early studies on children's home literacy experiences focused on umbrella characteristics such as family income and parents' levels of education (Sulzby & Teale, 1991). Results revealed positive relationships between these variables and reading

■ ■ ■ ■ ■ ■

BOX 4.1

DEFINITION OF TERMS

broad-spectrum instructional strategy: strategies that are effective and appropriate for a wide range of learner abilities.

environmental print (EP): includes the real-life print children see in the home or community, including print on food containers and other kinds of product boxes, store signs, road signs, and advertisements. Because the situation gives clues to the print's meaning, EP is often the first type of print young children recognize and understand.

functional literacy activities: reading and writing activities that accomplish real-life purposes, such as writing lists and reading directions.

functional print: print that guides everyday classroom activity (e.g., labels, lists, directions, sign-up sheets).

interactive writing: an extension of shared writing in which children share the pen with the teacher to write a text.

language experience approach (LEA)/shared writing: the teacher works with whole groups, small groups, or individual students to write down the children's oral language stories. These highly contextualized stories are easy for children to read.

literacy-enriched dramatic play centers: sociodramatic play centers that are enhanced with appropriate theme-related literacy materials, such as recipe cards, cookbooks, and food containers for the kitchen center.

shared book experience: the teacher reads a big book with enlarged print and encourages children to read along on parts that they can remember or predict.

achievement in the early grades. For example, children from middle-income families tend to be better readers than those from low-income families. Unfortunately, such findings do little to explain how these variables directly affect children's literacy growth.

More recent studies have narrowed their focus and have attempted to describe the actual literacy-related experiences that children have at home. These home literacy studies have identified several factors that appear to have important roles in early literacy acquisition. These factors are described in the sections that follow.

Access to Print and Books

To learn about literacy, young children must have opportunities to see lots of print and must have easy access to books. Plentiful home supplies of children's books have been found to be associated with early reading (Durkin, 1966), interest in literature (Morrow, 1983), and positive orientation toward schooling (Feitelson & Goldstein, 1986).

Because of the literate nature of our society, all children are surrounded by large amounts of environmental print. For example, they see print on product containers (Cheerios, Pepsi), street signs (Stop), and store signs (McDonald's, Pizza Hut).

Differences do occur, however, in children's exposure to books and other forms of reading materials. Bill Teale's (1986b) descriptive study of the home environments of twenty-four low-income preschoolers revealed that although some of the homes had ample supplies of children's books, other homes contained none. This finding is not to suggest that all children from low-income families lack exposure to reading materials at home (see Special Feature 4.1). Those children who do not have access to books at home, however, are at a great disadvantage in acquiring literacy.

Adult Demonstrations of Literacy Behavior.   Children also need to observe their parents, other adults, or older siblings using literacy in everyday situations (Smith, 1988). When children see their family members use print for various purposes— writing shopping lists, paying bills, looking up programs in the television listings, and writing notes to each other—they begin to learn about the practical uses of written language and to understand why reading and writing are activities worth doing. If their parents happen to model reading for pleasure, so much the better. These children see literature as a source of entertainment. Children's exposure to these types of functional and recreational literacy demonstrations has been found to vary greatly.

Supportive Adults.   Early readers tend to have parents who are very supportive of their early attempts at literacy (Morrow, 1983). Although these parents rarely attempt to directly teach their children how to read and write, they do support literacy growth by doing such things as (1) answering their children's questions about print; (2) pointing out letters and words in the environment; (3) reading storybooks frequently; (4) making regular visits to the local library; (5) providing children with a wide variety of experiences such as trips to stores, parks, and museums; and (6) initiating functional literacy activities such as suggesting that a child write a letter to grandmother or help make a shopping list.

The amount of such support that children receive during the preschool years varies greatly from family to family. These differences have been found to have a considerable effect on children's literacy learning during kindergarten and the elementary grades (Christian, Morrison, & Bryant, 1998).

Independent Engagements with Literacy

Young children need to get their hands on literacy materials and have opportunities to engage in early forms of reading and writing. Such exploration and experimentation allow children to try out and perfect their growing concepts about the functions, forms, and conventions of written language.

Independent engagements with literacy often take place in connection with play. Don Holdaway (1979) has described how, as soon as young children become familiar with a storybook through repetitive read-aloud experiences, they will begin to play with the books and pretend to read them. He believes that this type of reading-like play is one of the most important factors promoting early literacy acquisition.

SPECIAL FEATURE 4.1
The Home Literacy Experiences of Nonmainstream Children

The majority of the research on the home literacy experiences of young children has been conducted in white, middle-class homes. In recent years, however, increasing attention is being given to the home literacy experiences of nonmainstream children: children from low-income and ethnically diverse families. The findings are mixed and show a complex picture of these children's early experiences with language and literacy.

On one hand, some studies have shown that many poor families have had difficulty providing their children with the rich types of language and literacy experiences that middle-income families typically provide (Vernon-Feagons, Hammer, Miccio, & Manlove, 2001). The Hart and Risley (1995) study, described in detail in Chapter 2, reported that low-income mothers used fewer words and a more restricted vocabulary in conversations with their children. Other studies suggest that many low-income children may have less experience with rhyming activity (Fernandez-Fein & Baker, 1997) and are less likely than middle class children to visit public libraries (Baker, Serpell, & Sonnenschein, 1995).

Other studies have documented a wide range of home literacy environments and practices within nonmainstream families (Purcell-Gates, 1996; Taylor & Dorsey-Gaines, 1988; Teale, 1986b). For example, Vicki Purcell-Gates's study of twenty low-income families of differing ethnic backgrounds revealed great variability in the literacy experiences of children. The total number of literacy events in the low-income homes ranged from 0.17 to 5.07 per hour, meaning that some children had opportunities to experience more than twenty-five times the amount of literacy than

other children. Similarly, Teale's (1986b) study of low-income children in San Diego, California, revealed that the average number of minutes per hour that children engaged in literacy activities ranged from 3.6 to 34.72, almost a tenfold difference. Although on average the home literacy experiences of low-income children may not be as rich as those of the average middle-class children, some nonmainstream children do have frequent interactions with print.

Another study (Vernon-Feagons, Hammer, Miccio, and Manlove, 2001, p. 194) pointed out a shortcoming of research on nonmainstream children's home literacy environments: "Most studies of poverty have generally measured environmental factors in the home at the exclusion of measuring health and the larger discrimination in the larger society." For example, that study cited Lynne Vernon-Faegans's (1996) study of rural African American children in the Piedmont area of North Carolina, which found that, within this group of children, those with early nutritional deficits were at much greater risk of having problems acquiring literacy. Larger societal factors also enter the picture. Susan Neuman and Donna Celano (2001), for example, found that low-income families had much more restricted access to public libraries and places to buy books. In addition, the school libraries in low-income neighborhoods had fewer books per child, lower-quality books, less qualified librarians, and fewer computers than school libraries in more affluent neighborhoods. Thus, limited access to literacy materials and good places to read, caused by societal inequities, may be contributing factors to many low-income children's "at-risk" status.

Young children also incorporate writing into their play. Sometimes this play writing is exploratory in nature, with children experimenting with different letter-forms and shapes. At other times, emergent writing occurs in the context of make-believe play. Figure 4.1 is an example of this type of play-related writing. Four-year-old Ben was engaging in dramatic play in the housekeeping center.

FIGURE 4.1   Ben's Post-it note: "Gone to soccer practice. Be back at 4."

He wrote a Post-it note message to another child, who was acting out the role of his mother, informing her that he was at soccer practice.

Elizabeth Sulzby's (1985) research has revealed how children's early writing follows a loose developmental sequence, becoming more conventional over time. Sulzby (1990) has identified seven broad categories of early writing: drawing as writing, scribble writing, letter-like units, nonphonetic letterstrings, copying from environmental print, invented spelling, and conventional writing (see Figure 4.2).

Play provides children with highly pleasurable and meaningful opportunities to experiment with these early forms of writing. In addition, social interaction during play (such as when other players cannot read a shopping list written in scribble writing) may provide motivation for children to develop more conventional forms of script.

Young children also use literacy in functional, nonplay situations. An excellent example is Glenda Bissex's (1980) account of how her four-year-old son Paul, after failing to get her attention by verbal means, used a stamp set to write "RUDF" (Are you deaf?). He also attempted to secure his privacy by putting the sign "DO NOT DSTRB GNYS AT WRK" (Do not disturb genius at work) on his door.

Drawing as writing—Pictures represent writing.

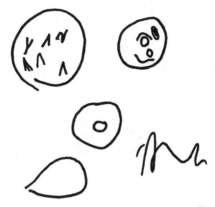

Context: Angela (age 4), who is playing in the housekeeping center, makes a shopping list for a trip to the supermarket.

Text: "Hamburgers [the two bottom circles] and chocolate chip cookies [the two top circles]"

Scribble writing—Continuous lines represent writing.

Context: Rimmert Jr. (age 6) writes a thank-you letter to a family friend.

Text: "Thank you for your letter from America."

Letter-like units—The child makes a series of separate marks that have some letter-like characteristics

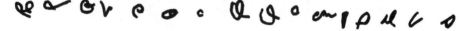

Context: Lauren (age 4) writes a story about a recent experience.

Text: "I buy the food at the store. I baked it, and I washed it and ate it."

Nonphonetic letter strings—The child writes strings of letters that show no evidence of letter–sound relationships. These can be random groups of letters or repeated clusters of letters.

Context: Debbie (age 4) writes in her journal about a recent school experience.

Text: "We play together, and Bobby fought with us. We fight with him, then we play again."

FIGURE 4.2   Sulzby's Categories of Emergent Writing

(continued)

Copying from environmental print—The child copies print found in the environment.

Context: Pierce (age 4), in the role of a veterinarian, writes a prescription for a sick teddy bear. He copies the words *apple juice* from a can he has retrieved from a nearby garbage can.

Text: "Penicillin" [invented spelling]
               "Apple juice" [copying]

Invented spelling—The child creates his or her own spelling using letter–sound relationships. This can range from using one letter per word to using a letter for every sound in each word (as in the example below).

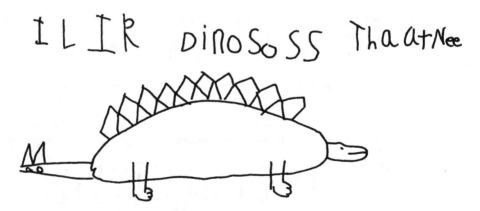

Context: Chris (age 5) writes in his journal.
Text: "I like dinosaurs. They are neat."

FIGURE 4.2   Continued

Conventional—The child uses correct spelling for most of the words.

Context: Johnny (age 5) writes in his journal.
Text: "This is a dog jumping over a box."

FIGURE 4.2   Continued

Opportunities to engage in these types of independent engagements with literacy depend on access to books and writing materials. As mentioned previously, research on children's home environments indicates that there are wide discrepancies in the availability of children's books and other reading materials. Similar differences also exist in the availability of writing materials. Teale's (1986b) descriptive study of the home environments of low-income preschoolers revealed that only four of twenty-four children had easy access to paper and writing instruments. He noted that these particular children engaged in far more emergent writing than did the other subjects in the study.

Storybook Reading

Storybook reading is undoubtedly the most studied aspect of home literacy. Quantitative studies have attempted to establish the importance and value of parents reading to their children. One meta-analysis of twenty-nine studies spanning more than three decades indicated that parent–preschooler storybook reading was positively related to outcomes such as language growth, early literacy, and reading achievement (Bus, van Ijzendoorn, & Pellegrini, 1995).

Other studies have attempted to describe and analyze what actually takes place during storybook-reading episodes and to identify the mechanisms through which storybook reading facilitates literacy growth (e.g., Altwerger, Diehl-Faxon, & Dockstader-Anderson, 1985; Heath, 1982; Holdaway, 1979; Snow & Ninio, 1986; Taylor, 1986; Yaden, Smolkin, & Conlon, 1989). These studies have shown that parent–child storybook reading is an ideal context for children to receive all the previously mentioned factors that promote literacy acquisition:

1. Storybook reading provides children with access to enjoyable children's books, which builds positive attitudes about books and reading.
2. During storybook reading, parents present children with a model of skilled reading. Children see how books are handled, and they hear the distinctive intonation patterns that are used in oral reading.
3. Parents provide support that enables young children to take an active part in storybook reading. Early storybook-reading sessions tend to be routine, with the parent first focusing the child's attention on a picture and then asking the child to label the picture. If the child does so, then the parent gives positive or negative feedback about the accuracy of the label. If the child does not volunteer a label, then the parent provides the correct label (Snow & Ninio, 1986). As children's abilities grow, parents up the ante, shifting more of the responsibility to the children and expecting them to participate in more advanced ways.
4. Storybook reading encourages independent engagements with literacy by familiarizing children with stories and encouraging them to attempt to read the stories on their own (Holdaway, 1979; Sulzby, 1985a).

Other researchers have studied how cultural factors affect the manner in which parents mediate storybook reading for their children. Shirley Brice Heath (1982) found that middle-class parents tended to help their children link book information with other experiences. For example, John Langstaff's popular, predictable book, *Oh, A-Hunting We Will Go* (1974, Macmillan), contains the following lines:

> *Oh, a-hunting we will go.*
> *A-hunting we will go.*
> *We'll catch a lamb*
> *And put him in a pram*
> *And then we'll let him go.*

To help the child understand the term *pram,* a middle-class parent might say, "The pram looks just like your sister's baby carriage." Working-class parents, on the other hand, had a tendency to not extend book information beyond its original context and would simply define the word *pram* for the child. Sulzby and Teale (1991) speculate that these differences in story-reading style may have a considerable effect on children's early literacy acquisition.

FUNCTIONAL LITERACY ACTIVITIES

A child's home reading experiences are usually functional in nature. Children watch their parents and older siblings use reading and writing to accomplish real-life purposes. They often join in these activities (e.g., reading food labels and signs in the environment). It is important that teachers provide opportunities for children to continue to learn about functional qualities of reading and writing.

In the vignette at the opening of this chapter, note how the helper necklaces in Isaac's classroom provide the same type of functional literacy experiences that children have at home. The print on the helper necklaces serves a real purpose and assists with everyday activities (classroom chores). The surrounding context—the chores that are done on a daily basis in the classroom—makes the print on the necklaces easy to recognize and understand.

Functional literacy activity is a broad-spectrum strategy that provides opportunities for children who are at different stages in their literacy development to learn new skills and concepts. For example, if Isaac is just beginning to learn about the meaning and functions of print, then the helper necklaces provide an opportunity to learn that print can inform him about his assigned chores and help him remember these chores. If he has already acquired this basic concept, then the necklaces provide opportunities to learn about the structure of print. For example, he may eventually learn to recognize some of the printed words on the necklaces (*runner, pencil, pet*) or to figure out some related letter–sound relationships (the letter *p* represents the sound that *pencil* and *pet* begin with).

In the sections that follow, we describe two types of print that can provide children with functional literacy activities. Environmental print exists in everyday life outside of school, and functional print is connected with classroom activities.

Bringing Environmental Print into the Classroom

Children begin to recognize environmental print—print that occurs in real-life contexts—at a very early age. Several researchers (e.g., Goodman, 1986; Lomax & McGee, 1987; Mason, 1980) have shown that many three- and four-year-olds can recognize and know the meanings of product labels (Colgate, Cheerios, Pepsi), restaurant signs (McDonald's, Pizza Hut), and street signs (Stop). Even if children do not say the correct word when attempting to read such print, they usually will come up with a related term. For example, when presented with a Coca-Cola can, the child might say "Pepsi."

Grocery stores are many children's first libraries

In recognizing environmental print, children attend to the entire context rather than just the print (Masonheimer, Drum, & Ehri, 1984). This *logographic reading* begins quite early. Yetta Goodman (1986) found that 80 percent of the four-year-olds in her study could recognize environmental print in full context; they knew that a can of Pepsi Cola said *Pepsi.* Typically, by the middle of kindergarten, many children learn to recognize a limited set of whole words without environmental context clues, using incidental cues such as shape, length, and pictures (Ehri, 1991).

Children often begin to recognize the letters of the alphabet at about the same time as they "read" environmental print. This ability varies considerably among children, with some children recognizing one third of the alphabet by age three (Hiebert, 1981) and others not learning any letters until they enter kindergarten (Morgan, 1987). As is explained later in this chapter, variations in children's home literacy experiences appear to be responsible for some of these differences.

Interest also appears to be a key factor in determining the specific letters that children learn first (McGee & Richgels, 1989). Children's own names and highly salient environmental print (EP) are often the source of initial letter learning. Marcia Baghban (1984), for example, describes how K (Kmart), M (McDonald's), and G (Giti) were among the first letters recognized by her two-year-old daughter Giti.

The ability to recognize letters is an important step in early literacy development. To grasp the *alphabetic principle* that underlies written English, children must realize that words are made up of individual letters. As explained later, this principle is an important prerequisite to invented spelling, decoding, and independent reading. Children's letter-recognition ability has been repeatedly shown to be a powerful predictor of later reading achievement (Adams, 1990). We present strategies for helping children learn the alphabet in Chapter 5.

Because the situation gives clues to the print's meaning, EP is often the first type of print that young children can recognize and understand. Because EP is so meaningful and easy to read, it should be available in all preschool and kindergarten classrooms. Unfortunately, EP tends to be rather scarce in school settings (Morrow, 2001). Teachers must therefore strive to make this type of print available to their students. Following are several strategies that can be used to bring real-world EP into the classroom.

EP Alphabet Chart. The teacher places pieces of chart paper around the room for every letter of the alphabet. Each day, children bring to class product labels that they can "read." During circle time, these labels are read and attached to the correct chart. For example, the Kix (cereal) label would go on the *K k* page. Then the group reads the labels on all the charts, starting with the *A a* page. After several months, when most of the chart pages are full, the teacher can use the product labels from the charts to make books such as "I Can Read Cereals."

EP Folders. Selected pieces of EP can be attached to file folders to make EP books (Anderson & Markle, 1985). For example, a pizza book could be made by pasting or laminating the product logos from pizza advertisements, coupons, and delivery containers onto the inside surfaces of a file folder (see Figure 4.3). Children can decorate the front cover with pizza-related illustrations. Other book possibilities include toothpaste, cookies, milk, cereal, and soft drinks. These EP folders should be placed in the classroom library so that children can show off to their friends how well they can read this type of contextualized print.

EP Walks. The strategy of EP walks involves taking a class for a walk in the neighborhood surrounding the school (Orellana & Hernández, 1999). Before leaving, the children are told to be on the lookout for EP. As examples of EP are encountered during the walk, they are pointed out by the teacher or by the children. After the children return to the classroom, they draw pictures of the print they could read on the walk. The pictures are put into a group book, which the teacher reads aloud to the class. The children can then take turns reading EP items in the book.

Individual EP Booklets. Magazine coupons or advertisements that feature products children are familiar with can be used to make personalized "I Can Read" books. Children sort through the ads or coupons, select the products they recognize, and then use glue sticks to secure the coupons to premade construction-paper booklets. The children can share their booklets with others and take them home to read to family members.

FIGURE 4.3   Folder

Literacy-enriched Dramatic Play.   As will be explained later in this chapter, EP can be used as props in children's dramatic play. For example, empty product boxes such as cereal containers and milk cartons can be used in the kitchen area of housekeeping or home centers. As children act out home-related themes such as making dinner, they will have opportunities to attempt to read the print on the containers.

Functional Print Connected with Classroom Activities

Unlike environmental print that is found in the world outside of school, functional classroom print is connected with everyday school activities. This print is practical as well as educational. The helper necklaces in the opening vignette help children remember their assigned chores, making the classroom run more smoothly. Simultaneously, the necklaces offer children opportunities to learn about the functions and structure of print. As with all functional print, the context helps children discover the meaning of the print.

Nancy Taylor and her colleagues (1986) observed the print in a number of preschool classrooms and used qualitative procedures to develop categories of written language displays, many of which involved functional uses. The major types of functional print that they discovered in classrooms are labels, lists, directions, schedules, calendars, and messages.

Labels. As illustrated by the helper necklaces in the vignette at the beginning of this chapter, labels may be used to delineate tasks that students are assigned to complete, such as line leader, pencil sharpener, pet feeder, and paper passer. Labels can also be used to help organize the classroom. For example, cubbies can be labeled with children's names so that students know where their belongings are stored. Containers can be labeled to designate their contents, and labels can be used on shelves to indicate where materials are to be stored. Labels can also be used to designate different areas of the classroom (library, home center, blocks, games, art), informing children about the types of activities that are supposed to take place in each location. Finally, labels can be used to convey information. For example, teachers often use labels to identify objects in displays (e.g., types of sea shells) and pictures ("This is a . . .").

Lists. Lists have a variety of practical classroom uses. Attendance charts can be constructed by placing each child's picture and name above a pocket. The children sign in by finding their name card in a box and by matching it with their name on the chart. After the children become familiar with their printed names, the pictures can be removed. In Trade Secret 4.1, a preschool teacher offers another way of using this approach to take attendance and document ongoing literacy development.

The teacher can use a second set of name tags to post jobs on a helper chart (Figure 4.4). This chart, which is an alternative to the helper necklaces described at the beginning of this chapter, contains a description of jobs needing to be done and display pockets that hold the children's name cards. When attendance and helper charts are used on a daily basis, children quickly learn to recognize their own names and the names of their classmates.

TRADE SECRET 4.1
Connecting Names and Faces

Ms. Martinez uses a visual approach to help her three- and four-year-old preschool students recognize their names and document their literacy growth over time. During the first day of school, Ms. Martinez takes an individual picture of each student using an instant camera. As the child's image emerges on the photo, she asks each child to write his or her name on a piece of construction paper. (If the child's writing is completely illegible, then she writes the child's name conventionally next to the child's personal script and explains, "This is how I write your name."). She places the child's picture above the name and places the page in a clear plastic protector. She places the pictures on a child's eye-level bulletin board. She uses the bulletin board to help the children take attendance (as the children enter the room in the morning they attach a brightly painted clothespin to their pictures).

In five or six weeks, Ms. Martinez repeats this process. She takes new pictures of the children and again asks them to print their names on a new piece of construction paper. In addition, she asks them to write anything else they would like to share. She is always amazed at how much the children's ability to print their names and their understanding about print has developed during the first few weeks. Instead of sending the first set of pictures home, she organizes the pages in a booklike fashion and places the "Our Class" book in the library. It is one of the children's favorite library books.

Ms. Martinez repeats this process four to five times during the year. By the end of the year, she has a visual record of her students' writing development throughout the school year.

Directions. Instructions can be posted for using equipment such as tape recorders and computers. Classroom rules (e.g., "We walk in our classroom") can be displayed to remind children of appropriate behavior. In addition, children can create their own personal directives. For example, a child may place a "Look, don't touch!" sign on a newly completed art project or block structure. At first, children will need help from the teacher or from peers in reading these types of directions. Soon, however, they will learn to use the surrounding context to help them remember what the directions say. Teachers can facilitate this process by constantly referring children to these posted directions. For example, if a child is running in the classroom, then the teacher could direct the child's attention to the "We walk in our classroom" sign and ask, "What does that sign say?"

Directions can also include recipes for cooking or instructions for art activities. The information can be put on wall charts. Even very young children can follow simple directions that use both words and pictures.

Schedules. A daily schedule can be presented at the beginning of class to prepare children for upcoming activities. Pictures can be used to help children remember

FIGURE 4.4   Helper Chart

the different segments of the day (Figure 4.5). When children ask what is going to happen next, the teacher can help them use the chart to figure it out.

Calendars.   A monthly calendar can be set up at the beginning of each month and used for marking children's birthdays, parties, and other special events (field trips, classroom visitors, when a student's dog had puppies, etc.). The teacher can encourage the children to use the calendar to determine how many more days until a special event takes place and to record events of importance to them.

FIGURE 4.5   Daily Schedule

Messages.   Often, unforeseen events change the day's plans. It's raining, so there can be no outdoor playtime. Instead of just telling children, some teachers write a message. For example:

> Circle time will be first thing this morning.
> We have a special visitor!
> She will share her cookies with us.

Because these messages inform children about activities that directly affect their day, even the youngest children quickly learn to pay close attention to these notices.

Sign-In and Sign-Up Lists. Children can write their names on lists for a variety of functional purposes. For example, kindergarten teacher Bobbi Fisher (1995) writes the date and day at the top of large nine-by-eighteen-inch piece of drawing paper and has her students write their names on the paper each morning when they first arrive in the classroom. Fisher and her assistant teacher also sign the list. During circle time, the list is read to the class as a means of taking attendance and to build a sense of community. As the students become familiar with each other's printed names, they take over the activity. Fisher periodically uses this sign-in procedure to assess the students' emerging writing abilities.

Lists can also be used to sign up for popular classroom centers and playground equipment. Judith Schickedanz (1986) describes how teachers at the Boston University laboratory preschool have children sign up on lists to use popular centers such as the block and dramatic play areas. If children do not get a chance to use the area on a given day, then they are first in line to use it the next day. Sign-up sheets are also used to get turns using tricycles on the playground.

Children should be encouraged to use emergent forms of writing. If a child's writing is completely illegible, then the teacher may need to write the child's name conventionally next to the child's personal script. The teacher can explain, "This is how I write your name." Once the child's name is recognizable, this scaffold can be discontinued.

Inventory Lists. Lists can also be used to create inventories of the supplies in different classroom areas. Susan Neuman and Kathy Roskos (1993) give an example of a chart that contains an inventory of the supplies in the art area. The list contains a picture and the name of each item as well as the quantity of each item available. The sign informs children that there are eight paintbrushes, twelve pairs of scissors, lots of paper, and so on. During cleanup, children can use this information to make sure the center is ready for future use.

SHARING LITERATURE WITH CHILDREN

As early as 1908, Edmond Huey wrote about children's acquisition of reading and noted that "the key to it all lies in the parent's reading aloud to and with the child" (p. 332). Today, after decades of research on the teaching of reading, we continue to agree with Huey. More recently, Marilyn Adams (1990) summarized what many educators believe and what research supports: "The single most important activity for building the knowledge and skills eventually required for reading appears to be reading aloud to children" (p. 46). This single act—parents and teachers reading aloud to children—has received more research attention than any other aspect of children's literacy development. The findings of this vast body of research support the claims of Huey and Adams.

What do we know about the benefits of parents or other adults reading aloud to young children? Come peek in on one of Joseph's story-reading events with his dad, Mike (Mowery, 1993). The reading begins with Mike inviting eighteen-month-old Joseph to pick a book "that Daddy hasn't read in a while" and Joseph eagerly climbing up into his daddy's lap. *Already Joseph knows that books are enjoyable; he even has favorites.* Dad waits for Joseph to snuggle in and turn the book so it is ready to be opened. *Already Joseph knows how to hold the book and that it needs to be held in a certain way to open,* skills Marie Clay (1985) would call important concepts about print. Joseph quickly moves beyond the title page; *he knows the story begins on the page with more print,* another concept about print. He looks up at his dad, perhaps signaling "I'm ready." *He knows what his dad will do (read) and he knows what he should do (listen),* although at this age, Mike doesn't always read and Joseph doesn't always listen. Sometimes Mike asks, "What's this?" as he points to a picture in the book. Joseph does his best to label the picture, and Dad says, " "Hey, it's a _____! And this is a _____." Joseph says, "Hey! _____!" *Joseph increases his vocabulary as he labels pictures in books and as he hears words read aloud in the context of a story.*

Today Dad reads a story that is one of Joseph's favorites, but one Mike has grown weary of reading. To hurry the reading along, Mike creates a sentence to accompany the picture on a page. Joseph says, "No! No! Read!" and he points to the words on the page. *Already Joseph knows about the stability of words in books; they tell the same story each time. He also seems to know that his dad reads the* words *on the page, not the pictures,* an atypical skill for an eighteen-month-old. As soon as Mike finishes reading the book, Joseph looks up at him and says sweetly, "Read it again, Daddy." *Joseph is learning to love books,* one of the most important gifts his family can give him.

Why is it that storybook reading is so important for young children's language and literacy development? The following points summarize select key research findings in this area.

- To succeed in school, children need experiences with decontextualized language. Decontextualized language is language for which there is no support available in the immediate environment to help children make meaning. Storybook reading provides children with models for decontextualized language (Dickinson, et al., 1992).
- Storybook reading exposes children to more complex grammar and to vocabulary that is not used in everyday conversations (Beck, McKeown, & Kucan, 2002; Brabham & Lynch-Brown, 2002).
- Read-alouds contribute to children's understanding of literary elements (Sipe, 1998).
- Storybook reading builds children's content knowledge (Leal, 1994).

The National Education Goals Panel (1997, p. 20) summarizes:

> Early, regular reading to children is one of the most important activities parents can do with their children to improve their readiness for school, serve as their child's first teacher, and instill a love of books and reading. Reading to children familiarizes them with story comprehension such as characters, plot, action, and sequence

("Once upon a time," "and they lived happily ever after"), and helps them associate oral language with printed text. Most important, reading to children builds their vocabularies and background knowledge about the world.

Unfortunately, not all children have equal access to this wonderful literacy-building experience. Data suggest that only about 45 percent of children below the age of three and 56 percent of three- to five-year-olds are read to daily by their parents (National Education Goals Panel, 1997). Recent research (Yarosz & Barnett, 2001) suggests that households in which reading experiences are the most infrequent exhibit three characteristics: (1) English is not spoken as a primary language, (2) the mother is Hispanic, and (3) the mother's educational level is below the twelfth grade.

This section is about how to share books with young children. We begin by explaining how teachers can set up inviting library centers in their classrooms and how they can effectively read stories to young children. Finally, we discuss how story-reading sessions can be an ideal context for assessing children's literacy growth.

Selecting Good Books for Children

Selecting the right book is the first step toward a successful story-reading session. Helen Ezell and Laura Justice (2005) suggest that there are three criteria teachers should use when selecting books: (1) narrative content (themes and topics need to be appropriate to young children and presented using vocabulary that children can understand), (2) print (the size needs to be large enough for the children to see and positioned to make the print prominent on the page in order to provide opportunities for adult and children to talk about the print), and (3) physical characteristics (the composition and shape, illustrations, and packaging need to be appealing and appropriate for the age of the child). The careful selection of quality picture storybooks can play be important in young children's development. According to Charlotte Huck, Susan Hepler, Janet Hickman, and Barbara Kiefer (1997, p. 250), quality picture storybooks can

> enlarge children's lives, stretch their imaginations, and enhance their living. The phenomenal growth of beautiful picture books for children of all ages is an outstanding accomplishment of the past fifty years of publishing. Children do not always recognize the beauty of these books, but early impressions do exert an influence on the development of permanent tastes for children growing up.

To help teachers with the task of making appropriate selections of quality books, we suggest two resources. First, we suggest readers consider obtaining a copy of Barbara Zulandt Kiefer, Charlotte S. Huck, Janet Hickman, and Susan Hepler's (2003) book, *Children's Literature in the Elementary School*. Although the title says "elementary school," the book is a rich resource for teachers of children of all ages. It alerts readers to title after title of outstanding literature, noting the likely age of children who would enjoy each book most. At the end of each chapter, readers will find pages and pages of recommended titles. The latest edition, the eighth edition, of this book reproduces many pages from quality picture books and picture storybooks for teachers' examination. This book is a *must* for every teacher's professional library.

Billie Enz, one of this book's authors believes that readers should be encouraged to discover: Frances S. Goforth's (1997) *Literature and the Learner*.

In addition to selecting high-quality books for sharing with children, teachers should ensure that they expose their young students to a variety of genres: counting books, alphabet books, predictable books, folktales, fantasy, narrative, poetry, and more, including informational books. Today, a growing number of informational (or expository) texts for young children, of research on the effect of informational texts on children's development of background knowledge and language, and of professional books for teachers on how and why it is important to include the sharing of informational books with children are published annually. Nell Duke and V. Susan Bennett-Armistead (2003, pp. 20–23) summarize several reasons teachers must include informational books in their story-reading sessions.

- The reading of informational texts will dominate the children's reading in their later schooling.
- This kind of text is ubiquitous to society; it is what people outside school read.
- Informational text is the preferred reading material of some children.
- Informational text builds children's knowledge of the natural and social world.
- Informational text may help build children's vocabulary and other kinds of literacy knowledge (e.g., graphical devices such as diagrams and tables).

Not only must teachers include informational books in the classroom libraries, but they also must read informational books aloud. Sadly, current survey data suggest that teachers read very few (less than 15 percent of all books read) informational texts in their read-aloud sessions (Yopp & Yopp, 2000). Through reading informational books, not only can teachers build children's background knowledge about a range of topics, but also they can introduce children to a range of text structures that are different from the narrative text structures (Vukelich, Evans, & Albertson, 2003). The range of expository text structures include the following:

- Description: Gives the reader a picture of what the subject under investigation looks like, acts like, sounds like, and feels like.
- Sequence: Explains the procedures or steps that produce a specific outcome or product.
- Compare and contrast: Describes the important similarities and differences in objects, events, or qualities.
- Cause and effect: Explains *why* something happened, the results of an action or undertaking.

- Problem and solution: Describes a problem and how it was solved.
- Exemplification (reason and example): Supports a main idea with reasons and examples.

Beginning to understand how texts are "knit together" helps children construct meaning (comprehension) of texts.

Finally, teachers should be sure to share tales representative of various cultures. Many resources locate high-quality multicultural literature. For example, the National Association for the Education of Young Children (1509 16th Street NW, Washington, DC 20036-1426) publishes a brochure, *African American Literature for Young Children,* developed by the National Black Child Development Institute. The most up-to-date information on multicultural books can be found on the World Wide Web. A variety of sites can be found using the descriptors "multicultural children's literature" with any of the major search engines.

Once appropriate selections have been made, the teacher's challenge is to organize the books to make them accessible to their students. Students should be encouraged to read, read, read voluntarily.

Classroom Library Centers

A key feature of a classroom for young children is a well-stocked, well-designed library center. Classroom libraries promote independent reading by providing children with easy access to books and a comfortable place for browsing and reading. Children have been found to read more books in classrooms with libraries than in ones without libraries (Morrow & Weinstein, 1982). As Stephen Krashen (1987, p. 2) has pointed out, this finding supports "the commonsense view that children read more when there are more books around."

The mere presence of a classroom library is not enough to ensure heavy use by young children, however. The library must contain an ample supply of appropriate and interesting books for children to read. Design features are also important. Lesley Morrow and Carol Weinstein (1982) found that children did not choose to use "barren and uninviting" library corners during free-play time. When the design features of centers were improved, however, children's library usage increased dramatically.

Unfortunately, classroom libraries are not a universal feature of early childhood classrooms, and many of the libraries that do exist were not designed well. Jann Fractor, Marjorie Woodruff, Miriam Martinez, and Bill Teale (1993) collected data on the libraries in eighty-nine kindergartens through second-grade classrooms and found that only 58 percent of classes had a library center. Only 8 percent of these classroom libraries were rated as being good or excellent (having large numbers of books, partitions, ample space, comfortable furnishings, book covers rather than book spines facing out on book shelves, and book-related displays and props). The vast majority of libraries were rated as basic, containing small numbers of books and few desirable design characteristics.

A well-designed library center invites children to read books

Books.   To attract and hold children's interest, a classroom library must be stocked with lots of good books to read. Experts recommend that classroom libraries contain five to eight books per child (Fractor et al., 1993). According to these guidelines, a class of twenty children would require 100 to 160 books. These books should be divided into a core collection and one or more revolving collections. The core collection should be made up of high-quality literature that remains constant and available all year. Included here should be books that appeal to most of the children in class and that most children will enjoy reading on more than one occasion. Lesley Morrow (2001) also recommends that the books be color-coded according to type. For example, all animal books could be identified with blue dots on their spines so they can be clustered together on a shelf marked *Animals.* Each category would be distinguished by a different color. Morrow also suggests a simpler alternative of storing books in plastic tubs or cardboard boxes, with labels on the front describing the type of book in the container.

Revolving collections change every few weeks to match children's current interests and topics being studied in class. For example, if several children become hooked on one author such as Tomie de Paola or Maurice Sendak, collections of that author's books could be brought into the library to capitalize on this interest. If the class were studying seeds and plants, then picture storybooks and informational books relating to these topics could be added. When student interest shifts to a new author or when a new topic is under investigation, the old sets of revolving books are replaced with new ones.

Quality and variety are also of utmost importance in selecting books for the classroom library (Fractor et al., 1993). To motivate voluntary reading and instill positive attitudes toward written texts, books must catch children's attention, hold their interest, and captivate their imaginations. Only high-quality literature will achieve these goals.

Physical Characteristics. A number of physical features have been identified that make libraries attractive to children and that promote book reading (Morrow, 1983, 2001):

- *Partitions*. Bookshelves, screens, large plants, or other barriers set the library center apart from the rest of the classroom, giving children a sense of privacy and providing a cozy, quiet setting for reading.
- *Ample space*. There should be room enough for at least five or six children to use the library at one time.
- *Comfortable furnishings*. The more comfortable the library area, the more likely it is that children will use it. Soft carpeting, chairs, old sofas, beanbags, and a rocking chair all help create a comfortable atmosphere for reading.
- *Open-faced and traditional shelves*. Traditional shelves display books with their spines out, whereas open-faced shelves display the covers of books. Open-faced shelves are very effective in attracting children's attention to specific books. Researchers have found that when both types of shelves are used, kindergartners chose more than 90 percent of their books from the open-faced displays (Fractor et al., 1993). Traditional shelves are also useful because they can hold many more books than open-faced shelves. Many teachers rotate books between traditional and open-faced shelves, advertising different books each week.
- *Book-related displays and props*. Posters (available from such sources as the Children's Book Council, 67 Irving Place, New York, NY 1003; the American Library Association, 50 East Huron Street, Chicago, IL 60611; and the International Reading Association, 800 Barksdale Road, Newark, DE 19711), puppets, flannel boards with cutout figures of story characters, and stuffed animals encourage children to engage in emergent reading and to act out favorite stories. Stuffed animals also are useful as listeners or babies for children to read to.
- *Label the center*. Like cordoning off the area from the classroom space, symbolic cues help define the space and identify appropriate activities for young children. Using print, "Library Corner," and symbols associated with the library—book jackets, a photograph of a child looking at a book—helps even the youngest child read the label for the corner.
- *Writing center*. Some teachers like to place a writing center near the library corner. This accessibility seems to prompt young children to make illustrations and write in their personal script or dictate a sentence to an adult about the stories they are reading.

Remember, the better designed the library corner, the more use children will make of it; that is, more children will choose to participate in book reading and literature-related activities during free-choice periods. Therefore, a classroom library corner that is voluntarily used by few children is suspected to be a poorly designed center. What might an enticing library corner look like? A drawing of a possible library corner for an early childhood classroom is shown in Figure 4.6.

Classroom Lending Library

We have already said it once: Reading aloud to young children is the single most important activity for building the knowledge and skills eventually required for their success in learning to read. Therefore, teachers regularly recommend that

FIGURE 4.6   Library Center

parents read to their young children. Unfortunately, many parents face great financial hardships and cannot provide high-quality reading materials in their homes (Becker & Epstein, 1982). While many communities have excellent public libraries with quality children's literature sections, some parents find it difficult to carve time from their busy schedules to visit the library; working to meet pressing financial needs understandably takes priority. Therefore, for parents to fulfill their roles as partners in literacy programs, teachers must work with these families to offer easy access to books (Brock & Dodd, 1994).

Many early childhood teachers have attempted to get quality literature into the homes of all their young students through the creation of classroom lending libraries. These libraries allow children to check out a book every day, thus ensuring that all parents have an opportunity to read to their children frequently.

A first step in the creation of a lending library is the acquisition of books. Because the children will exchange a book for a different book each week, a teacher in a twelve-month day care program with twenty children in her classroom would need at least fifty-two books in the classroom lending library. For a new teacher that is a lot of books, especially when that new teacher is also building the classroom library.

The rules that accompany the classroom lending library are simple. A child may borrow one book each week. When the book is returned, the child may check out another book. Teacher Carolyn Lingo puts a book and an activity appropriate for the book in a bag for her young learners. For example, one of her book bags is built around *Mouse Paint* (Walsh, 1989). The materials in the book bag include small vials of paint, a smock, newspaper to cover the table, a paintbrush, and mixing cups. First, the parent and child read the book together. Then they pretend they are the mice in the book; they are to mix the yellow, blue, and red paints, just like the mice in the book did.

Effective Story-Reading Strategies

Research suggests that the frequency with which children participate in shared reading during the preschool years has a positive influence on their language and early reading skills (Snow, Griffin, & Burns, 1998). Attention to quantity alone is insufficient, however. The quality of the story-reading sessions also is important.

The verbal interaction between adult and child that occurs during story readings has a major influence on children's literacy development (Cochran-Smith, 1984). Much of the research on effective story-reading techniques reports on the interactions between a parent and child during story reading.

Some of this research discusses the affective benefits of story reading. For example, researchers such as David Yaden, Laura Smolkin, and Laurie MacGillivray (1993, p. 60) describe story reading as a pleasurable activity: "Children learn very quickly that bringing a book to a parent or caregiver will begin a certain predictable and, for the most part, pleasurable activity." Teale (1986b) describes the exchange as a dance, a choreographed interaction between adult and child reader (sometimes the adult and sometimes the child) and listener (sometimes the adult and sometimes the child).

A growing number of researchers have studied preschool teachers' reading styles and the impact of their interaction style on their young learners' literacy development. Each of these researchers (e.g., Brabham & Lynch-Brown, 2000; Dickinson & Smith, 1994; Hargrave & Senechal, 2000; Lo, 1997; Reese & Cox, 1999) discovered that teachers who had children predict, analyze, generate word meanings, and draw conclusions *as they read* had a significantly positive impact on children's vocabulary development, memory abilities, and print skills. Key features of adult behaviors during reading include (1) encouraging children to participate while the adult is reading by using evocative techniques to assist the children in using language, techniques such as asking "wh" questions that require the children to engage in novel speech; (2) providing children with feedback in the form of instructive information by expanding what the children said, praising and correcting errors; and (3) adapting the reading style to the children's growing linguistic abilities, moving beyond what the children already know to new information.

Adult Behaviors While Reading.   The majority of researchers have concentrated on the human interactions during story reading. From this research, we learn about taking turns in story reading. Through story reading, very young children are guided into the turn-taking pattern inherent in all conversation: the adult (in this research the adult is usually a parent) talks, then the child talks, then the adult talks, and so forth.

It is within this verbal exchange that the dyad (parent and child) engages in its most significant negotiations: negotiating the meaning of the story. Obviously, the adults' understanding exceeds the child's understanding of the text. Through scaffolding, the adult gently moves the child toward the adult's understanding of the text. That is, the adult questions the child about the text's meaning. The child replies, and this reply gives the adult a cue. Based on the child's response, the adult adjusts the kind of support (the scaffold) provided. To aid the child's construction of the meaning, the adult behaves in three ways: (1) as a co-respondent who shares experiences and relates the reading to personal experiences, (2) as an informer who provides information, and (3) as a monitor who questions and sets expectations for the reading session (Roser & Martinez, 1985). Adults play these roles differently, depending on the child's response and age. (Figure 4.7 summarizes how adults read to children of different ages.)

Child Behaviors During Reading.   What do children do when a caring adult is reading to them? Several researchers (e.g., Baghban, 1984; Morrow, 1988) have studied young children's behavior, often their own children, during adult–child readings. These researchers tell us that even infants focus on the book. They make sounds even before they are speaking, as if they are imitating the reader's voice. They slap at the picture in the book. A little older child with some language facility begins to ask questions about the pictures. Children play the "What's that?" game,

FIGURE 4.7   Typical adult behaviors when reading aloud to children of different ages

12 Months or Younger	12 to 15 Months	15 to 36 Months	36 Months and Older
Adult does most of the talking. Adult labels the pictures ("Look, a train!") and answers ("Yup, it's a train."). Adult points to object.	Adult asks rhetorical questions ("Is that a bus, Kareen?"). Adults answer question ("Yup! It's a bus allright!").	Adult asks child to label the object ("What's that?"). If the child does not answer, the adult provides the answer ("It's a peach."). If the child provides the correct answer, the adult repeats and reinforces the child's correct answer ("Peach! Yeah! This is a peach."). As the child's competence increases, the adult asks for more ("What color is that peach?" "When do you eat a peach?").	Adult expects child to attend and listen to larger chunks of the text. Adult questions child about characters and story meaning ("Who brought the goodies to her grandmother?" "What did the wolf first say when he saw Little Red Riding Hood?"). Most questions are literal (the answers are in the text). Adult points to object. Adult encourages child to read a section of book with support ("What did the Gingerbread Man say to the Little Old Woman?" "Run, run, as fast as you can. . . .").

pointing and asking "What's dat? What's dat? What's dat?" almost without pausing for an answer.

David Yaden, Laura Smolkin, and Mark Conlon's (1989) longitudinal case studies of preschoolers, age three to five, revealed an interesting trend in the questions children ask during reading aloud at home. Initially, most of the children's questions were about the pictures in books. Over time, there was an increase in the number of questions about word meanings and the story being read, and a decrease in picture-related questions. The investigators concluded that "it is possible that after 4 years of age, children begin to pay more attention to the story itself and to the written displays than they do at age 3" (p. 208).

Cultural Variations in Story Reading.   Do children from nonmainstream families have similar early childhood home reading experiences? Shirley Brice Heath's answer to this question is no. In her book *Way with Words* (1983), Heath provides a rich description of the literacy experiences of working-class African American, working-class Caucasian, and mainstream families in the Piedmont area of the Carolinas. From her research, Heath learned that parents from the mainstream families read to their children well into elementary school; use a wide variety of complex questioning strategies to develop their children's understanding of story, plot event sequence, and characterization; and look for ways to connect the text information to their children's experiences. Parents from the working-class

Caucasian families also read to their children, but what they do while they read is different. They stress the sequence of the stories and ask children literal meaning questions ("What did the little boy do then?" "What's the hen's name?"). Further, they make few attempts to connect the events described in the books to their children's experiences. Finally, Heath learned that the African American families tell lots of stories, but reading is strictly for functional purposes. These families read forms, recipes, and the newspaper. They tend not to read books to their children. Of course, Heath's work cannot be generalized to all mainstream, Caucasian working-class, or African American families. As Teale (1987) notes, there is a great deal of variation among and within social and cultural groups. Teachers need to learn from their students' parents about the experiences their young children have had with books.

We believe that children who have had experiences with books and have experienced dialogic interactions with adults with books have an advantage over children who have no experiences with books and whose parents or early teachers have not shared books with them. Therefore, we strongly encourage teachers and parents of young children to read, read, read to their children.

Classroom Read-Alouds

When a parent and a child read together, the child typically sits in the parent's lap or snuggles under the parent's arm. Many parents establish a bedtime reading ritual, cuddling with the child for a quiet reading time before the child goes to bed. Teachers of the very youngest children, infants, and toddlers should follow parents' lead and apply what is known about how parents read to infants and toddlers to their reading to their young students. The low teacher–child ratio recommended by the National Association for the Education of Young Children for infant (one adult to one infant) and toddler (one adult to four toddlers) programs helps permit this kind of adult–child interaction, although with toddlers, such one-on-one reading together requires some careful arranging (Bredekamp, 1989). We recommend that teachers create a daily reading ritual. Some day care centers connect with church groups or nearby residential facilities for elderly citizens for the explicit purpose of adults coming to the center just before naptime to read to the children. Now, like at home, every child can have a lap, a cuddle, and a "grandparent" all alone.

The older the child, the larger the permitted-by-law number of children in the group. The typical kindergarten class, for example, is often one teacher and twenty (unfortunately, sometimes even more) children. Teachers of these children are challenged to keep read-alouds enjoyable, pleasurable experiences. Of course, selecting age- and interest-appropriate books is important. Read-aloud experiences are one means to ensure that high-quality literature is accessible to all students, something that is especially important for children who have had few storybook experiences outside school.

The *how* of reading is also important. Even when there are too many children for everyone to cuddle next to the adult reader, physical comfort is important.

Having a special carpeted area for reading to the group is important. This area is often next to the library center. Nancy asks her young learners to sit in a semicircle. Patty asks her young learners to sit on the X marks she has made with masking tape on the carpet. Lolita asks her three-year-olds to sit or lie wherever they like in the small, carpeted area, as long as they can see the pictures and the words. Each day a different child gets to snuggle with her. In all these classrooms, the teacher sits at the edge of the circle or the carpet on a low chair, holding the picture book about at the children's eye level. The chair the teacher sits in to read from is a special chair, used both for teacher read-alouds and for the children to read their own writing to the class. Each teacher calls this chair *the author's chair.* Nancy, Patty, and Lolita have mastered reading from the side. Thus, the children can see the illustrations and the print while the teacher reads. These teachers know the story they are about to read. They have carefully selected it and read it through in advance, practicing how it will sound when read aloud. They know how to read it with excitement in their voices. They are careful not to overdramatize, yet they use pitch and stress to make the printed dialogue sound like conversation. They show that they enjoy the story.

The following sequence describes the typical read-aloud strategies recommended by several groups of researchers based on their survey of research studies, reading methods textbooks, and books and articles about reading to children (Teale & Martinez, 1988).

- *Select high-quality literature.* A key element to a successful read-aloud experience is the book that is being read. Try to find books that will appeal to the children's interest, evoke humor, stimulate critical thinking, stretch the imagination, and so on. Although a good story is always effective, also try to include informational books and poetry written for young audiences. A great source for locating good read-aloud books is Jim Trelease's (2001) *The Read-Aloud Handbook.* Trelease's book is also available at www.trelease-on-reading.com/rah.
- *Show the children the cover of the book.* Draw the children's attention to the illustration on the cover ("Look at the illustration on this book!"). Tell the children the title of the book, the author's name, and the illustrator's name. ("The title of this book is. . . . The author is. . . . The illustrator is. . . .") Point your finger to the title, the author's name, and the illustrator's name as you read each. Remind the children that the title, author's name, and illustrator's name are always on the front cover of the book. Remember that these are new concepts for young children.
- *Ask the children for their predictions about the story* ("What do you think this story might be about?"). Take a few of the children's predictions about the story's content. ("Let's read to see what this story is about.")
- *Or, provide a brief introduction to the story.* An introduction can be given in a number of ways. You might provide background information about the story ("This story is going to be about . . ."), connect the topic or theme of the story to the children's own experiences, draw the children's attention to familiar

books written by the same author, draw the children's attention to the book's central characters, clarify vocabulary that might be outside the children's realm of experiences, and so on. Keep the introduction brief so that there is ample reading time.

- *Identify where and what you will read.* Two important concepts about print for young children to learn are that readers read the print, not the pictures, on the pages and where readers begin reading. Begin read-alouds by identifying where you will start reading and what you will read. Repeating this important information often ("Now, I'll begin reading the words right here") weaves it into the read-aloud. Be sure to point to the first word on the page as you say where you will begin. Eventually, the children will be able to tell you where to begin reading. After many exposures to this important concept, you might playfully ask, "Am I going to read the words or the pictures in this book?" and "Where should I begin reading?"
- *Read with expression and at a moderate rate.* When teachers read with enthusiasm and vary their voices to fit different characters and the ongoing dialogue, the story comes alive for children. It is also important to avoid reading too quickly. Trelease (1989), a leading authority, claims that is the most common mistake adults make when reading aloud. He recommends reading slowly enough that children can enjoy the pictures and can make mental images of the story.
- *Read stories interactively.* Encourage children to interact verbally with the text, peers, and the teacher during the book reading. Pose questions throughout the book reading to enhance the children's meaning construction and to show how one makes sense of text (Barrentine, 1996). Encourage children to offer spontaneous comments, to ask questions, to respond to others' questions, and to notice the forms and functions of print features (words, punctuation, letters) as the story unfolds. Use these during-reading book discussions to help children understand what to think about as a story unfolds. As indicated earlier, adults (teachers and parents) who use an interactive reading technique facilitate children's language, particularly vocabulary, and early reading development.
- *Read favorite books repeatedly.* Not every book you read has to be a book the children have never heard before. In fact, repeated readings of books can lead to enhanced comprehension, better postreading discussions, and children's acquisition of expressive and receptive vocabulary (Martinez & Roser, 1985; Morrow, 1988; Senechal, 1995). In addition, reading a book three or more times increases the likelihood that young children will attempt to select that book during free-choice time and will try to reenact or read it on their own (Martinez & Teale, 1988). Of course, the benefits of repeated reading should be balanced against the need to expose children to a wide variety of literature.
- *Allow time for discussion after reading.* Good books arouse a variety of thoughts and emotions in children. Be sure to follow each read-aloud session with a good conversation and with questions and comments ("What part of the

story did you like best?" "How did you feel when . . . ?" "Has anything like that ever happened to you?" "Who has something to say about the story?"). Such open-ended questions invite children to share their responses to the book that was read. After listening to a book read aloud, children want to talk about the events, characters, parts they liked best, and so forth. As children and teacher talk about the book together, they construct a richer, deeper understanding of the book. How might a teacher get children to talk about a story? In Trade Secret 4.2, Cory Hansen describes how Chris Boyd engages her kindergartners in discussions that help them jointly construct deeper meaning for the stories they are read.

When teachers follow the preceding guidelines, they can help ensure that their story reading has the maximum impact on children's literacy learning.

Shared Reading

Teachers usually read picture books to their classes by holding the books so that the children can see the illustrations and by pausing occasionally to elicit students' reactions to the stories or to ask story-related questions. This traditional whole-class read-aloud experience differs from parent–child storybook reading interactions in a very important way: Most children can see only the pictures, not the print. To remedy this situation, Holdaway (1979) devised the shared book experience, a strategy that uses enlarged print, repeated readings, and increased pupil participation to make whole-class storybook reading sessions similar to parent–child reading experiences. Today, the shared book experience has become an important component of a quality early literacy program.

To use this strategy, the teacher first needs to select an appropriate book. Andrea Butler and Jan Turbill (1984) recommend stories that have (1) an absorbing, predictable story line; (2) a predictable structure, containing elements of rhyme, rhythm, and repetition; and (3) illustrations that enhance and support the text. These features make it easy for children to predict what is coming up in the story and to read along with the teacher.

Once a book has been selected, an enlarged copy needs to be obtained, which can be done in several ways. The teacher can (1) rewrite the story on chart paper, using one- or two-inch tall letters and hand-drawn illustrations; (2) make color transparencies of the pages from the original picture book and use an overhead projector; or (3) acquire a commercially published big book (about twenty-four by twenty-six inches) version of the story. Scholastic and Wright Group/McGraw-Hill, for example, publish enlarged versions of a number of high-quality picture books. Initially, only picture storybooks were available in the big book size. Today, informational books also can be located in big book size. These ready-made big books have the advantage of saving teachers time by eliminating the need to make enlarged texts. Understandably, they are expensive because they include large versions of the original illustrations.

TRADE SECRET 4.2

Getting Children to Talk About Story

BY CORY HANSEN AND CHRIS BOYD

I had the opportunity to observe in Chris Boyd's kindergarten classroom on the day she read De Paola's *Strega Nona* (1975), a wonderful story of what happens when Big Anthony ignores good advice and overruns his town with pasta from the magic pasta pot. As Chris was reading the book, the carpet in front of her was scattered with children. Some were lying flat on their backs looking up at the ceiling; others were on their sides, only a finger wiggle away from good friends; and others were sitting up, cross-legged, their eyes never leaving the pages of the story. The last page of the story is wordless. Big Anthony's expression tells it all as he sits outside the house, his stomach swollen almost to bursting, with one last strand of pasta lingering on his fork. The children burst into laughter, and as Chris motioned with her index finger, they regrouped, calling out, "I think . . . , I think . . ." on their way to forming a large circle. For the next half hour, that was what was talked about: what the children thought about the story.

The conversation began with what the children thought was going to happen and comparing it with what actually did occur. Chris asked the children why they thought the way they did, and then the serious business of making meaning together began. She gradually lowered herself from the reading chair and joined in as one participant in this group talk about story: the one with a copy of the text and the one writing comments into a notebook. The kindergartners called on her only when they needed someone to reread part of the text to settle disputes. Chris did not enter the conversation unless the children lost sight of her one rule for talk about story or unless an opportunity to seize a literary teachable moment emerged.

After the group examined Big Anthony's motives and explored connections from this story to their own lives, Chris and I had an oppor-tunity to talk about how she structured and scaffolded meaningful talk about story with young children. My first question was why the children were all over the room as she read. She explained that she offered the children the opportunity to "go to wherever they could do their best listening." In this way, she believed that she respected the children's choices and could hold them accountable if they acted in ways that did not show good listening (by moving them to a different part of the room). By respecting their choices, focus was on listening and thinking, rather than on sitting or being still.

"So why," I was quick to ask, "do they form a sitting circle after the story?"

"Well, first, it is easier to hear what is being said if they are in a circle," Chris replied. "I teach them to look at the person who is talking. I think it encourages them to listen carefully and think through what others are saying. Also, when they are all in a circle, they begin to watch for nonverbal cues that show another person has something to add or introduce to the conversation."

I noticed that the kinds of questions Chris asked her kindergartners during the talk were different than those I had heard in other classrooms. When the children were arguing about why Big Anthony didn't know to blow the three kisses, Chris's question to the group was, "Was there any clue that that might have been a problem for him?" Matthew was quick to suggest that Chris should again read the part when Strega Nona was singing to the pot. The children listened very carefully as Chris reread that part of the story and used the information from the book to settle their disagreement. While that particular part of the conversation was going on, Chris was writing hurriedly in her notebook. I asked her why she recorded what the children were saying as they talked about story.

"When I write down what they say, they see and feel the importance of their words," she said. "They know I value what they say and what

---

TRADE SECRET 4.2 (continued)

they think is special enough to write down. It makes them realize how important talk about story really is. Also, I can bring the conversation back around to something a child said when everyone gets talking at once or if a soft-spoken or shy child makes a comment that may otherwise go unnoticed. For instance, when they were arguing about Big Anthony, Sara made a really smart comment about how the pot needed someone to be nice to it. Her comment was lost in the discussion, but later on, after the issue was settled, I could bring it up again and then the conversation started anew."

I wondered why Chris didn't just have the children raise their hands when they had something to say. She told me that, even though it takes a long time and lots of patience to teach

children to follow her one rule for talk about story–talk one at a time and talk to the whole group–they eventually learn more than just being polite. Chris found that if she had children raise their hands to talk, they just sat there, waving their arms, waiting to say what they wanted without listening to and considering what other people were saying or connecting their ideas to the book or the opinions of others. Even though it is loud and messy at times, the results are worth the effort.

The kindergartners in Chris Boyd's classroom obviously loved the chance to talk about story with each other. They used talk about story to learn more about how things worked in the world and, in the process, learned more about the world of story.

Unlike when regular-size books are shared with children, big books permit all children to see the print. Teachers may take advantage of the enlarged print by drawing young children's attention to the print in the same ways that a parent draws a child's attention to the print in a regular-size book during a read-aloud. Typically, teachers use a pointer to point to the words as they read big books and invite the children to read along, particularly to the words in a familiar text or to the refrain in a book. As children "read" along with the teacher, they internalize the language of the story. They also learn about directionality (reading from left to right with return sweeps), one important convention of print.

Through the use of big books, teachers can introduce children to other conventions of print: to letter–sound relationships (phonics); to the sequence of letter sounds in words (phonemic awareness); to the difference between letters, words, and sentences; to the spaces between words; to where to start reading on the page; to reading left to right; to return sweeps; to punctuation. In addition, through the use of big books, teachers are able to further children's development of important concepts about books (e.g., the front and back of a book, the difference between print and pictures, that pictures on a page are related to what the print says, that readers read the print, where to begin reading, where the title is and what it is, what an author is, what an illustrator is). In essence, using big books teaches skills in context. Read Trade Secret 4.3 to discover how kindergarten teacher Bernadette Watson uses big books with her young learners.

TRADE SECRET 4.3
Ms. Watson's Sharing of *Mrs. Wishy-washy*

Ms. Watson's kindergarten students read together every day. The following procedures describe how Ms. Watson engages in shared reading with her young students. She begins the reading with the big book on the special big book easel purchased by her school's PTA. The book is closed, and the cover is shown to the students.

■ The First Reading

"What do you see on the cover of this book?" she asks the children. Their responses range from "a picture of a lady" to "words" to "a title." With each suggestion, Ms. Watson confirms the response and points to the item on the cover.

"What do you think this story will be about?" Ms. Watson asks. With this question, she is attempting to activate the children's prior knowledge, knowledge that will help them understand this story. She is modeling what she hopes they will soon do on their own as independent readers. Today the children are all quite sure that the story is going to be about a "mad woman." Ms. Watson says, "Let's read and see if you are correct." As she reads, she points to each word using her special big book pointer, a stick with a small stuffed glove tied to the end with the index finger pointing out and the other fingers folded under. While she reads, she does not pause for questions or comments. She wants the children to hear the story and to focus on the words.

When she finishes reading, she asks, "So, were you right? Was this a story about a mad lady?" The children unanimously respond, "YES!"

■ The Second Reading

The next day, Ms. Watson reads the same story again. This time, she invites the children's comments and questions. She begins by reading the title and author from the cover. She asks, "Does anyone remember what the author does?" One child shouts out, "Writes the words." Ms. Watson

reads the title again and turns to the first page. "What do you think this page will be about?" she asks.

Immediately several children respond, "The cow."

"How do you know?"

A child tells her, "Because of the picture of the cow." Another child says, "I can read cow." Ms. Watson has that student use the pointer to point to the word *cow*.

Ms. Watson reads the words on the first two pages and continues the pattern of "What will this page be about?" and "How do you know?" Once she says, "Right! The picture on the page helps readers know what the words on the page will be. You are so smart!" On several pages, she asks the children whether they have any questions or comments about the story. On the next to the last page, she asks, "What do you think the cow, pig, and duck might be thinking?"

Her goal during this reading is for the children to become engaged with the print and the story. She invites talk about each page. She encourages the children's questions and comments. She is modeling that reading is about constructing meaning from the text. Readers think while they read. Readers make sense of stories by connecting what happens in the story with their experiences.

■ The Third Reading

Mrs. Watson begins, "Today how about if you read Mrs. Wishy-washy with me?" She points and reads Mrs. Wishy-washy. " 'Oh, lovely mud,' said the [she pauses] cow." Some children are "reading" all the words with her as she reads and points. More children join in more loudly She pauses. She continues this pattern, encouraging the children to use the picture cues to help them decode the word if they can not read or remember it.

TRADE SECRET 4.3 (continued)

"Now I'm going to cover a word. Let's see if you can figure out what it is." Using a Post-it note, she covers *mud* on page 4. "'Oh, lovely mud,' said the pig." She opens the book to that page and reads, "'Oh, lovely blank,' said the pig." "What might that word be?" Someone shouts, "Mud." Mrs. Watson asks, "How did you know?" The child "remembered." "How else could you figure out the word?" Someone says, "Pigs like mud." Mrs. Watson says, "Good. You used what you knew about pigs to make a guess. How else might you know?" She pulls the Post-it note back so the *m* is revealed. "What letter is this? What sound does it make? Could this help you figure out the word?" She stretches the sound of *m*, reveals the *u* and says its sound, and reveals the *d* and says its

sound. "Looking at the letters and saying their sounds can help you figure out the words. Let's try another mystery word." She does one more. "Remember, this book is in the library corner if any of you would like to read it. Oh, I also have five small copies of the book. If you'd like to take it home to read to your parents, just check it out with Missy, this week's class librarian."

Pointing to the words is very important. The message Mrs. Watson communicates is: You read the words, not the illustrations, when you read. Having all the children read together is important: no one fails, everyone can "read." She also taught (actually retaught since she had used these procedures before—and will over and over again) decoding strategies.

LINKING LITERACY AND PLAY

In Chapter 3, dramatic play is described as an ideal context for developing young children's oral language. Dramatic play can also offer a context in which children can have meaningful, authentic interactions with reading and writing in early childhood classrooms (Roskos & Christie, 2000, 2004; Yaden, Rowe, & MacGillivary, 2000). The following vignette, which involves four-year-old preschoolers, illustrates some of the advantages of integrating play and literacy:

> With some teacher assistance, Noah and several friends are getting ready to take a make-believe plane trip to France. The elevated loft in the classroom has been equipped with chairs and has become the plane, and a nearby theme center has been turned into a ticket office. Noah goes into the ticket office, picks up a marker, and begins making scribbles on several small pieces of paper. The teacher passes by with some luggage for the trip. Noah says, "Here Kurt! Here are some tickets." The teacher responds, "Oh great. Frequent flyer plan!" Noah then makes one more ticket for himself, using the same scribblelike script. The teacher distributes the tickets to several children, explaining that they will need these tickets to get on board the plane. As Noah leaves the center, he scribbles on a wall sign. When asked what he has written, Noah explains that he wanted to let people know that he would be gone for a while.

The most obvious benefit of linking literacy and play is that play is fun. When children incorporate literacy into their play, they begin to view reading and writing as enjoyable skills that are desirable to master. Yet there are benefits of linking play and literacy beyond fun. Kathy Roskos and James Christie (2004) report three additional claims regarding how play serves literacy. Following their critical review of the play and literacy research, they suggest three ways that play can serve literacy:

1. By providing settings that promote literacy activity, skills, and strategies
2. By serving as a language experience that can build connections between oral and written modes of expression
3. By providing opportunities to teach and learn literacy

The plane trip vignette illustrates how the nonliteral nature of play makes literacy activities significant to children. The pieces of paper that Noah produced would be meaningless in most situations. Within the context of a make-believe plane trip, however, Noah's scribbles represent writing and the pieces of paper signify tickets, not just to Noah, but also to the teacher and the other children. This make-believe orientation enabled Noah to demonstrate his growing awareness of the practical functions of print. He showed that he knew that printed tickets can grant access to experiences such as trips and that signs can be used to leave messages for other people.

The low-risk atmosphere of play encourages children to experiment with emergent forms of reading and writing. When children play, their attention is focused on the activity itself rather than on the goals or outcome of the activity. This means-over-ends orientation promotes risk taking. If outcomes are not critical, then mistakes are inconsequential. There is little to lose by taking a chance and trying something new or difficult. Noah felt safe using scribble writing to construct tickets and signs. In nonplay situations, the tickets and signs themselves would assume more importance, decreasing the likelihood that Noah would risk using a personal form of script to construct them.

Like functional literacy, linking literacy and play is a broad-spectrum instructional strategy that offers children many opportunities to learn a variety of skills and concepts. In addition, children can learn these skills in many ways, including observation, experimentation, collaboration, and instruction. As a result, there are great opportunities for children at different levels of development to learn new skills and to consolidate newly acquired skills that are only partially mastered. Unlike narrowly focused skill-and-drill activities, opportunities exist for every child in the classroom to advance his or her literacy development.

Literacy-Enriched Dramatic Play Centers

Nigel Hall (1991) recommends that classroom play areas be subjected to a print flood, an abundance of reading and writing materials that go along with each area's play theme. The goal is to make these play centers resemble the literacy environments that children encounter at home and in their communities. For example, a restaurant center might be equipped with menus, wall signs, pencils, and notepads (for taking food orders). These props would invite children to incorporate familiar restaurant-based literacy routines into their play. Research has shown that this print-prop strategy results in significant increases in the amount of literacy activity during play (Morrow & Rand, 1991; Neuman & Roskos, 1992, 1997).

Different types of literacy materials have been found to stimulate different kinds of literacy play. Lesley Morrow and Muriel Rand (1991) reported that unthematic literacy materials such as pens, pencils, felt-tip markers, and books encouraged children to practice and experiment with the form and structure of print. For example, children practiced writing letter characters or jotted down all the words they knew how to spell. These literacy activities tended to be unconnected with other play activities. Figure 4.8 shows an example of four-year-old Ryan's unthematic writing. He picked up a piece of paper at the writing center and proceeded to write his name and several random strings of letters and black dots. When asked what he was writing, he responded, "Letters and periods." He had just noticed this punctuation convention (in books or environmental print) and decided to include it in his writing.

In contrast, the thematic literacy props in a veterinarian play center tended to elicit reading and writing activities that were related to the play theme. The thematic literacy play activities appeared to focus on the functional uses of print rather than on its form and structure. For example, children acting in the role of

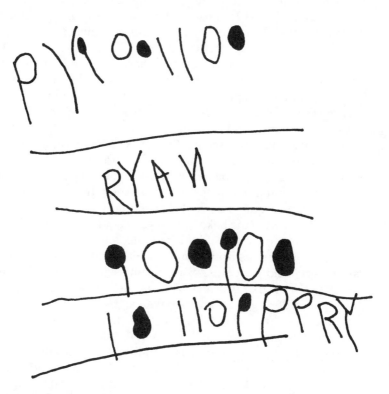

FIGURE 4.8   Unthematic play writing—Ryan writes "letters and periods."

doctor wrote make-believe prescriptions, jotted down notes on patients' charts, and filled out appointment cards for future checkups. Other children, in the role of pet owners, pretended to read the pamphlets in the waiting room while their pets were examined. Both thematic and unthematic literacy materials should be included so that children will be encouraged to explore the structural features and practical functions of print.

Besides writing implements such as pencils, markers, crayons, and pens, thematic and unthematic literacy materials that can be used with a variety of dramatic-play themes. Examples are given in Table 4.1 (Christie & Enz, 1992).

Preparatory Experiences

Matching the classroom settings to children's experiences outside the classroom is important. Children can play only what they know. Nigel Hall and Anne Robinson (1995), for example, used a mechanic's garage as a setting for classroom play and as a stimulus for multiple kinds of reading and writing. Prior to initiating the garage play theme, the children were taken on a field trip to a neighborhood mechanic's garage. This firsthand, direct experience greatly increased the children's understanding of what goes on in a mechanic's garage, helped them plan and construct a realistic garage play center, and enhanced their subsequent play.

Using Hall and Robinson's book as their guide, a group of undergraduate students at the University of Delaware designed a bakery play setting in their kindergarten field placement classroom. First, they took the kindergartners on a walk to the neighborhood bakery. There the children saw how bread, cookies, cakes, and so forth were made. They watched cakes and cookies being decorated. On clipboards they had carried with them, the children also recorded the kinds of environmental print they saw in the bakery. They watched the bakery's owner serve a customer. They heard about the importance of cleanliness when preparing food and of being certain to get the correct spelling of names for writing on cakes.

On return to the classroom, the undergraduate students talked with the children about setting up a bakery play setting. How could they create a display case? "Put some of that um, um paper you can look through on one side of those shelves [shelves open on both sides]." What should we call our bakery? "McVey Bakery." What do we need in the bakery? "Cakes, cookies, a cash register," and the list grew.

The next day, the undergraduate students had created a bakery. They brought cooking pans from home, posters borrowed from a bakery, foam circles of various sizes and paper disks of the same size that could be decorated with magic markers to look like cakes, a cash register, play money, checkbooks with blank checks, an order pad, cookbooks, wall signs, brown foam pieces that looked like doughnuts, and two chef hats. Together, the college students and the children set the limit on the number of children who could play at any one time—five—which necessitated a sign-up sheet. The children played and wrote orders, decorated cakes with messages ("Happy Birthday"), made signs advertising specials, wrote checks to pay for ordered cakes, wrote receipts, and so forth. The trip to the bakery clearly provided the children with lots of literacy-rich ideas for play.

TABLE 4.1   Literacy Materials Added to Play Settings in the Christie and Enz Study

HOME CENTER	BUSINESS OFFICE
Pencils, pens, markers	Pencils, pens, markers
Note pads	Note pads
Post-it notes	Telephone message forms
Baby-sitter instruction forms	Calendar
Telephone book	Typewriter
Telephone message pads	Order forms
Message board	Stationery, envelopes, stamps
Children's books	File folders
Magazines, newspapers	Wall signs
Cookbooks, recipe box	
Product containers from children's homes	
Junk mail	

RESTAURANT	POST OFFICE
Pencils	Pencils, pens, markers
Note pads	Stationery and envelopes
Menus	Stamps
Wall signs ("Pay Here")	Mailboxes
Bank checks	Address labels
Cookbooks	Wall signs ("Line Starts Here")
Product containers	

GROCERY STORE	VETERINARIAN'S OFFICE
Pencils, pens, markers	Pencils, pens, markers
Note pads	Appointment book
Bank checks	Wall signs ("Receptionist")
Wall signs ("Supermarket")	Labels with pets' names
Shelf labels for store areas ("Meat")	Patient charts
Product containers	Prescription forms
	Magazines (in waiting room)

AIRPORT/AIRPLANE	LIBRARY
Pencils, pens, markers	Pencils
Tickets	Books
Bank checks	Shelf labels for books
Luggage tags	("ABCs," "Animals")
Magazines (on-board plane)	Wall signs ("Quiet!")
Air sickness bags with printed instructions	Library cards
Maps	Checkout cards for books
Signs ("Baggage Claim Area")	

Notice how easy it was for the undergraduate students to provide the needed preparatory experience (the field trip) and gather the materials needed to create the bakery. Most items were inexpensive or free. To convert traditional play areas into literacy-enriched dramatic play centers requires a minimum of resources and effort. In return, children's play options are expanded and the children are presented with opportunities for meaningful engagements with reading and writing.

Teacher Involvement in Play

Lev Vygotsky (1978) has described how adult interaction can facilitate children's development within the children's zone of proximal development. That is, adults can help children engage in activities that go beyond their current level of mastery, which the children could not do on their own without adult mediation. Many opportunities for this type of adult scaffolding occur when children are engaged in dramatic play in literacy-enriched settings (Roskos & Neuman, 1993). Teachers can encourage children to incorporate literacy activities into ongoing play episodes and can help children with reading and writing activities that the children cannot do independently, both of which, in turn, can promote literacy growth. Carol Vukelich (1994) found that when adults assumed the role of a more knowledgeable play partner with kindergartners in print-rich play settings, the children's ability to read environmental print was enhanced.

The following vignette illustrates how one teacher used literacy scaffolding to enrich her four-year-olds' pizza parlor dramatization.

> Channing and several friends ask their teacher whether they may play pizza parlor. The teacher says yes and brings out a prop box containing felt pizza pieces, pizza boxes, menus, tablecloths, and so on. The children spend about ten minutes separating the pizza ingredients (olives, pepperoni slices, onions, and cheese shavings made out of felt) into bins. When they have finished, the teacher asks which pizza shop they would like to be today. They respond, "Pizza Hut." While the children watch, the teacher makes a sign with the Pizza Hut name and logo. Channing requests, "Make a 'Closed for business' sign on the back." The teacher turns over the paper and writes "CLOSED FOR BUSINESS." She then hangs the "CLOSED" sign on the front of the play center. The children spend another ten minutes rearranging furniture and setting up the eating and kitchen areas in their pretend restaurant. When the children have finished their preparations, the teacher asks, "Is it time to open?" Channing responds, "Yeah. Switch the sign now." The teacher turns the "CLOSED" sign over so that the Pizza Hut logo is showing. The teacher then pretends to be a customer, reads a menu, and orders a pizza with pepperoni, green peppers, onions, and lots of cheese. Once the cooks have piled the appropriate ingredients onto the pizza, the teacher carries it over to a table and pretends to eat it. When she finishes eating, she writes a make-believe check to pay for her meal.

The teacher played several important roles in this episode. First, she served as stage manager, supplying the props that made the pizza play possible. She also provided scaffolding, making signs that the children could not make on their own.

The "Pizza Hut" and "CLOSED" signs provided environmental print for the children to read and also created an opportunity for the children to demonstrate their growing awareness of the regulatory power of print. The pizza shop could not be open for business until the "CLOSED" sign was taken down.

The teacher also served as a coplayer, taking on a role and becoming a play partner with the children. Notice that she took the minor role of customer, leaving the more important roles (pizza cooks) to the children. While in the role of customer, the teacher modeled several literacy activities, such as menu reading and check writing. Several children noticed these behaviors and imitated them in future play episodes.

Research has revealed that teachers assume a variety of roles when interacting with children during play (Enz & Christie, 1997; Roskos & Neuman, 1993). As we illustrate in Figure 4.9, these roles form a continuum from no involvement to complete domination of play. The roles in the center of this continuum have been found to be the most effective for enriching the quality of children's play and encouraging play-related literacy activities:

- *Stage manager.* In the role of stage manager, the teacher stays on the sidelines and does not enter into children's play. From this position outside the play frame, the teacher helps children prepare for play and offers assistance once play is under way. Stage managers respond to children's requests for materials, help the children construct costumes and props, and assist in organizing the play set. Stage managers also may make appropriate theme-related script suggestions to extend the children's ongoing play.
- *Coplayer.* In the coplayer role, the teacher joins in and becomes an active participant in children's play. Coplayers function as an equal play partner with children. The teacher usually takes a minor role in the drama, such as a customer in a store or a passenger on a plane, leaving the prime roles (store clerk, pilot) to the children. While enacting this role, the teacher follows the flow of the dramatic

FIGURE 4.9 **Teacher's roles in play**

Uninvolved	Interviewer/ Narrator	Stage Manager	Co-Player	Play-Leader	Director
Out of room Engaged in other activities	Asks literal nonplay-related questions Engages in informal conversation, "chatting" Narrates activities	Gathers materials Makes props Constructs costumes Organizes set Script suggestions	Assumes role and within the role: Supports dialogue Guides plot Makes plot suggestions Defines roles and responsibilities of different characters	Introduces conflicts Facilitates dialogue Problem solving	Delegates props Dictates actions Directs dialogue

action, letting the children take the lead most of time. During the course of play, many opportunities arise for the adult to model sociodramatic play skills (e.g., role-playing and make-believe transformations) and play-related literacy activities (e.g., writing a shopping list, ordering food from a menu).

■ *Play leader*. As in the coplayer role, play leaders join in and actively participate in the children's play, but they exert more influence and take deliberate steps to enrich and extend play episodes. They suggest new play themes and introduce new props or plot elements to extend existing themes. For example, if the teacher has taken on the role of a family member preparing a meal, she might exclaim, "Oh my goodness, we don't have any meat or vegetables for our soup! What should we do?" This step creates a problem for the children to solve and may result in the writing of a shopping list and a trip to a nearby store center. Teachers often adopt this role when children have difficulty getting play started on their own or when an ongoing play episode is beginning to falter.

Other roles—uninvolved, interviewer (the teacher quizzes children about their play activities), and director, in which the teacher takes over control of the play and tells children what to do—tend to be less effective. These latter two roles tend to disrupt children's play rather than enhance it. When adults take over control of children's play and intervene with a heavy-hand, children lose interest and often stop playing.

The keys to successful play involvement are for teachers to observe carefully and to choose an interaction style that fits with children's ongoing play interests and activities. Kathy Roskos and Susan Neuman (1993) observed six experienced preschool teachers and found that they used a repertoire of interaction styles to encourage literacy-related play. These veteran teachers switched styles frequently, depending on the children who were playing and the nature of the play. The teachers' ability to switch styles to fit the children's play agenda appeared to be as important as the specific interaction styles the teachers used.

When teachers set up literacy-enriched play settings and become involved in play in appropriate ways, they provide children with opportunities for meaningful engagements with emergent reading and writing. They help children see different uses for familiar props and create new props, expand the children's repertoire of play themes and roles by exposing them to new experiences (through field trips, guest speakers, and carefully chosen videos), and help children use appropriate strategies to plan and carry out their play (Bodrova & Leong, 2003).

Play-related literacy activities go hand in hand with such functional, real-world writing activities as signing up to use a popular center, making an invitation to class parties or performances, writing a message to the custodians ("Plz du nt tch"), and so on. Both types of literacy engagements give children opportunities to form, try out, and perfect their own hypotheses about the function and structure of print.

Shared Enactments

In sociodramatic play, children make up their own stories as the play progresses. In shared enactments, on the other hand, the players enact a written story. This story can be composed by the children in the classroom or by an adult author.

Written Story to Dramatization.   Vivian Paley (1981) developed a strategy that combines storytelling and play, Children first dictate stories that are tape recorded and later written out by the teacher. The teacher reads the stories aloud to the class, and then the children work together as a group to act out the stories. This strategy promotes children's narrative skills—over time, their stories become better organized and increasingly more complex—and makes contributions to many aspects of their social, oral language, and cognitive development.

In her book *Boys and Girls: Superheroes in the Doll Corner,* Paley (1984, pp. 50–51) gives an example of a story written by one of her kindergarten boys:

> Superman, Batman, Spiderman, and Wonderwoman went into the woods and they saw a wicked witch. She gave them poisoned food. Then they died. Then Wonderwoman had magic and they woke up. Everybody didn't wake up. Then they woke up from Wonderwoman's magic. They saw a chimney and the wolf opened his mouth. Superman exploded him.

Notice how this story has a rudimentary narrative plot: the main characters encounter a problem (dying as a result of eating poison), an attempt is made to solve the problem (magic), and there is a resolution (waking up). Then a new problem comes along (the wolf), and the narrative cycle continues. Also, notice that this child has incorporated superheroes from popular media with elements from classic fairy tales to build his story: finding a cottage in the woods (*Hansel and Gretel*), a witch who gives poison food (*Snow White*), and a wolf and a chimney (*The Three Pigs*).

Greta Fein, Alicia Ardila-Rey, and Lois Groth (2000) developed a version of Paley's strategy that they call *shared enactment.* During free-choice activity time, the teacher sits in the classroom writing center, and children are encouraged to tell the teacher stories. The teacher writes down the children's words verbatim. When a child finishes with his or her story, the teacher asks if there is anything else he or she wishes to add. Then the teacher reads the story back to the child to make sure that it matches the child's intentions. The child decides whether to share the story with the group. If the child wants to share it, the writing is put in a special container called the story box.

Later, during shared enactment time, the teacher reads the story to the class, and the story is dramatized. Fein, Ardila-Rey, and Groth (2000, p. 31) describe a typical shared enactment session:

> The children gathered along two sides of a large space used for circle time and the teacher sits among them. The empty space before them became the stage. The teacher summoned the author to sit by her side and read the story out loud to the group. The teacher then asked the author what characters were needed for the enactment. The author identified the characters (often with the eager help of other children) and chose a peer to portray each one. When the actors had been assembled, the teacher read the story slowly as a narrator would, stopping to allow for action and omitting dialogue so that the actors could improvise. The players dramatized the story, following the lead of the author who acts as director. At the completion of the enactment and the applause, another story was selected for dramatization.

Fein and her colleagues used the shared enactment procedure with a class of kindergartners twice a week for twelve weeks and found that it resulted in a substantial increase in narrative activity (story enactment and storytelling) during free play. The investigators noted that this brief intervention appeared to penetrate the daily life of the classroom and promised to make important contributions to the children's narrative development.

Dramatization to Written Story.   Another version of combining play and storytelling for preschool children involves an observant teacher who witnesses an interesting drama emerging from the children's pretend play. At the conclusion of the dramatic play, the teacher privately asks these children if they would like to retell their drama with the class. If the children wish to share their pretend adventure, the teacher quickly writes the play down as the entire group listens. This strategy helps children realize how spoken words and actions can be written down and shared with others. The following is an example of dramatic play-to-written story told by three four-year-old girls.

> There were two mommies who were going to take their babies to the doctor 'cause their babies were sick from a sleeping spell. On the way to the doctor they got lost in the forest. Just then Xena came by on her big white horse. They all got on the horse together and they found Dr. Mary, Medicine Woman. The doctor gave the babies shots and medicine and the babies got better.

Notice how the children's story reflected a traditional plot line: a problem that needed to be solved, a crisis, and two heroines who saved the day. Once again the children had interwoven story elements from classic fairy tales (*Sleeping Beauty*) with current TV heroes.

LANGUAGE EXPERIENCE APPROACH
OR SHARED WRITING

The language experience approach (LEA), which became popular in the 1970s (Allen, 1976; Veatch et al., 1979), has children read texts composed of their own oral language. Children first dictate a story about a personal experience, and the teacher writes it down. The teacher reads the story back to the children and then gives them the opportunity to read it themselves. Sometimes the children illustrate their dictated sentences. This strategy is also referred to as shared writing.

The LEA or shared writing strategy is an excellent means for teachers to demonstrate the relationship between speaking, writing, and reading. It can help children realize (1) that what is said can be written down in print and (2) that print can be read back as oral language.

Like functional print and play-based literacy, the language experience or shared writing strategy presents children with many learning opportunities. At the most basic level, LEA/shared writing helps children learn that the purpose of written language is the same as that of oral language: to communicate meaning.

For other children, the strategy enables teachers to demonstrate explicitly the structure and conventions of written language. The children watch as the teacher spells words conventionally, leaves spaces between words, uses left-to-right and top-to-bottom sequences, starts sentences and names with capital letters, ends sentences with periods or other terminal punctuation marks, and so on. This method is an ideal way to show children how the mechanical aspects of writing work.

LEA/shared writing has the additional advantage of making conventional writing and reading easier for children. By acting as scribe, the teacher removes mechanical barriers to written composition. The children's compositions are limited only by their experiential backgrounds and oral language. Reading is also made easier because the stories are composed of the children's own oral language and are based on their personal experiences. This close personal connection with the story makes it easy for children to predict the identity of unknown words in the text.

Many variations of LEA/shared writing have been developed. In the sections that follow, three that are particularly appropriate for use with young children are described: group experience stories, individual experience stories, and classroom newspapers.

Group Experience or Shared Writing Stories

The group experience strategy begins with the class having some type of shared experience, such as the class takes a field trip to a farm, to a zoo, across the street to the supermarket, to see a play; the class guinea pig has babies; the class completes a special cooking activity or other project. Whatever the event, the experience should be shared by all members of the group so that everyone can contribute to the story.

The following is a description of how early childhood teachers might engage their children in a group shared story-writing experience. The "make-a-word" and "make-a-sentence" ideas described below are Pat Cunningham's (1995). Many early childhood teachers have begun to weave activities like these into their children's LEA/shared writing experiences. Many believe that their children are much more knowledgeable about print because of their use of Cunningham's ideas.

Teachers need to be selective about which activity to use in a single LEA/shared writing. To use all these activities in one LEA/shared writing might take too much time. It is important to keep the group's attention and ensure that this reading and writing activity remains enjoyable.

1. The teacher begins by gathering the children on the rug in the whole-group area to record their thoughts about the experiences and preserve what they recall in print. Teachers often begin with a request to "tell me what you remember about. . . ."

2. As children share their memories, the teacher records exactly what they say. The teacher does not rephrase or correct what a child says. The teacher records the children's language, just as they use it. The sentence structure, or syntax, is the child's. The spellings, however, are correct. As the teacher writes the child's comments on

a large sheet of chart paper with a marker in print large enough for all the children to see, the teacher verbalizes the process used to construct the text. (The teacher might choose to write on the chalkboard, an overhead transparency, or chart paper.) The following dialogue (sometimes a bit of a monologue) illustrates what the teacher might say as the child's language is recorded:

Our Trip to the Farm

> **LOLLIE:**   We went on a hayride.
>
> **TEACHER:**   *We*—because that word is the first word in Lollie's sentence, it needs to be capitalized.
>
> **TEACHER:**   Lollie's next word is *went.* I need to make a space between *We* and *went.* [Teacher reads: "We went."] How many letters are in *went*? Let's count them.
>
> **CHILDREN:**   1–2–3–4
>
> **TEACHER:**   *On.* Does anyone know how to spell *on*? No? *O—n. On* is spelled *o—n.* Another space before I write the *o.* Watch while I write an *n.* First I draw a straight line down, from top to bottom. Then I come to the top of the straight line, and I make a curved line like that. That's an *n.* Another space. *A.* Watch while I make an *a.* First make a circle, and then I make a line on the right-hand side of the circle, from top to bottom. *Hayride.* That sounds like two words, doesn't it? What two words, Marcus?
>
> **MARCUS:**   Hayride. [He says them together.]
>
> **TEACHER:**   That's right. *Hay* and *ride.* That's the end of Lollie's sentence. What do I need to put at the end of this sentence?
>
> **KRISTOL:**   A period.
>
> **TEACHER:**   Right. A period. [She makes a large dot and rereads Lollie's sentence. She points as she reads the whole sentence.]

Many concepts about the structure and conventions of print are taught during the creation of this single sentence: capitalize the first word of a sentence, put a space between words, form an *n* in this way, an *h* and an *n* are formed in the same way, letters make up words, and so forth. Every sentence in LEA/shared writing lends itself to exploring how our language conventions work, to introducing and reinforcing young children's knowledge of the mechanics of writing. In addition, by reading each word as it is written, the teacher promotes word recognition and one-to-one matching of speech and print.

Because of the amount of time spent on each sentence, the teacher takes sentences from only a small number of students. Taking sentences from all the children would make the sitting time too long for the young learners.

If a student's contribution is vague or unclear, then the teacher might have to ask the child to clarify the point or may have to do some *minor* editing to make the sentence comprehensible to the rest of the class. The teacher must exercise caution when a student's contribution is in a divergent dialect (e.g., "He be funny"). Changing this utterance to Standard English may be interpreted as a rejection of the child's language, which, in turn, might cause the child to cease to participate in future experience stories. In such cases, it is usually better to accept the child's language and not change it. As Nigel Hall (1987) points out, this dialect sensitivity does not need to extend to differences in pronunciation. If a child pronounces a word in a divergent manner (e.g., *bes* for *best*), the conventional spelling of the word can still be used. The child is still able to pronounce the word as *bes* when reading it.

3. When the whole story is created, the teacher rereads it from beginning to end, carefully pointing to each word and emphasizing the left-to-right and return-sweep progression. Then the class reads the story as a group (a practice called choral reading). Often a child points to the words with a pointer as the class reads aloud.

4. The teacher hangs the story in the writing center, low enough so that interested children can copy the story. Because the teacher wrote the story on chart paper (teachers' preferred medium for group stories), the story can be stored on the chart stand and reviewed periodically by the class. Sometimes the teacher rewrites each child's sentence on a piece of paper and asks the originator to illustrate his or her sentence. The pages are then collected into a book, complete with a title page listing a title and the authors' names, and placed in the library corner. These books are very popular with the children. Other times, the teacher makes individual copies of the story—via photocopying or word processing—for each child.

Interactive Writing

An extension of the group experience story approach is known as interactive writing. Like the creation of the group experience story described above, interactive writing follows a series of steps (Boroski, 1998). A significant difference is that the teacher shares the pen with the children, inviting them to write some of the letters and words on the chart paper. There are six recommended steps of interactive writing:

Step 1: Negotiate a sentence. The teacher and the children collaborate to write a meaningful sentence that can be read.

Step 2: Count the number of words on fingers. The teacher repeats the agreed-upon sentence slowly, putting up one finger for each word spoken. Then, the teacher and the children say and count the number of words in the sentence.

Step 3: Recall each word to be written and stretch the word. The teacher articulates each word slowly, stretching the word to help the children hear each phoneme of each word.

Step 4: Using a felt-tip mark pen, the teacher invites a child to volunteer to take the pen and write part of the word or the whole word on the chart paper.

Conventional spelling is used. When errors are made, as they likely will be, the teacher places adhesive labels or tape over the error to cover the mistake. Errors are treated as expected, natural occurrences. The teacher praises the child for the writing attempt.

Step 5: Point and read. The teacher or a child points to each word written on the chart, and everyone reads the word aloud.

Step 6: Recall the sentence and begin again at step 3. At step 5, there will now be two words to read.

Individual Language Experience Stories

In an individual language experience story, each student meets individually with the teacher and dictates her or his own story. As the child dictates, the teacher writes the story. Because the story is not intended for use with a group audience, editing can be kept to a minimum and the child's language can be left largely intact. Once the dictation is completed, the teacher reads the story back to the child. This rereading provides a model of fluent oral reading and gives the child an opportunity to revise the story ("Is there anything you would like to change in your story?"). Finally, the child reads the story.

A variety of media can be used to record individual experience stories, each with its own advantages. Lined writing paper helps teachers model neat handwriting and proper letter formation. Story paper and unlined drawing paper provide opportunities for children to draw illustrations to go with their stories. Teachers can also use the classroom computer to make individual experience stories. Children enjoy watching the text appear on the monitor as the teacher keys in their story. Word-processing programs make it easy for the teacher to make any changes the children want in their stories. Stories can then be printed to produce a professional-looking text.

Individual experience stories can be used to make child-generated books. One approach is to write children's stories directly into blank books (books made of sheets of paper stapled between heavy construction paper or bound in hard covers). Another approach is to staple completed experience stories between sheets of heavy construction paper. For example, books can be made up of one student's stories ("Joey's Book") or can be a compilation of different children's stories ("Our Favorite Stories" or "Our Trip to the Fire Station"). Child-authored texts can be placed in the classroom library for others to read. These books tend to be very popular because children like to read what their friends have written.

Individual experience stories have several important advantages over group stories. The direct personal involvement produces high interest and motivation to read the story. There is a perfect match between the child's experiences and the text, making the story very easy to read. Children also feel a sense of ownership of their stories and begin to think of themselves as authors.

The one drawback to this strategy is that the one-to-one dictation requires a considerable amount of teacher time. Many teachers make use of parent volunteers or older students (buddy writers) to overcome this obstacle. Another strategy is to have a tape recorder available for children to dictate their stories. Teachers can then transcribe the children's compositions when time allows. Of course, children miss out on valuable teacher modeling when tape recordings are used.

Classroom Newspaper

The classroom newspaper strategy (Veatch, 1986) begins with oral sharing in which individual children discuss recent events that have happened to them. For example, Bobby might say, "We went to the lake, and I saw a big fish swimming in the water. I tried to catch it, but I fell in and got all wet." After five or six children have shared their personal experiences, the teacher picks several of the most interesting to put in the classroom newspaper. The teacher then writes these experiences on a piece of chart paper and puts the date on the top. The teacher rephrases the children's contributions, polishing them up a bit and converting them to the third person. For example, Bobby's contribution might be edited into the following: "Bobby and his family went to the lake. He tried to catch a large fish and fell into the water. He got all wet!" Notice that Bobby's thoughts are preserved but that the text is transformed into third-person, newspaper-style writing.

Children then take turns reading the day's news. The charts can be saved and reviewed at the end of the week. Classroom news does not require a shared experience, making it easier to use this technique on a regular basis than to use the group experience story. This technique also can give quite an ego boost to the children whose experiences are reported. For this reason, an effort should be made to ensure that all children get a turn at having their stories included in the news.

The classroom newspaper is an excellent way to help shift children from first-person narrative style used in individual and group stories to the third-person narrative styles used in many magazines and adult-authored children's books.

SUMMARY

When most children enter preschool or kindergarten, they already possess considerable knowledge about reading and writing. Teachers can capitalize on this prior learning by using a number of effective yet remarkably simple instructional strategies that link home and school literacy learning. In this chapter, we discussed four strategies that form a solid foundation for an effective, developmentally appropriate early childhood language arts program: functional literacy activities, storybook reading, play-based literacy, and the language experience approach/shared writing.

   ■ *What are functional literacy activities, and how can teachers use these activities in a preschool or kindergarten classroom?*

Functional print (labels, lists, directions, and schedules) is ideal for beginning readers because the surrounding context helps explain its meaning. This contextualized print is easy for young children to read and helps them view themselves as real readers. In addition, functional literacy activities help develop the concept that reading and writing have practical significance and can be used to get things done in everyday life. This realization makes print more salient to children and provides important motivation for learning to read and write. Functional print also presents opportunities for children to learn to recognize letters and words in a highly meaningful context.

■ *How can teachers set up a well-designed library center?*

A well-stocked and managed classroom library should be a key feature of every early childhood classroom. To encourage young children to engage in book reading in this area, the classroom library must be well designed, with partitions, ample space, comfortable furnishings, open-faced and traditional bookshelves, and book-related props and displays. Teachers will know quickly if their classroom library meets the well-designed criteria; inviting classroom libraries are heavily used by the children.

■ *What are the characteristics of effective adult storybook reading?*

What adults say—the verbal interaction between adult (parent or teacher) and child—during story readings has a major influence on children's literacy development. During storybook readings, children learn about the turn taking inherent in all conversation. The adult helps the child negotiate the meaning of the text, assisting by relating the content to personal experiences, providing information, asking questions, and setting expectations. Who talks the most and the content of the talk varies with the child's age.

Specific read-aloud strategies have been recommended for use in early childhood classrooms. A general read-aloud structure includes the following: read aloud every day, select high-quality literature, show and discuss the cover of the book before reading, ask children to make predictions about the story, provide a brief introduction, identify where and what you will read, read with expression at a moderate rate, read some stories interactively, read favorite stories repeatedly, and allow time for discussion after reading.

Shared reading through the reading of big books is also recognized as a critically important practice in quality early childhood literacy programs. Big books permit all children to see the print, something not possible when teachers read aloud from a regular-sized book. By using big books, teachers can introduce children to the conventions of print and the concepts about books.

■ *How can dramatic play centers be used to encourage young children's literacy development?*

Dramatic play provides an ideal context for children to have meaningful, authentic interactions with print. Dramatic play offers children of all ages and abilities multiple low-risk opportunities to explore and experiment with reading and writing.

- *How does the language experience approach (or shared writing) increase a child's understanding of print and facilitate reading development?*

The language experience approach/shared writing strategy involves having the teacher write stories that children dictate. In interactive writing, the teacher and child share the pen, both writing to create the text (with the child doing most of the writing). The resulting experience stories are a dynamic means to demonstrate the connections among talking, reading, and writing. As the teacher writes the children's speech, the children immediately see the one-to-one correspondence between spoken and written words. Because the children are the authors of these highly contextualized stories, they can easily read the stories. Experience stories can be composed by either a single child or by a group of children. Group stories are more time efficient, but individual stories are more personalized and ensure a perfect match between reader and text. The classroom newspaper is a current-event variation of the LEA strategy and provides children the same opportunities to read print in highly contextualized, authentic situations.

LINKING KNOWLEDGE TO PRACTICE

1. Visit a preschool or kindergarten classroom and record the different types and ways functional literacy activities are used in the classroom. How did the children respond to or use functional print within classroom? Did the teacher refer to the functional print?

2. Observe a library center in an early childhood classroom and evaluate its book holdings and design features. Are there a large number and wide variety of books available for the children to read? Are any basic types of books missing? Does the library center contain partitions, ample space, comfortable furnishings, open-faced and traditional bookshelves, and book-related props and displays? Is there a writing center nearby?

3. Select a specific read-aloud strategy. Using this strategy, tape yourself during a read-aloud with a small group of children. Analyze your read-aloud style for the strategies suggested in this chapter. What goals would you set for yourself?

4. With a partner, design plans for a literacy-enriched play center. Select a setting appropriate for a group of children. Describe how this center might be created in a classroom. What literacy props could be placed in the play center? What functional uses of print might be used to convey information? What literacy routines might children use in this center? What roles might children and teacher play? How might you scaffold children's play and literacy knowledge in this play center?

5. Observe a LEA/shared writing activity. Describe how the teacher used this opportunity to teach children about the forms and functions of print.

CHAPTER 5

TEACHING EARLY READING AND WRITING

When Carol was three and four years old, she lived in California and her beloved Grammy lived in Minnesota. Whenever her mother wrote home, Carol wrote to her grandmother. When she had completed her letter, her mother always asked, "And what did you tell Grammy?" Carol pointed to the scribbles on the page, every scribble, and eagerly told her mother exactly what the letter said. Her mother listened intently, always ending with, "And you wrote all that?" Later, her clever mother inserted a slip of paper into the envelope telling Grammy the gist of Carol's message. Grammy's response to Carol's letter always arrived within a week or two. Carol and her mother snuggled together on the overstuffed green sofa to read Grammy's letter, over and over. When her father came home from work, Carol met him with, "It's a Grammy letter day!" Then, she'd "read" Grammy's letter to her Daddy.

As suggested in Chapter 1, there is a continuum of beliefs about how children learn written language. On one end of the continuum, some contend that children learn to read and write simply by having opportunities to see print in use and by engaging in activities in which literacy is embedded in the task, just like Carol did in the vignette above. These people believe that children learn without ever knowing they are learning. This view supports the implicit teaching of literacy. On the other end of the continuum are those who believe that children need to engage in activities that help them focus on the abstract features of our written language, such as letter names and sounds. This perspective supports the explicit teaching of literacy. We believe that children need both kinds of experiences: opportunities to see reading and writing in use and opportunities to experience the purposes of literacy. Children also need to be directly taught about the functions and features of print. The key is that the activities and experiences early childhood teachers offer young children must be appropriate for the children's age and stage.

Chapter 4 presented the core components of a blended early childhood language arts program:

- Daily storybook reading by the teacher
- Opportunities for children to attempt to read books on their own in the library center

- Functional reading and writing activities
- Literacy activities linked to play
- Language experience or shared writing activities

This chapter is about three other key components of a blended early literacy program: writing instruction, reading instruction, and assessment. The chapter begins with a description of developmentally appropriate strategies for teaching "core" early reading skills, including phonological awareness, alphabet knowledge, print awareness, word recognition, and phonics. Next, strategies for teaching early writing are discussed, including the writing center, the writing workshop, interactive writing, and publication. Finally, we describe how teachers can assess children's early literacy skills and knowledge.

BEFORE READING THIS CHAPTER, THINK ABOUT . . .

- How you learned the names of the letters of the alphabet. Did you learn by singing the alphabet song?

- How you learned the sounds letters make. Do you remember phonics workbooks or learning phonics rules (e.g., when two vowels go walking, the first one does the talking)?

- How you learned to write (not handwrite, but write). Do you remember writing messages to special people, maybe messages that were lines and lines of scribble? Do you remember writing on walls, much to someone's dismay?

FOCUS QUESTIONS

- Which reading skills should early childhood teachers provide in order to give their students an opportunity to learn?

- What is the difference between phonological awareness, phonemic awareness, and phonics? In what sequence do young children typically acquire these skills? What does this sequence suggest about classroom instructional strategies?

- How might early childhood teachers introduce young children to the letters of the alphabet?

- Why is a writing center an important area in the preschool classroom? How might an adult teach in the writing center?

- How does a teacher teach during a writing workshop?

- Why is it important to publish children's writing?

- What types of assessment methods are used to collect data about children's early literacy learning?

■ ■ ■ ■ ■

BOX 5.1

DEFINITION OF TERMS

alphabetic principle: the idea that that there is a relationship between alphabet letters, or groups of letters, and the sounds of oral language.

ongoing assessment: a form of assessment that relies on the regular collection of children's work to illustrate children's knowledge and learning. The children's products are created as the students engage in daily classroom activities. Thus, children are learning while they are being assessed.

onsets: the beginning parts of words.

phonemes: the individual sounds that make up spoken words.

phonemic awareness: the awareness that spoken words are composed of individual sounds or phonemes.

phonics: the relationship between sounds and letters in written language.

phonological awareness: the awareness of the sound structure of oral language.

rimes: the endings parts of words.

writing center: an area in the classroom that is stocked with materials (different kinds of paper, different writing tools) to invite children to write.

writing workshop: a time in the schedule when all children meet to study the art and craft of writing.

EARLY READING INSTRUCTION

As explained in Chapter 1, recent years have seen a remarkable increase in research focused on identifying the early reading skills that are most predictive of later reading achievement. (For a review of this research, see Scarborough, 1998, and Snow et al., 1998.) We now know that high-quality early education yields long-lasting benefits (Bowman, Donovan, & Burns, 2000; Shonkoff & Phillips, 2000).

Exactly *which* early reading skills should early childhood teachers provide to give their students an opportunity to learn? The National Early Literacy Panel was formed to synthesize the research on this question and to evaluate the role of teachers and families in supporting children's language and literacy development (Strickland & Shanahan, 2004). To date, this panel has identified eleven variables as important components of an early literacy program: alphabetic knowledge, print knowledge, environmental print, invented spelling, listening comprehension, oral language/vocabulary, phonemic awareness, phonological short-term memory, rapid naming, visual memory, and visual perception skills.

We described earlier how children begin to recognize environmental print at a very early age and how early childhood teachers can bring environmental print into their classrooms (see Chapter 4). Further, we described children's invented spelling (also called emergent writing and sometimes experimental writing) and how early childhood teachers can provide young children with opportunities to use their developing invented spelling skills in functional activities and play (also in Chapter 4). Finally, we described children's development of oral language in Chapter 2 and how to facilitate children's language learning in Chapter 3. We specifically addressed children's vocabulary development on pages 47 to 56. The sections that follow describe a number of strategies for teaching what Dorothy Strickland and Tim Shanahan (2004 p. 76) refer to as the "broader" early reading skills: phonological and phonemic awareness, alphabet knowledge, word recognition, and phonics.

Phonological and Phonemic Awareness

A "massive body of work has established that phonological awareness is a critical precursor, correlate, and predictor of reading achievement" (Dickinson et al., 2003, p. 467) and that discriminating units of language (i.e., words, segments, phonemes) is linked to successful reading (Carnine et al., 2004; National Reading Panel, 2000). Clearly, phonological and phonemic awareness are two closely related skills that play important roles in early literacy development. Phonological awareness is a broader term, referring to awareness of the sound structure of speech. Phonemic awareness, a subset of phonological awareness, involves awareness that spoken words are composed of individual sounds or phonemes (Yopp & Yopp, 2000). Both are important for all young children to possess if they are to become successful readers (Stahl, Duffy-Hester, & Stahl, 1998).

Marilyn Adams (1990) suggests that if children are to succeed at reading, especially if the reading program they meet in the primary grades relies heavily on phonics, phonemic awareness is the most crucial component of an early literacy program. Yet, again, the data challenge the use of highly structured training programs with young children (IRA/NAEYC, 1998). Therefore, early childhood teachers must look for ways to embed less formal activities within their classroom settings that will help their young students attend to the sounds in the language. It is a new challenge for early childhood teachers. In the past, the teaching of letter–sound associations (phonics) has dominated early childhood programs; for the most part, children have been denied phonological and phonemic awareness experiences. Now we know that before phonics instruction can be fully useful to young children, they need phonological and phonemic awareness experiences. Even after children begin to read, they need continued instruction in phonological awareness, phonemic awareness, and phonics.

Growth in phonological awareness begins in infancy, so even the teacher of the youngest child is a phonological awareness instructor. Initially, babies hear language "as one big piece of 'BLAH BLAH BLAH.' " As discussed in Chapter 2, however, babies quickly learn to hear the unique phonemes that make up their native language. These early speech lessons occur naturally because most adults use parentese (an exaggerated, slowed, and highly articulated form of speech that allows infants to see and hear their native language) to communicate with infants. Phonological awareness begins when young children are able to hear the boundaries of words (e.g., *Seethekitty* becomes *See the kitty*). As sounds become words that are frequently used in context to label specific objects, the acquisition of word meaning begins.

The ability to hear distinct words and make meaningful associations usually emerges between nine and eighteen months (Cowley, 1997), and children quickly become specialists in their native tongue. As children begin to hear and consistently produce the discreet sounds that comprise their language, however, the ability to hear and produce the phonemes of other languages accurately diminishes rapidly. Robert Sylvester (1995) calls this process "neural selectivity." The networks for phonemes that are not in the local language may atrophy over time because of lack of use. This situation creates a challenge for children who do not speak the language of instruction when they enter school because they often experience difficulty with hearing the phonemes and word boundaries of a second language. Therefore, oral language in the early childhood classroom is central and is a prerequisite to children's phonological and phonemic awareness development.

Normally developing children begin first to discriminate among units of language (i.e., phonological awareness) and then within these units (i.e., phonemic awareness) (Adams, 1990). Evidence suggests that children show sensitivity to rhyme and to syllables before sensitivity to phonemes (Whitehurst & Lonigan, 1998). Research is clear that phonological awareness and phonemic awareness are metalinguistic abilities (Adams, 1990). As such, children must not only be able to recite and play with sound units, but they also must develop and understand that sound units map onto whole or parts of language. Although children's entry into phonological awareness might be through recitations and playing with sound units, such activities appear to be insufficient. Explicit instruction is required (Snow et al., 1998). In addition, teachers are cautioned against focusing too much attention on rhyming because rhyming has not been found to be a significant predictor of children's reading skills (e.g., Mann & Foy, 2003; Muter & Diethelm, 2001).

So, what can a child who is phonologically aware do? According to Catherine Snow, Susan Burns, and Peg Griffin (1998, p. 52), a child who is phonologically aware can enjoy and produce rhymes, count the number of syllables in a word, and notice when words begin or end with the same sound. Recall from Chapter 1 that most states have adopted preschool language and early reading standards. For example, Virginia's Literacy Foundation Blocks identifies the following phonological and phonemic awareness skills as "appropriate" for their young citizens to demonstrate by the end of their preschool years:

- Successfully detect the beginning sounds in words.
- Listen to two one-syllable words and successfully blend to form the compound word (e.g., *rain bow* to *rainbow*).
- Identify words that rhyme and successfully generate rhymes.
- Listen to a sequence of separate sounds in words with three phonemes and correctly blend the sounds to form the whole word (e.g., /k/ /a/ /t/ = cat).

(*Source:* www.pen.k12.va.us/VDOE/Instruction/Elem_M/FoundationBlocks.pdf)

What kinds of preschool activities help children develop an appreciation of the sounds of spoken words? Adams and several colleagues recommend a sequence of instructional activities that starts by building the most basic concepts of phonological awareness and then moves toward awareness of smaller and smaller units of sound (Adams, Foorman, Lundberg, & Beeler, 1998):

- *Rhyming activities.* Plan activities that focus the children's attention on the sounds inside words. For example, invite the children to recite or sing well-known nursery rhymes such as "Jack and Jill," "Humpty Dumpty," or "Hickory Dickory Dock." Once children are familiar with the rhymes, repeat a rhyme leaving out the rhyming word. Ask the children to guess the missing rhyming words ("Humpty Dumpty sat on a wall. Humpty Dumpty had a big _____.") (Ericson & Juliebö, 1998).

- *Words and sentences.* Plan activities that develop children's awareness that language is made up of strings of words. For example, recite a familiar nursery rhyme and invite the children to join in. Explain that rhymes are made up of individual words. Recite the rhyme again, clapping as each word is spoken. Then construct the rhyme by inviting each child to say one word of the rhyme in sequence (The Wright Group, 1998). Activities in which children track print, such as the shared reading strategy described in Chapter 4, are also effective ways to help children discover the concept of words.

- *Awareness of syllables.* Plan activities that develop the ability to analyze words into separate syllables and to combine syllables into words. For example, clap and count the syllables in the children's first and last names. Start with several names with one syllable, then with multiple syllables. Say the names slowly, and clap for each syllable. Then ask the children to say the names and clap along. After each name has been "clapped," ask children how many syllables they heard.

Note that these phonological awareness activities are sequenced to provide progressively closer analysis of the units of sounds. Young children will need many of these kinds of activities. Teachers will need to be aware of when their students are ready for a new challenge.

Phonological awareness exercises build a base for phonemic awareness in which children become aware that the words in speech are composed of sequences of individual sounds or phonemes. This conscious awareness of phonemes sets the stage for children to discover the alphabetic principle that there is a relationship between letters and sounds. Learning these letter–sound relationships, in turn, facilitates the recognition of words that are in children's oral vocabulary but are not familiar in print (Stanovich, 1986). In addition, learning letter–sound relationships facilitates emergent writing. To use invented spellings in their writing, children need to be able to isolate sounds in words (Richgels, Poremba, & McGee, 1996).

Most children come to understand the phonological structure of speech gradually during their preschool years. Adults report observing children as young as two or three years of age playing with sounds. For example, young children rhyme words, (e.g., *bunny, sunny, funny*), or they mix words (e.g., *pancake, canpake*).

These children are exhibiting phonological awareness. According to Catherine Snow and her colleagues (1998), for most children phonemic awareness begins when they appreciate alliteration. That is, they understand that two words begin with the same sound (e.g., *baby* and *boy* begin with /b/). Not until children are five or six years old can the majority of them identify words that begin with particular phonemes. Those children whose oral language is the most proficient are the children whose phonemic awareness is the most developed.

Upon entering school, children's level of phonemic awareness is one of the strongest predictors of success in learning to read (Adams, 1990). In fact, phonemic awareness has been shown to account for 50 percent of the variance in children's reading proficiency at the end of first grade (Adams, Foorman, Lundberg, & Beeler, 1998).

Unfortunately, phonemic awareness is difficult for many young children to acquire. Adams and her colleagues (1998, p. 19) report: "Phonemic awareness eludes roughly 25 percent of middle-class first graders and substantially more of those who come from less literacy-rich backgrounds. Furthermore, these children evidence serious difficulty in learning to read and write."

One reason that phonemic awareness is difficult to learn is that there are few clues in speech to signal the separate phonemes that make up words (Ehri, 1997). Instead, phonemes overlap with each other and fuse together into syllabic units. Adams and her colleagues (1998) give the example of *bark*. They point out that this word is not pronounced /b/, /a/, /r/, /k/. Instead, the pronunciation of the medial vowel *a* is influenced by the consonants that precede and follow it. Because phonemes are not discrete units of sound, they are very abstract and are difficult for children to recognize and manipulate (Yopp, 1992).

Here are some activities that can be used to develop awareness of phonemes:

■ *Sound matching*. Plan activities that ask children to decide which of several words begins with a specific sound (Yopp & Yopp, 2000). For example, show children pictures of familiar objects (cat, bird, monkey) and ask which object's name begins with the /b/ sound.

■ *Sound isolation*. Plan activities in which children are given words and are asked to tell what sound occurs at the beginning, middle, or ending (Yopp, 1992). For example, ask, "What's the sound that starts these words: *time, turtle, top*?" Or, instruct children to "say the first little bit of *snap*" (Snow et al., 1998).

■ *Blending*. Plan activities that invite children to combine individual sounds to form words. For example, play "What am I thinking of?" (Yopp, 1992). Tell the class that you are thinking of an animal. Then say the name of the animal in separate phonemes: "/c/-/a/-/t/." Ask the children to blend the sounds to come up with the name of the animal.

■ *Segmentation*. The flip side of blending is segmentation, in which teachers ask children to break words into individual sounds (Stahl et al., 1998). Lucy Calkins (1994) calls the ability to segment words "rubber-banding," stretching words out to hear the individual phonemes. For example, provide each child with counters and Elkonin boxes (a diagram of three blank squares representing the beginning, middle, and ending sounds in a word). Ask the children to place counters in the boxes to represent each sound in a word. For the word *cat*, a marker would be placed in the left-hand square for /c/, another in the center square for /a/, and a third in the right-hand square for /t/. The concrete props often make this difficult task easier for children.

■ *Phonemic manipulation.* Ask the children to mentally add, delete, substitute, or reverse phonemes in words. For example, ask them to say a word and then say it again without the initial sound (*farm > arm*), to substitute initial sounds in lyrics of familiar songs (*Fe-Fi-Fiddly-i-o > De-Di-Diddly-i-o*) (Yopp, 1992), or to build words by substituting onsets or rimes (*c-ake, b-ake, sh-ake, m-ake*).

Other ways to increase phonemic awareness include reading children's books that play with sounds of language (see Opitz, 1998, for a list); reading alphabet books (Murray, Stahl, & Ivey, 1996); inviting children to use computer software such as *Reader Rabbit's Ready for Letters, Kid Pix, A to Z, Bailey's Book House,* and *The Playroom* (Snow et al., 1998); and encouraging children to use invented spelling (Stahl et al., 1998). A recent meta-analysis of the results of fifty-two research studies revealed that phonemic awareness instruction is more effective when it is taught along with the letters of the alphabet (Ehri, Nunes, Willows, Schuster, Yaghoub-Zadeh, & Shanahan, 2001). Once children begin to recognize letters, they can use them to manipulate and reflect on the sounds in oral language (Yopp & Yopp, 2000). The activities in the Alphabet Knowledge section below will also indirectly help them develop phonemic awareness.

Some words of caution: Such activities can become developmentally inappropriate if the teacher does not keep them playful, weaving them intentionally and regularly into the day's activities in ways that do not dominate the early childhood program. Also, some of these activities will be inappropriate for some children. Children who are ready for such experiences will have had many experiences with books.

Alphabet Knowledge

Research has shown that alphabet identification in kindergarten is a moderately strong predictor of later reading achievement (Snow et al., 1998). The National Early Literacy Panel identified alphabetic knowledge as a core component of early literacy instruction (Strickland & Shanahan, 2004). What do children seem to be learning when they begin to name and write alphabet letters? By the time young children say the alphabet letter names, they have begun to make discoveries about the alphabet. Children who have had experiences with print come to understand that the squiggles on the paper are special; they can be named. Toddler Jed, for example, called all letters in his alphabet books or in environmental print signs either *B* or *D* (Lass, 1982). At this very young age, he had already learned that letters were a special form of graphics with names. Three-year-old Frank associated letters with things that were meaningful to him. He argued with his mother to buy him the *Firetruck* (not just the car) because "It's like me!" He pointed to the *F*. (Incidentally, his argument was successful.) Giti pointed to the *z* on her blocks and said, "Look, like in the zoo!" (Baghban, 1984, p. 30). These three young children have learned to associate letters with things important to them.

Should early childhood teachers expect all children to say and write all letters of the alphabet by the time the children are five? Certainly not; even children who read and write before entering kindergarten might not know the names of all the letters of the alphabet (Lass, 1982). As with other literacy learning areas, there is wide variation in what each child in a group of children will know and be able to do. By the age of three, some children can name as many as ten alphabet letters (Hiebert, 1981), whereas others may not be able to name any. Classroom strategies selected to teach young children alphabet letter names must be sensitive to these individual differences.

Knowing that some young children who are accomplished readers cannot name all the letters of the alphabet is a significant discovery. It is clear that learning to say the alphabet names need not be the first literacy skill children learn. Maybe it makes more sense to help children learn some whole words first, words that are important to them (e.g., their names, stores). Then, the letters within the words, like Cara's *C*, might hold more meaning.

Two methods are widely used to teach children the alphabet: the alphabet song and letter-of-the-week activities. Both methods have been criticized.

The alphabet song is the way children are most often introduced to letters at home (Adams, 1990). Although there are some advantages to learning the names of letters in this fashion (e.g., the names give children a peg on which to attach perceptual information about letters), the song can also lead to misconceptions (e.g., that *lmnop* is one letter). In addition, Judy Schickedanz (1998) argues that learning to recite the alphabet from memory is a trivial accomplishment that contributes little to children's learning to read. Yet one report by the National Research Council (Snow et al., 1998) suggests that singing the alphabet song is one of many activities early childhood teachers should use to support children's literacy learning.

The letter-of-the-week strategy involves introducing children to a different letter each week. During that week, children engage in a variety of activities related to the target letter. For example, during *A* week, children might establish an ant farm, eat apples, read a book about antelope, and the like. This strategy has been criticized for focusing on letters in isolation from meaningful reading and writing, for being too slow (it takes twenty-six weeks to introduce all the letters), and for not capitalizing on children's interests and prior knowledge (Schickedanz, 1998; Wagstaff, 1997–98).

Rather than introducing letters in a fixed, arbitrary sequence, Lea McGee and Don Richgels (1989) believe that it is preferable to teach letters that match children's current interests and activities. Other researchers do not support the totally random nature of alphabet letter teaching proposed by McGee and Richgels. For example, Rebecca Treiman and Brett Kessler (2003) discovered that young children learn letters in about the same order. For example, *O* is one of the easiest letters for children between the ages of three and seven to recognize. Letters such as *D, G, K, L, V*, and

Y are more difficult for children and are typically among the last children recognize. In short, although children may learn to sing the letters of the alphabet in alphabetical order, they do not learn to recognize the printed letters in this traditional order.

Why some letters are more difficult to learn than others is not perfectly clear. One factor that may affect the learning of letter names is the extent to which the visual form of the target letter looks like that of other letters. Another possible factor is whether the shape of the letter is the same in uppercase and lowercase, as with *o* and *c*. Hence, Margo Bowman and Rebecca Treiman (2004) suggest that teachers should expose children to the printed letters in the order of difficulty, introducing the easiest letters first to build the foundation, followed by the more difficult letters.

We recommend the following types of alphabet learning activities:

- *Environmental print.* Bring environmental print items to class (empty cereal boxes, cookie bags, etc.) and encourage children to read the print's message and discuss prominent letters (e.g., the letter *C* on a box of corn flakes).

- *Reading and writing children's names.* As discussed in Chapter 4, printed versions of children's names can be used for a variety of functional purposes, including attendance charts, helper charts, sign-up lists, and so on. Names of classmates have inherent high interest. Take advantage of every opportunity to read these names and to call attention to letters in the names ("Look, Jenny's and Jerry's names both start with the same letter. What letter is it?").

- *Writing.* Whenever children engage in writing, on their own or with a teacher (e.g., shared writing), their attention can be drawn to the letters of the alphabet. Remember that even if children are using scribbles or another personalized form of script, they are attempting to represent the letters of alphabet and thus are learning about letters.

- *Alphabet books.* There are many types of alphabet books available. For young children who are just learning the alphabet, books with simple letter–object associations (e.g., illustrations that show a letter and objects that begin with the sound associated with the letter) are most appropriate (Raines & Isbell, 1994). Alphabet books offer an enjoyable way to introduce children to letters and the sounds they represent. Research has shown that repeated reading of ABC books can promote young children's letter recognition (Greenewald & Kulig, 1995). It is also beneficial for children to make their own alphabet books. These childmade ABC books typically have a letter at the top of each page. Children then draw pictures or cut and paste illustrations of objects that begin with the sound of each letter. They can also write any words they know that contain the target letter. An adult can label the pictures.

- *Alphabet games.* Schickedanz (1998) recommends two alphabet games in particular:

  - In alphabet-matching puzzles, children must match loose letter tiles with letters printed on a background board.

- In the alphabet clue game, the teacher draws part of a letter and then asks children to guess which letter he or she is thinking of. After children make their guesses, the teacher adds another piece to the letter and has the children guess again.

- *Special alphabet activities.* Young children enjoy finger painting letters, painting letters on the easel or on the sidewalk on a hot day with a brush dipped in water, rolling and folding clay to make letters, and making and eating alphabet soup or pretzels. All these activities provide meaningful, playful contexts within which young children can learn alphabet names.

- *Traditional manipulatives.* Many traditional early childhood manipulatives can be used to support children's alphabet letter name learning. These manipulatives include alphabet puzzles, magnetic uppercase and lowercase letters, felt letters, letter stencils, and chalk and chalkboards.

- *Computer-based activities.* Computer-based activities provide children with an opportunity to practice their alphabet knowledge skills. Dorothy Strickland and Judy Schickedanz (2004, p. 77) suggest that many alphabet activities are available on the Internet and give the following as examples of what is available

  - ABC Order: www.learningplanet.com/act/abcorder.asp
  - Big Bird Gets a Letter: www.sesameworkshop.org/sesamestreet/sitemap

Strickland and Schickedanz wisely advise teachers to *always* preview computer programs in advance.

Incidentally, Adams (1990) recommends that teachers help children identify uppercase letters first, followed by lowercase letters. She believes that uppercase letters are more familiar to children and are easier for children to discriminate between visually than their lowercase counterparts. A second reason it is appropriate to teach uppercase letters first is that lowercase letters are more visually confusable. The advantage for uppercase letters is greatest at ages four and five; by age six, children are typically able to manage learning both uppercase and lowercase letters (Bowman & Treiman, 2004).

Print Awareness

According to the National Research Council (1999, p. 27), "a child's sensitivity to print is a major first step toward reading." The earliest forms of print awareness entail understanding that print is everywhere in the environment and that reading and writing are ways to obtain ideas, information, and knowledge. In other words, children begin to develop print awareness by understanding the functions of print. One of the earliest discoveries that children make about written language is that print has meaning. Jerry Harste, Virginia Woodward, and Carolyn Burke (1984) found that many three-year-olds expect print to be meaningful. This understanding becomes evident when children point to words on signs, cereal boxes, or menus and ask, "What does that say?" Alternatively, after making marks on a piece of paper, children make comments such as, "What did I write?" or "This says. . . ."

A related discovery is that print is functional; it can be used to get things done in daily life. Children's knowledge of the practical uses of print grows substantially during the preschool years. Elfrieda Hiebert (1981) found that three-year-olds demonstrated limited knowledge of the purposes of several types of print, such as labels on Christmas presents, street signs, and store signs, but that five-year-olds showed much greater knowledge of these functions.

Children's knowledge of the functional uses of literacy frequently shows up in their make-believe play. For example, Marcia Baghban (1984) recounts how she took her daughter, twenty-eight-month-old Giti, out to eat at a restaurant. Upon returning home, Giti promptly acted out the role of a waitress, making marks on a pad of paper while recording her mother's food orders. Other researchers have reported numerous incidents of preschoolers engaging in a variety of functional literacy activities while engaging in dramatic play, including jotting down phone messages, writing checks to pay for purchases, looking up recipes in cookbooks, and making shopping lists (Neuman & Roskos, 1997; Vukelich, 1992).

Later, by about age three, children understand that it is the print that is read, not the pictures. Ask three-year-olds to draw a picture and write their names. Their markings when asked to draw a picture will likely be quite different from those made when they are asked to write their names. This distinction is important because it establishes a separate identify for print and allows children to begin learning about print's functions and structure.

Other print concepts that develop at this time include that print contains alphabet letters that are special kinds of visuals, that a sentence starts at the left and continues from left to right, that a sentence continues until a punctuation indicates that it ends, and that there are spaces between words. To this list many add concepts about books. The book concepts typically identified include identifying the front of books and locating the titles of books.

Unlike the other foundations of reading skill areas, there is only one study demonstrating the relationship of print convention skills and later reading (Tunmer, Herriman, & Nesdale, 1988). Rather, print conventions seem to be a more immediate indicator of children's familiarity with text.

Research identifies two instructional contexts for the teaching of print awareness, dramatic play and storybook reading. Dramatic play provides an environment for children to engage in a variety of functional literacy activities (Neuman & Roskos, 1997). We described how to integrate print into children's play in Chapter 4. Storybook reading provides a key means through which young children acquire general knowledge, language development, book concepts and print conventions (Lonigan & Whitehurst, 1998; Neuman, 1999). Effective story-reading techniques that provide children with opportunities to learn print awareness concepts as well as other important language and early literacy concepts were also described in Chapter 4.

Word Recognition

We used to believe that children needed to learn to recognize the letters of the alphabet before they were ready to learn to recognize and read whole words.

Emergent literacy research has shown us to be incorrect (see Chapter 4). We now know that many children learn to recognize personally significant words, such as their names and environmental print (*Pepsi*), before they learn to recognize the more abstract letters that make up these words. We recommend that teachers work on the two skills in a simultaneous and connected fashion: provide experiences that draw children's attention to highly meaningful words and, at the same time, point out key letters in those words.

We have already described several basic strategies that parents and teachers can use to help young children learn to recognize whole words:

- *Storybook reading.* When adults read favorite books to children over and over again, repeated exposure to a small number of words can lead to the beginning of word recognition.

- *Environmental print.* Words connected with environmental print (e.g., cereal boxes, beverage cans, road signs, billboards, and restaurant menus) are often among the first words that children recognize. As explained in Chapter 4, this type of print is easy to learn to recognize because the context gives clues to the print's meaning. Adults can assist this process by drawing children's attention to environmental print and by using the environmental print and functional print strategies described at the beginning of Chapter 4.

- To this list, Elizabeth Kirk and Patricia Clark (2005) would add the following word recognition activities that use the children's names (pp. 142–143):

  - *Name-photo match.* The teacher prints each child's name on one piece of card stock and glues a picture of each child on another piece of card stock; both cards are laminated. The children match the photo with the name.
  - *Name puzzle.* The teacher prints each child's name on card stock, laminates the card, cuts the letters apart, and places the letters in an envelope with the child's name on the outside. The children correctly organize the letters to make their names or their friend's names.

Although we have only referenced Kirk and Clark's ideas here, their article includes numerous activities for using children's names to facilitate their early literacy learning. In total, they describe some two dozen early literacy activities using the children's names, a very important word to young children.

In the following sections, we discuss two other strategies that are ideally suited for building young children's recognition of words: key words and word walls.

Key Words.   The key word strategy, developed by Sylvia Ashton-Warner (1963), is an excellent way to build young children's ability to recognize words. It is a very simple and elegant strategy: children choose words that are personally meaningful and that they would like to learn to read. Real-life experiences, favorite children's books, writing workshop, and language experience stories are primary sources for these key words. Children learn to recognize these words quickly because of their high meaning and personal significance.

Here is how the key word strategy works. The teacher asks each child in the class to pick a favorite word that he or she would like to learn to read. This word is written on a large card while the child watches. (This activity is sometimes done in circle time so that the whole class learns about each child's key word.) The children then write their key words plus any other words they remember. Finally, they engage in various games and practice activities with their key words.

The following are some of the key word games and practice activities recommended by Jeanette Veatch and her associates (Veatch, Sawicki, Elliot, Flake, & Blakey, 1979, pp. 30–32):

- *Retrieving words from the floor.* The children's words (with young children they will be the words of a partner or a small group) are placed face down on the floor. On the signal, each child is to find one of her or his own words, hold it up, and read it aloud.

- *Claiming the cards.* The teacher selects many words from the class, holds them up, and the child who "owns" each word claims it.

- *Classifying words.* The teacher selects categories that encompass all the words selected by the children. The categories are introduced, and labels are placed on the floor for each category. The children must then decide in which category their words belong. For example, the children who have animal words would stand next to the sheet of paper that says *animals.*

- *Making alphabet books.* Children record their words in the correct section of an alphabet book that is divided by initial letters. This strategy is a good example of how children can learn about words and letters simultaneously.

- *Illustrating.* The child can draw a picture about the key word, dictate the word to a teacher to write on a card, and then copy the word into a picture dictionary word book.

- *Finding words.* Children might find their key words in books, magazines, and newspapers.

Veatch and her colleagues recommend that children collect key words and keep them in a box or on a ring file known as a "word bank." Another possibility is to have children keep their key words in a word book as is illustrated in Trade Secret 5.1. In this variation, the teacher writes a word on a card for the child, and then the child copies the word into his or her word book. Notice how the teacher, Bernadette Watson, prompts Amanda to use letter–sound relationships when she writes Amanda's key word, *elephant,* on the card.

Periodically, the teacher can have children review the words in their word banks or word books. Besides providing opportunities for children to practice recognizing

TRADE SECRET 5.1
My Word Book

BY BERNADETTE WATSON

As the children entered the classroom, Ms. Watson greeted them, gave them a three-by-five-inch card, and asked them, "What is your word for today?" Children answered. Amanda said, "Elephant." Ms. Watson positioned her hand to write *elephant* on the card. Before she wrote the word, she asked Amanda how she decided on this word as her word for the day. Amanda had seen a program on television about elephants the night before and had decided, right then and there, that *elephant* would be her word today.

"So," asked Ms. Watson, "what letter do you think *elephant* begins with?"

"I don't know," responded Amanda.

"It's an *e*," said Ms. Watson. "What letter is next?" She stretched the sound, "L-l-l-l-l."

Amanda responded, "L!"

"You're right," exclaimed Ms. Watson, "and then it's another *e*, and a *p-h-a-n*. And what do you think the last letter is? T-t-t-t-t."

Amanda said, "T!"

"Absolutely," said Ms. Watson.

Amanda took her card with *elephant* written on it with her and set off to locate her word book. Having found it, she sat at a table to copy her word into her book. First, she drew a picture of an elephant. Above it, she copied the word *elephant*. At the beginning of the year, that is all she would have done. Now, she also wrote a sentence under the picture: "isnt.v" (I saw on TV).

When she was done, Amanda took her book to the library center. Here, she might read her words to herself or to a friend. The pictures she had drawn greatly help her remember her word for the day.

key words, word banks and word books serve other valuable functions. They provide children with a concrete record of their reading vocabulary growth. It is very motivating for children to see their collections of words grow larger and larger. In addition, the words can be used to help children learn about letters and the sounds each letter is associated with. For example, if children are learning the sound associated with *b*, the teacher can have children find all the words in their collections that begin with that letter.

Word Walls.   A word wall is a word collection for an entire classroom. Category labels are posted at the top of one or more bulletin boards, and then words are selected by the teacher or children and placed on the board under the appropriate label. ABC word walls are very appropriate for use with four- and five-year-olds. The category labels are the letters of the alphabet. Children's names, environmental print, words related to ongoing units or projects, and salient words from shared writing stories can be added, one at a time. For example, if the class is studying transportation, the words *truck* and *taxi* might be put under the letter *t*, along with the children's names, Terrance and Tammy. The ABC word wall helps children learn the alphabet and understand the concept of alliteration as well as promoting whole word recognition. Trade Secret 5.2 describes a variation of the ABC word wall that might be used at the preschool or kindergarten level.

TRADE SECRET 5.2
ABC Word Walls

At the beginning of the kindergarten year, Mrs. Burl begins each school day by asking her class to share any print items they brought from home. These items are usually packages or wrappers of products that the children's families use at home. She asks each child who brought an item to read the name of the item to the rest of the class. After the children have read their environmental print, Mrs. Burl selects one of the products, Aim toothpaste, and asks the children where they think the Aim toothpaste container should go on their ABC word wall. The children think for just a moment before Anissa suggests cutting the wrapper into two parts: one part for *Aim* to go under the letter *Aa* on the word wall and the second for *toothpaste* to go under the letter *Tt*. Mrs. Burl asks the class for a thumbs-up (for yes) or thumbs-down (for no) vote. The children give her a unanimous thumbs up. Mrs. Burl quickly cuts the package, circles the appropriate words, and asks the child who brought the wrapper to pin each word under the correct letter on the word wall.

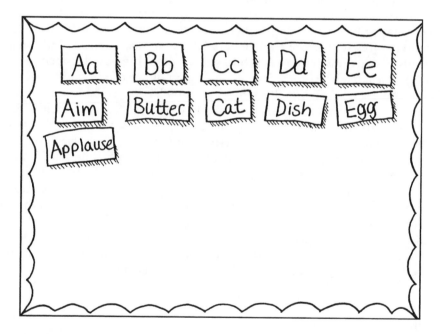

FIGURE 5.1 ABC Word Wall

Stories and rhymes can also be a source of word wall words. For example, Janiel Wagstaff (1998) describes a strategy in which the class focuses on a different poem or nursery rhyme each week. After the rhyme or poem is read for the first time, several words that begin with different letters are selected. For example, if the rhyme was "Jack and Jill," then *Jack*, *hill*, and *pail* might be selected as the focus words. The following sequence is used to familiarize children with these words and their initial sounds:

- The teacher emphasizes the beginning sound of each word, helping children hear and say the sounds.
- The words are written on colored pieces of construction paper and added to the word wall under the appropriate letter labels.
- The children engage in word play: putting thumbs up if words begin with the same sound as *Jack*, *hill*, or *pail* and thumbs down if they start with a different sound; finding other words that start with the /j/, /h/, or /p/ sounds; and substituting words that rhyme with words in the nursery rhyme "Back and Jill went up the pill to fetch a tail of water." The rhyme is reread, placing the words back into a meaningful context.

During the rest of the week, the rhyme can be revisited with shared reading, and the children can engage in different types of word play with the words on the word wall to build phonemic awareness and knowledge of letter–sound relationships.

Jane Katch (2004) suggests another variation on the word wall that she uses with her four-year-olds. The category labels for Ms. Katch's word wall are her students' names. She wrote each child's name on a three-by-five-inch card and taped the names in a horizontal row along the top of her classroom's large whiteboard. Each day, she asked one child, the day's line leader, to think of a special word for her to write on a blank card, which she taped beneath that child's name on the whiteboard. For example, when she asked Anna for a word, Anna softly said, "Kitty." She wrote *Kitty* on a three-by-five-inch card and placed it under Anna's name on the word wall. By the end of the month, each child had chosen a special word and had one word under his or her name on the word wall. It was Anna's turn again, and she said, "Mommy." Ms. Katch wrote the word on a card, posted it under Anna's name, and asked her if she wanted to read both of her important words, which Anna did proudly. As the year progressed and lists became longer, Ms. Katch incorporated a quick minilesson into the routine, such as teaching how to make a word plural by adding an *s* and asking the children to find all words on the whiteboard that began with the same letter as the new word.

Phonics

In English, the letters of the alphabet are related to the sounds of oral language. This feature of English is referred to as the alphabetic principle. Phonics involves using letter–sound relationships to decode printed words. These numerous relationships are somewhat complex. Once children grasp the alphabetic principle and learn some of the major letter–sound relationships, however, they can use this knowledge to "sound out" or decode unfamiliar printed words.

To learn phonics, children first need to make some headway in mastering phonemic awareness, the awareness that words are composed of individual sounds.

To match these sounds up with alphabet letter, children have to be aware of the individual sounds in words, which is one reason phonemic awareness is such a key early literacy skill. Of course, being able to name and identify letters also helps with learning these relationships.

Young children differ greatly in their need for instruction in this important decoding skill. Steve Stahl (1992, p. 620) explains: "Some will learn to decode on their own, without any instruction. Others will need some degree of instruction, ranging from the pointing out of common spelling patterns to intense and systematic instruction." Thus, as in all other aspects of literacy instruction, it is important that phonics teaching match the needs of individual students.

The children who learn phonics more or less on their own simply need to be provided with the types of meaningful reading and writing activities described in Chapter 4—shared reading and writing, literacy-enriched play, and functional literacy activities. As these children engage in purposeful literacy activities, they gradually discover the relationship between letters and sounds.

Those who need a moderate amount of assistance profit from what Lesley Morrow and Diane Tracey (1997) call "contextual instruction." This type of instruction also occurs in conjunction with the types of activities described above: shared reading and writing, literacy-enriched play, and functional literacy activities. The only difference is that while children are engaging in these activities, the teacher draws children's attention to letter–sound relationships that are present.

Morrow and Tracey (1997, p. 647) give an example of how one teacher, Mrs. M., drew her students' attention to the letter *m* and its sound during an activity that involved both shared writing and functional writing:

> Because her class had finished putting on a show for their grandparents, Mrs. M. thought it would be a good idea if they wrote a thank-you note to the music teacher who assisted them with the performance. The note was composed by the students with the teacher's help. She wrote the note on the board and sounded out each word to help the students with spelling. After they finished writing, Mrs. M. read the entire note and had the students read the note aloud:

> **MRS. M.:** How should we start this letter?

> **STUDENT:** Dear Mr. Miller.

> **MRS. M.:** Very good. [as she writes] "Dear Mr. Miller" has three words. *Dear* is the first word, *Mr.* is the second word, and *Miller* is the third word. I just realized that my name and Mr. Miller's name both begin with the same letter, *M*. Let's say these words together, "Mr. Miller, Mrs. Martinez."

This type of spontaneous teaching can occur in connection with all the literacy learning activities described in this chapter and in Chapter 4. Of course, such teaching requires a teacher who is on the lookout for teachable moments involving letter–sound relationships. Because most, if not all, preschool and kindergarten classes contain some children who need moderate assistance, teachers should take advantage of these types of teaching opportunities when they arise.

Another way to help children acquire knowledge about phonics is through writing (IRA/NAEYC, 1998; Stahl, 1992). Once children have reached the invented spelling stage in their writing development, they begin to use their knowledge of letter names and letter–sound relationships to spell words. During this stage, children spell words based on the way the words sound rather than on how they are conventionally spelled. For example, a child may spell the word *leave* with the letters *lev* because that is how the word sounds. When children use invented spelling, their attention is naturally focused on letter–sound relationships.

Research indicates that temporary use of invented spelling can promote children's reading development (IRA/NAEYC, 1998). For example, one study (Clarke, 1988) found that young children who were encouraged to write with invented spelling scored higher on decoding and reading comprehension tests than children who were encouraged to use conventional spelling.

Finally, by adapting the phonemic awareness, letter recognition, and word recognition activities discussed earlier so that they focus on letter–sound relationships, teachers can provide preplanned phonics activities to children who have developed some awareness of the sounds that make up spoken words and who can recognize some of the letters of the alphabet. We recommend that letter–sound relationships be selected that fit with ongoing class activities or that fit the needs of specific children, rather than using an arbitrary sequence (consonants first, short vowels second, long vowels third, etc.).

Several of the phonemic awareness activities described earlier can easily be modified to teach phonics by having children identify which letters represent the various sounds and then writing words so that children can see the letter–sound relationships. For example:

■ *Letter–sound matching.* Show pictures of familiar objects (cat, bird, and monkey) and ask children which begins with the /m/ sound. Then ask which letter *monkey* starts with. Write the word on chalkboard. Ask children for other words that start with the /m/ sound, and write these words on the board.

■ *Letter–sound isolation.* Pronounce words and ask children what sounds are heard at the beginning, middle, or end of the word. For example, ask the children, "What sound is in the middle of *man, cat,* and *Sam*?" Once the sound is identified, ask the children what letter represents the sound. The words can then be written on the chalkboard, along with other short-*a* words.

Letter recognition activities can also be modified to teach phonics by shifting the focus from letters to their sounds. For example:

■ *Environmental print.* Discuss letter–sound relationships that occur in environmental print. For example, if children have brought in cereal boxes from home, the teacher could ask, "What letters make the /ch/ sound in Cheerios?" Children could then be asked to identify other words that start with the /ch/ sound, and these words could be written on the chalkboard or added to an ABC word wall.

■ *Reading and writing children's names.* When referring to children's names in attendance charts, helper charts, and other places, call children's attention to letter–sound correspondences in their names. For example, the teacher might say, "Jenny's and Jerry's names start with the same sound. What letter is it?"

■ *Games.* Create games that enable children to reinforce their growing knowledge of letter–sound relationships in an enjoyable manner. A popular type of phonics game requires children to match letters with pictures that begin with letter sounds. For example, the letter *b* might be matched with a picture of a bird. To avoid confusion with other words that the picture could represent, be sure to tell the children the word that each picture represents when using this type of phonics matching game. In the example of the *b/bird* item, a child might justifiably believe that the picture of a bird represented the word *robin* or *sparrow* rather than *bird.*

Word banks and word walls, discussed in the section on word recognition, can also be invaluable aids in helping children learn phonics. The words in these collections are familiar to children and often have strong personal significance and meaning. These high-meaning words can serve as pegs on which children can attach letter–sound relationships. Teachers should routinely take advantage of these words by linking them with phonics activities and lessons. For example, if a teacher were trying to help children learn the /ch/ sound–symbol correspondence, children could be asked to find all the letters in their word banks or on the word wall that contain this letter combination.

Some children will need more direct instruction on letter–sound relationships, but not during the preschool years. Preschool and kindergarten children who need extensive help learning phonics really need more experience with phonemic awareness, letter recognition, and informal types of phonic instruction described in this chapter. These activities will build a foundation that will help these children benefit from more systematic approaches to learning phonics later.

Writing Instruction

Even the youngest of children like to write—not only on paper, but also on walls and floors. As Pam Oken-Wright notes, "The urge to make one's mark is such a strong one that it is manifest on many a bedroom wall, executed with whatever implement was handy or seemed exciting" (1998, p. 76). Early childhood teachers, then, must take advantage of this natural urge by providing a variety of writing materials to their young writers, learning to ask the right question at the right time, and providing the right instruction at the right time to nudge their young writers' development (Schickedanz & Casbergue, 2004). In this section, we explore the what and how of writing instruction in an early childhood classroom.

The Context for Writing: The Writing Center

A writing center is a special area in the classroom that is stocked with materials that invite children to write. When setting up such a center, teachers need to remember

Some children learn to write simply by engaging in meaningful writing activities. Others need direct instruction

that writing is a social act. Children want to share their writing with peers, know what their peers are writing, and ask for assistance with the construction of their text. For instance, a child might say, "Morning. How do you spell 'mororornnn-nnninggg'?" Teachers typically provide a table and chairs in the writing center because they know of children's need for talk while writing.

Gather the Needed Materials.   In addition to a table and chairs, teachers stock the writing center with materials that invite children to write and to play with writing materials. Such materials include but are not limited to the following:

- Many different kinds of paper (e.g., lined theme paper, typical story paper, discarded computer or office letterhead paper with one side clean, lots of unlined paper, paper cut into different shapes to suggest writing about particular topics, paper folded and made into blank books, stationery and envelopes, cards)
- Various writing tools (e.g., pencils, markers—be certain to purchase the kind that can withstand the kind of pressure young children exert as they write—crayons, felt-tip pens, a computer or computers with a word-processing program)
- Writing folders for storage of each child's writing efforts

- A box or file drawer in which to store the file folders
- Lists of children's names
- Children's names and photos laminated on card stock
- Magic slates
- Dry erase board and markers
- Three-by-five-inch cards
- Letter stamps and stamp pads
- Homemade blank books
- Hole punch, stapler, scissors, tape

Notice that oversized (fat) pencils and special primary-lined paper were not recommended as the only paper and pencils to be provided. For young children, Miriam Martinez and Bill Teale (1987) recommend unlined paper because it does not signal how writing is supposed to be done. Children are freer to use the emergent forms of writing—pictures used as writing, scribble writing, letterlike units, and so on—that do not fit on the lines of traditional lined writing paper or story paper (e.g., top half blank, bottom half lined).

In addition to these required items, many teachers include the following items in their classroom writing center:

- A bulletin board for displaying such items as samples of the children's writing, examples of different forms of writing (e.g., thank-you notes, letters, postcards, stories), writing-related messages (e.g., "Here's our grocery list"), messages about writing (e.g., "Look at this! Shawn's sister published a story in the newspaper"), and the children's writing
- Posters showing people engaged in writing
- Clipboards for children who want to write somewhere other than at the table
- Mailboxes (one for each child, the teacher, the principal or center director, and other appropriate persons, as determined by the children) to encourage note and letter writing
- Alphabet strips on the writing table so that children have a model readily available when they begin to attempt to link their knowledge of letter sounds with their knowledge of letter formations

Most teachers introduce the materials to the children gradually, that is, they do not place all these materials in the writing center on the first day of school, which young children would find overwhelming. They make the writing center new and exciting over the year by regularly adding new materials and tools. Pam Oken-Wright (1998) suggests that when new materials are added to the writing center, it is important not to substitute the new for the old; young children like the familiar along with the new.

Arrange the Materials.   With so many different materials in the writing center, keeping the supplies orderly and replenishing them can take up time. Some teachers label the places where the various tools and paper belong in the writing center, which helps all the children know where to return used materials and helps a child "clerk" know how to straighten the center at cleanup time. Further, labeling the places where the items belong permits a quick inventory of missing and needed items. Figure 5.2 provides an illustration of a well-equipped, well-arranged writing center.

Computers and Word Processing.   A growing number of early childhood classrooms have computers in the writing center. Early childhood computer expert Dan Shade highly recommends the following relatively new software packages for their user-friendly qualities; that is, young children can easily use them to write: *Orly's Draw-a-Story* (Shade's personal favorite), *Claris for Kids*, and *The Writing Center* (the new and improved version). Some older favorites include *Kid Works 2* (Davidson), *Storybook Weaver* (MECC), *Wiggins in Storybook Land*, and *The Incredible Writing Machine* (The Learning Company).

FIGURE 5.2   A Well-Equipped Writing Center

Marilyn Cochran-Smith, Jessica Kahn, and Cynthia Paris (1986) point out that all writers, regardless of age, require time at the computer when their attention is focused on learning word-processing skills. For example, Bev Winston, a kindergarten teacher, introduced her young students to word processing during the school's orientation days, those days that precede the first full day of school. Then she watched her students as they played with word processing during their free-play time and provided instruction as each child needed it. Word processing is a tool to preserve children's important first writings. It is important for teachers to keep that in mind. Young children need time to experiment with this tool just as children need time to experiment with pencils, pens, markers, and so forth.

Teachers' Role. Materials alone, however, even well-organized materials in beautifully arranged writing centers, are not enough. Children also need opportunities to interact with their teachers in the writing center. They need their teachers to sit beside them to support their writing efforts. Sometimes teachers will support by selecting a writing tool and paper and modeling a form of writing, such as writing a letter to a friend, writing a thank-you note, or making a sign for the coat cubbies asking the children to please put their snowboots in the bottom of their cubbies. While teachers engage in this modeling, they talk aloud, describing their thinking, stretching words to hear the letter sounds, asking for assistance, and so on. At other times, teachers will support a child's writing, particularly those students who have begun to associate sounds with letters, by helping the child stretch out the words to hear the letter sounds and select the correct letter to represent each sound. Just as in teachers' involvement with children during their play, such adult interactions can facilitate children's learning within their zone of proximal. Through such support, teachers can stretch children beyond their current level of knowledge, and children can do what they could not be independently. In turn, children's literacy growth can be promoted, both in terms of their knowledge about the purposes of writing and in terms of their understanding of how sound is mapped onto print in the language.

The Writing Workshop

By the time children reach kindergarten, many teachers add a writing workshop, with some direct teaching of writing, to the daily schedule at least once a week.

The writing workshop was first described by Donald Graves (1983) in his book *Writing: Teachers and Children at Work*. All members of the writing workshop meet to intensively study the art and craft of writing. The workshop typically has the following components:

- *Focus lesson*. A five-minute lesson to teach children about the writing process ("I want to make a change in my writing. I'm going to *revise*. Here's how I'll do it."); a procedural aspect of the writing program ("We help our friends while they write. We say things like, 'Tell me more about your dog. What color is he?'"); a quality of good writing ("I can tell more about my dog by adding his color, black.

So I'll write 'I hv a blk dg.' "); a mechanical feature of writing ("Always make *I* a capital, a big letter."); or about why people write ("We need to make a list.")

■ *Writing.* A ten- to fifteen-minute period during which children write and meet with peers and the teacher

■ *Group share.* A ten-minute period during which one or two children read their writing pieces to the group and receive positive feedback and content-related questions.

Although the writing workshop was originally designed for use in the elementary grades (see Chapter 8), it can be easily adapted for use with younger children. One kindergarten teacher, for example, has used variations of the workshop approach—focus lessons and group share time—to help her students develop as writers.

Focus Lessons.   Focus lessons, (also called minilessons) are short lessons that focus on an aspect of writing. In Trade Secret 5.3, kindergarten teacher Bernadette Watson uses focus lessons to teach her students how to match letter sounds with the correct letter symbols. In one lesson, she helped the children sound out the spellings of the words in the sentence "I went to New York." She stretched the words out (e.g., w-e-n-t) and focused the children's attention on the sound of each letter ("What letter makes the /w/ sound?") or letter cluster ("How about /ent/?"). Because she knows that her students will not fully understand the relationship between sounds and symbols as a result of one lesson, she weaves the content of this lesson into many lessons and reinforces this understanding when she talks with her young writers about their writing.

Writing Time.   The focus lesson is followed by a time for the children to write. Ms. Watson teaches in a public school and has an occasional parent as a teacher assistant. She presents a writing lesson on Monday. Five children begin their free-play time in the writing center, writing with Ms. Watson's support and reading their text to her before they leave the writing center. The other children proceed to centers of their choice. Tomorrow another five children will begin their free-play time in the writing center. Each child begins free-play in the writing center once each week. The children can choose to write on more than their writing day, but all children must write at least one day each week. Requiring the children to begin their play in the writing center one day each week allows Ms. Watson time to support and observe each child's writing development at least once each week.

While the children write, Ms. Watson and other adults who might be in the classroom meet with the young writers about their writing. The opportunity to talk while writing is a critically important component of writing workshop. The talk is about the content and the mechanics (usually the letter–sound relationships) of the piece. Through conferences, teachers can provide one-on-one instruction, providing the child with just the right help needed at that minute.

TRADE SECRET 5.3

**Teaching about Sound–Symbol Relationships:
An Invented-Spelling Focus Lesson**

BY BERNADETTE WATSON

Teacher: I didn't tell you this before. I went on a trip to New York this weekend. The New York Marathon, a running race, was on this weekend, so there was a lot of traffic! It took us a long time to get to New York. That's what I'm going to write about today. I'm going to start by drawing a picture. I'll just draw a road. That will help me remember what I'm going to write about. [Teacher draws a road.] I'm going to write "I went to New York City." Will you help me write the words? "I" Oh, that's an easy one. [Writes "I" on the board.]

W-e-n-t. [Stretches word.]
"w"-"w"-"w."
Child: "Y."
Teacher: It does sound like a "Y." We'll use "Y" for that sound. E-N-T.
Childern: "N!" "N!" [Teacher writes "N."]
Teacher: W-E-N-*T*-T-T
Childern: "T!" [Teacher writes "T."]
Teacher: to
Child: I know how to spell to—"t" "o."
Teacher: How do you know that?
Child: I don't know. I just do. [Teacher writes *to*.]
Teacher: [Reads, I went "to."] New. "N"-"N"-"N."
Child: It's like my name. "N."

Group Share Time.   The workshop is culminated by group share time. During the group share session, two or three children sit, one at a time, in the author's chair and share their pieces with the other writers in the class. (See Trade Secret 5.4 for a description of how one teacher uses the "author's chair" strategy.) Typically, the other children are gathered at the sharing writer's feet, listening attentively while the writer reads the piece and preparing to make comments or ask questions. The following describes one group share in Bernadette Watson's kindergarten classroom.

> **DEMETRI:**   I like your story.
>
> **MS. WATSON:**   Remember, Demetri, when we talked about how we tell the writer what we really liked about his or her story? Can you tell Aaron what you liked about his story?
>
> **DEMETRI:**   I really liked the part where you thought you would get a dog because I want a dog, too.
>
> **AARON:**   Thanks.
> [The classroom rule is that the writer calls on three children for a question or a comment. The first response is a comment. The other two must be questions. Ms. Watson uses this time to help her students begin to understand the difference between a comment (statement or sentence) and a

TRADE SECRET 5.4
The Author's Chair

Ms. Garcia has taken a regular classroom chair and taped the label "Author's Chair" on its backrest. The chair is placed in front of the carpeted area where her kindergartners sit during circle time. She uses this chair on a daily basis to read good literature to her class. Ms. Garcia also uses the Author's Chair to read stories that her students have written, treating them in the same manner as the adult-authored books. Her students also use the chair, taking turns reading their own writing from the Author's Chair.

Regardless of who is doing the reading (Ms. Garcia or her students) or what type of book is being read (adult authored or child authored), the children in the audience respond in the same way. First, they receive the story, making positive comments about their favorite part, what they liked best about the story (e.g., "It was funny!"), or their views of what the story was about. Then the students may ask questions, requesting additional information or inquiring about specific events in the story. If the book was written by a professional author, then Ms. Garcia and the children speculate on how the author might answer these questions.

The Author's Chair strategy, developed by Donald Graves and Jane Hansen (1983), provides a powerful incentive for young children to write. They know that selected pieces of their writing will be published by being read from the Author's Chair. Another advantage of this strategy is that the chair serves as a link between child and adult authors. When children sit in the chair and read their published books, their books are treated just like those of professional writers. They are received and questioned in the same manner, which adds status to their writing, helps them perceive themselves as being real authors, motivates them to write, and helps them develop a sense of authorship.

question. Learning the difference takes a lot of practice.] [Aaron calls on another child, Luisa, for a question.]

LUISA: Did you draw your picture and write, or write and draw your picture?

AARON: I drew the pictures and then wrote. [Aaron calls on Bill.]

BILL: I know how to spell *to*. Do you?

Aaron is unsure how to respond to Bill's question. He writes a string of letters with no match to letter sounds. According to Elizabeth Sulzby's categories of emergent writing, Aaron's writing is representative of nonphonetic letter strings (see page 119 for a description.)

Ms. Watson understands his confusion and comes to his rescue. She asks, "Bill can you write *to* on the chart paper for us? [Bill eagerly displays what he knows.] "Listen to Aaron's sentence. *I want to get a dog.* Count the number of words in Aaron's sentence," [Ms. Watson says the sentence and raises a finger for each word.] "I want to get a dog." [Children respond correctly.] "What Bill is saying is that Aaron's third word, I want *to*, is always written *t-o*. Should we add that to our word wall? Then you can look at the word wall when you need to write the word *to* in your sentences." [She takes a three-by-five-inch card, writes *to* on the card, and ceremoniously adds it to the classroom word wall.] "Thanks so much, Aaron and Bill. We learned about Aaron's hope for a birthday present and how to write the word *to* today. Who else would like to share?"

Through group shares, young children learn that writing is meant to be shared with others. Writers write to communicate their thoughts and ideas with their readers. Young children also learn how to share their writing with others (reading in a loud voice so that others can hear, holding their writing so others can see) and about the difference between a question and a comment. Teachers use children's texts and questions and comments as a context to teach about writing.

We return to the writing workshop in Chapter 8. There, we describe how the workshop is used in the elementary grades.

Journals and Interactive Forms of Writing

Teachers want to provide young children with opportunities to write for many different purposes and to use different forms (or modes) of writing. Ms. Murphy modeled writing a letter (a form or mode) to stay in contact with people (a purpose) in the writing center. Ms. Edwards demonstrated writing a list (a form or mode) to help her remember (a purpose) in a writing workshop minilesson. In this section, we describe three kinds of writing that are particularly beneficial for beginning writers: journals, dialogue writing, and pen pals.

Journals.   Journals focus on personal expression and learning. Children write to themselves about what is happening in their lives in and out of school, the stories they are reading, and what they are learning in different subject areas. The writer is his or her own audience. The "text" might be pictures and writing, or just pictures, or just print.

In Trade Secret 5.5, Phoebe Ingraham describes several kinds of journal writing that her kindergarten students use for many different purposes: creative journals, literature response journals, alphabet journals, theme journals, and learning logs.

Dialogue Writing.   By the time children are four or five years old, most have become quite proficient at oral dialogue. Teachers can capitalize on this strength by engaging children in written conversations (Watson, 1983). In written conversations, the teacher and child use shared writing paper or dialogue journals to take turns writing to each other and reading each other's comments. This strategy makes children's writing more spontaneous and natural by helping them see the link between written and oral language. In addition, the teacher serves as an authentic audience of children's writing, providing motivation for engaging in the writing process.

The teacher initiates these written conversations by writing brief messages to each student, who, in turn, reads what the teacher has written and writes a response to the teacher. The teacher then reads these responses and writes additional comments. This process continues in a chainlike fashion.

TRADE SECRET 5.5
Journal Experiences for Young Children

BY PHOEBE BELL INGRAHAM

Young children love to imitate adult behaviors, especially reading and writing. Before ever entering school, young children can be caught "reading" stories to baby dolls or teddy bears, writing grocery lists, or taking phone messages in typical adult, sloppy "cursive." Too often, this experimentation with everyday functions and forms of literacy vanishes once they begin school. Concerned parents, politically conscious school administrators, and stressed-out teachers in upper grades encourage kindergarten teachers to "get the children reading and writing" as soon as possible. The expectation to write using "real" words and read only what is on the page often chases away all enthusiasm for risk taking. So how do we merge these two philosophies, encouraging children to experiment with literacy while teaching them specific literacy skills at the same time?

Journals. I use a variety of journals with my kindergarten students. It gives me opportunities to scaffold their literacy skills, nudging them to use what they know and experiment with what is not secure. I can give minilessons to model literacy skills I see they are ready to begin using, and they can have a blank page of paper to try it out on their own.

Creative Journals. Open-ended creative journals can be purchased ready-made or put together with blank paper. Covers can simply be colored paper, with the children writing their name, the month, or drawing a picture of themselves. At the beginning of the year, I begin journaling with my students with a story. Sometimes, I tell a story about my life and then I draw a picture about it, making certain to include important details, such as the stripes on my favorite shirt or the color of my daughter's bicycle and the tassels that hang from the handle grips. On other days, I choose books about five-year-olds going

to school, being part of a family, having friends, enjoying holidays; we then have a discussion about one of their experiences that relate to the story. Then each writer goes off to develop their ideas into pictures and words so that they can be kept forever on the pages of their journal. Even the first few days, when these "translations" don't quite fit the image in their minds, my young students learn that their thoughts can be communicated and saved.

Later in the year, I move on to minilessons to help them include writing with their pictures. We might notice how the words and illustrations go together in a favorite book or how there are always spaces around words in text. As the year goes on, I may give a lesson on invented spelling, what we call the "sounding game" in my classroom. (I like to differentiate between writing the sounds we hear in words and actual spelling, which allows me to avoid a negative response to that question, "But is this spelled right?") On another day, we might brainstorm a list of sight words we can read and write independently to use in our journals. The children write them on chart paper, and we hang them in our writing center to use throughout the week.

As the year progresses, my students move from scribbled designs and pictures to including a few words and then a sentence. Their pictures begin to show a sense of story, and their writing begins to demonstrate their increasing literacy skills. When sharing their entries with the class, their vocabulary and oral language skills show signs of growth. It is slow progress, but it is secure and stable.

Literature Response Journals. My classes always love books. I don't give them much of an opportunity to think that books are anything but wonderful. We have a variety of ways to write about our favorites. During an author study, we might make a collection of journal entries to share our favorite stories the author has written. Such writings make a nice collection in a loose-leaf notebook to have in our library throughout the year.

Another favorite "group" journal activity is a take-home literature suitcase. A favorite book is sent home along with a journal. If the book has a stuffed animal, such as the bunny in Goodnight Moon or Curious George, then that item might also be placed in the suitcase or backpack. Simple instructions are secured to the inside lid of the suitcase with clear contact paper, telling the family to enjoy the book and then complete a page of the journal telling what they liked about the story or possibly what they did while their character was visiting.

Literacy Journals, Theme Journals, and Learning Logs. Special journals such as literacy journals, theme journals, and learning logs are linked specifically to our learning in other areas. I have found that although kindergarten students know many things, they often do not understand what they know or how to use it. They are not mature enough in the learning process to have a metacognitive framework for using their knowledge independently on other seemingly unrelated tasks. Writing in journals to record observations, questions, and insights helps children make important links between what they already know and what they are learning. Writing about what you want to know is a wonderful way to learn, even for adults.

Teachers usually begin by making declarative statements about personal experiences rather than by asking children questions. Questions have a tendency to result in brief, stilted replies from children (similar to their oral responses to verbal interrogation by a teacher). For example,

> **TEACHER:** Did you do anything nice over the weekend?
>
> **CHILD:** No.

On the other hand, when teachers write personal statements to the children, the students respond more spontaneously. Nigel Hall and Rose Duffy (1987, p. 527) give the following example:

> **TEACHER:** I am upset today.
>
> **CHILD:** What is the matr with you?
>
> **TEACHER:** My dog is sick. I took her to the vet, and he gave her some medicine.
>
> **CHILD:** I hop she get betr sun did the medsn wok?

Obviously, it is helpful if children are able to use legible forms of invented spelling to write their messages. This strategy, however, can be used even with children who are at the scribble or nonphonetic letter-string stage of early literacy. With these children, a brief teacher–child conference is needed so that children can read their personal script messages to the teacher.

Pen Pals.   Once children get used to engaging in written conversations with their teachers, they will naturally want to engage in written exchanges with their peers. Martinez and Teale (1987) describe how a "postal system/pen pal" program was successfully implemented in several Texas early childhood classrooms. Children in the morning half-day classes wrote weekly letters to pen pals in the afternoon classes; children in full-day programs were assigned pen pals in other full-day program classrooms. Children were purposely paired with partners who used different writing strategies. For example, a scribble writer was matched with an invented speller. Letters were exchanged once a week and placed in mailboxes located in the writing center. A teacher or aide was at the center to assistwhen children received letters they could not read. Teachers reported that student response was overwhelmingly positive. Here, real audiences and real purposes for writing were provided.

Publishing Children's Writing

"Helping children make and publish their own books taps into [their] love of creating and owning written words" (Power, 1998, pp. 31–32). Brenda Power suggests several reasons teachers should help young children publish their writing in books. Making their own books helps children learn the following:

- To hold the book right side up and to turn the pages correctly
- That books have covers, titles, and authors
- Letter and sounds through writing a book and how to decode words by reading their own words
- About the importance of an author and an illustrator to a book

To publish with young children is to take their written texts and do something special with them. To publish is to make the writing public, to present it for others to read. There are many different ways to publish young children's writing. For example:

- Ask each child to bring a clear, plastic eight-and-a-half-by-eleven-inch frame to school. (Of course, frames must be purchased for those children whose parents cannot provide them.) Have the children publish their work by mounting their selected pieces, one at a time, in their frames. Hang the frames on the back wall of the classroom on a Wall of Fame.

- String a clothesline across the classroom. Using clothespins, clip the children's writings to the clothesline.

- Punch a hole in the upper left corner of several pages. Construction paper can be used for all pages. If not, include a piece of colored construction paper or poster board on the top and bottom of the pile of pages for the book's cover. Thread string, yarn, or a silver ring through the hole to hold the book together.

■ Purchase a low-cost photo album with large, stick-on plastic sleeves. (They can be found at discount stores and occasionally at flea markets or rummage and garage sales.) Place one page of each child's writing in one of the plastic sleeves. The same photo album can be used again and again as one piece of writing can be substituted for another piece of writing.

■ While engaging in a special experience, take photographs of the children. Glue the picture to a piece of construction paper. Ask each child to select a photo. Ask the child to write about the chosen picture on a piece of white paper. Cut the white paper into an interesting shape and mount it on the construction paper below the photo.

■ Laminate each page and put the pages together with spiral binding.

■ Cover a large bulletin board with bright paper or fabric. In large cutout letters, label the bulletin board something like "Young Authors" or "Room 101 Authors." Divide the bulletin board evenly into rectangular-shaped sections, one section for each child in the class, using yarn or a marker. Label each section with a child's name. Encourage each child to mount one piece of writing in his or her special section each week. A staple or pushpin might be used to mount the writing.

These suggestions are but a few of the many ways that children's writing might be published. We repeat: Publishing with young children means making their writing public and available for others to read. It is developmentally inappropriate to require young children to revise or recopy their writing, although sometimes they are willing to add to their text. Most young children do not have the attention span or interest to make revisions or to recopy the text.

If the child's writing is a personal script—that is, if it is a form of emergent writing that needs the child's reading for meaning to be constructed—then the teacher might elect to include a conventionally spelled version of the message with the child's personal script version. It is important to include the child's personal script version on the page with the conventionally spelled version to avoid taking ownership from the child. Trade Secret 5.6 describes how kindergarten teacher Ginny Emerson publishes her children's emergent writing.

Handwriting

So far, we have focused on providing young children with opportunities to write. What about handwriting? Drilling young children on how to form the letters of the alphabet correctly also is a developmentally inappropriate practice. Forming letters correctly requires a good bit of manual dexterity, something most young children are developing. Teachers should provide young children with numerous opportunities to engage in activities that help develop their dexterity, such as puzzles, sewing cards, table games, cutting, and drawing. Models of appropriately formed letters should be available for the children's reference. Teachers should correctly form the uppercase and lowercase letters when writing for and with the

TRADE SECRET 5.6
Kid Writing

The kindergarten children in Ginny Emerson's kindergarten classroom are writers. Several years ago Ginny "converted" to Eileen Feldgus and Isabell Cardonick's (1999) *Kid Writing* program. As Feldgus and Cardonic suggest, Ginny introduces her students to written language through journal writing in a writing workshop format.

This classroom is rich with functional print. Ginny pays particular attention to posting words that the children might need in their writing. For example, the light switches are labeled *up* and *down*. The attendance chart is labeled *Boys* and *Girls*, with space for the children to sign in each day. The inside of the classroom door is labeled *inside*; the outside is labeled *outside*. Ginny often reminds the children to use the classroom print as a resource, asking, for example, "Where can you find the word *outside* in our classroom?" There is a word wall. The categories are letters of the alphabet. The words listed are high-frequency words, arranged alphabetically. Words are added to the "Words We Use a Lot" word wall as Ginny introduces them during minilessons.

Ginny watches her young writers to learn what minilessons (or focus lessons) they need. When she noticed that the children often needed the /ing/ sound in their writing, she followed the *Kid Writing* authors' suggestion and made a crown with /ing/ written on it. Each day during the writing workshop, a child is assigned to be the "King of /ing/." The child proudly wears the /ing/ crown. When the young writers want to write "shopp*ing*" or "go*ing*," they use the King of /ing/ to help them remember on to write *ing*. The

"Star of *are*" wears a hat with a star and the word *are* written on it. There is also a "Wiz of *is*" moving about the classroom.

All this activity, of course, comes after Ginny gets her kid writing program going, shortly after the first day of school. To kick off the program, she follows the description of the first day of writing found in *Kid Writing* (p. 33). She demonstrates for the children different ways of writing, from wavy lines to zigzag writing to magic lines to letterlike forms that resemble alphabet letters to alphabet letters. The children "write" in the air. With every stroke they make, Ginny reinforces what they know with encouragement such as, "You are such great wavy-line writers!" She follows this lesson with a minilesson on using a sound (the first most prominent sound) to write a word. Many subsequent lessons help children stretch out words, listening to the sounds, much like Bernadette Watson's minilesson. Other lessons, for example, teach children how to use a dash as a placeholder for a word they cannot spell or about using rime to help them spell.

Ginny's students write, share, and publish. Ginny celebrates what they can do, verbalizing that they are doing ("Oh, you made a capital *B* there, didn't you?), and seems always to be telling the children what good writers they are. She claims that nothing she does is "original"; she borrowed all her ideas from Feldgus and Cardonick. She encourages every teacher of young children to use *Kid Writing*. Kindergarten students *can* write, and the children in her classroom prove the accuracy of her belief.

children, and an alphabet chart of uppercase and lowercase letters should be available at eye level for the children's use in the writing center. When children have achieved some control, the teacher might work one on one with each child. Because the letters in a child's name are the most important, the teacher might choose to begin instruction by helping the child form these letters correctly. Do not expect perfection, and be sure to keep the instruction playful.

ASSESSMENT: DISCOVERING WHAT CHILDREN KNOW AND CAN DO

Formal assessment of children's language and early reading skills is becoming increasingly common at the preschool level and beyond. We provide information on formal assessment tools in Chapter 10. Whether or not your school or center requires the use of a formal assessment, we believe that it is critically important for teachers to take advantage of classroom's daily literacy activities to monitor and document their young students' development of the important early reading skills described in this chapter. By gathering data on an ongoing basis, assessment and instruction can be closely linked, a main tenet of quality instruction set forth in Chapter 1.

Ongoing, or classroom-based, assessment is an important means for teachers to gather information that can guide their literacy instruction. Ongoing assessment strategies include anecdotal notes, vignettes, conferencing, audio and video recording, and the collection of artifacts and work samples. These types of performance-based assessment are conducted while children are engaging in everyday types of classroom activities, and the resulting data are often organized and reported in portfolios that show a child's progress over time (see Chapter 10 for additional information on creating portfolios). In the following section, we provide several checklists, and descriptions of how to use them, to help teachers assess their young children's early reading skills.

Checklists

Checklists are one of the most commonly used types of ongoing assessment tools. These observational tools specify what to look for and provide a convenient system for keeping records. A variety of checklists have been published that can help teachers keep track of children's early literacy learning. For example, Figure 5.3 presents an adapted version of Elizabeth Sulzby, June Barnhart, and Joyce Hieshima's (1989) Forms of Writing checklist, which can help identify the forms of emergent writing that children use during play and other classroom activities.

FIGURE 5.3   Emergent Writing Checklist

Child's Name _____

Forms of Writing	Date(s) Observed	Situation
■ uses drawing (might be circular scribbles)	_____	_____
■ uses drawing and writing	_____	_____
■ uses linear scribble	_____	_____
■ uses letter-like shapes	_____	_____
■ uses random letters	_____	_____
■ uses invented spellings	_____	_____
■ uses conventional spellings	_____	_____

Teachers can also construct their own checklists to keep track of their data. Some years ago, the teachers at the St. Michael's Early Childhood Center constructed a literacy checklist. They knew that children's book-reading behaviors were important for them to understand, but they were not certain just which book-reading behaviors were important to track as their young learners moved through their center. They formed a study group to read and discuss professional literature on children's literacy development to understand better how they should conduct their read-aloud and shared reading sessions and on what they should focus during their observations of their students. One outcome of their study was a checklist. Following the publication of the National Research Council's report *Preventing Reading Difficulties in Young Children* (Snow, Burns, & Griffin, 1998), the teachers worked together to reconsider their checklist to ensure that they were appropriately following the children's literacy accomplishments. An edited version of their checklist is reproduced in Figure 5.4.

By using checklists such as those shown in Figure 5.3 and 5.4, a teacher can observe children as they work and play in the classroom and record their observations on the checklists. Certainly, observing a behavior once is insufficient to justify drawing the conclusion that the behavior is a part of the child's permanent repertoire. Teachers will want to look for repeated evidence that the child is habitually exhibiting these accomplishments. Teachers should indicate the dates of their observations on the checklist and make quick notes of the specific behaviors the child exhibited. At St. Michael's, the checklist follows the child from year to year as a part of the child's portfolio. Knowing when each child demonstrated each literacy accomplishment helps teachers and parents understand individual children's patterns of development. Reading each child's checklist informs the teacher of the child's strengths and the instructional program for that child. Collectively reading all children's checklists informs the teacher of the instructional needs of all the children in the class.

Performance Sampling

One problem with ongoing assessment is that teachers have to wait for literacy events to occur naturally and spontaneously. Teachers sometimes need to hurry things along a bit to gain the information they need to plan effective literacy instruction. They can do so by using performance sampling: setting up situations that enable the teachers to gather data about children's literacy abilities (Teale, 1990).

Performance samples of one-to-one storybook reading can provide insights into children's concepts about print. The first step is reading a familiar storybook to a single child. The teacher can ask the child to point to words that are being read, providing information about print-to-speech matching and directionality. Questions can also be asked to probe the child's understanding of concepts such as letters (e.g., "Show me a letter"; "Show me the letter *m*"), words (e.g., showing a scribble ask, "Is this a word?"; "Show me a word"), capitalization (e.g., "Show me a capital letter"; "Show me a lowercase, or small, letter"; "Show me a capital B"), and punctuation (e.g., "Show me a question mark"). This type of informal performance

FIGURE 5.4   Checklist for Assessing Young Children's Book-Related Understandings

_____can
(Child's name)

Concepts about Books	Date	Comments
look at the picture of an object in a book and realize it is a symbol for the real object	_____	_____
handle a book without attempting to eat or chew it	_____	_____
identify the front, back, top, and bottom of a book	_____	_____
turn the pages of a book correctly	_____	_____
point to the print when asked, "What do people look at when they read?"	_____	_____
show how picture and print connect	_____	_____
point to where a reader begins reading	_____	_____
point to a book's title	_____	_____
point to a book's author	_____	_____
recognize specific books by their covers	_____	_____
Conventions of Print		
show that a reader reads left to right with return sweeps	_____	_____
find a requested letter or provide the letter's name	_____	_____
ask questions or make comments about letters	_____	_____
ask questions or make comments about words	_____	_____
read words or phrases	_____	_____
read sentences	_____	_____
read along while adult reads familiar stories	_____	_____
Attitude toward Books		
participate in book-sharing routine with caregiver	_____	_____
listen to story	_____	_____
voluntarily look at books	_____	_____
show excitement about books and reading	_____	_____
ask adults to read to him or her	_____	_____
use books as resource for answers to questions	_____	_____

sample is preferable to the more standardized _Concepts about Print_ test (Clay, 2000) because it uses books that are familiar and highly meaningful to children (Goodman, 1981; Schickedanz & Strickland, 2004; Teale, 1990).

Performance sampling can be combined with a checklist to assess children's developing phonological awareness, including phonemic awareness, alphabet knowledge, and phonics understandings. For example, Figure 5.5 presents a checklist

FIGURE 5.5 **Phonological Awareness, Phonemic Awareness, and Phonics Checklist**

Child's name _____

Skills	Sample Performance Tasks	Date(s) Demonstrated
Rhyming words: recognition	Ask: "Do these two words rhyme?" (*house, mouse; cat, tree*)	
Rhyming words: production	Select a song or poem with rhyming words. Teacher says the words, pausing before the rhyme. The child fills in the missing rhyming word. Ask: "What rhymes with *boat? see? fish?*"	Note: Nonsense words count as correct.
Sentence segmenting	Say: "Clap the number of words you hear in this sentence." (I like dogs.) Note: Only use one-syllable words in the sentences.	
Syllable segmenting	Say: "Clap the number of syllables you hear in *bat*, wagon, *elephant, hippopotamus.*"	
Syllable blending	Say: "I'll say a word slowly, then you tell me what word I said." (Teacher: *rain-bow*; child: *rainbow*; Teacher: *ba-by*; child: *baby*; Teacher: *ab-so-lute-ly*; Child: *absolutely*)	
Beginning sound: recognition	Collect pictures of things or objects that begin with the same sound. Review names of objects with the child. Say: "Put all of the pictures (or objects) that begin like (sample object) in this pile."	
Beginning sound: production	Say: "What words can you say that begin like *b-aby? c*-at?"	
Onset rime*	Ask: "What words can you make that end in *–at*? I'll start: *f-at.*"	
Phoneme Isolation	Ask: "What sounds do you hear at the beginning of *foot, hop, run, yes*?"	
Phoneme Blending	Ask: "What word am I saying, *b-a-t*?" Child: "*Bat.*" "What word am I saying, *f-ee-t.*"Child: "*Feet.*"	
Phoneme segmenting	Ask: "Say each word slowly so that you can hear all of the sounds. What sounds do you hear in *bat*?" Child: "*b-a-t.*" "What sounds do you hear in *love*?" Child: "*l-o-ve.*"	
Phoneme substitution	Ask: "If we take the /k/ off of *cat* and put on a /h/ sound, what new word have I made?	
Connects beginning sounds with letters (phonics)	Say: "Help me write the word *Daddy.*" Record as the child says the letter names.	

*Some teachers may know onset rime as word families.

that can be used to record children's progress in phonological awareness, including phonemic awareness, and phonics. In general, the skills in this figure appear in order of difficulty, from the broad aspects of phonological awareness to phonemic awareness to phonics. As indicated, children need experiences with phonological and phonemic awareness skills prior to experiences with phonics. Because the checklist lays out the general order of children's acquisition of these two

FIGURE 5.6 Alphabet Knowledge Checklist

Child's Name _____

Uppercase Alphabet Letters	Start of the Year	Middle of the Year	End of the Year	Lowercase Alphabet Letters	Start of the Year	Middle of the Year	End of the Year
A				a			
B				b			
C				c			
D				d			
E				e			
F				f			
G				g			
H				h			
I				i			
J				j			
K				k			
L				l			
M				m			
N				n			
O				o			
P				p			
Q				q			
R				r			
S				s			
T				t			
U				u			
V				v			
W				w			
X				x			
Y				y			
Z				z			

important skills, teachers can use it not only to monitor children's acquisition of these important early reading skills but also as a guide to plan for instruction. We suggest that teachers record the date of the collection of the performance sample data on the line, rather than a use a checkmark. It is also possible to record natural and spontaneous observations of children's demonstration of these skills during large group or circle time, small group instruction, and center or activity time on this checklist.

Similarly, it is possible to assess children's alphabet knowledge by observing what they do during the ongoing classroom activities, such those described on pages 175 to 176. In addition, we recommend that early childhood teachers assess their children individually three times a year: at the beginning, middle, and end of the school year. To gather the performance sample information, teachers will need two sets of cards, one for the uppercase letters and one for the lowercase letters. Each letter must be written on a separate card. Arrange the cards in random order Because we know that children seem to learn the uppercase letters first (Trieman & Kessler, 2003), begin by assessing the child's knowledge of those letters. Present the letters to the child, one at a time, in the recommended order. Place a checkmark in the appropriate column next to each letter the child correctly names.

SUMMARY

Whereas Chapter 4 described activities that can implicitly teach children how to write and read, this chapter dealt with explicit literacy instruction. It described a variety of developmentally appropriate strategies that teachers can use to teach children to write and read. Each skill has been found to be important to children's success as readers and writers. What have you learned?

- *Which early reading skills should early childhood teachers provide in order to give their students an opportunity to learn?*

The National Early Literacy Panel was formed to synthesize the early literacy research to this question. To date, this panel has identified eleven variables as important components of an early literacy program: alphabet knowledge, print knowledge, environmental print, invented spelling, listening comprehension, oral language/vocabulary, phonemic awareness, phonological short-term memory, rapid naming, visual memory, and visual perception skills. Of this list, the "broader" early reading skills include phonological and phonemic awareness, alphabet letter recognition, phonics, word recognition, and print awareness. Early childhood teachers must ensure that they provide their young learners with opportunities to learn each of these key skills by using a variety of explicit and implicit teaching procedures and activities.

- *What is the difference between phonological awareness, phonemic awareness, and phonics? In what sequence do young children typically acquire these skills? What does this sequence suggest about classroom instructional strategies?*

Phonological awareness (realization that spoken language is composed of words, syllables, and sounds) is broader than phonemic awareness (realization that words are composed of phonemes). Both concepts are important for all young children to know if they are to become successful readers. Whereas phonological and phonemic awareness just involve sound, phonics involves learning the relationship between letters and the sounds they represent. The instructional sequence now recommended by research is to begin by helping children build the basic concepts of phonological awareness, then move toward helping children develop awareness that words are composed of phonemes, and finally help children develop awareness of letter–sound associations. Therefore, the instructional sequence is from broad concepts to smaller and smaller ones.

■ *How might early childhood teachers introduce young children to the letters of the alphabet?*

Some readers probably learned the names of the letters of the alphabet by singing the alphabet song. Today, the value of this activity gets mixed reviews. Some readers probably learned the names of the letters of the alphabet by studying a different letter each week. This approach receives some criticism today. Early childhood teachers should teach their young learners the names of the letters through explicit instruction. A teacher should remember that most children will not know the names of all the letters of the alphabet before they recognize and read whole words. A skillful teacher can link children's attention to highly meaningful words and key letters simultaneously.

■ *Why is a writing center an important area in the preschool classroom? How might an adult teach in the writing center?*

A writing center is that area of the classroom where the teacher has stocked materials (different kinds of papers, various writing tools, alphabet strips, computers) that invite children to write. The teacher is an important other in the writing center. As a cowriter, the teacher writes alongside the children and models the writing process, informally teaching children about the forms (letters, thank-you notes) and features (spelling, letter formation) of print. As a skilled writer, the teacher can teach children as he or she writes by casually talking about letter–sound relationships, how to begin a letter, or what might be said in a letter.

■ *How does a teacher teach during a writing workshop?*

Each writing workshop begins with a minilesson. The goal of such lessons is to teach children about some aspect of writing (e.g., how to make revisions, how to add describing words, how to spell words). The focus lesson is followed by writing time. During writing time, the teacher talks with individual children about their writing. Here, the teacher might help a child stretch words to hear sounds, add details to the child's drawing, or talk with the child about the topic of the piece. Through conferences, the teacher provides one-on-one instruction. After the writing time, two or three children will share their work with their peers and the teacher. Now, the teacher and the other children can ask questions about the writing.

■ *Why is it important to publish children's writing?*

Publishing helps young children understand that they write so that others can read their thoughts. Making young children's writing efforts public is important. The publishing process need not be complicated.

■ *What types of assessment methods are used to collect information about children's progress?*

Changes in what we know about literacy learning have necessitated major changes in our ways of measuring young children's literacy accomplishments and progress. Effective teachers use ongoing assessment procedures that are connected with a classroom's daily literacy activities. This ongoing assessment makes heavy use of systematic observation, checklists, and the collection of samples of children's work. The classroom library, writing center, and dramatic play areas are ideal settings for this type of assessment, and anecdotal notes, vignettes, and checklists provide effective ways to record data.

LINKING KNOWLEDGE TO PRACTICE

1. Visit a classroom set up for three-year-olds and a classroom set up for five-year-olds in an early childhood center. Draw a diagram of each classroom's writing center, and make a list of the writing materials the teacher has provided. Describe the differences between the writing center set up for three-year-olds and the one for five-year-olds. Observe the classrooms' teachers as they interact with the children in the writing center. Describe what they talk about with the children.

2. Create descriptions of several developmentally appropriate phonological or phonemic awareness activities, from the most basic concepts to the more advanced, that might be used with young children. Make copies of your activities for others in your class.

3. Create a description of several developmentally appropriate alphabet recognition activities for use with young children. Make copies of your activities for others in your class.

4. Interview a pre-K or kindergarten teacher about the information-gathering tools that he or she typically uses to collect information about children's literacy development. How does the teacher organize this information to share with parents?

5. Search the Internet for sites describing activities to help children develop each of the key early reading skills. Prepare a brief description of each site. Make copies of your discoveries for others in your class.

CHAPTER 6

READING: EXPANDING THE FOUNDATION FOR ONGOING LITERACY LEARNING

MARY F. ROE

Adam is in the sixth grade. He receives high grades in his language arts class, and his teacher considers him a capable reader, but he does not fare as well in his social studies class. Outside school, he has read every Harry Potter book and recently began reading Tolkien's trilogy.

Janet is just starting first grade. She enjoys listening to books read to her and can easily talk about them. She can identify her name and several words that frequently appear in her books, but is unable to read the simplest of texts independently.

Juan is bilingual. He speaks Spanish at home and learned to read in his native language. He started school in the United States in third grade. Now in fourth grade, he attends a class for second-language learners twice a week. In addition, he receives reading assistance from a Title I paraprofessional, a federal program established to provide assistance to students like Juan. His classroom teacher remains concerned about his reading achievement, especially his ability to contribute to classroom discussions about assigned texts from his basal anthology.

Each of these three students has a teacher who is responsible for helping them read better. To accomplish that goal, the teachers must hold a rich and deep understanding of reading. Armed with theoretical and practical understandings, the teacher can make the "just right" instructional choices that allow not only students like Juan, Adam, and Janet read better, but also myriad other readers the teacher will encounter in his or her professional journey. Today's classrooms do not hold readers who are cookie-cutter versions of each other. Therefore, helping all children read better demands responsive teachers who realize that as long as they teach, they will engage in life-long learning. The goal remains constant: intentionally selecting from myriad scientifically based possibilities those strategies that will help each student be a better reader. Parents and guardians turn to teachers for reading expertise and expect that teachers, whether novice or experienced, will not fail their children. Meeting this challenge demands more than enjoying the company of children. It depends on knowledge, versatility, and gumption. In this chapter, we help teachers begin the task of becoming a reading teacher scholar.

BEFORE READING THIS CHAPTER, THINK ABOUT . . .

- A text you recently read for pleasure. What type of text was it: a magazine, a newspaper, a novel, a historical account? Why did you find it pleasurable? Were you aware of the processes you used to obtain meaning from it?
- A text recently assigned for you to read. Did you find it easier or more difficult to read than the text you read by choice? Were you aware of the processes you used to obtain meaning from it? How did those processes compare with what you noticed when you read for pleasure?
- How you learned to read. Do you remember being taught to read, or did reading just magically begin? While in grades 1 through 6, what do you remember most about reading in and out of school? How do those reading contexts compare?

FOCUS QUESTIONS

- What are the components of the reading process?
- Beyond a reader's proficiency in the specific features of this process, what else contributes to reading achievement?
- What classroom events would you expect to see during the time assigned for reading?
- What attributes define a successful reading teacher?

UNDERSTANDING THE READING PROCESS

Reading is comprehending. Perhaps you have heard that statement before. It has upheld the test of time. This statement makes reading sound like a simple process when it is actually a complex, challenging process. We begin this chapter by briefly describing the history of reading and shedding light on past trends and current misconceptions.

Explanations of the process that supports reading comprehension have undergone many changes. In earlier times, comprehension was believed to rest on a reader's ability to say words quickly and accurately (Mathews, 1966). Reading in this era was viewed as no more complicated than understanding oral language. Break the code, say the words, and comprehension followed. More recently, this perspective became labeled as a *bottom-up* approach. By privileging the text (the

BOX 6.1
DEFINITION OF TERMS

comprehension: an ability to combine what you know (i.e., prior knowledge) with an author's words to understand a text.

comprehension strategies: approaches used by readers to assist their understanding of a text (e.g., visualizing, determining importance, monitoring and adjusting, predicting, making inferences, summarizing, analyzing, posing questions, using fix-up strategies).

flexible grouping: the formation of temporary groups to address student's specific reading needs.

sight vocabulary: words that are immediately and correctly pronounced and understood by a reader (i.e., known at the level of automaticity).

text structure: the organization of a text (i.e., narrative or exposition).

vocabulary: words that hold conceptual meaning for a reader and that he or she can appropriately understand when reading a text.

word identification strategies: cues used by a reader to pronounce an unknown word (i.e., contextual cues, morphemic cues, and graphophonic cues).

word meaning strategies: cues used by a reader to infer the meaning of an unknown word (i.e., definition, appositive, example, antonym, synonym, grouping, summary, and simile).

print on the page, i.e., starting from the bottom), reading experts believed that meaning resided in the words and a reader's ability to say them quickly and accurately. Classroom reading programs that reflected this stance revealed a heavy emphasis on word identification strategies such as phonics.

Move forward a few years and an alternative explanation was put forth. This perspective viewed comprehension as residing in the head of a reader. Within this view, typically called a *top-down* approach, a reader acquired a text's meaning by using his or her prior knowledge to understand it. Although decoding the words was essential, decoding alone was insufficient to signal comprehension. As the famous quote by John Locke suggests, it was the *thinking* that made the reader know the meaning of the words.

Driven by the early research conducted by educational psychologists and cognitive scientists (Anderson, Pichert, & Shirey, 1983; Bransford, Barclay, & Franks, 1972), a third perspective arose that views reading as an interaction between the text and the reader. Typically called an interactive or sociocultural view of reading (Au, 2006), this position holds that comprehension stems from an interplay between the words on the page and the understandings that a reader brings to them. A continuous and reciprocal action exists between what is in the reader's head and what is on the page. As Gretchen Owocki explains (2005, p. 5), "Socio-cultural theory of learning recognizes that children's life experiences provide a foundation from which all new learning occurs." This perspective allows a teacher to embrace the five key psychological components noted by the National Reading Panel (2000) (rate and fluency, phonemic awareness, phonics, comprehension, and vocabulary) as well as what Marjorie Lipson and Karen Wixson (2003) call learner and context factors. Four of these components of reading (fluency, phonemic awareness, phonics, and vocabulary) coalesce, and the result is comprehension. We discuss each component separately to help readers grasp the complexity of this process and the information a teacher needs to help all students read better.

PSYCHOLOGICAL CONTRIBUTORS TO READING

As previously mentioned, several text-driven processes allow a reader to access a text's message. Sometimes, the word is one the reader recognizes immediately; the word is in the reader's sight word vocabulary. At other times, readers need to draw on one of numerous word identification strategies to help them say the word. Once a word is pronounced, a reader must attach meaning to it. Of course, readers with large speaking vocabulary are at an advantage over readers with limited speaking vocabularies. When the reader does not know a word, he or she is prompted to use any of a number of word meaning strategies. Reading, however, is more than saying individual words and knowing their meanings. Readers must handle connected text. This requires the use of comprehension strategies. Expert readers initially make a decision and then adjust their thinking as necessary to maintain meaning. They perform these mental gymnastics (saying words, attaching meaning, and understanding the whole connected text) simultaneously and without pause. More novice readers, and those older readers who struggle, must work harder. To assist all readers, a teacher needs a rich and deep grasp of each piece a reader uses: word identification, vocabulary, and comprehension strategies.

Word Identification

Some readers possess a large sight vocabulary and recognize a word immediately. They can quickly turn their attention to the big ideas and nuances of the words as presented in the text. Of course, that is not true of all readers. Some readers are still developing large reading vocabularies. They must rely on several word identification strategies to assist them. Approaching word identification *strategically* rather than as a skill requires a plan for directing the entire process of saying words. It demands problem solving, a road map of sorts to guide a reader's actions. A strategy holds ongoing value for readers. In addressing word identification, readers have several options.

■ First, students with large speaking vocabularies find using context helpful. A reader who uses context predicts an unknown word by using the sense of the text. Consider the following sentence from *Knuffle Bunny* (Willems, 2004): *Then they left.* Previously, a dad and his daughter had gone to a Laundromat. This three-word sentence appears once they finish their laundry. If *left* is unknown, then readers who hold this word in their oral (i.e., speaking) vocabulary can reasonably infer this word's pronunciation.

■ Readers can also use a second strategy, graphophonic cues, which is often called phonics. Those who use this strategy must understand that words are composed of subsounds (phonemes); must know the sound that each letter represents (in the above example, the consonant sounds for *l, f,* and *t* and the short sound for *e*); must synthesize them or blend them to say the word; and then must check to make sure that the word makes sense. Good readers often combine these strategies. With the word *left*, a host of words would make sense in the general sentence (e.g., Then they played, danced, or sang). These words, however, do not cohere with this story's events and do not coincide with this word's first letter.

■ When using morphemic analysis for saying unknown words, a reader must first identify the affixes, expose the root, and then pronounce and recombine these pieces. Such analysis occurs, for example, with words like *helped*, which is also found in *Knuffle Bunny*. Although some novice readers may know the word *help*, they can become perplexed when they see *helped*. Identifying the suffix (i.e., *ed*) and exposing the root (i.e., *help*) is an example of morphemic analysis. Of importance, only a word's spelling confirms its pronunciation, and a reader should never be led to think otherwise. Because word identification cues are often misunderstood and inappropriately presented, a fuller explanation of each is warranted.

Graphophonic Cues.   Using cues driven by a word's spelling requires students to understand the sounds that letters generally represent, the unique sounds of some letter combinations, and generalizations that control letter sounds. Because phonics applies to syllables, when readers encounter multisyllabic words, they must first apply syllabication generalizations. (Refer to Table 6.1 for a listing of letter sounds, sound combinations, generalizations that control letter sounds, and syllabication generalizations.) The use of the term *generalizations* is intentional and important.

Parents who designate a bedtime rule, a teacher and students who compose classroom rules, or a school principal who posts playground rules expect their children or students to follow them without exception. Such is not the case with phonics. Exceptions exist. Good readers understand flexibility and good teachers promote it. Table 6.2 uses additional words from *Knuffle Bunny* to further underscore the helpfulness and complexity of using phonics.

Morphemic Analysis Cues.   As described above, readers who use morphemic analysis must be well grounded in commonly occurring prefixes and suffixes (collectively called affixes). A teacher's goal is to make sure his or her students identify affixes as a unit and pronounce them correctly. (Refer to Table 6.3 for a listing of common prefixes and suffixes.) For more novice readers, attending to *-s, -ed,* and *-ing* makes sense because these suffixes often appear in the simplest of words. It is important for novice readers to know that *-ed* can assume three pronunciations: /d/ as in *tied*, /t/ as in *stopped*, and /ed/ as in *acted*. Although a student's oral language often corrects a mispronunciation of this word ending, a teacher must be

TABLE 6.1   Using Phonics for Word Identification

LETTER SOUNDS	EXPLANATION	SAMPLE WORDS
consonant sounds	Letters other than a, e, i, o, and u are called consonants.	bet, cat, dog, four, gum, hat, jog, kit, like, me, no, pig, run, sun, tip, van, won, yes, zoo
		Note: /q/ typically represents the sound /kw/ as in quit, /x/ the sound /ks/.
short and long vowel sounds	a, e, i, o, and u are called vowels. Vowels can represent two sounds: short and long.	short vowel examples: cat, beg, ill, on, up
	At times, y and w can function as a vowel.	long vowel examples: ate, eel, ice, bone, use
ch, th, wh, ph, ng, sh	These consonant combinations, called consonant digraphs, represent a single sound.	chip, this, thin, when, phone, sang, ship
oi, oy, ou, ow	These vowel combinations, called diphthongs, represent a single sound.	boil, coy, out, owl

GENERALIZATIONS FOR LETTER SOUNDS	EXPLANATION	SAMPLE WORDS
c/g	c and g can represent two sounds: a hard sound as in *cat* and *go* and a soft sound as in *city* and *gym*. To guide a reader's initial decision, c and g usually represent their soft sound when followed by e, i, or y and their hard sound when followed by a, o, and u.	Soft sound: mice, cent, gem, page Hard sound: cut, come, gut, gave
r-controlled vowels	When an r appears after a vowel, one of three r-controlled sounds is possible.	car, fir, or
silent-e generalization	When a syllable or word ends in a single consonant and an e, the vowel usually represents its long sound and the e is silent (i.e., does not represent a sound).	tone, bake, cute, cite, muse, mete
double vowel generalization	When two vowels appear next to each other, the first vowel usually represents its long sound and the second is silent.	boat, seem, team, aim

(continued)

TABLE 6.1   Using Phonics for Word Identification (Continued)

GENERALIZATIONS FOR LETTER SOUNDS	EXPLANATION	SAMPLE WORDS
open syllables	When a syllable ends in a vowel sound, the vowel usually represents its long sound.	go, me, hi
closed syllables	When a syllable ends in a consonant sound, the vowel usually represents its short sound.	Bug, mat, set, hit, pot, tug

GENERALIZATIONS FOR SYLLABICATION	EXPLANATION	SAMPLE WORDS
VCCV	When two consonants appear next to each other, usually divide between the consonants.	matter (mat/ter) album (al/bum)
VCV	When two vowels are separated by a single consonant, the syllabication division usually occurs after the vowel.	cater (ca/ter) bison (bi/son)
Vcle	When a word ends in an le, the consonant before it usually stays with it and the -le is always pronounced /ul/.	sparkle (spar/kle) kindle (kin/dle)

Note: The following texts provide fuller accounts of decoding and phonics: P. M. Cunningham (2005), *Phonics they use* (Boston: Allyn and Bacon); B. J. Fox & M. A. Hull (2002), *Phonics for the teacher of reading* (Columbus, Ohio: Merrill); and D. D. Durkin (1981), *Strategies for identifying words* Boston: Allyn and Bacon).

prepared to understand this misstep and, if necessary, explicitly address it. An examination of the words in the texts that a student reads determines the affixes that matter at a particular point in time.

Context Cues.   Context cues come from two sources: syntactic cues (the grammatical use of a word) and semantic cues (the meaning of the text). For example, the following sentence appears in *Kira-Kira* (Kadohata, 2004, p. 9): *It was a sweltering day when Uncle Katsuhisa arrived in Iowa to help us move to Georgia.* Assuming that a reader was unable to pronounce *sweltering*, the reader might infer that the word must describe *day* and therefore serve as an adjective. Syntax provides

TABLE 6.2   Applying Phonics to Real Texts

WORDS	GENERALIZATIONS THAT APPLY	EXCEPTIONS
so, she, be	Individual consonant sounds Open syllable generalization Consonant digraph, sh Long vowel sounds Blending demand: two phonemes	to
as, did, not, went, but	Individual consonant sounds Closed syllable generalization Short vowel sounds Blending demand: two to four elements	put, was
home, time, those	Individual consonant sounds Consonant digraph, th Silent-*e* generalization Long vowel sounds Blending demand: three elements	whole, were
please	Individual consonant sounds double vowel generalization long vowel sounds Blending demand: three or four phonemes (depending on whether the reader perceives pl as a consonant cluster)	Said
daddy, fussy, mommy	Syllabication generalization (VCCV) dad/dy, fus/sy, mom/my Individual consonant sounds Closed syllable generalization Short vowel sounds y as a long-e sound	

that information. Then, if a reader also considers the time of year when this section of the story took place and the story's geographical setting, the reader could (and, one hopes, would) use semantic information to identify the word. Remember that the best readers combine strategies. In a closer consideration of *sweltering*, the reader could start with context and combine this word's spelling when making a final decision. If that proved unsuccessful, then the next step would require morphemic analysis: eliminating the suffix, *-ing*, to expose the root, *swelter*. From here, the reader would know to expect two syllables because this word has two letters that represent vowel sounds. Next, the reader would apply the vowel-consonant-vowel-consonant (VCCV) syllabication generalization, pronounce each syllable, and combine the pieces. Because *swelter* follows the applicable generalizations, a reader who took this path likely would succeed in pronouncing it.

TABLE 6.3   Common Prefixes and Suffixes

PREFIXES	SUFFIXES
ab-	-tion
ad-	-ment
de-	-ate
dis-	-ance
com-	-able
im-	-ity
pre-	-ous
pro-	-ence
per-	-ic
un-	-age
ex-	-tive
sub-	-ness
bi-	-ful
non-	-ism
retro-	-sion

Are you impressed with all that you are doing when you read to identify the words, many of them new to you? Identifying words is a challenging task for novice and struggling readers. As the above examples confirm, the use of word identification strategies is complex. Teachers must teach this area well, and students must strategically call upon the options available to them when they encounter an unknown word. Once readers understand their options, they can use a cue or combination of cues efficiently and successfully. If well taught, readers will develop what Marie Clay (1991) called a "self-extending" system. The options can be accessed without prompting or assistance and can be used successfully. In addition, if teachers maintain the important links between an attention to word identification and real reading, then readers will not fall into the trap of believing that reading is saying words with accuracy and speed or accepting a mindless response to the printed page.

Selecting a text for or by a student at a "just right" level of challenge will prevent word identification from overwhelming the reader. As a rule of thumb, a reader should encounter no more than four errors per hundred words of text. This maximum number of errors provides opportunities for a reader to be strategic in using word identification strategies and does not present so many roadblocks that meaning (and a student's enjoyment of reading) is sacrificed. One study (Shannon, 1988) found that the most successful readers of school-assigned materials made two errors per one hundred words read. The weakest readers, however, made at least eighteen errors per one hundred words. A teacher must continually monitor the texts that students read to make sure that students do not experience the discouragement that results in their need to employ word identification strategies too often. As Althier Lazar (2004) reminds us, "Children, even those who struggle with reading, can develop as readers when they are given lots of texts they can read and when they have highly knowledgeable teachers to guide their progress" (p. 18). Teachers who remember that reading is comprehending and who explain and model word identification strategies at just the right moment to students who make immediate use of the strategies make strides toward this important goal. (See Figure 6.1 for an example of a word identification lesson.)

Word Meaning

Although some students need to say words to read better (use appropriate word identification strategies), others need to increase the number of words that are meaningful to them. In other words, they must build their vocabularies, both reading and oral. Although acknowledging that readers must know word meanings may seem obvious, like word identification, careful examination of this obvious concept reveals its complexity.

For some students, especially those with large oral vocabularies, merely saying a word triggers its meaning. At other times, students' correct pronunciation of a word may lead a teacher to assume that the students know its meaning when in fact they do not. For these students, word meaning assistance is required. A student's needs can vary. For some words, readers need to know their multiple meanings and select the one that applies in the text being read. For example, a student reading the book *Sadako and the Thousand Paper Cranes* must understand that *crane* in this instance refers to a bird and not to a piece of construction equipment. The youngest of readers needs to understand homophones, words such as *to, too,* and *two* that sound the same but have different meanings. At some point, all readers will encounter a word for which they know the concept but not the label. An example is when a sixth-grade student reads a science text and encounters *platyhelminthes*. Students might understand flatworms, but they need to add this new scientific label for that concept. In addition, all readers eventually must learn a word and its concept simultaneously. For instance, this process might have occurred for you while reading this chapter and adding the term *phonemic awareness* to your professional language.

In addressing these various vocabulary needs, teachers have several choices. Of course, they can directly teach the unknown word. Although potentially helpful and appropriate, however, limitations exist for the number of words a teacher can select for this instruction. If a teacher decides to offer a definition, then the teacher should move beyond a simple statement. Instead, students benefit from an initial and student-friendly explanation of a word's meaning followed by opportunities to engage in applying its meaning. Teachers can accomplish that by having students respond to questions or complete activities that use the target words. For example, after addressing the words *meander, scamper, sprint,* and *saunter,* a teacher might ask students if a turtle would meander or scamper? Or, students might work in groups to place words with comparable meanings together.

FIGURE 6.1   A Word Identification Lesson

Declarative

"Today we're going to learn how to increase the accuracy of words that we say by using our understanding of what we're reading and a word's spelling."

Conditional

"Good readers say words quickly and correctly. Increasing your accuracy with pronouncing words can allow you to exhibit this attribute and, in some instances, improve your understanding of what you read."

Procedural

"Let's see how this works. The first thing I want to do is to confirm that the word I say matches the spelling of the word the author used. Let me use a sentence you recently encountered as an example."

[Show the student the sentence:]

> When Martin Luther King Jr. was a boy many laws would not allow black people to go to the same places as whites.

"I begin reading and say, When Martha—

"Then, I notice that the author's word ends in an /n/ and doesn't match the word I said, *Martha*. I look at the word more closely—*Mar–tin, Martin*.

"As I read further [return to the sentence], I have another reason to know that Martha would be incorrect since Martha is not a name typically given to a boy and this person is male.

"Let's do one together. Listen to these two words: presence, presentation. Do you expect them to be spelled the same?"

[Student response.]

"Okay, so if I read this sentence [show it to the student],

> Soccer had not been very popular in the United States up to this point, but Pele's presence had a dramatic effect.

"I would immediately know to look again at this word if I pronounced it *presentation*. Now I'm thinking, Do I know another word that matches this spelling and makes sense? Can you help me?"

[Student says *presence*.] "Let's try one more. You see this sentence." [show it to the student] He could not afford a soccer ball so he fashioned one.

"and read it this way:

> He could not afford a soccer ball so he finished one.

[I will say the sentence without showing it to the student.]

"Did you hear a word that did not match its spelling? Can you point to it?" [Student responds appropriately.]

(continued)

FIGURE 6.1   A Word Identification Lesson (Continued)

"Now, read the sentence silently and see if you can think of a word that matches its spelling and makes sense."

[Student begins using phonics, /f/a/sh/, and says *fashioned*.]

"Let's review. What are two things you want to do before you settle on a word's pronunciation?"

[Student responds appropriately: Make sure it matches the spelling of the word and makes sense.]

"Correct, so anytime you read, remember this important strategy. I will be checking with you to see how this strategy helps."

This future reading provides independent practice. Listen to the student read aloud on regular occasions to monitor the success.

Notes: Success with this strategy depends on the unknown or incorrect word being part of a student's oral vocabulary. In this lesson, the student held this information. Nonetheless, the teacher must be prepared to provide additional instruction if the student encounters words that are unknown conceptually (oral language) as well as in print (reading vocabulary).

The text examples for this lesson come from the *Qualitative Reading Inventory* (Leslie & Caldwell, 2006).

Beyond providing explanations and follow-up activities to learn new words, teachers can direct students to use a reference such as a dictionary or online source. The availability of an appropriate source limits the helpfulness of this option. As Bill Nagy and Judy Scott (2000) note, too often students find dictionary definitions confusing or misleading. As they explain:

> Definitions, the traditional means of offering concentrated information about words to students, do not contain the quantity or quality of information that constitutes true word knowledge. Students can gain some word knowledge from definitions, but generally only if they are given other types of information about the word and opportunities to apply this information in meaningful tasks. (p. 280)

Simply stated, instead of assisting readers' comprehension, definitions can further cloud it. In addition, and on a practical note, ask yourself whether you read with a dictionary at your side. Most readers do not. Taking time away from reading to access dictionary definitions becomes time consuming and intrusive.

A final option involves teaching readers to use context strategies for inferring the meaning of an unknown word. Although readers should not be expected to infer a perfect definition, unless that is the teacher's goal, they often can make a decision that allows them to keep reading without a comprehension break.

Expecting readers to use context to infer the meaning of an unknown word depends on the types of assistance an author makes available. This assistance can take several forms: definition, appositive, example, summary, synonym, antonym, grouping, and simile.

- *Definition.* The most helpful context provides a definition. Informational texts and textbooks often provide this level of help. Generally, definitions follow this pattern: X (the unknown word) is X (a definition). For example, in Chapter 1, you read that "Reading First is a component of the No Child Left Behind Act." As an expert reader, you easily and quickly linked the information on each side of the linking verb to obtain accurate information about Reading First. For some students, this mental act needs explicit instruction and modeling.

- *Appositive.* In appositive assistance, a reader encounters an unknown word followed by an appositive, a descriptive phrase set off from the rest of the sentence by commas. We just used this type of clue in the preceding sentence to explain an appositive. A reader needs to understand this grammatical structure to grasp that the phrase means the same thing as the word, typically a noun that comes before it. A student reading narratives often finds out more about a character through an appositional phrase, such as in the case in *Gooney Bird Greene* (Lowry, 2004) when the author uses this sentence: "Hello," Mrs. Pidgeon, the second grade teacher, said (p. 1). From this appositive, a reader learns that Mrs. Pidgeon *is* the second grade teacher. On other occasions, the appositional phrase defines a term of importance. Russell Freedman (1987) uses this structure in the following sentence to explain indentures: Often they sold themselves as indentures for a period of twenty years, a form of voluntary slavery, just to eat and have a place to live (p. 46). A reader who does not hold *indentures* in his oral vocabulary or who thinks that the word only applies to the use of paragraphs while writing now can use the appositional phrase to understand that *indentures* refer to voluntary slavery. Science, social studies, and math textbooks regularly rely on definitions with sentences such as: The *nucleus* is the center of the atom. Islands, bodies of land completely surrounded by water, can be found in the Pacific Ocean and other bodies of water.

- *Example.* When an author provides an example, the reader must think (i.e., infer) what the example suggests about an unknown word's meaning. For example, in the first chapter of *The Midwife's Apprentice* (Cushman, 1995), the word *stench* appears in the following sentence: Usually no one gets close enough to notice because of the stench (p. 1). Prior to using this sentence, the author talks about animal droppings, garbage, and spoiled straw. A reader familiar with these things who then links this information with the sentence in which the unknown word, *stench*, appears could infer that a bad smell, (the stench) kept people at bay. Examples can provide relatively straightforward assistance. Consider a reader who does not know the word *muffle* but who encounters this sentence from *The Slave Dancer* (Fox, 1973): I lay motionless, my hands over my mouth to muffle my laughter (p. 34). Visualizing what happens when people talk with their hands covering their face could support this reader's inference that the laughter would not be very loud. Other examples might demand more prior knowledge or background experiences. Any reader who uses examples must infer a meaning, and a teacher who explicitly presents and models how to use examples increases the chances for a reader's success with this strategy.

■ *Summary.* When an author uses a summary, a reader's understanding of an unknown word comes by integrating information provided across several sentences or longer paragraphs. Assuming that the word *championships* is unknown, the following summary offers assistance: The wrestlers had to win several matches to qualify for the final event. The final event had winners from each weight class. These *championships* were exciting to watch.

The following excerpt from *Walk Two Moons* (Creech, 1994) adds to our understanding of *pandemonium*:

> It was complete pandemonium at the Finneys'. May Lou had an older sister and three brothers. In addition, there were her parents and Ben. There were footballs and basketballs lying all over the place, and boys sliding down the banister and leaping over tables and talking with their mouths full and interrupting everyone with endless questions. (pp. 46–47)

With summaries and comparable to other types of assistance, the reader must understand how to capitalize on this information. A reader can best understand this mental process from a teacher who makes this thinking public.

■ *Synonyms.* Consistent with its attributes, synonym help comes from an author's use of a word that holds a comparable meaning to the unknown word.

■ *Antonyms.* An author who offers a word or phrase that means the opposite of an unknown word takes advantage of antonyms. In the following sentences from *Because of Winn Dixie* (DiCamillo, 2000), the author provides this type of clue for *cooped up*: My mama says you shouldn't be spending all your time cooped up in that pet shop and at that library, sitting around talking with old ladies. She says you should get out in the fresh air and play with kids your own age (p. 89). Here, a reader must link the term *cooped up* with *get out* and infer the contrast in word meanings. As this example indicates, a reader often gets the best assistance by reading further. When appropriate, a knowledgeable teacher would encourage a reader to consider more than the single sentence in which the unknown word appears.

■ *Groupings.* In using groupings, a reader encounters a series of words that hold shared features. Assume that a reader does not know the meaning of *perch* as used in the following sentence: Troy caught a salmon, perch, and trout. If Troy knows that salmon and trout are fish, then he can infer that perch is, too. He still could not distinguish a perch from another fish, but he does correctly understand its general classification. This general information is often all a reader needs to understand a piece of text.

■ *Simile.* A simile links shared features between two words by using *like* or *as.* For a simile to help with inferring the meaning of an unknown word, a reader must have a solid sense of the concept the author uses for comparison. For example, to gain an understanding of *parliament* from "Parliament is like our House of Representatives," a reader must be informed about the House of Representatives.

Looking across these options and examples, two features about using context for inferring the meaning of an unknown word become clear: (1) readers benefit from broad and rich conceptual understandings and known vocabulary and (2) the inferential load for a reader varies across and within the types of clues a reader might encounter. Hence, an important task for teachers is joining a text's vocabulary demands with a reader's vocabulary strengths and needs to determine the appropriateness of expecting a reader to use context to understand unknown words. If readers hold gaps in their general understanding of the process of using context or specific gaps in this strategy's options, then explicit instruction assumes importance. As Isabel Beck, Margaret McKeown, and Linda Kucan (2002) remind us, "Because of the unreliability of natural contexts, instruction needs to be presented as a process of figuring out meaning within an individual context, rather than focusing on the product—a word's meaning" (p. 115). (Figure 6.2 shows an example of an instructional plan that addresses using context for vocabulary learning.)

Beyond teaching specific words and helping students learn words independently, James Baumann, Ed Kame'enui, and Gwynne Ash (2003) propose that a comprehensive vocabulary program should also "help students to develop an appreciation for words and to experience enjoyment and satisfaction in their use" (p. 778). A word-rich classroom that includes word play can foster this final goal. To accomplish it, Camille Blachowicz and Peter Fisher (2004) recommend activities such as a variety of vocabulary games, word puzzles, riddles, Hink Pink (e.g., an angry father—mad dad), drama, and art.

Connected Text

Armed with a large sight vocabulary, the known meanings of a multitude of words, and strategies to use when a bump in the road appears, a reader's effort to comprehend is not complete. Comprehension also depends on the mental tasks inherent in reading an array of connected texts. In this chapter, we focus on the general demands a reader encounters as well as those unique to narrative and informational texts: comprehension strategies.

General Demands. Much of what we know about the general demands of understanding connected text comes from close studies of what real readers do. Mary's recent reading of *The Three Questions* (Muth, 2002) serves as an example. Overall, because she was reading a story, she knew to expect its features: setting, character(s), plot, and theme. Initially, the title prompted her curiosity about the nature of the questions mentioned in the title, what they entailed, and why they

FIGURE 6.2   An Example of a Vocabulary Lesson: Teaching a Contextual Cue for Word Learning

Declarative

"Today we are going to learn how to use groupings to figure out what an unknown word means."

Conditional

"The grouping strategy is helpful when there is a list of words and one word is unknown. Figuring out an unknown word helps you understand what you are reading."

Procedural: Information and Modeling

"First we need to understand what the grouping strategy is."

[Write the following sentence on the board: In Hawaii, you can buy pineapples, papayas, and coconuts.]

"I don't know what a papaya is, but I know that pineapples and coconuts are fruits. Therefore, I make an educated guess that a papaya is a fruit because it is in a list with other fruits."

Repeat with another example: I love the sound of a clarinet, saxophone, and oboe.

"I don't know what an oboe is, so I look at the rest of the words in the group, or list. I know that a clarinet and saxophone are instruments, so I can figure out that an oboe is probably an instrument also."

Guided Practice

Each student will receive a list with five sentences that include a group of items where one item is, most likely, unknown. Also have a copy of this list to use with a document camera or an overhead. Fill the sheet out as a group, having one student volunteer to discuss what he or she thinks the unknown word means and why. The questions after each sentence will be, "What do you think _____ means? What helped you figure out what that word means?

> My dad is in the garage working on the *carburetor*, tires, brakes, and steering wheel today.
> My new sweater is gray, blue, and *chartreuse*.
> The woman said she owned a dalmatian, golden retriever, and *Pekingese*.
> We have daisies, *hydrangeas*, and roses in our backyard.
> The store had a special on chicken, *veal*, and pork.

Independent Practice

The students' future reading will promote practice by the use of grouping to derive meaning from unknown words that are grouped with known words.

mattered. She also wondered who asked them and how they got answered. These initial musings gave her reading a purpose. The author immediately introduced her to Nikolai and his three questions: When is the best time to do things? Who is the most important one? What is the right thing to do? These questions resonated with Mary and she considered them in light of her own life. In other words, she linked what she was reading with her personal experiences and background knowledge. As she read on, she met other characters (in this case, a series of animals) whom Mary considered self-serving in their responses to Nikolai. She compared her response with that of Nikolai, who, although not quite as critical of his friends, did realize that their answers were "not quite right." So, along with Nikolai, Mary moved beyond her initial questions to wonder if another animal (or person) would offer a wiser response. Nikolai next asked his three questions of a turtle. As the story progressed, Mary altered her questions, posited many guesses about what might happen next, and made numerous inferences to link the text's ideas. For example, this text demanded that she follow the use of quotations marks to understand dialogue, link pronouns to their referents, use sequence words such as *then* to keep the story's events in order, and understand cause-and-effect relationships. In addition, she needed to give herself over to the possibility that animals can speak with humans. As she read, she created many mental images suggested by this story's events and the author's wording. In the end, she understood the satisfaction Nikolai must feel with all he learned about himself and his life. Her involvement with the story did not end when she finished the last word on the last page. Mary continued to think about its ideas and shared them with several friends.

This brief account pinpoints the aspects of understanding connected text that many scholars identify as important comprehension strategies (e.g., Cunningham & Shagoury, 2005; Duffy, 2003; Duke & Pearson, 2002; Keene, 2002; Sweet & Snow, 2002). Readers pay attention to the *features of text*. They hold *purposes* for reading. Readers *self-question*. They make numerous *inferences* and continually use the author's words to spark pictures in their head (i.e., *visualize*). In addition, they *summarize* as they go and *monitor* their understanding. Finally, although Mary did not experience this need, good readers use *fix-up strategies* when comprehension failures occur.

This example stems from reading a story, narrative text. Readers also read exposition, informational texts, however. Shifting from narration to exposition introduces an additional challenge: an ability to shift between organizational frameworks rather than tapping a single expectation. Specifically, and as previously mentioned, stories have a predictable grammar: characters in a specific location do something that all comes together in the end and leaves a reader with a message to ponder. Stories may vary in sophistication, such as a reading of *Knuffle Bunny* (Willems, 2004) compared with *The Giver* (Lowry, 1993), but a reader still knows to expect a setting, characters, plot, and theme. This expectation disappears when a reader switches to exposition. Now, an author chooses from an array of options: (1) simple listing or description, (2) cause and effect, (3) problem–solution, (4) sequence, or time order, and (5) compare–contrast (Alvermann & Phelps, 2005). The author also often frequently shifts structures, sometimes within the same paragraph. On top of this complicating factor, nonfiction authors often use different fonts, insert headings and subheadings, link ideas to graphs and charts, and offer various text elements such as a table of contents, index, or glossary. Many students who read stories well stumble when reading exposition. Starting early on, teachers must attend to narrative and informational reading. In Special Feature 6.1, Deanne McCredie describes several writing strategies she has found helpful when using informational texts with students.

In summary, good readers use an array of comprehension strategies before, during, and after they read. They predict what they think might happen next. Whether novice readers or more expert in their achievement, good readers anticipate meaning and revise their predictions. As the cycle of reading continues, good readers question and monitor. Good readers imagine, combining prior knowledge with the descriptions and wording used by the author to envision the text's events or ideas. Good readers know when to use look-backs or fix-up strategies to rectify comprehension lapses. Good readers synthesize, summarize, and draw conclusions. When reading a narration, they grasp its theme. When reading exposition, they determine its main idea. Ultimately, good readers evaluate, making judgments or forming opinions stemming from a text's ideas. And, with a great deal of frequency, good readers understand what an author implies but does not directly state. The inferential load varies from text to text and reader to reader. Readers who make inferences understand how a character feels, where a story takes place, the ordering of a story's events, or a main idea that an author does not explicitly specify. Simply stated, making inferences is at the heart of understanding connected text. (Figure 6.3 gives an example of a connected text instructional plan.)

For purposes of convenience and clarity, we discussed these psychological components (word identification, vocabulary, and connected text demands) individually. For real readers, however, these components do not occur as separate entities. Instead, they represent intersecting spheres of components. When readers use them efficiently and in concert, they understand and enjoy a text.

CLASSROOM EVENTS

Armed with the information about reading as a process and the elements inherent in it, we turn to the practical task of designing a classroom program. This task requires attention to many complex features. Although options exist for each decision point, an overarching consideration applies: Do the various decisions place students' needs as readers at the heart of the classroom reading program? At this point, you might wonder whether this proposal for a child-centered pedagogy contradicts an attention to a standards-guided curriculum. We, however, consider that maintaining a combined focus on students and standards is the heart of the challenge rather than an either/or competition. So, how do teachers develop a reading program for the students in their classroom?

SPECIAL FEATURE 6.1
Using Writing with Reading to Learn from Informational Texts

BY DEANNE McCREDIE

Language serves a central role in content learning in the elementary classroom because students read, write, speak, and listen to construct meaning. A student is content literate when he or she possesses the ability to use literacy strategies to acquire new content in a given discipline: learning how to use language to learn (McKenna & Robinson, 2002).

When confronted with new information, good readers and listeners look for opportunities to connect the new information to their prior knowledge, or schema, in meaningful ways. Because no one brings the same prior knowledge to a text, no one finds meaning in the same way or in the same places. Many content literacy strategies effectively facilitate students' interaction with content, but a classroom that links reading and writing "invites students to explore ideas, clarify meaning, and construct knowledge . . . in ways not possible when students read without writing or write without reading" (Vacca & Vacca, 2005, p. 353).

Writing in the content areas is sometimes discouraged, however, because teachers worry that the writing needs to be formally corrected or assessed. Writing need not always culminate in a polished, formal product. Simply recording rough thoughts on paper focuses students' thinking and prepares them to learn. The objective of the following before, during, and after learning activities is to use writing to maximize and motivate content learning, not to improve students' writing ability, although, as McKenna and Robinson (2002) point out, "this may follow as a by-product" (p. 12).

■ Before Reading

Quick-Write. The quick-write is a warm-up writing activity that helps students access their prior knowledge about a topic (Richardson &

Morgan, 2000). In one or two minutes, students write what they know about the topic, considering, developing, and organizing ideas as they think through writing. Writing is thinking. Therefore, when students have a record of their thoughts, they can see their thinking and further ponder and elaborate their ideas.

Student-Generated Questions. Another warm-up writing activity involves student-generated questions. In groups, students write questions that they would like answered about a topic (Richardson & Morgan, 2000). This activity not only helps students discover what they already know, but also peaks their curiosity about the topic as they generate questions. Of equal importance, because this prereading activity links writing, listening, and speaking, students refine and deepen their understanding of ideas through speaking and compare their thinking with what they hear from their group members through listening.

Factstorming and Brain Writing. During factstorming, in groups, or independently, students write down facts and associations about a topic (Richardson & Morgan, 2000). For example, during math class, students write anything they know about fractions.

Others (Brown, Phillips, and Stephens, as cited in Richardson & Morgan, 2000) suggest a variation of factstorming called brain writing. During this activity, students first jot down their ideas, and then small groups of students switch their lists and add to each other's thinking. For instance, in social studies, students write what they think about when they hear the word *freedom*. Once the brain writing activity is complete, students have a record of both their thinking and their group members' thoughts to consider before they engage with a written text.

Not only do these prereading activities help students explore what they know about a

(continued on next page)

topic, but they also help teachers to assess students' background knowledge and, if necessary, build that background knowledge for their students during subsequent instruction before or during reading.

■ During Reading

Write As You Read. When students "write as they read," they make connections to what they already know instead of being intimidated by what they don't understand. They can record their thoughts on copies of the reading material, on Post-it notes, on an overhead transparency, or in a journal. This strategy not only supports student learning, but also builds confidence. Everyone is an active participant. Jim Burke (2000) suggests "having students annotate or otherwise mark up texts is one of the most powerful ways of turning them into active readers" (p. 213).

Methods for this strategy might include:

- Underlining main ideas and topics
- Underlining ideas worth remembering
- Underlining ideas students might want to learn more about
- Underlining ideas students question and want to check
- Underlining parts students want to share with other learners
- Underlining ideas students agree with or disagree with
- Underlining ideas students wrestle with
- Writing definitions or synonyms for difficult words
- Writing notes about personal connections and feelings
- Writing about the text structure
- Writing opinions
- Writing questions
- Summarizing a section of the text

When students are given the opportunity to choose a method or methods to mark up texts, their annotations reflect their unique thinking processes and schema and provide teachers important insights into their students' learning. By collecting the annotated texts, teachers have evidence of their students' learning. For instance, they can identify sections of a text or vocabulary that their students didn't understand and reteach the concepts during whole-group or small group instruction. They can also assess their students' overall comprehension of the text by analyzing the sections of texts they underlined and/or the questions and paraphrasing they wrote in the margins.

Furthermore, following up with debriefing discussions encourages students to use their speaking and listening skills to spark new ideas about how to "write as you read" and how the strategy helped them interact with the text. These discussions give students opportunities to talk about their own reading processes and the thinking behind their annotations, and to learn from their peers' efforts. Through all these activities, students are actively engaged with a written text and constructing knowledge, "seeing how they think and how other kids' minds work" (Wilhelm, 1997, p. 142).

Crystal Ball. Another during-reading strategy is called Crystal Ball (Billmeyer and Barton, 1998). At a pivotal point in the reading, teachers direct students to stop and write a prediction about what will happen next. Teachers then encourage students to support their predictions by using information from the reading to explain their thinking and to return to reflect on their predictions when they complete the reading.

Student VOC Strategy. Learning vocabulary in the content areas is particularly challenging for students because it often means that they have no schema for the concepts. Rote memorization or use of a dictionary to look up definitions of words that are entirely new to them clearly does not help students build a meaningful understanding of the vocabulary. Students need time and practice learning how to relate vocabulary to experiences and ideas that are their own. Writing can assist them in this requisite but also provocative process.

The Student Voc Strategy (Billmeyer & Barton, 1998) uses writing to assist students in using context to analyze the meaning of words. After the teacher shares key vocabulary with students prior to reading, students identify the words that are new to them. They then use the VOC strategy while they read by

1. Writing the actual sentence in which the word appears
2. Writing a prediction about the word's meaning using the context of the sentence
3. Writing a definition of the word after consulting a friend, teacher, or other expert resource
4. Writing a sentence of their own exhibiting their understanding of the word's meaning

Rachel Billmeyer and Mary Lee Barton go on to recommend that students link the word and its meaning to one of their senses by drawing a picture, miming an action, or relating the word to another familiar text such as a song or story. Students then write about the connection they made under the sentence they crafted. When students are asked finally to explain their understanding of the word and sensory association with the word to a partner, they use their speaking skills to further make clear their grasp of the word's meaning.

■ **After Reading**

First-Person Summary. The National Reading Panel (2000) links students' successful summarization to improved comprehension. Despite its seeming simplicity, however, summarizing is a complex process that is often daunting for students. First-person summaries (Richardson & Morgan, 2000) allow students to work through the summarizing process by writing in their own words about a topic. Using the first person helps students become personally connected with the ideas so that they can distinguish between summarizing the important information and retelling

all the information in the text, and so that they can better remember what they've learned.

First-person summaries need not be limited to writing from the perspective of characters in a narrative text. This writing activity also works well in a science, social studies, or math class. For example, when students study fractions, they could explain the process of reducing a fraction from the fraction's point of view. In science, when reading about ecosystems, students could write how the snail plays an important role in its ecosystem from the snail's point of view. The goal of first-person summaries, in any content area, is to help students decide on the information and the details, determine which examples are key, continually organize the information, and finally present the information in a concise form.

Cinquain. Writing a cinquain is an engaging language activity for students of all ages (Richardson & Morgan, 2000). Cinquains are patterned five-line poems:

Line 1: a noun or the subject of the poem
Line 2: two adjectives that describe the first line
Line 3: three verbs or action words
Line 4: four words that express a feeling
Line 5: one word that refers back to line one, the subject of the poem

This activity requires focus and reflection as students exhibit their understanding of a concept through the careful composition of their poems.

"And the Winner Is . . .". According to Billmeyer and Barton (1998), the writing activity "And the winner is . . . " is particularly effective at the conclusion of a unit of study. Students begin by thinking about the following:

The publisher of the textbook we use wants student input on the content of the chapter we are studying. Specifically, the publisher wants to know which individual or concept

(continued on next page)

included in the chapter/unit has had the greatest impact on your life and why. (p. 157)

Students then write their argument in a letter to the publisher, explaining the effect the individual or concept has had on their lives. This authentic writing activity helps students reflect on their learning as they write to an actual audience. Not only does a real audience motivate students to do their best writing, but also their best thinking and learning.

Final Thoughts. Thinking through writing in the content areas helps facilitate conversations students have with themselves and others that reveal and clarify their understandings before, during, and after learning, as they broaden and refine their new knowledge. And that new knowledge will be better understood and remembered because it is explored, cultivated, and organized through language that is meaningful and personal as students use their language to learn.

Determining a Schedule

Teachers must set aside ample time for reading and its instruction. Some literacy blocks are divided by the students leaving the room for library, physical education, or music. Other teachers enjoy an uninterrupted time frame. Although research does not establish a time-allotment preference, some time ago Charles Fisher and his colleagues (1978) found that teachers averaged a ninety-minute time frame. We consider a ninety-minute period necessary and reasonable for today's classrooms.

Once the time is set, teachers must use it wisely. Some teachers cleanly divide their time between teaching reading and writing without setting aside the mutual benefits that occur when readers write and writers read. David Pearson and Rob Tierney (1984) established these important relationships years ago, and teachers remain wise to act on them.

Selecting and Using Materials

Most teachers use trade books (i.e., narratives and exposition written by published authors) but also have basal materials (i.e., teacher manuals and student anthologies created by a publishing company) available to them. Some teachers, especially those in schools that receive funding from Reading First, are often required to use published materials that this funding agency, the U.S. Department of Education, considers scientifically based. Other teachers combine their use of trade books and basal materials.

Research does not support basal readers or trade books over the other. In fact, the clear message from the First-Grade Studies (Bond & Dykstra, 1967) was that "children learn to read by a variety of materials and methods" (p. 67). No research today contradicts this conclusion. The choice of materials, however, does come with advantages and drawbacks. In some cases, published materials promote the use of a script rather than a responsiveness to readers' needs that we propose. Because teachers typically receive only grade-level basal readers, their students may find themselves expected to read books that are either too hard or too easy,

FIGURE 6.3   An Example of a Connected Text Lesson: Determining Setting

Declarative

Today we're going to learn how to determine a story's setting.

Conditional

Every story has a setting, so you should determine it for every story you read. Knowing the setting helps you better understand any story's events and how to interpret them.

Procedural: Information and Modeling

First, let's define setting. It includes two things: where and when the story took place. *Where* includes the general location that applies to the entire piece. Certainly, characters can move from place to place, but when we determine the setting of the story we consider it as a whole. *When* refers to the time of the story: in the past, relatively modern times, or in the future. With many of the books you've read, the author directly states the setting. For example, *The Snowy Day* provides the setting in its title and in the first sentence when the author says "it was a winter morning." *Little Nino's Pizzeria* takes place in a city where a man owns a pizza restaurant. The title provides the first evidence of the importance of the restaurant and then the first events take place in one. Several events suggest that it is a city location: the crowdedness of the restaurant, the alley behind it, and the availability of someone to finance a larger restaurant. Because nothing in either story suggests that they took place a long time ago or in the future, I can infer that the author intended a reader to consider it modern. Without these settings, none of the events in either story could have happened.

Other books and stories require you to use text information to infer the setting. To understand where and when these stories take place, you need to put together clues that the author provides. These clues often appear in the beginning of the story, but they can appear throughout it. Let me give you an example. In *Wringer*, the author includes a newspaper article that says Waymer. So, even though he never mentions this town in the book, I can infer that this is the name of the town because the newspaper article talks about its events. Then, the events in the story—wide use of hunting, lack of mention of city landscapes—help me understand that it is a rural town. Because the author mentions the American Legion, I also know it is in the United States. So, *Wringer* takes place in a small rural town. Since none of the events in the story places it in a past or future time, I can infer that it is relatively modern.

Before we work together to determine a story's setting, let's review. What does setting include? What does a reader do to understand a book's setting?

Guided Practice

Today, I asked you to read *Thank You, Ma'am,* a short story by Langston Hughes. To determine its setting, what two things do we want to know? So, does this story take place in the country or in a city? How do you know? Now let's consider the clues about when it took place. Was this a modern-day story or one that took place in years past? What clues help you make this decision? Now let's combine this information to state its setting: a city in past times. Of course, the action is divided between the street and the woman's apartment, but setting needs to capture the whole story.

Independent Practice

Review the new information before reminding students to use it to determine the setting of stories they read in the future in their independent practice.

mismatch their interests, or differ from their prior knowledge and experiences. On the other hand, teachers often find the sample lessons and curricular directions that these published materials offer helpful. Trade books allow a wider variety of choice and match "real reading." As real texts, they obviously demand the use of the psychological elements we previously explained. They easily lend themselves to instructional plans. Teachers must decide. Whatever their choice, a teacher must make certain that students read texts that allow them to grow and learn as readers and reading enthusiasts. In the end, we concur with Dolores Durkin (2004) that "every teacher must strive to become a knowledgeable decision maker, whether using basal materials or something else" (p. 333).

Considering Reading Options

Teachers have a variety of ways to read a text. First, they can *read to* students (a read aloud). In this option, teachers take great care in selecting a text and consider the students' oral language, prior knowledge, and interests. As the name of this option implies, students listen as their teacher orally presents the text to them. This oral presentation by the teacher provides a common text for students to discuss, allows students to appreciate a text that they are perhaps unable to read by themselves, and offers them a model of their teacher's fluent oral reading.

Second, teachers can *read with* their students (a shared reading). In a shared reading, the teacher and students contribute to the oral presentation. A teacher who selects a text with the students' practice needs in mind can provide many important opportunities for students to hone their strategy use in the company of their peers and teacher.

Finally, teachers can assign *independent* reading. During independent reading, students silently read a text that matches their reading achievement and personal interests. At times, this independent reading becomes a whole-class activity (including the teacher). Called SSR (silent sustained reading), DEAR (drop everything and read), or HIP (high-intensity practice), the teacher sets aside a specific amount of time for *everyone* to read. With younger readers, this independent reading might last for five minutes. Teachers of older readers might set aside a twenty-minute period. This type of independent reading might occur daily or weekly, depending on the time available for it and the other options a teacher uses.

On other occasions, teachers link independent reading to guided reading groups (Fountas & Pinnell, 2001). In guided reading groups, teachers work with children who are at about the same level of reading development. Although students still read the text silently, they meet with the teacher in small groups before and after they read. During these small group meetings, teachers address the readers' comprehension needs for understanding this text and assess their understanding of text after the reading. Irene Fountas and Guy Su Pinnell (1996) outline these core components of a guided reading lesson:

- The teacher chooses a book that is relatively easy for this group of children to read, but one that poses a few problems for them to solve.

- The teacher briefly introduces the book.
- The students then read the text to themselves.
- The teacher invites children to share their personal responses to the story.
- The teacher selects one or two teaching points to present to the group following the reading.
- Students may read this book again during free-choice reading. Occasionally, the teacher engages children in extending the story through art, drama, writing, or additional reading.

Other teachers prefer Book Clubs (Raphael & McMahon, 1994). In Book Clubs, students read their text independently for a minimum of fifteen minutes, use writing to reflect on their reading, and then discuss their texts in peer-led discussion groups. Ralph Peterson and Maryann Eeds's (1990) classic book, *Grand Conversations: Literature Groups in Action,* contains wonderful examples of the deep discussions elementary students can have about good literature.

Regardless of the options a teacher uses, teachers must set aside regular chunks of time for students to read and hear texts. Students at all grade levels benefit from these options (read alouds, shared reading, and independent reading). Time to read is insufficient without an instructionally supportive environment, however.

Providing Instruction

Previously, we outlined the word identification, vocabulary, and connected text strategies a teacher *might* teach. A student's reading of a specific text determines what and when a teacher *should* teach a strategy. In other words, teach what a student does not know and needs to know to comprehend a text successfully. Some students will need more support (often called scaffolding) than others.

Offering appropriate instruction depends on the formation of instructional groups. Sometimes an instructional group is composed of one student. On other occasions, the entire class or a small group of students benefit from a specific lesson. These options and varied needs lead teachers to consider *flexible grouping.* These groups are "flexible" in their composition (ranging from individual, small group, or whole-class membership), duration (lasting only as long as necessary for students to learn the unknown strategy), and topic (addressing what is unknown and necessary for the students to read a specific text). In addition to strategy instruction, teachers can also use flexible groups to accommodate students' mutual interests (reading everything available by a specific author or reading to understand a topic).

Once a teacher establishes the type of group and its membership, a teacher plans the instruction. As each example in this chapter shows, and influenced by the combined work of Scott Paris and his colleagues (1984) and David Pearson and Linda Fielding (1994), we propose that instructional plans have three features. First, teachers tell the students *what* they plan to teach. Called a *declarative statement,* this step allows students to focus their attention on a topic and tap the information they might already hold about it. Second, teachers tell students *why* learning this information matters (a *conditional statement*). Students now understand what they will learn (the declarative statement) and why (the conditional statement). Finally, teachers develop a *procedural* component. In this section, teachers *provide information* about the topic and then model its use. Then, students engage in guided practice where the teacher and students work together to use a strategy to understand a text. The sequence ends with independent practice. At this time, students read alone and use their newly acquired strategy as the need naturally arises. This progression from the teacher to the student is called the gradual release of responsibility. The teacher initially takes the stage to provide information about a strategy and model its use, is followed by the students and teacher working together to apply the strategy, and ends with the student using the strategy during the student's independent reading time. In other words, the responsibility for using a strategy begins with the teacher, shifts to the teacher and student working together, and ends with the student working alone.

We propose the use of declarative, conditional, and procedural components for preplanned instruction. Of course teachers also help students while they read. Mary Roe (2004b) calls these opportunities *real reading interactions*. Such interactions occur while students read. As a teacher roams the room and kneels at a student's side, the teacher responds to the student's needs of the moment. These interactions might last a few seconds or a few moments. For them to matter, and like planned instruction, they must be intentional (i.e., linked to a student's need and the teacher's overall reading goals) and helpful (quickly targeted to the student's comprehension need). Teachers who respond quickly and helpfully select from a broad and quickly accessible knowledge base. A preservice teacher compared this knowledge to a Rolodex. Each card would hold information about the psychological elements that we explained in this chapter and then be able to "spin" to the one that holds the information that matters at this time and for this student.

As teachers identify the needs of a student or group of students, they must carefully balance their individual time with some students with their availability to others. To personalize their instruction, some teachers make sure that all students are meaningfully engaged with reading or a reading-related activity.

Assessing

Teachers use assessments to determine the psychological component a student needs to read better. These assessments can take several forms. Standardized and norm-referenced tests provide guidance about students' relative reading success. Performance on state tests (and all states now use them) can further identify the successful from less successful readers. (See Chapter 10 for a description of one state's English language arts test development.) To personalize instruction, however, a teacher needs specific direction. For that, teachers turn to informal and classroom-based tools. Informal reading inventories such as the Qualitative Reading Inventory-4 (Leslie & Caldwell, 2006) provide a way for teachers to establish students' reading levels. This important information allows a teacher to match this reading level to a specific guided reading group placement or basal text. For teachers who use basal readers, these published materials often provide their own informal reading inventory. If so, using the basal version makes sense. To maintain a close understanding of students' decoding, teachers regularly use running records (a recording of students' oral reading using checkmarks for correct words and a coding system for errors) or miscue analysis (a follow-up analysis that compares students' pronunciations with the words in the text). Special Feature 6.2 gives directions on how to take a running record of a child's reading behavior.

To monitor more than decoding, teachers typically combine a word-error analysis with a retelling (a request for the readers to use their own words to retell a story or capture an informational text's central messages). Some districts provide specific texts and times for collecting these running record and retelling assessments. Teachers, however, can use them with any text at any time.

Beyond these formal and informal assessment tools, teachers benefit from viewing ordinary classroom events as assessment opportunities. For example, Peter Johnston (1997) reminds teachers of all the things they can learn from listening to students as they respond in the classroom and engage in personal conversations with their friends about books and reading. In addition, Beverly DeVries (2004) notes classroom products that also serve as assessment tools. For example, students' completion of classroom products such as written responses to a text or the completion of a graphic organizer evidence students' comprehension. Remember that one of this book's main tenets is that assessment offers a lynchpin between assessing and planning. For this goal to be practical and doable, teachers must remember that helpful assessment occurs systematically, develops over time, and taps an array of assessment tools. In combination, these assessments provide teachers with rich data about students' development as readers and supply information that can be used to direct instruction.

ATTRIBUTES OF A SUCCESSFUL READING TEACHER

The previous sections of this chapter suggest many attributes of the successful reading teacher. Successful reading teachers:

- Understand the reading process
- Articulate the psychological components that contribute to comprehension and understand the additional influences of attitude and motivation
- Create classroom environments that maximize the time available for reading and its instruction
- Tap a variety of reading options (read-alouds, shared readings, and independent reading)
- Select materials wisely and well
- Use assessments to guide instruction
- Have a familiarity with books appropriate for children in their classes to read

SPECIAL FEATURE 6.2
Running Records

The running record is a means of systematically observing and recording children's reading behavior (Clay, 1985). This procedure is very popular with classroom teachers because of its ease of use and the valuable information it provides. In a one-to-one setting, the student reads a brief passage from a book while the teacher uses a special symbol system to make a written record of what occurs: ticks (checkmarks) are used to record each correct response, and other symbols are used to note the errors and other behaviors that occur (see Figure 6.4). No special transcript of the passage is needed. The marks are made on a blank piece of paper. After the reading is finished,

comprehension can be checked by asking the student to retell the story in his or her own words.

After a running record has been taken, the written record can be analyzed to determine the accuracy of the student's reading. The first step is to subtract the number of countable errors (words supplied by the teacher and non-self-corrected substitutions, omissions, and insertions) from the number of words in the passage. Then divide this number by the number of words. The resulting percentage indicates the proportion of words that the student recognizes accurately and is an indication of the relative difficulty of the passage for that particular student:

✓	correctly read word	
ride / run	incorrectly read/substitution (error each time misread – proper name counted as error 1st time only)	error
/ r̲/r̲u̲n̲ / ri- / ride /	record all trials	1 error
/ r̲i̲d̲e̲/r̲u̲n̲ / ran / run / SC	*self-correct–child corrects error	no error
w̄a̅l̅k̅	omission	error
t̲o̲	insertion	error
T TOLD	child given word	1 error
/ ride / up and / R /	*repetition	no error
/ (slash)	*hesitation (errors of pronunciation not counted as reading error)	no error
ACCURACY	Running Words – Countable Errors / Running Words	
	*Not counted as an error	

FIGURE 6.4 **Conventions for Recording a Running Record**

SPECIAL FEATURE 6.2 (continued)

95 to 100 percent accuracy: *independent-level material,* suitable for pleasure reading

90 to 95 percent accuracy: *instructional-level material,* suitable for instruction

Less than 90 percent accuracy: *frustration-level material,* too difficult

This calculation gives the teacher an idea of the difficulty level of material that the student is capable of reading for different purposes. In the example running record in Figure 6.5, the student's accuracy is 90 percent, indicating that the passage is on the boundary between the frustration and the instructional level for this particular student. The only time that students should read material that is this difficult is when passage information is of particularly high interest or utility (e.g., needed for a class project).

Additional information about students' reading strategies can be obtained by using miscue analysis to analyze the errors contained on a running record (Goodman & Goodman, 1994). Miscue analysis involves examining errors in terms of cue systems and self-monitoring behavior. Errors are compared with their text counterparts and the surrounding context to determine whether students are attending to the following:

- *Graphophonic cues:* substituted words look like the text words
- *Syntactic cues:* substituted words are the same part of speech, and other errors maintain grammatical acceptability
- *Semantic cues:* errors make sense in the context in which they occur

In the example in Figure 6.5, most of the reader's substitutions look like the text words, but many do not make sense in terms of the preceding or subsequent context. Notice that several are also different parts of speech than their text counterparts. This analysis indicates that the reader is relying heavily on graphophonic cues (letter–sound relationships) but is not paying adequate attention to context cues. Only one of the serious, meaning-disrupting errors was self-corrected, hinting that the reader may not be self-monitoring her reading to make sure that what is read makes sense. Detailed instructions for conducting and interpreting miscue analysis can be found in the manual by Yetta Goodman, Dorothy Satson, and Carolyn Burke (1987).

TEXT

Jimmy was a little boy. He was walking home from school when he saw an old house on the corner. Jimmy and his dog Spot walked up to the old house. Jimmy knocked on the door, but no one answered. Jimmy was brave. He went inside.

Jimmy looked around the house, and he saw a door to his right. He opened the door and went inside. The room was very dark. Jimmy tried to find a light and he fell down. He sat on the floor and began to cry. Spot heard Jimmy crying and ran into the room, Spot found Jimmy and led him out of the dark room.

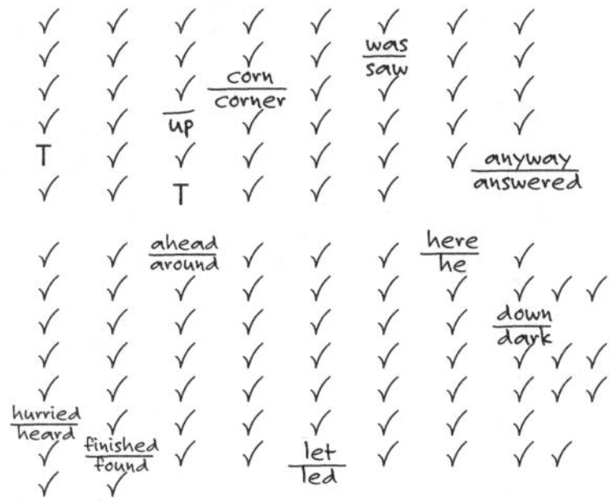

$$\text{ACCURACY} = \frac{110 \text{ (running words)} - 11 \text{ (countable errors)}}{110 \text{ (running words)}} = 90 \text{ percent}$$

FIGURE 6.5   Example Running Record

Now, consider the complex task of integrating these various features. In doing so, teachers must focus on the student. As Gerald Duffy (2003) reminds us, the overall goal is to "put students in control of their own efforts to make sense out of text" (p. 215). So, although teachers are "in charge," they should never remain center stage. They should strongly believe that all students can read better and openly share with their students the joy and wonder of reading.

SUMMARY

Readers benefit from teachers who are well versed in the reading process. They also benefit from teachers who design classroom environments that provide opportunities to engage in meaningful reading activities. While just reading, students can increase their fluency, add to their vocabulary, and practice many important reading strategies. Many students, however, rarely acquire all the strategies they need to be proficient readers from just reading. In addition, readers benefit from teachers who wed the opportunity to read with personalized strategy instruction. Finally, readers benefit from teachers who explain what they do in light of students' needs and in consideration of district and state standards. We designed this chapter and the others in this book to help you be that teacher.

- *What are the components of the reading process?*

The components of the reading process include several psychological pieces: (1) word identification, (2) vocabulary, and (3) connected text. For each component, a reader taps a number of strategies. For word identification, readers might use phonics, consider the context, or employ morphemic analysis. In addressing vocabulary, they might use strategies such as consulting a reference or using context. In addition, and when their strategy use is unsuccessful, readers might rely on their teacher's explicit instruction. For connected text, comprehension strategies include identifying a text's structure, understanding a purpose for reading, visualizing, posing questions, making inferences, and summarizing. Of importance, readers monitor their reading and use fix-up strategies when their understanding wanes.

- *Beyond a reader's proficiency in the specific features of this process, what else contributes to reading achievement?*

Especially in a school setting, a number of classroom events contribute to reading achievement. Specifically, the amount of time designated for reading (i.e., scheduling), the choice of materials (i.e., finding the "just right" book), the type of reading (i.e., independent, shared, or guided), and the quality of instruction add or detract from a student's reading success.

■ *What classroom events should occur during the time assigned for reading?*

Within a sufficiently long block of time (approximately ninety minutes), students should be seen reading an appropriate text, responding to that text, and receiving instruction from their teacher designed to help them read better.

■ *What attributes define a successful reading teacher?*

Good teachers hold a deep understanding of the reading process. Based on this they select appropriate assessments and interpret the assessment results to offer appropriate instruction. They create an environment that maximizes the students' opportunities to read appropriate books. To support this responsibility, they possess a broad understanding of books that allows them to choose materials wisely and well.

LINKING KNOWLEDGE TO PRACTICE

1. Interview several elementary grade teachers and ask them about their views of the reading process. Compare their responses with what you learned about the process of reading and its psychological components.

2. Observe an elementary grade teacher during the teacher's reading time. Record what the students and teacher do. Overall, consider the question, How do the teacher and students spend their time?

CHAPTER 7

EMBEDDED WITHIN A BALANCED READING PROGRAM: TEACHING MEANING AND SKILLS

When he was in sixth grade, Jim Christie recalls spending two hours every day engaged in round-robin oral reading of literary classics. He can still recall the "butterflies" that he got in his stomach as his turn to read approached. Every Friday, a lengthy multiple-choice test was given about the portion of the book that was read that week. He came to think of reading as unpleasant work, and it took years before he began reading books for pleasure again. Fortunately, fewer and fewer teachers are using this approach to literature.

Many adults remember reading experiences like Jim's. The teacher-assigned stories were followed by the teacher asking, actually reading, a set of very specific questions that typically had only one "right" answer. These "When did?" "Who did?" questions were designed to test the reader's comprehension of the story. Occasionally, the teacher varied this routine by requiring students to complete a fill-in-the-blanks test or to write a book report. Unfortunately, this approach to reading may have taught a number of lessons unintended by the teacher, as Nancy Atwell (1987, p. 152) describes:

- Reading is difficult, serious business.
- Literature is even more difficult and serious.
- There is one interpretation of a text: the teacher's.

Instead of a single "correct" interpretation of a piece of literature, the new approaches to the teaching of reading operate on the premise that individuals bring to the act of reading their unique prior experiences and beliefs that influence how they interpret the author's words. Likewise, a reader's interpretation may change and be influenced by ongoing life experiences (Rosenblatt, 1991). For instance, Billie remembers reading Laura Ingalls Wilder's *On the Banks of Plum Creek* (1937) when she was nine years old. In Chapter 8, Laura described Pa's reactions after she and Mary disobeyed Pa's instructions and continued to tumble down the tall straw stack that Pa had carefully raked:

PA: Did you slide down the straw-stack?

LAURA: No, Pa.

PA: Laura!

LAURA: We did not slide, Pa. But we did roll down it.

Pa got up quickly and went to the door and stood looking out. His back quivered. Laura and Mary did not know what to think (p. 60).

At nine, Billie believed Pa to be so upset with Mary and Laura that he was physically shaking with anger. Some twenty years later, however, when she was rereading this story to her class, her life experiences as a parent and teacher caused her to reevaluate her original view of Pa's reaction. Billie now believes that Pa was laughing at his children's silly antics! This example illustrates today's view of reading as being both transactive and interactive; in other words, understanding is a combination of what the reader brings to the text and what the reader takes from the text (Eeds & Wells, 1991). Thus, the act of reading is social in nature; minimally, it consists of a conversation between one reader and an author. Optimally, reading may be enhanced when several readers discuss their personal interpretations and construct shared understandings (Peterson & Eeds, 1990; Rascon-Briones & Searfoss, 1995).

In this book, we encourage teachers to use a blended approach to the teaching of reading as a way to help students interact with high-quality literature. The approach offers students an opportunity to

- Read independently and study texts of their own choosing
- Read independently and discuss communally
- Work in temporary small groups to learn specific skills
- Work one on one with their teacher in individual conferences to learn specific skills
- Work in a whole-class group to learn those skills the teacher sees all students needing
- Lead and participate in discussions in which each member of the group has equal status
- Work in cooperative groups, governed by rules of respect, with everyone's ideas or interpretations respected and valued
- Practice working in self-governing groups
- Talk, share ideas, build new understandings with peers, and consider and value others' divergent perspectives

In this chapter, we will describe how teachers use the ideas presented in Chapter 6 to help their students learn to construct a personal understanding of text. In addition, we discuss how they can teach specific decoding and comprehension skills within a blended approach to teaching reading. We begin with a rich description of three first grade teachers. In Special Feature 7.1, our colleague, Sara McCraw, provides this careful description of these three teachers' daily reading instruction. These teachers integrate a writing workshop (see Chapters 8 and 9) into their literacy time block. Therefore, the description also provides information about the teaching of writing in two first grades.

Teachers of older students also teach reading and help their students use their reading and writing skills to learn. Therefore, we invited a colleague, Deanne McCredie, to describe how she supported her third-grade students' use of their reading and writing skills within the context of the study of immigration in the United States (see Special Feature 7.2), and we provide a description of a sixth grade teacher's, Mr. Sousa's, reading and writing program. From Delaware to Washington to Arizona, teachers across the country are using these strategies to support their students' development as readers (and writers).

BEFORE READING THIS CHAPTER, THINK ABOUT . . .

- The type of reading instruction you experienced when you were in grade school. Were you in a reading group? Did you participate in round-robin reading, when one child read, and then another, and then another, until finally it was your turn?
- A favorite story that you read with your teacher and peers. Did you have a favorite book of poetry that you read again and again?
- How your teacher assessed your comprehension of the stories and books you read. Did you complete workbook pages? Were there weekly tests? Did you write book reports? Did you share your views with peers?

FOCUS QUESTIONS

- What organizational strategies do teachers use to implement a blended reading program?
- What types of grouping strategies are used in a blended reading program?
- How do teachers provide skill instruction in a blended reading program?
- How do teachers help students construct meaning and expand their understanding of text?

USING READING AND WRITING FOR LEARNING

Children learn through reading. Witness Mrs. Meszaros's students' learning about how horses sleep (standing up) from their reading of a book on horses. In recent years, many teachers have intentionally planned ways for their students to use

BOX 7.1
DEFINITION OF TERMS

book club: A time when a small group of students read the same book and gather to talk about their reading and strategy use (e.g., how they decoded a word, how they determined a word's meaning) and to clarify any questions.

individual conference: A time for a teacher to meet with a student individually to learn about reading strengths and needs and areas of interest, monitor book selection, and set goals.

running record: An ongoing assessment by which a teacher determines the level of word decoding accuracy a student has with a particular text.

schema: A reader's background knowledge on a specific topic or experience.

strategy-based guided reading: An instructional method whereby students are grouped by reading strategy need and teachers provide appropriate instruction. Students are usually reading on a similar level but are not confined to reading with only students on their specific level. These groups remain fluid; as student needs change, the group membership changes.

their reading and writing skills to support their learning of the social studies or science content. These teachers are heeding the advice of the National Council of Teachers of English (NCTE, 1993):

> Rather than working on subjects in isolation from one another, studying reading apart from writing, and apart from math, science, social studies, and other curricular areas, children learn best when they are engaged in inquiries that involve using language to learn, and that naturally incorporate content from a variety of subject areas.

When the language arts are woven into the very fabric of all subject matter areas, it is a classic win–win situation. Subject matter content and the language arts are both learned more effectively. As teacher Tarry Lindquist (1995, p. 1) points out:

> It is through the language arts that my students most often reveal their knowledge and apply their skills. Reading, writing, listening, and speaking are integral to all learning. Without language arts, the construction of meaning in specific topics is impossible.

In Special Feature 7.2, Deanne McCredie describes aspects of her students' study of immigration, highlighting how she used this social studies topic to support her students' literacy development.

SPECIAL FEATURE 7.1
Lessons from Three Experienced First Grade Teachers

BY SARA B. McCRAW

Sheila Roche-Cooper, Janelle Layton, and Chrissy Meszaros each knew that teaching from the reading series (sometimes called the reading anthology) was not enough for the students in their classrooms. It seemed to reach students who were just about on grade level, but first-graders who were below felt lost and left behind and those above felt bored. These teachers decided to meet every Thursday to see if they could teach differently. During these weekly meetings, they invited other staff members to share what was working for them, and they worked to uncover good resources for learning different ways to meet the needs of all their students in an engaging and motivating way. They also used this time to brainstorm and problem solve. They were willing to change their instruction if it was not benefiting their students. What these teachers learned was that through collaboration, not only did they create a dynamic learning environment in each of their classrooms where students were actually asking for more time to read, but they also formed a partnership that continues to grow and reduces the anxieties of trying to teach in an exciting different way. No longer must they teach in isolation.

Each teacher has a strong foundation in teaching and recognizes that students need both explicit and implicit instruction in decoding and comprehension strategies to become proficient readers. These teachers believe in a systematic yet responsive model of instruction designed around collecting ongoing assessment information on each student and designing instruction in each student's zone of proximal development (be it in whole groups, flexible small groups, or individually during reading conferences). These teachers continue to follow the district guidelines in terms of trimester goals to meet, and they continue to use the district-adopted reading materials and established assessments used in all first grades. They just use these materials and assessments differently from the ways they did in other years.

Mrs. Layton and Mrs. Meszaros share a classroom in a TAM (Team Approach to Mastery) model whereby students with special needs learn with general education students, while Mrs. Roche-Cooper has a general education class. They all work in an early childhood center located in a rural, mid-Atlantic state where the building services all kindergarten and first grade students in the district and those who qualify for prekindergarten. The average class size is twenty-three students, and these children come from a variety of backgrounds. Each student is viewed as a person who is capable and ready to learn and who also needs patience and guidance as they explore learning about themselves as readers, writers, and speakers. Because the teachers plan together, they have a similar daily schedule, which is described on the following pages. This responsive approach to literacy instruction incorporates a reading and writing workshop model and time for word study each day.

■ Beginning the Day (8:10–8:40)

Students trickle into the classrooms when they are dropped off by parents, arrive on the bus, or have finished eating breakfast in the school cafeteria. By the second week of school, these first-graders know the routine of turning in homework, making their lunch selection, returning the book brought home to read the night before, and settling in to one of their morning literacy stations. Here students spend time reading and discussing books on the same theme (typically the upcoming or current science or social studies theme), listening to books on tape, practicing their fluency by reading into a tape recorder, working on a computer program to enhance their reading skills, or pairing up with a partner to practice high-frequency words. Students transition by cleaning up their station and joining together in the meeting area. A few students share what they learned from reading a book in the theme tub (a plastic tub with books of varying levels of difficulty on a selected topic), and others share excitement about improved reading fluency and other successes.

■ **Thinking about Reading (8:40–9:10)**

The teachers constantly model how they think about what they read as they share their "think-alouds" during reading (which occurs throughout the day, across content areas). One morning, students in Mrs. Roche-Cooper's class gathered in the meeting area to listen to two stories about costume parades (it's October 31). Over the past two weeks, the students learned about text-to-self and text-to-text connections and how good readers get ready to read by activating their schema. At this point, students are very comfortable using the language of schema and connections correctly. More important, students have learned what kinds of connections help a reader understand (e.g., "I know what it feels like to lose a best friend. That happened to me when I moved.") versus ones that do not (e.g., "I have red shoes, too!"). The students learned about making connections using their reading series materials and other text. An excerpt from a comprehension lesson using picture books follows.

One boy sits up high on a chair facing the students yet watching the teacher; today is his special day to sit in the chair and help the teacher. She reads the story with the book facing her as the students listen and visualize what is happening. At the end of each page, she shows the pictures, and the students automatically discuss with each other what they see and think. An atmosphere of a conversation—versus "teacher talks, students raise their hands, and one responds"—is evident. In a conversational approach, all students have a chance to share their thinking and ask questions with their classmates as authentic audience members. Near the end of the story,

Mrs. Roche-Cooper stops and asks a prediction question, "Why did the boy Gilbert in this story wear a ballerina costume?" Immediately, the students turn to each other to respond, giggling about the question and sharing their own predictions. A few moments later, the teacher counts backward from five to indicate that it is time to stop talking and to listen. She continues to the end of the story, when the students take over the reading as they chant the poem told again and again in the story.

At the end of the story, the teacher facilitates the students sitting in pairs, knee to knee and eye to eye as they share their connections from the story. The students have close to two minutes to share. Mrs. Roche-Cooper follows up with compliments and specific language models, such as "Remember to use our phrase when sharing connections: When I heard the part about hmmmm it reminded me of hmmmm." Students are invited to share their connections. One student shares, "I remember when I sang the same song from the story last year in class." She acknowledges that some students may not have made a connection with the first story. Mrs. Roche-Cooper lets the students know that it is okay if they did not make a connection the first time but also mentions that they might with the second one or that they may even make a connection between the two stories.

She begins reading the second story, the book facing her as she reads and then sharing the pictures at end of each page. She compliments the students' listening behavior, "Thank you, Tyke and Jasmine, for listening politely." Mrs. Roche-Cooper naturally defines unfamiliar words during the reading experience and engages her class to see if they are familiar with each unfamiliar word. One student picks up on this habit and calls out "gloomy means dark" as the teacher reads the sentence with the word

(continued on next page)

gloomy. Other students look at her and nod in agreement. Interjecting is an accepted behavior when the comment or question is on topic and done so respectfully. Two thirds of the way through the second story, Mrs. Roche-Cooper prompts students to share their connections with their same partners from before. She immediately gets up and roams around the pairs, listening, coaching, and reminding. She brings them back together and compliments those students who used the language of connections.

Next, Mrs. Roche-Cooper asks students to determine the book they made more connections with and to stand in groups accordingly. She breaks these two groups into smaller groups of three to four and sends each group off with chart paper and markers to record their connections. One group (three girls and a boy) talks about what they are supposed to do. "You have to put a big T and a big S with an arrow in between." They end by taking up the entire paper with their big T and big S, and then one girl points and states what each letter stands for: "text-to-self connection." Two of the girls take charge while the boy stands up looking for the teacher and the third girl tries to write her own T and S smaller on the chart. About this time, Mrs. Roche-Cooper walks over and compliments their teamwork. She comments that the T and S are too large, so she flips the paper over and is more explicit about how the students should record their connections. She leaves and floats around to the other five groups, passing out compliments and facilitating when needed. The group of three girls and one boy is still having problems deciding how to share the writing experience. They each want to take turns writing one letter in each word. Mrs. Roche-Cooper returns and suggests that they pick one recorder. The students raise their hands and eagerly look at the teacher. She says that she will not pick the recorder and puts the responsibility back to the group to determine. She walks away, and one girl decides to be the recorder and starts writing. The other group members offer help with spelling, spacing, and other conventions of writing.

Each group is given the responsibility to determine how to organize the writing and sharing at the end of the writing event. Two groups share the pen and write one connection together, while the other four groups find a way to each record their own connections. No students complain that they cannot write or spell. They all have the confidence to record using their best spelling. About eight minutes later (the teacher continued to rotate between groups offering support and guidance when needed), Mrs. Roche-Cooper lets the students know that they will gather together soon by saying, "Put the caps on your markers and bring your chart back to the meeting area, and be sure to sit with your group." The students are so excited to share their charts that each holds a corner of the chart paper. Lots of chatter is heard in the room as the groups try to determine who will do the talking. Mrs. Roche-Cooper patiently reminds the groups to gather in the meeting area; then she calls up one group to share. She points out how well the group organized their work. "What do you notice about how they organized their connections?" Mrs. Roche-Cooper asks her class. One student comments, "They drew lines so they each had a place to write their own comment." The process of sharing continues until each group has had a chance to share. The teacher gives subtle reminders to look at the people speaking. She also compliments students for speaking clearly and sharing connections that helped others understand the story better. During transitions between groups, she asks the students if they made a similar connection to the last group that shared.

■ **Applying What They Learned (9:10–9:40)**

In previous years, these teachers used a centers approach where reading-related activities were placed around the room and the students moved independently from center to center, completing the various activities, so they could meet in small groups for guided reading. This approach was satisfactory, but the teachers believed that the time could be used better. They wanted their students to spend more time reading and less time practicing disconnected skills (e.g., busy work). As a result, the teachers began to study a different model for teaching reading (see Figure 7.1) and decided to use this approach in their classroom this year. They knew that it would take time to build stamina for reading, so they began the year with just five minutes of independent reading time. Each day, they extended the time until the students could read "just-right books" for ten minutes. At this point (about one week into the school year), the teachers began to meet with students for individual conferences. They interviewed students to learn about their interests and how each child viewed himself or herself as a reader. The second conference was more of an assessment at which the teacher took a running record (see Special Feature 6.1), checked for comprehension, and shared the results with the student including strengths and areas for growth. Together the teacher and student set a goal for the student's reading, a way to measure the goal, and a time to check progress. About five weeks into the school year, the students in both classes were able to read books from their book basket, a collection of books at each student's independent and instructional level (originally selected by the teacher, but later by the students once they recognized what a just-right book was). The teachers could then meet with three students individually for a conference. The conferences shifted from simply assessment to more instruction as teachers offered support when needed. During a Thursday after-school meeting, the teachers discussed what was happening during their reading workshop time, and one teacher commented:

"It's amazing! I cannot believe how engaged the students are in reading. Last year, I would never have believed that this could happen." The teachers realized that they knew more about their students' reading ability six weeks into the school year than they did all year in years past. An excerpt from a reading workshop follows.

A transition is made to reading workshop time by reviewing expectations, with the teacher saying, "We all want to be reading during this time." Mrs. Roche-Cooper reviews a few key strategies that students can use while reading to help figure out words and help with understanding. Then she asks the students to close their eyes and think about what their personal goal is for reading. "Remember that using strategies helps us remember the story, understand the story, and enjoy the story." Students get their reading basket of personal books at their independent level as she hands each student a rubric; they will use the rubric to score themselves at the end of reading workshop time. They all sing a song together as they move through this transition, "There is a child who likes to read and _____ is her/his name-o R-E-A-D read R-E-A-D read R-E-A-D read and _____ is her/his name-o!" Students eagerly go to their cubbies to get their book baskets; some even skip on the way. Each student finds a special place in the room to read (sitting on the ledge of the coat cubby, in a rocking chair, at a desk, at the writing center, under the table, on the floor with a carpet square, in the book closet with a pillow). Immediately, students pull out their books and begin reading (some read leveled books; others read from the reading series). One child has a hard time getting started. He roams around the room and watches other students until he finds a place to sit; only then does he begin by looking at his goal notebook to see what his latest goal is.

(continued on next page)

Mrs. Roche-Cooper watches as the students begin reading and then chooses the student with whom she will hold her first conference. She approaches Connor, listens to him read a few moments, and then asks if she can hold a conference with him. The rest of the class is reading (out loud as they are apt to do at this stage of development) and do not seem to notice the others. One child stops periodically in his reading and comments on what is happening in the story. "This walrus is a wimp, he doesn't want to get in the cold water," he giggles. At the end he says, to no one in particular, "This book is too easy for me." He reads a second book from his basket, and at the end he makes a text-to-self connection between the character and his own sister. Meanwhile, Mrs. Roche-Cooper finishes one conference in about four minutes and then approaches Wen Li and asks if she can have a conference. Mrs. Roche-Cooper begins by asking why Wen Li chose the book she did. Wen Li responds that it is the next story in the book (anthology) and that it is her goal to read all the stories in it. The teacher asks Wen Li to determine if the story is too hard, too easy, or just right. Wen Li is not sure, so she starts reading to decide. The teacher listens and occasionally records comments in Wen Li's conference notebook. When Wen Li needs help, Mrs. Roche-Cooper prompts her with, "What can you do to figure it out?"

Elsewhere in the room a boy is reading *The Wide-Mouth Frog* and another boy lingers and listens from behind, his eyes following the text as the reader reads. It is difficult to see the faces of the students in the room because they hold their book close to their eyes and concentrate on reading. Some are pointing to the words. Many squiggle and move their legs, feet, and bodies, but the entire time their eyes are focused on the book and they are reading. One boy walks to his cubby to find a book that was missing from his basket. Students in this room are reading books from a level 2 (just a few words on a page with high picture support and a repeated pattern) to a level 17 (beginning of second grade, with many words per page, past tense verbs, dialogue, and multisyllabic words). One student pulls out the word bank of words from his basket and goes through reading all his high-frequency words. He quickly makes a pile of the ones he knows and the ones he does not know. Another student is reading a "phonic book" that she made practicing short-*e* word families. Yet another child reads a class-generated book of a poem that he illustrated. Off in a corner a girl curls up and flips through all the books in her basket. She seems to crave the quiet, small space as she begins reading. From this point on, she does not seem to notice anyone or anything else in the room.

Mrs. Roche-Cooper moves to the third conference, this time with Thomas. He chooses a class-made book to read. She listens to his reading, supporting when needed but really trying to see what Thomas can do on his own. At the end, she points out what he did a good job in his reading: "At the beginning you had a hard time reading the word *pumpkin*, but later in the story you read it with no problem." She finishes by saying, "Thanks for letting me visit, and happy reading!" She moves to another conference while quietly letting two students know that they have a zero on their rubric for reading workshop at this point. She transitions the class to finish reading workshop by reminding them to choose a book from their basket to take home to read to someone at home for homework tonight. She also reminds them to score their rubrics and that they should have a score of two unless she spoke to them directly. The students gather in the meeting area to share their books and strategies used.

Eight weeks into the school year, all three teachers realize that some of their students are no longer making steady progress in their reading (an average of two levels every three weeks), so they decide that it is time to begin small group instruction. Realizing that "fair" does not always mean "equal" time for every student, Mrs. Layton and Mrs. Meszaros set up a weekly schedule that allows them to meet with students who are struggling the most three times a week in strategy-based, guided reading groups and three times a week for individual instruction later in the day. Students who are reading near the end of first grade level will meet in book clubs twice a week, and students who are reading on a level typical of this time of year will continue meeting individually with one teacher each week for a conference; the latter students will also meet once a week in a strategy-based guided reading group. The teachers are able to plan their instruction for small groups based on the information collected during individual conferences.

■ **Differentiating Instruction 9:40–10:10**

During the time that the teachers meet with their students individually for conferences, they also meet with small, guided reading groups based on student needs. At this time of year, Mrs. Layton and Mrs. Meszaros find themselves working with several groups of varying needs. Four students are already reading on a level near the end of first grade and participate in a book club. They read the same book and meet twice a week with a teacher to discuss the book, share strategies used, and increase their understanding. Three students in this inclusion class are still learning letter sounds and need to increase their phoneme manipulation skills. They meet as a small group for shared reading, phonics work, and phonemic awareness lessons four times a week. Four students are just beginning to apply voice–print–match skills and meet three times a week for guided reading. The rest of the class is reading on grade level, and these students also have different strengths and needs. A group of four students meets twice a week in a guided

reading group to strengthen their context clue use in combination with their strong decoding skills. Another group of five students uses context clues well but needs help with decoding; they also meet twice a week for guided reading. The other four students reading on grade level are balancing their use of context and decoding strategies and continue to meet with the teachers for individual conferences. A strategy-based, guided reading lesson with the group of on-level readers who need help with using context clues follows.

Five students and Mrs. Meszaros gather in a circle on the floor, each on their own carpet square. Some kneel and others sit with their legs crossed. Each student has his or her book box and is reading a self-selected book as a warm-up. Mrs. Meszaros listens to Zane read the new book from the last time they met and takes a running record to check his accuracy and strategy use. About three minutes into the meeting, Mrs. Meszaros asks the students to find a stopping place in their reading and then shares the strategies Zane used in his reading. She says,, "I like the way he went back and read the sentence again after he paused to sound out a word. It shows that he was paying attention to what the story was about." Then she asks, "Does anyone want to share a strategy they used when they got stuck on a word?" Oliva says, "I got stuck on a word so I looked at it and I saw the little word go inside. Then I figured out the word was *going*." "Great," says Mrs. Meszaros, and then she asks, "What else do good readers do when they get stuck on a word?" "Sound it out!" calls out Zane. "Look at the beginning sound and match it to the pictures," says Miles. Mrs. Meszaros continues by describing how good readers sometimes get stuck on a word. When sounding out or looking for chunks does not work, they reread the sentence from the beginning to recall what the text is

(continued on next page)

talking about and predict what word would make sense that has the same beginning sound. The group tries this technique with a few practice sentences (When will we b_____ our new jobs? School is the best place to l_____.). The students match their predictions to the spelling of the word.

After the strategy lesson, Mrs. Meszaros prepares the students for their new book, *Sleeping Animals*. She passes out a copy of the book to everyone, and they immediately begin taking a picture walk, looking at each page and predicting what the book will be about. Miles says, "It looks like horses sleep standing up. I wonder if that is true?" Olivia says, "Hey I knew bats sleep upside down. We learned that when we read the bat book last week." After the picture walk, Mrs. Meszaros reminds the students to use their strategies if they get stuck on a word and to check their predictions. Because the goal of guided reading is for students to learn how to read text on their own and rely on their strategies if they get stuck, she invites one member of the group at a time to begin reading. (The result is all students reading aloud, but not all students reading the same words at the same time.) Mrs. Meszaros listens and occasionally jots notes about each student on her lesson plan. These notes, in combination with the conference notes, will help her plan for the next guided reading lesson. Cole says, "I need help." Mrs. Meszaros asks, "What can you do to figure it out?" "I can chunk it," he says. "Okay," she replies. "Show me." Cole finds *ing* and *sleep* and says that the word *is* sleeping. His teacher smiles, and Cole continues reading.

Latisha finishes reading first, so Mrs. Meszaros prompts her to find a word in the book with which she had trouble and to be prepared to share with the group what she did to figure it out. As the others finish, they begin to talk about how animals sleep and confirm their predictions. "I was right! Horses do sleep standing up!" Miles says. "I don't see how they do that. Why don't their legs get tired from standing all the time?" Latisha asks. Cole says, "It's probably because that's how they were made. Yeah. Horses were made to stand up all the time, that's why." The students decide that they would like to learn more about horses and how they sleep, so they ask Mrs. Meszaros to find more information about horses for them. She says that they can look into it the next time they meet. Then she asks Latisha to share a strategy she used while reading. "I got stuck on this word, Latisha replies. "It was so big that I didn't know how to sound it out, so I tried reading the sentence again. Then the word popped into my head, *alligator*! That made sense and it matched the picture, but when I looked at the word again I knew it couldn't be alligator because the word starts with a *c*. So I looked at the word again, read the sentence again, and knew that the word must be *crocodile*." Two other students share the strategies they used to help them figure out a word.

Next, Mrs. Meszaros invites them to read the book again with a partner. She says, "Now that you have figured out all the words and learned some new facts, when you read the book this time, work on your fluency. You want your reading to sound smooth and your voice to go up and down some, like when Mrs. Layton reads aloud to us. Take turns reading with a partner. When it is your turn to listen, follow the words with your eyes and let your partner know if he or she is reading fluently. I am going to listen to Zane read and take a running record on his reading." The students begin reading and do not seem to notice those reading near them. Latisha sounds like her teachers when Olivia asked for help and Latisha replies, "What can you do to figure it out?" The students are learning how to rely on their own strategies while reading. When all are finished reading and commenting on each other's fluency, Mrs. Meszaros asks, "Would you recommend this book to other readers? Do you feel comfortable keeping this book in your book basket?" They all agree that other boys and girls would enjoy reading the book. Most want to keep it in their basket, but Cole decides that it is too hard, so he will not keep it in his book basket.

■ **Ready to Write 10:10–11:00**

At this point in the school year, the students understand the components and expectations of the writing workshop. On the day described below, the students are in the middle of writing a letter all about themselves to their special teacher, who is out on maternity leave. To prepare to write the letter, the class spent many weeks reading samples of different letters in literature, morning messages, and letters from home. The class then created a list of characteristics common to friendly letters and began writing letters in whole group and small group situations. Now the students are ready to produce their own letter.

Mrs. Layton reminds students who were publishing yesterday to return to the same computer and continue typing. She asks the class, "What can you do if you are finished with your letters or are waiting for a computer?" One student states that they can read a book or play on the computer. Mrs. Layton reminds him that it is not the time to play on the computer but that it would be a great time to begin a new piece of writing that is free choice. "You can write about anything you want. Maybe you could write a letter to someone else or make up a silly story," she suggests.

Mrs. Meszaros asks those students who have a note from her on their writing (the teachers had read through the student writing and had written comments to those who need to add more to their letters) to join her at the table. She is able to guide students' writing when they need help in the small group setting. Some of the students have special needs and some just need help. The teachers are able to provide support to any student who needs help at the time, versus only students with special needs.

Mrs. Layton confers with students who are ready to publish their letters individually. Together she and the student read through the letter, stopping periodically to see if the writing sounds right and makes sense. At the end of the letter, they check the planning web (the notes the student made before beginning to write) to make sure everything is included. The rest of the students not publishing on the computer or meeting with a teacher are working independently on their writing. Some are focused on writing a web for a new writing piece, and others are reading through and revising their writing after a conference. One girl has a hard time getting started on her own, so Mrs. Layton asks the girl to move closer so that she can help motivate and monitor the student's work.

Because they had read through the writing the day before, both teachers are very aware of each student's stage in writing and can constantly monitor their progress. Today is one of the first days that the students have a choice to start writing something new if they are done. During the first six weeks of school, they received a great deal of scaffolded support in writing about a similar topic together. The challenge of writing independently is too much for one girl, who just sits and "thinks" (tapping a finger on the side of her

(continued on next page)

head). When Mrs. Layton asks Kaitlyn what she is writing, her eyes tear up and she says that she has nothing to write about. Before Kaitlyn gets upset, Mrs. Layton joins her and helps her look through her writing folder to see if she has any unfinished writing or ideas of topics to write about. Kaitlyn smiles and pulls out a letter she had started before but has never finished.

In another part of the room, two boys sit side by side and work on separate tasks, yet they motivate each other with their level of focus. Mrs. Meszaros continues working with the same group of students who had notes on their letters. "It says here that you need to add more details to this part of the letter," she says. "I think Mrs. Sistare would like to know more about your family when she reads your letter." Then she leans across the kidney-shaped table to help other students with ideas, revisions, and stretching out words. She sends Abbey to the editing center and explains that there is a checklist of things to do. Abbey joins Karl on the carpet near the editor's checklist and begins to look through the list the class is creating together (adding items to check as they learn more ways to edit).

■ **Word Study Time 1:30–2:00**

Although there targeted skills will be tested on the district assessment, these teachers realize that understanding why words are spelled the way they are versus teaching students to simply sound out words at the phoneme level and memorize words for a spelling quiz is a more useful approach. A snapshot of a typical day of word study in Mrs. Meszaros and Mrs. Layton's class follows.

The students get a dry-erase board, marker, and eraser and gather together in the meeting area. Mrs. Layton explains that they will do a couple of examples together and then they will each get a

chance to do some on their own. She says, "I'm going to ask you to spell a word. What is the first thing you would do to get all the sounds on the paper? If it's a word you know how to spell, you can just write it. If you don't know how, what can you do?" "Sound it out," says Darnell. Mrs. Layton answers, "Right. Show me how you can sound out the word *man*." Together the class chorally segments the word /m/ /a/ /n/ as they count out the sounds on their fingertips. Mrs. Layton says, "Yes there are three sounds." She records three dashes on the chart paper. The class segments the sounds in *man* again, but this time they stop and decide what letter(s) represent each sound and fill it in on the chart. The /m/ sound was easy but the short /a/ was difficult, so they pay close attention to the sound in the word and determine that it was the letter /a/ making the short a sound. To clarify, Mrs. Meszaros showed the students how they can feel the difference between short /i/ and short /a/ by placing their hand under their chin and feeling how far their chin drops for the short /a/ sound but not for the short /i/ sound. They finish filling in the word together on the chart and start with the next word.

She continues, "Go ahead and count out how many sounds are in the word *grab*." The room fills with chatter as students segment the word and try counting out the sounds on their hand. Together the class segments the word into four sounds, and Janelle puts four dashes on the chart to represent the sounds. Then Mrs. Lawton prompts the students to do the same on their dry-erase boards and lets them try filling in the letters for the sounds. Both teachers move around to assist students as they segment the word grab, and then Mrs. Layton fills in the dashes with the appropriate letter on the chart for the students to check. She is very explicit in her modeling and guided instruction as she clearly articulates the sounds. "We just learned these *r* blend sounds this week, so I know that they are tough," she tells one worried-looking student. Mrs. Meszaros circulates around the class, but mainly sits with two students who are in the prealphabetic stage and are having trouble segmenting sounds.

Mrs. Layton prompts the class: "The next word is tricky, so listen carefully. The word is *trip*. How many sounds do you think it has?" The students again try to segment it. Then Mrs. Meszaros asks students to hold up enough fingers to show how many sounds are in it. A variety of fingers go up and she calls on one student to share what the first two letters are that make the sound /tr/. The class decides that there are four sounds, so each student records four dashes on the dry-erase board. Although the students were very excited about using the dry-erase boards and markers, they had used them enough before not to be too distracted by them. One boy has trouble focusing, so he is asked to stop using his marker for a short time. He is invited to try again when he is ready (and he immediately shows he is ready). Again Mrs. Layton prompts students to try recording the letters that correspond to the sounds. "Look at my mouth and listen to the sounds.," she says Many of you wrote 'i' but some wrote 'e'. The sounds are close together. Listen as I say the sounds. Put your hand under your chin and feel how your chin moves when you make the short /e/ sound but not with the short /i/ sound. You can try this when you are spelling and not sure what letter it should be.

"Everything's in my lap and my ears are listening," Mrs. Layton states to prompt the students to get ready to listen to a new word. "Okay, listen to my word. The word is *prop*. If I put my feet up, I could prop them on the chair. *Prop*. Okay, sound it out and show me with your fingers how many sounds you hear. This time I'm going to let you do it all on your own." Students begin to work on their own to spell the word while both teachers move around and assist as needed, but waiting first to see what students can do on their own. Mrs. Meszaros asks, "Jason, how many sounds did you hear in *prop*? Four? Okay, everyone, let's try it together." They all segment it out together. Then they spell the word together. Mrs. Layton says, "I must tell you it looks very impressive up here," as she refers to the students sitting near her who have written the word. She asks Mrs. Meszaros, who confirms that the same thing is happening in the back of the room.

Mrs. Layton continues: "Here are the directions. Listen carefully. I'm going to say the word, and you are going to sound out the word, count the sounds in the word, write that many dashes on your board, and then fill in the letters. Remember that every word has to have at least one vowel. The letters *a, e, i, o,* and *u* are vowels." She records these letters on the chart. "The word is *grin*." The chatter begins as students stretch out the word, talk about how many sounds they hear, and write. Jason shows his board to Mrs. Meszaros for affirmation. Dyson asks to hear the word again so that he can make sure he hears the end of the word correctly. "Let's tap it out together. Then I will have everyone help me spell it because everyone did an awesome job writing this word," Mrs. Layton says. The students grin with pride as they spell the word *grin* together. Students are dismissed individually to return their materials and get their books from their book baskets in anticipation of meeting with their book buddies.

(continued on next page)

SPECIAL FEATURE 7.1 (continued)

■ Reading with a Friend 2:00–2:30 (once a week)

Once a week, Mrs. Roche-Cooper's class joins Mrs. Layton and Mrs. Meszaros's class for book buddy time. At the beginning of the year, students chose a buddy from the other class, and they now share their books, which they can now read, with each other every week. The teachers designed this weekly meeting time to create an authentic purpose for students to practice reading familiar text and to create positive relations across classrooms.

> Mrs. Meszaros reminds her class, "After your buddy reads his or her book to you, ask a few questions to see if he or she understand what was read. I think your buddy will be surprised you ask questions, and I bet your buddy can tell you what he or she was thinking while he or she was reading." Students move to their book baskets to pick out just the right book to share with their buddy. Shaya carefully looks through each title, pulls one out, and then picks another book instead to share before returning her basket to her cubby above the coatrack. As the students wait for their buddy from the other class, they whisper to a neighbor what their book is about.
>
> Soon Mrs. Roche-Cooper's students eagerly enter the room, books held tightly to their bodies, looking around the room for their buddies. No more directions are needed as the students begin sharing. Some sit knee to knee and eye to eye, others sit side by side. They all find their own place to share their reading. The room is buzzing with first-graders' voices reading. "What's this word?" Byron asks Chloe. "No way, I didn't know that," Zack tells D.J. "I like your reading," James tells Sara. "Where do you want to sit?" Jaymen asks Tywon. One boy leans over to get a closer look at the pictures in another boy's book. Two girls sit on the floor and then they decide to lie down and look up at the books. While Susan reads, Tanika listens and helps her check her words when she needs help. Giggles come out when Cole reads *The Wide-Mouth Frog* to Bobby, who has never heard the story before. The students read and share books for ten minutes. Then Mrs. Meszaros counts backwards from ten, giving the partners a chance to finish talking and get ready to listen. Mrs. Meszaros shares compliments with the students. "I noticed Patrick and Dylon were sitting knee to knee and eye to eye and having a conversation about their book after reading," she says. Mrs. Roche-Cooper shares a compliment about how one student put his arm around his buddy, showing how he was really paying attention. Mrs. Layton shares how two sets of buddies found two different ways to sit together and invites them to model a "fishbowl" as the rest of the boys and girls stand in a large circle to watch and learn. "Okay, Antonio, pick a page to read so we can all watch what happens. Look at how Kyron put his arm around Antonio, looked at the words on the page, and was quiet. Kyron was really showing Antonio that he was interested," she says. A second set of buddies moves to the middle, ready to model. "Stand back and admire what these two students are doing," Mrs. Roche-Cooper prompts the students. The two girls sit facing each other. Samantha read one page and then turned the book to show her buddy, Manny, the pictures. Manny was looking right at Samantha and listening until she got to look at the picture. "Manny really showed Samantha that she was listening and paying attention to her good reading.," the teacher says.
>
> Mrs. Meszaro's and Mrs. Layton's students put their books away, unprompted, and return to their desks as Mrs. Roche-Cooper's class lines up and walks out.

"Bye, Darion," a buddy calls out. It was exciting to see the new friendships developing across the classrooms and the sense of community and mutual respect expanding beyond their own classroom. These students also share the same recess time each day and have another chance to develop relationships across classrooms.

All three teachers believe that students need to learn how to be self-determining in their literacy activities by taking over choice in what text to read, what to write about, and what to discuss. These teachers also understand that students this age need to see models and receive support until they are ready to take over the responsibility for some of their own learning events. They know that students need instruction in the skills of reading (decoding, comprehension, fluency). Their new approach to teaching reading allows them to do it all. Figure 7.1 provides a pictorial representation of these teachers' blended approach to teaching reading.

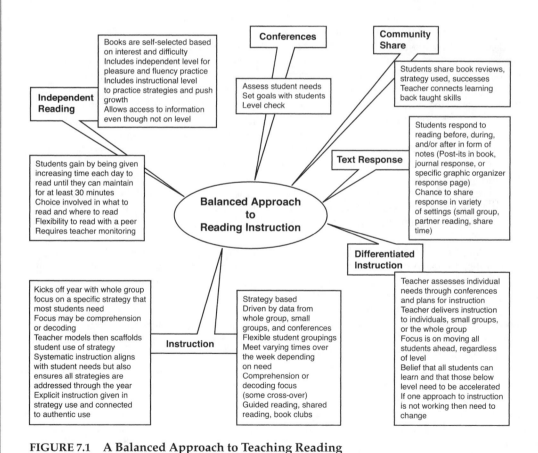

FIGURE 7.1   A Balanced Approach to Teaching Reading

SPECIAL FEATURE 7.2
The Immigrant Experience: An Integrated Unit

BY DEANNE McCREDIE

Over the year, my children had selected many topics for study. In this instance, however, topic selection was driven by my state's and district's standard curriculum-content mandates and by my interest in providing my students with meaningful multicultural experiences and learning events. Specifically, I wanted my students to consider America's ethnic diversity. This diversity is possibly America's greatest national challenge as people of all backgrounds learn to live together and to appreciate one another's contributions to American life. One reason that the United States is so diverse is that it was settled by immigrants; everyone who lives in the United States is an immigrant or a descendent of an immigrant. I wanted my students to understand that their own family history is part of the story of America's immigration.

During the period of 1820 to 1920, the United States experienced the largest wave of immigrants in its history. I wanted my students to understand these immigrants' experiences, why the immigrants chose to leave their homelands, and to realize that immigrants continue to come to the United States in search of a new life for many of the same reasons immigrants came nearly a century ago.

What did my students already know about immigration? I began the unit with an introductory discussion to assess their existing knowledge about the topic. I learned quickly that my children knew very little about immigration. Therefore, defining what they wanted to learn was difficult. I decided to begin the unit by having the students engage in the behaviors of social scientists—historians—by examining primary sources of historical information and by recording and interpreting their findings. As the students acquired some knowledge about immigration, I asked them what *else* they wanted to learn, and I used their questions and discoveries to guide the direction of our investigations.

I wanted the students to understand that primary sources give us a firsthand look at the past and that studying primary sources helps us experience history. These students were eight- and nine-year-olds, though. How might we begin? I decided to begin by examining primary sources that were significant to these children. I sent a letter to the children's parents requesting that they consider sending an item from their families' history to school for their child to share with the class. I suggested that the primary sources might include artifacts such as letters, journals, documents, photographs, and art.

The next day, the children arrived with many different pieces of their families' histories for sharing. A great deal of talk ensued. The artifact of greatest interest was an old glass bottle, probably dating from the Civil War. The students excitedly guessed whom the bottle might have belonged to and how it came to be buried in the ground. I closed this sharing session by asking, "Has anyone read *Homeplace* by Crescent Dragonwagon, which was written in 1993? It's a story about a family who discovers several artifacts buried in the ground and imagines to whom the items might have belonged. You'll find a copy of it in the library corner."

In addition to *Homeplace*, the children found many other books in the library corner dealing with the topic of immigration. During the class's reading workshop, the children read books they chose from among the books in that corner. As always, I conferred with the children, discussing their selections, learning what they had learned, and listening to them read selections they chose. The children also gathered in literature circles to discuss their books with other students. In addition, they raised questions, copied quotes they particularly liked, wrote drafts of letters to authors, and wrote drafts of letters to peers recommending their book (regular reading-response activities) in their reading-response journals.

In addition to their independent reading, my read-aloud sessions played a significant role in building the children's knowledge. I believed that the inclusion of children's literature would be crucial to the students' understanding of the immigrants' experiences. I selected books for specific purposes, all about children who had immigrated to the United States. Each time we read a story, we wrote the child's name on his or her homeland's flag, attached it to the child's homeland on a large map, marked the map indicating where the child landed in the United States, and connected the two locations with a string.

For example, I read and we discussed *Gooseberries to Oranges* (Cohen, 1982). First, however, we brainstormed a list of reasons why immigrants might choose to leave their homeland. What I thought would take five minutes took twenty minutes. The children had many thoughtful ideas on why people might leave their homeland. On another day, I read *Klara's New World* (Winter, 1992). The children commented on the similarities and differences between these two stories. To visualize the commonalities and differences, we created interconnecting circles, much like a Venn diagram.

I planned to have the children use learning logs to record their findings during our study. To illustrate how historians record their findings, I showed a slide of immigrants arriving on Ellis Island (photos, still and video, are important primary sources) and modeled how historians record their findings. I looked carefully at the slide. "What did this picture tell me about these immigrants?" I asked. I voiced some of my findings. I provided justification for each finding. I asked for the children's help. Together, we constructed a list of findings from this one slide, and I recorded our findings on the board. Then it was their turn. Over the remainder of our study, as we carefully considered the information in slides, in print, and in oral forms, we recorded our findings in our logs. Always, as the students wrote in their logs, I circulated about the classroom, speaking with them about their findings and learning much about their developing understandings of immigration.

By chance, there was a piece on the evening news about people immigrating from Mexico into the United States. Our focus to this point had been immigrants of the past; this news clip connected our study to today. As homework, the children were directed to skim newspapers and to watch the evening news broadcasts for information on immigration. (I brought copies of newspapers for those children who did not have access to them at home; none of my students lacked access to television.) Copies of the newspaper articles and notes taken while observing the news broadcasts were mounted on a classroom bulletin board. These became the topic of our morning current-events discussions. These articles and broadcasts verified that the items on our brainstormed list of reasons people immigrated to the United States in the past were equally relevant today. We decided that this discovery was important to record in our learning logs.

One child observed that it seemed as though when people immigrate, they do not bring much with them. "What would you choose to bring with you?" I asked. I brought a trunk to school the size of the trunks used by nineteenth-century immigrants. "If you could only bring what would fit in a trunk this size, what would you bring and why?" I asked. In groups, the children considered the possibilities. All groups concluded that money was important—even if it was not the currency of the new country—because any currency could be exchanged for appropriate currency. Perhaps stimulated by some of the family artifacts they had seen, the groups thought it would be important to bring things to remind them of their homeland and family (e.g., photographs, special gifts, favorite toys—small ones, of course). Also, they thought they would need food. One group thought that carrots would be a good idea; the thinking was that because no one likes them very much, they would not have to worry about their being stolen.

As the number of pieces of strings on our classroom map grew, the children's conversations around the map naturally turned to "My Pop-Pop immigrated [they liked to use that word,

(continued on next page)

immigrated] from Sweden, just like Klara." Children made mental and written notes to check on their families' heritages. The children suggested making flags with their names on them and attaching the flags to the map to denote their own families' original homelands. Soon, conversations around the map indicated that the children were noting the many different original homelands represented by the children in the class: Puerto Rico, someplace in Africa, Poland, Croatia, Ireland, England, and many more.

I had wanted to introduce the children to the conditions that early African immigrants (i.e., unwilling immigrants) faced when they were brutally forced to come to this country. The children's interest in their families' countries of origin provided a reason for this discussion. I read excerpts from *Days of Slavery* (Kallen, 1990); *The Story of the Henrietta Marie* (Sullivan, 1994), showing the photographs of the actual shackles from the sunken slave ship; and Alex Haley's *Roots* (1974), the section describing the conditions of the slave ship that brought Kunta to America. Many of the students' recordings in their learning logs indicated their genuine concern regarding the conditions on the slave ships.

A colleague's middle-school students had been studying the slave experience. The day following our examination of the evidence of the conditions of the slave ships, three of her students came to our class to make brief speeches summarizing their research on life in the United States for the African Americans who were sold into slavery and how people such as Harriet Beecher Stowe helped some slaves escape to freedom. We ended this session with the reading of *Nettie's Trip South* (Turner, 1987), an excellent story told from the point of view of a ten-year-old girl, and the singing of "Follow the Drinking Gourd" (Winter, 1988), an African American freedom trail song. (The drinking gourd is the Big Dipper, which points the direction northward at night.) Again, the children's learning logs indicated their concern with the plight of the early African immigrants. Throughout the unit, I contin-

ually reinforced the connection between the immigrant experience and the slave experience so the children would understand that both groups contributed to the hopes and dreams that have built the United States.

One reason that people have immigrated to this country has been to worship their god or gods as they pleased. (We had noted this reason on our early brainstorming list, an indication that the children recalled our Thanksgiving-time discussion of why the Pilgrims came to America.) I decided to reread *Molly's Pilgrim* (1983), a book the children had enjoyed in November. Before reading the story, I wrote the Yiddish words used in the story on the board: *malkeleh, shaynkeit, paskudnyaks*. As I pronounced them, Zoe proudly told the class what they meant. As I read the book, we stopped often to discuss such points as why Molly's English was not perfect, why the other children teased Molly and how that must have made Molly feel, who the Cossacks were, why Molly's family left Russia, what her class learned from Molly's doll, and Molly's definition of *Pilgrim*. I ended the presentation by indicating that we were going to make our own immigrant dolls to symbolize all the different people who came to live in the United States. Each student would select a different country and a specific person to research to understand how people in that country dressed when this immigrant came to the United States. They would use this information to dress their immigrant dolls. They would complete an immigration identification card for their dolls, with details such as the name of the immigrant, how old the immigrant was, the country of origin, the year of arrival, the reason(s) for immigrating, the conditions during their immigration journey, and the challenges faced when living in the United States. Finally, the students would use their research to write a piece that would tell their peers about their immigrant's journey. I closed the session with, "Think about the country of your choice overnight."

The next day, I posted a sign-up sheet for the students to note their selected countries. I provided

SPECIAL FEATURE 7.2 (continued)

sheets of poster board with the outline of a child traced on each board; various kinds of materials gathered from every neighbor of mine who sewed or knitted, to use for clothing and hair; informational books; an encyclopedia on CD-ROM; passes for trips to the library; and the children were off. Of course, I conferred, guided, formed discussion groups to resolve common problems or to consider clothing-customs discoveries made by children working on immigrants from similar parts of the world, negotiated material selections, conferred with writers, listened in on peer writing conferences, did minilessons addressing the needs I observed in the children's writing and researching, and so forth. The draft of one child's piece is presented in Figure 7.2.

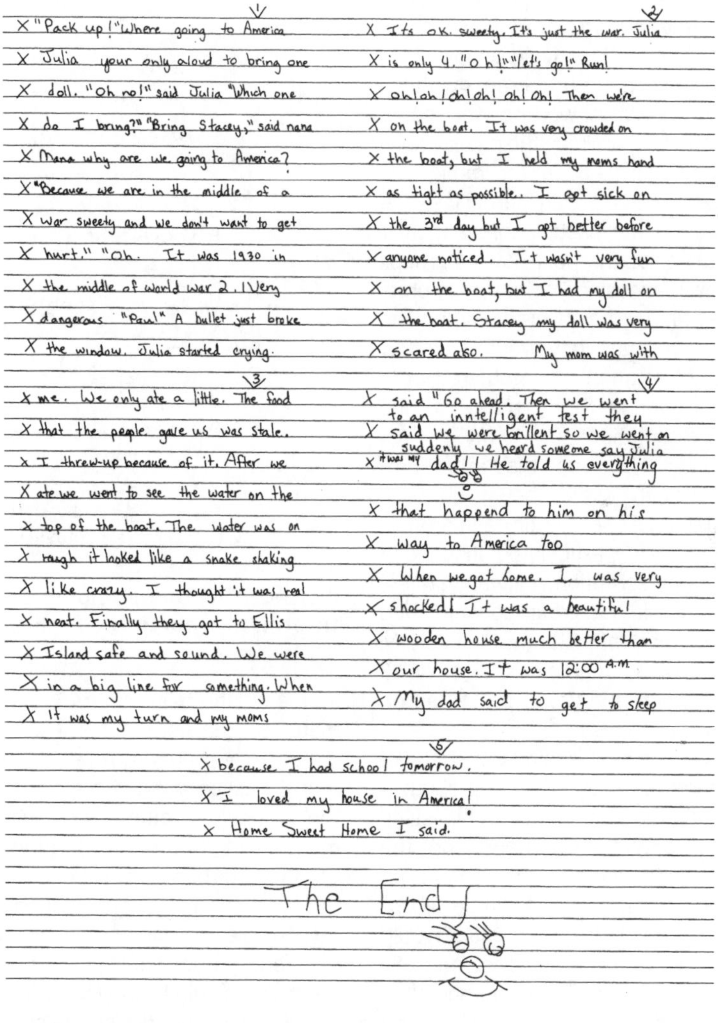
1
"Pack up!" "Where going to America
Julia your only aloud to bring one
doll. "Oh no!" said Julia "Which one
do I bring?" "Bring Stacey," said nana
Mana why are we going to America?
"Because we are in the middle of a
war sweety and we don't want to get
hurt." "Oh. It was 1930 in
the middle of world war 2. Very
dangerous "Paul" A bullet just broke
the window. Julia started crying.

2
It's ok. sweety. It's just the war. Julia
is only 4. "Oh!" "let's go!" Run!
oh! oh! oh! oh! oh! oh! Then we're
on the boat. It was very crowded on
the boat, but I held my moms hand
as tight as possible. I got sick on
the 3rd day but I got better before
anyone noticed. It wasn't very fun
on the boat, but I had my doll on
the boat. Stacey my doll was very
scared also. My mom was with

3
me. We only ate a little. The food
that the people gave us was stale.
I threw-up because of it. After we
ate we went to see the water on the
top of the boat. The water was on
rough it looked like a snake shaking
like crazy. I thought it was real
neat. Finally they got to Ellis
Island safe and sound. We were
in a big line for something. When
It was my turn and my moms

4
said "Go ahead. Then we went
to an inntelligent test they
said we were brillent so we went on
suddenly we heard someone say Julia
it was my dad!! He told us everything
that happend to him on his
way to America too
When we got home. I was very
shocked! It was a beautiful
wooden house much better than
our house. It was 12:00 A.M.
My dad said to get to sleep

5
because I had school tomorrow.
I loved my house in America!
Home Sweet Home I said.

The End

FIGURE 7.2 **The Story of Julia's Coming to America**

(continued on next page)

Our culminating experience for the unit was to take a bus trip to Ellis Island. Although everything we had studied and learned was in preparation for this trip, I wanted to review the use of photographs as primary historical sources. I marked three photographs in each of several different books (*Ellis Island: New Hope in a New Land* by W. J. Jacobs [1990], *Ellis Island: Echoes from a Nation's Past* edited by S. Jonas [1989], *Ellis Island: A Pictorial History* by B. Benton [1985], *Keepers of the Gate: A History of Ellis Island* by T. M. Pitkin [1925]), divided the children into eight groups, and gave each group three overhead transparencies. The children were to work cooperatively as historians, examining the photographs and recording their findings about the immigrants pictured on the overhead transparencies. The transparencies would be used to present their discoveries to the class the next day. As groups finished their observations and writing, they practiced their presentation. The children worked one day longer than I thought they would, carefully considering the information they gathered from the photographs, writing their sentences, and practicing their presentations.

One day later, the groups made their presentations. Photographs were shown; observations were read and justified. After each group's presentation, the class participated in an oral evaluation of their presentation, answering questions such as "What did this group do well?" and "What might they do better next time?" Generally, the presentations were marvelous. (Figure 7.3 shows the information one group presented on its overhead transparencies.)

Because we would be seeing the Statue of Liberty, we needed to learn something about it before we boarded the buses. I began by asking the children what they already knew about the Statue of Liberty. I listed the few known points on the board. I read *The Story of the Statue of Liberty* by Betsey and Guilio Maestro (1986). "Would the Statue of Liberty fit in this classroom?" I asked. Showing the students a meterstick, I asked the students to estimate the height of the

1st picture.   ELLIS ILAND

1. The first thing we noticed was that you can not fit another person on the ship

2. Next we saw that most women are wearing scarfs on their heads.

3. Most of the men are wearing top hats or some sort of hat on his head, because of his religion.

4. We also noticed that the ship was huge! (As you can see.)

5. You know, if I were on that ship I would be so confused!! (Just think how they feel.)

2nd picture.

1. The thing we really noticed most about this picture was that there is a huge American Flag on top of the front wall.

2. The Immigrants are waiting on benches or standing in long lines inside the railings

3. We also noticed that the ceiling is large and round, like a dome.

4. These are lots of huge windows.

FIGURE 7.3   Using Photographs to Gather Information about the Past

Statue of Liberty in meters. I recorded their estimates on the board. Then I told them that the statue is one hundred meters tall. "How tall is that?" I asked. Although guesses were offered, the students seemed very unsure. We would measure the Statue of Liberty to exact scale on the grass outside the school building. I divided the class into four groups and made each group responsible for laying out a section of the statue (e.g., one group would mark the distance from the statue's chin to the top of the flame, another the distance from the statue's waist to its chin).

I gave each group a container of Popsicle sticks. They were to place their meterstick on a beginning line and insert the Popsicle stick into the ground at the end of the meterstick. Then they would butt the meterstick to the Popsicle stick and place a second Popsicle stick at the end of the meterstick. The process would be repeated until they had reached the top of their section. Then the group cut a piece of twine exactly as long as from their beginning line to their last Popsicle stick. When all groups had completed their tasks, we carefully laid the four pieces of twine end to end. The students exclaimed, "Wow! That's how big the Statue of Liberty is!" and "It looks as big as two eighteen-wheelers!!"

Fortunately, I had enlisted the assistance of several middle school students to help with our measuring. This hands-on measurement activity was meaningful to the children, but they definitely needed helpers. The next day, I used the middle school students' participation to teach the students about the social convention of writing a thank-you note when someone does something that pleases you. We talked about what might be included in a thank-you note. Interested students wrote thank-you notes.

Before leaving the unit, I wanted to pull the discussion back to our classroom and the twenty-four people who lived in it. During a read-aloud session, I read *Make a Wish, Molly* (Cohen, 1995). We live in a pluralistic culture in our society and in our classroom. We talked about what that meant.

We also talked about several metaphors that describe our pluralistic culture: salad bowl, melting pot, and patchwork quilt. We decided that our classroom was a patchwork quilt. Our class was composed of different students with different backgrounds. We decided to make a patchwork quilt to symbolize our cohesiveness. Alone, each square would be lovely; together, all the squares would be a wonderful illustration of how we work together, just like how all the immigrants had to work together to make our country. The children decorated their squares with symbols telling about themselves and their heritage. Once the squares were sewn together, we proudly displayed the quilt in our classroom.

At the end of May, we boarded the buses for the long bus ride to Ellis Island and the Statue of Liberty. Throughout this unit of study, my students read, wrote, listened, talked, and observed. The materials in the classroom and in the school's library supported their investigations. Although the classroom schedule suggested reading workshop, writing workshop, social studies, and so forth, from the children's perspective, the day was seamless. Our investigation of immigration flowed across and was embedded within the various curriculum content areas. Although I had outlined goals and objectives for this interdisciplinary unit, the students' questions and observations guided our study as we learned together about the dreams and hopes that have built the United States.

LESSONS FROM AN EXPERIENCED SIXTH-GRADE TEACHER

Teaching writing in the ways described above does not just "happen." Teachers must thoughtfully consider the many instructional aspects discussed in Chapter 6. In this section, readers will observe how Mr. Sousa organizes and conducts his reading program with his sixth-grade students. We again encourage readers to make text-to-text connections between this description of the teaching of reading to upper elementary students with the previous descriptions of the teaching of reading to first-grade and third-grade students. How does the students' ages affect the teacher's teaching? How does the upper grade experience reflect the blended practices presented in Figure 7.1?

Mr. Sousa is part of a sixth-grade team that organizes the students' day into two major parts: the humanities class, which teaches the Arizona State social studies, and language arts standards, which are taught through careful curriculum integration (Figure 7.4) and the math–science inquiry lab. During the two-hour humanities block, Mr. Sousa teaches reading, writing, and oral communication skills by using social studies as the vehicle for this content. He has found this approach to be highly effective and efficient because it makes the best use of the limited time he has available to teach the course objectives for all these subjects.

He teaches this content to two sets of students: one class of thirty students in the morning and one class in the afternoon. On Monday and Tuesdays, he uses his time for text study and independent related reading. On Wednesdays and Thursdays, he uses his time for writers' workshop and research writing, and on Fridays, he uses his time for multiple assessment and group project work. He shares the students with Ms. Selina, who teaches the math and science content also using two, two-hour daily time blocks. The students come from predominately lower-socioeconomic homes, and, for many, English is their second language. The students' reading levels range from a third-grade to a ninth-grade level. The students are heterogeneous grouped overall, but both teachers often group homogenously to teach specific skills.

Typical Monday and Tuesday Schedule

8:15–8:30.   Attendance, lunch count, settling in.

8:30–8:45.   During the last two weeks, the students read the sixth-grade social studies text, which provided a basic foundation for the study of early civilizations. Mr. Sousa begins each day with a focused minilesson or a minilesson review. Today, during this time, he reviews the use of a graphic organizer to help the students' structure and summarize the information presented in the text (Figure 7.5). He also shows them how the graphic organizer helps them compare and contrast the different components of information.

8:45–9:00.   Independent reading. Because of the students' different reading levels and competency in speaking and reading English, Mr. Sousa found that they focus better on the social studies text when he organized their independent reading time into fifteen-minute segments. During this fifteen-minute segment, he asks the students to use their Post-it notes to identify unknown vocabulary words.

9:00–9:15.   After a few minutes of finalizing their Post-it notes, Mr. Sousa asks the students to share their vocabulary words. He writes their words on large word cards and asks all students to provide definitions. In most cases, someone in the class will offer an appropriate definition. Mr. Sousa gives the student who offers the correct definition the word card; that student gets to put the definition on the

FIGURE 7.4 **Sixth-Grade Language Arts, Social Studies Curriculum Map: First Quarter**

Student Skills	Teacher Methodology	Social Studies Content

Reading

Decode new words in print

Decoding multisyllable words (Prefix, suffix, root word, dividing in syllables, and context clues)

Use comprehension skills

Vocabulary development
Self-monitoring strategies
Individual comprehension strategies

- Visualizing
- Summarizing
- Predicting
- Questioning to check for understanding
- Questioning to clarify
- Identifying big ideas and themes
- Making text-to-text connections
- Making text-to-self connections
- Making text-to-world connections
- Identify the main idea
- Cause and effect
- Description
- Compare and contrast
- Use of charts, graphs, sidebars, and structure (mainly with expository text)
- Mapping (graphic organizers)

Teacher Methodology

- Reciprocal teaching
- Independent reading
- Guided reading (teacher directed)
- Shared reading (partners)
- Paired reading
- Read-alouds
- Rereading
- Literature circles (substantive discussion)
- Whole group (substantive discussion)
- Guess the covered word
- Graphic organizers
- Response journals
- Active reading activity (Post-it notes)

Social Studies

Comparing early civilizations

- Aztec
- Egyptian
- Roman
- Greek
- Incan
- Chinese
- Informational texts

How did early civilizations develop:

- Architecture
- Agriculture
- Domesticate animals
- Transportation

What innovations and inventions did these civilizations develop?

What religion did these civilization practice?

What supported these civilizations' economic system?

- Money
- Trade

Did these civilizations have a form of writing?

(continued)

FIGURE 7.4   (Continued)

Student Skills	Teacher Methodology	Social Studies Content

Writing

Grammar

- Adverbs (develop)
- Conjunctions (developing)
- Prepositions (developing)
- Pronoun agreement (developing)
- Quotations (developing)

- Generate, draft, revise, edit, publish different forms of written expression
  - Fiction
  - Research papers/reports
  - Comparative/contrast
  - Paragraph writing (topic sentence, supporting details & concluding sentence)
  - Short stories (Project Read Story form)/ Narrative
  - Book reviews

Oral Presentation

- Organize, sequence, practice, and deliver an oral presentation on the social studies project incorporating the skills of voice, projection, inflection, fluency and appropriate nonverbal language.
- Use courtesy and consideration in communication situations.

Grammar

- Language book
- Teacher created activities
- District grammar book

Writing

- Writer's Workshop (writer's process)
  - Brainstorm
  - Graphic organizer
  - First draft
  - Conference (teacher & peer)
  - Revise
  - Second draft
  - Edit)
- Journal writing
- Modeling
- Minilessons

Writing

- Social studies project and research paper

Spelling

Content vocabulary will be added to spelling lists

- Social Studies presentations

FIGURE 7.5   Graphic Organizer

Civilization	Where Located	Time Frame of Civilization	Type of Government	Innovations and Inventions	Religious Beliefs and Practices
Aztec					
Roman					
Greek					
Incan					
Chinese					
Egyptian					

card and then sign his or her name. (To encourage the students to identify unknown vocabulary, Mr. Sousa gives the students extra credit points for each word card.) If the class cannot offer a definition, then Mr. Sousa uses the dictionary to find the definition. He reads the various definitions, and the students select the most appropriate response. Mr. Sousa believes that this extra effort to build vocabulary has had a positive effect on the students' oral language and reading comprehension. He also uses these words to build the unit spelling list.

9:15–9:30.   Mr. Sousa asks the students to work in pairs to complete the components of the graphic organizer. While they do so, he circulates among the students, occasionally redirecting student behavior. For the most part, however, he offers vocabulary and language support to various students. Mr. Sousa has discovered that when the students know that they will be discussing their reading, they pay more attention to the text. For the students who are less confident in reading and English, the opportunity to talk helps them comprehend the text.

9:30–9:45.   Once again, Mr. Sousa redirects his students to the text. Once again, they use their Post-it notes, but this time he has directed them to focus on the question, What innovations and inventions did the Egyptian culture developed? Mr. Sousa believes that by guiding their reading through the use of focus questions, he helps them learn to take notes, which also provides a basis for small group discussion. As the students read, Mr. Sousa monitors their behavior and offers decoding help where needed.

9:45–10:00.   Mr. Sousa asks the students to complete their graphic organizer for the Egyptian section. He encourages the students to work in pairs and to compare their answers. As the students work, he circulates to make sure that they are staying focused on the task at hand. After a few minutes, he draws the class's attention to the large graphic organizer chart he has placed on the wall. The class shares their responses as Mr. Sousa writes the information in the appropriate squares.

10:00–10:30.   Related independent reading time. The students have already determined which civilization they wish to study. They have already gone to the library and/or downloaded information from the computer to study their civilization further. Some students are reading historical fiction, others are reviewing expository texts. Each group of five or six students meets together to briefly review what they are reading and to read further. The students' use an independent reading guide (Figure 7.6) to help them document and guide their reading.

During this time, Mr. Sousa monitors the groups briefly to make sure that the students are focused on their task. After the students begin reading, Mr. Sousa calls one or two students back to conduct a running record. His goal is to conduct a running record on each student every month. Although it is a daunting task, Mr. Sousa believes that it helps him guide his students to select appropriate difficulty-level texts and also helps him determine the content of the focus lessons he may conduct.

By 10:30, the students need to pack up their materials and go to other classes. The independent reading text and the reading guide go into their backpacks. Their reading guides are reviewed by Mr. Sousa and their peers each Friday. Independent reading at home is expected.

FIGURE 7.6   Independent Reading Guide

Name_____ Date_____

I'm reading

Text Title	Author	Publication Date
What pages have you read? Identifying big ideas and themes.		
What text-to-text connections can you make?		
What text-to-self connections can you make?		
What text-to-world connections can you make?		
What vocabulary do you need help with?		

Typical Wednesday and Thursday Schedule

8:15–8:30. Attendance, lunch count, settling in.

8:30–9:00. The civilization groups begin to meet to review their research projects. Each person in the group is responsible for one of the following topics:

a. What innovations and inventions did this civilization develop?
b. What religion did this civilization practice?
c. What supported this civilization's economic system?
d. Did this civilization have a form of schooling, writing, numbers?
e. What was life like for a commoner in this civilization?

The students have been collecting information about these subjects. They have gone to the school library, have conducted searches in the school's computer lab, and have visited the public library, where they checked out materials (including some DVDs and videos) about the topic. During this half hour, Mr. Sousa has given them the task of sharing the materials and information they have collected. The student groups buzz (somewhat loudly) as they share the information they have collected. Across the room, Mr. Sousa hears "I read that, too!" or "I found something that you could use." One group approaches Mr. Sousa to see if it could schedule a DVD player to review a program together.

9:00–9:30. Mr. Sousa reviews the parts of a research paper (Figure 7.7). To help the students learn about the parts of the paper, he has given them a copy of an excellent research paper that was written last year. He reviews the components of the paper step by step. The students are somewhat overwhelmed by the total research paper, but he reminds them to "take one step at a time."

9:30–10:00. After reviewing the parts, Mr. Sousa returns to paragraph writing. He puts a good example of a paragraph on the overhead projector. He highlights

FIGURE 7.7   Parts of a Research Paper

- Title page
- List of figures
- Abstract
- Outline
- Body of the report
  - An introduction
  - Background information
  - Body of the paper
  - A conclusion
- Appendices
- Works Cited

the parts of the paragraph (topic sentence, supporting details, and concluding sentence) in different colors. Next, he gives the students a worksheet that has three different paragraphs. He asks them to identify the topic sentences in each paragraph. As the group moves to identifying supporting detail sentences, they realize that the second paragraph is very weak. Mr. Sousa asks the students to work in pairs to write supporting details. Within a few minutes, the students offer examples of supporting detail sentences. Finally, Mr. Sousa talks about the importance of a concluding sentence. The students once again find that one of the examples is very weak, and he asks them to rewrite the sentence and share with a partner.

10:00–10:30.   Mr. Sousa asks the students to begin to draft the first part of their reports, using their outlines that they developed last week. He reminds the students that they are in the first draft mode. He encourages them to get their ideas on paper and reminds them that tomorrow they will have time to work with a peer editor.

Typical Friday Schedule

8:15–8:30.   Attendance, lunch count, settling in.

8:30–9:00.   Spelling assessment and vocabulary matching. The words were selected by the students (see Monday–Tuesday schedule). Students complete the test, grade each other's work, and turn the papers in to Mr. Sousa.

9:00–10:30.   On Fridays, Mr. Sousa conducts writing conferences and running records as needed. The students sign up for ten-minute blocks of time. The remainder of the time the students work to complete the first drafts of each segment of their research report.

At the beginning of the semester, Mr. Sousa had difficulty managing student behavior during Friday work sessions, yet he continued to persist in his work expectations. Likewise, he also assigned lunch detention for students who misbehaved during this time. Within a month, nearly all the behavior challenges had faded.

SUMMARY

Implementing a high-quality reading instructional program requires thoughtful planning, management, and organization as well as an ongoing and ever-changing understanding of student strengths, interests, and needs. For a blended approach to reading instruction like those described in this chapter to be successful, the teacher must purposefully structure a classroom environment that supports complex literacy and language communities and addresses each student's instructional needs. High-quality blended reading programs include all the features, carefully organized so that the teacher looks more like an orchestra conductor, identified in Figure 7.1.

■ *What organizational strategies do teachers use to implement a blended reading program?*

Teachers thoughtfully organize large blocks of time to begin to organize their teaching of reading. Teachers need to develop weekly schedules that consistently structure time for independent reading; whole group, small group, and individual instruction; and community sharing. Teachers must also offer a number of procedural lessons that help students learn to be contributing members of the classroom learning community.

■ *What types of grouping strategies are used in a blended reading program?*

Teachers who use the blended approach to reading instruction usually use both homogeneous (students with similar needs and abilities) and heterogeneous (students with different skills and abilities) grouping strategies. Teachers may also use whole group or small group instruction, or provide individual instruction, depending on the needs of the students and the content that needs to be taught.

■ *How do teachers provide skill instruction in a blended reading program?*

Teachers usually deliver skill instruction through lessons. These lessons evolve from readers' immediate needs and concerns, or they may be based on teacher choice or district goals and objectives. There are three broad categories of lessons, including procedures for managing the instructional time, such as how to choose interesting books; and how to select "just-right" books or skill lessons, such as what students can do when they meet an unknown word or how to determine the main idea.

■ *How do teachers help students construct meaning and expand their understanding of text?*

High-quality reading instruction provides limitless possibilities for observant teachers to extend children's understanding of text. It can be accomplished during all components of a blended reading program: one-on-one teacher conferences, small group instruction, and whole group instruction.

LINKING KNOWLEDGE TO PRACTICE

1. Interview a teacher about grouping practices for reading instruction. How does this teacher determine his or her students' reading abilities? Does this teacher use a running record to evaluate a student's independent and instructional reading levels? How often does the teacher assess student progress? How does the teacher use these data to create groups?

2. Visit a classroom during the time designated for reading instruction. Take field notes like those gathered by Sara McCraw. Compare your notes with those taken by Sara. Did the students engage in independent reading? Did the teacher hold individual conferences with the students? Were small groups of students pulled together for instruction based on their skill needs? In what ways did the teacher differentiate instruction? What conclusions can be reached about the observed teacher's teaching of reading? Are these students being offered a blended reading program?

3. Observe a classroom during the teaching of social studies or science. What reading, writing, and speaking skills has the teacher integrated into the social studies or science lesson?

···· ▬▬▬▬▬▬▬▬▬▬▬▬▬▬▬▬▬▬▬▬▬▬▬▬▬▬▬▬▬▬▬▬▬

CHAPTER 8

TEACHING WRITING
THE WORKSHOP WAY

Writing and writers are important in Deirdra Aikens's classroom. Ms. Aikens invites her students to join her on the rug for a writing lesson. She begins by saying, "I know you've been waiting for this! I'm going to reveal the next great beginning. Ta-dah!!" She uncovers the next great beginning statement on the Great Beginnings chart and reads:

SETTING THE MOOD/CREATING THE SETTING

Example: It was a deep, dark, snowy Christmas Eve and presents were under the tree.

Referring to the example, she asks, "Where do you see it happening?" The students respond. "What could come after that?" Again, the students respond. She continues: "I've pulled together some beginnings from three of our favorite books. I really like how these authors started their pieces by setting the mood and creating an image of the setting. I'll read each beginning. You tell me where you see the story happening and how it feels." With that, she reads the opening sentence of Tar Beach *by Faith Ringgold. "What did you see when you heard this sentence?" she asks. The students offer responses about the image the sentence created in their minds. Ms. Aikens accepts their answers and then shows the illustration that accompanies the sentence. "Was the picture in your head like the image created by the illustrator?" She moves on and repeats the process with the two other stories. "This is a different kind of beginning, isn't it? It's different from the other beginnings on our list. When you go back to your writing folders today, take a look at an old piece. Could using this kind of beginning to make one of your old pieces better? If you start a new piece, think about using this kind of a beginning. Will this beginning work in all pieces?" The students answer no in unison. "Of course not!" Ms. Aikens says. "You've got to think like a writer and make decisions about which kind of beginning to use. Team leaders, please get the writing folders out. Green folder writers, let's do a quick status of the class." Ms. Aikens calls on each green folder writer, gets a response ("start a new piece," "edit my piece"), and sends the writers off to write. The writing lesson is over.*

Writers return to their desks, where their writing folders have been placed. Some sit down, others move to be near a friend. One student selects the sharing chair as her writing place. In less than two minutes, all writers are writing. Students talk with each other while they write. Ms. Aikens begins a conference with a red folder writer; Monday is red folder writers' teacher–student conference day. Too quickly, the writing time ends and the students return their bulging folders by color group to the hanging file, all except the blue folder writers.

Blue folder writers share today. A blue folder writer sits in the sharing chair. His team leader stands beside him. The writer reads his piece. The team leader calls on a student to summarize. A student responds, and then several students and Ms. Aikens offer their comments. The team leader calls on another student to praise the author. The student responds, and then several students offer specific examples of what they like about the piece. The team leader calls on another student to question the author. The student responds, and then other students and Ms. Aikens state their questions. The team leader calls on a student to offer a suggestion. This student responds, and then another student offers a suggestion. Writing workshop is over.

This is writing workshop as it happens in Ms. Aikens's classroom every day for forty-five minutes. During writing workshop, the students use the writing process, the same process used by young and old writers. Some are prewriting. Some are looking off into space to discover what they know enough about to write about. Some immediately begin writing; they seem not to know what they have to say until they see the words appear on the paper. Some look at the list of topics they made for days like this one, days when they need an idea on what to write about. Others are making a graphic organizer or a list. Other students are writing their "sloppy copy" or first draft. While they write, they pause to read and reread what they wrote. Still other students cross out words; they draw arrows to shift the position of sentences. These students are revising. They change the spelling of a word. These students are editing. Finally, other students are recopying their revised and edited piece; they are publishing or doing their final draft. These students are using the writing process to write their ideas.

These students know what it means to be a writer.

BEFORE READING THIS CHAPTER, THINK ABOUT . . .

- Yourself as a writer. How do you prewrite? Do you make an outline or a graphic organizer, mull your thoughts over in your mind for several days, or just begin writing? Do you have a favorite writing tool, such as a special pen or the computer? Do you make lots of revisions while you write? Do you edit while you write?

- Writing instruction in your elementary school years. Did you write about topics of your choice? Did you share your writing with your peers? Did your teacher confer with you about your writing? Did you publish your writing?

- The kinds of writing you did in your elementary school years. Did you write stories? Did you write research reports? Did you write persuasive essays?

■ How your writing was graded. Did your teacher write congratulatory words like "Good job!" or use a rubric to give you specific feedback about how effectively you used various writing traits? DId your teacher put a grade on your paper? Did your teacher encourage you to self-assess your writing?

FOCUS QUESTIONS

■ What are the essentials of writing workshop?
■ What are the components of writing workshop?
■ How do teachers teach and what kinds of lessons might they teach during writing workshop?
■ What is the structure of a writing conference?
■ How might teachers assess their students' writing development?

■ ■ ■ ■ ■

BOX 8.1
DEFINITION OF TERMS

analytical scoring: Scoring each key component of a piece of writing, trait by trait (organization, development or ideas, sentence variety, voice, mechanics).

conference: Conversation between a teacher and a student, or between or among peers, about a piece of writing.

criteria: Language used to describe how the writing traits look at various performance levels.

editing: Correcting mechanical errors in writing, such as spelling, punctuation, and grammar.

focus lesson: Whole-class lessons on writing that typically occur at the beginning of writing workshop.

holistic scoring: Scoring by considering how all the qualities of the writing (organization, ideas or development, voice, mechanics) work together to achieve an overall effect. Scorers judge the piece based on their general impression of the piece.

primary trait scoring: Scoring based on the degree of presence of the primary, or most important, traits within the piece of writing. The primary traits vary by purpose (to persuade, to express, to inform) and audience.

revising: Making changes (adding, moving, deleting) in the content of a writing piece.

rubric: Criteria that describe student performance at various levels of proficiency.

trait: Qualities of writing (ideas, organization, voice).

writing process: The recursive behaviors all writers, regardless of age, engage in (prewriting, writing or drafting, revising, editing, final draft or publishing).

writing workshop: a time in the schedule when all students meet to study the art and craft of writing.

THE ESSENTIALS OF WRITING WORKSHOP

"Writing workshop" was first described by Donald Graves (1983) in his book *Writing: Teachers and Children at Work*. During writing workshop, all members of the workshop meet to study intensively the art and craft of writing. Recently, Graves (2004) reviewed the fundamentals of the teaching of writing and identified the constants that two decades of research have confirmed are central to the teaching of writing. In the following section, we describe these essential features of a quality writing program.

Children Need Time to Write

Children need a block of time to write. Donald Graves (1983) and Lucy Calkins (1983) recommended that teachers provide at least three, although five would be better, writing workshops each week, with each workshop lasting from forty-five to sixty minutes. Regular, frequent times for writing are required to help children develop as writers. When children know to expect writing workshop, they begin to rehearse their writing ideas between workshops. They come to school with ideas for topics and text construction. As Katie Wood Ray (2001) explains:

> It takes lots and lots of time over the course of years for writers to get the experience they need to become good writers. Along the way, writers need time to just write and write—a lot of it won't be very good, but all of it gives writers experience When it comes to TIME, quantity is what matters. (pp. 9–10)

Some teachers groan, "*Where* can I find time in my already overloaded daily schedule? There is no room for yet another activity!" Ralph Fletcher and JoAnn Portalupi (2001) suggest that, if the schedule is truly full, then teachers figure out what activities writing workshop could replace. Instead of teaching punctuation, capitalization, spelling, or handwriting as separate subjects, these teachers could use the time previously devoted to these language arts skills for writing workshop. They will see their students gaining competence in these mechanical skills because their students will be using the skills again and again as they construct texts for different purposes and audiences. In addition, in writing workshop teachers will see their students listening, speaking, and reading. Here all the language arts are integrated into one meaningful, purposeful activity: writing.

Children Need Regular Response to Their Writing from the Teacher, Their Peers, and Others

Writing is a social act. Through interactions with others, writers come to understand the needs of their audience. Because writers write about things they know, they make decisions about what information to include from their knowledgeable perspective. In sharing their writing with an audience, writers sometimes come to understand what information is needed to make their topic clear to an audience, or they watch the glazed look in their listeners' eyes and realize that too much detail has been provided, or they recognize the need to rearrange the information. Children want to share their writing with peers, know what their peers are writing, and ask for assistance with the construction of their text. Knowing this, writing workshop teachers cluster children at tables or at desks that have been moved together. Most writing and *conferring* (talking with peers about writing) occur among the children in these clusters. This talk is not just any kind of talk; it is talk about the writers' texts. Writers need listeners who stop their writing, listen intently, and say, "Oh, your description of your dog is really good" or "Your characters' talk, your dialogue? Well, it sounds just like what teenagers would say" or "Hmmm. I don't get it. I'm confused here."

Children also want, and need, to talk with their teachers about their writing. They need to talk with a teacher who listens carefully to them, who makes considered honest responses to the writer's questions and statements, who asks genuine questions, and who supports the writer to become a better writer. Later in this chapter, we provide details of how teachers can engage in meaningful conversations, how to confer, with their young writers.

Children Need to Publish Their Writings

A key element of a quality writing program—that children need to publish their writings—is closely related to the above fundamental element. Writing is meant for others to read. Yes, we write for ourselves, but few of us would sustain our effort if no one ever read our writings, if no one ever said, "Hey, I really enjoyed reading that piece!" Publishing need not be a complicated procedure. Children can publish by mounting their writings on a specially labeled bulletin board, by printing the final draft in a format that would allow the pages to be folded into a book, by joining with other writers to create a newsletter or newspaper, by stapling pages between two sheets of construction paper, and so forth. In Trade Secret 8.1, Gaysha Beard provides several suggestions of magazines that accept children's writing.

By writing for real audiences, children come to think of themselves as authors. Further, writing for an unknown audience, one that is not present to ask clarifying questions, results in children developing an understanding for others' point of view.

Children Need to Choose Most of the Topics They Write About

Writers write about things they know. For those just beginning to be writers, the personal narrative (telling their own stories) is the easiest kind of writing. Children need teachers who help them see that they can write about the everyday

TRADE SECRET 8.1
Magazines That Accept Children's Work

BY GAYSHA BEARD

Acorn (The)
1530 Seventh St., Rock Island, IL 61201. (Grades K–12.) Publishes fiction, poetry, and artwork.

Bear Essential News for Kids
1037 Alvernon Way, Suite 150, Tucson, AZ 85711. (Grades Pre-K–7.) Distributed without charge to children in Arizona, California, and Georgia. Publishes all types of children's creative writing. www.bearessentialnews.com.

Bitterroot Poetry Magazine
P.O. Box 489, Spring Glen, NY 12483. (Grades K12.) Publishes poetry, and black and white art.

Boodle: By Kids for Kids
P.O. Box 1049, Portland, IN 47371. (Ages 6–12.) Formerly called *Caboodle*, this quarterly magazine is full of funny, imaginative stories, poetry and drawings. There are more than fifty contributions per issue.

Boy's Life
1325 Walnut Hill Lane, Irving, TX 75038. (For all boys.) Official youth magazine of the Boy Scouts of America. Publishes stories, jokes, and poems. www.boyslife.org.

Children's Better Health Institute
1100 Waterway Blvd., Indianapolis, IN 46202 (Ages 2–12.) Publishes seven magazines for children readers— *Turtle*, *Humpty Dumpty*, *Children's Playmate*, *Jack and Jill*, *Child Life*, *Children's Digest*, and *U.S. Kids*. Each award-winning magazine is devoted to an instructional approach that combines fun with learning. Publishes children's poems, jokes, artwork, and much more. http://cbhi.org/cbhi/magazines/index.shtml.

Children's Express
20 Charles St. New York, NY 10014. (Ages 8–18.) Through a unique learning through journalism program, young people research and write stories on issues that are important to them for publication in national and local newspapers, magazines, television, and radio. The twice-weekly column is distributed by UPI to 2,500 newspapers around the world. www.childrens-express.org/.

chixLIT
P.O. Box 12051, Orange, CA 92859. (Ages 7–17.) Publishes poems, short stories, reviews, rants, raves, love letters, song lyrics, journal entries, artwork, photography and more. www.chixlit.com.

Cobblestone
30 Grove Street, Suite C, Peterborough, NH 03458. (Ages 8–14.) Issues examine a part of America's past. Publishes children's nonfiction writing experiences related to a monthly theme. www.cobblestonepub.com/.

Creative Kids
P.O. Box 8813, Waco, TX 76714-8813. (Ages 8–14.) Provides students with an authentic experience. Contains the best stories, poetry, opinion, artwork, games and photography by kids. www.prufrock.com.

Custom Education Inc.
P.O. Box 340596, Tampa, FL 33694-0596. (Ages 6–12.) Publishes fiction, nonfiction, poetry, recipes, crafts, artwork,

(continued on next page)

and photography. This magazine wants to inspire, educate, and create an outlet in which students can display their creativity. www.customed.com.

Dragon Fly: E/W Haiku Quarterly
Middlewood Press, P.O. Box 11236, Salt Lake City, UT 84118. (All ages.) Publishes students' original haikus and written articles about haikus.

Dream/Girl
P.O. Box 51867, Durham, NC 27717. (Girls 18 and younger.) Provides girls with the most informative and interesting arts and literary information around. Publishes stories, poems, book reviews, essays, and artwork for this bimonthly arts magazine. www.dgarts.com.

Highlights for Children
803 Church St., Honesdale, PA 18431. (Grades Pre-K–12.) Publishes children's letters and original drawings, poetry, and stories. Accepts jokes and riddles selected by readers. www.highlights.com.

National Geographic Kids
1145 Seventeenth St. NW, Washington, DC 20036-4688. (Ages 8–14.) Publishes children's artwork, jokes, and captions. www.nationalgeographic.com/ngkids.

New Moon: The Magazine for Girls & Their Dreams
New Moon Publishing Inc., 34 Superior St., Duluth, MN 55802. (Ages 8–14.) Publishes to educate and excite girls and teens about the wonders of the world. Accepts nonfiction, fiction, artwork, and photography by girls. www.newmoon.org.

Potato Hill Poetry
6 Pleasant Street South, Apt. 2, Natick, MA 01760. (Grades 1–12.) Publishes poems in this quarterly magazine. www.potatohill.com/.

Potluck Children's Literary Magazine
P.O. Box 546, Deerfield, IL 60015. (Ages 8–16.) A not-for-profit quarterly magazine. Publishes fiction, nonfiction, poetry, and book reviews. www.potluckmagazine.org.

Skipping Stones
Multicultural Children's Magazine, P.O. Box 3939, Eugene, OR 97403-0939. (Children younger than 18.) International, minorities, and underrepresented populations receive priority. Publishes fiction short stories, plays, nonfiction articles, interviews, letters, history, descriptions of celebrations, poems, jokes, riddles, and proverbs. www.skippingstones.org.

Sports Illustrated for Kids
Children's work: Time and Life Building, 1271 Avenue of the Americas, New York, NY 10020. (Grades 3–7.) Publishes children's letters, poems, jokes, and drawings. www.sikids.com.

Spring Tides
824 Stillwood Dr., Savannah, GA 31419. (Ages 5–12.) Accepts submissions of original literature and artwork from school children across the United States. Publishes autobiographical experiences, poems, and fiction.

Stone Soup
The Magazine by Young Writers and Artists, Children's Art Foundation, P.O. Box 83, Santa Cruz, CA 95063-0083. (Children 13 and under.) Accepts students' stories, poems, artwork, and book reviews. Contains information for contributors in each issue. www.stonesoup.com.

The Writers' Slate
The Writing Conference, Inc., P.O. Box 669, Ottawa, KS 66067. (Grades K–12.) Provides students to read quality literature written by other students. Publishes

TRADE SECRET 8.1 (continued)

fiction, nonfiction, poetry, prose, and artwork. www.writingconference.com.

Word Dance Magazine

34 Barnard St., Newark, DE 19711. (Grades K–8.) Publishes stories, poems, and artwork four times a year. www.worddance.com.

Young Voices

P.O. Box 2321, Olympia, WA 98507. (Ages 6–18.) Quarterly publication of children's stories, poems, photography, and drawings. https://secure.westhost.com/secure/youngvoicesmagazine/submissionreg. html.

things that happen to them. Graves (1993) suggests that teachers need to help children discover those topics for which they "have a passion for the truth" (p. 2). In Trade Secret 8.2, Christine Evans describes how she helps young writers find a topic about which they have knowledge and maybe passion.

Yet there is more to writing than writing personal narratives. Children need teachers who help them build their background knowledge about topics of their choosing and then use what they know to write fiction, nonfiction, poetry, and more by selecting a corner of the topic to write about. In Graves's words, children need teachers who help them "penetrate a subject . . . enabling them to understand what it means to know in an unusual way (writing *as* Joan of Arc instead of *about* Joan of Arc, for example)" (2004, p. 90).

Children Need to Hear Their Teachers Talk Through What They Are Doing as They Write

What do writers think about as they create text? Irene Fountas and Gay Su Pinnel (1996) suggest that one kind of support teachers can provide their young writers is "modeled writing." In this method, teachers demonstrate or model how expert writers write. As they write, they say aloud what they are thinking. With the students watching, they engage in the writing process. They select a topic that they know something about and have some passion for writing about. They talk about how they might begin their piece (e.g., "I want to begin in a way that makes readers want to read my piece. I think I'll begin with a question."). They talk about making changes, revising their text, and why they think a different word or sentence or order would be better. They fix their spelling of a word (e.g., "Oops! That doesn't look right. Let me try it again.") and check their punctuation. Teachers use modeled writing to show how experienced writers write and solve problems as they write. In this way, writers see (and hear) what is behind the print they read on the page. They catch a glimpse of the behind the scenes thinking.

Children Need to Maintain Collections of Their Work to Create the Portrait of Their Writing History

The only way to understand children's development as writers is to study the writings they produced over a period of time. By placing the writings in chronological order and looking closely at how the writer controls the traits or crafts of writing (e.g., organization, development, voice, conventions) over time, the teacher and the writer can understand the writer's development over time.

To Graves's list of the fundamentals of teaching writing, we add one more.

Children Need Teachers Who TEACH Writing, Not Just Make Writing Assignments

Teaching kids how to write is hard because writing is not so much one skill as a *bundle* of skills that includes sequencing, spelling, rereading, and supporting big ideas with examples. These skills, however, are teachable (Fletcher & Portalupi, 2001, p. 1).

Sometimes teachers say, "Oh, my students write every day." Yes, writing every day is important, but it is not enough. Teachers need to *teach* writing every day. Teaching happens in several different ways. Teachers pull the whole class together to teach. Teachers pull groups of children who need the same information together and teach them in a small group. Teachers confer with their students and teach them one on one. Students confer with each other, working in small groups and one on one. The class comes together to respond to students' writings and teach through their responses. The label given to this teaching and writing time is *writing workshop*. Teachers teach about where writers get ideas, about how to write great leads that make readers want to read more, about how to punctuate and capitalize correctly, about how to write different kinds of pieces for different purposes (letters to persuade, reports to inform, stories to entertain), and so on.

In the following section, we detail how teachers teach writing during writing workshop.

SETTING THE STAGE FOR WRITING

First, though, we consider what teachers must do to set the classroom stage to support their students' writing.

Gather the Needed Materials

Like younger writers, students in elementary school need materials to support their writing efforts. Return to page 186 in Chapter 5 to review the list of materials needed to support our youngest writers' writing efforts. Elementary school students also need many different kinds of paper (add stationery and envelopes to the list, various writing tools, writing folders, and a box or file drawer in which to store their writing folders. These students will need two writing folders with pockets, one for works in progress and one for completed works. Figure 8.1 gives suggestions on the use of the inside covers of the works in progress folders. These students also need samples of different writers' work on a bulletin board, posters, clipboards, and mailboxes. In addition to these items, elementary-aged students need the following:

- Tools for revising their writing (e.g., scissors, tape, staples, staplers, correction fluid, glue sticks, paper clips, gum-backed paper, Post-it notes, highlighters)
- Writer's notebooks for recording special language heard or read that they may want to use in their writing or ideas thought of when they are not writing
- Materials for bookmaking (e.g., construction paper, wallpaper, or poster board for making book covers; colored paper in various sizes; a long-arm stapler for binding; clear plastic covers with colored plastic spines)
- Reference materials (e.g., dictionaries, thesauri, spelling books and electronic spellmasters, style handbooks)
- Teacher-made charts to guide their writing efforts (Figure 8.2 shows several charts that hang in Deirdra Aikens's classroom writing center)

Determining how to make effective use of the classroom's computers is an even greater challenge for teachers of older students than it is for teachers of younger children. Older children's writing pieces are longer; consequently, it takes longer to compose a first draft, revise, edit, and create a final draft. Older students tend to make more changes in their writing and need computer time to make these revisions. Some teachers assign a group of students to the computers. When this group completes writing, another group begins to use the computers. While some students write with paper and pencils, others write with the computer. Some teachers connect writing with word processing with a particular kind of writing, such as a research report. When all the students have completed their research reports, a new kind of writing will be introduced, and all will again have a turn with the word processor. Many teachers respond to their students' cries for more time at the word processor by permitting them access before school, during class meetings, during recess, and whenever else time permits. The effect is that writing begins to pervade the school day. Very fortunate teachers and writers have word processors for every student or every two students. Readers might consider attempting to secure simple word processors, such as Dreamwriters, for their students' use (http://www2.edc.org/NCIP/library/laptops/dreamwriters.htm).

Arrange the Materials.   Return to page 188 to look again at Figure 5.2. Like their colleagues who teach younger children, some teachers of elementary-aged children also place the classroom's shared writing materials in a writing center (or area). One difference is that elementary school teachers tend not to put a table and chairs in their writing centers. Instead, they ask their students to collect the materials they need from the writing center and to use them at their table or desk.

Topics I could write about:

*1 My Dog Lucky!

*2 School!

3 Christmas!

4 My Dog Lucky ran away from home.

5 playing with my friend: poem
6 the big monster in mrs. Hull's room
7 music

8 war

9 on the bus
10 a trip to Jenny's
11 going to gym

Skills I can use:

① I capitalize "I."
② I capitalize Christmas.
③ I use 's to show belonging.
④ I usually capitalize people's names.
⑤ I use !

FIGURE 8.1   Use the inside covers of the "Work in Progress" folders to record valuable information

Be Different!

Give a

R = Restate the question

A = Answer it!

R = Reasons! Reasons!

E = Examples! Examples!

The Best Endings

1. Surprise Ending
2. Emotional Ending
3. Circular Ending
4. Express your Feelings

and the rest are covered. Ms. Aikens hasn't taught them yet

Editing #1

⬭ misspelled word

My (frend) is here.

Editing #2

add a space

#
Mycat is smart.

Editing #3

∧ add this

new
Ihave a bike.
      ∧

Editing #4

⚡ no capital

My scHool is cool.

Editing #5

≡ needs a capital

Ms. aikens is here.
       ≡

Great Beginnings!

1. Question
      "Have you ever seen a cat?"
2. Arresting sentence
      "She stole my mom's present!"
3. Astonishing Fact
      The Sun is 93 million miles from earth.
4. Spoken Words
      "Daddy is coming home today, Ben."
5. Setting the Mood (setting)
      It was a deep, dark, snowy Christmas.

FIGURE 8.2   **Examples of Charts in Deirdra Aikens's Writing Center**

Because people are known to forget to return borrowed items to their appropriate storage places, we strongly recommend that teachers create an inventory of the shared writing materials, post the inventory in the writing center, and assign a student to the task of checking the materials in the area against the inventory following each writing workshop. Other teachers of elementary-aged students make a "tool chest" (a plastic container) of regularly needed writing supplies (pencils, pens, scissors, tape, stapler and staples, paper clips) for each grouping of desks or each table. A student at each table or cluster of desks is responsible for ensuring that the shared supplies are returned to the tool chest and returned to the writing center at the end of writing workshop.

THE COMPONENTS OF THE WRITING WORKSHOP

Nancie Atwell (1987) credits Graves (1983) with helping her discover a structure that was successful with her students. Teachers across the nation (world, really) have adopted and adapted this structure. Each writing workshop has three or four components. Although the components may be arranged differently on any given day, each writing workshop contains these components. In most classrooms, they happen in the order described here.

Focus Lesson

In the early days of writing workshop, each session always began with a minilesson (a five- to ten-minute teacher presentation). Today, writing workshop experts are less concerned with the time factor, so they, like Ray (2001), have shifted to calling the writing lesson a "focus lesson." As Ralph Fletcher's and JoAnn Portalupi's (2001) book verifies, the categories of these lessons remain the same (procedural, process, qualities of good writing, and mechanical skills); only the title has changed.

Writing Time

During writing time, students write while the teacher moves about the room conferring with the writers. Students might also confer with other students. While the teacher confers with students at the students' writing place, peer conferences might occur with those around the writer or two or more writers might move to a special section of the room.

Sharing

Each writing workshop ends with the students gathering together for a share. Here two or three students share their pieces of writing and receive feedback in the form of content-related questions and comments from their peers. Sharing might be done as a whole group, in smaller groups, or in pairs.

Some teachers insert a *status-of-the-class report* between the whole-group lesson and the students' writing time. During status-of-the-class, the teacher quickly checks what each writer plans to do that day. Will the writer be beginning a draft of a new piece? Editing a piece? Making revisions to a piece based on peer feedback?

Some teachers have created a system to check on their students' writing plans for the day. For example, some teachers ask students to report on their writing plans by attaching a clothespin, one per student with the student's name on it, to a circular wheel depicting a combination of the writing process and the classroom writing workshop procedures (Figure 8.3). Students move their clothespins as they move from the whole-group focus lesson area to their table or desk to begin writing. Karen Bromley (1998) describes a different status-of-the-class procedure used by Karen Wassell. Ms. Wassell staples five library pockets to a bulletin board. Each pocket has the label of a stage in the writing process written on it (e.g., planning, drafting, revising, editing, and publishing). Each child is given a Popsicle stick with his or her name written on it. The students insert the sticks into the pocket that correctly describes their writing activity of the day.

How does a teacher get writing workshop going in a classroom? In Trade Secret 8.2, third-grade teacher Christine Evans describes how she helps her young writers determine what they might write about. Like so many third-graders, Ms. Evans's students came to her without previous writing workshop experiences. Their first- and second-grade teachers had told them what to write about. Now, Ms Evans wanted them to write about topics that were important to them, topics they wanted others to know about. A writer's notebook, with teacher modeling of how to use it, is an effective strategy. In each writing workshop, Ms. Evans follows this sequence: the lesson, writing, and then group sharing. In the following sections, each of the parts of the writing workshop is examined more closely.

Focus Lessons

Focus lessons are direct instruction lessons that teach students something about writing. Carl Anderson (2005, p. xiii) describes these lessons as "usually part of a *unit of study,* a sequence of lessons on one aspect of writing that last two to six weeks." When writing workshop first began, teachers selected focus lesson topics using a "little of this and a little of that" approach. Every day, teachers presented lessons on a different topic: today a lesson on writing a strong lead, tomorrow a lesson on a revision strategy. Over the years, teachers have discovered that this approach is not nearly as effective as organizing their lesson topics into units of study. For two to six weeks, teachers focus on teaching lessons on a single topic.

The lessons are focused in three ways. First, they are focused on a specific need the teacher has determined the students have. That is, a good focus lesson has a very clear objective. Ray (2001) points out that sometimes this objective is behavioral (the students should be able to do something after the lesson), and other times the objective is more cognitive (the students should have a better understanding of some aspect of writing after the lesson). The teachers' task, then, is to determine what their group of students needs to help the group members write better and to plan a lesson focused on this need. No one lesson can tell the writers everything they need to know about the topic. Therefore, a cluster of les-

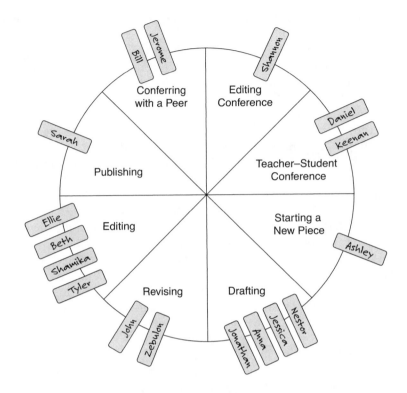

Clothespins with Names

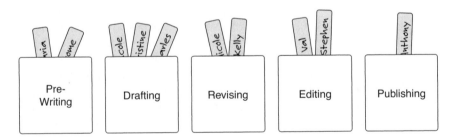

FIGURE 8.3   Status-of-the-Class Procedures

sons, say for a week's time, is focused on a particular need. For example, if the students need help adding rich, telling details to their pieces, then the teacher would provide focused, direct instruction on this topic every day for a week. Each day's lesson would build on and extend the writers' knowledge of how to add rich, telling details. That is the second way the lessons are focused. The goal is to offer

TRADE SECRET 8.2
Getting Started: Topics That Matter

BY CHRISTINE EVANS

Eight-year old Peter stands by the writing center, new writing notebook and sharpened pencil in hand, listening to some of his friends as they talk about topics for their writing. It's Friday of the first week of third grade, and Peter, not unlike many others in the class, has difficulty finding topics for his writing. Peter's other teachers assigned topics, so he didn't need to have good ideas for his writing. And, like others in the class, Peter didn't like to write.

I wanted my third-graders to be motivated about writing, but so many didn't know where to begin to find ideas for good topics. I wanted them to be eager to develop personal topics and be passionate about their writing. I wanted them to share themselves through their writing. I wanted them to talk to each other about writing. So many "wants," but where should I start? How would I teach my students to find good topics? It dawned on me that I was asking my students to do something that I didn't do: write about myself. I wrote memos to the third grade team, letters to my son's teacher, notes to my friends at Christmas time, but I never wrote a piece on a topic that was important to me. So I decided it was time for me to "walk the talk." That year I began to keep a writer's notebook.

Each year writing workshop in my class begins with me sharing my notebook. I show my students the wonderings, reflections, quotes, and lists that fill its pages. I explain to my students that my notebook is the place where I write down, sometimes quickly, funny things that happen, curious things that I wonder about, and even favorite words or sentences from books I am reading. Students notice that my notebook is always close at hand whenever I read aloud, and they watch as I enter the colorful words or images that authors use. I explain to my students that they are the ones who decide what goes in their notebooks. I tell them that the writing bits that fill their notebook pages will later become "seed ideas" for their pieces. These notebooks will hold the beginnings of longer pieces of writing; writing that matters.

Afterward, I invite my students to eavesdrop on my thinking as I page through my notebook and evaluate different ideas for my first writing piece. I mention three possibilities. Each one I consider individually, and then I decide on one. I let students "see" how I make the decision to write about my cat, Lotus. Then I share with students an entry from my notebook. I say, "Last night, when I got home from work, Lotus ran to the hallway closet and meowed and meowed. She wouldn't stop! So, I opened the closet door and remembered that was where I kept her favorite toy. I took it out and played a game with her. Well, I couldn't believe that a cat would 'talk' and play like that so I decided to write about it in my notebook." *Sitting in my favorite chair, I waved the bird toy in circles over Lotus's head. Lotus leaped and somersaulted trying to get the bird in her mouth. One time she landed on her back and went skidding across the rug. It made me belly laugh to see her flipping and rolling while trying to catch the bird.*

My students learn how this entry becomes the seed for my first writing of the year. Together, the students and I write, revise, and edit my Lotus piece as I teach them both the process and the crafts of writing.

Like Peter, some of my students experience writer's block and need help gathering ideas. To help them get started, I might read a particularly thought-provoking picture book (*The Memory String* by Eve Bunting, *Charlie Anderson* by Barbara Abercrombie, *Faithful Elephants* by Yukio Tsuchiya, or *The Other Side* by Jacqueline Woodson) or a poem and have students do a "quick write" (students write quickly and freely for about two minutes everything that the text brings to mind) in their notebooks. Because quick writes capture what is important or interesting,

(continued on next page)

TRADE SECRET 8.2   (continued)

students often recover from their writer's block and develop these entries into polished pieces.

By the end of the year, my third-graders have filled their notebooks with facts, descriptions, stories, poems, and responses to literature. They have learned the power of the notebook—learning to write by writing. Many of the entries will never be used for topics of their published pieces but more importantly, students have developed the writing habit. They have learned not only to write about their world but also to look closely at it.

the writers pointers that they can consider as they construct their texts. Finally, a series of these lessons might be focused on the primary traits of a particular genre, such as historical fiction, memoir, poetry, persuasive essay, or nonfiction. Because the primary traits of each genre are different, the lessons (in addition to the students being immersed in reading quality pieces in each genre and engaging in the close study of the genre and several key authors of this genre) are aimed at helping students craft texts of their own in this genre.

Remember that the content of the lessons will be reinforced and reconsidered in other components of the writing workshop. In particular, the teacher–student conferences offer this opportunity.

Regardless of grade level, topic selection is one of the first writing workshop focus lessons. Using Evans's (see Trade Secrets 8.2) and Atwell's (1987, pp. 76–83) topic-selection lessons as models will make the first day successful, but what about all the days after the first day? Lessons for these days group themselves into four categories (procedural, craft or qualities of writing, writing process, and mechanical skills), as noted above.

Procedural Lessons.   It is natural for many of the beginning-of-the-year lessons to be procedural lessons. These lessons help the students learn about the teacher's expectations for their behavior and about what they can expect from the teacher. Procedural lesson topics include discussions about such items as conferences, editing, and publishing.

1. *Where and how to confer with peers.* Some teachers ask their students to confer with those peers seated around them. Others designate spots (e.g, in the library corner, behind the teacher's desk) in the room for conferring. The lesson might include information on (a) the volume of the voice permitted when conferring with peers; (b) the need to be kind and to remember that the piece belongs to its author, so revision decisions are the writer's; and (c) the type of questions listeners might ask of authors. Once peers begin conferring, the teacher is no longer the only teacher of writing in the classroom. Now there are twenty to twenty-five teacher assistants. A goal of this lesson is to alert the students to their awesome responsibility to be helpful to their fellow writers.

2. *How teacher–student content conferences will occur.* An important component of the teaching of writing is the teacher–student conference about the content of the students' writing. These conferences will occur while the students are writing. The lesson should inform the students about two elements of teacher–student conferences. First, the lesson should describe how writers will be selected for a conferences. Teachers report that it works well for them to go to the writer rather than have the writer come to them. By going to the student, teachers can control the length of the conference. Atwell (1987) describes how she carried a child-sized chair and zigzagged about the room, randomly selecting students with whom to confer. By intentionally moving from one side of the classroom to the other, she was able to monitor all the students' behavior.

Second, the lesson should tell the students about the teacher's and the students' roles during the conference. The students should know that the teacher will be an attentive listener, an audience genuinely interested in learning about the topics they have chosen; that they will be asked to read their piece to the teacher; that the teacher will be asking questions to learn more about their topic and proposing suggestions for their consideration; and that the conferences will be short (two to three minutes) so that they can get back to their writing. In addition, students understand the procedures better when the teacher models a teacher–student conference during the lesson.

3. *Classroom editing procedures.* Pieces that are to be published must be edited prior to publication. Writers edit by searching for the mechanical errors in their pieces and attempting to correct them. Directions on how to edit pieces and what will occur during the teacher–student editing conference should be presented in a focus lesson. (See the description of one teacher's procedure on pp. 339–340.) Teachers should wait to present this lesson until some of the students are ready to publish their first piece.

4. *How publishing will be done in the classroom.* Publishing includes preparation of the pieces for others to read. It is an important component of the writing process because most writing is meant to be read by an audience. There are many ways to publish students' writings. One teacher asked each student to bring a clear, plastic eight-by-eleven-inch picture frame to school. (She purchased frames for those children whose parents could not provide frames.) Her students published their work by mounting their selected pieces in their frames. The frames hung on the back wall of the classroom on the "Wall of Fame." A teacher of older students purchased plastic covers with colored spines. Her students published by mounting their pieces in these covers. JoAnne Deshon's third-graders publish their writing in books. Many other ideas are suggested in Sandra Brady's (1992) book, *Let's Make Books.*

Besides making books, teachers might consider making a class newspaper or magazine. Perhaps some pieces will be appropriate for submission to magazines with a broader circulation than the classroom. (See Trade Secret 8.1.) Specific kinds of writing dictate publication in culturally defined ways (e.g., business letters, personal letters, invitations, thank-you notes). Each new way to publish means that the teacher must provide a lesson describing and illustrating the procedure for the children.

Crafts or Traits of Good Writing Lessons.   The second kind of lesson, crafts or traits of good writing, should make up the majority of the lessons presented during the year. These lessons cover what Shelley Harwayne (1992) calls the "power of language" and are about the content of the children's pieces and what makes writing good.

Teachers of writing—such as William Zinsser, Donald Murray, and Ralph Fletcher—and pieces of good children's literature are the excellent sources for ideas for these focus lessons. From Zinsser (1998), teachers have gathered many ideas. For example, use leads to suck readers into the piece and make them want to read on, select a *corner* (a small and interesting aspect) of the subject and focus on it, give the last sentence a special twist and make it a surprise, use action verbs, eliminate clutter, and watch the use of adjectives. From Murray (1990), they have learned about choosing vivid, precise descriptive words; describing the sights, sounds, and smells so that readers will be put into the scene; using dialogue to enliven the piece; and writing in the present tense. From Fletcher (1993), teachers have learned about the art of writing with specificity, creating a character, writing with voice, creating dramatic leads, using various kinds of endings, creating tension in pieces, designing the setting, focusing, and choosing the best language.

In addition to these teachers of writing, a growing number of authors are providing accounts of their writing process. For example, Stephen King (2000), in *On Writing*, describes his writing process. In explaining the *why* of his books, King says, "Many of us [popular novelists] care about the language, in our humble way, and care passionately about the art and craft of telling stories on paper. What follows is an attempt to put down, briefly and simply, how I came to the craft, what I know about it now, and how it's done" (p. 9). From King, teachers can learn about what writers need in their "toolbox": qualities of writing such as do not use long words just because you are a little ashamed of your short words; begin with the situations and then develop the characters; if you want to be a writer, then read a lot; and do not be afraid to imitate your favorite authors.

To present these ideas to their students, teachers typically use their own writing or children's literature to illustrate the point. For example, Maryanne Lamont, a first-grade teacher, noticed that her students were writing unfocused pieces. To help her young writers think about how to select a corner on a topic, she prepared a lesson using pieces she wrote to illustrate her point. Her lesson plan is presented in Trade Secret 8.3. Ms. Lamont fussed about writing something on her students' level, in a sense an artificial piece, to illustrate the use of focus. Unfortunately, however, her lessons showing how to draw a map of a writing plan and illustrating how children's literature authors focus their writing on a corner of their topic

TRADE SECRET 8.3
Selecting a Corner of the Topic: Writing Pieces with a Focus

MARYANNE LAMONT

"It is important for authors to choose topics that they know a lot about. It is also important for authors to write about one part of their topic. Today I need your help with a piece I've been working on. It's a piece about school. I know a lot about school! This is the first piece I wrote last night. The title of my piece is *All About School.*

> School is fun.
> We read books.
> We have three recesses.
> We make books.
> We do math.
> We eat lunch in the cafeteria.
> Our principal is Mr. Householder.
> I like school.

"When I read it over, I thought, 'Wow, I wrote about a lot of things that we do in school but I didn't really write an interesting piece because my topic was just too big. I just have one sentence about each thing I mentioned.' I decided that I needed to revise my writing. The first thing I had to do was choose one of these things to write about. Hmmm. Should I write about the cafeteria? I knew I could write about any of these things. I decided to write about recess because I had been thinking about something that happened last year on the playground."

"Listen to my revised piece. Its title is 'An Accident on the Playground':

It was Monday morning. Mrs. Jones and I had recess duty. I was watching the children on the swings. Suddenly, I heard a scream! I turned around and saw Jimmy slip and fall off the monkey bars. I raced over to see if he was alright. He was crying and couldn't move his arm. All the children came rushing over to see what had happened. Jimmy's arm really hurt. I sent John in to get the nurse. When the nurse came out and looked at Jimmy's arm, she discovered that it was broken. She took Jimmy to her office and called his mother. Jimmy's mother came to school to pick him up. She had to take him to the hospital to get a cast on his arm. When Jimmy came to school the next day, he let everyone sign his cast.

"What do you think? Does the second one tell you a lot about just one thing that happened in school—about one adventure on the playground? Do you know what happened to Jimmy? I think I'm happier with this piece. I'll keep working on it."

"When you work on your writing today, read it over and decide whether you chose a giant topic or if you focused your topic. If you chose a giant topic, think about what you might do to focus on one part of your topic. When we come together for sharing time, I'll be asking some of you to show us how you decided to focus in on one aspect of your topic. Perhaps you could read us your piece and your revised piece to help us see how your writing is different."

did not help her students focus their own writing. (Remember that many topics will need to be revisited and presented using various kinds of materials.) Later, she discovered what Harwayne (1992) reports having discovered: Young writers are good at discovering what is wrong with poor writing when the good and the poor are placed side by side. For that reason, she wrote a good piece and a poor piece, to use side by side in her lesson.

Does Ms. Lamont's lesson "show" as Ray (2001) says teachers should during a lesson? Ray suggests ways a lesson can *show* (2001, p. 147):

- Provide advice from a professional writer that explains some process of writing
- Illustrate with an example from a published text, a piece of student writing, or a piece of teacher writing that shows how some crafting technique works
- Report on the conversation of a teacher–student conference with one student that will help the other students
- Illustrate by having the teacher write during the lesson (on the spot)
- Use a story or metaphor to help students understand the point of the lesson

Who does most of the talking, the students or the teacher? Typically, the teacher will do most of the talking. The teacher will draw the students into the lesson by using their names or asking them for their advice. The key, however, will be to stay focused and brief so that the students have time to write. Will the students ever try something out, "have a go," during a lesson? Certainly, they can, but remember that they are working on a piece of their own writing. Notice how Ms. Lamont ended her lesson. She made the connection between the topic of her lesson and their writing; she told her young writers to "have a go" with their writing. So, there was a try-it-out time, a practice time, later.

Do children actually come to understand the qualities of good writing from such illustrations, using teacher's writing or children's literature? Harwayne (1992, p. 278) suggests that teachers reconsider the use of a sequence of lessons, such as one day teaching of "telling details, the next [of] good leads, [the following] of fresh language, [and another of] lots of showing, not telling." She suggests that students do not learn about the qualities of good writing with quick, even dynamic, teacher focus lesson presentations. Some lessons might involve the teacher and students investigating in an interactive way how various authors, including the students, craft their writing or how a trait is used in a specific genre. In writing workshop classrooms, the serious study of authors' literary techniques begins to pervade the children's interactions with text. The qualities of good literature begin to be considered not only during the lessons before the students write but also when the teacher shares literature with the students and when the children engage in conversations about pieces they have read. The result is seamless reading and writing instruction: writers becoming better readers by writing, and readers becoming better writers by reading. As Harwayne (1992, p. 337) says, "[While] there is no one way to run a writing workshop, [high-]quality texts are nonnegotiable." How right she is! The teaching of writing occurs every time the teacher and students engage in honest discussions about literature. Lessons on the qualities of good writing then serve to highlight the points garnered from these authentic interactive literary discussions.

Fletcher and Portalupi know that teachers can sometimes use help creating their focus lessons. So few teachers had good writing instruction when they were in school; most teachers do not have a lot to draw on when they start to think about the teaching of writing. Fletcher and Portalupi's first book, *Craft Lessons* (1998), contains numerous lessons on the qualities of good writing, arranged by grade cluster (K–2, 3–4, and 5–8). Their goal in writing *Nonfiction Craft Lessons: Teaching Information Writing K–8* (2001) was to help teachers teach "the kind of writing that draws less on students' stories, memories, and histories, and more on the concrete 'out there' world" (p. 2). They know that teachers must teach their students how to write good informative pieces because this kind of writing is a crucial tool for students as they learn about the world around them.

More recently, Lucy Calkins and her Teachers College Reading and Writing Project colleagues wrote *Units of Study* (2003). This resource provides lessons to guide teachers in the teaching of the traits of personal narrative, nonfiction, and poetry. In addition, Nell Duke and V. Susan Bennett-Armistead (2003) provide a step-by-step, day 1 to day 8, description of Pam Richardson's approach to teaching informational writing in her first-grade classroom. Others, like Barry Lane and Gretchen Bernabei (2001), provide idea development, organization, voice, word choice, and sentence fluency lessons for teaching persuasive writing. A growing number of resources are available to help teachers teach their students the traits (idea development, organization, voice, word choice, sentence fluency) of good writing in each genre.

Writing Process Lessons.   Writers engage in several behaviors as they write. When asked to describe their writing process, writers speak about where they get their ideas, how they draft their pieces (e.g., how many drafts they actually write; whether they use typewriter, longhand, or computer; where they write), how they revise, and how their pieces are published. Writers make it clear that the process of writing is *not* a linear process. It is not even safe to suggest that writers begin with an idea because, as Peter Elbow (1973) suggests, some writers begin by writing and discover their idea through their writing. Similarly, it is not safe to suggest that writing ends in publication. Not all pieces written are worthy of publication; many die in the drafting stage. Hence, in lessons on the writing process, teachers want to show their writers the *behaviors* of writers, and make visible a process that is mostly invisible.

Some teachers find it helpful to children to share writers' descriptions of their writing process. Two of many helpful books are *Worlds of Childhood: The Art and Craft of Writing for Children* by William Zinsser (1990) and *How Writers Write* by Pam Lloyd (1987). Some teachers share the videotapes produced by Houghton-Mifflin/Clarion (n.d.), showing the writing process as described by various well-known children's book authors (e.g., *A Visit with Russell Freedman*). *Booklinks*, a magazine published by the American Library Association, regularly contains interviews with authors. In addition, teachers and students can access interviews, even sometimes participate in live interactions with authors, through the writers' or the writers' publishers' Web sites. For example, Scholastic (http://teachers. scholastic.com authorsandbooks) advertises that teachers and students can meet their favorite authors and discover new ones through live interviews, classroom activities, and author profiles. Other teachers invite local authors into the classroom to write with the students, which has the advantage of making an author come alive for the students.

In addition to descriptions of writers' writing behaviors, children need to be shown how to make revisions to their text. To revise a text means to change the meaning, content, structure, or style; to edit is to make surface changes to the text, to fix the spelling, punctuation, capitalization, or grammar. Revision does not just occur when the writer thinks the piece is finished; rather, it happens throughout the writing process. Teaching writers about the need to revise can be tricky. None of us likes to hear that the piece that we thought was "done" needs additional work. As Georgia Heard (2002) points out, when someone says, "I think you should add more," we translate it to mean, "My writing is not good enough." In her 2002 book *The Revision Toolbox: Teaching Techniques that Work,* Heard provides teachers with numerous strategies for helping children revise. A few of her strategies are summarized in Table 8.1, and we encourage readers to obtain a copy of her book, which illustrates these strategies using students' writings, for additional ideas.

Another excellent source of revision strategies and lessons is Barry Lane's (1993) *After the End.* In Trade Secret 8.4, teacher Jane Ragains describes how she used one of Lane's revision strategies, "snapshot," in a lesson with her fifth-graders.

Mechanical Skills Lessons.   Finally, there are the lessons about the conventions of language: punctuation, grammar, usage, handwriting, capitalization, and spelling. Teachers can discover which mechanical skill lessons need to be presented through various sources. As with all lessons, the best source is the students' writing. What conventions do students need to use that they are not using correctly? They use dialogue, but is it incorrectly punctuated and capitalized, without quotation marks? If so, the topic of at least one lesson is clear. Often, school districts have identified specific mechanical competencies that are to be covered at each grade level. Teaching these skills in lessons and then incorporating them into the editing stage of the writing process provides students with many practice opportunities. In districts in which a language arts textbook is issued, teachers often examine the textbook to discover the mechanical skills they are responsible for ensuring their students encounter. These skills are then taught through the lessons and reinforced as a part of the editing process in much the same way as the district-specified competencies were taught. Even when district competencies or a textbook are used as sources for mechanical-skill topic suggestions, teachers teach the skill *when their students' writing indicates a need for that skill* rather than following the order in which the skills are presented in the textbook or on the competency list. When students have a reason to learn particular skills and when the skills are taught in a meaningful context, students learn the skills much more quickly.

As with other kinds of lessons, the content of mechanical-skills lessons may need to be repeated. One mechanical-skills lesson, how to write using your best guess of how to spell each word, for example, may need to be repeated often, particularly with kindergarten and first-grade students. Teachers of older students will want to present a similar lesson to their students, although their reason will be different. These teachers want their writers to use the words in their oral vocabulary in their writings. Hence, they need to convince their students that spelling every word correctly is *not* important in their rough drafts and to show them how

TABLE 8.1   Selected Revision Strategies

REVISION TOOLS	PURPOSE	STRATEGIES
Cracking open words	To help students eliminate the use of words such as *fun*, *nice*, *pretty*, *wonderful*, and *scary* and replace them with words that bring a particular picture to the readers' mind	Ask students to create a list of tired, worn, and overused words and sentences from their writing. Then ask them to close their eyes and see or feel what *fun* or *nice* really looked or felt like and to write what they saw.
Collecting words	To help students expand the collection of words that they know so that they can access these words when they write	Ask students to begin a collection of "treasure" words in a notebook.
Give a yard sale for extra words	To help students obtain concise writing by cutting out extra unnecessary words in their writing, which will also help them understand which details of a story are essential	Have students practice cutting out extra words from a book excerpt, explaining to leave only the details that are really essential for the piece of writing. Then ask them to choose a piece of their own writing, cut out what they can, and share with the class.
Specificity of words	To help students learn how to write with detail, allowing them to express their specific thoughts in their writing correctly	Ask students to select a piece of their own writing and underline or highlight the verbs. Ask them to brainstorm or look in the thesaurus to replace those highlighted verbs with more detailed ones. Then ask students to repeat this exercise and underline nouns instead of verbs.
Reseeing: Two-column writing	To help students observe and "resee" different objects or events with specificity and help them learn how to write with this kind of observational eye	Ask students to make a T-chart, labeling one side "ordinary" and the other side "poetic." Then ask them to observe a natural object and put the first words that come to mind under the "ordinary" column. Under "poetic," ask them to transform the "ordinary" descriptions into poetry by using metaphors and similes describing exact details. Then have them try writing the poetic side of the T-chart as a poem.
Asking questions, adding details	To help students discover what details they might need to add to their writing	Ask a student to choose a piece of writing in need of revision. Then, ask him or her to read the writing aloud while the rest of the class listens and jots down any questions they might want to ask the author. The class can then ask questions about the writing to the author, getting the author to think about what he or she might want to add to the story.

(continued)

TABLE 8.1   Selected Revision Strategies (Continued)

REVISION TOOLS	PURPOSE	STRATEGIES
Opening the front door: The lead	To help students write interesting and appropriate introductory sentences	Ask students to reread a piece of writing and underline a sentence or part that might serve as a compelling lead. Another strategy is to ask students to write three or four alternative leads before choosing one they will finally use.
Playing with time flashback	To help students discover ways to use the flashback strategy in their writing	Ask students to make a time line of a favorite book or poem. Then ask them to select a story or poem that they have written and create a time line of the big events and actions, paying attention to the elements of time. If their stories are chronological, then ask them to begin their stories at the end of their time line and flash back to the beginning to see how this new structure transforms their stories.
Looking through a magnifying glass: Expanding writing	To help students expand their descriptions of particular experiences, details, or people in their writing	Ask students to free-write a brief autobiographical synopsis of themselves, up to a full-page long. Then ask them to underline one sentence that is most interesting to them and expand that sentence into a full-page description. Tell them to use their imagination to fill in some of the details.
Rearranging the furniture: Cut and tape	To help students discover new ways to begin or end their stories and help students discover a new way to tell their story or poem	Ask students to select a piece of writing that they want to revise. Ask them to chunk the main parts of the writing and then cut each part out with scissors. Next ask them to rearrange the chunks: move the end to the beginning, begin with an image or dialogue from the middle of their writing, and so forth
Leaving the house: Endings	To help students be more specific and creative with the endings of their writing	Ask students to reread a piece of writing they have already written and explore one of the following three endings: circular ending, emotional statement, and surprise ending.
Point of view	To help students learn how to write through different points of view	Ask students to select a piece of writing and experiment with the three points of view: first person, second person, and third person.

TRADE SECRETS 8.4
Yes, You Can Get Your Students to Revise!

JANE RAGAINS

"No, I don't want to write any more."
"I'm Done!"
THE END

Do these comments sound familiar? Many students respond in these ways when asked to revise their pieces of writing. Even if they are willing to revise, they don't change leads, add details, or clarify any ideas. They fix spelling, punctuation, and any other conventions that seem appropriate to them. From our frustration with the response "THE END," revision strategies need to emerge.

In order to be successful in having our students even consider revising, we need to create a classroom community of learners—students who feel comfortable enough with one another to offer constructive ideas to make writing better. This can be accomplished by showing that we value our students' work. Find something of substance that is positive about the students' work. Be sincere in the compliment. Accentuate the positives in all aspects of classroom life. Encourage all ideas as worthy of sharing. Teach students ways to listen to each other. This community needs to be established early in the year and fostered with each passing month. As this happens, students will feel comfortable sharing their work with the teacher and their peers. They will be more willing to take risks and look for ways to improve in all facets of their academic life. There is also a carryover to the unstructured moments during recess, lunch, and related art classes.

While this atmosphere of caring is being nurtured, begin teaching focus lessons that will develop procedures to make revision easier—skip lines as you write, leave wide margins, and write only on the front of the paper. It is always wise to number the pages in any piece just in case that ten-page masterpiece is dropped to the floor and scatters in many directions. It will take several reminders to make sure students adhere to these guidelines, but they are absolutely necessary in the art of successful revision.

A favorite revision strategy comes from *After the End* by Barry Lane (1993). A "snapshot" is a description of an event using physical details. A wonderful example can be found in Laura Ingalls Wilder's *Little House in the Big Woods*:

> Ma kissed them both, and tucked the covers in around them. They lay there awhile, looking at Ma's smooth, parted hair and her hands busy with sewing in the lamplight. Her needle made little clicking sounds against her thimble, and then the thread went softly, swish! through the pretty calico that Pa had traded furs for.

After reading this to your students, you may want to ask them about the physical details Wilder considered as she was writing this paragraph. Ask them to take a series of "snapshots" of the scene. One picture might be of Ma tucking the girls into bed. Another might be of Ma's head as she bent over her sewing. The last photo might be of her hands as she pushes the needle through the calico. Have the students tell you the details they see.

Students should then be able to take a closer look at their own work. Where can they take a snapshot? How can they describe an event in more detail? A "bed-to-bed" piece, one in which the author writes an account from morning to night of an event in his or her life, can be turned into several great vignettes using the snapshot technique. Below is an example of such a piece. As you read it, look for places where Chris might give the reader a closer look.

■ The Trip to Nagshead

(retyped exactly as written by the student)
It was early in the morning around 6:30. When we heard a knock. I ran to the door. I opened the door.

(continued on next page)

It was my cousins! Megan brought her stuff in. Steven did not. At 7:00 we packed up the car and we were off to Nagshead.

There was a lot of food with us. There were snacks with us.

We drove onto a bridge. There were tunnels that we drove threw. They went underwater. There was a rest stop on the bridge. We got out of the car and went to the bathroom. We had lunch there. It was good. We got back in the car, and we were off again.

We met our cousin and Grandpa at a rest-stop. We ate some snacks. Then we went to the house. We got there too early. So my brothers, cousin and I went swimming. We went swimming because we were hot from the long ride.

Then the house was clean. We discovered the house was big. I went exploring with my cousin while the moms put away the food. First, we went to my mom and dad's room. It was big. Then we went into my aunt and uncle's room. Then we went into my girl cousin's room. Then the boy's room. It was all ready a mess.

Then we went down into the garage. We found a big raft. We ate pizza for dinner and then went to sleep.

The next day was nice. There were big waves. We got the raft out and went swimming. Everybody went down to the beach today. David and I got in the water with the raft.

Then my cousin got on the raft with us. We waited for a wave to come. My mom was video taping us when a big wave came. It hit us on my dad's head. I did a back flip off my dad's head. My brother was up in the air. He landed on the raft. My dad put my cousin down and she went in.

A big wave came right after the other one. I went under the water. I came up too early. I got caught in the raft. I got dragged up to the shore. Then David and I went back.

There was a sandbar in the water. Then right when we got out therecrash!! The wave knocked me back off the sandbar. My brother got me and took me back to the sandbar.

That night we went in the hot tub. It was nice. Then I watched a move and went to sleep.

Two days later we went home, unpacked and we went inside.

The End *(YES! Chris actually wrote these two words.)*

We might want to guide Chris to the part where he describes going over the Chesapeake Bay Bridge and Tunnel. He could tell us about that specific part of his trip—give us the physical details. Perhaps he would draw a picture. What more might he tell us about their rest there? Another part on which we might have him focus is his experience with the waves. How did he feel? What did it look like? Encourage him to think about how the event might have looked if someone had taken photographs of each action he described. Using pictures or words, Chris could give the reader a better idea of what really happened.

Find a particularly vivid example of physical description from the work of your students and share it with the entire class. Nothing inspires a writer more than sharing his or her work with others.

Just as dialogue is not the only way to begin a piece of writing, snapshots are not the only revision strategy. Students also need to learn how to take conference questions and insert their answers. Improving word choice is another way to enliven any piece. Once students decide where they wish to revise their piece, we can show them how to draw arrows, cut, paste, and rearrange.

It is not enough to teach revision strategies once or twice. Students need to be encouraged to routinely reread their work or share it with a friend. Teaching and reviewing ideas for revising should be an ongoing process. You will know that you have succeeded when you no longer see

THE END.

Lane, B. (1993). *After the end*: Teaching and learning creative revision. Portsmouth, NH: Heinemann.

to spell the words the best they can so that they can read them later. After all, the students are the only persons reading their rough drafts.

Status-of-the-Class Report

When teachers use a status-of-the-class report following a lesson, they need to make the transition to the writing portion of the writing workshop. For example, they can ask, "What are you planning to do today?" or "What will you be working on today?"

This report provides the teacher with valuable information. First, it provides clues about which students might need a teacher–student conference. Students who seem unsure of their plans need to be seen first so as to provide support to help them proceed with the writing challenge. Students who are struggling to make their pieces say what they want them to say may need the teacher's assistance as soon as possible. Second, it tells the teacher where the writers are in the writing process. Who is beginning a new piece? Who is publishing a piece? Who is continuing to write on a topic? The report provides a snapshot of each writer's behavior during the writing workshop.

The status-of-the-class report also provides writers with valuable information. Hearing what colleagues are doing helps teach them about appropriate writing workshop behaviors and gives them the vocabulary to describe their own writing activities. Hearing colleagues' writing topics often results in another child saying, for example, "Oh, I'm going to write about my birthday party!"

Writing Time

As the students move from the status-of-the-class report to writing, many teachers require five minutes of silent writing before peer and teacher–student conferences begin. Like the status-of-the-class report, this five-minute period serves as a transition from the noise of students moving about the room to the seriousness of the writing task. Writers need time to reread yesterday's writing or rehearse today's topic in their minds before writing or to start writing to learn what is known about a topic. Many teachers also use this time to write themselves, thus providing students a model of a writer.

The teacher who looks around the classroom during this component of the writing workshop will observe writers engaged in various aspects of the writing process. Some students will be selecting new topics, so they will be thinking, talking (after the five-minute period of silence), writing, or observing. Others will be writing, with pauses to reread what they have written, reconsider their topic, or confer with the teacher or a colleague about the topic or the text. Others will be editing pieces in preparation for publication. Yet others will be publishing. In each writing workshop, young writers will be engaged in the writing behaviors of all writers. The only differences will be the physical size and the experience of these writers.

Teacher–Student Conferences.   From Carl Anderson's (2000) perspective, conferences are conversations. Anderson believes that conferences are conversations because they share the characteristics of a conversation.

- Conferences and conversations have a point to them; the point of a conference is to help the student become a better writer.
- Conferences and conversations have a predictable structure; the structure of a conference is to talk about the work the student is doing as a writer and how the student can become a better writer.
- In conferences and conversations, listeners pursue the talkers' (or readers') line of thinking; the line of thinking in a conference is driven by the student's concerns and the text.
- In conferences and conversations, speakers engage in a pattern of exchange: one talks and then the other talks, one leads and then the other leads; in conferences, the student sets the conference's agenda by describing what he or she is working on and then the teacher takes the lead to help the student write better.
- In conferences and in conversations, listeners show they care about each other; in conferences, teachers show students that they care by nodding, smiling, and celebrating what they did well.

Conferences might proceed in the following way:

- *Writer's intent.* The teacher might begin the conference with an opening such as, "Tell me about how your writing is going. What are you trying to do?" The teacher's goal is to discover the student's intentions. As the student speaks, the teacher listens intently. For example, is the writer working to tell this story in the clever way, to keep the readers' attention? Is the writer working to create a really engaging lead? Is the writer working to put spaces between the words? In this "research" or "understand the writer" part of the conference, the teacher searches for the way to match the teaching during the conference with the writer's goal for this piece of writing (Fletcher & Portalupi, 2001; Ray, 2001).

- *Writer's need.* Knowing the writer's goal helps the teacher know the right questions to ask and how to focus the conversation in ways that will help the student become a better writer. In Ray's terms (2001, p. 163), the teacher is making a "what-does-this-student-need-to-know" decision. So the second part of the conference is assessing the writer's need and deciding what to teach. Remember that the goal of a writing conference is to help the student become a better writer, not just to make this piece of writing better. The challenge for the teacher is to figure out on the spot what will help this student as a writer now. Fletcher and Portalupi remind teachers to figure out just *one* thing that will help this writer be a better writer, one strategy, skill, or technique. All the writer's needs cannot be "fixed" in a single conference.

- *Teach the writer.* Once the teacher has decided what would help the student be a better writer, the teacher teaches. Beware, however: conferences are not minilectures. The teacher might grab a book to illustrate a quality of writing that this writer needs ("Hmmm. I wonder if this lead will really grab your reader's attention. What leads have you tried? Can you think of any stories we have read recently that had a really great lead? Let's take a look at these three or four books."). The teacher might let the writer know that something is missing ("I got confused right here. As you were reading me this section, I couldn't figure out what you made out front when you write, 'Then I made one in the front.' "). Or, the teacher might label what the writer is trying to do ("Ah, so you are trying to write this piece from the perspective of your cat and you're having trouble always seeing things from your cat's perspective? Let's think about a story we have read recently where the author did just what you are trying to do.") or may teach a revision strategy ("Here's how you might add this information without rewriting your whole piece. Please get scissors and tape from the writing center. Now, where do you want to add more information? Right here? So, take the scissors and cut your piece apart right there. Now write the new section on this piece of paper. I'll return in a few minutes to help you insert what you write into your piece."). (Trade Secret 8.4 showed one teacher's experiences teaching revision, using one of Barry Lane's strategies, to a fifth-grade writer.) Exactly what the teacher says will be dependent on the writer's intent. What is this writer is trying to do? What can the teacher teach this writer now that will help the writer achieve his or her intent? What can the teacher teach now, what strategies or techniques, that the student can use not only in this piece but also in subsequent pieces? The teacher does not teach to make *this* draft wonderful. A perfect lead in this draft or the use of brilliant dialogue—without learning a strategy for discovering a perfect lead or making dialogue brilliant—is of little use to the writer.

- *Writer's plan.* What did the writer understand the teacher to say? What will the writer do now? How will the writer use the conversation to make the writing better? Ray (2001, p. 168) ends her conferences with, "Say back to me what I just talked to you about." Teacher Deanne McCredie ends her conferences by asking, "What will you do now? How will you use what we talked about?" Teacher Deirdra Aikens ends her conferences by saying, "So, what we talked about was ..." and the student fills in the blank. Ms. Aikens then records a few key words from the student's summary on a piece of paper and staples it to the inside of the student's writing folder. She and the student now have a record of the content of the conference. Making a note about the content of the conferences helps remind Ms. Aikens and the student what was taught during the conference. Ms. Aikens departs from each conference by saying, "I'll check back with you in a few minutes to see how you are doing." In this way, her students know that they are to "have a go" at whatever strategy or technique she taught during the conference.

Teaching the writer whose primary language is not English can sometimes be challenging. Teachers need to be aware of the textual organizational structures

The role of a teacher in a teacher–student writing conference is to listen carefully to the writer, to respond honestly to the writer's questions, and to offer suggestions that will help the student become a better writer

and cultural norms that might affect their students' writing. In Special Feature 8.1, Barbara Lutz offers some cautionary notes to teachers whose classrooms include students whose primary language is not English.

Like Ms. Aikens, most teachers record what they taught during each conference with each student. Not every teacher staples the note to the student's writing folder. Terry Analore, for example, records her notes on three-by-five-inch index cards. Following one conference she wrote "10/26—By reading the end of her piece, Constance saw that the last sentence didn't fit. She crossed it out and thought of a new ending." Here Ms. Analore taught the strategy of reading a piece aloud to hear how it sounds, which can help writers determine what needs revision. When a student's card is filled with her notes, Ms. Analore puts it in the student's working portfolio (see Chapter 10). Other teachers record their notes on computer labels, the kind on eight-by-eleven-inch sheets. They write each child's name on a label. As they confer with their students, they record their notes on each student's computer label. At a glance, they can tell who they have conferred with and who might be in need of her support. As a student's computer label is filled with her notes, they are removed from the sheet and attached to a sheet of paper in the student's working portfolio.

Anderson (2005) suggests that teachers use an individual learning plan form to record their observations about each student. In the first column, he suggests

English as a Second Language: How Can We Help?

BY BARBARA GAAL LUTZ

Teachers sometimes view the pieces written by English as a second language (ESL) learners as being written in another language. Sometimes these students seem to make random word choices. Grammatical errors pepper their papers; in particular teachers see verb tense errors, article omissions, and the incorrect use of prepositions. Teachers often question, "What is the purpose of this paper?" because the paper seems to digress in several directions. Red pen in hand and with the intent of being helpful, teachers attack ESL learners' papers, editing heavily. Yet is this strategy the best? Teachers should know the *why* behind ESL writers' decisions.

Writing Personal Opinions. The assignment asked the students to write about their personal opinion on a topic under discussion in the classroom. U.S. students enjoy expressing their opinions, even when they are not well versed on the topic. Our educational system nurtures self-expression and individualism. For some ESL students, however, expressing personal opinions poses difficulties. In some cultures, students conform to the group, "subordinating the self for the 'we'" (Harris, 1994, p. 102); they are encouraged to voice those opinions that are commonly shared by the culture rather than express their personal views. Thus, an assignment that requires a personal opinion becomes an agonizing task for these students. Rather than take a stand, some students will persist in writing generalities, thereby avoiding personal comments or experiences to support specific points. Of course, other ESL students may be quite happy to write from a personal opinion, but they may not understand the need to defend their position by providing supporting evidence. In such cases, merely expressing their opinions would be enough to satisfy their assignments in their own classroom cultures.

Taking these cultural differences into account when preparing assignments will greatly alleviate difficulties for both the ESL student and the teacher. For example, rather than one prompt for a writing assignment, teachers might consider several prompts, with each requiring a different kind response. In this way, both native speakers and ESL students could select the prompt that works best for them. In addition, directions that request the types of support the teacher expects to see in the development of the piece (e.g., examples from the textbook, examples from two outside sources, examples from real life) can be given.

Focus. English composition convention dictates that most pieces begin with a thesis in the first paragraph, clearly announcing the author's purpose. This pronouncement of purpose, which is continued in the piece with topic sentences, is a prominent feature of American discourse. For many ESL students, however, this convention does not exist. In fact, just the opposite rhetorical style may be employed. Long before the piece's main point is divulged, the writer may provide extensive background information to establish context and subtle suggestions that hint at the topic to be discussed. Only after such steady buildup does the writer arrive at the key point of the essay. Clearly, such a contrast in rhetorical styles can result in misreading and misunderstandings.

One way to overcome such differences in a piece's construction is to read the piece completely, resisting the urge to stop and search for the thesis. In doing so, the essay will unfold gradually, eventually revealing the writer's point. Once the main idea is clear, the teacher can then show the student how to work the main point closer to start of the piece. Another method is to ask the student how arguments and essays are constructed in the student's native language (Minett, 2004). Then, the teacher could explain the structure used in American writing. By comparing and contrasting ways in which texts are constructed, the student will come to see that by

(continued on next page)

---

merely reorganizing an essay the meaning will be made clear for the American audience.

Coherence and Organization. When digression within the paper's paragraphs interferes with the American expectation for getting to the point, a handy exercise, called *topical structural analysis*, may help. Working through one paragraph at a time, the teacher and the student underline the subject of each sentence. These underlined "topics" are then placed in an outline diagram to determine the overall focus of the paragraph. This way, students can see the coherence and sequence of ideas in each paragraph and will be better able to make changes so that the paragraphs are developed for specific topics (Connor and Farmer, 1990).

Grammar and Form. A good way to view ESL grammatical errors is to view ESL writing as "a kind of foreign accent, only in writing instead of speech"(Leki, 1992, p. 129). As with accents in pronunciation, we can only expect modest improvement over time and, in many cases, no improvement at all. Thus it is with grammar. Correcting surface grammatical errors, even when the student wishes for such correction and when the teacher feels compelled to do so, will, according to research findings, produce "insignificant improvement in subsequent writing tasks" (Leki, 1992, p. 128). What is a teacher to do? The most beneficial help would be to focus on a few aspects of form in each paper. For example, if the overwhelming difficulty for the reader of the ESL piece comes from verb tense shifts, then let this one area be the focus of subsequent revision expectations.

Finally, it is important to note that some types of errors are usage rather than rule based and thus will not be something that a student will understand or learn simply by correcting in a single piece. On the other hand, rule-based errors will be the ones that practice and correction will eliminate to some degree over time. Overall, teachers cannot expect ESL students to write perfect papers. Teachers can, however, encourage them by valuing their ideas and assisting them in learning the conventions of American English writing.

---

that teachers describe what they learn about each student writer in response to the question: *What am I learning about this student as a writer?* In the second column, he suggests that teachers describe what they need to teach their students in response to the question: *What do I need to teach this student?*

Conferring with student writers, with any writer actually, is not easy. Students sometimes resist the teacher's suggestions, creating tensions (Nickel, 2001). Teachers need time to develop the skills needed to teach writers a new strategy or technique in a way that keeps ownership of the piece with the writer. Following each conference, it is important that teachers step back and reflect on what they did and why they did it, and what the writer did and how the writer felt. Ray (2001) suggests that teachers form a study group with colleagues and read Anderson's book, *How's It Going?* (2001), which is about conferring. She offers these words of advice (p. 171): "Conferring is very challenging, and you will probably struggle with it for quite some time before you begin to feel at ease. But most things in teaching—as in all of life—are like that, aren't they?"

Peer Conferences.   In addition to teacher–student conferences, peers will confer with peers, using the procedures determined by the teacher and taught in a procedural focus lesson. As students have increasing numbers of conferences with their teacher, their conferences with their peers will improve. Experience is the best teacher, and social interaction with peers influences the kinds of writing strategies children internalize and use independently (Neuman & Roskos, 1991a; Rowe, 1989; Vukelich, 1993).

The ultimate purpose of teacher and peer conferences is to help the writers learn about the kinds of questions they might ask themselves when considering their audience's needs. As several writers (e.g., Calkins, 1986; Graves, 1983; Harwayne, 1992) have suggested, the teacher's goal is to put herself or himself out of a job. Yet can young writers learn to consider their audience's needs? After all, they are still quite egocentric.

Teachers organize peer conferencing in a variety of ways. As noted earlier, some teachers encourage the students to talk with the writers at their table or group of desks. M. Colleen Cruz (2004) describes a more complicated system. She had three kinds of peer writing groups functioning in her fourth-grade classroom. A "salon" consisted of six to eight writers. Salons were organized by the students and, for the most part, the groups stayed together for the entire year. A "writing club" consisted of three to five writers and lasted from one to eight weeks. Again, writing clubs were organized by the students. The third kind of writing group, "partnerships," consisted of two writers, were organized by the teacher or the student, and lasted from five minutes to a full year.

Students will not automatically know how to confer with their peers. While the teacher models conferring in the teacher–student conference, modeling likely will be insufficient to help students develop the necessary skills to offer constructive criticism. Cruz (2004) approached the teaching of conversational skills within a conference in the following ways. First, she generated a list of "some things writers talk to each other about" (p. 100), which included such things as asking advice, giving advice, identifying things that are going well and not so well, plot ideas, character traits, confusing parts, and word choice. Then, she sent her students off to talk as she walked around the room, eavesdropping on her students' conversations. Later, she realized that her students needed a model of how providing thoughtful criticism might sound. The model she provided her students included four points (p. 102):

- Start with a sincere compliment.
- Be honest, but be kind.
- Make suggestions that the writer can try right away.
- Use examples from other authors' work.

Then, using a piece of her writing (yes, the best teachers of writing are writers themselves), she invited the students to use the model to critique her draft. When using this model, she noticed significant positive changes in her students' peer conferences.

What about the student who just does not want to join a community of writers? Cruz's advice is to expose the writer to partnerships, clubs, and salons, but then to allow the student to do what works best for him or her. These students will be a member of the larger community when the class meets for group focus lessons.

They will be members of the small groups that the teacher will bring together for a lesson on a topic of specific need to this small group. Finally, they will confer with the teacher. They also will participate in group share sessions. Hence, they will receive feedback to their writing.

Using Technology to Respond to Writers. Today technology can be used as an additional means for teachers and peers to provide response to a writer and for collaboration among writers in the creation of texts. In Special Feature 8.2, Patricia Scott describes several ways to use technology to foster a collaborative, interactive environment that nurtures the writing process.

Group Share Sessions

Each writing workshop ends with a *group share session*. These sessions are a bit like the teacher and peer conferences from the writing portion of the writing workshop. An important difference is that during the group share session, two or three students sit, one at a time, in the author's chair and share their pieces with the other writers in the class. With young writers, the other writers typically gather at the sharing writer's feet. Older writers tend to remain at their desk or table. Regardless of the seating arrangement, the other writers listen attentively while the writer reads the piece, or a portion of the piece, preparing to ask meaning-related questions. The purpose is for the author "to receive help on what is and is not working in their writing and what, if anything, they might consider doing next" (Harste, Short, & Burke, 1988, p. 221). Trade Secret 8.5 describes group sharing in Jackie Shockley's classroom.

Teachers might organize several different kinds of group share meetings in their classrooms. Many of these ideas originated some time ago with Calkins (1983). The typical group share session is like the sessions described in this chapter (e.g., see Trade Secret 8.5). In this kind of ten- to fifteen-minute share session, called a *share meeting,* as many writers as possible share their drafts and receive their peers' and teacher's questions. Some teachers select students who volunteer to be the presenters. Other teachers select those whom they have identified as having made a significant discovery to be the presenters. For example, teacher Margaret Hull asked student Charlie to share his piece about his fishing trip because he discovered how to use parentheses to explain words possibly unknown to his readers. Still other teachers ask writers who tried the strategy or technique taught in the focus lesson to share their revised draft and talk about how they used that strategy or technique. Deirdra Aikens invites all the students with a particular color folder to share on the same day. Many use a combination of these means of selecting writers for group share presentations.

A second kind of group share session is *writers' circle.* In this kind of share session, the teacher divides the class into several small groups of five or so students. Writers then simultaneously share pieces with their peers. Obviously, many experiences with share meetings are needed before young students can be expected to independently and effectively run writers' circles. Some educators

SPECIAL FEATURE 8.2
Integrating Technology into Writing

BY PATRICIA G. SCOTT

Research suggests that the effective use of technology fosters a collaborative, interactive environment that nurtures the writing process and supports the social perspective on learning (Hewett, 2000; Kamil, Intrator, & Kim, 2000; Karchmer, 2001; Leu, 2000; Selfe, 1999). Networked computers open the possibility to encourage a true sense of audience by cultivating an online community in which writers and readers are communicating and collaborating with each other. In an online community, students see a genuine purpose for the writing, beyond the assignment (Hawisher et al., 1996; Spitzer, 1990).

Below I describe a few technology ideas to foster the social process of writing.

■ **Software Programs**

Often, educators are searching for the perfect fix to help students write. Most educators seem not to know that there is a program installed, for free, on most school computers that facilitates the writing process. When a student completes a writing piece on the computer, the writer often prints the document for the teacher and peers to read and respond, a step that is no longer necessary. Microsoft Word, a Microsoft Office product, comes installed with two revising tools: comments and track changes. Teachers should ask their students to electronically send them or their peers their writing piece (e-mail, shared network drive, jump drive, CD). Once received, the teacher or peers open the document and opens *track changes* (Figure 8.4). (*Track changes* is located under *Tools* on the top tool bar. By clicking on *track change*, both *track changes* and *comments* will be engaged.) To insert a comment, the teacher or peers will click on the *yellow folder*.

With *insert comment* engaged, the teacher or peer is able to write detailed comments to guide the writer through the revision process by moving the cursor and clicking at the spots in the document where he or she wishes to make a comment and typing the comment. Figure 8.5 gives an example of how the *insert comments* works. With *track change* engaged (the

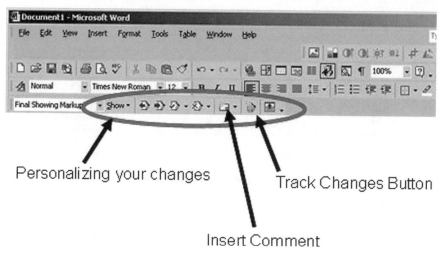

FIGURE 8.4

(continued on next page)

SPECIAL FEATURE 8.2   (continued)

background of the *track change* icon is orange), teachers and peers can make suggested revisions directly in the writer's piece. Figure 8.6 shows how *track changes* allows readers to make suggested changes directly in the writer's piece.

When the teacher or peers have responded, they will return the document via e-mail or jump drive to the writer. As soon as the writer opens the document, the feedback is obvious and easy to read.

■ Wikis and Blogs

Wikis and blogs are two examples of online applications to encourage writers to collaborate on the Internet. Wiki, the Hawaiian name for quick, is defined by Wikipedia (http://en.wikipedia.org/wiki/Wiki) as a Web application that allows users, anyone with a browser, to freely add and edit content on the Web. The idea behind wiki use in the classroom is for students to collectively author write by simply clicking on the link "Edit This Page." Go to the Wikipedia site, an online wiki encyclopedia, for an example of how wikis enhance the community of learners. With the ease of creating, editing, and publishing pages immediately, wikis provide a simple way for asynchronous collaboration.

Another collaborative opportunity on the Internet is the blog or Web log, often referred to as online journals. This description, however, often ignores the interactive potential. A blog allows a writer to publish and permit readers to post comments in response to the original entry, idea, or question. Kennedy (2003, para.2) identifies how a blog can enhance the social process of writing:

> Web publication gives students a real audience to write to and, when optimized, a collaborative environment where they can give and receive feedback, mirroring the way professional writers use a workshop environment to hone their craft. Creating online communities where student writing takes center stage means inviting audiences to read and reflect on published work.

In a blog, the audience and the writers are able to connect to each other more interactively in time and space, fostering and supporting a community of writers for bloggers to comment and give feedback to other bloggers, link to other bloggers, and create an interactive organization. Blogs in the classroom provide opportunities for students to write in a personal space and also

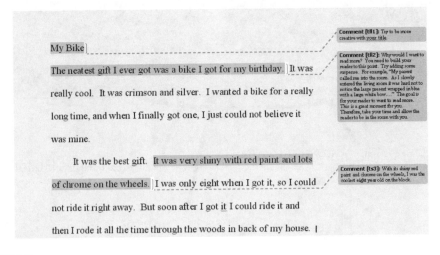

FIGURE 8.5

My ⎟Bike

_____The neatest best gift I ever got was a bike I got for my

birthday. It was really cool. It was croimsoncrimson and kind of

silver, but mostly red.

_____I wanted a bike for a really long time, and when I finally got

one, I just could not believe it was mine. It was the best gift I ever

got for a birthday presentmy birthday.

FIGURE 8.6

write in a collaborative space where ideas are shared, questions are asked and answered, and social cohesion is developed (Huffaker, 2004).

The ways in which we write and learn with technologies need to shift from thinking about the hardware to thinking about the designs, set of activities, and the environments of technology that engage students to be active, constructive, authentic, and collaborative (Jonassen et al., 1998). The effective use of blogs and wikis is an example of how to think about technology as an environment to engage students in meaning-making processes. Writing with multimedia is another way.

■ Digital Storytelling

Teaching and learning with multimedia have a rich history in education. Instructional technology such as film, video, slides, and tapes has been used in the classroom for many years. The introduction of multimedia software in schools during the late 1980s, however, provided teachers an ability to capture, synthesize, and manipulate audio, video, and special effects with traditional media of text and images. Jonassen, Peck, and Wilson (1998, p. 88) define multimedia as "the integration to more than one medium (audio, video, graphics, text, and animation) into some form of communication." Digital storytelling is a way to write using a variety of multimedia practices. For the student, digital storytelling is an opportunity to share personal stories about the events, people, and places in their lives. For teachers, digital storytelling provides the media for students to find their voices, communi-

cate their stories, and connect with peers in a very special way.

What are the materials used and how do they create a story package? Although there are many software packages to purchase to create digital stories, often a program is already installed on the computer. Movie Maker 2, a program installed on computers with Microsoft Office XP, or iMovie, for Macintosh computers, is more than enough for students to create digital stories. Additional hardware might include a microphone, speakers, and a scanner. Before using the technology, there are excellent resources that provide teachers with student samples, adult samples, and lesson plans to learn more about digital storytelling. Listed below are a few "musts" in resources to investigate:

A Must List of Resources

- Digital Storytelling in Scott County: www.scott.k12.ky.us/technology/digitalstorytelling/ds.html
- Center for Digital Storytelling: www.storycenter.org/
- Digital Storytelling Cookbook: www.storycenter.org/memvoice/pages/cookbook.html
- Digital Stories by Students and Teachers: www.digitalstories.org/

The focus of digital storytelling is the storytelling. Technology provides the environment and tools to create a story rich in voice and message.

Regardless of the technology, such as software programs, blogs, wikis, email, instant messaging, or digital storytelling, online and multimedia writing challenges the way we interact, communicate, and think with writing. If technology matters to the social process of writing, then a central issue in the classroom use of computer technologies for literacy (specifically writing) and learning is how can classroom teachers integrate technology into the content and social context of the writing classroom as a means to support the writing process.

TRADE SECRET 8.5
Group Sharing

JACKIE SHOCKLEY

I glanced at the classroom clock—2:50.

"Boys and girls, writing time is over for today. Please put your folders away unless it is your turn to share, and meet us on the rug." Share time begins in Room 206.

The first author reads his piece in its entirety. He concludes; his audience applauds. Several hands shoot up. The author calls on a student: "I really like how you said you felt like biting him back. I liked hearing how you felt." The author smiles, replies with a thank you, and calls on another student. "I heard a lot of ands in your piece. Maybe you should go through and see if you need all of those ands." Sitting in the back of the group, I record that comment on a small piece of notepaper. The author again declines comment but calls on another student: "I liked your story a lot." I interrupt the student and ask, "What exactly did you like about it? Be specific so you can help the author." The student responds that she liked how he wrote about his gerbil because she has one, too.

I tell the audience that I really like how they are helping each other when they make comments that are specific and refer to our focus lessons. I request another round of applause for our author and hand him the notes I wrote, asking, "Here are the suggestions that were made, but who's the boss of this piece?"

Two more authors read their pieces; each reading was followed by more comments and applause. Precious learning moments have occurred and have been reinforced during the ten-minute period. So ends a typical share time in my room.

There is concrete evidence that helpful comments during share time have a positive impact on the students' writing. During a small-group share, a writer (Kip) was reading a piece about a camping trip. In his attempts to be explicit, he included the time each activity began and ended. After one reading, a member of the audience commented, "Wow, you told the time on everything." He responded, "I know. I didn't like how it sounded. I think I'll take it out." I was thinking, "Hooray!" only to hear another member of the group saying, "I like it. I think you should leave it in." The discussion continued. Kip wavered but prior to publishing decided to include only a few of the times. His final decision is not really the issue here. What is important is that these writers were thinking critically about the piece.

(e.g., Harste, Short, & Burke, 1988) insist that each participant in this kind of share session bring a piece of writing to the writers' circle.

A third share session is a *quiet share*, which requires the listeners to have access to paper; a writing tool; and a desk, table, or clipboard. When each of the two or three writers has finished reading a piece, the listeners write their questions or comments. They may or may not sign them. The comments are then given to the writers for their consideration.

In *focused shares*, the teacher asks the writers to read a specific aspect of their pieces. For example, the teacher might ask the students to gather to read their leads, titles, or sentence or sentences that describe the setting of their piece, or to show how they focused their topic. Sometimes, teachers link focused shares with the day's focus lessons (as Maryanne Lamont did). On the day when the topic of her focus lesson was the writing of focused pieces, Ms. Lamont decided that the group share session would be a focused share, during which time some of her young writers would read their old pieces and their revised pieces to illustrate how they had revised to focus on one aspect of their topic.

Occasionally, teachers will use the group share session for a *process share.* During these kinds of group share sessions, the students may be asked to bring illustrations of revisions they made in their texts and to be prepared to tell about why they made the changes. The students may also be asked to share their notes (like brainstorming webs), created to help them discover what they know about a topic, or their handling of problems they have solved in their pieces (such as Charlie's use of parentheses).

Giving or *celebration shares* are unlike all other group share sessions. During these share sessions, writers share the pieces they have published. Because the writers have completed their writing of these pieces, only comments are offered by the listeners. These authors' works then join those by other published authors (writers such as Maurice Sendak, Chris Van Allsberg, Tomie de Paolo, and Eric Carle) in the classroom library corner. Like all other books in that corner, these works are available to be checked out and read by an appreciative audience. Like the other books in a library, these books need to have a library checkout card and a pocket in which to keep the card.

ASSESSMENT: DISCOVERING WHAT STUDENTS KNOW AND CAN DO

An observant reader of this book has already realized a teacher's important role in implementing a writing program. Central to teachers' implementation of a high-quality writing program is their ability to answer the following kinds of questions: What do these writers need? Do they need information on how to pull their readers into their pieces, on good leads? Do they, perhaps, need information on how to make their writing come alive, using dialogue? When children use dialogue, do they know how to punctuate their texts? By examining the pieces in the students' writing folders or writing notebooks, rereading the anecdotal notes made during teacher–student conferences and the vignettes of significant breakthroughs demonstrated by their writers, and reading and evaluating their students' writing pieces, teachers can acquire the information they need to make instructional decisions. This information will also help teachers judge their writers' development and accomplishments.

Anderson (2005, p. 2) encourages teachers to "take an assessment stance" and assess student writers every day. He is *not* suggesting that teachers *test* student writers every day by having them write to a prompt. Rather, Anderson suggests that good teachers gather information about their student writers by observing them, talking with them, and studying their writing pieces. By observing, teachers can gather information about the students' initiative, what the students know about writing well, and about the students' writing process. By conferring, teachers can learn what the students are thinking about as they write as well as what they know about writing and their writing process. By studying the writing pieces (not just the finished pieces but all the drafts), teachers can learn what the students do well, what revising strategies they use, and what their editing shows that they know about the English language system. Using these strategies, good writing teachers learn about their students' writing strengths and weaknesses, how to tailor their conversations with their students during conferences to meet each student's needs, and how to design focus lessons and units of study that best meet the collective needs of the class of writers.

Using Writing Rubrics

Rubrics are an important tool teachers use to evaluate their students' finished piece. Rubrics help teachers answer the questions: How good is this piece of writing? What qualities of good writing did this writer use effectively in crafting this piece? (The answer to this question helps teachers know what to celebrate in their students' writing, and celebrating what is good is as important as uncovering each writer's instructional needs.) What qualities of good writing did this writer not use as effectively in crafting this piece? (The answer to this question helps teachers know what lessons to teach this student.) Rubrics, then, help teachers understand their students' development. They provide the "criteria that describe student performance at various levels of proficiency" (O'Neill, 1994, p. 4). Rubrics enable teachers (and students) to assign a score or rating (beginning, developing, proficient) to a piece of writing. Classic writing rubrics typically describe student writing in several areas (writing traits), such as organization, development or ideas, sentence variety, word choice, voice, and conventions. Descriptors outline the expectations or criteria for each of the possible point values or performance levels, usually on a three- to six-point scale, for each area. The clearer the criteria, the more likely the student writers will know what is expected of them in each writing trait. Vicki Spandel (2001, p. 21), for example, describes the level of detail needed to describe the *organization* writing trait. She suggests that the criteria describing proficient organization might be: "(1) inviting, purposeful lead; (2) effective sequencing; (3) smooth, helpful transitions; (4) good pacing; and (5) effective conclusion that makes the reader think." The criteria describing developing performance might be: "(1) introduction and conclusion present, (2) sequencing sometimes works, (3) transitions attempted, and (4) pacing sometimes too rapid or too slow." Finally, the criteria for beginning organization might be: "(1) no real lead or conclusion yet, (2) sequencing creates confusion, and (3) pacing slows reader down— or pushes the reader too hard." Notice how these criteria are clearly written, identify significant aspects of an important writing trait, give clear distinctions among the three performance levels, and describe what the writer should do. The students could use these criteria to guide their development of their writing, and they and their teachers could use this rubric to judge the quality of this writing trait (organization) in the students' writing pieces.

Three kinds of scoring rubrics for teachers and students are in use today:

- *Primary trait scoring rubrics* vary with the writing's purpose and audience. If the writers are to write to persuade a person in authority, for example, then the traits that are central to putting forth an argument might be to articulate a position and to prepare a well-written discussion on the reasons for the position, taking into account the knowledge of the audience about the topic. Because the audience is a person in authority, an additional trait might be to offer a counterargument for at least one of the audience's possible positions on the topic. An example of a primary trait scoring rubric is presented Figure 8.7. Using this rubric, how would you score the persuasive letter in Figure 8.8?

- *Holistic scoring rubrics* require raters to consider how the writer used all the writing traits (organization, ideas or development, voice, word choice, sentence variety, mechanics) in harmony in a piece to achieve an overall effect. In essence, the scorer reads the piece and gets a general impression of how well the writer has used the writing traits in the crafting of the piece. To help scorers, exemplars (or anchor papers) are selected to illustrate typical performance at each score point. The scorers, then, can compare the piece they are reading against the anchor papers to help them arrive at a single score

FIGURE 8.7   Primary Trait Scoring Rubric for Persuasive Writing

---

6   **Extensively elaborated.** In these pieces, students articulate a position for or against the topic, or they suggest a compromise, and they present an extended, well-written discussion on the reasons for their position. These responses may be similar to "5" responses, but they provide an extended discussion of the reasons for their position.

5   **Elaborated.** In these responses, students articulate a position for or against the topic, or they suggest a compromise, and they provide an extended discussion of the reasons for their position.

4   **Developed.** In these responses, students take a position for or against the topic, or they suggest a compromise, and they discuss the reasons for their position. Although the reasons may be more clearly stated than in papers that receive lower scores, the discussions may be unevenly developed.

3   **Minimally developed.** In these responses, students state or imply a position for or against the topic. Rather than support their position with reasons, however, these papers tend to offer specific suggestions or to elaborate on the students' opinions.

2   **Undeveloped.** In these responses, students state or imply a position for or against the topic, but they offer no reasons to support their point of view.

1   **Off-topic or no response.** In these responses, students do not take a position or write nothing.

Jason

I think you Shouldn't give us homework becusase I think we should have a free break. becusase I think you Should Let us have a break becusase Spring it's our time off. and plus I'm going to west Vrginia with my dad

FIGURE 8.8   Jason's Persuasive Letter

Three Rubrics: Basic, Proficient, Advanced

Pieces rated as basic *should exhibit the following characteristics:*

- The piece has a good topic sentence.
- Piece focuses on one topic.
- The sequence of the events is appropriate.
- The description of the setting (where the event occurred) might be stated or implied.
- The piece has a beginning, a middle, and an end. The beginning and middle probably are more developed than the end.
- The transition between sentences and paragraphs is typically clear.
- The piece has a title that is consistent with its main idea.

Pieces rated as proficient *should exhibit the preceding characteristics, with some elaboration, and the following characteristics:*

- The setting is stated and developed, probably through the use of an adjective or two.
- The piece has a beginning, a middle, and an end that exhibits more development (particularly of the middle) than pieces rated as basic. One event may be detailed, or there may be brief details for multiple events.
- The vocabulary is selected to create a picture of the event or events, the character, the setting, and so on. Fresh adverbs and adjectives are often used.

Pieces rated as advanced *should exhibit the following characteristics:*

- The lead is catchy; grabbing the readerís attention and making him or her want to read on.
- The setting is explicitly described, using imagery.
- The beginning catches the readerís attention, arousing his or her interest and helping him or her to anticipate the middle. It provides the information necessary to understand the rest of the narrative. The middle sustains interest by depicting events with details. The piece ends with an effective ìbangî that reveals the outcome.
- The dialogue provides insights into the character's (or characters') thoughts and feelings, in addition to advancing the plot/storyline.
- The writer uses appropriate words to signal transitions.
- There is cohesion within the paragraphs (each idea is developed in a paragraph) and coherence across paragraphs. One event moves smoothly to another.
- Multiple events are described. Events, details, and dialogue are carefully chosen with the purpose of telling the story.
- The writer selects and sustains
    —a language natural to the narrative,
    —a point of view appropriate to the narrative, and
    —a tense (or tenses) consistent with the flow of the narrative.

FIGURE 8.9   **Teacher-Designed Expressive Rubric**

for this piece. Unlike primary trait scoring rubrics, the same holistic scoring rubric can be used to score writing in all discourse categories (persuasive, expressive, information, narrative). An example of a holistic scoring rubric developed by a group of teachers is shown in Figure 8.9. Consistent with suggestions regarding how a rubric should be created, these teachers researched

There once was a very tiny
family. The largest one was six inches tall.
They all had tals they lived in the walls
of the Bigg family. Nobody ever noticed
them. One Halloween the 2 yongest ones
were thinking of something to scare there
family with. The oldest was listening to
the radio. The little boy told his plan to
scare his family with to his Sister. They
wen to the microphone on the radio
If this tiny family was discoverd they
would be destroyed. The little boy turned
on the microphone and said "There has
been discoverd a Small family living inside
the walls. If you think you have them
call this Number 738-9828 we will
Send you a destroer for them. The whole
family went wild they Started packing
there things The yongest 2 told them
it was just a joke They unpacked
there things and settled down.

                                    True story

                          T.H.

          The day I went to the Carnival in wildwood

                    One day I went to wildwood and we
stayed in a motel in wildwood for 20 days in the summer
I went in the Spooky house and It was Fun My brother
My cousin they went Into It was Fun we went pass Dracula
My cousin thought that It was a staten so he said Boo!
that Dracula said Boo! back to him and we jumped We
almost jumped and the water. It was all over a man at
the door was beating the door and I never went in a
Spook house again And we had fun. That all I can
Say now By
                          The
                              End

FIGURE 8.10 Two Third Graders' Stories

the characteristics of expressive texts and read published pieces when preparing a list of the important characteristics exhibited by these kinds of texts. They incorporated these characteristics into the highest category, which they labeled "advanced," on their rubric. Using this rubric, how would you score the writing in Figure 8.10?

- *Analytical scoring* "acknowledges the underlying premise that, in writing, the whole is more than the sum of its parts, but it adds that, if we are to teach students to write, we must take writing apart—temporarily—in order to focus on one skill at a time" (Spandel, 2001, p. 26). An analytical scoring rubric, then, takes each significant writing trait and describes, using specific language and criteria, what each trait looks like at various levels of proficiency. For example, Ruth Culham (2003) describes a 6 + 1 analytic scoring rubric used by many teachers to describe students' writing. The traits on this rubric include *ideas* (the content), *organization* (the internal structure, the logical pattern of the ideas), *voice* (the writer's style, what makes the writer's feelings and convictions come out through the words), *word choice* (the rich, colorful, precise language that moves the piece), *sentence fluency* (the flow of the language), and *conventions* (the level of correctness), plus *presentation* (the form and layout of the writing). Culham then defines the qualities of each trait at five levels of performance. For guidance in how to focus on each trait to score students' writing, see Culham's book and complete the exercises on scoring samples of students' papers.

The analytical scoring rubric is the most useful rubric for teachers. By scoring students' writing along each significant writing trait, teachers can determine each student's writing needs and the class's writing needs. Now, the teacher knows what to teach and what the topics of the classroom's focus lessons should be. In Trade Secret 8.6, Peggy Dillner describes this critical link between assessment and instruction. An example of an analytical scoring rubric is shown in Figure 8.11. Using this rubric, how would you score the writing in Figure 8.12?

Rubrics not only help teachers, but they also help students if they are taught how to use the rubric for self-assessment purposes. In fact, George Hillocks Jr. (1986) suggests that of all the methods used to teach writing over the past decades, well-defined criteria is one of the two research-supported instructional techniques (the other instructional technique is providing good models). To make the state's scoring rubric useful for their students, the teachers at Jennie Smith Elementary School rewrote the language of the criteria of the state's rubric into "kid-friendly language" (Figure 8.13). The principal then contracted with the district's vocational students to make poster-size rubric charts to hang in each classroom's writing center. In addition, the teachers placed a copy of the kid-friendly rubric in each student's writing folder. Through teacher–student conferences and the group sharing session at the end of writing workshop, the teachers teach the students to use the language of the rubrics to describe their writing.

Ray (2001) suggests that teachers form a study group around Anderson's book on conferring. Once the study group has read and discussed Anderson's book on conferring, they can read and discuss at least one on assessment, such as Spandel (2001), Anderson (2005), and Culham (2003). Teachers also should visit www.nwrel.org/assessment, which provides numerous support materials for teachers attempting to integrate six-trait assessment into their classrooms.

TRADE SECRET 8.6
From Assessment to Instruction

BY MARGARET PHILLIS DILLNER

"Look at this paper," the disgruntled English language arts teacher muttered in the faculty room. "She did not skip lines as I requested, the spelling is atrocious, and I just spent a significant amount of time teaching the proper punctuation of direct quotations, which she has totally ignored. Humph! And she had the audacity to tell me I was going to love this piece."

How was this teacher going to assess this student's piece of writing? Would the teacher's disappointment with the student's weakness in conventions sway the evaluation? Why did the student think that the teacher would love the writing sample? Was there a writing rubric to be used in scoring? What would the teacher do to improve this student's writing? What *is* the link between assessment and instruction?

Assessing writing using a rubric has been around for many years. Many teachers of writing are using a holistic rubric now, and some states have adopted holistic rubrics for state writing tests. Teachers may also use analytic rubrics to define specific strengths and weaknesses within writing pieces. Some states give this kind of feedback to students as well. Many researchers and teachers agree that evaluations using rubrics are clearer and more objective than subjectively assigned grades (Baldwin, 2004, Saddler & Andrade, 2004). Continued staff development will help ensure that all teachers understand and use good rubrics (Spandel, 2001).

Assessment with a rubric in only the beginning of the cycle, however. If the assessment is to be truly meaningful, then it must drive instruction (Hansen, 1996). By looking at an individual student's writing, and the class's writing as whole, the teacher will make instructional decisions. Such decisions may involve quick individual lessons given during a conference, several children who exhibit the same weakness, or an instruction to the entire class about a need they all share. The subtlety is between telling students what is wrong with their writing versus telling students how to improve their writing.

In assessment, one of the biases to which teachers are prone is to note the errors in conventions and stop the assessment at that point (Spandel, 2001). Faulty grammar, missing punctuation, and poor spelling jump out at teachers, jangle their nerves, and undoubtedly point to instructional needs. Weaknesses in development, organization, word choice and style, and sentence structure, however, also point to instructional needs. These writing characteristics, particularly development and organization, are less likely to be targets of instruction despite exhibited needs in student writing.

Teachers must assess and instruct in all areas, focusing on areas of greatest need. Teachers need to force themselves to examine closely the needs exhibited by their students' writing according to a reliable rubric. Then instruction can focus on one or two weaknesses at a time. Many students will be overwhelmed if expected to fix everything. Following instruction, there should be immediate application as students return to their writing.

The following ideas are for focus lessons appropriate for weaknesses in organization, development, word choice and style, and sentence structure. A weakness in conventions is not listed because most teachers have an excellent repertoire of lessons on spelling, punctuation, and grammar.

■ Organization
Problem: Lacks unity and smooth transitions
Possible lesson: Find a well-written published piece that illustrates unity with good use of transition words or phrases. Such an example is from pages 24–25 in *Spinning Spiders* by Melvin Berger. For older students, one could use page 20 of *The Midwife's Apprentice* by Karen Cushman. Retype either passage in discrete sentences and cut the sentences apart. Have students work in groups to put their paragraph back together.

TRADE SECRET 8.6 (continued)

Discuss how they knew the sequence into which to arrange the piece. Then have students return to their own writing pieces and read them, looking for unity and transition for possible revision.

■ Development

Problem: Many irrelevant details

Possible lesson: Have students list everything they know about a particular subject (e.g., the *Titanic*, basketball, MTV, the local mall). Then have that list divided into two: one for critical information and the other for trivial information. Discuss what would be included in a good paper on this topic. Remind them of the quotation by Elmore Leonard, "I try to leave out the parts that people skip." Have them return to their writing. If necessary, have them list on another piece of paper all the details about their subject that are in their piece. Then have them determine if all these details belong in a critical information column or if some belong in the trivial information column.

■ Word Choice/Style

Problem: Lacks distinctive tone or character

Possible lesson: Pick one of the biographies written by Russell Freedman (about Marian Anderson, Louis Braille, Confucius, Crazy Horse, Martha Graham, Abraham Lincoln, Eleanor Roosevelt, Franklin Delano Roosevelt, or the Wright Brothers). Read a section from the Freedman biography and then part of an encyclopedia article about the same individual. Discuss the difference. Have students return to their pieces to see if they believe that their distinctive voice shines through.

■ Sentence Formation

Problem: Choppy sentences

Possible lesson: Select a passage from a published author that illustrates compound and complex sentences as well as sentences of varying length. Helen Griffith's book, *Dinosaur Habitat*, chapter 2, paragraph 1, is a possibility. For more advanced students, one could use page 1 of *Jip* by Katherine Paterson, which also includes direct quotations. In a teacher-guided discussion, have student(s) examine each sentence in this paragraph for the number of words, type of sentence, and variety of sentence. Then have someone read it aloud to hear the flow of the paragraph. Students should return to their piece to see if they can change any sentences to add variety and fluidity.

The best practice is for teachers to use pieces of student work (with the student's permission, of course) and/or quality literature from their classroom in development of focus lessons. The above suggestions can all be adapted to many grade levels with many pieces of appropriate literature. The reading–writing connection is crucial for students to understand (Atwell, 1998). So much good literature is available today to enrich our students' literary world, and it can be easily woven into lessons on writing strategies. Besides, one of our great chroniclers of southern life, William Faulkner, said

> "Read, read, read. Read everything—trash, classics, good and bad, and see how they do it. Just like a carpenter who works as an apprentice and studies the master. Read! You'll absorb it. Then write. If it is good, you'll find out. If it's not, throw it out the window." (Faulkner, 2005)

Instruction based on the needs of students is where constructivist research says to begin (Herman, 1992). One then builds on the learner's prior knowledge to enable movement forward. Assessing a student's writing to determine instructional needs and making decisions on how to best meet those needs are what good teachers of writing do.

FIGURE 8.11   Analytical Scoring Rubric

The following characteristics determine the success of the response in meeting the needs of the audience and fulfilling the writing purpose.

		Score of 5	Score of 4	Score of 3	Score of 2	Score of 1
Organization		*Score point 5 meets all the criteria listed in score point 4. In addition, a paper receiving this score shows an exceptional awareness of readers' concerns and needs.*	Unified with smooth transitions, a clear and logical progression of ideas, and an effective introduction and closing.	Generally unified with some transitions, a clear progression of ideas, and an introduction and closing.	Minimally unified and may lack transitions or an introduction or closing.	Lacks unity.
Development		*The student may have shown an exceptional use of:*	Sufficient, specific, and relevant details that are fully elaborated.	Specific details but may be insufficient, irrelevant, or not fully elaborated.	Some specific details but may be insufficient, irrelevant, and/or not elaborated.	No or few specific details that are minimally elaborated.
Sentence Formation		*Development strategies specific to the purpose for writing*	Consistently complete sentences with appropriate variety in length and structure.	Generally complete sentences with sufficient variety in length and structure.	Some sentence formation errors and a lack of sentence variety.	Frequent and severe sentence formation errors and/or a lack of sentence variety.
Style/Word Choice		*Distinctive style, voice, tone* *Literary devices*	A consistent style with precise and vivid word choice.	Some style and generally precise word choice.	Sometimes general and repetitive word choice.	Often general, repetitive, and/or confusing word choice.
Lang. Conventions		*Compositional risks*	Few, if any, errors in standard written English that do not interfere with understanding.	Some errors in standard written English that rarely interfere with understanding.	Several kinds of errors in standard written English that interfere with understanding.	Frequent and severe errors in standard written English that interfere with understanding.

Source: Delaware Department of Education.

LARGE-SCALE ASSESSMENTS

In the previous section, we described how teachers might use rubrics to judge their students' writing performance. In addition to teachers assessing their students' writing performance, a growing number of states assess students' writing performance. In some states, they are high-stakes tests. The results not only reflect on the school but also determine the student's promotion to the next grade level or the ability to attend a school of the student's choice. Because of the No Child Left Behind Act (see Chapter 1), states now must assess their young citizens in grades 2

Do you know how to play soccer? Well, Matt and I do. This is how you start. First, you sign up. Then you get your coach. After that, the coach gets the whole team together and you have your first practice. Then you practice all the kicks and moves. Now we are going to tell you how to do them.

(1)

First we will tell you the way you should use your feet. You use the inside of your feet to dribble, pass and score. Also, you use the inside of your feet to block the ball.

Now we will tell you about kicks. One kick is the dribble and kick. It is when you dribble and then you kick the ball.

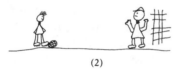

(2)

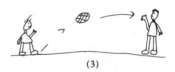

(3)

Since we have been talking about dribbling, we will tell you how to dribble. You use the inside of your feet. Then you kick it with the inside of your feet. If you kick it with your toes, sometimes it will hurt. Also if you kick it with the outside of your foot, the person can steal the ball. Also you might twist your ankle. But if you want to kick the ball like that you should be a professional or if you had a lot of experience. If you want to, you can try it; but we're just telling you that you shouldn't try it.

Now we will tell you more kicks. This play is called the "give and go." First, you dribble the ball. Then you pass it to your teammate. Then their teammate kicks the ball and makes a score.

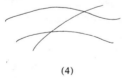

(4)

(5)

Now we will tell you about the banana kick. The banana kick is when the defender is charging. You should strike the ball with the outside of your foot. It will curve around him to your teammate. The banana kick is a very famous kick because it is made by famous Peli.

(6)

Now we will tell you how to act on the field. First, you be kind to your teammates. If you yell at the ref, you will get a yellow card. If you yell at the ref again, you will get another yellow card. That means you got a red card and you will get kicked out of the other next game.

(7)

FIGURE 8.12 How to Play Soccer by Matt and Scott

(continued)

Now we will tell you about the tournaments. Later on in the season, there will be tournaments. Your coach will sign your team up and you will go on the day that it is done. You also will play lots of teams. There will be an ice cream truck at the side walk. There will also be a concession stand and it will have hot dogs and candy bars and lots of other candy. Then there will be more tournaments later on. Just so you know, a tournament is a scrimmage too,

Soccer is one of the best games in our state. If you like football, you should like soccer too. That's how soccer is.

by Scott Myers and Matt Hearn

(8)

(9)

FIGURE 8.12   Continued.

through 8. On a specific day, typically in the spring, all students at those grade levels are required to produce a piece of writing. The procedures for gathering this sample of students' performance are standardized. Typically, teachers across the state, at each of the grade levels, present their students with the same prompt. For example, the students might be directed to write to the following prompt (from the Delaware Department of Education): The editor of your newspaper is putting together a student section of the newspaper. Students have been asked to write about their favorite holiday or tradition for this section. Write an article about your favorite holiday or tradition to send to the newspaper. Once the allotted time has passed, the teachers box the students' writing samples and deliver them to the school's office. The office staff then forwards the test to the district office or the state for scoring by trained scorers. (For additional prompt suggestions, see Spandel, 2001, pp. 32–33.) This kind of writing is different from what typically occurs in writing workshops. In writing workshops, students write about topics in which they have vested interests. Real audiences read their writing. Students have time to prewrite, write, revise, edit, and write a final copy. Students use the resources (e.g., dictionary, thesaurus, spell checker) they need. Perhaps it is not surprising that, given such differences, all teachers are not enthusiastically supportive of such large-scale assessments. Some teachers find them threatening and intimidating, especially when their students' performance is used to judge their teaching or their school's or education's performance.

How do teachers survive, and flourish, in this accountability climate? One suggestion is to volunteer to serve as a scorer, prompt writer, or selector of anchor papers. Typically, the state will bring teachers from across the state together to engage in each of these activities. Teachers who participate in such activities repeatedly declare that their participation provided them with excellent information, knowledge they can use in their classroom with their instruction and assessment

FIGURE 8.13   Kid-friendly Writing Rubric

Organize	Develop	Sentences	Words
4	**4**	**4**	**4**
My writing is in an order that makes sense.	My details are all about my topic.	I use complete sentences.	I use many exciting, sparkling words.
I use words to connect the beginning, middle, and end.	My details are important to my topic.	I use different words to start my sentences.	I use many powerful action words.
I always stay on topic.	I use many details to tell about my topic.	I use long and short sentences.	I use many different words.
My piece's beginning tells about the topic in an exciting way.			
My writing has an effective ending.			
3	**3**	**3**	**3**
My writing is mostly in an order that makes sense.	My details are mostly about my topic.	I usually use complete sentences.	I use some exciting, sparkling words.
My writing has a beginning, middle, and end.	I use some details to tell about my topic.	I usually use different words to start my sentences.	I use some powerful action words.
I usually use words to connect the beginning, middle, and end.	My details are good.	I use long and short sentences.	I use a lot of different words.
My writing has a good ending.			
2	**2**	**2**	**2**
My writing might be in an order that is confusing.	I use just a few details to tell about my topic.	I sometimes use complete sentences.	I use a few exciting, sparkling words.
My writing might be missing a beginning, middle, or end.	Some of my details might not tell about my topic.	I start most of my sentences the same.	I use few powerful action words.
My writing might include sentences that are not about the topic. My ending is just "The End."		My sentences are short.	Many of my words are the same.
1	**1**	**1**	**1**
My writing is in an order that is confusing.	I have few or no details.	My sentences might not be complete.	I do not use exciting sparkling words.
I might have written about more than one topic.	My piece is very short.	I might use the same words to begin my sentences.	I do not use powerful action words.
My writing may be missing a beginning, middle, or ending.		My sentences are short.	I often use the same words.
			I leave out words.

Source: Jennie Smith Elementary School.

practices. Remember that the large-scale assessment is just one assessment of students' writing. The students' writing folders or notebooks will house multiple other indicators of their day-to-day efforts. Most states have developed a process whereby teachers can provide classroom evidence to support their claim that a student's writing score is atypical to that student's day-to-day writing performance. In addition, teachers should periodically ask the students to respond to a prompt like one on the state test. (In fact, Ray, 2001 suggests teaching writing to a prompt as a "genre" study before the large-scale assessment test.) Score the students' responses using the state's writing rubric. Ask them to score their own writing using the state's writing rubric. Talk about what the students could have done to make their writing better.

Large-scale assessment has served to remind everyone—students, teachers, administrators, the public—of the importance of writing. It has provided a strong reason for teachers to find time in their already-packed daily schedules to teach, not just assign, writing. It has provided a reason for students to attend to how they might make their writing better. Sadly, it is the *how* of doing the assessment that does not always match good writing instruction.

SUMMARY

To become a competent teacher of writing in a writing workshop context will require considerable effort. Not only is this approach to the teaching of writing likely different from what most readers experienced as elementary students themselves, most elementary school teachers do not believe that they know much about good writing. Readers are encouraged to begin collecting models of good writing in all genres and to add copies of the many new books on the teaching of writing to their personal professional library. Entire books have been written on conferring, focus lessons, evaluating, and, these days, teaching writing the writing workshop way.

■ *What are the essentials of writing workshop?*

Before writing workshop begins, teachers need to make preparations. They need to consider their daily schedule. Where will forty-five to sixty minutes of writing workshop each day fit into the schedule? They need to arrange the classroom environment for talk among peers and for quiet writing. They need to create an area where all the writers can gather to share their drafts and finished pieces. They need to gather the needed materials and determine how to arrange these materials for the writers' easy access. They need to make plans to teach their students how to write.

■ *What are the components of writing workshop?*

In most classrooms, the components of writing workshop happen in the following order each day: a focus lesson in which the teacher teaches the students something about writing or writing workshop procedures; writing time during which the students write, confer with the teacher, and confer with each other; and group sharing time during which two or three students share their writing with the group and receive responses. Some teachers insert a status-of-the-class report between the focus lesson and writing time and quickly check on what each writer plans to do that day during writing workshop.

- *How do teachers teach and what kinds of lessons might they teach during writing workshop?*

Teachers teach through focus lessons, which might be procedural lessons in which students learn the teachers' expectations for their behavior during writing workshop; the craft or qualities of good writing lessons in which students learn about what makes writing good; writing process lessons in which students learn about the recursive nature of the writing process (prewriting, drafting, revising, editing, publishing) and how to use this process themselves; or mechanical-skills lessons in which students learn the rules of capitalization, punctuation, grammar, or usage. Teachers can teach these same lessons, one on one, during teacher–student conferences. They can reinforce these lessons through the group share at the end of writing workshop.

- *What is the structure of a writing conference?*

Conferences have a predictable structure. The teacher begins by attempting to discover the student's intentions. Here, the teacher is searching for the way to match the teaching during the conference with the writer's goal for this piece of writing. Knowing the writer's goal helps the teacher decide what the writer needs to achieve the goal. The second part of the conference is assessing the writer's need so as to decide what to teach. The third step is to teach the writer a needed strategy or skill. The teacher teaches something the student needs now but also something that will be useful in subsequent pieces of writing. The fourth step is to create a plan with the writer. What did the writer understand the teacher to say and what will the writer do now? The teacher then records the student's plan.

- *How might teachers assess their students' writing development?*

In their classrooms, teachers gather evidence about students' writing development every time they confer with a student. Most teachers make judgments about their students' writing performance through the use of analytical, holistic, or primary trait rubrics. Rubrics help not only teachers but also students if they are taught how to use rubrics for self-assessment. In addition to classroom-based assessments, many states require that students at particular grade levels participate in the state's large-scale assessment. Here students respond to prompts, someone other than the teacher scores the students' writing, and the teacher and student (and the student's parents) receive a score or rating of the student's performance.

LINKING KNOWLEDGE TO PRACTICE

1. Visit a classroom to observe a writing workshop. Make field notes of your observations of the classroom environment (the materials, the furniture arrangement, the writing area), the procedures used to implement writing workshop, the topic and content of the focus lesson, the models provided for the writers, how the teacher confers with the students, how peer conferring occurs, the availability of rubrics for the students' use, and how group sharing happened. Compare your observation data with your colleagues' data.

2. Use the rubrics to rate the writing pieces in this chapter. In addition to the rating, make a written record of your reasons for your rating. Share your ratings and rationales with your colleagues. Did you agree? Why or why not?

3. Teaching writing through writing workshop likely will be different from what most students' parents experienced in elementary school. Using the information in this chapter, work with a colleague to write a brochure or handout for parents describing this approach to teaching writing.

4. Begin a writing support group with a group of colleagues. Challenge each other to write pieces in various genres. Gather models in each genre to "teach" you about the genre. Aim to publish your pieces.

5. Use Microsoft Word's two revising tools, comments and track changes, to revise a piece of your own writing or to respond to a colleague's or a student's writing.

CHAPTER 9

EMBEDDED WITHIN WRITING WORKSHOP: TEACHING SKILLS AND MEETING SPECIAL NEEDS

Zebulon is ready to publish his story on his piece about his trip to Virginia Beach. He knows the classroom editing procedures. He collects the classroom's editing checklist from the writing center. With a blue pen, he circles any words he thinks might be misspelled. Then he searches his story to be certain he has put a punctuation mark at the end of each sentence, capitalized the first word in each sentence, indented the first word of each paragraph, capitalized the important words in the title, and capitalized the names of people and places. When he finishes with his search, he staples the editing checklist to his story and places both in "The Editing Box" in the writing center. He knows that before the next writing workshop his teacher will examine his edited piece and maybe will write him some notes, notes like "I see two more words that are misspelled. Can you find them?" or "I see three sentences in your second paragraph. Can you find them?" His teacher will also add the mechanical skills he used correctly to the list of skills he knows how to use on the inside cover of his writing folder (see Figure 9.1). The next day during writing workshop, Zebulon will take a green pen and search the piece again to see if he can make the corrections the teacher's notes suggested. He can ask a friend to help him if he wishes. Following this search, he will sign up for an editing conference with his teacher. When he confers with his teacher, his teacher will celebrate the mechanical skills that he used correctly and teach him one or two additional skills. Then, he will publish his story by rewriting it on special theme paper using a felt-tip pen. He'll make a cover page with the title and his name. Then he'll insert the final draft and cover into a plastic sleeve and select a colored spine to hold it in place. His story will be placed in the library center, alongside the work of other published authors.

Recall Ralph Fletcher's and JoAnn Portalupi's (2001) suggestion that to "fit" writing workshop into the daily schedule teachers might need to determine what activities writing workshop could replace. Instead of teaching punctuation, capitalization, spelling, or handwriting as separate subjects, teachers can teach most of these important mechanical skills of writing within the context of the classroom's writing workshop. As explained in Chapter 8, some focus lessons will be on topics in these areas. But focus lessons alone are insufficient; students will not learn these skills by hearing their teachers talking about or seeing their teachers demonstrating their use. These skills come to the forefront during editing conferences, after the students have made the content of their pieces as good as they can. Thus, the teaching of mechanical skills is embedded in the writing workshop and in the writing process itself.

In the sections that follow, the mechanical skills of writing—capitalization, punctuation, handwriting, spelling, and grammar—are temporarily removed from their supporting context (the writing workshop) and examined in isolation. This chapter highlights one additional significant feature embedded within the writing workshop: meeting the special needs of students, particularly bilingual and second-language learners who come to school exhibiting varying degrees of competence in writing in English. Today in the United States, native speakers of Spanish compose the largest group of these learners. Special Feature 9.1 (by Sarah Hudelson and Irene Serna, presented later in this chapter) provides suggestions on how to support these students' writing development within the writing workshop.

BEFORE READING THIS CHAPTER, THINK ABOUT . . .

- How you learned to spell words. Did you learn to spell words by studying lists of words—the same list your peers studied—for Friday spelling tests?
- How you learned the rules of capitalization, punctuation, and grammar. Did you complete practice exercises?
- How you learned to form the letters of the alphabet. Did you practice by writing a page of *a*'s just like a model and then a page of *b*'s just like a model?
- How you might support bilingual and second-language learners' writing development.

FOCUS QUESTIONS

- When will students learn about the mechanics of writing—spelling, grammar, capitalization, punctuation, and handwriting—in writing workshop?
- Given a choice, which handwriting style and form should teachers use? How should teachers teach students to form the alphabet letters correctly?
- Is writing workshop and teaching the mechanical skills of writing within writing workshop appropriate for nonnative speakers of English?

THE MECHANICAL SKILLS OF WRITING

If you answered "yes" to the questions in the "Before You Read This Chapter, Think About . . ." section, you were taught the mechanical skills of writing through a *drill and practice* approach. By drilling you on the skills, your elementary school

■ ■ ■ ■ ■

BOX 9.1
DEFINITION OF TERMS

cursive-style writing: flowing form of writing in which the strokes of the letters in each word are joined

early phonemic spelling: children represent one or two phonemes in words with letters

editing conference: time when the teacher discusses the mechanical rules a student used correctly and teaches one or two rules he or she did not learn correctly

letter-name spelling: children break words into phonemes and choose letters to represent the phonemes based on similarity between the sound of the letter names and the respective phoneme

manuscript-style writing: vertical form of writing with letters made with circles and straight lines

prephonemic spelling: children form letters correctly, but they have not yet discovered that letters represent the sounds or phonemes in words

transitional spelling: children write words that look like English words, though the words are not all spelled correctly

teachers hoped you would be able to apply your knowledge to your writing. In all likelihood, you did not.

Today instruction occurs in a variety of ways. Teachers help students learn to spell by helping them understand how words work—the conventions that govern the structure of words and how these structures signal sound and meaning. Rather than studying lists of words, students pull words out of the immediate contexts of reading and writing in order to examine and explore them for common patterns. Today teachers teach students the capitalization, punctuation, and grammar rules in focus lessons and by helping them correct errors in the pieces they plan to publish. The rules taught are those that the students need, as demonstrated by errors in the pieces they are ready to publish.

As you read the following sections, you will find that we often suggest that correcting a writing piece's mechanical problems will occur in an editing conference. These are conferences that teachers hold with their students who have selected a piece to publish. Many teachers ask their students to examine their pieces, using an editing checklist to support their searching, before an editing conference. Typically the editing checklist includes punctuation, capitalization, and grammar rules that the teacher has taught during focus lessons. When students hunt through their writing pieces to discover whether or not they have used each rule correctly, the act of hunting is a way to reinforce the skills the teacher has taught. As the teacher teaches new skills, the editing checklist changes and the number of items on the checklist grows. Readers will find an example of an editing checklist in Figure 9.1.

Editing Checklist

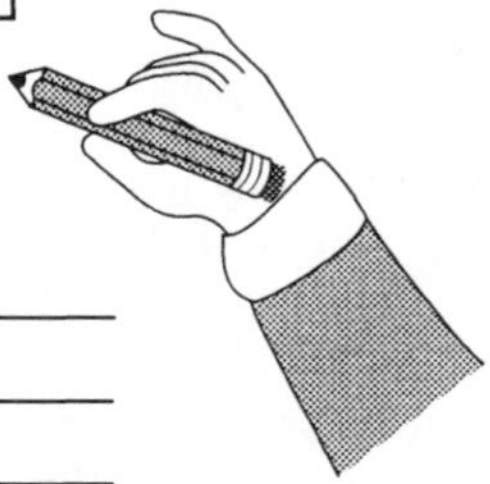

Title _____

Name _____

Date _____

Are you ready to publish?

Check ✓ your piece for the following:

____ 1. Have you circled all the words you think might be misspelled?

____ 2. Have you punctuated the end of each sentence? (? ! .)

____ 3. Does each sentence begin with a capital letter?

____ 4. Have you capitalized the names of people and places?

____ 5. Did you indent the first word of each paragraph?

____ 6. Is your title capitalized?

____ 7. Have you read your piece aloud to check for errors?

Editing Marks

⬭   Circle misspelled words

∧   Add word(s) or punctuation

≡   Capitalize a letter

¶   Begin a new paragraph

FIGURE 9.1   Editing Checklist

Spelling

Learning to spell words correctly is important. However, until children demonstrate sufficient understanding of how the English language works, teachers must permit their writers to use their best guesses to construct their texts. Encouraging children to use invented (or temporary or experimental) spellings means that every word in the children's oral vocabulary can be used in their written texts. To insist that children use correct spellings, look up the words they cannot spell in a dictionary, or seek help in spelling unknown words, will result in their abandoning their use of sophisticated words they do not know how to spell in favor of simple words they do know how to spell. The early school years are a time for experimentation, a time to risk making a mistake, a time for students to use the linguistic principles they know to construct their texts. So the time for fixing the spelling in texts—like the time for fixing handwriting, punctuation, and capitalization—is after the writing, as a part of the editing process.

After the students are confident that the content of their texts is as they wish it to be, their attention can turn to spelling. They can, as Zebulon did, circle the words that they think are misspelled when they edit their pieces. When teachers hold editing conferences with their writers, they can *teach* them spelling strategies (e.g., write the word several different ways until you discover the one that looks correct) and patterns or rules (e.g., [long vowel]–[consonant]–*e*, as in *take* or *bite*). In addition, teachers can pull words from the children's writing to explore the patterns that can be detected in sound, structure, and meaning features.

How Children Learn to Spell. Encouraging children to use invented spellings in their writings is a concern to some parents. Teachers who know how children learn to spell can better explain the role of children's use of invented spellings to these concerned parents.

As explained in Chapter 4, children's emergent writing starts as pictures or scribbles and gradually becomes similar to conventional writing. Elizabeth Sulzby (1990) has identified seven broad categories of emergent writing: drawing as writing, scribble writing, letterlike units, nonphonetic letter strings, copying from environmental print, invented spelling, and conventional spelling (see Figure 4.2). For primary-grade teachers, invented spelling is the category of greatest interest because most children go through the multistage transition between invented and conventional spelling between ages six and eight years (described later in this chapter).

A number of studies have focused solely on invented spelling, providing very detailed information about this stage of spelling development. These studies have provided important information to assist teachers in explaining invented spelling and in determining how to help children develop their ability to spell words conventionally. The following three points briefly summarize this research:

1. Children who have had many experiences with print learn about how written language works through a process of discovery and experimentation. Children construct their own knowledge of written language as they interact with print and with people in everyday situations. Among the factors that contribute to children's discoveries about writing are being read to regularly, seeing adults who are important to them writing, and having access to writing tools. According to J. Richard Gentry and Jean Gillet (1993, pp. 22–24), three of children's first discoveries are that "print stays the same," that "writing is arranged horizontally" and moves from left to right across a page, and that "print is made up of certain kinds of marks."

2. At an early age, most children are able to detect the phonetic characteristics of words. They break words into their individual sounds and find a letter to represent each phoneme. These "finds," as Charles Read (1971, 1975) discovered, are not random. English-speaking children spell words by

- using letter names (e.g., *C* for see, *LADE* for *lady*),
- using only consonant sounds (e.g., *GRL* for *girl*),
- omitting nasals within words (e.g., *ED* for *end*),
- using phonetically based spelling patterns to represent artifacts (e.g., *chr* for *tr* as in *CHRIBLES* for *troubles*),
- substituting *d* for *t* (e.g., *prede* for *pretty*).

Children also employ several different strategies to spell words with short vowels, based on the place of articulation in the mouth. Short *i*, for example, is represented with an *e* (e.g., *FES* for *fish*), and short *o* is represented with an *i* (e.g., *CLIK* for *clock*).

3. Children's invented spelling changes as they become aware of the many rules and patterns that govern the English language. Most children pass through the different stages of spelling in the same order. The five stages (using Temple, Nathan, Temple, & Burris's 1993 categories and labels) are as follows:

   a. *Prephonemic stage*—Children can form letters correctly, but they have not yet discovered that letters represent the sounds or phonemes in words. Letters are strung together randomly. This stage is typical of three- to five-year-olds (for example, "RAVRDJRV" may be used for "ocean road").

   b. *Early phonemic stage*—Children attempt to represent phonemes in words with letters, but they usually only represent one or two letters in words. Typically, the initial and the final sound are represented. This stage is typical of five- and six-year-olds (for example, "MNMDF" may be used for "me and my dad fishing").

   c. *Letter-name stage*—Children break words into phonemes and choose letters to represent the phonemes based on the similarity between the sound of the letter names and the respective phonemes. This stage is typical of six-year-olds (for example, "I WAT TO MAI FRNDZ BRATHDAY WE MAD AOI ON SUNDAY" for "I went to my friend's birthday. We made our own sundae.").

   d. *Transitional stage*—Children write words that look like English words, though the words are not all spelled correctly. Typically, each syllable has a vowel. Unlike children in the earlier stages, transitional spellers no longer rely mostly on sounds to present written words; transitional spellers use a morphological and visual strategy also (e.g., *eightee* instead of *ate* for *eighty*). The child has a visual memory of spelling patterns. This stage is typical of seven- and eight-year-olds (for example, "Out back thar is a pass. it is hils. and thar is a huj hil. and I krassd on my bike." may be used for, "Out back, there is a pass. It is [between] hills. And there is a huge hill. And I crashed on my bike.").

   e. *Correct spelling stage*—Children spell nearly all words correctly, though like all of us, assistance may be needed with occasional troublesome words. Children typically reach this stage by age eight or nine years. (For example, "I am nice, talented and aspeily smart BECAUSE I moved up to second grade. The week was very easy in first grade and just right in second grade. I really like second grade. In lunch a fly landed on Allen's nose today and it went buzzzzzzz!")

So learning to spell begins in the early years of children's literacy development. Children's early years, when they play with the forms and functions of print, are important because they lay the groundwork for children's later exploration of the alphabetic layer of spelling. By the early phonemic stage, children have some knowledge of the names of the alphabet letters and some awareness of sounds within spoken words. Now they can invent their spellings as they write. Notice how children are using consonants almost exclusively in the early phonemic stage. In English, according to Shane Templeton and Darrell Morris (1999), consonants emerge first in children's invented spellings because they are more salient acoustically and the children can feel their articulation. Vowels emerge later, in the letter-name stage.

By the time children move into the transitional stage of spelling, they have begun to understand how groups or patterns of letters work together to represent sound. A key indicator that children have progressed to this point is their use of silent letters in their invented spellings to represent long-vowel sounds. For example, for *tied* they might write *tide*. From letter patterns within single syllables, children will progress to understanding syllable patterns. Now, they grasp the understanding of "consonant-doubling/e-drop principles as it applies to simple base words and suffixes" (Templeton & Morris, 1999, p. 106). Understanding how syllables and suffixes work in spellings leads students to attending to the role of meaning in spelling. Now they correct words by relating words to the base. For example, they might write *oppisition*, look at it, see the word *oppose*, and understand how to correct their error.

By closely examining students' writings, teachers can understand the strategies children are using to construct written words. Each word can be categorized into one of the five spelling stages, and the percentage of words spelled using prephonemic, early phonemic, letter-name, transitional, and correct spelling strategies can be calculated. For example, if the word looks a lot like conventional English spelling, with a vowel in each syllable (e.g., "EGLE" for "eagle"), then the teacher knows the child used the sounds in the word and a visual pattern (*gle*) in constructing the word—strategies characteristic of a transitional speller. By engaging in this kind of analysis and calculating the percentage of words written at each stage, the teacher can identify the student as *primarily* exhibiting the strategies of a particular stage of spelling. (Children typically do not use strategies of one stage only.) Comparing two or more of a student's writing samples, written at different times during the year, helps the teacher understand the child's growth in spelling knowledge. With this information, the teacher can answer the question, is the child becoming a better speller?

Helping Children Become Better Spellers. Will children learn to spell words correctly by discovery on their own? Today's spelling experts (e.g., Gentry & Gillet, 1993; Temple, Nathan, Temple, & Burris, 1993; Templeton & Morris, 1999) suggest that independent discovery is not enough; children need instruction to become expert spellers.

While the theoretical and descriptive research has been "quite rich in describing what is happening cognitively as children learn to spell," the literature on what adults should *do* to assist children's development only has begun to be clarified recently. In the past, there was considerable disagreement about how spelling skills were best acquired. Would these skills be acquired by immersing children in a literacy-rich environment, where they have numerous opportunities to read and write for real purposes and audiences? Or do children need instruction in order to acquire these mechanical skills? The natural learning approach advocates argued with the direct instruction advocates. We have chosen a blended approach, an approach that recognizes the importance of children's immersion in a literacy-rich environment *and* of teachers providing their students with direct instruction in important mechanical skills. Below we detail some strategies that the literature currently recommends. We believe instruction should vary, depending on the students' needs.

Prephonemic and early phonemic spellers need help learning more about how alphabet writing works. Appropriate goals for these young spellers include learning letter names and sounds, developing a stable concept of what constitutes a word, and discovering both how to break words into their constituent parts—to phonemically segment words—and how to represent the parts with letters. Bernadette Watson's minilesson on invented spelling is an example of an appropriate activity (see Trade Secret 5.3). As Bernadette wrote her piece on traveling to New York, she helped her young students break words into sound segments and select the best letter to represent these parts. She left spaces between the words and told the children why (e.g., "I need to leave a space here between these two words. The space tells me where this word ends and where this word begins"). As her children worked at writing their own pieces, Bernadette provided one-on-one instruction in these important skills as she conferred with each child.

These same kinds of activities are appropriate for letter-name spellers. As children move into this stage and have had many experiences with segmenting words and selecting the best letter to represent the spoken parts of each word, their accuracy will increase. More sounds are heard, including vowels. Occasionally, teachers might do as Elizabeth Sulzby has recommended. When a child says *went* is spelled *YNT*, the teacher might suggest that *YNT* is the way many children spell *went*, but soon they will learn that adults spell it a little differently—WENT.

Lawrence Sipe (2001) suggests another strategy, using an organizer such as Elkonin boxes to help students stretch out the phonemes or individual sounds in the words. As they stretch out the sounds and identify the corresponding letters, they fill in the individual sound boxes to complete the word. For example, to write the word *trap,* the teacher might present the child with three boxes.

tr	a	p

The use of such a strategy gives students a visual representation of how phonemes are combined to make words. It also emphasizes the number of letters that are used to make each word.

Teachers might also wish to help each child at the letter-name stage to construct a personal dictionary of those words frequently misspelled in the child's writing. In some classrooms, these dictionaries are small spiral-bound notebooks, with one page per letter. In other classrooms, the dictionaries are three-by-five-inch note cards. In still other classrooms, some teachers create a word wall where they list words frequently used and misspelled by members of the class. Typically, these teachers have each letter of the alphabet posted on the wall, and words troublesome to many students in the class are written on cards under the letter. Copying the correct spelling of frequently misspelled words from a personal dictionary when the words are needed in a piece of writing helps to establish the children's memory bank of how the words look and are spelled.

As letter-name spellers begin to move into the transitional stage, it is appropriate to begin asking the students to study a short list of not more than ten words per week (Temple et al., 1993). Recall that, for the typical speller, this will occur sometime during the second half of first grade. Other children do not reach the transitional stage until later in the primary grades.

So, which words exactly? Shane Templeton and Darrell Morris (1999) suggest several principles that teachers might use in the selection and organization of spelling words. First, the words selected should reflect the spelling features that students use but confuse when they write. For example, if the students are using but confusing short-vowel spellings, then they should work with words with this pattern. Attempting to teach these students long-vowel patterns would not be productive. Students who are using but confusing one-syllable long-vowel patterns should be studying these words; it would be inappropriate to ask them to study polysyllabic words.

Secondly, the words should be organized according to spelling patterns. Younger students might explore vowel patterns; older students might explore syllable patterns or spelling–meaning relationships (like *oppisition* and *oppose*). For younger students, the words should be organized around common features or patterns, for example the CVC short-vowel pattern.

Thirdly, at the primary level (grades 1 through 3) the students should be able to read the words automatically as sight words. At the upper grade levels, the students should be familiar with most words, but some new words might be included.

Recall our earlier statement that today teachers help students learn to spell by helping them understand how words work—the conventions that govern the structure of words and how these structures signal sound and meaning. A team of colleagues—Donald Bear, Marcia Invernizzi, Shane Templeton, and Francine Johnston (2003) recently provided teachers with specific helpful suggestions for, first, determining their children's developmental spelling level, and then, providing developmentally appropriate instruction, aimed at helping the children understand the patterns and structure of the English language, that addresses each level. Such instruction is important not only because it helps children become better spellers but also because it improves their skills as readers. In Trade Secret 9.1, Gaysha Beard describes how she found her way to providing developmentally appropriate spelling instruction in her classroom using their ideas. We echo Ms. Beard's suggestions: readers should obtain copies of the *Words Their Way* materials for use in their classrooms.

TRADE SECRET 9.1

Using *Words Their Way* to Find My Way to Improved Spelling Instruction

GAYSHA BEARD

I wanted my classroom instruction to be based on students' individual needs. As a developing educator, I knew the importance of instructing at my students' developmental level. Naturally, in reading, I grouped my students based on their specific skill needs. For some reason, it took me some months before I made this link to spelling instruction. I like to think of *Words Their Way* (Bear, Invernizzi, Templeton, & Johnston, 2003) as the book that gave me that "aha" moment.

Words Their Way is a resource that every classroom teacher should own. This book was created on the principle that literacy development occurs in stages. Bear and his colleagues (2003) suggest that children develop knowledge of word features on a continuum. As students explore the English spelling system and make qualitative shifts from stage to stage, they use distinct spelling patterns and make distinct spelling errors. On average, K-3 teachers will find students working within the emergent, letter-name alphabetic, and within word pattern stages. At the beginning of the *emergent stage,* spellers' writing takes on the form of drawing and scribbling, and by the end students are spelling words representing the most salient sounds. *Letter-name alphabetic* spellers begin this stage accurately representing initial and final sounds, but eliminating vowels. As students approach the end of this stage their writing accurately represents short vowel patterns, digraphs, and blends. Students' writing during the *within word pattern* stage shows some confusion with long vowel patterns, and by the end of this stage students are accurately using complex vowel teams, and learning two- or three-letter complex consonant patterns. As children progress to the *syllables and affixes* stage, their writing suggests that they understand such concepts as silent *e,* other long vowels, and complex

consonant patterns. However, they appear to be confused about the adding of suffixes and spelling multisyllabic words. The assessment tool provided in *Words Their Way* makes it relatively easy for a classroom teacher to assess and place each child in an appropriate instructional group.

I began, as recommended, by administering the *Words Their Way Spelling Inventory* to my entire class. The book provided user-friendly guidelines to administer and score the assessment. I said something like the following:

> Today, boys and girls, all of you have a chance to help me become a better teacher. I want each of you to show me how well you can spell. Even if you cannot spell every word correctly, what you write on your papers are clues for me. These clues will teach me how to help you become an even better speller. Is everyone willing to help me become a better teacher?

The assessment took no longer than fifteen to twenty minutes. It took me about one hour to score my classroom set.

I scored the papers using the Feature or Error Guide. The data chart revealed my students' developmental spelling stage. I grouped children with similar needs into small groups for instructional purposes. For example, children who made errors with short vowels were grouped together, and students who understood the silent *e* pattern but confused the other long vowel patterns were grouped in the "other long vowel patterns" spelling group.

After these groups were formed, my spelling instruction could begin. Because I could differentiate my instruction based on need, my students were not required to take the same twenty-word spelling test on Friday. I learned, for example, which children were not developmentally ready to spell multisyllabic words. Teaching spelling in this way begins with what children *know* and moves forward to advance their knowledge of how words work.

Other than the assessment tool, the second best component of the *Words Their Way* book is the resources for teachers. Now teachers might feel a little overwhelmed if they discovered that they needed to create four different lesson plans for their various spelling groups. Not a problem! *Words Their Way* is divided into the literacy stages and provides examples of activities, word sorts, word lists, and reproducibles that teachers can easily adapt to their individual classroom needs. That's what I did. I provide a few examples of these authors' suggestions in the table at the end of this article. (See the table below for a list of sample activities that can be used for emergent to syllables and affixes spellers based on children's developmental needs.) The table is organized by developmental spelling stages, which I have learned are very important to keep in mind when designing any lesson. Each activity is designed for small-group instruction. In addition to the activities suggested in *Words Their Way*, Francine Johnston, Donald Bear, and Marcia Invernizzi recently published a set of additional teacher-friendly books with many activities for use with children at each stage.

Now that I have been using this approach to guide my spelling instruction, I see a difference in my students' spelling abilities. They now have discovered spelling patterns and are knowledgeable about how words work. As a class, we have moved from memorization to understanding!

Sample Word Study Activities Based on Students' Developmental Needs

Developmental Stage	Developmental Stage	Developmental Stage	Developmental Stage
Emergent Late	Letter-Name Alphabetic Early Middle Late	Within Word Pattern Early Middle Late	Syllables and Affixes Early Middle Late
Areas of Need	**Areas of Need**	**Areas of Need**	**Areas of Need**
Initial Sounds	Final Sounds Short Vowels Consonant Digraphs Consonant Blends	Consonant Blends Long Vowel Patterns Other Long Vowel Patterns	Other Long Vowel Patterns Multisyllabic Patterns Easy Prefixes & Suffixes

(continued on next page)

Sample Word Study Activities Based on Students' Developmental Needs (continued)

Activities	Activities	Activities	Activities
SORTS	**SORTS**	**SORTS**	**SORTS**
■ pictures or objects focusing on the beginning sounds; give students columns and ask them to sort the pictures ■ students complete concept sorts (e.g., sorting buttons) to develop their ability to compare and contrast	■ begin with pictures and then introduce word sorts (focusing on final sounds, short vowels, digraphs, and blends); give students columns and ask them to sort the pictures and words ■ sort should include what the child knows and the new skill that they will learn	■ word sorts beginning with what the child knows and adding a new skill (focusing on silent -e, r-controlled vowels, diphthongs, & vowel teams); allow students to discover the pattern by creating their own columns for the sort; semantic sorts (compare and contrast word meanings, and content-specific words)	■ word sorts beginning with what the child knows and adding a new skill (focusing on adding -ing, doubling consonants, comparing open & closed syllables, comparing words that end in –er and –ure; allow students to discover the pattern by creating their own columns for the sort; semantic sorts (compare and contrast word meanings, and content-specific words)
RHYME & ALLITERATION ■ Games (bingo, Concentration; reading poetry; name game) **LITERATURE** ■ share children's literature that reinforces alliteration and rhyme	**ACTIVITIES** ■ board games (focusing on key concepts at this stage); word hunts looking for words that follow the patterns; word hunts looking at word families (add new words to personal dictionaries); Concentration **LITERATURE** ■ share children's literature that reinforces learned skills	**ACTIVITIES** ■ board games (focusing on key concepts at this stage); word hunts looking for words that follow the patterns; word hunts looking at word families (add words to personal dictionaries); playing Concentration using homophones; Jeopardy **LITERATURE** ■ share children's literature that reinforces learned skills	**ACTIVITIES** ■ board games (focusing on key concepts at this stage); word hunts looking for words that follow the patterns; create a word study notebook); playing Concentration using homophones; Jeopardy including vocabulary and key features at this stage **LITERATURE** ■ share children's literature that reinforces learned skills

Explicit Instruction Once Students Become Fluent Writers. According to J. Richard Gentry and Jean Gillet (1993), formal instruction in spelling should possess six characteristics: self-selection, student ownership, self-monitoring, collaboration, feedback, and needs-based direct instruction.

In the past, the words to be studied were selected by textbook writers. Today, the recommendation is for teachers and students to select the words to be learned. Which words should be chosen? Two teams of researchers (i.e., Gentry & Gillet, 1993, and Temple, Nathan, Temple, & Burris, 1993) provide comparable advice: Some words should come from each student's reading and writing. To this advice, Shane Templeton and Darryl Morris (1999) add that, at the primary level, the words should be known as sight words in reading. As indicated above, words should be selected that the student will use frequently, which show a particular spelling pattern (e.g., [long vowel]-[consonant]-*e: name, hide, cute*), or which follow a consistent spelling generalization with no more than two different spelling patterns being evident in a student's weekly list. Good sources for these words include the books the student is reading, the student's personal dictionary, and the student's personal writings. A key is that the words should reflect features that the student uses but confuses in their own writing. Using these personalized words as the base, the teacher should add two or three words that share the same spelling pattern (e.g., *cat* and *fat* with *sat*), meaning pattern (e.g., synonyms and antonyms), or visual pattern (e.g., *ough* in *rough, cough,* and *enough*). Because the teacher and the student selected the initial words to be studied from the student's reading and writing, self-selection and student ownership is inherent in the word-selection process. How many words should be selected for study each week? Templeton and Morris recommend ten to twelve words as appropriate for second- and third-grade students and about twenty words for fourth graders and beyond.

Collaboration occurs when students study their selected words with peers. Working with others helps students discover patterns in the spelling of words. Peers might study their words in pairs or they might administer tests of their words to each other. Working with other students reduces the tedium of studying for all students, learning disabled and non–learning disabled. Some teachers suggest pairing students in the class (Burks, 2004), while others recommend at least occasionally pairing with older "buddies" because the older student can serve as a positive model and provide signficant support and scaffolding (Buschman, 2003). J. Richard Gentry and Jean Gillet (1993) and Charles Temple and his colleagues (1993) recommend using the following five-day schedule:

- *Monday*—Each student's words should be called out, and each student should attempt to write the correct spellings. Obviously, because each student's list of words is different, the teacher cannot possibly call out each student's list. Students can work in pairs, taking turns calling out each other's list. Then each list should be returned to its owner so that the owner can compare the correct spellings against his or her spellings. Words spelled incorrectly should be crossed out, and the correct spelling should be written beside each incorrectly spelled word. The processes of collaboration, feed-back, and self-monitoring are evident.

- *Tuesday, Wednesday, and Thursday*—The students can work to learn those words they misspelled on the Monday pretest. Lynnette Bradley and Peter Bryant (1985) and Cassandra Keller (2002) that students be taught to study their words using a multisensory study technique such as the one outlined in the following eight steps (a technique that provides image feedback and a lot of self-monitoring):

  1. **Look** at the word, and **say** it aloud.
  2. **Read** each letter in the word.
  3. **Close** your eyes, try to **picture** the word, and **spell** it to yourself.
  4. **Look** at the word. Did you spell it correctly?
  5. **Say** each letter of the word as you **copy** it.
  6. **Cover** the word, and **write** it again.
  7. **Look** at the word. Did you write it correctly?
  8. If you made any mistakes, **repeat** these steps.

On these days, the teacher might also bring together the students who are working on words with a common pattern for some group work. Games and exer-cises that play on the spelling patterns of the group's words can be profitable and fun. Thursday might also be a practice-test day. This instruction is clearly direct and based on needs. It is also fun.

- *Friday*—Students are tested on the words they selected (with the teacher's assistance) for studying that week. Tests are administered and corrected, as they were on Monday. The new words each student has learned to spell are celebrated. The students can record the words they learned to spell correctly in a personal record-keeping book. Words that the student misspelled might be returned to the list for additional study next week or retired to be reviewed at a later appropriate time. Self-monitoring, immediate positive feedback, and student ownership evident.

This test–study–test method works equally as successfully with good and poor spellers, although the efficacy of this procedure has not been specifically examined with learning-disabled students. Of course, the presumption is that the students can spell some of the words on the pretest. Otherwise, imagine the resent-ment against taking such tests. Further, the procedures suggested for studying the spelling words are equally effective with learning-disabled students as with non–learning-disabled students. However, some data suggest that testing the stu-dents daily is an effective means of supporting daily practice (Graham, 1999).

This kind of spelling program—one that focuses on each student's word needs, that provides direct instruction based on the students' spelling stage and demonstrated knowledge, that celebrates each student's growth without compar-ing a student's growth against that of other class members, that supports invented spellings as developmentally appropriate for writers and not as errors—provides support for growing writers and spellers, helping them to tackle the challenges of writing and learning to spell with confidence and enthusiasm.

Remember that each of the strategies described here is equally appropriate for learning-disabled children as it is for non–learning-disabled students. As Steve Graham (1999, p. 96) notes: "teachers of learning disabled students need to explicitly teach [spelling] skills while simultaneously capitalizing on incidental and less formal methods of instruction. It is important to realize that an overemphasis on meaning, process, or form in writing instruction is not in the best interest of the child." The good news is that the spelling instruction described above not only improves students' spelling abilities but also improves students' reading word attack skills, specifically their ability to pronounce words correctly and decode unknown words (Graham, Harris, & Chorzempa, 2003).

Grammar

Children come to school knowing a lot about how language works. By the age of six years, they know the basic grammar of the language used in their home. They have internalized the rules for creating language. Their grammatical knowledge is *implicit*—that is, children cannot tell their teachers the rules they are using, but they can intuitively use the rules to construct their oral texts. As Neil Daniel and Christina Murphy (1995, p. 226) point out, "All normal humans have full control of the grammar they use every day."

For some children, the grammar that works well at home is different from the grammar they meet at school. School's grammar is "a set of conventions, collectively known as usage, that govern written [and oral] discourse" (Daniel & Murphy, 1995, p. 226). School's grammar is an arbitrary system of rules, rules to be learned and demonstrated by students.

In the past, teachers tried to teach their students the rules of grammar or usage through drill. Readers may recall filling in tedious workbook exercises such as, **"The children _____ (was or were) playing."** Years of researching the effectiveness of this approach to teaching grammar led diverse scholars to the same conclusion: Students make almost no connection between this traditional grammar instruction and the production of their own texts (Hillocks, 1986). Even those students who successfully completed the exercises and scored well on the Friday tests rarely used what they had learned in their own writing and speaking. The main predictable outcome was that most students developed an aversion to studying grammar. A new method of teaching grammar was clearly needed. Note that the question was not, to teach grammar or not to teach grammar. As Constance Weaver, Carol McNally, and Sharon Moerman (2001) suggest, "That is *not* the question."

The constructivist perspective suggests that grammar should be taught as children engage in meaningful uses of language. More than anything else, humans need to be engaged with significant tasks (Csikszentmihalyi, 1990). Within these meaningful tasks, grammar instruction can help children understand that there are many ways of saying the same thing. As George Hillocks Jr. (1986) suggests, teachers should show writers how to use a variety of syntactic structures (word orderings) and how to select the most effective structure for the current situation.

For example, the grammatical structures used in writing a letter for publication in a newspaper are different from those used to write a letter to a grandmother.

The teaching of grammar, then, does not mean requiring students to memorize a collection of do's and don'ts! It does mean helping students learn how to manipulate language. For example, students can be assisted in selecting words to modify nouns, or they can learn to combine sentences by discovering the processes of embedding, deletion, substitution, and rearrangement of elements (Brosnahan & Neuleib, 1995). Yes, teachers should expose their students to grammar's vocabulary: *noun, verb, adjective, adverb,* and *clause,* yet students need very little of this to learn the conventions of written English. The difference today is that grammar's vocabulary and the structure of the language is studied within the context of a meaningful task.

The writing workshop provides a meaningful context within which to facilitate students' study of grammar. A significant component of the writing workshop is helping students use the writing process used by all writers. Within the writing workshop, writers produce products that are published in various forms for others to read. As Wendy Bishop (1995, p. 187) points out, "There is nothing like [publishing] to make us try to make ourselves and our writing presentable!" The opportunity to publish supplies considerable motivation for students to follow the conventional rules of grammar.

The components of the writing workshop—focus lesson, writing and conferring (content and editing conferences), and group sharing—provide grammar teaching and learning opportunities. For example, during a focus lesson, Deanne McCredie shared with her students a piece that she had written about her dogs. She finished by saying, "You remember I was working on this last week? Well, I thought it got kind of boring. It was funny when it happened, but my story didn't sound funny. I remembered the story of the wolf's view of his adventures with the three little pigs, and I thought, 'Why don't I try this piece from my dogs' perspective!' Here's what it sounds like now." Her students agreed that the story from the dogs' perspective made it "funnier"—though they professed to like the story from her perspective also. The lesson continued with a brief comparison of the two perspectives. Ms. McCredie ended by saying, "When you work on your pieces today, you might think about writing about your topic from one of the characters' perspective." So, as Weaver and her colleagues suggest and Deanne McCredie demonstrates, the important question to ask is, "What aspects of grammar can we teach to enhance and improve students' writing, and when and how can we best teach them (p. 19)?" Dawn Downes (see Trade Secret 9.2) would respond, "in the context of writing in writing workshop." The goal is to see students incorporating the grammatical constructions teachers teach into their writing, to see them using the grammatical constructions in their writing.

Focus lessons on grammatical constructions can take many forms. For example, teachers might model and ask students to generate sentences with particular kinds of grammatical constructions like those found in literature, or they might show students how to use the five senses in their writing to sharpen the details in their descriptions of objects and experiences in their writing. Carol McNally

TRADE SECRET 9.2
Building Language: A Constructivist Approach To Grammar

DAWN DOWNES

The first year that I initiated a writing workshop in my classroom my students drafted writing, conferred with each other, and published their writing in a class anthology. I gave focus lessons on topics, leads, revision, poetry, organization, and other parts of the writing process. I felt good about what was happening in my classroom. The kids were writing, and I felt like I was making a difference in the literate lives of my students. Several weeks into the workshop, however, one of my students came up to me and very innocently asked, "When are we going to do English?"

After I recovered from the surprise of her question, I stammered that we were doing English. To write is to accomplish what all of those grammar skills add up to. Satisfied with my less than polished answer, Sarah walked away to join her writing circle, but she left me with a nagging question in the back of my head that wouldn't go away: What was I doing about grammar?

I knew that many teachers teach formalized grammar lessons because they believe that it improves the quality of their students' writing. They also think that learning grammar makes language empirical, promotes "mental discipline," improves standardized test scores, facilitates the learning of a foreign language, improves social status, and makes our students better users of language (Weaver, 1996).

In reality, *more than fifty years of research suggest that teaching the grammar book in a traditional manner does not improve the quality of students' writing*. In fact, "if schools insist upon teaching concepts of traditional school grammar (as many still do), they cannot defend it as a means of improving the quality of writing" (Hillocks, 1986, p. 138). Moreover, "the conclusion can be stated in strong and unqualified terms: the teaching of formal grammar has a negligible or, because it usually displaces some of the instruction and practice in actual composition, even a harmful effect on the improvement of writing" (Braddock, Lloyd-Jones, & Schoer, as quoted in Calkins, 1986, p. 195). Such strong words confirm what I had known instinctively all along: teaching the grammar book is a waste of instructional time.

To teach grammar in the context of student writing means that we follow a constructivist approach to teaching. In traditional grammar curricula, the language (or whole) is broken down into a system of rules (parts) that describe and prescribe how we use language. English teachers hope that their students will manage somehow to apply these "rules" and transfer their writing (and speech). However, students enter school with a knowledge of some version of English (a grammar), and learn best when their teachers help them to apply what they already know about the language in their writing, and then instruct them on those aspects they don't know. This contrasts sharply with a traditional grammar classroom where students are overwhelmed with rules and structures that are not directly applied to their writing and cannot be internalized. The rules and patterns may be momentarily memorized for a test or quiz, but in the end they are lost. Instead, in a constructivist classroom, students build their knowledge by learning in the context of authentic tasks. Students have the opportunity to write, and as the teacher sees a need for grammatical coaching, a lesson is taught. However, since the grammatical rule and its authentic application are taught simultaneously, the new knowledge will be valued and attached to the existing knowledge about composition. Instead of learning the grammatical skills in isolation, they will be attached to meaningful texts in a powerful way (Brooks & Brooks, 1993).

(continued on next page)

There are four different kinds of grammar lessons that can be embedded in writing workshop. All of these lessons start with student work; the teacher assesses the work, determines the grammatical needs of the writing, and plans lessons (coaching sessions) around those needs.

Incidental Lessons are lessons that are not taught through direct instruction. They take place during a student conference or casually as the teacher moves about the room, coaching students on their writing. The emphasis is on exposing students to the rules of grammar at the moment of greatest impact: right when they find that they don't know how to do or say something. The application is immediate and meaningful (Weaver, 1996).

Inductive Lessons are some of the most powerful lessons that students can learn. This is when students are presented with a collection of data (like student work) and they draw conclusions and formulate a rule based on the work (Weaver, 1996). As suggested by Brooks & Brooks, inductive lessons require students to construct knowledge and come to their own conclusions based on their own observations. Because the lesson came out of students' needs, the application of the rule derived inductively is immediate.

Focus Lessons are short, five- to ten-minute lessons. Several lessons in a sequence may be used to teach larger concepts. In general, the students are not required to practice the skill immediately, outside of the context of their writing, and the skills that are presented are not tested in isolation from the student writing.

Extended Focus Lessons should take place when a concept is complex and the students would benefit from some practice of the idea. The teacher teaches a regular focus lesson and then the students are asked to apply it in a short activity. The focus of the practice is to clarify the concept, not necessarily to master it. Again, the students will not be tested in isolation on this topic. Instead, the teacher should assess whether or not the students grasp the ideas based on their writing.

Altogether, grammar lessons that are taught in this manner fit into a curriculum in which the application of grammatical patterns is contextualized in response to student work and taught in an active learning curriculum. I was misguided in my original application of writing workshop. I thought that writing was the cumulative activity that grows from the application of other discrete skills. I was approaching the workshop from a parts to whole pedagogy. The students were "doing English" by using their grammar in writing.

Now I approach English and grammar from a different perspective. Students must use their prior knowledge of grammar to create a new piece of writing. Then, as a coach, I study their writing and create a grammar game plan that teaches them the grammar that they need to know in the context of when they need to know it. Grammatical knowledge makes writing effective and purposeful. I am not afraid to teach grammar. My students will learn grammar as they craft their writing around meaningful experiences, playing with language inside and outside the rules of grammar, searching for a clear voice to express their thoughts and ideas.

(Weaver, McNally, & Moerman, 2001) used Lois Lowry's *The Giver* (1993) in one of her focus lessons. She selected a paragraph from Chapter 9 and, "through a regression process," turned it into a piece of writing that sounded just like what her students wrote (p. 24). When her students read the passage, they thought it was "too choppy." So they combined sentences, rewrote the altered passage, and revised the paragraph to make it sound like what they thought Lowry would have written. Then they compared what they had written with what Lois Lowry wrote. Ms. McNally encouraged her students to think about how they might incorporate what they had learned about how to combine sentences in their own writings. What she discovered was increased use of participial phrases, appositives, and subordinate clauses in her students' writing—all without telling them they were studying grammar. So grammatical constructions can be topics of focus lessons.

During teacher–student conferences, teachers can discuss the decisions their students make about their sentences or the perspective they decide to take on their topic, or many of the other grammatical and stylistic decisions writers must make to construct text. During editing conferences, teachers can help their writers consider the conventions of grammar needed to meet the demands of this text's situation. Is it going to the writer's grandmother or to the newspaper? As different grammatical constructions are taught in focus lessons, they can be added to the editing checklist. Joan Berger (2001) did this. As well as providing instruction during focus lessons, Ms. Berger's peer editor's checklist gave specific directions on what peers should look for as they edited each other's papers. For example, items on this checklist included, "Commas are used correctly after adverb phrases or with compound sentences. Place a check mark in the margin where commas are not used or used incorrectly." Through focus lessons, her students had the "verbal equipment" to recognize "adverb phrases" and "compound sentences" (p. 47).

This kind of grammar teaching provides support for growing writers and users of the language. It helps them to tackle the challenges of writing and to begin "to share in what every writer knows is grammar's 'infinite power' " (Hunter & Wallace, 1995, p. 246).

Now, it is possible that some readers are feeling moderately unsure that the grammar instruction *they* received helped *them* recognize adverbial phrases and compound sentences. For assistance with personal grammar questions, readers might wish to visit the Guide to Grammar and Writing site maintained by Charles Darling (http://webster.commnet.edu/grammar/index.htm). Readers who find themselves overwhelmed with all the information on this site might turn to the Big Dog's Grammar site, a bare bones guide to English (http://aliscot.com/bigdog/). For numerous other sites to support teachers' teaching of grammar in the context of meaningful language activities, we recommend Nancy Patterson's article in *Voices from the Middle*, March 2001.

Capitalization and Punctuation

Students who learned capitalization and punctuation rules as needed in the context of their own writing perform equally as well on a standardized test as students who are taught using the more traditional skill-and-drill method (e.g., Calkins, 1980; Cordeiro, Giacobbe, & Cazden, 1983). Lucy Calkins (1980) also discovered that the students who learned the rules as needed within the context of their writing used more kinds of punctuation correctly within their pieces and explained the reasons why punctuation is used more clearly than did students taught using the traditional approach. Further, Pat Cordeiro, Mary Ellen Giacobbe, and Courtney Cazden (1983) discovered that teaching the rules in the context of the students' writing actually seems to provide students with *more* opportunities to practice using the rules than does the language-arts book and workbook they might have used.

Once a rule is introduced in Deirdre Aiken's classroom, it becomes an item on the classroom's editing checklist. As with all items on this checklist, writers search the pieces they have selected for publication for words that should be capitalized that are not or words that are capitalized that should not be, as well as for punctuation that is missing or is used incorrectly. The practice of searching for errors and correcting them in one's own work provides instruction. Additional instruction occurs during the editing conference. The teacher can reinforce the rule supporting each self-correction made by the student and can call the student's attention to one or two words incorrectly capitalized or one or two punctuation marks used incorrectly. As in handwriting instruction, during the editing conference, the teacher has the opportunity to provide direct instruction on those rules of capitalization and punctuation the student needs.

Unfortunately, however, a student's piece typically has many capitalization and punctuation errors. The teacher cannot teach all rules simultaneously! Which rule should the teacher focus upon first? Teacher Judy Patton used her school district's language-arts textbook to guide her decision making. Ms. Patton decided to teach those punctuation and capitalization rules that her students' writings indicated they needed and that her district (by its selection of the language-arts textbook) identified as important. Teachers who have no textbook to guide their decisions have the advantage of focusing solely on their students' needs, selecting those most in need of attention, as determined by frequency of use in the students' pieces. Teachers may wish to use resources like *The Elements of Style* (Strunk & White, 2005), *Writers Express* (Kemper, Nathan, & Sebranek,1994) or *The Write Track* (Kemper, Nathan, & Sebranek, 1995) to guide their recall of capitalization and punctuation rules.

Handwriting

Does it really matter how students form letters? In the past, the idea of teaching letter formation was pushed away. Today, the data clearly indicate that teaching handwriting improves students' writing. Further, teachers, test readers, potential employers, and others form impressions of the student as a writer based on the quality of the handwriting. On scored writing pieces, the student with the poorer handwriting typically scores considerably lower than the student with better handwriting (Graham, Harris, & Fink, 2000). Because handwriting instruction facilitates learning to write, more and more educators believe teachers should provide their students with handwriting instruction.

Before considering how to help students learn to make legible alphabet forms, teachers need to decide which handwriting style and form to use: manuscript or cursive style, vertical or slanted manuscript form.

Manuscript or Cursive Style?   Prior to the 1920s, U.S. children of all ages were taught only the cursive style (Hackney, n.d.). Marjorie Wise's 1921 arrival in the United States from England marked the commencement of U.S. children being taught the manuscript style. Wise's introduction of the manuscript style, a vertical form with letters made with circles and straight lines, was quickly embraced by teachers as the writing style most appropriate for young children. Several reasons have been put forth to support the teaching of the manuscript style to young children (Barbe & Milone, 1980; Duvall, 1985; Farris, 1982; Graham, 1993–1994, 1999; Hackney, n.d.). These include the following:

- Manuscript letters are very similar to the print forms used in books. Only two lowercase letters, *a* and *g*, are different in type than in handwriting.
- The print in children's world outside the classroom (e.g., "STOP," "SCHOOL BUS") is mostly in manuscript style.
- The manuscript style is easier to produce than is the cursive style.
- The basic strokes (mostly circles and lines) used in the manuscript style parallel young children's perceptual and motor development; the basic shapes are in their drawings.

The typical pattern has been to introduce students to the manuscript style first and then to the teach them cursive style in second or third grade.

Vertical or Slanted Form?   Which manuscript form: vertical or slanted? The title of Steve Graham's (1993/1994) article, "Are Slanted Manuscript Alphabets Superior to the Traditional Manuscript Alphabet?" summarizes the debate. Beginning in the 1960s, some educators began to question children's introduction to the vertical manuscript alphabet— a form like that used by the Zaner-Bloser Company in their handwriting program, *Hand-writing: A Way to Self-Expression* (1993) (see www.zaner-bloser.com/html/HWgen.html). (Directions for how to form Zaner-Bloser's manuscript and cursive letters can be found in Figure 9.2.) Two concerns have been raised most frequently: (1) Young children often reverse some of the very similar lowercase letters (e.g., *b* and *d*), and (2) young children are being required to learn two distinctly different handwriting forms in the span of only two or three years. Concerns such as these resulted in the introduction of slanted manuscript alphabets, a manuscript form purportedly more similar than the vertical form to cursive writing. Today, for example, Donald Thurber's D'Nealian slanted manuscript alphabet is used in the Scott, Foresman (1999) handwriting program *D'Nealian Handwriting* (see www.dnealian.com/).

Do the slanted alphabets really ease children's transition from the manuscript to the cursive style? Does the use of a slanted alphabet truly help children become better cursive writers? Several researchers (e.g., Duvall, 1985; Farris,

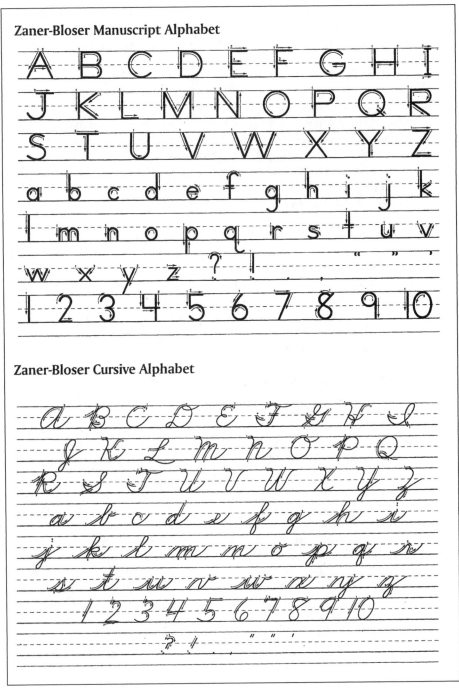

Zaner-Bloser Manuscript Alphabet

Zaner-Bloser Cursive Alphabet

FIGURE 9.2   **Zaner-Bloser's Manuscript and Cursive Handwriting Forms**

1982; Graham, 1992, 1993/1994, 1999; Ourada, 1993) contend that there is insufficient evidence to support the claims made by the supporters of slanted alphabets of the benefits of this form to writers. Instead, their findings indicate the following:

- The use of slanted alphabets does not help children to learn cursive more easily or quickly.
- The slanted alphabets' manuscript and cursive letter forms are, like the vertical manuscript and cursive forms, dissimilar.
- There is no evidence that using the slanted alphabets' continuous strokes to form manuscript letters resulted in children having a better writing rhythm, a faster writing speed, or a smaller number of reversed letters than when using single strokes.
- Slanted alphabets require young children to engage in fine-motor motions that are beyond their physical developmental level.

Hence, the present evidence seems to suggest that, if given a choice, teachers should choose to introduce their students to the vertical manuscript style like that from the students' environment outside the school. Learning the vertical manuscript style is also recommended for students with learning disabilities, even though there is no research examining the effectiveness of different scripts with these special needs students (Graham, 1999). Steve Graham adds a word of caution, however. Regardless of which script teachers teach their students, children will develop their own style. Teachers ought not to insist on a strict adherence to any particular model.

Teaching Students How to Form Letters.   Attention to how letters have been and should be formed is part of the editing stage of writing. The procedures used by first-grade teacher Donna Hutchins provide an illustration of how handwriting instruction can be woven into this stage of the writing process. When her first-graders are ready to publish their pieces, they compare their letters against models and circle the letters that they think are formed incorrectly. When Ms. Hutchins meets with each student during an editing conference, she selects a letter or two from among those circled by the student. Sometimes the letters selected are those that are most illegible; often they are those in the student's name; sometimes they are the two letters that appear most frequently in the student's piece.

Once the letters are identified, Ms. Hutchins provides *direct instruction* in how to form these few selected letters. She uses a procedure recommended by researchers such as Beatrice Furner (1985) and Karl Koenke (1986). She gives verbal directions for how each of the two letters should be formed; models how to construct the letters; observes as the student repeats the steps in making the letters while saying the directions softly; and provides the student with corrective feedback and reinforcement. Ms. Hutchins observes as the student forms the selected letters three or four times each. Then she asks the student to select the best formed letter.

The exception is with her learning-disabled students; she does not ask them to verbalize the steps for forming a letter while learning it. What seems to work best with learning-disabled students is to have them examine a model of the letter marked with numbered arrows and then to reproduce the letter from memory (Berninger et al., 1997). All students seem to benefit from the brief kind of supervised practice Ms. Hutchins provides for her students.

This procedure provides direct instruction in correct letter formation. Rather than introducing all students to each letter, instruction is individualized, focusing only on those letters each student needs assistance in learning to form. This teaching approach demands that the teacher maintain careful records of which letters have been introduced to which student and which letters each student writes correctly. Usually, a checklist is used to help the teacher track the students' handwriting progress and to recall which letters have been introduced to which students. When the teacher notices that some students have been introduced to the correct way to form a letter more than once, but they persist in forming that letter incorrectly, these students can be brought together for a brief session of direct instruction and practice in the formation of the problematic letter.

An increasing number of school districts are purchasing handwriting programs to teach their elementary students correct letter formation. A program with growing popularity is the *Handwriting Without Tears* program (see http://www.hwtears.com/method.htm). Other school districts are turning to technology to teach letter formation. Programs like WriteOn! (http://www.incrediblekid.com/about.htm) and KIDPAD (http://www.penman.com/prodinfo.html) have received positive response from teachers and children.

Left-Handed Writers.   Given that 10 to 15 percent (a percentage that is growing) of the population is left-handed, most teachers will have at least some left-handed students in their classrooms. Instruction for left-handed students is only slightly different from the instruction provided for right-handed students. First, it is important for the teacher to determine each student's hand preference. Most children develop a preference for their left or right hand sometime during the first four years of life (Bloodsworth, 1993). When unsure of the student's choice, the teacher can ask the student to throw a ball, to cut with scissors, to paint, to string beads, or to hold a pencil or crayon. These will provide clues regarding the student's hand preference. Sometimes these observations will provide conflicting information. Carol Vukelich, one of the authors of this book, writes with her left hand, holds a tennis racket in her right hand, paints walls with her right hand, throws a ball with her right hand, manipulates puzzle pieces with her right hand, pours water with her left hand, and pours sand with her right hand. Fortunately, her first-grade teacher, Ms. Peggar, permitted her to choose which hand she preferred to use to write.

Three instructional adjustments are recommended for left-handed writers (Hackney, n.d.; Howell, 1978):

- Left-handed writers might wish to hold their writing tools an inch or more farther back from the tip than right-handed writers. This change permits them more easily to see what they have just written.
- Left-handed writers should tilt the paper to slope downward slightly to the right about 30 to 40 percent, with the lower right corner pointed toward their midsection. (Right-handed writers tilt the paper slightly upward and to the left.) Too severe a tilt results in a backward slant to the letters.
- Teachers should permit left-handed writers to slant their handwriting slightly backward.

Of the three suggestions, the paper tilting is the most critical (see Figure 9.3). If the left-handed child fails to position the paper correctly, the child may end up writing with a hooked wrist, a problem that affects legibility and fluency and can cause erasure or smudging of what has been written. Carol Vukelich knows about these problems from personal experience. She has received many smudged notes

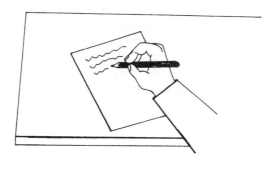

FIGURE 9.3   Correct Paper Slant for Right- and Left-Handed Writers

from her left-handed father, whose teacher, Ms. Peggar, would not let him tilt his paper to the right. Fortunately, a generation later, when Ms. Peggar was Carol's first-grade teacher, she had changed her approach to teaching handwriting and allowed Carol to tilt her paper in the proper direction.

The kind of support needed by developing writers comes from handwriting instruction that focuses on each student's letter-formation needs, provides direct instruction in how to form the selected letters, and adapts to student's hand preferences.

SPECIAL POPULATIONS

Recall that one of the underlying themes of this book is respecting the tremendous diversity of children who are enrolled in today's schools. It is not surprising, therefore, that the general strategies we have recommended will sometimes need to be modified to meet the needs of specific children.

As explained throughout this book, ongoing assessment is a key requirement for providing this type of individualized instruction. Another important requirement is for teachers to be aware of the needs of special populations—groups of students who face common problems and challenges.

This section contains information on adapting instruction to meet the needs of two groups of students—bilingual second-language learners and students with various types of disabilities. Teachers will undoubtedly encounter many members of both groups of students during their teaching careers. Tailoring instruction to meet the needs of linguistically and developmentally diverse students is one of the hallmarks of excellent teaching. The special features that follow give practical tips to assist teachers in this challenging task.

Bilingual and Second-Language Learners

Currently, more than one in seven students in U.S. schools speak English as a second language (Barone, 1998), and the proportion is much higher in some areas such as California and other parts of the Southwest. In addition, the percentage of second-language learners tends to be higher in the earliest grades, forecasting even greater linguistic diversity in future classrooms. For example, one survey of Head Start programs reported that 22 percent of the students spoke Spanish at home and that 4 percent came from families who spoke one of 139 other languages (Tabors & Snow, 1994)! It is vitally important for early childhood educators to be prepared to help these students learn to speak, read, and write English. These students also need to be helped to learn content knowledge in subjects such as math, science, and social studies. Whenever possible, second-language learners should also be helped to continue to master their native languages.

In Special Feature 9.1, Sarah Hudelson and Irene Serna describe how the writing workshop can be adapted for use with second-language learners. As you

SPECIAL FEATURE 9.1
Meeting Special Needs of Bilingual and Second-Language Learners

SARAH HUDELSON AND IRENE SERNA

Question: How applicable is the writing workshop approach to nonnative speakers of English? Answer: Totally! Bilingual programs (especially Spanish-to-English programs) have used this approach to teaching writing and have found that bilingual children can and do engage in writing for multiple purposes and audiences. These children need the same kinds of opportunities as nonbilingual speakers do. Through this kind of instruction, non-English-speaking children discover both the forms and the functions of their native written language (Edelsky, 1986; Flores, Garcia, Gonzalez, Hidalgo, Kaczmarek, & Romero, 1985; Freeman & Freeman, 1992, 1994b; Serna & Hudelson, 1993).

Developments in the field of English as a second language (ESL) teaching also support the workshop approach to the teaching of writing. At one time, ESL pedagogy advocated the sequential introduction of listening, speaking, reading, and *finally* writing and suggested devoting substantial amounts of time to children's oral language development before worrying about their reading and writing development. This traditional ESL writing instruction prescribed the writing of words, then phrases, then sentences, and finally paragraphs from models. The assumption was that second-language learners needed extended, structured practice with the language before they could be asked to create text. When this method was used, these learners were never given the opportunity to write their own pieces. Fortunately, brave teachers began to test the use of the writing workshop with ESL students. Virginia Allen (1991) and Sarah Hudelson (1989) summarize these teachers' discoveries:

- Young ESL learners can write from early on in their second-language learning experiences, while they are developing oral proficiency in the language.

- Young ESL writers' texts display features similar to those seen in native speakers' texts, providing evidence of ESL learners' experimentation with the new language, English.
- The texts produced reflect the learners' abilities in English at a particular time. As the learners' competence grows, the learners' texts change, offering evidence of how the learners are constructing and reconstructing the written language.
- Young ESL learners learn to write in English (a) by engaging in writing with varied audiences, for varied purposes; and (b) by having others respond to what they are writing—just as native speakers do.
- Like native speakers of the language, young ESL speakers are able to respond to the writing of others and to make changes in their writing.
- Writing ability in the native language facilitates writing in the second language.
- The teacher's role is crucial. ESL children are extremely sensitive to the teacher's beliefs about writing.

Given this new knowledge, what are the best practices in the teaching of writing to bilingual and second-language learners? How can teachers use the writing workshop to meet the special needs of ESL and bilingual students?

Facilitating First-Language Competence. Encourage and support children to become competent writers in their *first* language. There is substantial evidence that time spent in becoming a writer of one's native language is time well-spent (Freeman & Freeman, 1994a; Hudelson, 1987, 1989). The reasons for this benefit are many. Writing is the creation of meaning from

(continued on next page)

one's intellectual and linguistic resources and activity. Construction of meaning will be enhanced if writers are able to use well-developed linguistic resources (the native language) rather than resources that are not as well developed (the second language). When ESL children write in their native language, their knowledge of how written language functions can be more easily constructed from a strong foundation in the spoken language (the native language) rather than from the weaker language (the second language). Native language writing provides children with opportunities to experience what writing is and does, how it functions for writers, and the uses or purposes it serves. Native language writing also gives children confidence in themselves in writers. Once ESL children know what writing is, how it functions, and how it can be used, they begin to experiment with writing in their second language, English. The specific time for this experimentation will be different for each young writer. Teachers should be guided by each student's timetable, not the calendar.

Teachers who speak and read the same language as the students can encourage and respond to their students' native language writing, even if they are not nearly as proficient in that language as they are in English. If the teachers do not know the students' native languages, then they might enlist the help of parents or community volunteers or other older children in the school. Response is important.

Encouragement of First-Language Use. When ESL learners begin to write in English, allow and encourage them to continue to use their native language to mediate their learning. There is considerable evidence that it may take second-language learners from four to six years to achieve full proficiency in English (Ramirez, Yuen, & Ramel, 1991). To deny access to the first language is to deny children the broadest, most complete access to learning. Additionally, if children are able to use both their native language and English, they may be able to articulate more completely what they know.

Benjamin, a Spanish-speaking second-grader, illustrates the importance of allowing ESL learners to use their native language freely. In the spring of second grade, Benjamin's bilingual second-grade class was studying China. Each student was to choose a topic of interest related to China, collect information about that topic, and prepare a report. Benjamin chose kung fu as his topic. School and public library resources were limited to English language materials, so Benjamin read about his topic in English. Then he switched into Spanish to write what he had learned. He needed to articulate what he had understood about his topic from his reading in English into his native language:

Benjamin's text in Spanish:	The English translation of Benjamin's text (Hudelson & Serna, 1994, p. 292)
Como pelean ConFoo	How do they fight kung fu?
ai muchos typos de CongFu.	There are many types of kung fu.
TiHe I CongFu	Tai chi and kung fu
En Ti He tocas con quien estas peleando	In tai chi you touch the person you're fighting with.
Kungfu si pegas a las personas	In kung fu you hit the people.

Third-grader Juan provides a second illustration. Juan chose to prepare a report on polar bears. His learning-log notes—notes taken from his readings, his interview of a zookeeper, and his viewing of a documentary—were written in both Spanish and English. After conferring in English with his teacher, Juan added information to his notes, which he then orally reviewed in Spanish with a group of peers. Juan was able to explain more coherently in Spanish than in English how the polar bear adapted to the Arctic. Juan then wrote the first draft of his report in Spanish. After peer and teacher response, he wrote a final draft in English. (The students chose whether to produce their final drafts in English or in Spanish.) Juan's Spanish writing facilitated construction of an informative text, which he wanted to write in English.

Juan's first draft written in Spanish:	Juan's second draft written in English:
Los osos polares viven in en artico donde hace mucho fio. Hay mucho hielo y nieve. Ellos tienen pel muy greso para que o tengan frio. El piel is negro y cuando el sol le pega se pone caliente para que no tengan frio.	Polar bears live in the Arctic in the north where it is very cold. day jave thick fur so day won't be cold. Polar Bears jave blak skin when the sun hits the fur ut terns warm so the polar Bear esn't cold.
Las garras y el pelo entre los dedos les ayundan andar en el hielo y nieve sin rebalarse. Osos polares tiene piel entre los dedos. El piel les ayuda a nadar porque pueden mover mas agua.	polar bears jave big claws and fur between their toes so they won't slip of the ice when they're walking. Polar Bers hae skin bituin their toes which helps them muve more water and that's whi they're good suimrs.
Pueden nadar abajo agua por dos minutos. Cuando estan nandando no tiene frip porque el pelo es muy greso. Los senores los estan matando porque quieren	

su piel para chamaras. Han matado muchos y por eso estan en peligro.

Multiplicity of Opportunities for Authentic Uses of Second Language. Recognize that children need multiple, authentic opportunities and purposes for writing in English. Children should not be asked to write in English simply for the sake of writing in English. Real reasons occur naturally within classroom life, particularly within the writing workshop; reasons do not need to be invented (Hudelson & Serna, 1994). For example, in Benjamin's second-grade classroom, there were both Spanish speakers and English speakers. When one of Benjamin's English-speaking friends moved to another school, Benjamin missed him a lot. He decided to write to him. Because he knew that Jimmy did not know Spanish, Benjamin wrote in English:

Benjamin's letter to Jimmy:	Conventional spelling (Hudelson & Serna, 1994, p. 283)
Dear jimmy, I mist jou sow moch ver du eu Lib uiarnt yu coming bac we d misiu Tichur ddyt tu Hector Tu I lov iu	Dear Jimmy, I miss you so much. Where do you live? Why aren't you coming back? We all miss you. Teacher did too. Hector too. I love you,
jemmy sensirali	Jimmy. Sincerely.

Benjamin used a considerable amount of Spanish orthography in his letter, but he wrote in English because he wanted to communicate with Jimmy, and he knew that to do so, he needed to write in English (Hudelson & Serna, 1994). Later in the year, Benjamin's teacher

(continued on next page)

established a pen-pal program, pairing Spanish-speaking students from her class with English-speaking students from another school and English-speaking students in her classroom with Spanish-speaking students from the other school. This provided all the students another opportunity to engage in communicating through writing, and it offered the Spanish-speaking students another opportunity to communicate in English.

Other examples of pen-pal programs are described in the ESL literature. For example, teachers have paired intermediate-grade native English speakers with primary-grade ESL learners in dialogue journal-writing programs (Bromley, 1995). In a third-grade class, students made biweekly visits to nursing-home residents. At Christmastime, the students wanted to make cards for their senior "buddies." One student who had been reluctant to write in English produced the following card, her first English writing. She knew the card had to be written in English because her buddy could not read Spanish.

Child's card:	Conventional spelling:
Dar Arty,	Dear Arty,
I lav u dices	I love you because
u ar nas tu mi.	you are nice to me.
I lav yu tu.	I love you too.
Ga old ar u?	How old are you?
I em 8. I lac u	I am 8. I like you
tu mah	too much.
fam _____	From _____.

These examples demonstrate that young ESL learners are very much aware of the contextual demands on their spoken and written language and illustrate how they respond to these demands.

Interdependence of Language Processes. Acknowledge that the language processes of listening, speaking, reading, and writing in a second language develop simultaneously and interdependently. That is, writing should not be isolated from the other language arts. Rather, writing is, and should be, connected to talking, to reading literature, and to study of content (such as thematic units or theme cycles).

Acceptance of All Attempts at Writing Communication. During children's early ESL writing experiences, be especially encouraging and accepting of all their efforts, encouraging the learners simply to write, to become comfortable and fluent as second-language writers. If second-language writers are to become better at the craft of writing, they need to be willing to take risks, to experiment, to ask questions, and to make mistakes. They will be more willing to adopt this stance of experimentation if they receive encouragement, and if their efforts are acknowledged and celebrated (Peyton & Reed, 1990).

First-grader Catalina, for example, came to school knowing no English. She began writing in her journal after a month in school. She started by drawing pictures and labeling them with words that she copied from around the room. She asked her teacher for help with her writing. Her teacher accepted Catalina's efforts, assisted her, and always responded to her entries, but she also kept encouraging her to try writing independently. For several months, Catalina insisted on writing only words that she could spell accurately by copying or by asking an adult or a peer. The consequence was that her writing took on the form of patterns, such as "I drink milk for dinner. I drink milk for breakfast." It was not until the end of March of her first-grade year that she took a risk and wrote independently, using invented spelling.

Catalina's writing:	Conventional spelling (Peyton & Reed, 1990, p. 86):
Friday I psie a psow the psow is read and Today I pie a crayons to.	Friday I buy a pencil. The pencil is red. And today I buy a crayons too.

Catalina's teacher celebrated the fact that Catalina finally had taken a risk in her writing and wrote back to her, "I didn't see your new red pencil. I did see your new crayons. Now you can do good work." This was a turning point for Catalina. Now, freed from the constraints of standard spelling, she could write about whatever she wanted. Her teacher continued to encourage her and to support her efforts. By the end of the school year, Catalina had added imaginative stories, science journal entries, and letters to her friends to her repertoire of writing. When interviewed before starting second grade, Catalina indicated that when she first started school she was afraid to write and always asked for help. Now, however, she judged herself to be a good writer who could figure out the answers to her own questions. Catalina had gradually developed confidence as a writer, and her teacher's attitude played a crucial role in that evolution.

Providing Special Assistance. Adapt practices (such as writing workshop, dialogue and literature response journals, and learning logs) to meet the specific needs of second-language learners. While it has been demonstrated, for example, that young ESL learners are able to participate meaningfully in writing workshop (Samway, 1992; Peyton, Jones, Vincent, & Greenblat, 1994), they may need more assistance with their writing than native speakers. They may benefit from extended talking about their chosen topics before and during drafting. They may need assistance with vocabulary and contextual cues such as how to use pictures or planning webs. They may be more successful with writing that is connected to a topic the class is studying rather than a personal experience since class activities may have provided more schema within which to write. Initially they may be less comfortable revising than native speakers or make more revisions that are word-based. A teacher's goal is to meet the needs of all her students within writing workshop, to provide the support each student needs to become a better writer.

Keeping Corrections to a Minimum. Recognize that young ESL learners are individuals with individual personalities, interests, varying degrees of interest in and commitment to writing, and varying rates of learning the second language. All learners do not learn at the same rate or in the same way. All ESL learners will not begin writing in English at the same time or under the same circumstances. Be patient. Be encouraging. Be supportive. Be reasonable about correcting the child's text—making the corrections fit the writing purpose and learner's language abilities. As with any writer, overcorrection will probably result in a decrease in the writer's interest in writing. How much correction should be done? What would be helpful to and manageable for this student? As was suggested earlier this chapter, choose one or two variations from conventional English, and focus on helping the learner correct those one or two errors. Think of this writing as learning in progress; over time, the student's writing will change and will move toward becoming more conventional. Also, over time, as ESL students develop more proficiency in English through many experiences writing, talking about their writing, hearing other students' writing, and talking about other students' writing, they will become competent writers of English texts.

will see, the writing workshop is ideally suited to the needs of students learning English as a second language. The main adaptation is to allow opportunities for children to become competent writers in their native language and then provide authentic opportunities and purposes for writing in English. The students' writing in their native language will mediate and facilitate their acquisition of written English.

Children with Special Needs

Legislation has mandated that students with disabilities be placed in the least restrictive environment. The goal is inclusion, allowing each student with special needs to have the maximum amount of integration into general education class-rooms that is possible. The resulting mainstreaming of students with special needs into regular classrooms has radically changed the role of classroom teachers at all grade levels. Teachers are now expected to work as part of a multidisciplinary team (along with special education teachers, psychologists, and other specialists) to develop an individualized education program (IEP) for each student with iden-tified special needs.

While this movement toward full inclusion has generated new challenges and responsibilities for teachers, it has also created wonderful new opportunities for students with disabilities. Koppenhaver, Spadorcia, and Erickson (1998, p. 95) explain:

> The importance of inclusive instruction for children with disabilities is that they receive instruction from the school personnel who have the greatest knowledge of literacy theory and practice, the most training, and the greatest print-specific resources. They are surrounded by models of varied print use, purposeful reading and writing, frequent peer interaction and support, and the expectation that chil-dren can, should, and will learn to read and write.

These types of positive literacy experiences are especially important for children with disabilities. Marvin and Mirenda (1993) investigated the home lit-eracy experiences of children enrolled in Head Start and special education pro-grams. They found that the parents of children with special needs placed a much higher priority on oral communication than on learning to read and write. Parents of preschoolers with disabilities reported less adult-initiated lit-eracy activity in the home, less exposure to nursery rhymes, and fewer trips to the library.

In Special Feature 9.2, Karen Burstein and Tanis Bryan describe how teachers can make accommodations to promote language and literacy learning for students with a variety of special needs. These adaptations, when combined with the activi-ties described in this book, should enable teachers to get all students off to a good start in learning language and literacy.

On Your Mark, Get Set, Go: Strategies for Supporting Children with Special Needs in General Education Classrooms

KAREN BURSTEIN AND TANIS BRYAN

Previous chapters in this book have described how to set up and implement a blended language and literacy program for young children. In this special feature, two early childhood special needs experts describe strategies for supporting children with special needs in such programs.

■ On Your Mark

Teachers in preschools, kindergartens, and the primary grades are increasingly likely to have students with special needs in their classrooms. Typically, the majority of these children have speech and/or language impairments, developmental delays, and learning disabilities. A smaller number of these children have mental and or emotional disturbances, sensory disabilities (hearing or visual impairments), and physical and health impairments. The latter reflects increases in the number of children surviving serious chronic conditions (e.g., spina bifida, cystic fibrosis) and attending school as well as increases in the number of children with less life-threatening but nonetheless serious health (e.g., asthma) and cognitive (e.g., autism) problems.

Public policy and law, including the 1997 Individuals with Disabilities Education Act (IDEA), along with humane and ethical considerations dictate that children with disabilities receive optimal educational programs, given our knowledge bases and resources. Further, IDEA stipulates that children with special needs be provided their education in classes with their age-same peers to the greatest extent possible.

One of the primary goals of early education is to prepare all young children for general education classrooms. Making this a reality for children with special needs requires that teachers make accommodations and adaptations that take into account the individual student's special needs. Teachers' willingness to *include* students with disabilities and their skillfulness in making adaptations are critical determinants of effective instruction. This special feature outlines strategies and suggestions for teachers who have young students with special needs in their classrooms. Our purpose is to provide suggestions for making adaptations so that teachers feel comfortable, confident, and successful including these students in their classrooms.

■ Get Set

Cognitive, physical, sensory, developmental, physical, emotional—there are so many variations in development! It is not reasonable to expect general education teachers or special education teachers to be experts on every childhood malady. The primary lesson to remember is that children are far more alike than they are different from one another. Whatever their differences, children desire and need the company of other children. They are more likely to develop adaptive behaviors in the presence of peers. Children with special needs can succeed academically and socially in mainstreamed settings (Stainback & Stainback, 1992; Thousand & Villa, 1990).

Setting the stage for an inclusive classroom takes somewhat more planning. Effective planning includes input and support from the school administration, other teachers, parents of children with special needs, and possibly the school nurse. Early and frequent collaboration with your special education colleagues is particularly helpful. There are significant differences between general and special education teachers' perspectives on curriculum and methods of instruction. Sometimes they differ in expectations for children.

Collaboration works when teachers constructively build on these different points of view. Collaboration produces multiple strategies that can be tested for effectiveness (as in the proverbial "two heads are better than one"). For collaboration to work, teachers have to respect different points of view, have good listening skills, and be

(continued on next page)

willing to try something new. It also requires systematic observation and evaluation of strategies that are tested. Teachers have to ask, "How well did the strategy/adaptation work? What effect did it have on the students in the class?" Here are some strategies for collaboration:

- Attend the student's multidisciplinary team meeting.
- Keep a copy of the individual family service plan (IFSP) or individualized education plan (IEP) and consult it periodically to ensure that short- and long-term goals are being achieved.
- Arrange to have some shared planning time each week with others who work with students with special needs.
- Brainstorm modifications/adaptations to regular instructional activities.
- Identify who will collect work samples of specific tasks.
- Assess the student's language, reading, and writing strengths, and give brief probes each week to check on progress and maintenance.
- Share copies of student work with your collaborators and add these artifacts to the student's portfolio.
- Collaborate with families. Parents are children's first and best teachers. Additionally, they possess personal knowledge of their children that far surpasses any assessment data we may collect.

■ Go

As previously mentioned, the majority of children with special needs have difficulties in language, reading, and written expression. Research indicates that these problems stem from deficits in short-term memory, lack of self-awareness and self-monitoring strategies, lack of mediational strategies, and inability to transfer and generalize learned material to new or novel situations. Hence, many students with special needs may have difficulty in classroom settings that utilize a high degree of implicit teaching of literacy. These

students typically can benefit from explicit instruction. Here are some general teaching strategies that teachers can use to support students with special needs:

- Establish a daily routine on which the student with special needs can depend.
- Allocate more time for tasks to be completed by students with special needs.
- Structure transitions between activities, and provide supervision and guidance for quick changes in activities.
- Adapt the physical arrangement of the room to provide a quiet space free of visual and auditory distractions.
- Plan time for one-on-one instruction at some point in the day.
- Use task analysis to break learning tasks into components.
- Recognize the different learning styles of all students, and prepare materials in different ways—for example, as manipulatives, audio recordings, visual displays, and the like.
- Try cross-ability or reciprocal peer tutoring for practice of learned material.
- Begin teaching organization skills such as the use of a simple daily planner.
- Teach positive social behaviors to all students.
- Consistently implement behavior change programs.
- Recognize and help students with special needs deal with their feelings.
- Encourage all students to respect and include students with special needs in their academic and play activities.
- Establish a routine means of communication with parents.
- Locate strategies that help parents select materials that are developmentally and educationally appropriate for their students.

■ Speech Development

When children come to school, they are expected to be able to communicate. Language is the ability to communicate using symbols; it includes comprehension of both oral and written expression. Speech is one component of oral expression. Many young children come to school with delays in speech and language (comprehension and expression). Speech problems such as misarticulations and dysfluencies are frequently seen in young children with and without special needs. Less obvious are problems understanding others' speech. Fortunately, the majority of children with language problems are able to successfully participate in all aspects of general education with a few modifications to the environment or curriculum.

Frequently, children with language problems receive special education services provided by a speech and language pathologist. However, the classroom teacher also has important roles to fulfill: (1) monitoring students' comprehension of instructions and classroom activities, and (2) providing opportunities for oral language practice and interaction with peers and adults.

The following are strategies that classroom teachers can use to help promote speech development in students with oral language delays:

- Collaborate with the speech and language pathologist in selecting activities, materials, and games that promote language development.
- Model appropriate grammar, rhythm, tone, and syntax.
- Keep directions simple, brief, and to the point.
- For students who have difficulty expressing themselves, do not rely solely on open-ended questions. Use yes or no questions that are easier to answer.
- When students with speech problems speak, give them your full attention and ensure that other students do the same.
- Errors should not be criticized. Pay attention to the content of the student's message. Do not call attention to misarticulations, especially dysfluencies, as the problem may become more serious if

attention is called to it (Lewis & Doorlag, 1999).

- Students who stutter may have improved speech quality if alternate styles of communication are used, such as whispering, singing in a higher or lower pitch, or choral reading.
- Give students with special needs multiple opportunities across the day to converse with you.
- Encourage parents to routinely engage in conversations using students' new words, experiences, and relationships.

Special strategies are also needed to help language-delayed children learn the meanings of new words (receptive vocabulary) and be able to use these new words in their speech (expressive vocabulary):

- Teach vocabulary in all subjects: math, science, social studies, health, and so on.
- Assess the student's prior knowledge before introducing a new topic.
- Have the student develop a word book of new words for practice. Pair these words with pictures.
- Encourage students to ask about words they do not understand. Pair these new words with concepts already known.
- Have the students paraphrase new words they are acquiring.
- Use physical demonstrations of words, such as verbs and prepositions, that are difficult to explain. Show students the meanings of these words.
- Have the students physically demonstrate the meanings of words.
- Use manipulatives that students can handle to teach new words.
- Give multiple examples of word meanings.
- Teach students to use picture dictionaries to locate unfamiliar words.
- Keep parents informed of these special strategies and urge them to continue their use outside of school.

(continued on next page)

For children with more severe special needs, secure the services of a specialist in augmentative communication. These individuals have specific skills in communication boards, electronic communication devices, and computer voice synthesis. For more information about this special area, contact the Assistive Technology On-Line Web site at http://www2.lib.udel.edu/atc/asstechn.htm, sponsored by the DuPont Hospital for Children and the University of Delaware.

■ Reading Assessment and Instruction

For many young children with or at-risk for special needs, reading is a very difficult task. Many of these children benefit greatly from explicit instruction in the basic tools of reading (Chall, 1989; Slavin, 1989; Stahl & Miller, 1989) using a direct instruction model. Assessments of children's phonemic awareness (Torgesen, 1994) provide valuable information about the student's skills and deficits in basic manipulation of phonemes. Additionally, it is essential for teachers to match reading materials to the skills of students with special needs.

Once a student's instructional reading level has been identified and appropriate reading materials have been obtained, teachers can use the following strategies to help promote the reading development of the student with special needs:

- Use books without words to provide early readers with an overview of the sequence of story content.
- Teach students to use the context clues available in the text such as the title and pictures.
- Use cross-age tutors, pairing older children such as second-graders with kindergarteners, for drill and practice of sight words and newly learned words.
- Increase fluency by having students repeat readings often.
- Have students use a straightedge under a line of text to eliminate visual distractions and keep place and pace.

- Have students use their finger to point and keep place and pace.
- Tape text read by the teacher or other students. Have the student follow along and read aloud while listening to correct pronunciation, expression, phrasing, and punctuation.
- Echo read with the students. Sit behind and to the side of the student out of his or her line of sight. Read the text with the student softly into his or her ear, providing a model of pacing, pronunciation, and corrective feedback.

■ Writing Instruction

Most young children with special needs do not have physical impairments. However, many may experience delays in both fine and gross motor development. These delays may affect a child's ability to effectively grasp a pencil or shape letters and numbers. Large or ball-shaped crayons are often effective writing tools for children who have not developed a pencil grip. Many commercial built-up pencils or pencil grips are also available. When using these grips, be sure to instruct the child in the proper finger and hand placement on the pencil. For very young children with special needs, tracing letters in sand is a good place to start. Practicing letter structure in fingerpaints or liquid soap is also effective. Paper used by young children can be brightly colored in order to produce a contrast between the writing and the background. Initially, plain paper without lines is preferable to that with lines, as printing is similar to drawing. Using successive approximation of the appropriate size and shape of letters can be accomplished with wide-lined paper with different colored lines. These lines serve as cues for the child to stop or go. Young children with more severe special needs may require the support and services of occupational therapists. These therapists can provide you with expertise and specialized equipment to promote fine motor development.

Written expression by young student with special needs may present several problems for

---

the teacher and the student, as writing is both a process and a product that requires physical and cognitive skills. The written product should be assessed using observable and measurable goals that correspond with the strengths and weaknesses of the student. Teachers need patience and repeated observations of students' written work in order to effectively evaluate and plan for writing instruction. The following are strategies for promoting written expression by young students with special needs:

- Allocate time for writing each day.
- Have students create simple stories from tangible objects that they can touch and manipulate, rather than asking for a memory or a concept. For example, give a ball to the student and ask the student to tell you about this ball. Have an adult serve as a scribe for the student and take dictation, writing down the story as it is composed. When the student is able, ask the student to copy the dictated copy and draw a picture of the ball.

- Compliment students on the content of their stories. Ask for more information about the topic and help them expand their stories.
- Develop a template for writing—for example, putting name and date on a specific area of the paper.
- Celebrate the student's successes!
- Exhibit examples of all students' work.

Including young students with special-needs in the general education setting can be a rewarding experience for the students and their teachers. Assisting students to meet their potential is a teacher's responsibility. These strategies have proven to be effective for teachers supporting students with special needs in special and general education classrooms. However, the most effective tool for teachers is shared planning and collaboration. We urge teachers in all settings to share their skills, experience, and techniques with one another and celebrate the diversity of learners in the schools of this new century.

SUMMARY

As we mentioned in the introduction to this chapter, the way in which skills are taught in the writing workshop is quite different from the way these skills were taught in the past. This change often makes parents uncomfortable and leads them to question whether handwriting, spelling, and grammatical conventions are being given adequate attention. Assure parents that skills are addressed in a writing workshop program. In fact, skills are being taught more effectively now than they were when the parents were students. Years of researching the drill-and-test approach to teaching skills have shown that students rarely used what they were believed to have learned in drill exercises in the texts they wrote! The writing workshop method is a definite improvement over the old method.

- *When will students learn about the mechanics of writing—spelling, grammar, capitalization, punctuation, and handwriting—in writing workshop?*

Instruction in the mechanics of writing is embedded in the writing workshop. First, students are provided instruction on the mechanics of writing during the focus lessons that begin each writing workshop. The students' needs determine which mechanical skills are taught. For example, the observant teacher notices when many of the students are not capitalizing the names of the months in their pieces and teaches a lesson on the importance of capitalizing the name of each month. Or the teacher might notice that the students write in short, choppy sentences and decide to teach a lesson on sentence combining. Second, when the writers have decided that the content of their pieces is just right, and they wish to publish their pieces, they then turn their attention toward the mechanical details. They search their piece, attempting to discover their errors. They circle the words they think are misspelled. They look for words that should be capitalized that are not or words that are capitalized that should not be. They look carefully at how their letters are formed, circling those they think look odd. They search for places that need punctuation marks. They look carefully at the grammatical structures they have used. They might search with a friend after they have searched alone for their errors. Then, the students and the teacher edit the pieces to be published, and the teacher provides one-on-one direct instruction on one or two rules the students need in order to correct mistakes in their pieces because the pieces will be read by a particular audience.

- *Which writing skills require not only teaching within the context of writing workshop but also more direct teaching?*

Those writing skills are spelling and handwriting. When children begin to write, it is important that they are encouraged to use what they know about words and their sounds to write their pieces. Becoming a competent speller is a developmental journey, with all children progressing through five stages at their own rate. At each stage, children need to be provided with spelling instruction; formal spelling instruction—being assigned particular words to study each week—will begin when the child reaches the fourth stage. The words the students will study will be constructed from their writing and reading. The teacher will also add some words that share the same spelling pattern (e.g., if a particular student needs to learn to spell *cough,* then *rough* and *tough* might also be added to the week's spelling list). There will be spelling tests on Friday for students who receive formal spelling instruction. There is some evidence that spelling instruction embedded in writing workshop and taught directly yields greater gains in spelling performance than either one alone. This is true for students who are learning-disabled and those who are not. This is also true for nonnative English-language speakers.

- *How should teachers teach students to form the alphabet letters correctly?*

Students *do* need instruction in how to form letters. Some teachers will provide this instruction during the editing stage of the writing process. They will select one or two letters that the student seems to be having difficulty forming correctly. They will give verbal directions for how to form each of the two letters, model how to construct the letters, and observe the student as the student repeats the steps in making the letters while saying the directions softly. They will provide the student with corrective feedback and observe while the student correctly forms the letters three or four times. They will ask the student to select the best-formed letter. With learning-disabled students, they will not ask them to verbalize the steps for forming a letter while learning it. Instead, they will have them examine a model of the letter marked with numbered arrows and then reproduce the letter from memory. Other teachers will find that their school district has purchased a handwriting program or technology tools as a guide for teaching its students to form letters correctly.

- *Given a choice, which handwriting style and form should teachers use? Manuscript or cursive style? Vertical or slant form?*

The answers are manuscript and vertical for students who are learning-disabled and those who are not.

- *Is writing workshop and teaching the mechanical skills of writing within writing workshop appropriate for nonnative speakers of English?*

Absolutely! Nonnative speakers of English have the same needs as native speakers of English. The focus of the writing workshop is to address the needs of each student. Hence, within the writing workshop, teachers can meet the needs of many different kinds of learners. Through writing workshop, second-language learners can and do engage in writing for multiple purposes and audiences, at first in their native language and then later in English. In the process, they learn about written language and about how to use it effectively.

LINKING KNOWLEDGE TO PRACTICE

1. Work with a colleague to develop a focus lesson plan on capitalization, punctuation, or grammar for a group of students.

2. Write the letters of the alphabet in manuscript vertical form. Check your letter formations against the letters in Figure 9.2. Repeat the task with cursive letters.

CHAPTER 10

ASSESSMENT: DETERMINING WHAT CHILDREN KNOW AND CAN DO

In the preceding chapters we have presented strategies for implicit and explicit instruction in literacy. While these instructional activities form the core of an effective reading, writing, and speaking program, they cannot stand alone. To ensure that the instructional strategies meet the needs of every student in the class, teachers need to assess whether these activities achieve their intended aims.

We begin this chapter by discussing the goals literacy professionals have identified as those that teachers should help their students to meet. Then we consider the two general assessment approaches that teachers might use to gather information about their students' literacy development: ongoing or classroom assessment and on-demand or standardized assessment. In the last edition of this book, we focused mostly on ongoing assessment because this was the approach that teachers used most frequently to gather information about their students' learning progress and needs. We continue to believe in the power of ongoing, classroom assessment and encourage teachers to use the various assessment strategies we have described in the previous chapters. However, since the publication of the last edition of this book, standardized assessments, in the form of large-scale statewide testing and mandated district-level testing, have become increasingly prevalent across the country. Therefore, we also believe that teachers need to be familiar with standardized assessment. As the editors (Short, Schroeder, Kauffman, & Kaser, 2002, p. 199) of *Language Arts* said in the issue focused on literacy testing, "Language arts educators can no longer afford to ignore these tests since the results are often used to make life-altering decisions about students and curriculum and to evaluate teachers and programs."

BEFORE READING THIS CHAPTER, THINK ABOUT . . .

- How your teachers assessed your literacy progress. Did you take a spelling test on Fridays? Did you read stories and answer comprehension questions? Did you ever evaluate your own progress? Did you keep a portfolio?

- How information about your literacy progress was shared with your parents. Did your parents learn about your progress by reading your report card? Did your parents attend conferences? Were you involved in sharing information about your progress with your peers or your parents?
- The on-demand tests you have taken. Did you take reading and writing tests throughout elementary school? Were you required to take a test, like the Scholastic Aptitude Test or the Graduate Record Examination, and score above a minimum level to gain admission to your undergraduate or graduate program?

FOCUS QUESTIONS

- What is important for teachers to know about children's literacy development?
- What are the two general approaches teachers might use to assess their students' literacy learning?
- What are the differences between working and showcase portfolios?
- How do teachers use the information they collect?

WHAT IS IMPORTANT FOR TEACHERS TO KNOW ABOUT CHILDREN'S LITERACY DEVELOPMENT?

Sheila Valencia (1990) and Grant Wiggins (1993) agree on a primary component in assessment: Teachers must begin assessment by determining what they value. "Only after goals have been established and clarified can attention turn to the appropriate tasks and contexts for gathering information" (Valencia, Hiebert, Afflerbach, 1994, p. 10). Teachers must answer the question, what is important for us to know about our children's development as readers, writers, speakers, and listeners?

The ideas in every chapter in this book help readers to answer this question. In addition, readers can use one or more of the sets of English language-arts *content standards* (or *outcomes, goals,* or *accomplishments*; the terms are used interchangeably) that are available. School districts from Bellevue, Washington, to Dover, Delaware, have prepared goals for their students. Most states have defined *content standards*—what their young citizens (grades pre-K–12) should know and be able to do at specific benchmark years (e.g., grades 3, 5, 8, and 10). (See Figure 1.2 in Chapter 1 for an illustration of the early language and literacy standards developed by teachers for one state's pre-K citizens.) Representatives of the two major literacy organizations, the International Reading Association (IRA) and the National Council of Teachers of English (NCTE), have worked collaboratively to construct a set of content standards for the whole nation.

In addition, the Committee on the Prevention of Reading Difficulties in Young Children, a committee appointed by the National Research Council, has provided educators interested in students' literacy learning with a list of accomplishments that successful learners are likely to exhibit each year (Snow, Burns, & Griffin, 1998).

■ ■ ■ ■ ■ ▬▬▬▬▬▬▬▬▬▬▬▬▬▬▬▬▬▬▬▬▬▬▬▬▬▬▬▬▬▬▬

BOX 10.1

DEFINITION OF TERMS

achievement test: a standardized test designed to measure how much a student has learned and to compare this student's learning with a standard or norm

analytic scoring: a type of rubric scoring that separates the whole into categories of criteria that are examined one at a time. For example, a rater might judge a piece of writing in the categories of organization, development, sentence sense, word choice/style, and mechanics, one score per category

assessment: the process of observing; describing, collecting, recording, scoring, interpreting, and sharing with appropriate others (like parents) information about a student's learning

benchmark: examples of actual student performance that illustrate each point on a scale and then are used as exemplars against which other students' performance can be measured

criterion-referenced test: a test used to compare a student's progress toward mastery of specified content, typically content the student had been taught. The performance criterion is referenced to some criterion level such as a cutoff score (e.g., a score of 60 is required for mastery)

evaluation: use of information from assessments to make a decision about continued instruction for a student

holistic scoring: assigning a single score based on the overall assessment of the student's performance

on-demand assessment: a type of assessment that occurs during a special time set aside for testing. In most cases, teaching and learning come to a complete stop while the teacher conducts the assessment. *See also* standardized test

ongoing assessment: a form of assessment that relies on the regular collection of student work to illustrate students' knowledge and learning. The students' products are created as they engage in daily classroom activities; thus, students are learning while they are being assessed

performance task: an activity that allows students to demonstrate what they know and can do

rubric: a scoring guide that describes the characteristics of performance at each point on a scale

showcase portfolio: samples of student work that illustrate the student's efforts, progress, and achievements. The showcase portfolio is shared with others, usually the student's parents

standardized test: The teacher reads verbatim the scripted procedures to the students. The conditions and directions are the same whenever the test is administered. Standardized tests are one form of on-demand testing

working portfolio: where the student and teacher place work that is reflective of the student's achievement. Both the student and the teacher may place work in the working portfolio

Similarly, the International Reading Association and the National Association for the Education of Young Children (NAEYC) have jointly issued a position statement on developmentally appropriate reading and writing practices that includes a list of what children of various ages and grade levels likely can do (IRA/NAEYC, 1998). The authors of this book strongly encourage readers to obtain copies of these important national publications.

English Language Arts Content Standards

Standard One: Students will use written and oral English appropriate for various purposes and audiences.

Standard Two: Students will construct, examine, and extend the meaning of literary, informative, and technical texts through listening, reading, and viewing.

Standard Three: Students will access, organize, and evaluate information gained through listening, reading, and viewing.

Standard Four: Students will use literary knowledge gained through print and visual media to connect self to society and culture.

(Indicators of required performance for each standard at four grade clusters—K-3, 4-5, 6-8, and 9-10—are provided. One such set of indicators for K-5 students for one standard, Standard One, is detailed below.)

Performance Indicator for the End of K–Grade 5

Writers will produce texts that exhibit the following textual features, all of which are consistent with the genre and purpose of the writing:

Development: The topic, theme, stand/perspective, argument, or character is fully developed.

Organization: The text exhibits a discernible progression of ideas.

Style: The writer demonstrates a quality of imagination, individuality, and a distinctive voice.

Word Choice: The words are precise, vivid, and economical.

Sentence Formation: Sentences are completed and varied in length and structure.

Conventions: Appropriate grammar, mechanics, spelling, and usage enhance the meaning and readability of the text.

Writers will produce examples that illustrate the following discourse classifications:

1. **Expressive** (author-oriented) texts, both personal and literary, that
   a. reveal self-discovery and reflection;
   b. demonstrate experimentation with techniques, which could include dialogue;
   c. demonstrate experimentation with appropriate modes, which include narration and description;
   d. demonstrate experimentation with rhetorical form.
2. **Informative** (subject-oriented) texts that
   a. begin to address audience;
   b. exhibit appropriate modes, which could include description, narration, classification, simple process analysis, simple definitions;
   c. conform to the appropriate formats, which include letters, summaries, messages, and reports;
   d. contain information from primary and secondary sources, avoiding plagiarism.
3. **Argumentative and persuasive** (audience-oriented) texts that
   a. address the needs of the audience;
   b. communicate a clear-cut position on an issue;
   c. support the position with relevant information, which could include personal and expert opinions and examples;
   d. exhibit evidence of reasoning.

Speakers demonstrate oral-language proficiency in formal and informal speech situations, such as conversations, interviews, collaborative group work, oral presentations, public speaking, and debate. Speakers are able to

1. **Formulate** a message, including all essential information.
2. Organize a message appropriately for the speech situation.
3. **Deliver** a message,
   a. beginning to control volume, tone, speed, and enunciation appropriately for the situational context;
   b. using facial expression to reinforce the message;
   c. maintaining focus;
   d. creating the impression of being secure and comfortable, and in command of the situation;
   e. incorporating audiovisual aids when appropriate.
4. **Respond** to feedback, adjusting volume and speed, and answering questions.

FIGURE 10.1   Delaware's English Language-Arts Content Standards and the Performance Indicators for the End of K–5

Further, in response to the No Child Left Behind Act described in Chapter 1, recently states have brought teachers together to define what students at each grade level should know and be able to do. These Grade Level Expectations (GLEs) aim to help teachers measure their students' progress toward the state's benchmark year expectations (e.g., grades 3, 5, 8, and 10). (For an example of one state's Grade Level Expectations, see http://www.doe.state.de.us/englangarts/elahome.html.)

When such lists of standards were first developed, they likely had an impact on classroom instruction. For example, teachers not previously teaching students how to write persuasively probably began to do so. Also, teachers probably introduced their students to the criteria that would be used to judge the quality of their work. Today states aim to ensure that the standards impact teachers' teaching by administering annual standardized achievement tests—as mandated by NCLB at grades 2–8—linked to each state's standards. As described in Chapter 1, each school must meet annual yearly progress goals, with 100 percent of the school's students "meeting the standards" in reading and mathematics by the 2013–2014 school year. Each state will make the determination of whether or not every student in each school has met the state's reading and mathematics standards by examining each school's students' performance on the statewide standardized achievement test.

There are two kinds of assessments that teachers use to measure their students' progress toward the achievement of the state standards: ongoing and on-demand. Below, we describe these two kinds of assessments. Charlene Cobb (2003, p. 386) uses an analogy to describe the difference between the two forms.

> A visit to the doctor's office is to [ongoing] assessment what an autopsy is to [on-demand assessment]. Let's say you see a doctor, for either a perceived need or a regular checkup. The doctor examines you, makes a diagnosis, and provides a treatment based on his or her discovery and your needs. This is a form of ongoing assessment. Suppose you come home from the doctor and find out that your neighbor has suddenly died. You're told that nobody knows what happened, but an autopsy is planned. An autopsy is [like an on-demand assessment.] [On-demand assessments] are done to determine what happened. . . .

As Peter Johnston and Paula Costello (2005) suggest, ongoing assessment is an assessment *for* learning while on-demand assessment is an assessment *of* learning. One looks forward, the other looks back. Just like a routine visit to the doctor and an autopsy.

ONGOING ASSESSMENT

Ongoing assessment relies on teachers' regular collection of artifacts to illustrate students' knowledge and learning. It is the regular gathering and interpreting of data to inform action. The artifacts are gathered while the students engage in their daily classroom activities, such as those described in every chapter in this book. The products of these activities, then, serve the dual purposes of instruction and assessment. Because ongoing assessment occurs at the classroom level, it often is referred to as "classroom-based assessment" or formative assessment, or "assessment for learning" (Johnston & Costello, 2005, p. 259).

Ongoing assessment exhibits the following features:

- Students work on their products for varying amounts of time, and the procedures or directions probably vary across all students in a classroom or across classes in the building.
- What each student selects as evidence of literacy learning may be different, not only across the students in the school but also across students in a teacher's class.
- The classroom teacher analyzes each student's performance on each of the tasks and makes judgments about each student's learning.
- The students know the criteria against which their products will be judged, and examples of students' work are often displayed to help them understand the criteria.
- The students engage in making judgments about how their work compares with the criteria. The students' self-evaluation is seen as an integral component of the process.
- The teacher's and student's judgments are used immediately to define the student's next learning goal. The assessment, then, has an immediate impact on instruction for each student.
- The assessment of the work produced over time in many different contexts permits the teacher and the student to gather more than a quick snapshot of what the student knows and is able to do at a given moment.
- The central purpose of ongoing assessment is not to grade students, but rather for the teacher to know how to modify instruction or to provide students with detailed feedback. The key intent is to achieve enhanced learning outcomes.
- Ongoing assessment, then, exhibits a strong reciprocal relationship among curriculum, assessment, and instruction. As the editor of *Educational Leadership* proclaims, it "blurs the line between instruction and assessment. Everything students do . . . is a potential source of information about how much students understand" (Scherer, 2005, p. 9).

Ongoing assessment, then, permits both the teacher and the student to examine the students' knowledge and learning so that the teacher can plan appropriate learning activities for each student. First-grader Phyllis shares what this means as she uses her journal to describe her growth as a reader and writer.

> I comed to this school a little bit nervous, you know. Nothin'. [She shakes her head for added emphasis.] I couldn't read or write nothin'. Look at this. [She turns to the first few pages of her writing journal.] Not a word! Not a word! [She taps the page

and adds an aside.] And the drawin's not too good. Now, look at this. [She turns to the end of the journal.] One, two, three, four. Four pages! And I can read 'em. Listen. [She reads.] Words! [Nodding her head.] Yup! Now I can read and write alotta words!

Information-Gathering Tools

Phyllis's journal is one of several tools her teacher uses to gather information about Phyllis's literacy learning. Like Phyllis, her teacher can compare the writing at the beginning and at the end of the journal to learn about Phyllis's literacy development over time. Each tool used permits teachers to gather information about their students' literacy learning while the students perform the kinds of activities described in this book. Readers were introduced to several of these tools in previous chapters.

Anecdotal records.   These are a teacher's notes describing a student's behavior. Peter Winograd and Harriette Johns Arrington (1999) suggest that teachers make their anecdotal notes as they "kidwatch," a term coined by Yetta Goodman (1978). They suggest that teachers often find it helpful to focus on a series of questions like the following: "What can this student do? What does this student know? What kinds of questions does the student have about their work? What does the student's attitude reveal about his/her growth and progress?" (p. 231). Fairfax County Public Schools (1998) offers additional suggestions for ways to avoid making the writing of anecdotal notes overwhelming. This school system suggests that teachers decide on a focus for their note taking. For example, in reading, teachers might focus on how fluently the students are reading, or how well the students are comprehending the text, or the students' interest in reading as reflected in their free-choice book selections. In writing, teachers might focus on how the students are organizing their pieces, or how the students are incorporating voice into their pieces. Undoubtedly, these questions link to the state's English language arts content standards. The school system also suggests that teachers begin their note taking by focusing on those students whose progress most concerns them.

Teachers use many different kinds of paper (e.g., computer address labels, notepads, paper in a loose-leaf binder, index cards, Post-it notes) to make their anecdotal records of students' behavior. Figure 10.2 shows an inexpensive flip chart a teacher developed to aid her anecdotal note record-keeping. The teacher used a clipboard and three- by five-inch index cards. She wrote each student's name on the bottom of a card, arranged the cards in alphabetical order, then, starting at the bottom of the clipboard, taped the student's card whose name began with the last letter of the alphabet onto the clipboard, so that the bottom of the card was even with the bottom right-hand corner of the clipboard. Then she placed the card of the student whose name began with the next-to-last letter of the alphabet on the clipboard slightly above the first card. She mounted it so that the name of the other student was still visible. She continued this process with the remaining cards. When she finished, she had constructed an inexpensive flip chart.

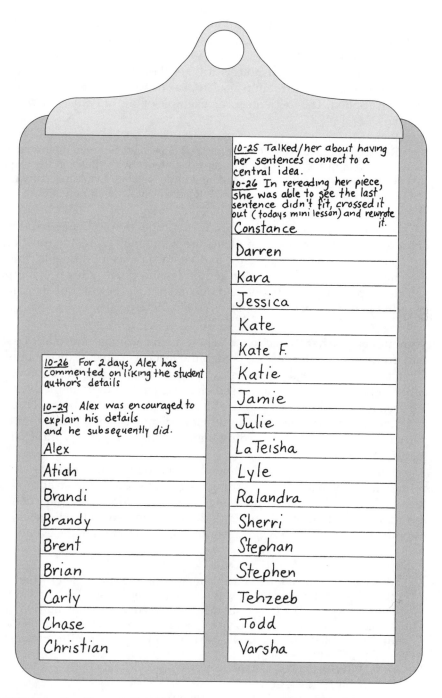

FIGURE 10.2   One Record-Keeping System: An Inexpensive Flip Chart

Patty Kopay writes anecdotal notes on computer address labels. In addition to the student's name and date, she describes the specific event or product exactly as she saw or heard it. Lynn Cohen (1999, p. 27) suggests that a teacher's goal when writing an anecdotal note is to "get the basic story and most significant details, keeping the information as factual as possible" with no judgment or interpretation applied. The following is an example of one of Patty's anecdotal notes:

> Ronnie 10/12
> Read self-selected book (*The Biggest, Best Snowman*). Skipped unknown words, read to the end of the sentence, and reread sentence with filling in the skipped word. When done, he said, "I know just how Little Nell felt. Everyone in my house thinks I'm too little to do everything, too!" Read s-l-o-w-l-y, haltingly!

Teachers use anecdotal notes to describe the strategies students use to decode words, the processes students use while they write, the functions of writing students use while they play, and characteristics of students' talk during a presentation to the class. "Taken regularly, anecdotal notes become not only a vehicle for planning instruction and documenting progress, but also a story about an individual" (Rhodes & Nathenson-Mejia, 1992, p. 503).

Vignettes or Teacher Reflections.   These are recordings of recollections of significant events made after the fact, when the teacher is free of distractions. Because vignettes are like anecdotal notes except that they are prepared sometime after a behavior has occurred and are based on a teacher's memory of the event, vignettes are used for purposes such as those identified for anecdotal notes. These after-the-fact descriptions or vignettes can be more detailed than anecdotal notes and are particularly useful when recording literacy behavior that is significant or unique for a specific student.

For example, Karen Valentine observed one of her students attempting to control his peers' behavior by writing a sign and posting it in an appropriate place. Because she was involved with a small group of students, she did not have time to record a description of the student's behavior immediately. However, as soon as the students left for the day, she recorded her recollection of the event:

> Jamali 3/7
> For days, Jamali had been complaining about the "mess" left by the children getting drinks at the classroom water fountain after recess. "Look at that mess! Water all over the floor!" At his insistence, the class discussed solutions to the problem. While the problem wasn't solved, I thought there was less water on the floor. Evidently, Jamali did not. Today he used the "power of the pen" to attempt to solve the problem. He wrote a sign:
> BEWR!! WTR SHUS UP
> ONLE TRN A LITL
> (Beware! Water shoots up. Only turn a little.)
> He posted his sign over the water fountain. This was the first time I had observed him using writing in an attempt to control other students' behavior.

Vignettes, then, are recollections of significant events. As such, they look much like an anecdotal note, except they are written in the past tense. Also, because teachers can write vignettes when they are free of distractions, they can be more descriptive about the student's concern that drove the literacy-oriented behavior, and they can connect this event to what is known about the student's previous literacy-oriented behaviors.

Checklists.   These are observational aids that specify which behaviors to look for and provide a convenient system for keeping records. They can make observations more systematic and easier to conduct, and can be used in a variety of instructional contexts.

Checklists are useful because they provide lists of items that teachers can see at a glance, showing what students can do. Teachers have learned that (1) students sometimes engage in a behavior on one day that does not reappear for several weeks, and (2) many different variables can affect the literate behaviors students show (e.g., the storybook being read and the other children in the group). Hence, teachers are careful to record the date of each observation and to use the checklists many times over the year in an attempt to create an accurate picture of students' literacy development.

The number of checklists available to describe students' literacy development seems almost endless. The writers of this textbook have provided several examples in previous chapters (see, for example, Figures 3.2 and 9.1).

Conferencing or Interviewing.   A conference is a conversation between a teacher and an individual student. Teachers confer to obtain information they cannot uncover any other way. Sometimes it permits the teacher to uncover the students' conception of literacy. Sometimes it is difficult to determine the significance of a literacy behavior. For example, a teacher observed several young students playing airport. They were cutting dollar-size pieces of paper and writing on each piece with scribbles.

> **TEACHER:**   I wonder what you guys are making. Is it money? Are you making a lot of money?
>
> **BUDDY:**   These aren't money. They're tickets for the airplane!

Note how this brief, informal interview cleared up the teacher's initial misconception about the make-believe identity of the pieces of paper.

Conferences can be quick and informal, like the one above, or more structured and systematic. Regardless of length, conferences must be conducted in a "secure and comfortable manner so that students feel encouraged to take risks and share their ideas" (Winograd & Arrington, 1999, p. 234); otherwise, the data gathered will be highly suspect. Scott Paris (1995) suggests that comfort occurs if the teacher does not ask too many questions; if the student does most of the talking; if the teacher appears interested and enthusiastic; and if the teacher celebrates the student's strengths.

Whether long or short (and conferences typically are short, about five to ten minutes), teachers begin the conference with a clear purpose in mind. Purposes might include asking questions to understand: (1) what the student is learning or has learned and would like to learn next, (2) the student's interests and attitudes, (3) the strategies the student is using to decode or comprehend text, and (4) what the student sees as difficult. The teacher should make a written record of each conference, noting the purpose of the conference, the student's thinking, and any conclusions reached. To this list, Diane Fu and Linda Lamme (2002) would add the following tips that they gathered from Ruth Hubbard and Brenda Power: (1) listen actively and (2) if the child looks puzzled by the question, don't hesitate to rephrase it or ask another.

Teachers must take great care in how they structure conference questions. Peter Johnston (1992) suggests that there are three kinds of questions teachers might ask: (1) descriptive questions (e.g., "What happens during the writing workshop in your classroom?" "What do you usually do during the readers' workshop?"); (2) structural questions (e.g., "Do you read during the writing workshop? Can you tell me about when and how?"); and (3) contrast questions (e.g., "Who are your two favorite authors? How are their stories the same? How are their stories different?"). To Johnston's list, we could add Graves's (1983) process questions (e.g., "I see you made a change here in your writing; you added some new information. I wonder why it was important to add this information? How did you know to add this information?"). Notice that all of these questions are open-ended questions.

Johnston noted that teachers might want to consider adding a pretend audience for the question. For example, teachers might say, "Suppose a new student was added to our classroom. What things would you tell him or her about reading to help him or her know what to do and how to be good at reading?"

Video and Audio Recordings.   Teachers often use audiotaping to document students' progress. To assess their students' reading ability, for example, teachers record their students' oral reading. In this way, teachers learn about their students' fluency in reading a text. Teachers also record students' retellings of stories that were read previously and literature-group discussions to study their students' comprehension of texts.

Teachers use videotaping to capture students' literacy behaviors in a variety of contexts. Some teachers focus the camera lens on an area of the classroom, such as the dramatic-play area or the writing center, to gather information about the students' literacy-related social interactions during their play and work. Viewing of the tapes provides valuable information, not only about the students' knowledge of context-appropriate oral language and their ability to engage in conversations with others, but also about the students' knowledge of the functions of writing.

Running Records.   Running records are used to document students' reading behaviors. In Chapter 6, readers were introduced to how to make a running record on a student's reading of a piece of text. As Peter Johnston suggests, "learning to record oral reading errors and figure out what they [mean]" takes practice (1992, p. 69). The recording and interpretation of oral reading errors are very important skills for teachers to develop. Once teachers have learned the procedures, they can record their students' oral reading behaviors at any time, from any book, without any preparation such as photocopying of the story's pages or having extra copies of the book available.

Products or Work Samples.   Some products, such as samples of students' writing, can be gathered together in a folder. If the students' original works cannot be saved (e.g., a letter that is sent to its recipient), a photocopy can be made of the product. Other products, such as structures the students have created, might not be conveniently saved. In these cases, a photograph—still or video—can be made. Because memories are short, the teacher or the student should record a brief description of the product or the activity that resulted in the product.

Many teachers find that folders with pockets and with center clasps for three-hole-punched paper serve as better storage containers than file folders. Interview forms, running-record sheets, and other similar papers can be three-hole-punched, thus permitting their easy insertion into each student's folder. When anecdotal notes and vignettes are written on computer mailing labels, the labels can be attached to the inside covers of each student's folder. When these notes are written on index cards, the cards can be stored in one of the folder's pockets. Also, a zip-top sandwich bag might be stapled inside each student's folder to hold an audio-tape. The self-sealing feature of the bag means that the tape can be securely held inside the folder. The class's folders might be housed in a plastic container or in hanging files in a file cabinet.

Typically, products or work samples demonstrate students' literacy knowledge and skill in performing an authentic, real-world literacy task. The students might write a report on their favorite animal, design a poster encouraging other students not to pollute the environment, create a commercial for a new cafeteria offering, or write a persuasive letter to the principal for more recess time, and so forth. Each of these products is different; each requires a different set of criteria to judge the product's "goodness." David Cooper and Nancy Kiger (2001) suggest that teachers use general criteria similar to the following to guide their assessment of such products. Teachers need to

- *first,* think through the strategies, skills, and knowledge the product will require the students to use. Which strategies and skills have the students already been taught? Which strategies and skills will the students need to be taught? The answer to this question will impact the immediate instructional plans.

- *second,* describe the task. This might be done alone or with the students. What is it that the students need to produce?

- *third,* develop a rubric, or scoring guide, of the specific criteria, to evaluate the product. The teacher alone or with the students should clearly identify and define the criteria to be used to judge whether or not each objective on the rubric has been met. Varying degrees of meeting the objective might also be described. Students should know what is expected before they begin creating their product. Samples of products produced by other students that illustrate varying "degrees to which an individual has attained something," in other words "anchor products," give students points of reference for their work. (See Special Feature 10.1 on constructing rubrics.)

■ *fourth,* share the rubric with the students. Do the students understand what they are being asked to do?

■ *fifth,* once the products have been created, invite the students to self-evaluate their product.

■ *sixth,* compare your assessment with each student's assessment and meet with each student to discuss this comparison. Consider which criteria were not met because additional teaching was needed, and which criteria were not met because the student needed to work harder. Plan for future teaching and learning.

The development of rubrics for assessing quality is a difficult and time-consuming—but worthwhile—task. Finding the correct language to describe the different performance levels for each facet is a challenge. In Special Feature 10.1, we describe a set of procedures for constructing a rubric.

Often, rubrics are developed by teachers for use by and with their students. Two teacher-developed rubrics used to judge the quality of students' writing were presented in Chapter 8 (see Figure 8.10 and 8.14). Rubrics might also be developed by teachers with their students. The NSP (1994) suggests that this is the way to begin. The teachers involved in the NSP say that constructing a rubric with students helps the students to understand the expectations for their behavior and helps them know what needs improvement to meet the required performance level.

Rubrics, then, provide criteria against which students can compare their work to determine how good it is and to select their best work for their portfolios.

Rubrics also provide the means by which teachers use portfolios to inform their instruction, to establish future learning goals for each student, and to report to parents or to school and district administrators. Comparing each student's performance against the appropriate rubrics permits the teacher to make ongoing determinations about the student's literacy development. For example, consider the teacher who uses an appropriate rubric for assessing a student's letter to the principal, attempting to convince her that he and his classmates need more than 20 minutes for lunch. By comparing the student's writing against an appropriate writing rubric, the teacher can identify the strengths and weaknesses in the student's writing of a persuasive letter. The resulting analysis informs the teacher of the instruction this student needs, and it defines learning goals for the student.

It is not just the teacher who uses rubrics to make informed judgments. Teachers report that students learn to "understand and internalize the criteria in a rubric, using the criteria to assist their peers in revising work and [in assessing] their own work" (O'Neill, 1994, p. 5). Knowing the criteria especially helps students to acquire the language they need in order to offer specific feedback to their peers. Many teachers ask their students to rate their work before the teachers assess the product. Even teachers of young students have discovered that students can be accurate in their assessment of their performance.

SPECIAL FEATURE 10.1
Developing Item-Specific Rubrics

■ **Considerations**

- Scoring Levels (degrees of performance)
- Outcome(s)
- Descriptors (qualities for each outcome at each scoring level)

■ **Scoring Levels**

Decide on the number of scoring levels. An even number of levels (four works well) requires the scorer to discriminate above or below a midpoint or average score.

	Four-Point Rubric	Two-Point Rubric
Score Point 4	complete and thorough, sufficient and relevant, specific	
Score Point 3	adequate, accurate, some	
Score Point 2	limited/sketchy, few	accurate and complete, appropriate and thorough, logical
Score Point 1	attempted, irrelevant, insufficient	incomplete, illogical

■ **Outcomes**

The outcome(s) indicate the product that the student is expected to generate. Some items may require students to produce more than one outcome. When possible, the outcome should be a noun or a noun form of the verb used in the wording of the item. For example, if the item says "Explain the reasons for the author's decision," the outcome would be stated as an "explanation." Here's a verb/noun list to consider when writing items and rubrics:

Adapt/Adaptation	Demonstrate/	Express/Expression	Predict/Prediction
Analyze/Analysis	Demonstration	Identify/Identification	Propose/
Apply/Application	Describe/Description	Integrate/Integration	Proposition
Appraise/Appraisal	Determine/	Interpret/	Reflect/Reflection
Clarify/Clarification	Determination	Interpretation	Represent/
Compare/	Differentiate/	Investigate/	Representation
Comparison	Differentiation	Investigation	Select/Selection
Consider/	Evaluate/Evaluation	Justify/Justification	Support/Support
Consideration	Examine/Examination	List/Listing	Synthesize/Synthesis
Contrast/Contrast	Explain/Explanation	Modify/Modification	Utilize/Utilization
Define/Definition	Explore/Exploration	Organize/Organization	

■ **Descriptors**

The descriptors are words that indicate the various degrees of performance across the scoring levels. They describe depth, breadth, quality, scope, extent, complexity, degree, and/or accuracy of the response. Here are some examples:

■ **Steps**

1. Determine the number of **scoring levels** to be used when evaluating responses.
2. Determine the learner **outcome(s),** and prioritize them if multiple outcomes are expected.

3. Write the **descriptors** for each outcome at the highest level of performance. Focus on terms of qualification rather than quantification, and avoid stating descriptors in the negative.

(continued on next page)

SPECIAL FEATURE 10.1 (continued)

4. Write the **descriptors** for each outcome at each of the lower levels of performance. Focus on words or phrases that clearly capture the actual differences among the levels of performance, and avoid the overuse of adjectives and adverbs.

5. Don't fall in love with the rubric. Chances are, once you actually use it to score stu-dent work, you'll discover ways to **revise and improve** the rubric, the item, or both.

■ **Rubric Development Template and Example**

Item: Although they are friends, Sheila and Michael are very different. Using information from the story, explain how they are different.

Template

Score Point	Outcome 1	Descriptors 1	Outcome 2	Descriptors 2	Outcome 3	Descriptors 4
4	Explanation	Thorough	Support	With sufficient, relevant details from the text		
3	Explanation	Adequate	Support	With some relevant details from the text		
2	Explanation	Limited	Support	With few, if any, relevant details from the text		
1	Explanation	Mostly inaccurate	Support	With irrelevant details, if any, from the text		
0	Explanation	Inappro-priate or incorrect	Support	Totally irrele-vant or incorrect		

Final Rubric

Score Point	Description
4	Response is a thorough explanation of how the characters are different, supported by sufficient, relevant details from the text.
3	Response is an adequate explanation of how the characters are different, supported by some relevant details from the text.
2	Response is limited explanation of how the characters are different, supported by few, if any, relevant details from the text.
1	Response is a mostly inaccurate explanation of how the characters are different, supported by irrelevant details, if any, from the text.
0	Response is totally inappropriate or inaccurate.

Adapted from materials provided by Michael C. Kelly at www.doe.state.de.us

Creating Portfolios: Working and Showcase

What exactly is a portfolio? F. Leon Paulson, Pearl Paulson, and Carol Meyer (1991, p. 60) define a portfolio as "a purposeful collection of [a sample of] student work that exhibits the student's efforts, progress, and achievements." The purposes of portfolios, as defined by Frank Serafini (2001b, p. 388), are "to uncover the possibilities for students, to understand each child as a whole, and to attempt to provide a window into a student's conceptual framework and ways of seeing the world."

There are at least two kinds of portfolios: the working portfolio and the showcase portfolio. The working portfolio should provide a description of how a student is developing (Gronlund, 1998). The work samples, anecdotal notes, and so forth described above will be housed in each student's working portfolios. The items housed in working portfolios are not representative of the student's best work. Rather, the items housed in working portfolios evidence a student's typical, everyday performance. From the working portfolios, students and their teachers select specific pieces for inclusion in each student's showcase portfolio. The items in the showcase portfolio exhibit the best work the student has produced.

What each portfolio will look like will vary from teacher to teacher and school to school. Some teachers maintain a folder on each student. For example, the majority of teachers in a Delaware portfolio project used expandable file folders for their students' portfolios. Manila folders were placed inside each expandable file folder. Each class's portfolios were placed inside a large plastic container with a lid. These teachers liked having a lid on their portfolio boxes because it helped to reduce the amount of classroom dust on the students' portfolios.

Other teachers have created different kinds of portfolios. For example, a Colorado teacher used gallon-size zip-top bags, bound together with large metal rings. The teacher's students decorated poster board covers, which the teacher then laminated (Wilcox, 1993). Some teachers use pizza boxes decorated by the students. One teacher used a handmade fabric wall-hanging with a pocket for each student. Some teachers help their students prepare digital portfolios. Still other teachers ask their students to decide what they want their portfolios to look like.

Deciding what to use is the practical starting point with portfolio assessment. There is no one right storage scheme for students' portfolios. Teachers might use one kind of system for their students' working portfolios and another for their students' showcase portfolios.

Selecting Artifacts for Inclusion.   Maintaining a classroom portfolio system does not mean saving everything the student does and sending nothing home. The pieces placed in a working portfolio are selected because they show students' everyday performance related to the literacy accomplishments or standards the teacher or school district or state has determined the students should know and be able to do. The pieces placed in the showcase portfolio are selected from the working portfolio because they show the student's best accomplishment relative to the literacy accomplishments.

Having a specific reason for selecting each artifact is critically important. What are the specific reasons? Recall that content standards (or goals, outcomes, or accomplishments) drive teachers' decisions about which data to gather. These same content standards drive the teachers' and the students' decisions about what should be selected for inclusion in the students' portfolios. For example, to demonstrate each student's accomplishments relative to state English language arts standards, teachers and students might include artifacts like those described in Figure 10.3 in students' working portfolios. The teacher and the students will select the artifacts that best illustrate the students' behavior relative to each literacy accomplishment for inclusion in the showcase portfolios.

Sharing Information on Artifact Selection for Showcase Portfolios.   To encourage the thoughtful selection of items, portfolio advocates suggest that an entry slip should be attached to each artifact included in the students' showcase portfolios. "Writing the entry slips is a way for students to reflect on their work, as well as to give the background for the work to others" (New Standards Project [NSP], 1994, p. 12). Entry slips require students to engage in a "dialogue with their inner, critical selves" (Wilcox, 1993, p. 20). The NSP teachers and Carol Wilcox agree: An entry slip helps readers of students' portfolios know the importance of the work selected for inclusion. "Why do I want this artifact in my (or this student's) portfolio? What does it show about me (or this student) as a reader, a writer, a learner, a literate individual?"

Just what does an entry slip look like? See Figure 10.4 for an example of an entry slip used by the five-, six-, and seven-year-olds in a multiage classroom. Notice that entry slips are dated. Many teachers have discovered that it is helpful to have a date stamp, like those used by librarians, readily available in the classroom in the area where the portfolios are stored. Dating each item selected for inclusion in portfolios permits the teacher and the student to arrange the items in chronological order to show changes or learning over time.

Frequency of Artifact Selection for Showcase Portfolios.   The NSP recommends that the selection of items for inclusion in students' portfolios should occur at least three times a year. The NSP teachers have discovered that too much accumulated work overwhelms students, making it difficult for them to be selective, so it seems wise to follow this rule: the younger the student, the more frequently the artifacts should be selected. Perhaps once every four weeks would be a prudent guide. However, a key to the decision regarding frequency of selection will be the number of artifacts the student and their teacher have created and stored in their various storage bins. Too few items also limits the students' and teacher's ability to select.

Another variable in determining when to select items will be the school's identified times for reporting to parents through report cards and parent–teacher, parent–teacher–student, or parent–student conferences. The portfolio items will serve as the information base for these reporting systems.

Sharing Portfolios with Others.   Carol Wilcox (1993, p. 33) reports teacher Karen Boettcher as saying, "The heart of portfolios is sharing." Following are some ways in which the information in portfolios can be shared with others.

FIGURE 10.3 **Possible artifacts for inclusion in students' working portfolios linked to a state's content standards**

Content standard	Students will	Possible artifacts
Standard One	use written and oral English appropriate for various purposes and audiences.	Writings illustrating different stages of the writing process (e.g., drafts, edited pieces, published pieces) Examples of writing in three discourse categories (e.g., expressive, informative, and persuasive) Best writing in September and in May All drafts from one piece to show changes within a piece of writing Notes from teacher/student conferences Videotape of a presentation Drafts of a speech from initial planning to final draft Teacher's anecdotal notes of student's speaking behavior Peer and teacher evaluations of oral presentations Checklist of oral discussion skills
Standard Two	construct, examine, and extend the meaning of literary, informative, and technical texts.	Reading response log entries Text-based writing responses Teacher anecdotal notes of reading or discussion observations Running records Retellings Attitude surveys Literature discussion checklist List of books read Reading strategy checklist
Standard Three	access, organize, and evaluate information gained through listening, reading, and viewing.	Research reports with graphs and figures Teacher anecdotal notes on computer skills; narrowing research topics; reading of graphs, tables, charts Copies of graphic organizers of information gained Samples of notes taken while reading
Standard Four	use literary knowledge gained through print and visual media to connect self to society and culture.	Teacher anecdotal notes of self-to-text and text-to-text connections Reading response log entries

Sharing with Peers.   One important audience for portfolios is the students' class-mates. "Sharing portfolios is a powerful tool for building community within the classroom" (Wilcox, 1993, p. 33). Wilcox has elaborated this statement by noting that by sharing, students learn unique things about their classmates. They learn about the learning strategies their colleagues have used successfully. They learn what peers are

Portfolio Entry Slip

Name __Matt__   Date __5/3/95__

I chose this piece because it shows: __Improvement since the begining of the year. It also shows I can spell better and I don't have to be corected as much.__

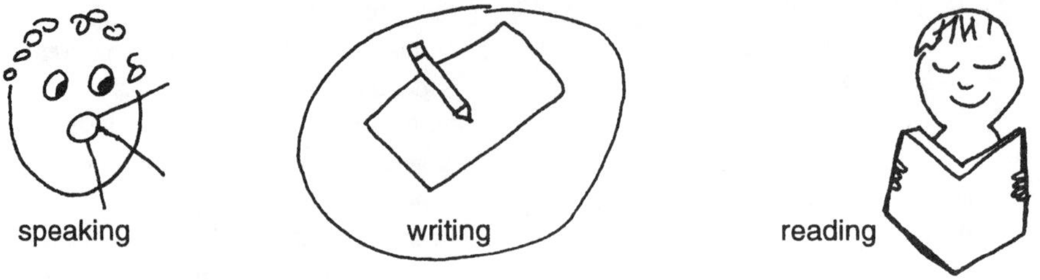

speaking   writing   reading

What did I learn: __I learned the storys are as fun to write as fiction storys. And I learned Paragraphs.__

FIGURE 10.4   Sample Portfolio Entry Slip

struggling to learn, and they learn to offer assistance in their peers' struggles. They learn about peers' special talents. They learn about books they might read, new ways of writing their own pieces, and new goals they might set for themselves.

Teachers can structure different kinds of ways for peers to share. Here are some options:

- Students are asked to share something that teaches others about them as a reader, that shows a new skill they have learned to use in writing, or that shows how they have changed as a reader, writer, or speaker.
- Students form a circle with an artifact of their choice from their portfolio in hand, each sharing the artifact and receiving the audience's response.
- Students take selected artifacts or their portfolios to another class at the same or a different grade to share with members of this other class. The children might meet in pairs, for example, to consider what development as a reader looks like in first and second grade. What better way to introduce first-graders to what to expect in second grade?

In addition to teaching students how and what to share, teachers need to teach students how to respond to their peers' portfolios. Carol Wilcox (1993) has described how second-grade teacher Kathy Busick had her students generate a list of statements they could use to help them respond to each other's portfolios. The list included statements such as,

> I learned about you.
> I like how you showed
> I never knew that

Sharing with Parents.   Parents (interpret this term broadly to mean the significant adults in each child's life) are another important audience for portfolios. Of course, teachers will use the students' portfolios during parent–teacher conferences. Sometimes students will join in these conferences to provide their own perspective on their own development as readers, writers, and speakers. At other times, students will independently use their portfolios to explain their literacy development to their parents. Even Bernadette Watson's kindergartners ran their own portfolio conferences for their parents! (Ms. Watson and other teachers have discovered that it is important to have student practice how they plan to share their portfolios with their parents before they actually do so.) See Chapter 11 for details of a conference where a portfolio is used to share a description of the student's literacy development.

Teachers not only need to teach students how to respond to their peers, but also to inform parents how to respond to their students' portfolios. Carol Wilcox (1993) has detailed the story of Michael, a six-year-old, who had a devastating experience when sharing his portfolio with his parents. Their response focused on his poor spelling and handwriting performance, rather than on his accomplishments and his literacy development. He was not, after all, spelling words conventionally!

Students may not always be present during the sharing of their portfolios. When the student is not to be present when her or his portfolio is examined by the parents, the student might write a letter explaining the portfolio to the reader. We present an example of a letter written by a third-grader to his portfolio's readers in Figure 10.5. This student's awareness of his learning is clearly evident in his letter to his readers.

Many school districts continue the policy of having four reporting periods per year, with two of these reports being oral and two being written. Teachers who use portfolios in their classroom as the means of tracking their students' literacy development can be frustrated if their district requires them to use a letter-grading system in their written report to parents. To translate the students' rich portfolio data into a single letter grade seems a formidable task. These teachers prefer to report progress to parents using a conference (see details of how in Chapter 11), and, when a written report is required, they prefer to use a narrative report. Peter Afflerbach (1993) has provided a hint about why teachers using portfolios prefer narrative reports over letter-grade reporting systems. He suggests that "within a narrative report, teachers can provide detail about [a] student's development. The narrative can include relatively detailed information about a student's strengths and needs, personal challenges and accomplishments, and describe the variety of a student's experiences" (p. 461).

Dear Reviewer,

   I think my story about the tiny family is my best piece. I organized the story real good. I tried to help my readers know how worried the tiny family would be when it heard the news that the police were coming for them. I thought I gave it a good ending. I wrote it around April Fool's Day. That's how I came up with the idea of the ending. I had two other ideas for endings, but this was the one I liked best. I liked when my friends said, "That's good!" when they heard my ending. I like to get good responses to my pieces from my friends.

   I think my writing has really improved this year. In September, I wrote short pieces. I wrote a lot about playing with my friends. Now I write about lots of different topics. I like writing stories. I'm good at paragraphing now. I used to just start writing. Now, I think about what I'm going to write about before I fall asleep. I come to school ready to write. I really like writing time. But I don't think I'll be a writer when I grow-up. I want to be a soccer player.

   Do you like my writing?

   Sincerely,

FIGURE 10.5   A Letter Written to Introduce a Student's Portfolio to Readers

Sharing with School Administrators.   Center directors, principals, and central-office administrators (e.g., the superintendent, the center's advisory board, the school board, the language-arts supervisor) want to know about the progress that all the students in each classroom or school are making toward the defined standards, outcomes, or goals. A data-collection form often is created, on which classroom teachers can summarize their students' portfolio information and arrive at a conclusion about how their students are progressing as a group. An example of such a form is presented in Figure 10.6. Using the information on this form, it is possible to aggregate the data across all students in a classroom or the school. Comparing the data from the fall to the spring permits school administrators to see changes in the percentages of students in each category within each teacher's classroom, within each grade level, and within the school who have met the standard or achieved the goal. Central-office administrators can calculate this information across all schools in the district. In this way, the portfolio

Teacher's Name _____ Grade _____
School _____ Date _____

Key:
✔ Meets or exceeds standard
★ Approaching standard
● Significantly below standard

> Teachers within the school or district will have defined what students at each grade level need to know and be able to do to earn each rating.

Standards	Students				
	Adam	Ainya	Collin	Shane	and other students in the class
I. Writer produces texts that exhibit the following textual features:					
• Development: The topic, theme, stand/perspective, argument, or character is fully developed.					
• Organization: The text exhibits a discernible progression of ideas.					
• Style: The writer demonstrates a quality of imagination, individuality, and a distinctive voice.					
• Word Choice: The words are precise, vivid, and economical.					
• Sentence Formation: Sentences are complete and varied in length and structure.					
• Conventions: Appropriate grammar, mechanics, spelling, and usage enhance the meaning and readability of the text.					

> Additional standards and indicators as defined by the district or state would be added to the form.

FIGURE 10.6 Sample Portfolio Data Summary Form

data can become an integral component of the school's and the school district's accountability system.

DOING ONGOING ASSESSMENT

Doing ongoing assessment well is critically important. As Dylan Williams (in Lynn Olson's article, 2005, p. 7), is quoted as saying, "A focus on 'assessment for learning' can yield 'radical effects.' I think we've got a clear view of what it is we want teachers to be doing. The challenge is to get teachers doing this at scale." A quote from a literacy mentor working in an early literacy initiative highlights the challenge:

> At first I felt everyone was just collecting . . . information, but why? Just putting numbers to fill out forms? I just pulled out the checklist when I was required to do it again.
> Heidemann, Chang, & Menninga, 2005

So how does a project or school "get it right"? In any effective assessment system, teachers will be using multiple measures or tools as described above (e.g., anecdotal notes, vignettes, checklists, work samples), sometimes along with on-demand assessment, to guide their instruction. Simply directing teachers to use the tools is not sufficient. Teachers must be taught how to make sense of the data and to use the data to drive their classroom instruction.

Words Work!, an early literacy initiative in St. Paul, Minnesota, did it this way (Heidemann, Chang, & Menninga, 2005). The project hired outside evaluators to help them determine if the project was meeting its goals. These evaluators met with the staff twice each year to share data and elicit the staff's analysis of the data. These meetings required the staff to reflect on the results and their teaching strategies. Further, at these meetings, the evaluators shared the aggregated data with the teachers, and the teachers set goals based on the data. This was the first time that the teachers saw the data for all their students aggregated across each classroom and then each site. Now the teachers could clearly see how groups, not just individual students, were progressing in their acquisition of early literacy skills. Now the teachers began to understand how to interpret the data. The evaluators helped the teachers to reflect on and understand student data by asking questions like the following (p. 90):

- Where do the children score the highest/lowest?
- Do you see any patterns?
- What factors contribute to this pattern?
- In what categories do you see the biggest growth?
- What do you do in the classroom to contribute to this growth?

Now teachers could begin to form goals, lesson plans, and learning experiences to meet the students' needs. With strong support, the teachers learned to engage in data-driven planning. In the end, the teachers' effective use of assessment translated into literacy success for the students. (For more information on Words Work!, visit their Web site: http://saintpaulfoundation.org/impact/wordswork.)

ON-DEMAND ASSESSMENT

There is another kind of assessment that teachers use, or are required to use, to understand their students' literacy learning: on-demand assessment. This kind of assessment also is referred to as summative assessment, the assessment of learning (Johnston & Costello, 2005). (Each of the following examples illustrates a kind of on-demand assessment.

> A teacher pulls each of her students aside, one at a time, to have them read the same book, a book unknown to all of them. While each student reads, the teacher records the student's reading errors. When the student finishes reading, the teacher asks the student to retell the story. Later, the teacher might use a miscue analysis system to analyze the students' reading errors and a story structure form to analyze the students' retellings. The teacher analyzes every student's reading and retelling exactly the same way.
>
> A group of students finish reading *Charlotte's Web* by E. B. White (Harper Collins, 1952). The teacher has participated occasionally in the group's book discussions so the teacher has a sense of the group's understanding of the story. However, the teacher wants to know more about each student's understanding of the text. The teacher develops a set of four open-ended questions to which all students will respond in writing and identifies the criteria to be used to score the students' work. All students in the group take the test on the same day, writing for as much time as they need, and are given the same directions: to use details from the story to support their answers. To score the test, the teacher compares what the students wrote and the degree to which they supported their ideas (rarely to thoroughly and sufficiently) against the previously defined criteria.
>
> On two days in March, all third-, fifth-, eighth-, and tenth-graders in the state read several passages and demonstrate their understanding of the passages by bubbling-in answers to multiple-choice questions and writing answers to open-ended questions. The multiple-choice questions are scored by machine; the open-ended questions are scored by trained raters using a rubric written by and anchor papers selected by teachers. (Because the items on the test have been linked to the state's content standards, this on-demand assessment would be called a "standards-based state-mandated" assessment because it is linked to the state's standards and mandated by the state's legislators.)

Notice the shared features of these on-demand assessments. A central feature is that during on-demand assessments the teacher stops instruction and the students stop their learning to demonstrate what they know and are able to do. The students are, as the name implies, required to show what they know "on-demand." (Recall that, in ongoing assessment, assessment and instruction were interwoven.)

The increased importance of the use of on-demand assessments has not been without educators expressing their concerns. We identify a few of these concerns below:

1. Current standardized assessments tend to focus on a narrow sampling of all-purpose skills and strategies. Literacy is more than a set of skills and strategies. Therefore, current assessments undersample the full range of literate behaviors.

For example, the current literacy assessments fail to assess such literate disposi-tions as reciprocity or the "willingness to engage in joint learning tasks, to express uncertainties and ask questions, to take a variety of roles in joint learn-ing enterprises and to take others' purposes and perspectives into account" (Carr & Claxton, 2002, p. 16). Current literacy assessments fail to assess resilience or the willingness to "focus on learning when the going gets tough, to quickly recover from setbacks, and to adapt" (Johnston & Costello, 2005, p. 257).

2. Literacy assessment practices affect teachers' instructional practices. When the standardized test focuses on a narrow set of skills and strategies, and teachers' salaries, student retention, student graduation, and more are affected by the students' performance on the test, teachers eliminate the more complex instructional practices from their repertoire (Rex & Nelson, 2004). Educators fear that only those skills assessed on the test will be taught. Further, they fear that these skills will be taught solely in the format of the test. Test practice becomes the reading curriculum (Santman, 2002).

3. Current assessment policies are too focused on accountability; assessment should be used as a tool for teachers to diagnose children's learning needs so that instruction can be adjusted to meet the children's needs (Olson, 2005).

4. Teachers are unsure about "whether to teach *to* the content of the test, teach students *about* the genre of tests, and test-taking, teach . . . students to take a stance *against* the test, or all of the above" (Short, Schroeder, Kauffman, & Kaser, 2002, p. 199).

STANDARDIZED TESTS

Many on-demand assessments, such as those in the third example above, are administered, scored, and interpreted in the same way for all test takers. Each stu-dent taking the test reads the same passages, answers the same questions, and hears the same directions or writes to the same prompt in the same amount of time. When all variables are held constant, the assessment would be known as a "standardized" on-demand test. In Table 10.1, we provide a description of several of the standardized assessments in reading currently in use. For example, the *Dynamic Indicators of Basic Early Literacy Skills (DIBELS)* is used in most Reading First programs across the United States.

There are two types of standardized tests:

1. **Criterion-referenced tests** are developed using a specific set of objectives that reflect district and state learning standards. For instance, the district or state has a standard that fourth-grade students should be able to identify the main idea of a passage. Mrs. Bette, a fourth-grade teacher, has taught a specific unit on com-prehending the main idea. Two weeks later Mrs. Bette administers the district cri-terion-based test that focuses on several reading comprehension skills, including identifying the main idea. The test has fifty items; ten items deal directly with identifying the main idea. The students read a short passage and choose the correct multiple-choice answer that identifies the main idea from each passage.

TABLE 10.1   Standardized Reading Measures

TITLE/PUBLISHER	PURPOSE	DESCRIPTION	WHEN TO USE IT
Diagnostic Assessment of Reading Publisher: Riverside, Houghton Mifflin	To identify students' strengths and weaknesses to determine future instructional needs	Assessments that identify students' specific reading abilities—from foundation skills through comprehension in just twenty to thirty minutes. Comprises six individually administered tests: word analysis, oral reading, silent reading, comprehension, spelling, and word meaning	Beginning first grade (age six years) for students not demonstrating adequate progress
Dynamic Indicators of Basic Early Literacy Skills (DIBELS)— Letter Naming Fluency	To assess fluency with which children identify letter names. To identify children at risk of reading difficulty early, before a low reading trajectory is established	Individually administered, timed phonemic awareness task. Randomly ordered lower- and uppercase letters are presented to children for one minute: children are instructed to name as many letters as they can	Beginning kindergarten through fall of first grade or until children are proficient at accurately producing forty to sixty letter names per minute
Nonsense Word Fluency	Measures knowledge of letter sounds and ability to use them to read nonsense words. To identify children at risk of reading difficulty early	Individually administered, one-minute timed word-reading fluency task. Children are presented with three-letter nonsense words that can be segmented by phonemes or blended and read as whole words	Beginning first grade through the end of the first grade. May be appropriate for monitoring the progress of older children with low skills in letter-sound correspondence or blending
Phonemic Segmentation Fluency Publisher: CBM Network, School Psychology Program, College of Education, University of Oregon http://dibels.uoregon.edu/	Assess children's ability to segment orally presented words into phonemes. To identify children who may be at risk of reading difficulty	Individually administered, timed phonological awareness task. Words are orally presented to children for one minute; children are instructed to segment each word into individual phonemes (i.e., sounds)	Winter of kindergarten through first grade or until children are proficient at accurately producing thirty-five to forty-five phonemes per minute

(continued)

TABLE 10.1   Standardized Reading Measures (Continued)

TITLE/PUBLISHER	PURPOSE	DESCRIPTION	WHEN TO USE IT
Early Reading Diagnostic Assessment Publisher: Harcourt	Diagnostic information specifying strengths and needs	Individually administered diagnostic test. Provides specific information about a child's reading skills	Grades K–3. Individually administered
Gates MacGinite Reading Tests, Third Edition Publisher: Riverside Publishing Company	Commercially published test designed to identify specific strengths and weaknesses in reading comprehension	Achievement test designed to assess a child's knowledge of important background concepts of reading, identify strengths and weaknesses in the area of beginning reading, and serve as a measure of reading skills for children who make less than average progress in reading by the end of first grade	Level "PRE" and "R" for use with beginning kinder gartners to assess background concepts; Level "R" for measuring reading skills of students who are not making adequate progress; other seven levels used to provide a general assessment of reading achievement
IDEA Proficiency Test (IPT) Publisher: Ballard & Tigh	To determine the English language skills of students who have a non-English language background	Children are assessed on oral language abilities, writing, and reading. Asked to write their own stories and respond to a story	Administered to children K–12
Individual Growth and Developmental Indicator (IGDI) www. getgotgo.net	To identify children's phonological awareness strengths and weaknesses	Three components to the test: picture naming, rhyming, and alliteration. Takes approximately five minutes to administer	Used for ages three to five
PALS Pre-K http://pals. virginia. edu/PALS-Instruments/ PALS-PreK.asp	To provide information on children's strengths and weaknesses	Measures name-writing ability, upper- and lowercase alphabet recognition, letter sound and beginning sound production, print and word awareness, rhyme awareness, and nursery rhyme awareness	Used in fall of pre-K and can be used as a measurement of progress in the spring

TABLE 10.1   Standardized Reading Measures (Continued)

TITLE/PUBLISHER	PURPOSE	DESCRIPTION	WHEN TO USE IT
Peabody Picture Vocabulary Test-III (PPVT-III) Publisher: American Guidance Service	To measure receptive vocabulary acquisition and serve as a screening test of verbal ability	Student points to the picture that best represents the stimulus word	Beginning at age two-and-a-half years to ninety-plus years
The Phonological Awareness Test (PAT) Publisher: LinguiSystems	To assess students' phonological awareness skills	Five different measures of phonemic awareness (segmentation of phonemes, phoneme isolation, phoneme deletion, phoneme sub-stitution, and phoneme blending) and a measure of sensitivity to rhyme	Beginning the second semester of kindergarten through grade 2
Word-Attack Subtest of the Woodcock Reading Mastery Test-Revised Publisher: American Guidance Service	To assess children's ability to apply knowl-edge of letter-sound correspondences in decoding complex nonwords	Individually administered test consisting of a series of increasingly complex nonwords that children are asked to sound out as best as they can	Kindergarten through Grade 12 as a screening measure

To demonstrate their mastery of this skill, students must correctly identify the main idea for eight out of ten passages. A second example emanates from the national level. The Department of Health and Human Services, under the National Reporting on Child Outcomes plan, requires that all Head Start students be tested twice annually on such skills as their ability to recognize a word as a unit of print, identify letters of the alphabet, associate sounds with written words, and so on. In the fall and spring, children are individually administered a test to assess their Head Start entry and exit reading skills. In Special Feature 10.2, we describe a criterion-referenced ongoing assessment procedure used by an Early Reading First project in Yuma, Arizona. The goal in criterion-referenced tests is for all student to demonstrate mastery of the information and skills they have been taught.

2. Norm-referenced tests are designed to measure the relative accomplishment of one student to the whole class, or to compare one classroom of fourth-grade students to another classroom within the same school, or to compare all fourth-grade classrooms in a district, or to compare all fourth-graders across the country. Norm-referenced standardized tests can be used to determine whether a school's

SPECIAL FEATURE 10.2

Curriculum-Based Assessments: Ongoing, Standardized, Criterion-Referenced Assessments

Curriculum-based assessments (CBM) are specific to the content of the curriculum. CBM has been shown to be an effective tool in monitoring students' progress so that students needing additional assistance can be identified and instruction can be modified. They are conducted regularly (i.e., weekly, biweekly) by the classroom teachers. Teachers follow a standardized procedure in their administration of the assessment. Through the use of the CBM, the teacher monitors the progress the students are making on specific skills. For example, teachers in the Yuma, Arizona, Early Reading First project are using the Doors to Discovery (McGraw-Hill, 2002) language and early reading program. To assess their young students' progress in the areas of vocabulary (receptive and expressive), phonological awareness, and alphabet letter knowledge, the project's leaders (Karen Burstein, Tanis Bryan, James Christie, and Jay Blanchard) developed a CBM. During each unit, the teachers focus on target letters, vocabulary, and alliteration. The CBM was designed to assess the young learners' acquisition of these same skills. The CBM procedures are as follows:

- The students participate in a weekly CBM. The CBM is individually administered by the teacher or teacher assistant. The weekly CBM includes letter identification of one or two uppercase letters; picture/vocabulary identification (receptive) of four words from the week's shared reading book; vocabulary production (oral vocabulary) from the Doors to Discovery picture vocabulary cards specific to the week's instruction; and identification of initial sounds from words from the week's vocabulary.
- The teachers are directed to administer the CBM as follows:

- Using the uppercase letter cards, show the alphabet letters to each student, one at a time. Ask the student to produce each letter's name. Record each students response on that student's data sheet.
- Using appropriate materials from the unit (vocabulary cards, interactive book, posters), ask each student to point to the picture of a select target vocabulary word (receptive vocabulary) (e.g, "Show me going *through* the tunnel"). Do this for the four selected words. Record each student's response on that student's data sheet.
- Using appropriate materials from the unit, point to a picture of a select target vocabulary word and ask each student to name (expressive vocabulary) the item (e.g., "Tell me what this is." "*Taxi*."). Do this for the four selected target words. Record each student's response on that student's data sheet.
- Using appropriate materials from the unit, say a word (e.g., *fire* truck) and say, "Point to a picture of something that begins with the same sound as *fire* truck (phonological awareness). What is that a picture of?" Record each student's response on that student's data sheet.

At the end of every other unit (quarterly), all students are assessed using the CBM procedures and data recorded on each student's data sheet and entered into the data management system. The teachers are coached to use the weekly and quarterly CBM to assess students' progress toward educational outcomes and to make decisions about their instructional practice.

curriculum reflects national expectations of what students should know at a specific grade level and to compare students to one another.

As readers have read, it is now common practice for states to mandate that students take a standards-based standardized test, typically in the spring of the academic year. The state's aim is to gather information on how a school and the school district are achieving with respect to all standards. In Special Feature 10.3, Bonnie Albertson describes the process used by one state to develop and implement its statewide, mandated test, a test driven by the state's English language arts content standards.

Lucy Calkins, Kate Montgomery, and Donna Santman (1998) suggest that teachers hired to teach in a new district ask questions like the following to help them understand the district's testing policies:

- Is the district's test norm-referenced or criterion-referenced and standards-based?
- How are the students' scores reported to the public? Raw scores? Percentile scores? Cut-score percentages (below standard, meets the standard, above the standard)?
- Is the school's score compared with that of other schools used to rank the school? Are all students' (special education, bilingual) scores counted in the school's ranking?

Preparing Students for On-Demand Assessments. Each state's department of education expects its mandated standardized achievement test to impact the state's teachers' classroom teaching practices. Of course, when the test is directly linked to the state's content standards, both the classroom curriculum and instruction and the test are driven by the standards. In theory, if teachers are teaching to the standards (providing learning opportunities that help their students develop the knowledge specified in the content standards), their students should do well on the test. Even so, teachers, like Donna Santman (2002), pause from their rich units of study to teach their students the test genre. Note that Ms. Santman does *not* spend the year teaching to the test. Rather, her rich reading and writing curriculum builds the knowledge her students require to perform well on the test. So the pause is to teach her students the particular challenges of reading associated with the test—to approach the test as a kind of genre and to teach her students how to negotiate the unique qualities of the test genre. Ms. Santman recommends teachers use the following test genre teaching strategies:

- Begin by having the students work in groups to create lists of what they already know about this genre. From previous years' experiences, what do they remember about the test? This provides teachers with information on what their students already know about the test.
- Immerse the students in materials *exactly like* the format of the test they will take. Many test publishers sell practice books. Some states (e.g., www.doe.k12. de.us/AAB/DSTP_ELA_Reading_Samplers_2005.html) provide item samplers for teachers' use with their students.

SPECIAL FEATURE 10.3
The Evolution of a Test

BY BONNIE R. ALBERTSON

Much has been written about the shortcomings of high-stakes assessment, accountability based on one-shot tests, and the negative impact that these tests have on students, teachers, and classroom practice in general. Researchers agree that when assessments have high stakes and high visibility, for both individual and program accountability, they influence teacher practice and often determine what will be taught (e.g., Hillocks, 2002; Mabry, 1999; Madaus, 1988; National Commission on Testing and Public Policy, 1990). However, this is not necessarily all bad; in fact, many assessment and literacy scholars (e.g., Black and Wiliam, 1998; Huot, 2002; Weigle, 2002) note that the future of such assessments lies in their potential to inform instruction. Similarly, many scholars argue for more local control of assessment systems and getting teachers involved in all aspects of assessment design (e.g., Huot, 2002; Winograd & Arrington, 1999). Calls for local control are based on a situated, contextual view of learning *and* assessment. Increased local control allows for open-ended dialogue among educators and helps to balance power relationships. These are the kinds of collaboration supported by the teacher-change literature (e.g., Anders & Richardson, 1992; Winograd & Arrington, 1999).

If we know that high-stakes assessments can lead to "teaching to the test," it stands to reason that at the very least, stakeholders should make sure that they are aware of what teaching to the test actually looks like (see Guthrie, 2002, for information about the role test-taking strategies and familiarity with the test format have on test performance). To this end, having teachers involved in every stage of the assessment process increases teachers' knowledge about what content is being tested, what the test looks like, and how it is scored. Surely this is important knowl-

edge if we want to give students every opportunity to truly show what they "know and can do" in reading and writing. The development of literacy assessment in one state, Delaware, has indeed evolved into a system that has influenced instruction in many of the ways promoted by scholars (e.g., Black & Wiliams, 1998; Huot, 2002).

Delaware's decade-old assessment system is not 100 percent "local"; it is, in fact, a hybrid. It calls for a partnership between the "client" (Delaware) and the test "vendor" (Harcourt Assessment Inc., of San Antonio, Texas). What does such a system look like and what are the positive elements of assessment systems such as Delaware's DSTP (Delaware Student Testing Program)?

■ Nuts and Bolts

This partnership is time-consuming; indeed, shared ownership is both a burden and a privilege. Exactly what roles do teachers play in Delaware's assessment system? In fact, teachers are involved in virtually every phase from passage selection to scoring resolution and publication of released items and anchor papers:

Teacher Selection. Teachers are nominated to serve on test development "steering committees." These teacher committees represent all three of Delaware's counties. In addition, every attempt is made to have committees reflect the makeup of Delaware's school population (gender, ethnic, racial) and represent a cross-section of students.

Test Development. Delaware teachers write the writing prompts; they locate, select, and screen reading passages; they write all the comprehension items (multiple choice, short answer, and extended responses). Committee members also conduct local passage and item "classroom trials" and student/teacher interviews to assess informally passage and item appropriateness. Throughout the development phase, Harcourt staff provide constant feedback.

Field Test and Scoring Protocols. Following the item development phase, the process moves to field testing and scoring. Harcourt selects a range of papers from reading and writing field tests. From these they arrange a preliminary set of "proposed anchors" for every written reading and writing test response. They make notes regarding the initial assessment of these pieces. These sets are brought to Delaware on designated days (for English Language Arts [ELA], usually three full days are allotted). Teachers are released from their schools to participate, although benchmarking often also runs into Saturdays. For each grade level, there are two representatives from Harcourt and several teachers, including steering committee members. Participants take turns recording careful notes about scoring discussions.

The first task is to read through the proposed set of anchors and come to consensus on them. This can take four to five hours of "lively" debate but always results in a "Delaware-sanctioned" anchor set. Then teachers turn their attention to additional "Training Sets" and "Decision Sets," to be used to train scorers once the Harcourt trainers are back in Texas.

At the end of these grueling sessions, the two trainers for each grade level leave with the anchor/training/decisions sets and two sets of notes. But Delaware's teachers leave with even more: they return to their respective districts declaring that participation in these sessions constitutes "the best staff development opportunity they've ever had," at least for the test. Individual scoring biases are exposed, overall student strength and weaknesses become evident, teachers learn about curriculum initiatives across the state, and they learn about what other teachers value in terms of content knowledge.

Live Scoring. Following the "live" assessment in March, Delaware Department of Education (DOE) staff and steering committee members travel to Texas to oversee the "training of scoring leaders." Districts are also invited to send representatives (often department chairs, curriculum leaders), and many do take advantage of this opportunity. These educators observe the scoring training and the actual scoring process. The Harcourt staff assigned to "the Delaware project" explain thoroughly the scoring process, covering everything from read-behind protocols to computer features that allow scorers to reverse-image for easier visibility—all information that reassures Delaware educators: "Yes, we all *do* have college degrees," and "No, lightning will *not* strike if a student writes his/her answer a bit outside the boxed lines."

Even after Delawareans have returned home, Harcourt stays in touch with DOE. They send odd papers, seeking Delaware's decision about papers that do not "fit" the anchors. The following account illustrates the process:

> One particularly difficult reading passage was selected by the tenth-grade Steering Committee to develop for the reading assessment. In keeping with Delaware's stated desire to have "authentic" texts whenever possible, and the ELA standard's stated goal of including some informative/ technical text, the committee chose to develop a brochure about the Cape May (New Jersey)–Lewes (Delaware) Ferry. One of the questions asked students to propose an itinerary for a hypothetical trip to the area, using information about both towns in the proposal. The ferry runs across the Delaware Bay, at the mouth of the inlet leading to the Atlantic Ocean. The two towns are in New Jersey and Delaware, across the river from one another. Both are resort towns. There was no apparent problem with the question during the initial

(continued on next page)

anchor-setting activities. However, when it came time for "live" scoring, the Harcourt folks noticed a scoring anomaly. Scorers became confused by a few responses that used the terms "beach" and "shore" when referring to Delaware and New Jersey respectively. Since neither of those terms is used in the brochure, and because the ferry runs across a river, the scorers were puzzled by words that referred to a sandy beach/sea shore. Delaware teachers, however, were not the least bit puzzled. It's common knowledge—among Delawareans and Jerseyites, that is—that when one says she is going to "the beach," she is going to one of Delaware's coastal resorts; when one says he is going to "the shore," he is undoubtedly headed for New Jersey. Once we explained the regionalism, a "scoring note" took care of the apparent dilemma. However, without a mutually respectful relationship between "client" and "vendor," many students would have received lower scores due to the inclusion of what a non-Delawarean would consider "irrelevant" information.

Other Teacher Resources. Teachers have access to a wealth of information on the DOE/DSTP Web site. Information about the reading and writing test configuration, item specifications used by item writers to compose the test, and sample items with benchmarked answers are all available to teachers and parents. The writing prompts and anchor papers for prompts dating back to 1998 are also released and available for teachers to download and use instructionally. In fact, teachers can access their own students' writing samples.

■ Conclusions

Testing is still testing, and the purpose of this section is not to paint an unrealistically rosy picture. However, we agree with Winograd and Arrington who note that "no particular assessment is a best practice in and of itself; rather, the quality of assessments lies largely in how wisely they are used" (1999, p. 214). Furthermore, the purpose of this section is not to argue for or against high-stakes assessments. Rather, this section explores the ways in which teacher participation influences one state's large-scale assessment system. What educational changes can be linked to Delaware's assessment system?

Finally, DSTP has changed the discourse of teachers. Across the state, teachers use the same terms to describe student performance, set achievement goals, and write curriculum. At the very least, consistency and clear expectations are positive outcomes of the DSTP. In addition, teachers have the power to define what is valued. Remember that it is Delaware teachers who "sanction" anchor sets; therefore, teachers make the decisions so teachers do not need to "guess" about the features that make up top scoring responses. They don't have to guess whether the five-paragraph essay is privileged or penalized (neither is true); whether students must restate the question in the answer (no) or cite specific information from the text (yes) to earn top scores on the reading test. And finally, although it may be too early to make any predictions about the long term performance of Delaware's schoolchildren, Delaware's National Assessment of Educational Progress scores have steadily increased over the last ten years.

└──┘

Note: Delaware's English Language Arts standards were adopted in 1995 along with an "interim" assessment, and the DSTP has been in place for the end-of-cluster grades (3, 5, 8, and 10) since 1998 (grades 2, 4, 6, 7, and 9 were added in 2002). Accountability, for school, teacher, and students, was gradually implemented over the next five years. The DSTP English language arts "test" is composed of reading (with both multiple choice and constructed response questions) and writing (composed of a "stand-alone" writing prompt and a text-based writing prompt). Learn more about the DSTP on the Delaware Department of Education Web site: www.doe.k12.de.us.

- Invite the students to explore (e.g., read through the test passages to consider how they are organized and the types of questions asked) the materials.
- Time the students as they work through a number of passages, if the test is a timed test. If not, invite them to read and respond to a number of passages. Then, talk about the strategies they used to read and respond to the questions.
- Role play the strategies *you* use when taking a test. Do you, for example, avoid looking ahead so that you are not overwhelmed by all that is left to do? Do you stop between sections to give yourself a short break in order to feel refreshed and ready to proceed? Do you change pencils to help you feel refreshed? Tell them what works for you and invite them to share their successful strategies.
- Focus on the test questions. Ask the students to work in groups to identify "tricky phrases." Translate the generated lists into words the students know and have been using all year.
- Focus on the test answers. Show the students how to avoid overanalyzing and to check the passage for answers to the questions.
- Invite the students to "act as if they are test writers" (p. 210). Being a test writer themselves will help them look at the questions and answers from a new perspective.

Reconsidering Teaching Practices

It is unacceptable if a teacher is still teaching the same way she/he was teaching twenty years ago. We, as a profession, have learned incredible amounts about how students learn best. . . . If [we] teach well, maintain best practices, make instructional decisions based on [our] students' needs, and make decisions that are reflective of [the principles of learning we hold], [our] students will learn. They will learn well, and they will pass the test. (Buckner, 2002, p. 215)

The authors of this book acknowledge that no single test score should be used alone to judge a student's progress in reading and writing. However, *if* most of the students in the classroom do not perform as expected on a standardized test, then teachers must be prepared to reconsider their methods of teaching reading and writing. Teachers need to ask themselves, "What could I have done better or differently?" Others certainly will raise this question. "Is it the reading curriculum?" A district administrator might recommend that a new basal anthology be purchased. Someone, maybe even a state legislator, might mandate that phonics be taught to all kindergarten through third-graders for thirty minutes a day. Teachers must be able to respond by defending their teaching practices and by learning what legitimately needs revising to support students' development as readers and writers. Teachers at each grade level and within each school need to study the reported testing data to understand what their students could do well and what was challenging for their students. These data can guide teachers' examination of their teaching practices.

SUMMARY

In the earlier chapters in this book, we presented the instructional strategies that create the framework for an effective language and literacy program. However, these strategies by themselves are not sufficient to construct a program that ensures optimal language and literacy learning for all students. In this chapter, we present information on a key ingredient—assessment.

- *What is important for teachers to know about children's literacy development?*

Teachers need a thorough knowledge of the language and literacy accomplishments or goals or objectives that have been judged by the professional community and the public as important. This information may be obtained from several sources, including state and local school district guidelines. In addition to information provided throughout this text, the authors also recommend reports prepared by the Committee on the Prevention of Reading Difficulties in Young Children, the joint position paper issued by the International Reading Association and the National Association for the Education of Young Children (IRA/NAEYC), and the joint standards issued by the International Reading Association and the National Council of Teachers of English (IRA/NCTE).

- *What are the two general approaches teachers might use to assess their students' literacy learning?*

Changes in what we know about literacy learning have necessitated major changes in our ways of measuring students' literacy learning. There are two general approaches teachers might use to gather information about their students' literacy development: ongoing assessment and on-demand assessment. Ongoing assessment makes use of such information-gathering tools as anecdotal notes, vignettes or teacher reflections, checklists, conferences, surveys, video and audio recordings, running records, and the collection of students' work samples. These artifacts of students' literacy learning are produced while the students engage in their daily classroom activities and the teacher is teaching. The artifacts, then, serve the dual purpose of instruction and assessment. These artifacts are stored in portfolios. Hence, ongoing assessment is often called "portfolio assessment." On-demand assessment occurs when the teacher stops teaching to assess the students' performance and asks them to demonstrate what they know and can do. The students are required to show what they know "on-demand." Typically, on-demand assessments are administered, scored, and interpreted in the same way for all test takers. In reality, the two approaches work hand-in-hand in the classroom. Teachers gather ongoing data while instructing about students' daily performances and on-demand data periodically in order to form a comprehensive picture of each student's literacy learning.

■ *What are the differences between working and showcase portfolios?*

The goal of the working portfolio is to provide documentation of how the student is growing and developing. The items housed in the working portfolio are evidence of a student's typical, everyday performance. From the working portfolio, the teacher and student will select specific pieces for inclusion in the student's showcase portfolio. The items housed in the showcase portfolio will exhibit the best work the student has produced.

■ *How do teachers use the information they collect?*

Teachers (and students) collect information and store it in the working portfolios. Teachers (and students) analyze the products and information contained in the working portfolio to assess each student's progress over time. These types of authentic assessment provide just the type of information that teachers need to know to provide effective literacy learning experiences for students.

Teachers also use the information they collect in portfolios to share with parents. Parents need to know how their students are progressing, and most parents need concrete examples with explicit information provided by the teacher, so teachers share the working and the showcase portfolios with students' parents.

Teachers also share information with parents that has been gathered through on-demand assessment. Teacher-made and district-mandated on-demand assessment data is housed in the students' showcase portfolios. The teacher uses these data to show what the student can do independently, unsupported by the teacher and peers.

LINKING KNOWLEDGE TO PRACTICE

1. One way teachers determine what they want and need to know about students' literacy development is by reviewing national, state, and local standards. Search the state's Web site or contact the state or a school district to obtain a copy of the state or local standards of language arts. Given what you have learned about students' literacy development in this textbook, do these standards appear reasonable goals for language arts instruction at the grade level of your choice? Why or why not?

2. Interview a teacher about the information-gathering tools that he or she typically uses to collect information about students' literacy development. How does the teacher store the information gathered? How does the teacher organize this information to share with parents?

3. Interview a principal, teacher, or someone from the state's Department of Education. What are the district-mandated on-demand assessments? What are the state-mandated on-demand assessments? How are these tests constructed? Ask the questions Lucy Calkins and her colleagues (see page 391) suggested that teachers new to a district ask.

4. The use of standardized tests has increased dramatically in recent years. Search your state's Web site or contact a school district for information on required state reading assessments. Contact a local Head Start for information on the mandatory twice-yearly testing of Head Start children.

CHAPTER 11

PARENTS AS PARTNERS IN LITERACY EDUCATION

Nestling close on Grandma's big, soft, feather bed, Grandma reads Billie her favorite book,
The Little Engine That Could. *Grandma barely finishes the last word in the book when Billie asks her to read it again. As Grandma rereads, Billie echoes the refrain, "I think I can, I think I can, I think I can!" After the story, Grandma always says, "If you think you can, you can do anything." To this day, whenever Billie is challenged to learn new concepts or deal with difficult situations, she remembers Grandma saying, "Just think you can, just think you can!"*

If you share memories like Billie's, you are indeed fortunate. Research demonstrates that a family's role in a child's language and literacy development is directly related to the child's communicative competence (Hart & Risley, 1995), positive attitudes toward reading and writing, and literacy achievement (e.g., Christian, Morrison, & Bryant, 1998; Nord, Lennon, Liu, & Chandler, 2000: Epstein, 1986; Sulzby, Teale, & Kamberelis, 1989).

BEFORE READING THIS CHAPTER, THINK ABOUT . . .

- Your early literacy experiences. Do you remember precious moments snuggling with a special person and sharing a book? Do you remember talking with an adult who provided you with many experiences and the words to describe these experiences? Do you remember an adult helping you read words in your environment?
- Your memories of a parent's report of a parent–teacher conference about your classroom behavior and learning. Do you remember if your parents always heard positive reports about your learning? Do you remember what happened if the teacher made suggestions for home learning activities?
- News flashes, newsletters, and other written communication you carried home from school. Do you remember these being posted in your home, perhaps on the refrigerator door? Do you remember them helping you answer the question, what did you do in school today?

When parents and teachers share information, the child benefits

FOCUS QUESTIONS

- What is known about the relationship between what parents do and children's literacy development?
- In what ways might early childhood teachers communicate personally with parents? How might teachers run a parent–teacher conference?
- In what ways might teachers communicate with parents in writing?
- What resources might an early childhood teacher provide to parents and parents provide to teachers to support young children's early literacy learning?

WHAT ROLES DO FAMILIES PLAY?

Collin (1992, p. 2) refers to the parents' nurturing role in their child's literacy development as "planting the seeds of literacy." Almost all parents want to plant these seeds, but many are unsure of the best way to begin. Similarly, most parents and other primary caregivers vastly underestimate the importance of their role in helping children become competent language users (McNeal, 1999). In this chapter, we discuss strategies teachers can use to inform parents of all cultures and other primary caregivers about the critical role they play in their child's language and literacy development, and how parents and teachers can work together to enhance language and reading and writing opportunities in the home. Special Feature 11.1, "Parental Involvement in Bilingual/Second-Language Settings," provides a multicultural perspective on this issue.

■ ■ ■ ■ ■

BOX 11.1
DEFINITION OF TERMS

developmental spelling: another name for invented spelling, where children use two or three letters to phonetically represent a word (e.g., *happy* might be spelled as *hape*).

Reading and Writing Acquisition

Parents play a critical role in helping children learn about print. Many children learn about literacy very early. This task is accomplished quite naturally as children sit on the laps of parents, other family members, or caregivers sharing a storybook. Surrounded by love, these children easily learn about the functions of print and the joys of reading. Being read to at home facilitates the onset of reading, reading fluency, and reading enjoyment. Unfortunately, a growing number of studies have documented a lack of parent–child reading opportunities, especially in low-income homes (Christian, Morrison, & Bryant, 1998; Griffin & Morrison, 1997). Lesley Morrow (1988) surveyed parents of children in three preschools serving poor families (incomes of less than $10,000, 40 percent minority, 75 percent single-parent headed). Ninety percent of these parents indicated that they read to their children only once a month or less! This lack of parental involvement may have a significant effect on the children's learning throughout their schooling. For example, Billie Enz's (1992) study of 400 high school sophomores revealed that 70 percent of the remedial readers could not recall being read to by their parents as children, while 96 percent of the students in advanced placement courses reported that their parents had read to them regularly. In essence, it appears that a child's future literacy and subsequent success in school depend on parents' ability and willingness to provide the child with thousands of planned and spontaneous encounters with print (Enz & Searfoss, 1995).

Parental involvement also has an important effect on children's writing development. In the following example, notice how four-year-old Timeka's early attempts at writing are subtly supported by her mother:

> Sitting at a table with crayon in hand, Timeka is engrossed in making squiggly lines across a large paper. Timeka's mother, sitting across from her, is busy writing checks. After Timeka finishes her writing, she folds her paper and asks her mother for an envelope so she can "pay the bank, too." As mother smiles and gives Timeka the envelope, she remarks, "Good, our bank needs your money."

This brief example illustrates how Timeka is taking her first steps to becoming literate. While most children need formal instruction to learn to read and write conventionally, children who have parents who guide and support their beginning literacy efforts learn to read and write more quickly. As Timeka observes her parents and other adults writing, she discovers that these marks have purpose and

SPECIAL FEATURE 11.1
Parental Involvement in Bilingual and Second-Language Settings

BY SARAH HUDELSON AND IRENE SERNA

This chapter discusses the importance of involving parents in their children's education. In the home setting, parents are their children's first teachers. There is no reason for this role to cease when children begin their formal schooling. In this special feature, the perspective already developed in this chapter is extended by exploring several issues that are particularly important to keep in mind when planning for the involvement of parents who are native speakers of a language other than English.

■ The Problem of Stereotyping

Even in the 1990s, when educators worked to be more sensitive to diversity (Brandt, 1992), comments about parents, especially parents of color, parents who do not speak English, and parents who are not middle class were heard.

> "Those parents are poor and uneducated; they don't have any idea of how to help their children."
> "The parents at my school don't value education; they don't even come to parent-teacher conferences."
> "Some parents can't even speak English and read and write themselves. How are they supposed to help their kids?"
> "These poor babies come from homes with no books; no wonder they are so behind. They have no understanding of literacy before they come to school."

Comments such as these reflect stereotyping and negative attitudes toward some parents. Some non-English-speaking parents have not been fortunate enough to complete even elementary school; some have had limited opportunities to develop literacy. Some are uncomfortable in the school setting because they do not speak English; some have difficulty attending school functions because they are holding down two or three poorly paying jobs in order to support their families. The presence of these challenging obstacles does not mean that parents are unable and unwilling to participate in their children's education. In fact, non-English-speaking parents are especially concerned about education because they view education as the key to a better life for their children.

Studies conducted over the past two decades (Allexsaht-Snider, 1991; Delgado-Gaitan & Trueba, 1991; Schieffelin & Cochran-Smith, 1984; Vasquez, 1991) (e.g., of home literacy practices in working-class, non-English-speaking, immigrant families) have found that these families do engage in a variety of literacy practices. However, these practices tend to be focused on literacy for daily life, survival, and communication with relatives in their native countries, rather than on more middle-class purposes for reading (for example, literacy for pleasure or to pass leisure time). Reading for pleasure or leisure is difficult when a parent is working multiple jobs.

Therefore, educators must avoid making assumptions about non-English-speaking parents. Instead teachers are encouraged to (1) acknowledge and understand parental and family realities; (2) work to establish relationships with parents that will allow them to feel valued for who they are; and (3) help parents recognize the important contributions they make to their children's continued education.

■ Understanding Different Cultural Norms Regarding Schooling

For individuals raised in mainstream, middle-class settings, parental involvement in education may be considered a given. Parents assume that they are welcome at school and that they ought to have a say in their children's educational experiences. However, such assumptions are not

(continued on next page)

necessarily the case in all communities, and they are particularly unlikely in culturally and linguistically diverse settings.

In the Miami community of Little Haiti, for example, Creole-speaking parents from Haiti historically had been excluded from the French-language schools their children attended. Parents viewed the schools as places where they sent their children to do as the schools instructed, with no input from parents. The schools, in turn, emphasized learning via memorization rather than through active construction of knowledge (Hudelson, 1990).

Similarly, in many communities populated by Mexican and other Latin American immigrants, parents believe that when they send their children to school, they turn over the responsibility for the child's education to that institution. Traditionally, there has been a separation of functions. The parents' role is to instruct their children to behave and to listen carefully to their teachers. The parents' job is also to discipline children who misbehave in school. The teachers' function is to teach (Delgado-Gaitan & Trueba, 1991). Additionally, Mexican and Mexican-American parents have not been schooled in the constructivist perspective advocated by so many educators today. These parents may hold views of literacy learning that may be much more traditional than those of the teacher. Also like most parents, they may be reticent to participate in pedagogies that they have not experienced (Enz & Searfoss, 1995; 1996).

Authoritarian views of schooling and the separation of parents from schools and teachers, then, have been experiences that parents from many cultural backgrounds may have shared. Given such socialization, it is understandable that parents may initially be uncomfortable seeing themselves in formal teaching roles and working in more interactional ways. They may also believe that they should come to school only for disciplinary reasons. It is important, therefore, to appreciate that parents may have been socialized to view schools and teacher-parent roles in ways that significantly differ from the views that the teacher expects. Teachers need to learn from community members what parents' views about schools and about experiences with schools have been so that they may more effectively invite parents to work with them.

■ Encouraging Native Language Use

One of Irene Serna's most vivid memories of her own elementary schooling is having a teacher tell her parents that they should not use Spanish with her in their home. If her parents continued to speak Spanish to her, they were told, Irene would be retarded in her academic development. The way to help Irene was to use English. More than thirty years later, this advice continues to be given to parents who are not proficient users of English. Simply stated, this advice is wrong.

In Special Feature 2.4 accompanying Chapter 2, you read about immigrant parents' problems in communicating effectively with their young children who no longer acknowledged their native languages. How were these adults who spoke little or no English to raise their children to be decent human beings if they could not use the language they spoke fluently (Fillmore, 1991)? In addition, think about what language means to humans, what humans use language for. People use both spoken and written language for a broad spectrum of purposes: to provide information, to persuade others to a point of view, to argue, to tell jokes, to share stories, to scold, to ask questions, to share opinions, to make interpersonal connections, to express emotions, and so on. Language is a powerful force in our lives.

In order to understand language's potential, children need to be exposed to a wide range of language uses (Heath, 1986). Such exposure is much more likely to happen when adults interact in a language they control (i.e., their native language), rather than in a language they are still struggling to learn. Unless second-language learners have achieved high levels of proficiency in the second language, they will not use this newer tongue for the full range of uses in which they will use the native language. To deny children access to this full range of language functions is to impoverish children's language and to put them at risk for lower achievement in school. David Dolson (1985) has demonstrated that children who come from monolingual homes where a language other than English is spoken perform better in school than children from homes where parents try to use their second language, English, with their children.

Therefore, parents who are more proficient in their native language than in English must be encouraged to use the native language with their children, thus providing the young learners with demonstrations of a broad range of possibilities of language use. Learners then take these understandings into the second-language setting.

Expanding Our Views of the Roots of Literacy

As this book has demonstrated, one place where children learn about reading and writing is the home, where the children see their parents engage in reading and writing and where they themselves engage in a variety of literacy events. One such event is storybook reading. Because storybook reading has been found to be a predictor of later success in reading (Wells, 1986), suggestions to parents for assisting their children to become literate generally include reading out loud.

For many non-English-speaking parents, economic circumstances and limited availability of materials in their native languages often mean that storybook reading is limited. However, in many cultures, a tradition of oral storytelling exists. Research has demonstrated that the elements of story, as well as the strategies or ways of thinking about or responding to text that schools expect (for example, sequencing, evaluating, elaborating, clarifying) are developed during these storytelling events (Guerra, 1991; Pease-Alvarez, 1991; Vasquez, 1991).

Juan's family is an example. Juan came from a home in which oral storytelling was a family ritual that took place as Juan's mother prepared the family dinner. Juan's mother would tell a story, and then the children were expected to tell stories. This home literacy practice provided Juan with a sophisticated understanding of story development. His stories demonstrated a complexity and creativity that many of his classmates (who did not engage in such storytelling) did not have. For example, during kindergarten, Juan created "Los Osos Malos" (The Bad Bears). In Juan's story, some bad bears chased him, even turning themselves into ghosts in an effort to capture him. However, through a series of moves and countermoves, Juan finally escaped. Juan's story was by far the most complex of any produced by the kindergarten children, and this, at least in part, can be attributed to his background in hearing and then telling stories.

Non-English-speaking parents who come from cultures with strong oral traditions should be encouraged to tell stories at home. Parents could be invited to tell stories at school. By broadening our base of understanding of what contributes to children's school literacy success, another avenue is provided for meaningful participation by non-English-speaking parents.

Family Literacy Demonstrations

The present chapter makes a series of excellent suggestions for providing workshops for parents on aspects of curriculum. The workshop format allows parents to participate in and try out some classroom instructional strategies that promote literacy. Educators involved with parents in bilingual and second-language settings also have worked in this hands-on way, but they have found particular success in organizing the workshops somewhat differently. They have involved parents and young children together in carrying out the kinds of activities and strategies that are a part of the children's ongoing literacy development; thus, the focus is on family and intergenerational literacy (Weinstein-Shr & Quintero, 1995).

(continued on next page)

SPECIAL FEATURE 11.1   (continued)

In an elementary school in central Phoenix, Arizona, primary-grade bilingual teachers have invited parents and children to participate in literature study groups with high-quality picture books. The teacher begins by reading the story aloud, followed by opportunities for adults and children to share their responses to the book. Often, parents and children then choose other books to take home. While this activity is usually carried out in Spanish, a variation of it could involve parents and children in listening, one time or several times, to a carefully selected predictable book in English. Parents who are ESL learners have reported that they themselves learn more English when they listen to predictable stories.

In a family literacy project involving Spanish-speaking mothers and their four-year-old preschoolers, experienced early childhood educators engaged parents and children in hands-on activities, followed by language-experience-type dictation. These parent- and child-generated stories became comprehensible reading material for the workshop participants. Teachers also urged the mothers to encourage their young children's experimentations with written language, even though the writing was not conventional (Macías-Huerta & Quintero, 1990).

In a project in Atlanta, Georgia, ESL parents with some ability in English came together with their children so that the parents could share stories of their lives in their various homelands. Teachers involved in the program helped put these stories into written English narratives, which then became a source of reading material for children and their parents. This project also utilized computers, motivating adults and children to learn to use the computer so that they could produce final versions of their stories.

Consider bringing parents and children together in workshop sessions that will both facilitate better understanding of your philosophy and pedagogy and contribute to children's and adult literacy.

■ **Use Parental Knowledge**

There is substantial evidence indicating that working-class immigrant families engage in a variety of home literacy practices. However, because these events often do not match the schools' views of literacy, family literacy practices may go unacknowledged or may even be viewed as standing in the way of children's academic development. For several years, educator Luis Moll and some of his colleagues have been working with teachers both to investigate literacy practices in U.S. and Mexican households and to develop innovations in literacy teaching in the schools based on these practices, related to what Moll calls "funds of knowledge" (Moll, Amanti, Neff, & González, 1992). Moll has used the term *funds of knowledge* to describe bodies of skills and knowledge that accumulate in all communities and households. He and his colleagues contend that family and local community knowledge and skills can be tapped strategically by teachers and used to promote academic achievement (González, 1995).

Early childhood education teacher Marla Hensley (1995) wrote about how she applied the concept of funds of knowledge to her kindergarten classroom. Hensley chose the family of one of her students for a series of extended home visits in which, with the assistance of a questionnaire, she learned about this family in depth. As she got to know the child's father, she discovered that he was an expert gardener, and she recruited him to help her class prepare and plant both a vegetable and a flower garden. As she continued to visit in the home, Hensley found that the father had excellent communication skills and that he was a skilled musician, playing both keyboard and guitar and composing original songs. This parent agreed to write some children's songs and to help create a musical based on the folktale "The Little Red Hen." Then Hensley and this parent worked together to help the children learn the songs and later to rehearse and perform the musical.

SPECIAL FEATURE 11.1 (continued)

Learning in detail about the talents and abilities of one parent gave this teacher an appreciation for parental funds of knowledge in general. This teacher developed a sensitivity to the possibilities of making use of parental experts across her school curriculum.

It may not be feasible for you to spend extensive amounts of time visiting families and conducting in-depth interviews with parents. Nonetheless, it is still possible to learn something about the kinds of knowledge and skills possessed by the parents of your learners. Parent-teacher conferences might be one venue for asking parents about their talents and interests. You may want to send a letter home asking parents to jot down hobbies, areas of expertise, and so on that they would be willing to share with the children. Listen to your children as they talk about the activities they engage in at home. Bring parental expertise into the classroom. Make parents' real-life knowledge an integral part of your curriculum, thus providing children with the opportunity to use spoken and written language to accomplish real-world learning.

meaning. Timeka then imitates, to the best of her ability, this process. Since the adults in Timeka's life also regard her efforts as meaningful, Timeka is encouraged to refine both her understanding of the functions of print and her writing skills. In that regard, Timeka's scribbles are to writing as her babbling was to talking. Because her parents approve and support her attempts instead of criticizing or correcting them, Timeka practices both talking and writing. This dual effort also simultaneously develops her understanding that words and thoughts can be expressed both orally and in print (Fields, Spangler, & Lee, 1991; Sulzby, Teale, & Kamberelis, 1989). Parents who value their children's growing literacy abilities also encourage their development. The following example demonstrates how ten-year-old Jeffery and his dad use Jeffery's literacy ability to accomplish an exciting task of putting together a mini-car using parts from the lawn mower engine.

DAD: Jeff, reread that last part of the directions again.

JEFFERY: It says to bolt the gasoline engine to the metal crossbars at right angles Dad. But Dad, what we have doesn't look like the drawing. (Both Jeffery and Dad study the diagram and go back to read the previous steps.)

DAD: Good going, Son!

Jeffery and his dad are using their ability to read to accomplish a task that is of great interest to both of them. Dad's reliance and genuine appreciation of his son's literacy reinforces reading as a great tool to achieve a big goal.

Dilemmas Facing Modern Families

The "family in America—Black, White, Hispanic, and Asian—is actually in the throes of basic upheaval" (Carlson, 1990, p. xv). As evidence, Carlson cites the three factors most likely to affect school performance: the employment of both parents in more than 70 percent of nuclear families, the high divorce rate, and the increase in single-parent families. Research indicates that 40 percent of today's schoolchildren will have lived with a single parent by the time they reach the age of 18 (Flaxman & Inger, 1991). The financial and psychological stresses many single-parent families face may not allow parents either the time or emotional energy to sustain conversation or read to their children on a regular basis.

Another significant factor is the cycle of poverty and undereducation. Research consistently reveals that a child whose parent has poor literacy skills is at great risk of repeating the illiteracy cycle (Nord, Lennon, Liu, & Chandler, 2000: Christian, Morrison, & Bryant, 1998; Lonigan & Whitehurst, 1998). Likewise, Betty Hart and Todd Risley's (1995) study clearly demonstrates that welfare parents often transmit their limited vocabulary and lower oral communicative competence to their children.

Two factors span socioeconomic and cultural differences. First, as educators we must help parents understand the crucial role they play in helping their children become successful communicators, readers, and writers (Epstein, 1995). Secondly, we must build parents' knowledge of how to support their child's language and literacy development. How else will parents be able to fulfill their role as their child's first and most important teacher?

HELPING PARENTS AND PRIMARY CAREGIVERS BECOME EFFECTIVE FIRST TEACHERS

Helping parents become successful language and literacy models is one of a teacher's most important tasks. To fulfill this responsibility, teachers at all grade levels must interact with parents constantly! However, this role may be more challenging than many teachers initially anticipate. In this chapter, we describe two categories of communication efforts—personal interactions and classroom instructional publications.

Personal Interactions

Personal interactions are opportunities for parents, other family members, and early childhood teachers or caregivers to share information about a child's individual needs in two-way conversations. Personal interactions also offer unique opportunities for modeling communication and literacy strategies. These personal interactions include home visits, parent workshops, parent–teacher conferences, and telephone calls.

Today's teachers need to be aware that English may not be their children's parents' dominant language; therefore, a teacher may need to have a translator help with communication during personal interactions. Regardless of how teachers choose to communicate, observation shows that whatever the content, medium, or language, any message is enhanced if it is delivered warmly, respectfully, and with genuine concern.

Home Visits.   Perhaps the best way to reach parents prior to children's formal entry into preschool or kindergarten is through home visits.

> "We are going to be heroes today," Dana Donor said as she sat down on the couch in the living room of the Youtie family. She was met by four-year-old Tate and three-year-old Darrin. They watched as Dana opened the children's storybook *One Duck Stuck.*
>
> "Are you ready to help?" Dana asked as she sat between Tate and Darrin. For the next 15 minutes, Dana and Marie, the children's mother, take turns reading to the children and encouraging them to interact with the pictures in the book. "How many frogs are trying to help this silly duck? Let's count them," Marie suggests, and Tate and Darrin use their fingers to count the fearless frogs. Dana asks, "What animal do you think will try to help next? How many animals do you think will be on the next page? How would you have helped the duck?" After they had read the story, two very happy children asked to have it read again!
>
> After the second reading, Dana passes out crayons and paper and asks the children to draw their favorite animal. "I'm gonna write my name," says Tate. "See T-A-T-E." Tate has recently begun using conventional print to write her name. Darrin announces loudly, "Me too!" Darrin uses scribble writing for his name. As the children work on their pictures, Dana and Marie step back to engage in a brief conversation about the children's stage of development in the writing process. After the children complete their pictures, they tape them to the refrigerator.
>
> Dana Donor is a teacher-demonstrator in a well-documented parent–child home program that has a long track record of helping at-risk families. Her job is to help bring stories to life for children as young as two. The demonstrator also helps parents learn how to make reading fun. During the twice-a-week visits, Marie is able to observe Dana model story-reading strategies, encourage language interactions, and support beginning writing opportunities. Marie and Dana also discuss age-appropriate language and literacy behavior (see Table 11.1). After several weeks of participating in the program, Marie is more confident and has begun to try some of these techniques using the storybooks Dana leaves in the home for between-visits use. Marie is pleased that she is learning how to keep her children actively engaged during storytime.

Teachers of school-age children also need to continue their efforts to help parents support their child's rapidly growing reading and writing skills. Table 11.2 offers age-appropriate activities that parents can use at home.

Since the 1970s, these types of home-visit programs have increased in number, especially as states and communities refocus attention and resources on young children. The programs can have long-term benefits, by offering maternal and child health care, parenting education, school readiness skills, guidance on how to create a literate home environment, and a direct link to other social services (Jacobson, 1998).

Parent Workshops.   Another strategy for involving and directly informing parents of preschool and kindergarten students about how to support their children's language and literacy learning is through parent workshops. The purpose of the

TABLE 11.1 Age-Appropriate Language and Literacy Activities: Birth to Age 5

		LANGUAGE	PRINT RECOGNITION	
Months		*Speaking/Listening*	*Receptive/Reading*	*Expressive/Writing*
0–6	CD	Babbling, extensive sound play.		
	PS	Talk to baby. Sing to baby. Make direct eye contact with baby when speaking. Use parentese.		
6–12	CD	Echolia, vocables, first words.	Is able to listen to short stories. Wants to handle books.	
	PS	Label objects. Scaffold child's language efforts.	Provide cloth and cardboard book. Read to your child.	
12–24	CD	Begins to use words and gestures. Responds to simple requests.	Begins to recognize environmental print/logos.	Begins to use writing implements to make marks.
	PS	Listen and actively respond. Read stories. Engage in frequent conversations.	Confirm print recognition, "Yes, that is Coke." Read to your child.	Offer chalk/chalkboard, paper, and crayons.
24–36	CD	Uses simple sentences, adds new words rapidly, and experiments with inflection.	Attends to pictures—describes pictures, then begins to form oral studies reflecting pictures.	Knows print has meaning and serves practical uses. Uses scribble marking.
	PS	Engage child in complex conversations frequently. Listen to child.	Read, read, read to your child. Ask child to label characters and objects.	Provide access to many type of writing implements/paper.
36–48	CD	Proficient language user. Engages in dramatic play. Likes to learn songs.	Attends to pictures. Repeats familiar story phrases.	Print recognition—may write letterlike units, and nonphonetic letterlike string.
	PS	Serve as coplayer in dramas. Teach new songs. Ask child questions to encourage two-way dialogue.	Reread familiar stories. Ask open-ended questions. Begin home library.	Model writing process. Demonstrate your interest in your child's writing efforts.
48–60	CD	Uses language to obtain and share information.	May begin to recognize individual words.	Conventional writing emerges as letter–sound relationship develops.
	PS	Offer logical explanations. Listen and respond thoughtfully and thoroughly.	Shared reading. Frequent visits to library and expand home library. Demonstrate your enjoyment of reading.	Begin writing notes to child. Read your child's writing.

CD: Child's development
PS: Parental support

TABLE 11.2   Age-Appropriate Literacy Activities: Age 6–12

AGE	LITERACY ACTIVITIES
6–7	Develop a shopping list with child's input During the shopping trip, ask child to find specific items on the aisle you are currently shopping. Write/draw a card to send to relatives. Find specific items in a pantry. Read storybooks to child; ask child to read to you.
8–10	Ask child to sort coupons for shopping trip. Ask child to review the *TV Guide*. Ask child to find a phone number in the phone book. Ask child to look up a word for you in the dictionary. Ask child to read to younger sibling(s). Ask child to read directions for a recipe.
11–12	Ask child to write shopping list will you dictate. Ask child to find specific sites on the Internet. Ask child to read movie reviews. Ask child to read a short article from the newspaper. Read a brief magazine article to child.

workshops is to share explicit information about the children's development and the class curriculum, and to provide practical suggestions that parents may use at home to support their child's learning (Brown, 1994).

To begin, the teacher should design a needs assessment survey to determine parents' special interests and needs. In Figure 11.1, we provide an example of a survey that covers possible workshop topics, meeting times, and child care needs.

After the survey has been returned and the results tallied, the early childhood teacher should publish and advertise the schedule of workshops. We recommend selecting the top two or three topics and identifying the time(s) and day(s) listed as convenient for most of the parents. Generally the most convenient meeting place is the classroom or the school's or center's multipurpose room. Scout troops, parent volunteers, or older students may provide child care. Teachers should be sure to have parents confirm their participation in the workshop (see Figure 11.2). This will allow the teacher to prepare sufficient materials and secure appropriate child care arrangements. Send reminders the day before the workshop. Don't be surprised if only a few parents attend initially. Parent workshops may be a new concept, and it might take a little time for parents to become comfortable with this approach to parent–teacher interactions.

Teachers must prepare for a parent workshop. They need adequate supplies. They may need to organize the room. They need to set up refreshments. (Parent–teacher organizations or center budgets can often reimburse teachers

Dear Parents,

   Did you know you are your child's first and most important teacher? One of my responsibilities as a teacher is to work and share all my teaching colleagues for the benefit of the special student we share—your child. I would like to conduct several workshops this year, and I need to know what topics you are most interested in learning about. Please complete the survey and have your child return it by _____. Place "X" by topics you would like to attend.

____Storytelling techniques   ____Linking Play and Literacy

____Writers Workshop   ____Kitchen Math and Science

____Rainy Day Fun   ____Learning Motivation

____Other_____
_____

What is the most convenient day? What time is the most convenient for you to attend a workshop?

____Monday   ____Tuesday   ____9:00am   ____4:00pm   ____7:00pm____

____Wednesday   ____Thursday

____Friday   ____Saturday

Would I use a child-care service if one was provided?

____Yes—list number of children needing care ____.

____No.

FIGURE 11.1   Needs Assessment Survey

for refreshments.) Teachers need to prepare name tags, double-check child care arrangements, develop an evaluation form for the workshop, and create a detailed lesson plan!

   There are several points for teachers to remember when running a parent workshop. First, the workshop should begin promptly. Second, start with a get-acquainted

Dear Parents:

The topics that most most of you wanted to learn more about were
Writing Workshop, Kitchen Math and Science, and Rainy Day Fun!

The times that were convenient for most of you were:

Wednesdays at 7:00 p.m. and Saturdays at 9:00 a.m.

I have used this information to create a schedule of workshops for the Fall semester. Please fill out the personal information and put an X by the workshops you plan to attend. All workshops will be in my classroom. Refreshments will be served. Dress comfortably as we might be getting messy. Children will be cared for in the cafeteria by the Girl Scouts and their leaders.

Name_____ Phone_____

Number of children needing child care_____.

_____Writers Workshop—Wednesday, October 2, 7:00–8:30 p.m.
_____Kitchen Math and Science—Saturday, November 4, 9:00–10:30 a.m.
_____Rainy Day Fun—Wednesday, November 9, 7:00–8:30 p.m.

FIGURE 11.2 Workshop Confirmation Form

activity to put people at ease and begin the workshop on a relaxed, positive note. Third, remember that parents should not be lectured to; instead, they should experience hands-on, highly engaging activities. After the parents have engaged in the activity, provide brief, specific information about the theory underlying the process. Most importantly, remember to smile. When the teacher has a good time, the parents will also! Finally, have parents complete the workshop evaluation form; this will help to continually refine the quality of the workshops (see Figure 11.3).

Phone Calls.   Another powerful tool for communicating with parents is the telephone. Unfortunately, phone calls have traditionally been reserved for bad news. However, successful teachers have found that brief, positive, frequent telephone conversations help establish a strong partnership with parents (Fredericks & Rasinski, 1990). When parents receive a phone call about something exciting at school, they immediately sense the teacher's enthusiasm for teaching their child and are more likely to become involved in classroom activities. Thus, whenever possible, the phone should be used as an instrument of good news. Whenever a call is made and for whatever reason, it is important to have the parents' correct surname; there are many stepfamilies in today's schools. All calls to parents should be documented. A phone log can be effective method to manage and maintain a record of phone conversations (see Figure 11.4). This log should contain a separate page or section for each student in the class, making it easy to trace the contacts with specific parents (Enz, Kortman, Honaker, 1993).

Parent–Teacher Conferences.   Children are complex, social individuals who must function appropriately in two very different cultures—school and home. Parents need to understand how a child uses his or her social skills to become a productive member of the school community. Likewise, experienced teachers appreciate the student's home life and recognize its significant influence on a student's behavior and ability to learn. Partnerships reach their full potential when parents and teachers share information about the child from their unique perspectives, value the student's individual needs and strengths, and work together for the benefit of the student.

The best opportunity teachers have for engaging parents in this type of discussion is during parent–teacher conferences. Conferences should feature a two-way exchange of information. There are generally two types of parent–teacher conferences—preestablished conferences that review the child's classroom progress, and spontaneous conferences that deal with a range of specific concerns that occur throughout the year.

Progress Review Conference.   The progress review conference is an opportunity for parents and teachers to share information about children's social interactions, emotional maturity, and cognitive development. One way to help a parent and teacher prepare to share information during the conference is a preconference questionnaire. The teacher sends the questionnaire home to the parent to complete and return prior to the conference. In Figure 11.5, we present the notes made by Manuel's mother as she prepared for her conference with Ms. Jones, her son's kindergarten teacher. The information Mrs. Rodriguez provides also tells Ms. Jones what concerns she has; therefore, Ms. Jones has a better idea about how to focus the conference. Remember, it may be necessary to have this letter and questionnaire translated into the language spoken in the home.

Workshop Name_____ Date_____

List two activities you enjoyed or learned the most about.

1.

2.

List any information that was not useful to you.

The workshop was (mark all that apply):

____clear   ____confusing   ____enjoyable   ____boring

____too short   ____too long ____informative

Any other comments?

Thanks for attending!

FIGURE 11.3   Workshop Evaluation

During the progress review conference, the teacher, of course, will share information about the student's academic progress. In Chapter 10, we discussed how to develop and maintain assessment portfolios and document observational data for each student. The portfolio allows the teacher an opportunity to document the student's development over time. In addition to academic progress, most

SPECIAL FEATURE 11.2

Teaching with Word Walls—A Workshop for Families

BY ANNAPURNA GANESH

It is 7 p.m., and Mrs. G. opens her door; several families begin to fill her first grade classroom. The children begin to show their parents and siblings the word walls, which are the subject of the workshop tonight.

Mrs. G offers monthly family workshops that reinforce her literacy program at a highly diverse school. She has realized that by including the whole family she encourages more families to participate; since they don't need to worry about child care for younger siblings, they are more likely to attend. Mrs. G also knows that the older siblings of her first graders are excellent tutors and often help to reinforce instructional concepts at home.

Mrs. G opens her workshop by briefly explaining that word wall activities are a tool designed to reinforce words that young children frequently see when reading and use when writing. Tonight she illustrates how the word walls work, by using rhyming word families (at, bat, cat, fat, rat, etc.). She explains that the purpose of the word wall activities is to help children learn to spell high-frequency vocabulary words and begin to use them in their writing (Cunningham, 1999).

To begin, she gives the families three sets of word family cards (at, ag, et) and asks the parents to shuffle the cards and to lay them on the table–with the words facing up. This variation of a card-game approach allows parents to play word wall activities at home without having to use wall space. Mrs. G continues by explaining that there are several goals for using the word wall interactively:

- Support the teaching of important general principles of words and how they work.
- Foster reading and writing.
- Provide reference support for children during their reading and writing.
- Promote independence as students work with words in reading and writing.
- Provide a visual map to help children remember patterns in words.

- Develop a vocabulary bank for reading and writing.

The first game Ms. G. teaches families is *Be a Mind Reader.* She demonstrates the game and gives them a handout with the "rules." First the parent thinks of a word on the wall and then gives five clues to that word.

- "It's one of the words on the table." (always the same clue)
- "It has _____ letters." (number of letters in the word)
- "It begins with _____" (the beginning sound)
- "It has a _____" (a clue about the word)
- Use the word in a sentence.

The families practice the game two or three times, choosing a different word each time. Mrs. G. circulates among the table and encourages the families.

The second game Mrs. G introduces is the *Word in a Jar.* She models the game with two of the children. Sharma and Kim put their word cards in a jar and then add several cards that have "SORRY" printed on them. Sharma pulls a card out of the jar. If she recognizes the word and says it correctly she gets to keep the card. If Sharma misses the word, then Kim has a chance to recognize and say the word on the card. If someone draws a SORRY card, they must put all their word cards back into the jar. The game is played for five minutes, and the winner is the person who has the most cards.

Another more difficult variation of this game includes spelling the word. For example, when Sharma draws the card, she reads the word on the card to Kim. Then Kim must spell the word. If Kim spells the word correctly then she gets to keep the word card. If not then Sharma shows Kim the card and they spell the word together, but the word goes back into the jar. This game is also played for five minutes and the winner has the most word cards. Mrs. G explains that one of the reasons the children like this game so much is the element of chance that the SORRY cards add. You can know all the words but if you get the SORRY card, you lose!

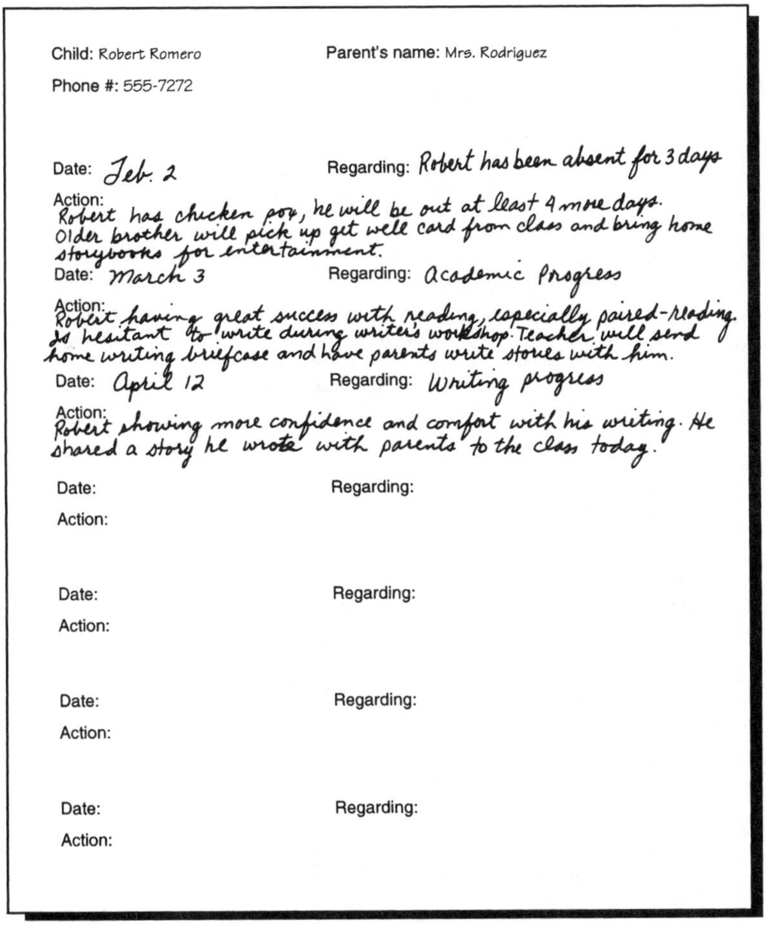

Child: Robert Romero

Parent's name: Mrs. Rodriguez

Phone #: 555-7272

Date: *Feb. 2*   Regarding: *Robert has been absent for 3 days*

Action:
*Robert has chicken pox, he will be out at least 4 more days.
Older brother will pick up get well card from class and bring home
storybooks for entertainment.*

Date: *March 3*   Regarding: *Academic Progress*

Action:
*Robert having great success with reading, especially paired-reading.
Is hesitant to write during writer's workshop. Teacher will send
home writing briefcase and have parents write stories with him.*

Date: *April 12*   Regarding: *Writing progress*

Action:
*Robert showing more confidence and comfort with his writing. He
shared a story he wrote with parents to the class today.*

Date: Regarding:

Action:

Date: Regarding:

Action:

Date: Regarding:

Action:

Date: Regarding:

Action:

FIGURE 11.4   Phone Call Log

parents want to know about their children's social interactions and classroom behavior. The observational data that the teacher has recorded helps provide a more complete picture of the student in the classroom context.

When working with parents, teachers are encouraged to use a structured format during the progress review conference. The structure keeps the conference focused and increases the chance of both teachers' and parents' concerns being adequately discussed. Billie Enz and Susie Cook (1993) recommend that progress review conferences be structured as follows:

- *Positive statement and review conference format*—The teacher's first sentence helps establish a foundation for a proactive conference. Positive statements are sincere and usually personal—for example, "Martha is so eager to learn."

Dear Parent,

    To help us make the most of our time, I am sending this questionnaire to help facilitate our progress review conference. Please read and complete the questions. If you have any other concerns, simply write them down on the questionnaire and we will discuss any of your inquiries during our time together. I look forward to getting to know both you and your child better.

1. How is your child's overall health?
   Good, but Manuel gets colds alot.

2. Are there specific health concerns that the teacher should know about? (include allergies)
   Colds and sometimes ear infections.

3. How many hours of sleep does your child typically get?
   About 9

4. Does your child take any medication on a regular basis? If so, what type?
   He takes penicillin when he has ear infections.

5. What are the names and ages of other children who live in your home?
   Maria, 9; Rosalina, 7; Carlos, 3.

6. How would you describe your child's attitude toward school?
   He likes school.

7. What school activity does your child enjoy most?
   P.E. and art

8. What school activity does your child enjoy least?
   Math

9. What are your child's favorite TV shows?
   Power Rangers, Ninja Turtles

   How many hours of TV will your child generally watch each night?
   Three

10. What is the title of your child's favorite storybook?
   Where the Wild Things Are.

11. How often do you read to your child?
   His sisters read to him most nights.

12. What other activities does your child enjoy?
   Playing soccer.

Other concerns:
   I can't read his writing. His sisters' was good in Kindergarten.

FIGURE 11.5   Preconference Questionnaire

Next, the teacher should briefly review the three steps of the conference: (1) parent input, (2) teacher input, and (3) closure. Reviewing the conference process relieves stress and actually helps keep the conference moving in a positive direction.

- *Ask for parental input*—"First, I am going to ask you to share with me what you have observed about your child this year that makes you feel good about his learning and then what concerns you have about his progress." It is important for parents to focus on their child's academic and social strengths when they meet with you. It is also important for you to know the parents' view of their child's major academic and social concerns.

- *Offer teacher input*—"Then I will share some of your child's work with you and my observations about his progress. We'll discuss ideas that will continue to encourage his learning."

■ *Closure*—"So let's review the home and school (or center) activities that we think will best help your child continue to progress."

The success of the parent–teacher relationship depends on the teacher's ability to highlight the child's academic and social strengths and progress. When areas of concern are discussed, it is important to provide examples of the child's work or review the observational data to illustrate the point. Often the issues the parents reveal are directly related to the concerns the teacher has. Whenever possible, connect these concerns, as this reinforces the feeling that the teacher and the parents have the same goals for helping the child learn. It is essential to solicit the parents' views and suggestions for helping the child and also to provide concrete examples about how they might help the child learn.

To make sure both teacher and parents reach a common understanding, briefly review the main ideas and suggestions for improvement that were discussed during the conference. Allow parents to orally discuss their views of the main ideas of the conference, and check the parents' perceptions. Finally, briefly record the parents' oral summary on the conference form. Figure 11.6 is a progress review conference form from Manuel's conference.

Student–Parent–Teacher Conferences. A rather new innovation in progress review conferences is the inclusion of the student. The student participates equally—sharing work, discussing areas in which he or she has noticed improvement, and establishing academic and/or social goals. This type of conference requires that the students are active participants in selecting what work will be featured in their portfolios. In addition, the teacher must begin to help students develop the skill to evaluate their own performance. For example, an editing checklist, such as the one described in Chapter 9, may be created with the students for use in the writing workshop. The checklist also serves as an instructional guide. Students consult the checklist to make sure they have used correct punctuation, have begun sentences with capital letters, or have asked another student to proofread their work. Student–parent–teacher conferences are a natural outgrowth of frequent student–teacher conferences.

Because a three-way conference may be a new experience for parents, it is important for the teacher to establish guidelines for parents and students. A letter sent home explaining the format of the conference and discussing each person's role is essential. Parents are encouraged to ask open-ended questions, such as:

"What did you learn the most about?"
"What did you work the hardest to learn?"
"What do you want to learn more about?"

Questions such as these encourage students to analyze their own learning and also help them to set new goals. Parents should not criticize their child's work or focus on any negative aspect of any material that is presented during the conference. Negative comments, particularly from parents, will only inhibit learning and dampen excitement about school.

Student's name: *Manuel Romero*   Parent's name: *Mary Romero*

Conference date: *Nov. 1*   Time: *4:30 p.m.*

Positive Statement: *Manuel is so eager to learn*

Review Conference steps:
Our conference today will consist of three parts. First, I will ask you to review your child's progress, sharing with me both academic/social strengths and areas of concern. Next, I'll review Manuel's work with you and discuss his academic/social strengths and areas in which we will want to help him grow. Finally, we will discuss the main points we discussed today, and review the strategies we decided would help Manuel continue to make progress.

1. Ask for Parent Input: What have you observed about Manuel this year that makes you feel good about his learning? (Take notes as parent is sharing)

Manuel likes school, drawing, friends, stories.

What are your main concerns?

His writing looks like scribbles. He's not reading yet but he likes stories read to him.

2. Teacher Input: I would like to share some observations about Manuel's work and review both areas of strengths and skills that need to be refined. *Manuel interest in reading is wonderful. He is eager to write in class journal. Though his printing is still developing, he is beginning to use "invented" spelling. Look at this example in his portfolio.*

MT MpN PR RG2

Mighty Morphin Power Rangers

Notice how he is separating the words. Ask him to read his work for you if you are having difficulty decoding or deciphering it. His printing skills will improve naturally with time and encouragement. He is really progressing well. Sometimes young girls develop finger muscles sooner. We need to support his efforts. Manuel enjoys sharing his writing in class with his friends and his art work is full of detail. Manuel has many friends and gets along easily with others.

3. Closure: Let's review those things we talked about that will facilitate continued success. (Teacher needs to write down this information as the parent talks)

a. *Manuel's printing is "okay" for him.*

b. *Manuel is writing. I am surprised to see that he really is writing. I just need to have him read for me. Then it's easier for me to figure out what his*

c. *letters say.*

FIGURE 11.6   Progress Review Conference Form

The following is a brief excerpt of a three-way conference at the last conference of the year. Notice that six-year-old Manuel does most of the talking:

MOTHER: Manuel, what have you worked hardest to learn?

MANUEL: My writing. I can do it faster and all of my friends can read my stories now. I draw really good ill-stra-suns—everybody likes them.

> **TEACHER:** Manuel, can you read your parents a favorite story you wrote? [Manuel begins to read his five-page, illustrated story with great confidence. He underlines the words with his fingers and reads with great fluency. His parents smile and are impressed with their son's comical pictures.]
>
> **TEACHER:** Manuel, what else have you been working on?
>
> **MANUEL:** My counting and adding. I can add really good and I helped Shelly and Robbie put together the 100 number board. [Manuel proudly takes his parents over to the 1–100 number board.]
>
> **FATHER:** Manuel, what do you want to learn next year?
>
> **MANUEL:** I want to read more big books [referring to the multichapter books]. I want to get my own library card. I want to learn the number tables, you know, like María [his fourth-grade sister] can do. I want to write more books about the rangers and stuff.

Student-Led Conference. The older child may actually run the conference with the teacher serving as conference recorder (see Figure 11.7). Once again it is important to prepare the parents for their role in the student-led conference.

The following is a brief excerpt of a student-led conference being conducted by Jasmine Jackson, who is a student in a fourth- and fifth-grade multiage classroom.

> **JASMINE:** Mom, Dad, this term we studied fantasy as a genre. We studied the features of popular stories like the J. K. Rowling's Harry Potter series and *The Lion, The Witch and the Wardrobe* by C. S. Lewis. After we analyzed the features we began to write our own fantasy stories. I cowrote and illustrated with Amee this story, "The Witch's Wand."
>
> **TEACHER:** Jasmine, what part of this project pleased you most about your progress? Why?
>
> **JASMINE:** It made it easier to write a good fantasy story after we studied the parts of a good fantasy and talked about the story elements.
>
> **MR. JACKSON:** You really wrote a good story. The illustrations are also really good, honey.

Specific Problem Conference. Occasionally, concerns will emerge that require the teacher to work with the family immediately. The following case studies illustrate how teacher and parents worked together to help identify and resolve a specific problem in the home that was creating tension in the child's school life.

Sibby. Four-year-old Sibby started preschool as a happy, confident child. She loved storytime and had memorized several stories that she had heard her family read to her over and over again. Sibby had learned to print her name and was excited about writing her own letters and stories (scribble writing and some letterlike streams). Sibby was interested in environmental print and often brought empty product boxes and wrappers to preschool because she was proud

Student name _____   Date: _____

Parent Name _____   Teacher's Name _____

Grade Level _____   School _____   District _____

_____, discussed the following topics during the conference:
(student's name)

1.

2.

3.

_____ was pleased with his/her progress in the following area(s):

Area _____   Reason _____

Area _____   Reason _____

Area _____   Reason _____

_____ is working to improve his/her progress in the following area(s):

Area _____   Plan _____

Area _____   Plan _____

Area _____   Plan _____

FIGURE 11.7   Student-Led Conference Summary Form

that she recognized words and specific letters. She loved playing in the dramatic play center and frequently demonstrated her understanding of the many practical functions of print. After winter break, Sibby's behavior changed abruptly. She said she didn't know how to read when she went to the library center, and she refused to write during journal time. Her teacher, Mrs. Role, quickly called Sibby's parents.

Mr. and Mrs. Jacobs came to preschool the following day. Mrs. Role described the dramatic change in Sibby's behavior and asked the Jacobses if they had any ideas about what may have caused the change. The Jacobses had also noticed a change in Sibby's confidence. After discussing her behavior, they mentioned that Sibby's grandmother, a retired high school English teacher, visited their home over winter break. They were surprised that Sibby's grandmother had been critical of their display of Sibby's stories on the refrigerator. Grandmother stated, "That youngster needs to know the correct way to write!" She felt that "praising Sibby's scribbles kept her from wanting to learn the right way to form letters," but they were sure Sibby had not overheard any of these comments. However, they remembered that Grandmother babysat Sibby one afternoon just before her visit was over. Mrs. Jacobs promised she would talk to Grandmother about the babysitting episode.

The following week, Mrs. Jacobs reported that Grandmother had decided "it was time someone taught Sibby how to print her letters properly." During the afternoon Grandmother and Sibby were together, Sibby had spent most of the time practicing making letters correctly. In addition, Grandmother required Sibby to say the letter sounds as she repeatedly wrote each letter. Grandmother told Sibby that she "would not be able to read and write until she knew all her letters and their sounds."

The Jacobses and Mrs. Role attributed Sibby's reluctance to read and write to her grandmother's inappropriate instructional efforts. Sibby was going to need a great deal of encouragement and support from her parents and her teacher to regain her confidence.

Steven. Mrs. Garcia, Steven's mother, called Mr. R., Steven's third-grade teacher. Mrs. Garcia was concerned that, for the past few mornings, Steven, a new student, had complained of a stomachache. On this morning, Steven had begun to cry and stated that he did not want to go to school. Mr. R. suggested that Mrs. Garcia come to school that afternoon for a conference. During the day Mr. R. observed Steven carefully. As Mr. R. watched Steven, he noticed that Steven could easily read and comprehend the materials during a running record, yet during paired reading, he seemed less confident in his oral reading and hesitant to participate in the story discussion. Mr. R. was puzzled. During recess, he watched to see whom Steven was playing with. Mr. R. soon realized that Steven was not playing with the students; instead, he just walked around the perimeter of the playground or watched the others play. During center time in class, Steven again worked by himself.

That afternoon, when Mrs. Garcia came to the conference, Mr. R. thanked her for calling. Mr. R. asked Mrs. Garcia whom Steven played with at home. Mrs. Garcia named one boy, who was in the fourth grade. Mr. R. then told Mrs. Garcia about his observation. He told Mrs. Garcia that he suspected that, because Steven was new to the neighborhood and school, he had not had a chance to make new friends. Steven might be feeling self-conscious and lonely. Mr. R. felt that Steven would eventually make friends in class and would regain his confidence. Mr. R. was planning to move Steven's desk closer to two very friendly children in the class. However, he wondered if Mrs. Garcia could help by encouraging Steven to invite one or two of the children in the class home to play. Mrs. Garcia agreed that Steven was sometimes shy and had difficulty making new friends. She also felt that she could talk to Steven about his feelings about being the new kid at school. Both Mr. R. and Mrs. Garcia agreed that Mrs. Garcia would call Mr. R. the next week to again share information about Steven's adjustment.

Classroom Instructional Publications

Classroom instructional publications are designed to describe the students' learning activities or directly inform parents about specific literacy concepts. They may include informal news flashes, weekly notes, and a more formal monthly newsletter that features regular columns such as Dear Teacher, Family Focus, and Center Highlights. With the growing number of homes with computers and Internet access, some teachers may be able to publish their classroom instructional publications on a classroom Web site or Listserv. Of course, teachers must check with their students' parents to learn which homes have access to these services. Sadly, those teachers who work with young students from low socioeconomic families likely will find few families with Internet access. The digital divide is widening, rather than narrowing, in the United States. Communities are struggling to learn how to increase Internet access to families of modest financial means.

Informal Weekly Notes.   Because consistent communication helps create a sense of community, the authors strongly recommend weekly, or at minimum, bimonthly notes. Frequent communications allow teachers the opportunity to

- provide a bond between school and home experiences,
- extend parents' understanding of developmentally appropriate curricula,
- involve parents in assessing the student's growth and development,
- encourage parents to reinforce and enrich students' learning, and
- strengthen the working partnership between parents and teacher.

Weekly notes are typically one page in length and generally include (1) information about upcoming events; (2) items about students' achievements; (3) explanations about the curriculum that help parents understand how children learn to read and write; (4) practical and developmentally appropriate suggestions for working with students; and (5) recognition of parents who have helped support classroom learning—for example, parents who accompanied the class on a field trip (Gelfer, 1991).

It is important for informal weekly notes to be reader-friendly and brief and to suggest successful activities for parents and students to do together. These suggestions typically are well received if they are stated in a positive, proactive manner—for example, "Reading to your child just ten minutes a day helps your child become a better reader," not, "Your child will not learn to read unless you read to her or him."

Figure 11.8 is a sample of an informal weekly note. Observe how Ms. Jones reviews the previous week's activities, taking the opportunity to thank parents who have provided supplies or support. Next she describes the focus of this week's curriculum and provides suggestions that will help parents reinforce this information at home. Notice how Ms. Jones uses friendly, everyday language to introduce and explain new concepts, and suggests realistic, content-appropriate literacy activities that encourage parents to become involved in classroom learning. Trade Secret 11.1 presents another way that students can participate in sharing

Dear Parents:

Last week our field trip to the hospital was exciting and we learned even more about how doctors and nurses serve our community. Have your child read you the story he or she wrote and illustrated about what we learned on our hospital journey. One of the most exciting stops in the hospital was the nursery. All of the children were interested in their own first stay at the hospital. Perhaps you will be able to share your memories about that event. A great big thank you to Mrs. Delgato and Cecille Ortiz for helping to chaperon. They also helped our students write their stories.

This week we will discuss fire safety at home and school. Our first lesson is called "Stop, Drop, and Roll," which teaches us what to do if our clothes catch on fire. Next, we will discuss the proper use and storage of matches and lighters. We will also map a safe exit from our room in case of fire and review appropriate behavior during an emergency (no talking, listen to teacher's directions, leave all possessions, walk the planned escape route). We will actually have a schoolwide fire drill to practice these skills. Because you and your child's safety is so important, I am asking that you work with your child to draw and label a map of your house and design the best fire escape route. Drawing the map and labeling the rooms of your house teach your child vocabulary words and reinforce the fire safety concepts I am teaching in school. On Friday we will go to our local fire station. Attached to this note is a permission slip. Since this is a walking field trip, I will need at least four parent volunteers. I hope you can join us. To help all of us learn more about fire safety, the Fire Marshall will provide the children and their families with a booklet called "Learn Not To Burn." The book is available in Spanish also. If you would like additional copies, let me know. Please review this informative and entertaining booklet with your child.

To learn even more about fire safety and fire fighters, you might wish to read the following books to your child. These books are available in the classroom, school, and local public library.

EL Fuego, by Maria Ruis and Josep McParramon, Harron's.
Pumpers, Boilers, Hooks and Ladders: A Book of Fire Engines,
by Leonard Everett Fisher, Dail Press.
Fire Fighters, by Ray Brockel, Children's Press.
Curious George at the Fire Station, by Margret and H.A. Rey, Houghton Mifflin.
Puedo Ser Bombero, by Rebecca Hankin, Children's Press.
The Whole Works: Careers in a Fire Department, by Margaret Reuter, Children's Press.

If you have any personal experiences in the area of fire safety, please let me know and you can be an Expert Speaker for our classroom.

Sincerely, Mrs. Jones

FIGURE 11.8   Informal Weekly Note

their views of the week—a child-authored "Student Note" that summarizes their perceptions of what they have learned.

News Flashes.   There are times when events occur that require immediate publication or an upcoming activity warrants attention, such as reminding parents that their children will attend school for only a half day because of parent–teacher conferences or alerting parents that their children will be on the TV news tonight. Teachers may use news flashes to inform parents about TV programming that is relevant to curriculum the class is currently studying. News flashes might also be used to tell a parent about a noteworthy event in the student's life that day (e.g., Zack wrote his first letter today!).

TRADE SECRET 11.1
Student Notes

BY DAWN FOLEY

As a third-grade teacher, I have found another way that children can communicate about what they are learning in school with their parents: a personal weekly summary letter called a "note." For example, in Figure 11.9, Abby describes her view of things that she has learned during the week, ranging from the concept of probability in math to the literature she is reading. The letter is written in a form that leaves space for the teacher to make comments also. In this case, I commented on the fact that Abby won first place in our Academic Fair Project.

Fantastic Week!!

Dear Mom & Dad,

This week in March we did probability. We took a couple of time tests too. Also we learned about counting change. It was fun.

In reading we red Mrs. Piggie Wiggie. We read a few. They were called Mrs. Piggie Wiggie and the radish cure, Mrs. Piggie Wiggie and the selfishness cure, Mrs. Piggie Wiggie and the tiny bitetaker. They were really good books.

I can't wait till we get to make T-shirts . This was so fun!!! Do you think we'll do that in fourth grade? I hope so.

It was fun wearing P.J.'s to school.

We have a mistery and we're trying to find out who is the mistery guest is? We have a few clues. I don't remember what the clues are but I think it might be Mrs. Gayhart. But I'm not quite sure. I have a mother day gift for you but I'm not telling what it is.

Love,
Abby

I am so proud of you and your Academic Fair Project!! WOW, WAY TO GO Abby 1st Place!!! Yeah!!!

FIGURE 11.9   Abby's Note to Her Parents

Monthly Newsletters.　　Like weekly notes, monthly newsletters create a sense of community. The goal of monthly newsletters should be to provide parents with specific information about children's literacy development. In addition, monthly newsletters offer parents an opportunity to preview the curriculum and classroom projects for the upcoming month. As most parents have extremely busy schedules, monthly newsletters help them plan ahead and thus increase the likelihood that they will be able to participate in school activities. Monthly newsletters are generally two or three pages in length and typically use a two- or three-column format. Regular features, such as Dear Teacher, Family Focus, Curriculum Overview, Center Highlights, and Monthly Calendar inform parents in a direct, but fun and interesting, manner. In Figure 11.10, we provide a sample kindergarten newsletter written for the month of October. Notice the regularly featured columns.

Dear Teacher Letters.　　As the sample newsletter demonstrates, parents frequently have questions about reading to their children. An effective way to address these inquires is through Dear Abby–type letters. The teacher frames the questions based on common concerns she hears from the parents. The following are examples of typical parent questions, answered by advice based on Jim Trelease's (1989) work.

> **DEAR TEACHER:**　My three-year-old often becomes restless when I read stories to him. What can I do to keep his interest? *Signed, Wiggle-Worm's Mom*
>
> **DEAR WIGGLE-WORM'S MOM:**　While most children enjoy having stories read to them, most young children also have a short attention span. Hence, younger children need to be actively involved in the reading. Asking your son to predict what he thinks will happen next or asking him to point to a character or discuss some aspect of the illustration is an excellent way to keep his attention.
>
> **DEAR TEACHER:**　I have three children, and our evenings are hectic to say the least! I also work, so the time I have is limited. When is the best time and for how long should I read to my kids? *Signed, Watching the Clock*
>
> **DEAR WATCHING:**　Excellent question! Many parents have multiple responsibilities, and time is always an issue. The best time is whenever you can consistently schedule about fifteen to twenty minutes alone. For most parents, that time appears to be just before bed. However, some parents report that they find time right after the evening meal. Whenever you feel rested and can give your children fifteen to twenty minutes of undivided time is the best time to read to them.
>
> **DEAR TEACHER:**　My four-year-old son wants to hear the same story over, and over, and over. Is this normal? Shouldn't I read a new book each night? *Signed, Repeating Myself*
>
> **DEAR REPEATING:**　As adults we tend to like variety, but most young children between the ages of two and seven have a favorite story, and this storybook may be as comforting to them as their best-loved stuffed toy.

Ms. Jones' October Newsletter

Kindergarten Curriculum

 It's October and the Kinder-gartners in Ms. Jones' class are learning about our 5 senses— Halloween style! During this month we will learn about sight: how our eyes work, and eye health and safety. We will also have our vision tested. We will study the super sense of smell: How the nose and olfactory nerves work, and how smell and memory are related. We will learn how the ear hears and discover how hearing aids work. We will test our tongues to determine how the sense of taste works to detect sweet, salty, sour, and bitter. Finally, we will learn about the largest organ on our bodies—our skin! The sense of touch can teach us many things about our world.

Dear Teacher: Questions about Reading.

Dear Teacher,
Hola! Both my husband and I speak and read Spanish. Though our son speaks both languages, would it confuse him if we read him story books in Spanish?
Signed, Bilingual/Biliterate

Dear Bi-double L,
How wonderful it is that your son is already speaking two languages! It is perfectly fine to read books written in Spanish to him in Spanish—just as you would read books written in English to him in English. While he is learning to read in both languages, he will also begin to write in English and Spanish.

Parent Partnership: Your Child Learns to Write.

DR TUTH FRE ILS MI TUTH
PLS HEL ME FD et

Can you read this? This is a note to the tooth fairy. It was written by a child who lost her first baby tooth. Let's decode this note together.

DR TUTH FRE ILS MI TUTH

Dear Tooth Fairy, I lost my tooth.

PLS HEL ME FD et

Please help me find it.

As adults, we have been conditioned to read only conventional spelling. On first glance, this note may resemble only a string of letters. On closer inspection, we detect that its writer is trying to convey an important message. When young children begin to use print, their parents and teachers should encourage all attempts. Treating a child's scribbles or letter streams as important and meaningful encourages the child to continue her efforts. As she experiments with reading and writing, her understanding of the rules of our language increases. Eventually, develop-mental or invented spelling matures into more conventional spelling. To read more about this process you might want to read *Spell. . . is a four letter word* by J. Richard Gentry, (1987) from Heinemann Publishing Company in Portsmouth, New Hampshire.

(cont.)

FIGURE 11.10   Monthly Newsletter

So the question becomes how to have both variety and comfort. At this age, favorite books tend to be short, so one suggestion is to read two or three books at storytime. Try reading the new books first and the favorite book last. When your child begins to read along with you, this is the per-fect time to have him read this favorite book to you or to another child in

Preparing for Parent/Student/Teacher Conferences

Conferences are wonderful opportunities for parents, student, and teacher to sit beside one another to share the students' work and review their progress. In our class each student will share the contents of his/her portfolio with both parents and teacher.

In the first half of the 20-minute conference, students will display and discuss their writing and perhaps read some of their stories. They will explain why certain products were included in the portfolio and why they believe these particular pieces best demonstrate their learning efforts. The students will also show the parents and teacher some of the work they completed at the beginning of the school year and compare it to how they are performing today. During this part of the conference, it is important for parents to listen to the student's self-evaluation. Parents are encouraged to ask open-ended questions, such as:

- What did you learn the most about?
- What did you work the hardest to learn?
- What do you want to learn more about?

These questions encourage students to analyze their own learning and also help them set new learning goals for themselves. Parents should not criticize the child's work or focus on any negative aspect of any material that is presented from the portfolio. Negative comments will only inhibit learning and dampen excitement about school. During the last ten minutes of the conference, the student will be excused so that parents and teacher have an opportunity to talk about any concerns the parents may have. Be sure to complete the Preconference Questionnaire and return it prior to the conference so that the teacher may be better prepared to discuss your concerns.

October Calendar

3rd	– Visit with the eye doctor: vision testing
7th	– Visit the audiologist: hearing tests
15th	– My Favorite Smells Day: bring in your favorite smell
18th	– Taste-testing day
19th	– School pictures day–dress bright
23rd	– Touch and tell day
28th–29th	– Parent/Student/Teacher Conference
31st	– Halloween/5 senses party

Remember: Weekly notes will provide details for each event.

Story Books for October

Georgie's Halloween, by Robert Bright (Doubleday)

The Teeny-Tiny Woman, by Paul Galdone (Clarion)

The Berenstain Bears: Trick or Treat, by Stan and Jan Berenstain (Random House)

Clifford's Halloween, by Norman Bridwill (Scholastic)

ABC Halloween Witch, by Ida Dedage (Garrard)

Who Goes Out on Halloween, by Sue Alexander (Bank Street)

It's Halloween, by Jack Prelutsky (Greenwillow)

FIGURE 11.10 Continued.

your household. Frequently a child's favorite book becomes the first one he will read independently.

DEAR TEACHER: When I read my five-year-old daughter a book at story-time, I worry about her comprehension skills. Should I ask questions? *Signed, Just the Facts*

DEAR FACTS: I'm so glad you asked that question. The stories you read will frequently inspire your child to share many of her thoughts, hopes, and fears. These discussions are obviously more important than reciting any particular detail. In fact, quizzing children about story details will only make storytime an unpleasant activity for both of you. Instead, ask open-ended, opinion questions, such as "Which was your favorite part?" or "Why do you think Max stared at the Wild Things?" Storytime will also motivate your children to ask you questions! Take your time, share your views, and allow your child to hear your thought process. This activity will do more to teach them about story interpretation than 1,000 fact questions! P.S. Did you know that Sendak's relatives served as the model for the Wild Things?

Family Focus.   Because many parents have a number of questions about how their child will learn to write, it becomes essential for teachers to proactively communicate information about the normal developmental process of writing. To help parents learn about emergent writing, teachers may wish to use a more formal, direct instruction approach, such as a Your Child Learns to Write column in the monthly newsletter, like the example in Figure 11.10. We recommend that before any student's writing is sent home, the teacher educate parents about the developmental writing stages. The following is an example of the most common questions parents ask about their child's writing development. The answers provide a sample of the tone and depth of information the column should contain.

■ *When does my child really start to write?* We live in a culture where print is used to communicate. Therefore, children begin to read and write informally long before they enter school. By the time children are able to pick up a pencil or crayon and draw or scribble, they are demonstrating their knowledge that these marks mean something, and the first step toward written communication has begun.

■ *When my child draws or scribbles, does that mean that I should begin to teach him or her how to hold the pencil and form letters correctly?* When your child first began to sing songs, did you start teaching him to play the piano? No, of course not! But you did enjoy the songs he or she sang, and you sang along. This is exactly the approach parents should take when their child first begins to draw or scribble write. Say, "Tell me about what you wrote about." Listen to the answer and compliment the effort.

■ *How can I encourage my child's writing?* When children watch adults write a grocery list or a letter or pay bills, they are often motivated to imitate this writing. Usually, all children need are the writing materials—paper, markers, crayons, pencils—and they will take the ideas from there. Occasionally, you could suggest that they might wish to write a letter to Grandmother or leave a note for the tooth fairy. Another perfect opportunity to encourage writing is during their dramatic play. When children play house, they can write grocery lists or leave phone messages—all you need to do is provide the writing materials and praise.

A particularly exciting activity is to have your child choose a favorite stuffed animal. The stuffed animal takes a field trip to Grandmother's house or to preschool with the child. That night, parents and child may write about and illustrate a story about "The Adventures of _____ at _____." Children will write frequently if they feel their attempts to communicate are accepted and valued as meaningful.

■ *Isn't handwriting practice important for learning to read and write?* Learning the correct written form of a letter is called *handwriting.* It is an opportunity for children to gain control of the small muscles in their fingers and hands. However, handwriting drills do not teach children how to read and write. A child who exhibits excellent penmanship will not necessarily learn to read or communicate in written form any faster than the child whose writing still resembles scribbles. Critical comments about a child's handwriting efforts can stifle the joy of communicating. When a new scribe begins to learn the "how" of writing, it is far better to praise the efforts. This will encourage the child to write more.

■ *How do I read my child's written work?* Start by asking your child to tell you what was written. The information provided will give you context. These clues should enable you to figure out what the scribble, shapes, or letters represent. Children tend to progress through predictable developmental stages on the way to conventional spelling. This progression may proceed from scribbles, to letter strings, to single letters representing whole words or thoughts, to invented spelling, to conventional spelling. Invented spelling is using two or three letters to phonetically represent a word—this is sometimes called developmental spelling.

H fi   hpe fi   hapy fi   happy
(happy)   (happy)   (happy)

■ *Should I correct my child's invented/developmental spelling?* Have you ever changed what you wanted to write simply because you were unsure of the spelling of a word? Research reveals that children write less and use only a limited vocabulary of known words if their spelling is criticized. However, young children of six or seven who are encouraged to use their invented spelling will often write extensive stories with complex vocabularies. Parents may help children sound out phonetic words or spell more difficult words if the child asks for assistance.

Student-Authored Newsletters.   Teachers of older students may wish to involve their classes in writing their own monthly newsletter. This provides students with an authentic purpose for writing and allows them to share their perceptions of important events at school. In Trade Secret 11.2, middle-school teacher Michelle Gary describes how she helps her students produce a monthly newsletter.

Thus far, this chapter has provided a number of communication strategies and highlighted the importance of ongoing communications to parents. One-shot publicity campaigns (e.g., read to and write with your child) do not provide parents with sufficient information or the long-term motivation they need to become

TRADE SECRET 11.2
Student-Authored Monthly Newsletter

BY MICHELLE GARY

Most intermediate-grade-level teachers assume that, because their students are older and more verbal, they will share pertinent information about their classes with their parents. This is simply not the case. Likewise, many intermediate-grade-level teachers believe that most parents are not as interested in what their children do in school as the parents of younger children are. This, too, is a false assumption. I have found that most parents of intermediate students feel out of touch with the activities and requirements of the classrooms and greatly appreciate newsletters that inform them of school activities.

I have found that monthly newsletters create a sense of community and offer parents an opportunity to preview the curriculum and classroom projects for the coming month. The monthly sixth-grade language arts class newsletters are generally one to two pages in length. The students include features such as "What I Learned" and "From a Student's Eye View." I supply the calendar for the coming month and curriculum overview.

At the middle-school level, I involve students in the following ways:

1. The last fifteen to twenty minutes on Friday, my students review the week's learning and suggest their views of the most important and interesting events.
2. I list their responses on the board.
3. Each of my students then chooses a topic from the list and writes a short descriptive paragraph.
4. I collect the paragraphs and select several to use in the newsletter.

The student-authored monthly newsletter has several positive features:

- It serves as a closure and summarization activity each Friday.
- My students have an opportunity to practice journalistic writing.
- Each of my students can author at least one article during the year.
- Parents receive frequent communications about classroom activities from the students' perspective.
- My students have an opportunity to publish their works for others to read and appreciate.

involved in a meaningful literacy program. Instead, consistent, frequent, positive information that includes highly practical suggestions will help parents support their child's education. Beyond communicating, however, teachers may also need to provide other types of support to help parents fulfill their role as their child's first teachers. In the remainder of this chapter, we discuss the teacher's role as educational resource and community connection.

TEACHERS AND SCHOOLS AS PROFESSIONAL RESOURCES

"In some schools there are still educators who say, 'If the family would just do its job, we could do our job.' And there are still families who say, 'I raised this child; now it is your turn to educate her'" (Epstein, 1995, p. 702). Most often, students who need the most help come from families that need the most support. Schools and centers that wish to make a significant difference in the lives of these students must find ways to offer support and forge successful school–family partnerships (Gardner, 1993–1994). Fortunately, most educators believe that educating a child requires at least two teachers—the one at school or the center and the one at home. Following are concrete suggestions that teachers may use to help parents fulfill their role as first teacher.

Sharing Instructional Materials and Offering Guidance

Teachers frequently recommend that parents read to their children (Becker & Epstein, 1982). Unfortunately, many parents face great financial hardships and cannot provide a large number of quality reading materials in their homes. Further, parents may not know how to encourage and engage their children's interest in reading (Richgels & Wold, 1998). To help parents to fulfill their role as partners in literacy programs, it is vital for teachers to work with these families to offer easy access to both books and writing materials (Brock & Dodd, 1994) and guidance in how to use them (McGee & Richgels, 1996).

Classroom Lending Library. Susan Neuman's 1999 study examined the effect of flooding more than 330 child care centers with storybooks. The results of her study confirm that children who have access to high-quality storybooks and teachers who are trained to support students' storybook interactions score significantly higher on several early reading achievement measures than students who have not experienced high-quality storybooks and trained teachers. In other words, it is critically important for children to have easy access to high-quality storybooks. Further, it is essential that parents and child care providers know how to support a child's early interactions with print. Though most public schools possess libraries, students generally are restricted to borrowing only one or two books a week. Some child care centers use public libraries with similar restrictions. While this may be appropriate for older students who can read chapter books, this quantity is insufficient for young students who are learning how to read. Young children should have the opportunity to have at least one new book an evening. One way to ensure early literacy development at home and foster the home–school connection is through a classroom lending library. A classroom lending library allows students to check out a new book each day, thus ensuring that all parents have an opportunity to read to their child frequently.

The acquisition of quality books for daily checkout is the first step in establishing a classroom lending library. Since the students will exchange their book each day, all a teacher needs to begin a library is one book per child.

Managing the classroom lending library requires that all books contain a library pocket and identification card. The teacher needs to create a classroom library checkout chart. When a student borrows a book, she simply removes the book's identification card and replaces it in her name pocket on the classroom checkout chart. The teacher can easily see what book each student has checked out at a glance.

The rules that accompany the classroom lending library are simple. A child may borrow one book each day. When the book is returned, the child may check out another. Teaching the children to manage the checkout routine is easy. When the children enter the classroom in the morning, they return their books to the library by removing the book's identification card from their name pocket. They place the identification card back in the book's library pocket, and they place the book back on the shelf. The children may select new books anytime throughout the day.

Writing Briefcase.   Another popular option that may be included as part of the classroom lending library is the writing briefcase. The briefcase can be an inexpensive plastic carrying case or a canvas portfolio. Inside the briefcase, the teacher may provide writing paper, colored construction paper, markers, pens and pencils, glue, tape—anything that might stimulate a student to write a story, make a greeting card, design a book cover, or create whatever they can imagine. Depending on the size of the class, teachers may have seven or eight writing briefcases—enough so that four or five students may check out the materials each day, and two or three extras so that the teacher has time to replenish the briefcase supplies frequently and conveniently. The briefcases are numbered, and each has a library pocket and identification card. The checkout procedures follow the same routine as for library books.

The writing briefcase may also contain explicit suggestions that encourage parents to use writing to communicate with their children.

Book Bags.   Yet another way to encourage family participation and successfully engage and guide parents' literacy interactions with their children is through book bags (Barbour, 1998–1999). Like writing briefcases, book bags may be checked out of the classroom lending library for a week at a time. Book bags contain a collection of high-quality books and offer informal, interactive activities for extending children's language and literacy acquisition. When designing the bags, teachers need to consider their students' developmental stages, interests and experiences, and literacy levels. The book bags (nylon gym bags) typically contain three or four books and activities inspired by a specific theme (see Figure 11.11 for sample book bag themes). In addition, each bag contains two response journals (one for the child and one for the parent). Some bags contain tape recorders and the tapes that accompany the books. The tapes and tape recorders are particularly important for parents who may not be able to read English. Each bag also contains an inventory that helps parents and children keep track of and return materials assigned to each bag.

Teachers typically initiate the program by sending home a letter describing the program. In addition to the introductory letter, each family also receives a contract. The terms of the contract are simple: Parents promise to spend time regularly reading to their children; students promise to spend time with the books and activities and treat each bag with care; and teachers promise to instill a love of reading in students and to manage the program. All three participants sign the contract.

FIGURE 11.11   Sample Book Bag Themes

Counting Theme

Hillanbrand, W. (1997). *Counting Crocodiles.* Orlando: FL: Harcourt Brace.

Kirk, D. (1994). *Miss Spider's Tea Party.* New York: Scholastic Editions Inc.

Barbieri-McGrath, B. (1998). *Hershey's Counting Board Book.* Wellesley, MA: Corporate Board Book.

Alphabet Theme

Wilbur, R. (1997). *The Disappearing Alphabet.* New York: Scholastic.

Alexander, M. (1994). *A You're Adorable.* New York: Scholastic.

Martin, B., & Archambault, J. (1989). *Chicka, Chicka, Boom Boom.* New York: Simon & Schuster Children's Publishing.

Rhyming Books

Goldston, B. (1998). *The Beastly Feast.* New York: Scholastic.

Slate, J. (1996). *Miss Bindergarten Gets Ready for Kindergarten.* New York: Scholastic.

Wood, A. (1992). *Silly Sally.* Orlando: FL: Harcourt Brace.

Getting Dressed

Degen, B. (1996). *Jesse Bear, What Will You Wear?* New York: Simon & Schuster Children's Publishing.

London, J. (1997). *Froggy Gets Dressed.* New York: Viking Children's Press.

Regan, D. (1998). *What Will I Do if I Can't Tie My Shoe?* New York: Scholastic.

The book bag project has been highly successful in many teachers' classrooms. The book bags supply parents with the appropriate materials and explicit guidance, which in turn

- empower and motivate them to become teachers of their own children,
- encourage them to provide supportive home learning environments, and
- expand their knowledge of how to interact with their children.

Videotape.   As more schools have access to video cameras, another option to consider is creating a videotape lending section for the classroom library. Videotape has the potential to become an exceptional tool for teaching parents about storybook reading skills. The teacher may wish to videotape himself or herself reading an exciting storybook. While reading a book to the students, the teacher has the opportunity to demonstrate oral fluency, enthusiasm, and the use of different voices to make the story characters come alive. In addition, the teacher can illustrate how open-ended, predictive questioning strategies can facilitate students' active involvement during storytime. Likewise, using retelling prompts, the teacher can demonstrate how students discuss story events with each other and share their unique and meaningful perspectives. These informal instructive videos may significantly help parents improve and expand their own story-reading skills. Students may check out both the videotape and the storybook. The video and accompanying storybook may be stored in a large self-sealing plastic bag. The same checkout procedures as for the library books or writing briefcases may be used.

Schools as Community Resources

Because literacy is a critical component for success in all aspects of community life, schools are beginning to extend opportunities for all community members to become involved in producing literate citizens. In extending our view of literacy beyond the classroom, we also expand our views of the traditional roles of schools. In the past decade, an increasing number of schools have chosen to provide for the social, medical, and educational needs of the families in their community (Liu, 1996; Patton, Silva, & Myers, 1999). In Special Feature 11.3, readers will find a discussion of the major components of family resource schools.

Teacher as Community Contact

Teachers also need to think beyond the classroom and consider the many ways reading, writing, talking, and listening enhance all facets of a person's life in the home, school, church, and workplace. Teachers then must consider how they can provide opportunities for students to learn about community literacy activities.

VIP Program.   The VIP, or very important person, program is an effective strategy for involving community members in classroom activities. Community members of all types—secretaries, politicians, lawyers, construction workers, computer programmers, maids, chefs, firefighters, flight attendants, store clerks, doctors, farmers, and professors—are invited to visit the classroom. When they arrive, they may read their favorite childhood story or perhaps an appropriate story that provides information about their career. After the VIP reads the story, she or he may wish to tell how reading and writing are used in the job. Students are sometimes surprised to hear how all types of jobs require literacy.

Another version of VIP is "Very Important Parents." As the name implies, this program features the students' parents. Parents may read their favorite childhood story to the class, share a favorite oral story, engage in a cooking activity using a favorite recipe, or perform another interesting activity.

Business Adoption Programs.   In this type of community involvement program, the school or classroom is adopted by a business in the community. Businesses often provide some financial support for the purchase of books or writing briefcases. In addition, employees of the businesses may be encouraged to be VIPs or help arrange a field trip to see business literacy in action (Rasinski & Fredericks, 1991).

SPECIAL FEATURE 11.3
Family Resource Schools

The way schools care about children is reflected in the way schools care about the children's families. If educators view children simply as students, they are likely to see the family as separate from the school. That is, the family is expected to do its job and leave the education of children to the schools. If educators view students as children, they are likely to see both the family and the community as partners with the school in children's education and development (Epstein, 1995, p. 701).

The major goal of family resource schools (also called *learning community schools*) is to strengthen the social and economic foundations of the neighborhood community. This goal is accomplished by providing extensive support to families, both before and after school. Family resource schools offer a broad range of services, including:

Student achievement and activity programs, such as

- community study hall with volunteer tutors,
- family read-alongs and family math classes,
- physical activity classes (gymnastics, dance, etc.),

- fine arts classes (arts and crafts, chorus, guitar, etc.),
- community garden.

Adult education and skill building, such as

- adult basic education,
- general equivalency diploma,
- English as a second language,
- Spanish as a second language,
- conflict management seminars,
- employment workshops.

Parent education courses, such as

- parenting education programs,
- positive discipline workshops,
- sex education workshops,
- gang prevention workshops.

Family support services, such as

- on-site case management,
- alcohol and drug prevention programs,
- before- and after-school child care,
- baby-sitting co-ops,
- food and clothing banks,
- primary health care,
- mental health services.

Children viewing the work of adults may be inspired to imitate and practice many of the reading and writing activities they see performed. Teachers may capitalize on this interest by creating dramatic play centers where the adopted business is a play theme, including all the literacy props and activities the children observed.

Community Tutors. Perhaps the most inclusive and dynamic method for involving adult community members in your classroom is as volunteer reading tutors. Retirees in particular enjoy the role of classroom grandparents. Classroom tutors regularly volunteer each week to cuddle with and read to a child. This consistent involvement is pleasurable for the volunteer and benefits the students. The value of spending individual time with another caring adult is beyond calculation.

Buddy Reading Programs.   To make a significant improvement in family literacy practices, it is essential that educators begin to develop the skills of tomorrow's parents. Older students may benefit greatly by participating in a parent apprenticeship program called Buddy Reading. Unfortunately, many older students do not have strong reading skills themselves. One major strength of the Buddy Reading program is that it has the potential to simultaneously improve older students' skills while supporting young students as they learn to read.

Primary, middle, or high school teachers may arrange to have their students work with preschool children during the school day, during lunch or recess, or in an after-school program. Whatever the time arrangement, the older reading buddies need to

- learn appropriate read-aloud behaviors, such as using an expressive voice, sharing and discussing pictures and print, and facilitating comprehension;
- identify characteristics of appropriate trade books, such as predictable books with repetitive, cumulative, rhythm and rhyme, and/or chronological patterns; and
- determine the younger reading buddy's interests and how to select appropriate books of interest to the child.

Sharing your literacy program within the school and throughout the local community is a win-win proposition. Older students learn how and why it is important to read to young children, while community members learn to appreciate the work of students and teachers in the schools. The following is a list of agencies that teachers may contact for more information and specific brochures about family involvement in the literacy process:

Association for Childhood Education International
The Olney Professional Building
17904 Georgia Avenue, Suite 215
Olney, MD 20832
www.acei.org/

National Association for the Education of Young Children
15009 16th Street, NW
Washington, DC 20036-1426
www.naeyc.org/

American Library Association
50 E. Huron Street
Chicago, IL 60611
www.ala.org/

International Reading Association
800 Barksdale Road
Newark, DE 19714
www.reading.org/

Reading Is Fundamental
P.O. Box 23444
Washington, DC 20026
www.rif.org/

SUMMARY

Families play a critical role in nurturing young children's literacy learning. Teachers must be prepared to reach out to parents to form two-way partnerships aimed at building parents' awareness of the important role they play in their children's literacy learning and providing them with strategies for nurturing their children's early reading, writing, and speaking development. Here, we return to the questions posed at the beginning of the chapter and briefly summarize the information presented.

■ *What is known about the relationship between what parents do and children's language and literacy development?*

Research demonstrates that when parents converse a great deal with their young children, the children's vocabulary and language fluency increase. Likewise, if parents consistently engage their children in storytime and storytelling, there is a greater likelihood that their children will enjoy reading and become interested in and knowledgeable about the reading process. Parents who support young children's early reading and writing attempts encourage their children to begin to read and write. In short, what parents do makes a great deal of difference in their children's literacy learning and success. The data suggest that many parents need their children's teachers' assistance in understanding the crucial role they play in helping their children become successful readers, writers, and speakers and that all parents need teachers to share strategies for nurturing their young children's early literacy learning.

■ *In what ways might early childhood teachers communicate personally with parents?*

Communication is the key to successful parent–teacher partnerships. True two-way communication must take place between parents and teachers. Teachers can communicate personally with parents through regular phone calls and conferences. Phone calls should be used to communicate good news, not just troubling news. Regularly scheduled progress review conferences offer opportunities for parents and teachers to share information about factors influencing students' reading and writing development. Specific problems conferences are needed when difficulties arise between regularly scheduled conferences. Sharing information about the student's literacy development might occur during a home visit, another forum for personal communication. Home visits also can be used to share information with parents on how to support their children's literacy learning. While teachers can share information one on one with parents during home visits, groups of parents can learn and interact together during parent workshops.

■ *How might teachers run a parent–teacher conference?*

Structuring the parent–teacher conference keeps the conference focused and increases the chance of both the teacher's and the parents' concerns being addressed. The teacher might begin with a positive statement and review the conference format, then ask for the parents' input, then offer input, and finally summarize points agreed on in the conference.

■ *In what ways might teachers communicate with parents in writing?*

Teachers can send home a variety of written publications including informal weekly notes, news flashes, and monthly newsletters. News flashes might be about classroom-related events, or they might be about something special the student has done that day. Some teachers might be able to use electronic mail to communicate with parents.

■ *What resources might an early childhood teacher provide to parents and parents provide to teachers to support young children's early literacy learning?*

Teachers are an important resource for parents. Through the use of classroom lending libraries, book bags, and writing briefcases, teachers can provide parents with the materials needed for home literacy activities. In addition, teacher-made videos can be sent home to show parents what they might do during an activity, like storybook reading, to help their child get the most from the activity.

Parents can be an important resource for teachers also. Teachers can recruit parents and other community adults to assist them in their efforts to offer students the best literacy education possible. Parents and members of the community might come to the classroom to read favorite stories to the class; local businesses might adopt the school or center and offer material and people resources; senior citizens might serve as classroom volunteers, offering a lap and cuddle for one-to-one sharing of a story; and older students might be reading buddies. Bringing parental and community expertise into the classroom does much to help build powerful partnership links between home and classroom and between classroom and community. These links are critical for all students. They offer young children the opportunity to use spoken and written language to accomplish real-world learning.

LINKING KNOWLEDGE TO PRACTICE

1. With a group of colleagues, plan a workshop for parents on some aspect of children's language and literacy learning. Write a letter to invite parents to the workshop. List the supplies you will need. List the refreshments. Develop an evaluation form. Create a detailed lesson plan. Offer your workshop to a group of parents.

2. Based on a classroom experience, write a one-page weekly note for parents.

3. Work with a group of colleagues to write a monthly newsletter for your class (the one for which you are reading this book).

4. Write a Dear Teacher question-and-answer for inclusion in a classroom newsletter. Make a photocopy for everyone in your college class.

5. Visit a school or public library. Question a librarian about the check-out policy for children. If this library allows children to check out only one book per week, write a letter to convince the librarian that this is inappropriate for children.

6. With a colleague, develop a bookbag around a theme for use by parents with their children.

REFERENCES

Adams, M. (1990). *Beginning to read: Thinking and learning about print.* Cambridge, MA. MIT Press.

Adams, M. (1991). A talk with Marilyn Adams. *Language Arts, 68,* 206–212.

Adams, M., Foorman, B., Lundberg, I., & Beeler, T. (1998). The elusive phoneme: Why phonemic awareness is so important and how to help children develop it. *American Educator, 21*(1 & 2), 18–29.

Afflerbach, P. (1993). Report cards and reading. *The Reading Teacher, 46,* 458–465.

Allen, R. (1976). *Language experiences in communication.* Boston: Houghton Mifflin.

Allen, V. (1991). Teaching bilingual and second language learners. In J. Flood, J. Jensen, D. Lapp, R. Squires (Eds.), *Research in the teaching of the English language arts* (pp. 356–365). New York: Macmillan.

Allexsaht-Snider, M. (1991). Family literacy in a Spanish-speaking context: Joint construction of meaning. *The Quarterly Newsletter of the Laboratory of Comparative Human Cognition, 13,* 15–21.

Allington, R. (1983). The reading instruction provided readers of differing reading abilities. *Elementary School Journal, 87,* 548–559.

Allington, R., & Woodside-Jiron, H. (1999). The politics of literacy teaching: How "research" shaped educational policy. *Educational Researcher, 28,* 4–13.

Allington, R. (2002). Setting the record straight. *Educational Leadership, 61,* 4, 22–25.

Allington, R. (2002). You can't learn much from books you can't read. *Educational Leadership, 60*(3), 16–19.

Altwerger, B., Diehl-Faxon, J., & Dockstader-Anderson, K. (1985). Read-aloud events as meaning construction. *Language Arts, 62,* 476–484.

Alvermann, D. E., & Phelps, S. F. (2005). *Content reading and literacy* 4th edition. Boston: Allyn and Bacon.

Anders, P. & Richardson, V. (1992). Teacher as game-show host, bookkeeper, or judge? Challenges, contradictions, and consequences of accountability. *Teachers College Record, 94,* 382–396.

Anderson, C. (2000). *How's it going?* Portsmouth, NH: Heinemann.

Anderson, C. (2005). *Assessing writers.* Portsmouth, NH: Heinemann.

Anderson, G., & Markle, A. (1985). Cheerios, McDonald's and Snickers: Bringing EP into the classroom. *Reading Education in Texas, 1,* 30–35.

Anderson, R., Heibert, E., Scott, J., & Wilkinson, I. (1985). *Becoming a nation of readers: The report of the Commission on Reading.* Washington, DC: National Institute of Education.

Anderson, R., & Pearson, P. D. (1984). A schema-theoretic view of basic processes in reading comprehension. In P. D. Pearson (Ed.), *Handbook of reading research* (pp. 255–291). New York: Longman.

Anderson, R., Wilson, P., & Fielding, L. (1988). Growth in reading and how children spend their time outside of school. *Reading Research Quarterly, 23,* 285–303.

Anderson, R. C., Pichert, J. W., & Shirey, L. L. (1983). Effects of reader's schema at different points in time. *Journal of Educational Psychology, 75,* 271–279.

Armbruster, B. B., Lehr, F., & Osborn, J. (2003). *A child becomes a reader: Birth through preschool.* Jessup, MD: The National Institute for Literacy.

Armbruster, B. B., Lehr, F., & Osborn, J. (2003). *A child becomes a reader: Kindergarten through grade 3.* Jessup, MD: The National Institute for Literacy.

Armbruster, B. B., & Osborn, J. (2001). *Put reading first: The research building blocks for teaching children to read.* Jessup, MD: The National Institute for Literacy.

Archbald, D., & Newman, F. (1988). *Beyond standardized testing: Assessing authentic academic achievement in secondary schools.* Washington, DC: National Association of Secondary School Principals.

Ashton-Warner, S. (1963). *Teacher.* New York: Simon & Schuster.

Atwell, N. (1987). *In the middle.* Portsmouth, NH: Heinemann.

Atwell, N. (1990a). *Coming to know.* Portsmouth, NH: Heinemann.

Atwell, N. (1990b). *Workshop 1: By and for Teachers* (Vol. 1). Portsmouth, NH: Heinemann.

Atwell, N. (1998) *In the middle, new understandings about writing, reading, and learning,* 2nd ed. Portsmouth, NH: Heinemann.

Au, K. (1993). *Literacy instruction in multicultural settings.* Fort Worth, TX: Harcourt Brace Jovanovich.

Au, K., Carroll, J., & Scheu, J. (1997). *Balanced literacy instruction: A teacher's resource book.* Norwood, MA: Christopher–Gordon.

Au, K., & Jordan, C. (1981). Teaching reading to Hawaiian children: Finding a culturally appropriate solution. In H. Tureba, B. Guthire, & K. Au (Eds.), *Culture and the bilingual classroom.* Rowley, MA: Newbury House.

Au, K., & Kawakami, J. (1991). Culture and ownership: Schooling of minority students. *Childhood Education, 67,* 280–284.

Au, K. (2006). *Multicultural issues and literacy achievement.* Mahwah, NJ: Lawrence Erlbaum Associates.

Auerbach, E. (1993). Reexamining English only in the ESL classroom. *TESOL Quarterly, 27,* 9–32.

Auerbach, E. (1995). Which way for family literacy: Intervention or empowerment. In L. Morrow (Ed.), *Family literacy: connections in schools and communities,* 11–28. Newark, DE: International Reading Association.

Aukerman, R. (1984) *Approaches to beginning reading.* New York, Wiley.

Avery, C. (1993). *And with a light touch: Learning about reading, writing, and teaching with first graders.* Portsmouth, NH: Heinemann.

Baghban, M. (1984). *Our daughter learns to read and write.* Newark, DE: International Reading Association.

Baker, L., Serpell, R., & Sonnenschein, S. (1995). Opportunities for literacy learning in the homes of urban preschoolers. In L. Morrow (Ed.), *Family literacy: Connections in schools and communities* (pp. 236–252). Newark, DE: International Reading Association.

Baldwin, D. "A Guide to Standardized Writing Assessment." *Educational Leadership, 62,* 72–75.

Barbe, W., & Milone, M., Jr. (1980). *Why manuscript writing should come before cursive writing* (Zaner-Bloser Professional Pamphlet No. 11). Columbus, OH: Zaner-Bloser.

Barbour, A. (1998/99). Home literacy bags: Promote family involvement. *Childhood Education, 75*(2), 71–75.

Barone, D. (1998). How do we teach literacy to children who are learning English as a Second Language? In S. Neuman & K. Roskos (Eds.), *Children achieving: Best practices in early literacy* (pp. 56–76). Newark, DE: International Reading Association.

Barrentine, S. (1996). Engaging with reading through interactive read-alouds. *The Reading Teacher, 50,* 36–43.

Barrera, R., Ligouri, O., & Salas, L. (1992). Ideas a literature can grow on: Key insights for enriching and expanding children's literature about the Mexican American experience. In V. Harris (Ed.), *Teaching multicultural literature in grades K–8* (pp. 203–243). Norwood, MA: Christopher-Gordon.

Bateson, G. (1979). *Mind and nature.* London: Wildwood House.

Baumann, J. F., Kame'enui, E. J., & Ash, G. E. (2003). Research on vocabulary instruction: Voltaire redux. In J. Flood, D. Lapp, J. R. Squire, J. M. Jensen (Eds.), *Handbook of research on teaching the English language arts* (2nd ed., pp. 752–785). Mahwah, NJ: Erlbaum.

Bear, D., Invernizzi, M., Templeton, S., & Johnston, F. (2003). *Words their way: Word study for phonics, vocabulary, and a spelling instruction.* Upper Saddle River, NJ: Merrill.

Bear, D. R, Invernizzi, M., & Johnston, F. (2003). *Words their way: Letter and picture sorts for emergent spellers.* Upper Saddle River, New Jersey: Pearson, Merrill, Prentice Hall.

Beck, I., & McKeown, M., (2001). Text Talk: Capturing the Benefits of Read-Aloud Experiences for Young Children. *Reading Teacher 55,* 10–20.

Beck, I., McKeown, M., & Kucan, L. (2002). *Bringing words to life: Robust vocabulary instruction. Solving problems in the teaching of literacy.* New York, NY: Guildford Publications, Inc.

Beck, I. L., McKeown, M. G., & Kucan, L. (2002). *Bringing words to life: Robust vocabulary instruction.* New York: Guilford Press.

Beck, I., McCaslin, E., & McKeown, M. (1981). Basal readers' purpose for story reading: Smoothly paving the road or setting up a detour? *The Elementary School Journal, 81,* 156–161.

Becker, H., & Epstein, J. (1982). Parent involvement: A study of teacher practices. *Elementary School Journal, 83,* 85–102.

Benton, B. (1985). *Ellis Island: A pictorial history.* New York: Facts on File.

Berger, J. (2001). A systematic approach to grammar instruction. *Voice from the Middle, 8,* 43–49.

Berger, M. (2003) *Spinning spiders.* Illus. by S. D. Schindler. New York: HarperCollins.

Berninger, V., Abbott, S., Reed, E., Greep, K., Hooven, C., Sylvester, L., Taylor, J., Clinton, A., & Abbott, R. (1997). Directed reading and writing activities: Aiming intervention to working brain systems. In S. Dollinger & L. DiLalla (Eds.), *Prevention and intervention issues across the life span* (pp. 123–158). Hillsdale, NJ: Erlbaum.

Bhavnagri, N., & Gonzalez-Mena, J. (1997). The cultural context of infant caregiving. *Childhood Education, 74,* 2–8.

Billmeyer, R., & Barton, M. L. (1998). *Teaching reading in the content areas: If not me, then who?* (2nd ed.). Aurora, CO: McRel.

Bird, L. B., Goodman, K. S., & Goodman, Y. M. (1994). *The whole language catalog: Forms for authentic assessment.* Santa Rosa, CA: American School Publishers.

Bishop, R. (Ed.). (1994). *Kaleidoscope: A multicultural booklist for grades K–8.* Urbana, IL: National Council of Teachers of English, 1994.

Bishop, W. (1995). Teaching grammar for writers in a process workshop classroom. In S. Hunter & R. Wallace (Eds.), *The place of grammar in writing instruction: Past, present, future* (pp. 176–187). Portsmouth, NH: Boynton/Cook Publishers.

Bissex, G. (1980). *GNYS AT WRK: A child learns to read and write.* Cambridge, MA: Harvard University Press.

Blachowicz, C. L. Z., & Fisher, P. (2004). Keep the "fun" in fundamental: Encouraging word awareness and incidental word learning in the classroom through word play. In J. F. Baumann & E. J. Kame'enui (Eds.), *Vocabulary instruction: Research to practice* (pp. 218–237). New York: Guilford Press.

Black, J. E. (2003). Environment and development of the nervous system. In M. Gallagher & R. G. Nelson (Eds.). *Handbook of psychology Vol. 3: Biological psychology* (pp. 655–668). Hoboken, NJ: Wiley.

Black, J., Puckett, M., & Bell, M. (1992). *The young child: Development from prebirth through age eight.* New York: Merrill.

Black, P., & Wiliam, D. (1998). Assessment and classroom learning. *Phi Delta Kappan, 80*(2), 139–148.

Blanchowicz, C., & Fisher, P. (2000). Vocabulary instruction. In M. Kamil, P. Mosenthal, P. D. Pearson, & R. Barr (Eds.), *Handbook of reading research* (vol. 3, pp. 503–523). Mahwah, NJ: Erlbaum.

Bloodsworth, J. (1993). *The left-handed writer.* Arlington, VA: ERIC Document Reproduction Service, ED356494.

Bodrova, E., & Leong, D. J. (2003). Building language and literacy through play. *Early Childhood Today,* 34–43.

Bond, G. L., & Dykstra, R. (1967). The cooperative research program in first-grade reading instruction. *Reading Research Quarterly, 2,* 5–141.

Boroski, L. (1998). The what, how, and why of interactive writing. In S. Collom (Ed.). *Sharing the pen: Interactive writing with young children.* Fresno, CA: San Joaquin Valley Writing Project.

Bortfeld, H., James, M. L., Golinkoff, R. & Rathbun, K. (2005). Mommy and me: Familiar names help launch babies into speech-stream segmentation. *Psychological Science, 16*(4), 298–304.

Bosma, B. (1992). *Fairy tales, fables, legends and myths* (2nd ed.). New York: Teachers College Press.

Bowman, B., Donovan, M. S., & Burns, M. S. (Eds.). (2000). *Eager to learn: Educating our preschoolers*. Washington, DC: National Academy Press.

Bowman, M., & Treiman, R. (2004). Stepping stones to reading. *Theory into Practice, 43,* 4, 295–303.

Brabham, E. G., & Lynch-Brown, C. (2002). Effects of teachers' reading-aloud styles on vocabulary acquisition and comprehension of students in the early elementary grades. *Journal of Education Psychology, 94,* 3, 465–472.

Bradley, P., & Bryant, L. (1985). *Children's reading problems*. New York: Oxford University Press.

Brady, S. (1992). *Let's make books*. Dubuque, IA: Kendall/Hunt.

Brandt, R. (1992). Overview: A caring community. *Educational Leadership, 49,* 3.

Bransford Barclay, J. R., & Franks, J. J., J. D., Barclay, J. R., & Franks, J. J. (1972). Sentence memory: A constructive versus interpretive approach. *Cognitive Psychology, 3,* 193–209.

Bravo-Villasante, C. (1980). *Historia y antologia de la literatura infantil iberoamericana* (Vols. 1 and 2; 2nd ed.). Madrid: Edita Doncel.

Bredekamp, S. (1989). *Developmentally appropriate practice.* Washington, D.C.: National Association for the Education.

Brice-Heath, S. (1993). Inner city life through drama: Imagining the language classroom. *TESOL Quarterly, 27,* 177–192.

Brock, D., & Dodd, E. (1994). A family lending library: Promoting early literacy development. *Young Children, 49*(3), 16–21.

Bromley, K. (1988). *Language arts: Exploring connections*. Boston: Allyn & Bacon.

Bromley, K. (1995). Buddy journals for ESL and native-English-speaking students. *TESOL Journal, 4*(3), 7–11.

Brooks, J., & Brooks, M. (1993). *In search of understanding: The case for constructivist classrooms.* Alexandria, VA: Association for Supervision and Curriculum Development.

Brosnahan, I., & Neuleib, J. (1995). Teaching grammar affectively: Learning to like grammar. In S. Hunter & R. Wallace (Eds.), *The place of grammar in writing instruction: Past, present, future.* Portsmouth, NH: Boynton/Cook.

Brown, J. (1994). Parent workshops: Closing the gap between parents and teachers. *Focus on Early Childhood Newsletter, 7*(1), 1.

Brown, M. (1947). *Goodnight moon*. New York: Scholastic.

Bruer, J. T. & Greenough, W. T. (2001). The subtle science of how experience affects the brain. In D. B. Bailey Jr., J. T. Bruer, F. J. Symons, & J. W. Lichtman (Eds.), *Critical thinking about critical periods* (pp. 209–232). Baltimore: Paul H. Brookes.

Bruner, J. (1980). *Under five in Britain*. Ypsilanti, MI: High/Scope.

Bruner, J. (1983). Play, thought, and language. *Peabody Journal of Education, 60*(3), 60–69.

Buckner, A. (2002). "Teaching in a world focused on testing." *Language Arts, 79,* 212–215.

Burke, J. (2000). *Reading reminders: Tools, tips and techniques*. Portsmouth, NH: Heinemann.

Burks, M. (2004). Effects of classwide peer tutoring on the numbers of words spelled correctly by students with LD. *Intervention in School and Clinic, 39,* 301–304.

Burns, M. S, Griffin, P., & Snow, C. E. (Eds.). (1999). *Starting out right: A. guide to promoting children's reading success*. Washington, DC: National Academy Press

Bus, A., van Izendoorn, M., & Pellegrini, A. (1995). Joint book reading makes for success in learning to read: A meta-analysis on intergenerational transmission of literacy. *Review of Educational Research, 65,* 1–21.

Buschman, L. (2003). Buddies aren't just for reading, they're for spelling too! *The Reading Teacher, 56,* 747–752.

Butler, A., & Turbill, J. (1984). *Towards a reading-writing classroom*. Portsmouth, NH: Heinemann.

Calderón, M., & Slavin, R. E., (Eds). (1999). Building community through cooperative learning. *Theory into Practice, 38.*

Calkins, L. (1980, February). Punctuate! Punctuate! Punctuate! *Learning Magazine,* 86–89.

Calkins, L. (1983). *Lessons from a child: On the teaching and learning of writing*. Portsmouth, NH: Heinemann.

Calkins, L. (1986). *The art of teaching writing.* Portsmouth, NH: Heinemann.

Calkins, L. (1991). *Living between the lines.* Portsmouth, NH: Heinemann.

Calkins, L. (1994). *The art of teaching writing.* Portsmouth, NH: Heinemann.

Calkins, L. (2001). *The art of teaching reading.* Portsmouth, NH: Heinemann.

Calkins, L., & Harwayne, S. (1987). *The writing workshop: A world of difference.* Portsmouth, NH: Heinemann.

Calkins, L., Montgomery, K., Santman, D., with Falk, B. (1998). *A teacher's guide to standardized reading tests.* Portsmouth, NH: Heinemann.

Cambourne, B. (1988). *The whole story: Natural learning and the acquisition of literacy in the classroom.* Auckland, New Zealand: Ashton Scholastic.

Canizares, S. (1997). Sharing stories. *Scholastic Early Childhood Today, 12*(3), 49–52.

Carey, S. (1979). The child as word learner. In M. Halle, J., Bresnan, & G. Miller (Eds.), *Linguistic theory and psychological reality* (pp. 264–293). Cambridge, MA: MIT Press.

Carlile, E., (1996). *Little Cloud.* New York, NY: Scholastic.

Carlson, A. (1990). *Family questions.* New Brunswick, NJ: Transaction.

Carnegie Corporation. (2004). *Achieving state and national goals, a long uphill road.* New York: Rand Corporation. Available: www.rand.org/publications/TR/TR180

Carnine, D., Silbert, J., & Kameenui E. (2004) Direct Instruction Reading NJ: Prentice Hall.

Carr, J., & Harris, D. (2001). *Succeeding with standards: Linking curriculum, assessment, and action planning.* Alexandria, VA: Association for Supervision and Curriculum Development.

Carr, M., & Claxton, G. (2002). Tracking the development of learning dispositions. *Assessment in Education, 9*(1), 9–37.

Carra, C. (1995). Reflecting on the rain forest in the third grade. In P. Cordeiro (Ed.), *Endless possibilities: Generating curriculum in social studies and literacy.* Portsmouth, NH: Heinemann.

Cazden, C. (1976). Play with language and meta-linguistic awareness: One dimension of language experience. In J. Bruner, A. Jolly, & K. Sylva (Eds.), *Play: Its role in development and evolution* (pp. 603–608). New York: Basic Books.

Cazden, C. (1988). *Classroom discourse.* Portsmouth, NH: Heinemann.

Chall, J. (1967). *Learning to read: The great debate.* New York: McGraw-Hill.

Chall, J. (1989). *Learning to read: The great debate* 20 years later—A response to "Debunking the great phonics myth." *Phi Delta Kappan, 70,* 521–538.

Chomsky, C. (1969). *The acquisition of syntax in children from 5 to 10.* Cambridge, MA: M.I.T. Press.

Chomsky, N. (1965). *Aspects of the theory of syntax.* Cambridge, MA: The MIT Press.

Christian, K., Morrison, F., & Bryant, F. (1998). Predicting kindergarten academic skills: Interaction among child-care, maternal education, and family literacy environments. *Early Childhood Research Quarterly, 13,* 501–521.

Christie, J. F., Roskos, K., & Vukelich, C. (2002). *Literacy in Play. Doors to Discovery: An Early Literacy Program.* Bothell, WA: McGraw-Hill/The Wright Group.

Christie, J. (1987). Play and story comprehension: A critique of recent training research. *Journal of Research and Development in Education, 21,* 36–43.

Christie, J. (1991). *Play and early literacy development.* Albany: State University of New York Press.

Christie, J. (1995). *Linking literacy and play.* Newark, DE: International Reading Association.

Christie, J., & Enz, B. (1992). The effects of literacy play interventions on preschoolers' play patterns and literacy development. *Early Education and Development, 3,* 205–220.

Christie, J., Johnsen, E. P., & Peckover, R. (1988). The effects of play period duration on children's play patterns. *Journal of Research in Childhood Education, 3,* 123–131.

Christie, J., & Stone, S. (1999). Collaborative literacy activity in print-enriched play centers: Exploring the "zone" in same-age and multi-age groupings. *Journal of Literacy Research, 31,* 109–131.

Chukovsky, K. (1976). The sense of nonsense verse. In J. Bruner, A. Jolly, & K. Sylva (Eds.), *Play: Its role in development and evolution* (pp. 596–608). New York: Basic Books.

Clark, E. (1983). Meanings and concepts. In J. Flavell & E. Markman (Eds.), *Handbook of child psychology: Vol. 3.* Cognitive development (4th ed., pp. 787–840). New York: Wiley.

Clark, M. (1976). *Young fluent readers.* London: Heinemann.

Clarke, A., & Kurtz-Costes, B. (1997). Television viewing, educational quality of the home environment, and school readiness. *Journal of Educational Research, 90,* 279–285.

Clarke, L. (1988). Invented spelling versus traditional spelling in first graders' writing: Effects on learning to spell and read. *Research in the Teaching of English, 22,* 281–309.

Clay, M. (1972). *Reading: The patterning of complex behaviour.* London: Heinemann.

Clay, M. (1975). *What did I write?* Auckland, New Zealand: Heinemann.

Clay, M. (1985). *The early detection of reading difficulties* (3rd. ed.). Portsmouth, NH.: Heinemann.

Clay, M. (1989). Telling stories. *Reading Today, 6*(5), 24.

Clay, M. (1991). *Becoming literate.* Portsmouth, NH: Heinemann.

Clay, M. (2000). *Concepts about print: What have children learned about the way we print language?* Portsmouth, NH: Heinemann.

Clay, M., & Cazden, C. (1990). A Vygotskian interpretation of Reading Recovery. In L. Moll (Ed.). *Vygotsky and education: Instructional implication and application of socio-historical psychology* (pp. 206– 222). New York: Cambridge University Press.

Cobb, C. (2003). Effective instruction begins with purposeful assessment. *The Reading Teacher, 57*(4), 386–388.

Cochran-Smith, M. (1984). *The making of a reader.* Norwood, NJ: Ablex.

Cochran-Smith, M., Kahn, J., & Paris, C. (1986, March). *Play with it; I'll help you with it; Figure it out; Here's what it can do for you.* Paper presented at the Literacy Research Center Speaker Series, Graduate School of Education, University of Pennsylvania.

Coerr, E. (1977). *Sadako and the thousand paper cranes.* New York: Yearling.

Cohen, B. K. (1995). *Make a wish, Molly.* New, York, NY: Bantam Doubleday Dell Publishing Group.

Cohen, L. (1999). The power of portfolios. *Early Childhood Today, 13*(5), 23–29.

Coley, R. J., & Coleman, A. B. (2004). *The fourth grade reading classroom.* Princeton, NJ: Educational Testing Service. Available: www.ets.org/research/pic/reading.pdf

Collin, B. (1992). *Read to me: Raising kids who love to read.* New York: Scholastic.

Collins, J. J. (1987). *The effective writing teacher: 18 strategies.* Andover, MA: NETWORK.

Collins, M. (1997). Sounds like fun. In B. Farber (Ed.), *The parents' and teachers' guide to helping young children learn* (pp. 213–218). Cutchoque, NY: Preschool Publications.

Connor, U., & Farmer, M. (1990). The teaching of topical structural analysis as a revision strategy for ESL writers. In B. Kroll, (Ed.). *Second language writers: Insights for the classroom.* New York: Cambridge University Press.

Cooper, J., & Kiger, N. (2001) *Literacy assessment: Helping teachers plan instruction.* New York: Houghton Mifflin Company.

Copeland, J. & Gleason, J. (1993). *Causes of speech disorders and language delays.* Tucson, AZ: University of Arizona Speech and Language Clinic.

Corballis, M. C. (1991). *The lopsided ape: Evolution of the generative mind.* New York: Oxford University Press.

Cordeiro, P., Giacobbe, M., & Cazden, C. (1983). Apostrophes, quotation marks, and periods: Learning punctuation in the first grade. *Language Arts, 60,* 323–332.

Corkum, V. & Moore, C. (1998). The origins of joint visual attention in infants. *Developmental Psychology, 24*(1), 28—38.

Cowley, F. (1997, Spring/Summer). The language explosion. *Newsweek: Your Child* (special edition).

Creech, S. (1994). *Walk two moons.* New York: Harper Collins.

Cruz, M. C. (2004). *Independent writing: One teacher–thirty-two needs, topics, and plans.* Portsmouth, NH: Heinemann.

Crystal, D. (1995). *Cambridge encyclopedia of the English language.* New York: Cambridge.

Csikszentmihalyi, M. (1990). *Flow, the psychology of optimal experience.* New York: Harper.

Culham, R. (2003) *6 + 1 Traits of Writing, the Complete Guide Grades 3 and Up.* New York: Scholastic.

Cunningham, A., & Shagoury, R. (2005). *Starting with comprehension: Reading strategies for the youngest learners.* Portland, ME: Stenhouse Publishers.

Cunningham, A., & Stanovich, K. (1998). What reading does for the mind. *American Educator, 21*(1 & 2), 8–15.

Cunningham, P. M. (1995). *Words they use: Word for reading and writing.* New York: Harper Collins.

Cunningham, P. M., Hall, D. P., & Sigmon, C. M. (1999). *The teacher's guide to the four blocks : A multimethod, multilevel framework for grades 1–3.* Greensboro: NC, Carson-Dellosa Pub. Co.

Cushman, K.(1995) *The Midwife's Apprentice.* New York: HarperCollins.

Cuyler, M. (1991). *That's Good! That's Bad!* New York, NY: Henry Holt.

Dailey, K. (1991). Writing in Kindergarten: Helping parents understand the process. *Childhood Education, 3,* 170–175.

Daniel, N., & Murphy, C. (1995). Correctness or clarity? Finding answers in the classroom and the professional world. In S. Hunter & Ray Wallace (Eds.), *The place of grammar in writing instruction: Past, present, future* (pp. 225–240). Portsmouth, NH: Boynton/Cook.

Daniels, H. (1994). Literature circles: Voice and choice in the student-centered classroom. York, ME: Stenhouse.

Danst, C., Lowe, L., & Bartholomew, P. (1990). Contingent social responsiveness, family ecology, and infant communicative competence. *National Student Speech-Language-Hearing Association Journal, 17*(1), 39–49.

Degroff, L., & Galda, L. (1992). Responding to literature: Activities for exploring books. In B. Cullinan (Ed.), *Invitation to read: More children's literature in the reading program* (pp. 225–240). Newark, DE: International Reading Association.

Delacre, L. (1989). *Arroz con leche: Popular songs from Latin America.* New York: Scholastic.

Delaware Department of Public Instruction. (1995). *New directions: English language arts curriculum framework.* Dover, DE: Author.

Delgado-Gaitan, C., & Trueba, H. (1991). *Crossing cultural borders: Education for immigrant families in America.* Philadelphia, PA: Falmer Press.

Delpit, L. (1988). The silenced dialogue: Power and pedagogy in educating other people's children. *Harvard Educational Review, 58,* 280–298.

Delpit, L. (1997). Ebonics and cultural responsive instruction. *Rethinking School Journal, 12*(1) 6–7.

Demo, D. (2000). *Dialects in education* (ERIC/CLL Resources Guide online). Washington, DC: ERIC: Clearinghouse on Language and Linguistics.

DePaola, T. (1975). *Strega Nona.* New York, NY: Prentice Hall.

DePaola, T., (1978). *Pancakes for breakfast.* New York, NY: Harcourt Brace Jovanovich.

DeVries, B. A. (2004). *Literacy assessment and intervention for the elementary classroom.* Scottsdale, AZ: Holcomb Hathaway Publishers.

Dewey, J. (1938). Experience and education. New York: Collier.

DiCamillo, K. (2000). *Because of Winn Dixie.* Cambridge, MA: Candlewick Press.

Dickinson, D. K., Temple, J. M., Hirschler, J. A., & Smith, M. W. (1992). Book Reading with Preschoolers: Coconstruction of Text at Home and at School. *Early Childhood Research Quarterly, 7,* 323–346.

Dickinson, D. K., McCabe, A., Anastaspoulos, L., Peisner-Feinberg, E. S. & Poe, M. D. (2003). The comprehensive language approach to early literacy: The interrelationships among vocabulary, phonological sensitivity, and print knowledge among preschool-aged children. *Journal of Educational Psychology, 95*(3), 465–481.

Dickinson, D. & Smith, M. (1994). Describing oral language opportunities and environments in Head Start and other preschool classrooms. *Early Childhood Research Quarterly, 9,* 345–366.

Dickinson, D., & Smith, M. (2004). Long-term effects of preschool teachers' book readings on low-income children's vocabulary and story comprehension. *Reading Research Quarterly, 29,* 104–122.

Dickinson, D., & Tabors, P. (2001). *Beginning literacy with language: Young children learning at home and school.* Baltimore: Paul H. Brookes.

Dodge, D., & Colker, L. (1992). *The creative curriculum for early childhood education.* Washington, DC: Teaching Strategies.

Dodici, B. J., Draper, D. C., & Peterson, C. A. (2003). Early parent-child interactions and early literacy development. *Topics in Early Childhood Special Education, 23*(3), 124–136.

Doiron, R. (1994). Using nonfiction in a read-aloud program: Letting the facts speak for themselves. *The Reading Teacher, 47*, 616–624.

Dolson, D. (1985). The effects of Spanish home language use on the scholastic performance of Hispanic pupils. *Journal of Multilingual Multicultural Development, 6*, 135–155.

Downing, J., & Oliver, P. (1973–74). The child's concept of a word. *Reading Research Quarterly, 9*, 568–582.

Dragonwagon, C. (1993). *Homeplace.* New York: Alladin Books.

Drake, S. (1998). *Integrated curriculum: A chapter in the Curriculum Handbook.* Alexandria, VA: ASCD.

Drake, S. (2001). Castles, Kings . . . and Standards. *Educational Leadership, 59*, 38–42.

Duffy, G. G. (2003). *Explaining reading: A resource for teaching concepts, skills, and strategies.* New York: Guilford Press.

Duke, N. K., & Bennett-Armistead, V. S. (2003). *Reading & writing informational text in the primary grades: Research-based practices.* New York, NY: Scholastic.

Duke, N., & Pearson, P. D. (2002). Effective practices for developing reading comprehension. In A. E. Farstrup & S. J. Samuels (Eds.), *What research has to say about reading instruction* (pp. 205–242). Newark, DE: International Reading Association.

Dunn, L., & Dunn, L. (1997). *Peabody Picture Vocabulary Test III. Circle* Pines, MN: American Guidance Service.

Durkin, D. (1966). *Children who read early.* New York: Teachers College Press.

Durkin, D. (1984). Is there a match between what elementary teachers do and what basal manuals recommend? *The Reading Teacher, 37*, 734–744.

Durkin, D. (1987). *Teaching young children to read* (4th ed.). Boston: Allyn & Bacon.

Durkin, D. (2004). *Teaching them to read* (6th ed.). Boston: Pearson.

Duvall, B. (1985). Evaluating the difficulty of four handwriting styles used for instruction. *ERS Spectrum, 3*, 13–20.

Dyson, A., & Genishi, C. (1983). Children's language for learning. *Language Arts, 60*, 751–757.

Early Childhood-Head Start Task Force. (2002). *Teaching our youngest: A guide for preschool teachers and child-care and family providers.* Jessup, MD: U.S. Department of Education.

Early Childhood Research Institute on Measuring Growth and Development. (2000). Individual Growth and Development Indicator (IGDI).

Edelsky, C. (1986). *Writing in a bilingual program: Habia una vez.* Norwood, NJ: Ablex.

Edelman, G. (1995, June) Neuroscience Institute, La Jolla, California cited in J. Swerdlow, Quiet Miracles of the Brain, *National Geographic, 187*(6).

Eeds, M., & Wells, D. (1989). Grand conversations: An exploration of meaning construction in literature study groups. *Research in the Teaching of English, 23*, 4–29.

Eeds, M. & Wells, D. (1991). Talking and thinking and cooperative learning: Lessons learned from listening to children talk about books. *Social Education, 55*(2), 134–137. Elbow, P. (1973). *Writing without teachers.* New York: Oxford University Press.

Ehri, L. (1991). Development of the ability to read words. In P. D. Pearson (Ed.), *Handbook of Reading Research* (Vol. II, pp. 383–417). New York: Longman.

Ehri, L. (1997). Phonemic awareness and learning to read. *Literacy Development in Young Children, 4*(2), 2–3.

Ehri, L., Nunes, S., Willows, D., Schuster, B., Yaghoub-Zadeh, Z., & Shanahan, T. (2001). Phonemic awareness instruction helps children learn to read: Evidence from the National Reading Panel's meta-analysis. *Reading Research Quarterly, 36*, 250–287.

Elbow, P. (1973). *Writing without teachers.* Oxford, England: Oxford University Press.

Elkind, D. (1990). Academic pressures–Too much, too soon: The demise of play. In E. Klugman & S. Smilansky (Eds.), *Children's play and learning: Perspectives and policy implications* (pp. 3–17). New York: Teachers College Press.

Ellis, R. (1985). *Understanding second language acquisition.* New York: Oxford University Press.

Elster, C. (1998). Influences of text and pictures on shared and emergent readings. *Research in the Teaching of English, 32*, 43–63.

Enright, D. (1986). Use everything you have to teach English: Providing useful input to young second language learners. In P. Rigg & D. Enright (Eds.), *Children and ESL: Integrating Perspectives* (pp. 113–162). Washington, DC: Teachers of English to Speakers of Other Languages.

Enright, D., & McCloskey, M. (1988). *Integrating English: Developing English language and literacy in the multilingual classroom.* Reading, MA: Addison-Wesley.

Enz, B. (1992). *Love, laps, and learning to read.* Paper presented at International Reading Association Southwest Regional Conference, Tucson, AZ.

Enz, B. J., Kortman, S., & Honaker, C. (1993). *Ready, Set, Teach:* A *Blueprint for the First Year.* Kappa Delta Pi, Indianapolis, IN.

Enz, B., & Christie, J. (1997). Teacher play interaction styles: Effects on play behavior and relationships with teacher training and experience. *International Journal of Early Childhood Education, 2,* 55–69.

Enz, B., & Cook, S. (1993). *Gateway to teaching: From pre-service to in-service.* Dubuque, IA: Kendall-Hunt.

Enz, B., & Searfoss, L. (1995). Let the circle be unbroken: Teens as literacy teachers and learners. In L. Morrow (Ed.) *Family literacy: Multiple perspectives* (pp. 115–128). Reston, VA: International Reading Association.

Enz, B., & Searfoss, L. (1996). Expanding our views of family literacy. *The Reading Teacher, 49,* 576–579.

Epstein, J. (1986). Parents' reactions to teacher practices of parent involvement. *Elementary School Journal, 86,* 277–294.

Epstein, J. (1995). School/family/community partnerships: Caring for the children we share. *Phi Delta Kappa, 76,* 701–712.

Ericson, L., & Juliebö, M. (1998). *The phonological awareness handbook for kindergarten and primary teachers.* Newark, DE: International Reading Association.

Ernst, G. (1994). "Talking circle:" Conversation and negotiation in the ESL classroom. *TESOL Quarterly, 28,* 293–322.

Espinosa, C., & Fournier, J. (1995). Making meaning of our lives through literature: Past, present, and future. *Primary Voices, 3*(2), 15–21.

Ezell, H., & Justice, L., (2005). *Shared storybook reading.* Baltimore, MD: Brookes Publishing.

Fairfax County Public Schools. (1998). *Expanding expectations: Assessing.* Annandale, VA: Author.

Faltis, C. (2001). *Joinfostering* (3rd ed.). Upper Saddle, NJ: Prentice Hall.

Farris, P. (1982). *A comparison of handwriting strategies for primary grade students.* Arlington, VA: ERIC Document Reproduction Service.

Faulkner, W. *Brainy Quote.* Retrieved 2005, October 13. www.brainyquote.com/quotes/quotes/w/williamfau151710.html

Fein, G., Ardila-Rey, A., & Groth, L. (2000). The narrative connection: Stories and literacy. In K. Roskos & J. Christie (Eds.). *Play and literacy in early childhood: Research from multiple perspectives* (pp. 27–43). Mahwah, NJ: Erlbaum.

Feitelson, D., & Goldstein, Z. (1986). Patterns of book ownership and reading to young children in Israeli school-oriented and nonschool-oriented families. *The Reading Teacher, 39,* 924–930.

Feldgus, E. G., & Cardonick, I. (1999). *Kid writing: A systematic approach to phonics, journals, and writing workshop.* Bothell, WA: McGraw-Hill/The Wright Group.

Fernandez-Fein, S., & Baker, L. (1997). Rhyme and alliteration sensitivity and relevant experiences among preschoolers from diverse backgrounds. *Journal of Literacy Research, 29,* 433–459.

Ferreiro, E., & Teberosky, A. (1982). *Literacy before schooling.* Exeter, NH: Heinemann.

Fessler, R. (1998). Room for talk: Peer support for getting into English in an ESL kindergarten. *Early Childhood Research Quarterly, 13,* 379–410.

Field, T., Woodson, R., Greenberg, R., & Cohen, D. (1982). Discrimination and imitation of facial expressions by neonates. *Science, 218,* 179–181.

Fields, M., Spangler, K., & Lee, D. (1991). *Let's begin reading right: Developmentally appropriate beginning literacy.* New York: Merrill-Macmillan.

Fillmore, L. (1976). *The second time around: Cognitive and social strategies in second language acquisition.* Unpublished doctoral dissertation, Stanford University.

Fillmore, L. (1982). Instructional language as linguistic input: Second language learning in classrooms. In L. Wilkinson (Ed.), *Communicating in the classroom.* New York: Academic Press.

Fillmore, L. (1983). The language learner as an individual: Implications of research on individual differences for the ESL teacher. In J. Handscombe & M. Clarke (Eds.), *On TESOL '82: Pacific perspectives on language learning and teaching* (pp. 53–67). Washington, DC: Teachers of English to Speakers of Other Languages.

Fillmore, L. (1991). When learning a second language means losing the first. *Early Childhood Research Quarterly, 6*(3), 323–346.

Fisher, B. (1995). Things take off: Note taking in the first grade. In P. Cordeiro (Ed.), *Endless possibilities: Generating curriculum in social studies and literacy.* Portsmouth, NH: Heinemann.

Fisher, C. W., Filby, N. N., Marliave, R., Cahen, L. S., Dishaw, M. M., Moore, J. E., & Berliner, D. C. (1978). *Teaching behaviors, academic learning time, and student achievement.* (Technical Report V–1). San Francisco: Northwest Regional Lab.

Flanigan, B. (1988). Second language acquisition in the elementary schools: The negotiation of meaning by native-speaking and nonnative-speaking peers. *The Bilingual Review/La Revista Bilingue, 14* (3), 25–40.

Flaxman, E., & Inger, M. (1991). Parents and schooling in the 1990s. *ERIC Review, 1*(3), 2–5.

Fletcher, R. (1993). *What a writer needs.* Portsmouth, NH: Heinemann.

Fletcher, R., & Portalupi, J. (1998). *Craft lessons: Teaching writing K–8.* York, ME: Stenhouse.

Fletcher, R., & Portalupi, J. (2001). *Writing workshop: The essential guide.* Portsmouth, NH: Heinemann.

Flood, J., Lapp, D., Flood, S., & Nagel, G. (1992). Am I allowed to group? Using flexible patterns for effective instruction. *The Reading Teacher, 45,* 608–616.

Flores, B., Garcia, E., Gonzalez, S., Hidalgo, G., Kaczmarek, K., & Romero, T. (1985). *Holistic bilingual instruction strategies.* Chandler, AZ: Exito.

Foley, D & Enz, B. (2004) Supporting the love of reading and learning: a multi-media approach. www.onlineopinion.com.au/view.asp?article=2305

Fountas, I. C., & Pinnell, G. S. (2001). *Guiding readers and writers: Grades 3–6.* Portsmouth, NH: Heinemann.

Fountas, I., & Pinnell, G. (1996). *Guided reading: Good first teaching for all children.* Portsmouth, NH: Heinemann.

Fournier, J., Lansdowne, E., Pastenes, Z., Steen, P., & Hudelson, S. (1992). Learning with, about and from children: Life in a bilingual second grade. In C. Genishi (Ed.), *Ways of assessing children and curriculum: Voices from the classroom* (pp. 126–168). New York: Teachers College Press.

Fox, B. J., & Hull, M. A. (2002). *Phonics for the teacher of reading.* Columbus, Ohio: Merrill.

Fox, P. (1973). *The slave dancer.* New York, NY: Random House, Inc.

Fractor, J., Woodruff, M., Martinez, M., & Teale, W. (1993). Let's not miss opportunities to promote voluntary reading: Classroom libraries in the elementary school. *The Reading Teacher, 46,* 476–484.

Fradd, S. H., & McGee, P. L. (1994). *Instructional assessment: An integrative approach to evaluating student performance.* New York: Addison Wesley.

Fredericks, A., & Rasinski, T. (1990). Involving the uninvolved: How to. *The Reading Teacher, 43,* 424–425.

Freedman, R. (1987) *Lincoln: a photobiography.* New York: Clarion.

Freedman, R. (1990) *Franklin Delano Roosevelt.* New York: Clarion.

Freedman, R. (1991) *The Wright Brothers: How they invented the airplane.* Illus. with original photographs by Orville and Wilbur Wright. New York: Holiday House.

Freedman, R. (1993) *Eleanor Roosevelt: a life of discovery.* New York: Clarion.

Freedman, R. (1996) *The life and death of Crazy Horse.* illus. By Amos Bad Heart Bull. New York: Holiday House.

Freedman, R. (1997) *Out of darkness: the story of Louis Braille.* Illus. by Kate Kiesler. New York: Clarion.

Freedman, R. (1998) *Martha Graham: a dancer's life.* New York: Clarion.

Freedman, R (2002) *Confucius: the golden rule.* illus. by Frederic Clement. New York: Arthur A. Levine.

Freedman, R. (2004) *The voice that challenged a nation: Marian Anderson and the struggle for equal rights.* New York: Clarion.

Freeman, D., & Freeman, Y. (1992). *Whole language for second language learners.* Portsmouth, NH: Heinemann.

Freeman, D., & Freeman, Y. (1994a). *Between worlds: Access to second language acquisition.* Portsmouth, NH: Heinemann.

Freeman, Y. and Freeman, D. (1994b). Whole language learning and teaching for second language learners. In C. Weaver, *Reading process and practice: From sociopsycholinguistics to whole language.* Portsmouth, NH: Heinemann.

Fu, D., & Lamme, L. L. (2002). Assessment through conversation. *Language Arts, 79*(3), 241–250.

Furner, B. (1985). *Handwriting instruction for a high-tech society: Will handwriting be necessary?* Paper presented at the annual spring conference of the National Council of Teachers of English, Houston, TX.

Galda, L., Cullinan, B., & Strickland, D. (1993). *Language, literacy, and the child.* Fort Worth: Harcourt Brace Jovanovich.

Gallas, K. (1992). When the children take the chair: A study of sharing in a primary classroom. *Language Arts, 69,* 172–182.

Gambrell, L., & Mazzoni, S. (1999). Principles of best practice: Finding the common ground. In L. Gambrell, L. Morrow, S. Neuman, & M. Pressley (Eds.), *Best practices in literacy instruction* (pp. 11–21). New York: Guilford.

Gambrell, L., Wilson, R., & Gantt, W. (1981). Classroom observations of task-attending behaviors of good and poor readers. *Journal of Educational Research, 74,* 400–404.

Gardner, S. (1993–94). Training for the future: Family support and school-linked services. *Family Resource Coalition, 3*(4), 18–19.

Garvey, C. (1977). *Play.* Cambridge, MA: Harvard University Press.

Garvey, C. (1984). *Children's talk.* Cambridge, MA: Harvard University Press.

Gavelek, J., Raphael, T., Biondo, S., & Wang, D. (2000). Integrated literacy instruction. In M. Kamil, P. Mosenthal, P. D. Pearson, & R. Barr (Eds.), *Handbook of reading research* (vol. 3, pp. 587–607). Mahwah, NJ: Erlbaum.

Gelfer, J. (1991). Teacher-parent partnerships: Enhancing communications. *Childhood Education, 67,* 164–167.

Geller, L. (1982). Linguistic consciousness-raising: Child's play. *Language Arts, 59,* 120–125.

Genishi, C. (1987). Acquiring oral language and communicative competence. In C. Seefeldt (Ed.). *The early childhood curriculum: A review of current research.* New York: Teachers College Press.

Genishi, C., & Dyson, A. (1984). *Language assessment in the early years.* Norwood, NJ: Ablex.

Gentry, J., & Gillet, J. (1993). *Teaching kids to spell.* Portsmouth, NH: Heinemann.

Gesell, A. (1928). *Infancy and human growth.* New York: Macmillan.

Gettinger, M. (1993). Effects of invented spelling and direct instruction on spelling performance of second-grade boys. *Journal of Applied Behavior Analysis, 26,* 281–291.

Gilbert, J. (1989). A two-week K–6 interdisciplinary unit. In H. Jacobs (Ed.), *Interdisciplinary curriculum: Design and implementation* (pp. 46–51). Arlington, VA: Association for Supervision and Curriculum Development.

Glass, G., McGaw, B., & Smith, M. L. (1981). *Meta-analysis in social research.* Beverly Hills, CA: Sage.

Gleason, J. (1967). Do children imitate? In C. Cazden (Ed.) *Language in early childhood education.* Washington, DC: National Association for the Education of Young Children.

Goals 2000: Educate America Act (1994). H.R.1804. www.ed.gov/legislangion/GOALS2000/TheAct/Index.html.

Good start, grow smart: The Bush administration's early childhood initiative. (2002, April). Washington, DC: The White House.

Goforth, F. S., (1998). *Literature and the learner.* Belmont, CA: Wadsworth Publishing Company.

Golinkoff, R. (1983). The preverbal negotiation of failed messages: Insights into the transition period. In R. Golinkoff (Ed.), *The transition from prelinguistic to linguistic communication* (pp. 57–78). Hillsdale, NJ: Erlbaum.

Golinkoff, R. M. & Hirsh-Pasek, K. (1999). *How babies talk: The magic and mystery of language in the first three years of life.* New York: NY: Dutton Publishers

González, N. (1995). The funds of knowledge for teaching project. *Practicing Anthropology, 17*(3), 3–7.

Gonzalez-Mena, J. (1997). *Multicultural issues in childcare* (2nd ed.). Mountain View, CA: Mayfield.

Goodlad, J., & Oakes, J. (1988). We must offer equal access to knowledge. *Educational Leadership, 45,* 16–22.

Goodman, K. (1970). Reading: A psycholinguistic guessing game. In H. Singer & R. Ruddell (Eds.), *Theoretical models and processes of reading* (pp. 259–271). Newark, DE: International Reading Association.

Goodman, Y. (1978). Kidwatching: an alternative to testing. *Journal of National Elementary School Principals, 574:*22–27.

Goodman, Y. (1981). Test review: Concepts about print test. *The Reading Teacher, 34,* 445–448.

Goodman, Y. (1986). Children coming to know literacy. In W. Teale & E. Sulzby (Eds.), *Emergent literacy: Writing and reading* (pp. 1–14). Norwood, NJ: Ablex.

Graham, S., Harris, K., & Chorzempa, B. (2003). Extra spelling instruction: Promoting better spelling, writing, and reading performance right from the start. *Teaching Exceptional Children, 35,* 66–68.

Graham, S., Harris, K., & Fink, B. (2000). Is handwriting causally related to learning to write? : Treatment of handwriting problems in beginning writers. *Journal of Educational Psychology, 92,* 620–633.

Graham, S. (1992). Issues in handwriting instruction. *Focus on Exceptional Children, 25,* 1–4.

Graham, S. (1993/94). Are slanted manuscript alphabets superior to the traditional manuscript alphabet? *Childhood Education, 70,* 91–95.

Graham, S. (1999). Handwriting and spelling instruction for students with learning disabilities: A review. *Learning Disability Quarterly, 22,* 78–98.

Graves, D. (1983). *Writing: Teachers and children at work.* Portsmouth, NH: Heinemann.

Graves, D. (1993). Children can write authentically if we help them. *Primary Voices K–6, 1,* 2–6.

Graves, D., & Hansen, J. (1983). The author's chair. *Language Arts, 60,* 176–183.

Graves, D. (2004). What I've Learned from Teachers of Writing. *Language Arts, 82*(2), 88–94.

Greenewald, M. J., & Kulig, R. (1995). Effects of repeated readings of alphabet books on kindergartners' letter recognition. In K. Hinchman, D. Leu, & Kinzer, C. (Eds.), *Perspectives on literacy research and practice: Forty-fourth yearbook of the National Reading Conference* (pp. 231–234). Chicago: National Reading Conference.

Greenough, W. T. & Black, J. E. (1999). Experience, neural plasticity, and psychological development. In N. Fox, L. Leavitt, & J. Warhol (Eds.), *Proceedings of the 1999 Johnson & Johnson Pediatric Round Table, "The role of early experience in infant development"* (pp. 29–40). Johnson & Johnson Consumer Companies, Inc.

Griffith, H. (1998) *Dinosaur habitat.* Illus. by Sonza Lamut. New York: Greenwillow Books

Griffin, E. & Morrison, F. (1997). The unique contribution of home literacy environment to differences in early literacy skills. *Early Child Development and Care, 127–128,* 233–243.

Griggs, M. C., Daane, Y. J., & Campbell, J. *Improving comprehension instruction* (pp. 80–105). San Francisco: Jossey Bass.

Gronlund, G. (1998). Portfolios as an assessment tool: Is collecting of work enough? *Young Children, 53,* 4–10.

Guerra, J. (1991). The role of ethnography in the reconceptualization of literacy. *The Quarterly Newsletter of the Laboratory of Comparative Human Cognition, 13,* 3–8.

Gump, P. (1989). Ecological psychology and issues of play. In M. Bloch & A. Pellegrini (Eds.), *The ecological context of children's play* (pp. 35–36). Norwood, NJ: Ablex.

Guthrie, J. T. (2002). Preparing students for high stakes testing in reading. In *What research has to say about reading instruction*. Newark, DE: International Reading Association.

Guthrie, J., & Wigfield, A. (2000). Engagement and motivation in reading. In M. Kamil, P. Mosenthal, P. D. Pearson, & R. Barr (Eds.), *Handbook of reading research* (vol. 3, pp. 403–422). Mahwah, NJ: Erlbaum.

Hackney, C. (n.d.) *Standard manuscript or modified italic?* Columbus, OH: Zaner-Bloser, Inc.

Hakuta, K. (1986). *Mirror of language: The debate on bilingualism.* New York: Basic Books.

Haley, A. (1974). *Roots: The saga of an American family.* New York: Doubleday.

Hall, N. (1987). *The emergence of literacy.* Portsmouth, NH: Heinemann.

Hall, N. (1991). Play and the emergence of literacy. In J. Christie (Ed.), *Play and early literacy development* (pp. 3–25). Albany, NY: State University of New York Press.

Hall, N. (1999). Real literacy in a school setting: Five-year-olds take on the world. *The Reading Teacher, 52*, 8–17.

Hall, N., & Duffy, R. (1987). Every child has a story to tell. *Language Arts, 64*, 523–529.

Hall, N., & Robinson, A. (1995). *Exploring writing and play in the early years.* London: David Fulton.

Halliday, M. (1975). *Learning how to mean: Explorationsof the development of language.* London: Edward Arnold.

Han, M., Chen, Y., Christie, J. & Enz, B. (2000). *Environmental Print Assessment Kit.* Tempe, AZ: Arizona State University.

Hansen, J. "Evaluation: The Center of Writing Instruction." *The Reading Teacher, 50*, 188–195.

Hansen, C. (1998). *Getting the picture: Talk about story in a kindergarten classroom.* Unpublished doctoral dissertation, Arizona State University.

Hansen, J. (1994). Literacy profiles: Windows on potential. In S. Valencia, E. Hiebert, P. Afflerbach (Eds.), *Authentic reading assessment*. Newark, DE: International Reading Association.

Hansen, J. (1996) Evaluation: The center of writing instruction. *Reading Teacher, 50*, 188–195

Hargrave, A. C., & Senechal, M. (2000). A book reading intervention with preschool children who have limited vocabularies: The benefits of regular reading and dialogic reading. *Early Childhood Research Quarterly, 18*, 1, 75–90.

Harp, B. (1996). *The handbook of literacy assessment and evaluation.* Norwood, MA: Christopher-Gordon.

Harris, M. (1994). Individualized writing instruction in writing centers: Attending to cross-cultural differences. In J. A. Mullin & R. Wallace (Eds.). *Intersections: Theory-practice in the writing center.* Urbana, Illinois: NCTE.

Harris, D., & Carr, J. (1996). *How to use standards in the classroom.* Alexandria, VA: ASCD.

Harris, V. (Ed.). (1992). *Teaching multicultural literature in grades K–8.* Norwood, MA: Christopher-Gordon.

Hart, B., & Risley, T. (1995). *Meaningful differences in the everyday experience of young American children.* Baltimore, MD: Paul H. Brookes.

Harste, J., Short, K., & Burke, C. (1988). *Creating classrooms for authors: The reading-writing connection.* Portsmouth, NH: Heinemann.

Harste, J., Woodward, V., & Burke, C. (1984). *Language stories and literacy lessons.* Portsmouth, NH: Heinemann.

Harwayne, S. (1992). *Lasting impressions.* Portsmouth, NH: Heinemann.

Hawisher, G. E., LeBlanc, P. L., Moran, C., & Selfe, C. L. (1996). *Computers and the teaching of writing in American higher education, 1979–1994: A history.* Norwood, NJ: Ablex.

Hazen, K. (October, 2001). *Teaching about dialects.* Educational Resources Information Center, ERIC: Clearinghouse on Language and Linguistics. EDO-FL-01-01.

Heald-Taylor, G. (1987). Predictable literature selections and activities for language arts instruction. *The Reading Teacher, 40*, 6–12.

Healy, J. (1994). *Your child's growing mind: A practical guide to brain development and learning from birth to adolescence.* New York: Doubleday.

Healy, J. (1997, August-September). Current brain research. *Scholastic Early Childhood Today, 12*(1), 42–44.

Heard, G. (2002). *The revision toolbox: Teaching techniques that work.* Portsmouth, NH: Heinemann.

Heath, S. (1982). What no bedtime story means: Narrative skills at home and school. *Language in Society, 11,* 49–76.

Heath, S. (1983). *Ways with words.* Cambridge, England: Cambridge University Press.

Heath, S. (1986). Sociocultural contexts of language development. In Bilingual Education Office, California State Department of Education (Ed.), *Beyond language: Social and cultural factors in schooling language minority students.* Los Angeles: Evaluation, Dissemination and Assessment Center, California State University.

Hedrick, W., & Pearish, A. (1999, April). Good reading instruction is more important than who provides the instruction or where it takes place. *The Reading Teacher, 52,* 716–725.

Heidemann, S., Chang, C., & Menninga, B. (2005). Teaching teachers about assessment. *Young Children, 60*(3), 86–92.

Helm, J. (1999). Projects! Exploring children's interests. *Scholastic Early Childhood Today,* 24–31.

Hensley, M. (1995). *Funds of knowledge for teaching.* Unpublished paper, University of Arizona.

Herman, J. L., Aschbacher, P. R., & Winter, L. (1992). *Linking assessment and instruction: A practical guide to alternative assessment.* Alexandria, VA: Association for Supervision and Curriculum Development.

Hewett, B. L. (2000). Characteristics of interactive oral and computer-mediated peer group talk and its influence on revision. *Computers and Composition, 17,* 265–288.

Hidi, S. (1990). Interest and its contribution as a mental resource for learning. *Review of Educational Research, 60,* 549–571. Hiebert, E. (1981). Developmental patterns and interrelationships of preschool children's print awareness. *Reading Research Quarterly, 16,* 236–260.

Hillocks, G., Jr. (1986). *Research on written composition: New directions for teaching.* Urbana, IL: National Conference on Research in English.

Hillocks, G., Jr. (2002). *The testing trap: How state writing assessments control learning.* Berkeley, CA: National Writing Project.

Holdaway, D. (1979). *The foundations of literacy.* Sydney: Ashton Scholastic.

Hong, L. (1981). Modifying SSR for beginning readers. *The Reading Teacher, 34,* 888–891.

Howard, S., Shaughnessy, A., Sanger, D., & Hux, K. (1998). Lets talk! Facilitating language in early elementary classrooms. *Young Children, 53*(3), 34–39.

Howell, H. (1978). Write on, you sinistrals! *Language Arts, 55,* 852–856.

Huck, C., Hepler, S., Hickman, J., & Kiefer, B. (1997). *Children's literature in the elementary school.* New York: Holt, Rinehart, & Winston.

Hudelson, S. (1987). The role of native language literacy in the education of language minority children. *Language Arts, 64,* 827–841.

Hudelson, S. (1989). *Write on: Children writing in ESL.* Englewood Cliffs, NJ: Prentice-Hall.

Hudelson, S. (1990). Bilingual/ESL learners talking in the English classroom. In S. Hynds & D. Rubin (Eds.), *Perspectives on talk and learning.* Urbana, IL: National Council of Teachers of English.

Hudelson, S. (1994). Literacy development of second language children. In F. Genesee (Ed.), *Educating second language children: The whole child, the whole curriculum, the whole community.* New York: Cambridge University Press.

Hudelson, S., Fournier, J., Espinosa, C., & Bachman, R. (1994). Chasing windmills: Confronting the obstacles for literature based reading programs. *Language Arts, 71,* 164–171.

Hudelson, S., & Serna, I. (1994). Beginning literacy in English in a whole language bilingual program. In A. Flurkey & R. Meyer (Eds.), *Under the whole language umbrella: Many cultures, many voices.* Urbana, IL: National Council of Teachers of English.

Huey, E. (1908). *The psychology and pedagogy of reading.* New York: Macmillan.

Huffaker, D. (2004). The educated blogger: Using weblogs to promote literacy in the classroom. *First Monday, 9*(6) (June 2004), Retrieved September 5, 2005 from http://firstmonday.org/issues/issue9_6/huffaker/index.html

Hunt, L. (1971). Six steps to the individualized reading program (IRP). *Elementary English, 48,* 27–32.

Hunter, S. (1995). Afterword. In S. Hunter & R. Wallace (Eds.). *The place of grammar in writing instruction: Past, present, future* (pp. 243–246). Portsmouth, NH: Boynton/Cook.

Huot, B. (2002). *(Re)articulating writing assessment.* Cedar City, Utah: Southern Utah University Press.

Huttenlocher, J. (1991). Early vocabulary growth: Relations to language input and gender. *Developmental Psychology, 27,* 236–248.

Huttenlocher, P. (1999). Synaptogenesis in human cerebral cortex and the concept of critical periods. In N. Fox, L. Leavitt, & J. Warhol (Eds.), *Proceedings of the 1999 Johnson & Johnson Pediatric Round Table, "The role of early experience in infant development"* (pp. 15–28). Johnson & Johnson Consumer Companies, Inc.

International Reading Association and National Association for the Education of Young Children. *Learning to read and write: Developmentally appropriate practices for young children.* Newark, DE: IRA.

Invernizzi, M., Meier, J., Swank, L. & Juel, C. (1999). *Phonological Awareness Literacy Screening Teacher's Manual.* Charlottesville: University Printing Services. 2nd edition.

Invernizzi, M., & Johnston, F., & Bear, D. R. (2006). *Words their way: Word sorts for within word pattern spellers.* Upper Saddle River, New Jersey: Pearson, Merrill, Prentice Hall.

IRA. (1999). *Using multiple methods of beginning reading instruction: A position statement of the International Reading Association.* Newark, DE: International Reading Association.

IRA. (2000). Teachers' choices for 2000. *The Reading Teacher, 54,* 269–276.

IRA/NCTE. (1994). *Standards for the assessment of reading and writing.* Newark, DE & Urbana, IL: International Reading Association & National Council of Teachers of English.

IRA/NAEYC. (1998). Learning to read and write: Developmentally appropriate practices for young children. *Young Children, 53*(4), 30–46.

Jackman, H. (1997). Early education curriculum: A child's connection to the world. Albany, NY: Delmar.

Jacobs, B. Schall, M., & Scheibel, A. B. (1993). A quantitative dendritic analysis of Wernicke's area in humans: II. Gender, hemispheric, and environmental factors. *Journal of Comparative Neurology, 327,* 97–111

Jacobs, H. (1989). *Interdisciplinary curriculum: Design and implementation.* Alexandria, VA: Association for Supervision and Curriculum Development.

Jacobs, W. (1990). *Ellis Island: New hope in a new land.* New York: Scribner.

Jacobson, L. (1998, February 11). House calls. *Education Week,* 19–27.

Jacobson, R., & Faltis, C. (Eds.). (1990). *Language distribution issues in bilingual schooling.* Clevedon, UK: Multilingual Matters.

Jalongo, M. (1995). Promoting active listening in the classroom. *Childhood Education, 72*(1), 13–18.

Jaramillo, N. (1994). *Grandmothers' nursery rhymes/Las nanas de abuelita.* New York: Henry Holt.

Johnson, D. (2001). Vocabulary in the elementary and middle school. Boston, MA: Allyn & Bacon.

Johnson, J., Christie, J., & Yawkey, T. (1999) *Play and early childhood development* (2nd ed.). New York: Allyn & Bacon/Longman.

Johnston, F., Bear, D. R, & Invernizzi, M. (2006). *Words their way: Word sorts for derivational relations spellers.* Upper Saddle River, New Jersey: Pearson, Merrill, Prentice Hall.

Johnston, F., Bear, D. R, & Invernizzi, M. (2006). *Words their way: Word sorts for letter name-alphabetic spellers.* Upper Saddle River, New Jersey: Pearson, Merrill, Prentice Hall.

Johnston, F., Bear, D. R, & Invernizzi, M. (2006). *Words their way: Word sorts for syllables and affixes spellers.* Upper Saddle River, New Jersey: Pearson, Merrill, Prentice Hall.

Johnston, P. (1997). *Knowing literacy: constructive literacy assessment.* York, ME: Stenhouse Publishers.

Johnston, P., & Costello, P. (2005). Principles for literacy assessment. *Reading Research Quarterly, 40*(2), 256–267.

Johnston, P. (1992). *Constructive evaluation of literate activity.* White Plains, NY: Longman.

Johnston, P., & Allington, R. (1991). Remediation. In R. Barr, M. Kamil, P. Mosenthal, & P. D. Pearson (Eds.), *Handbook of reading research* (Vol. 2, pp. 984–1012). New York: Longman.

Jonas, S. (Ed.) (1989). *Ellis Island: Echoes from a nation's past.* Montclair, NJ: Aperture.

Jonassen, D. H., Peck, K. L., & Wilson, B. G. (1998). *Teaching with technology: A constructivist perspective.* Upper Saddle River, NJ: Merrill.

Jones, E. & Reynolds, G. (1992). *The play's the thing: Teachers' roles in children's play.* New York: Teachers College Press.

Joyce, B. (1999). Reading about reading: Notes from a consumer to the scholars of literacy. *The Reading Teacher, 52,* 662–671.

Juscyzk, P. W. (1997) *The discovery of spoken language.* Cambridge, MA. MIT Press.

Juscyzk, P. W., Luce, P. A., & Charles-Luce, J. (1999). Infants' sensitivity to phonontactic patterns in the native language. *Journal of Memory and Language, 33,* 630–645.

Kadohata, C. (2004). *Kira-kira.* New York: Atheneum Books.

Kalb, C. & Namuth, T. (1997, Spring/Summer). When a child's silence isn't golden. *Newsweek: Your Child* (special edition).

Kallen, S. (1990). *Days of slavery: A history of black people in America.* Edina, MN: Abdo & Daughters.

Kamil, M. L., Intrator, S. M., & Kim, H. S. (2000). The effects of other technologies on literacy and literacy learning. In Kamil, M., Mosenthal, P., Pearson, P. D., & Barr, R. *Handbook of reading research, Volume III* (pp. 195–206). Mahwah, NJ: Lawrence Erlbaum Associates.

Karchmer, R. A. (2001). The journey ahead: Thirteen teachers report how the Internet influences literacy in their K–12 classrooms. *Reading Research Quarterly, 36,* 4, 442–460.

Karmiloff-Smith, A. (1979). Language development after five. In P. Fletcher & M. Garman (Eds.), *Language acquisition.* Cambridge, England: Cambridge University Press.

Kashen, S. (2005). False claims about literacy development. *Educational Leadership, 61,* 4, 18–21.

Katch, J. (2004). The most important words. *Educational Leadership, 61,* 4, 62–65.

Katz, L., & Chard, S. (1993). *Engaging children's minds: The project approach.* Norwood, NJ: Ablex.

Keene, E. O. (2002). From good to memorable: Characteristics of highly effective comprehension teaching. In C. C. Block, L. B. Gambrell, & M. Pressley (Eds.).

Keller, C. (2002). A new twist on spelling instruction for elementary school teachers. *Intervention in School and Clinic, 38,* 3–7.

Kemper, D., Nathan, R., & Sebranek, P. (1995). *The Write Track.* Burlington, WI: The Write Source.

Kemper, D., Nathan, R., & Sebranek, P. (1994). *Writers express.* Burlington, WI: The Write Source.

Kennedy, K. (February 15, 2003). Writing with web logs. *Techlearning.* Available online at www.techlearning.com/db_area/archives/TL/2003/02/blogs.html.

Kiefer, B. Z., Huck, C., Hepler, S., & Hickman, J. (2003). *Children's literature in the elementary school.* New York: Holt, Rinehart, & Winston.

King, S. (2000). *On writing.* New York: Scribner.

King, S (2000) *On writing, a memoir of the craft.* New York: Simon & Schuster.

Kirk, E. W., & Clark, P. (2005). Beginning with names: Using children's names to facilitate early literacy learning. *Childhood Education, 81,* 3, 139–145.

Klein, A. (1991). All about ants: Discovery learning in the primary grades. *Young Children, 46,* 23–27.

Koenke, K. (1986). Handwriting instruction: What do we know? *The Reading Teacher, 40,* 214–216.

Koppenhaver, D., Spadorcia, S., & Erickson, K. (1998). How do we provide inclusive early literacy instruction for children with disabilities? In S. Neuman & K. Roskos (Eds.), *Children achieving: Best practices in early literacy* (pp. 77–97). Newark, DE: International Reading Association.

Kotulak, R. (1997). Inside the brain: Revolutionary discoveries of how the mind works. Kansas City, MO: Andrews McMeel.

Krashen, S. (1982). *Principles and practices in second language acquisition*. Oxford, England: Pergamon.

Krashen, S. (1987). Encouraging free reading. In M. Douglass (Ed.), *51st Claremont Reading Conference Yearbook*. Claremont, CA: Center for Developmental Studies.

Kuhl, P. (1993). *Life language*. Seattle, WA: University of Washington.

Kuhl, P. (1999). The role of experience in early language development: Linguistic experience alters the perception and production of speech. In N. Fox, L. Leavitt, & J. Warhol (Eds.), *Proceedings of the 1999 Johnson & Johnson Pediatric Round Table, "The role of early experience in infant development"* (pp. 101–125). Johnson & Johnson Consumer Companies, Inc.

Laminack, L., & Lawing, S. (1994). Building generative curriculum. *Primary Voices K–6, 2*, 8–18.

Lane, B. (1993). *After the end: Teaching and learning creative revision*. Portsmouth, NH: Heinemann.

Lane, B., & Bernabei, G. (2001). *Why we must run with scissors*. Shoreham, VT: Discover Writing Press.

Lass, B. (1982). Portrait of my son as an early reader. *The Reading Teacher, 36*, 20–28.

Lazar, A. M. (2004). *Learning to be literacy teachers in urban schools*. Newark, DE: International Reading Association.

Leal, D. (1994). Storybooks, information books, and informational storybooks: An explication of the ambiguous gray genre. *The New Advocate, 6*, 61–70.

Leki, I. (1992). *Understanding ESL writers: A guide for teachers*. Portsmouth, NH: Boynton/ Cook.

Leslie, L., & Jett-Simpson, M. (1997). *Authentic literacy assessment: An ecological approach*. New York: Addison Wesley Longman.

Leslie, L. & Caldwell, J., (2006). *Qualitative Reading Inventory-4*. Allyn & Bacon.

Lessow-Hurley, J. (1990). *Foundations of dual language instruction*. New York: Longman.

Leu, D. J. (2000). Literacy and technology: Deictic consequences for literacy education in an Information Age. In Kamil, M., Mosenthal, P., Pearson, P. D., & Barr, R. *Handbook of reading research, Volume III* (pp. 195–206). Mahwah, NJ: Lawrence Erlbaum Associates.

Levin, D., & Carlsson-Paige, N. (1994). Developmentally appropriate television: Putting children first. *Young Children, 49*, 38–44.

Lewis, R., & Doorlag, D. (1999). *Teaching special students in general education classrooms*. Columbus, Ohio: Prentice Hall.

Lindfors, J. (1987). *Children's language and learning* (2nd ed.). Englewood Cliffs, NJ: Prentice-Hall, Inc.

Lindquist, T. (1995). *Seeing the whole through social studies*. Portsmouth, NH: Heinemann.

Lipson, M. Y., & Wixson, M. Y. (2003). *Assessment and instruction of reading and writing difficulty*. New York: Allyn and Bacon.

Liu, P. (1996). Limited English proficient children's literacy acquisition and parental involvement: A tutoring/family literacy model. *Reading Horizons, 37*(1), 60–74.

Lloyd, P. (1987). *How writers write*. Portsmouth, NH: Heinemann.

Lo, D. (1997). *Individual differences in the social construction of knowledge with children over a storybook reading*. Paper presented at the Annual Meeting of the American Educational Research Association. Chicago. (ERIC Document Reproduction Service No. ED410519).

Lomax, R., & McGee, L. (1987). Young children's concepts about print and reading: Toward a model of word reading acquisition. *Reading Research Quarterly, 22*, 237–256.

Lowry, L. (1993). *The Giver*. New York, NY: Houghton Mifflin Company.

Lowry, L. (2004). *Gooney Bird Greene*. New York, NY: Dell Yearling.

Lyon, G. R., & Chhabra, V. (2004). The science of reading research. *Educational Leadership, 61*(6), 13–17.

Lubitz, D. (1995). Unpublished field notes. Tempe, AZ: College of Education, Arizona State University.

Luke, A., & Kale, J. (1997). Learning through difference: cultural practices in early childhood language socialization. In E. Gregory (Ed.), *One child, many worlds: Early learning in multicultural communities* (pp. 11–29). New York: Teachers College Press.

Lynch, P. (1988). *Using predictable books and big books*. New York: Scholastic.

Mabry, L. (1999). Writing to the rubric. *Phi Delta Kappan, 80,* 673–679.

Macias-Huerta, A., and Quintero, E. (1990). *All in the family: Bilingualism and biliteracy. The Reading Teacher, 44,* 306–314.

MacLean, P. (1978). A mind of three minds: Educating the triune brain. In J. Chall & A. Mirsky (Eds.), *Education and the Brain, 77th Yearbook of the National Society for the Study of Education.* Chicago: University of Chicago Press.

Madaus, G. F. (1988). The influence of testing on curriculum. In L.N. Tanner (Ed.), *Critical issues in curriculum: Eighty-seventh yearbook of the National Society for the Study of Education* (pp. 83-121). Chicago, IL: University of Chicago Press.

Maestro, B., & Maestro, G. (1986). *The story of the Statue of Liberty.* New York: Lothrop, Lee & Shepard.

Mann, V. A. & Foy, J. G. (2003). Phonological awareness, speech development, and letter knowledge in preschool children. *Annals of Dyslexia, 53,* 149–173.

Manning, M., Manning, G., & Long, R. (1994). *Theme immersion: Inquiry-based curriculum in elementary and middle schools.* Portsmouth, NH: Heinemann.

Manning-Kratcoski, A., & Bobkoff-Katz, K. (1998). Conversing with young language learners in the classroom. *Young Children, 53*(3), 30–33.

Maras, L., & Brummett, B. (1995). Time for a change: Presidential elections in a grade 3–4 multi-age classroom. In P. Cordeiro (Ed.), *Endless possibilities: Generating curriculum in social studies and literacy.* Portsmouth, NH: Heinemann.

Marcus, G. (2003). *The birth of the mind: How a tiny number of genes creates the complexities of human thought.* NY: Basic Books.

Martinez, M., & Roser, N. (1985). Read it again: The value of repeated readings during storytime. *The Reading Teacher, 38,* 782–786.

Martinez, M., & Teale, W. (1987). The ins and outs of a kindergarten writing program. *The Reading Teacher, 40,* 444–451.

Martinez, M., & Teale, W. (1988). Reading in a kindergarten classroom library. *The Reading Teacher, 41,* 568–572.

Marvin, C., & Mirenda, P. (1993). Home literacy experiences of preschoolers in Head Start and special education programs. *Journal of Early Intervention, 17*(4), 351–366.

Mason, J. (1980). When do children begin to read? An exploration of four-year-old children's letter and word reading competencies. *Reading Research Quarterly, 15,* 203–227.

Masonheimer, P., Drum, P., & Ehri, L. (1984). Does environmental print identification lead children into word reading? *Journal of Reading Behavior, 16,* 257–271.

Mathews, M. (1966). *Teaching to read: Historically considered.* Chicago: University of Chicago Press.

McAleer-Hamaguchi, P. (1995) Childhood speech, language, and listening problems: What every parent should know. New York: NY. John Wiley Publishers.

McCardle, P., & Chhabra, V. (2004). *The voice of evidence in reading research.* Baltimore: Brookes.

McCaslin, N. (1987). *Creative drama in the primary grades.* New York: Longman.

McCracken, R., & McCracken, M. (1978). Modeling is the key to sustained silent reading. *The Reading Teacher, 31,* 406–408.

McGee, L., & Richgels, D. (1989). "K is Kristen's": Learning the alphabet from a child's perspective. *The Reading Teacher, 43,* 216–225.

McGee, L. & Richgels. D. (1996). *Literacy's beginnings: Supporting young readers and writers* (2nd ed.). Boston, MA: Allyn & Bacon.

McKenna, M.C., & Robinson, R.D. (2002). *Teaching through text: Reading and writing in the content areas* (3rd ed.). Boston: Allyn & Bacon.

McNeal, R. B., Jr. (1999). Parental involvement as social capital: Differential effectiveness on science achievement, truancy, and dropping out. *Social Forces, 78*(1), 117–144.

Menyuk, P. (1988). *Language development: Knowledge and use.* Glenview, IL: ScottForesman.

Miller, S. (1997). Family television viewing: How to gain control. *Childhood Education, 74*(1), 38–40.

Miller-Lachman, R. (Ed.). (1995). *Global voices, global visions: A core collection of multicultural books.* New Providence, NJ: R. R. Bowker.

Minett, A. J. (2004). Earth aches by midnight: Helping ESL writers clarify their intended meaning. In S. Bruce & B. Rafoth (Eds.). *ESL writers: A guide for writing center tutors.* Portsmouth, NH: Boynton/Cook.

Moffett, J., & Wagner, B. (1983). *Student-centered language arts and reading, K–13: A handbook for teachers* (3rd ed.). Boston: Houghton Mifflin.

Moir, A. & Jessel, D. (1991). *Brain sex: The real differences between men and women.* New York: Carol.

Moll, L., Amanti, C., Neff, D., & González, N. (1992). Funds of knowledge for teaching: Using a qualitative approach to connect homes and classrooms. *Theory into Practice, 31*(2), 132–141.

Morgan, A. (1987). The development of written language awareness in black preschool children. *Journal of Reading Behavior, 19,* 49–67.

Morisset, C. (1995). Language development: Sex differences within social risk. *Developmental Psychology, 31,* 851–865.

Morrow, L. (1983). Home and school correlates of early interest in literature. *Journal of Educational Research, 76,* 221–230.

Morrow, L. (1985). Reading and retelling stories: Strategies for emergent readers. *The Reading Teacher, 38,* 870–875.

Morrow, L. (1988). Young children's responses to one-to-one story readings in school settings. *Reading Research Quarterly, 23,* 89–107.

Morrow, L. (2001). *Literacy development in the early years: Helping children read and write* (4th ed.). Boston: Allyn & Bacon.

Morrow, L., & Rand, M. (1991). Preparing the classroom environment to promote literacy during play. In J. Christie (Ed.), *Play and early literacy development* (pp. 141–165). Albany, NY: State University of New York Press.

Morrow, L., & Tracey, D. (1997). Strategies used for phonics instruction in early childhood classrooms. *The Reading Teacher, 50,* 644–651.

Morrow, L., Tracey, D., Gee-Woo, D., & Pressley, M. (1999). Characteristics of exemplary first-grade literacy instruction. *The Reading Instructor, 52,* 462–476.

Morrow, L., & Weinstein, C. (1982). Increasing children's use of literature through program and physical changes. *Elementary School Journal, 83,* 131–137.

Morrow, L., & Weinstein, C. (1986). Encouraging voluntary reading: The importance of a literature program on children's use of library centers. *Reading Research Quarterly, 21,* 330–346.

Mowery, A., (1993). *Qualifying paper on early childhood parent education programs.* Unpublished manuscript, University of Delaware, Newark, DE.

Murray, D. (1990). *Write to learn.* New York: Holt, Rinehart, and Winston.

Murray, B., Stahl, S., & Ivey, M. (1996). Developing phoneme awareness through alphabet books. *Reading and Writing: An Interdisciplinary Journal, 8,* 307–322.

Muter, V. & Diethelm, K. (2001). The contribution of phonological skills and letter knowledge to early reading development in a multilingual program. *Language Learning, 51*(2), 187–219.

Muth, J. J. (2002). *The three questions.* New York: Scholastic.

Nagy, W. (1988). Teaching vocabulary to improve reading comprehension. Newark, DE: International Reading Association.

Nagy, W. E., & Scott, J. A. (2000). Vocabulary processes. In M. L. Kamil, P. B. Mosenthal, P. D. Pearson, & R Barr (Eds.), *Handbook of Reading Research Volume III* (pp. 269–284).

Nation at Risk (1983). *An Imperative for Educational Reform.* National Commission on Excellence in Education. Retrieved January 3, 2006, from http://www.ed.gov/pubs/NatAtRisk/index.html.

National Institute for Literacy (NIFL). (n.d.). Retrieved July 22, 2005, from www.nifl.gov.

National Reading Panel. (2000). *Report of the National Reading Panel: Teaching children to read.* Bethesda, MD: National Institute for Child Health and Human Development. Available: www.nichd.nih.gov/publications/nrp/smallbook.htm.

National Reading Panel. (2000). *Teaching children to read: An evidence-based assessment of the scientific research literature on reading and its implications for reading instruction.* (National Institute of Health Pub. No. 00-4769). Washington, DC: National Institute of Child Health and Human Development.

National Research Council. (1999). *Starting out right: A guide to promoting children's reading success.* Washington, DC: National Academy Press.

National Council of Teachers of English. (1993). *Elementary school practices: Current research on language learning.* Urbana, IL: Author.

National Education Goals Panel. (1997). *Special early childhood report.* Washington, DC: Department of Education.

National Reading Panel. (2000). *Teaching children to read: An evidence-based assessment of the scientific research literature on reading and its implications for reading instruction.* Washington, DC: U.S. Government Printing Office.

NCLB Act of 2001. www.ed.gov/nclb/overview/intro/edpicks.jhtml?src=ln.

Neuman, S. (1995). *Linking literacy and play.* Newark, DE: International Reading Association.

Neuman, S. (1998). How can we enable all children to achieve? In S. Neuman & K. Roskos (Eds.), *Children achieving: Best practices in early literacy* (pp. 5–19). Newark, DE: International Reading Association.

Neuman, S. (1999). Books make a difference: A study of access to literacy. *Reading Research Quarterly, 34*(3), 286–311.

Neuman, S., & Celano, D. (2001). Access to print in low-income and middle-income communities: An ecological study of four neighborhoods. *Reading Research Quarterly, 30,* 8–26.

Neuman, S., & Roskos, K. (1991a). Peers as literacy informants: A description of young children's literacy conversations in play. *Early Childhood Research Quarterly, 6,* 233–248.

Neuman, S., & Roskos, K. (1991b). The influence of literacy-enriched play centers on preschoolers' conceptions of the functions of print. In J. Christie (Ed.), *Play and early literacy development* (pp. 167–187). Albany, NY: State University of New York Press.

Neuman, S., & Roskos, K. (1992). Literacy objects as cultural tools: Effects on children's literacy behaviors during play. *Reading Research Quarterly, 27,* 203–223.

Neuman, S., & Roskos, K. (1993). *Language and literacy learning in the early years: An integrated approach.* Fort Worth, TX: Harcourt Brace Jovanovich.

Neuman, S., & Roskos, K. (1997). Literacy knowledge in practice: Contexts of participation for young writers and readers. *Reading Research Quarterly, 32,* 10–32.

Neuman, S., & Roskos, K. (Eds.). (1998). *Children achieving: Best practices in early literacy.* Newark, DE: International Reading Association.

Neuman, S., & Roskos, K. (2005a). The state of the state prekindergarten standards. *Early Childhood Research Quarterly, 20,* 125–145.

Neuman, S., & Roskos, K. (2005b). What ever happened to developmentally appropriate practice in early literacy? *Young Children, 60*(4), 22–26.

New Standards Project. (1994). *Elementary English Language Arts Teacher Portfolio Handbook: Field Trial Version, 1994–1995.* Urbana, IL: Author.

Nickel, J. (2001). When writing conferences don't work: Students' retreat from teacher agenda. *Language Arts, 79,* 136–147.

Noguchi, R. R. (1991). *Grammar and the teaching of writing: Limits and possibilities.* Urbana, IL: National Council of Teachers of English.

Nord, C. W., Lennon, J., Liu, B., & Chandler, K. (2000). *Home literacy activities and signs of children's emerging literacy, 1993 and 1999* [NCES Publication 2000–026]. Washington DC: National Center for Education Statistics.

Norris, A., & Hoffman, P. (1990). Language intervention with naturalistic environments. *Language, Speech, and Hearing Services in the Schools, 21,* 72–84

Noyce, R., & Christie, J. (1989). *Integrating reading and writing instruction in grades K–8.* Boston, MA: Allyn & Bacon.

Nurss, J., Hough, R. & Enright, D.S. (1986). Story reading with limited English children in the regular classroom. *The Reading Teacher, 39,* 510–515.

Nurss, J., & McGauvran, M. (1976). *Metropolitan readiness tests.* New York: Harcourt Brace Jovanovich.

Oates, J. & Grayson, A. (2004) *Cognitive and language development in children* 3rd ed. Cambridge, Mass. Blackwell Publishers.

Ogle, D. (1986). KWL: A teaching model that develops active reading of expository text. *The Reading Teacher, 39,* 564–570.

Oken-Wright, P. (1998) Transition to writing: drawing as a scaffold for emergent writers. *Young Children, 53*(2), 76–81.

Olson, L. (October 19, 2005). Purpose of testing needs to shift, experts say. *Education Week.*

O'Neill, J. (1994). Making assessment meaningful: "Rubrics" clarify expectation, yield better feedback. *ASCD Update, 36,* 1, 4–5.

Opitz, M. (1998). Children's books develop phonemic awareness—for you and parents, too! *The Reading Teacher, 51,* 526–528.

Opitz, M., & Ford, M. (2001). *Reaching readers: Flexible & innovative strategies for guided reading.* Portsmouth, NH: Heinemann.

Orellana, M., & Hernández, A. (1999). Taking the walk: Children reading urban environmental print. *The Reading Teacher, 52,* 612–619.

Ourada, E. (1993). Legibility of third-grade handwriting: D'Nealian Versus traditional Zaner-Bloser. In G. Coon & G. Palmer (Eds.), *Handwriting research and information: An administrators handbook* (pp. 72–87). Glenview, IL: Scott Foresman.

Ovando, C., & Collier, V. (1998). Bilingual and ESL classrooms: Teaching in multicultural context. New York: McGraw-Hill.

Owocki, G. (2005). *Time for literacy centers.* Portsmouth, NH: Heinemann.

Paley, V. (1981). *Wally's stories.* Cambridge, MA: Harvard University Press.

Paley, V. (1984). *Boys and girls: Superheroes in the doll corner.* Chicago: University of Chicago Press.

Paley, V. (1990). *The boy who would be a helicopter.* Cambridge, MA: Harvard University Press.

Pappas, C. (1993). Is narrative "Primary"? Some insights from kindergartners' pretend readings of stories and information books. *Journal of Reading Behavior, 25,* 97–129.

Pappas, C., & Brown, E. (1987). Learning how to read by reading: Learning how to extend the functional potential of language. *Research in the Teaching of English, 21,* 160–177.

Paris, S. (1995). *Coming to grips with authentic instruction and assessment.*

Paris, S. G., Cross, D. R., & Lipson, M. Y. (1984). Informed strategies for learning: A program to improve children's reading awareness and comprehension. *Journal of Educational Psychology, 76,* 1239–1252.

Paris, S., Wasik, B., & Turner, J. (1991). The development of strategic learners. In R. Barr, M. Kamil, P. Mosenthal, & P. D. Pearson (Eds.), *Handbook of reading research* (vol. 2, pp. 609–640). New York: Longman.

Paterson, K. (1996) *Jip: His Story.* New York: Dutton. Presentation sponsored by the Education Center, Torrance, CA.

Patterson, N. (2001). Just the facts: Research and theory about grammar instruction. *Voices from the Middle, 8,* 50–55.

Patton, M., Silva, C., & Myers, S. (1999). Teachers and Family Literacy: Bridging Theory to Practice. *Journal of Teacher Education, 50,* 140–146.

Paulson, F., Paulson, P., & Meyer, C. (1991). What makes a portfolio a portfolio? *Educational Leadership, 48,* 60–63.

Pearson, P. D., & Tierney, R. J. (1984). On becoming a thoughtful reader: Learning to read like a writer. In A. Purves & O. Niles (Eds.), *Becoming readers in a complex society.* Chicago: National Society for the Study of Education.

Pearson, P. D., & Fielding, L. (1994). Reading comprehension: What works? *Educational Leadership, 51*(5), 62–67.

Pearson, P. D., & Raphael, T. (1999). Toward an ecologically balanced literacy curriculum. In L. Gambrell, L. Morrow, S. Neuman, & M. Pressley (Eds.), *Best practices in literacy instruction* (pp. 22–33). New York: Guilford.

Pease-Alvarez, L. (1991). Oral contexts for literacy development in a Mexican community. *The Quarterly Newsletter of the Laboratory of Comparative Human Cognition, 13,* 9–13.

Peck, S. (1978). Child-child discourse in second language acquisition. In E. Hatch (Ed.), *Second language acquisition: A book of readings* (pp. 383–400). Rowley, MA: Newbury House.

Peterson, R., & Eeds, M. (1990). *Grand conversations: Literature groups in action.* New York: Scholastic.

Peyton, J., & Reed, J. (1990). *Dialogue journal writing with non-native English speakers: A handbook for teachers.* Alexandria, VA: Teachers of English to Speakers of Other Languages.

Peyton, J., Jones, C., Vincent, A., & Greenblatt, L. (1994). Implementing Writer's Workshop with ESL students: Visions and realities. *TESOL Quarterly, 28,* 469–488.

Piper, T. (1993). *Language for all our children.* New York: Macmillan.

Pitkin, T. (1975). *Keepers of the gate: A history of Ellis Island.* New York: New York University Press.

Portalupi, J., & Fletcher, R. (2001). *Nonfiction craft lessons: Teaching information writing K–8.* Portland, ME: Stenhouse.

Power, B. (1998). Author! Author! *Early Childhood Today, 12,* 30–34.

Preschool Curriculum Evaluation Research (PCER). (n.d.). Retrieved July 22, 2005, from http://pcer.rti.org

Pressley, M. (2000). What should comprehension instruction be instruction of? In M. Kamil, P. Mosenthal, P. D. Pearson, & R. Barr (Eds.), *Handbook of reading research* (vol. 3, pp. 545–561). Mahwah, NJ: Erlbaum.

Purcell-Gates, V. (1989). What oral/written language differences tell us about beginning reading instruction. *The Reading Teacher, 43,* 290–294.

Purcell-Gates, V. (1996). Stories, coupons, and the *TV Guide*: Relationships between home literacy experiences and emergent literacy knowledge. *Reading Research Quarterly, 31,* 406–428.

Raines, S., & Isbell, R. (1994). *Stories: Children's literature in early education.* Albany, NY: Delmar.

Ramirez, D., Yuen, S., & Ramel, D. (1991). *Executive summary: Longitudinal study of structured English immersion, early-exit, and late-exit transitional bilingual education programs for language minority children.* San Mateo, CA: Aguirre International.

Raphael, T. E., & McMahon, S. I. (1994). Book Club: An alternative framework for reading instruction. *The Reading Teacher, 48*(2), 102–116.

Rascon-Briones, M., & Searfoss L. (1995, December). *Literature study groups in a preservice teacher education class.* Paper presented at the meeting of the National Reading Conference, New Orleans.

Rasinski, T., & Fredericks, A. (1991). Beyond parents and into the community. *The Reading Teacher, 44,* 698–699.

Ray, K. (2001). *The writing workshop: Working through the hard parts (and they're all hard parts).* Urbana, ILL: National Council of Teachers of English.

Read, C. (1971). Pre-school children's knowledge of English phonology. *Harvard Educational Review, 41,* 1–34.

Read, C. (1975). *Children's categorization of speech sounds in English.* Urbana, IL: National Council of Teachers of English.

Reese, E., & Cox, A. (1999). Quality of adult book reading affects children's emergent literacy. *Developmental Psychology, 35,* 20–28.

Reutzel, D. R. (1999). Organizing literacy instruction: Effective grouping and organizational plans. In L. Gambrell, L. Morrow, S. Neuman, & M. Pressley (Eds.), *Best practices in literacy instruction* (pp. 271–291). New York: Guilford.

Reyes, M., & Franquiz, M. (1998). Creating inclusive learning communities through English language arts: From chanclas to canicas. *Language Arts, 75,* 211–220.

Reyes, M., Laliberty, E., & Orbansky, J. (1993). Emerging biliteracy and cross-cultural sensitivity in a language arts classroom. *Language Arts, 70,* 659–668.

Rex, L. A., & Nelson, M. C. (2004). How teachers' professional identities position high-stakes test preparation in their classrooms. *Teachers College Record, 106,* 1288–1331.

Rhodes, L., & Nathenson-Mejia, S. (1992). Anecdotal records: A powerful tool for ongoing literacy assessment. *The Reading Teacher, 45,* 502–509.

Rice, M., Huston, A., Truglio, R., & Wright, J. (1990) Words from Sesame Street: Learning vocabulary while viewing. *Development Psychology, 26,* 421–428.

Richardson, J. S., & Morgan, R. F. (2000). *Reading to learn in the content areas* (4th ed.). Belmont, CA: Wadsworth/Thomson Learning.

Richgels, D., Poremba, K., & McGee, L. (1996). Kindergarteners talk about print: Phonemic awareness in meaningful contexts. *The Reading Teacher, 49,* 632–642.

Richgels, D. & Wold, L. (1998). Literacy on the road: Backpacking partnerships between school and home. *The Reading Teacher, 52,* 18–29.

Roe, M. F. (2004b). Real reading interactions: Identifying and meeting the challenges of middle level unsuccessful readers. *Childhood Education, 81*(1), 9–15.

Roe, M. F. (2004a). Professional learning catalysts: An examination of one teacher's developing literacy practices. *Reading Research and Instruction, 44*(1), 32–61.

Rosenblatt, L. (1985). The transactional theory of literary work: Implications for research. In C. Cooper (Ed.), *Researching response to literature and the teaching of literature* (pp. 33–53). Norwood, NJ: Ablex.

Rosenblatt, L. (1991). Literacy theory. In J. Flood, M. Jensen, D. Lapp, & J. Squire (Eds.), *Handbook of research on teaching the English language arts* (pp. 57–62). New York: Macmillan.

Roser, N. (1998, February). Young children as competent communicators. *Scholastic Early Childhood Today, 9*(6), 45–47.

Roser, N., & Martinez, M. (1985). Roles adults play in preschoolers' response to literature. *Language Arts, 62,* 485–490.

Roskos, K., & Christie, J. (2001).Examining the play-literacy interface: A critical review and future directions. *Journal of Early Childhood Literacy, 1,* 59–89.

Roskos, K. (1995, October). *Integrated curriculum: Criteria for assessment.* Personal conversation.

Roskos, K., Burstein, K., Bryan, T., Christie, J., Ergel, C., & Han, M. (2005, April). *Rare word vocabulary growth in at-risk preschool English language learners.* Annual meeting of the Society for Research in Child Development, Atlanta, GA.

Roskos, K., & Christie, J. (Eds.). (2000). *Play and literacy in early childhood: Research from multiple perspectives.* Mahwah, NJ: Erlbaum.

Roskos, K., & Christie, J. (2004). Examining the play-literacy interface: A critical review and future directions. In E. Zigler, D. Singer, & S. Bishop-Josef (Eds.), *Children's play: The roots of reading* (pp. 95–123). Washington, DC: Zero to Three Press.

Roskos, K., & Neuman, S. (1993). Descriptive observations of adults' facilitation of literacy in play. *Early Childhood Research Quarterly, 8,* 77–97.

Routman, R. (1991). *Invitations: Changing as teachers and learners K–12.* Portsmouth, NH: Heinemann.

Routman, R. (1996). Literacy at the crossroads: Crucial talk about reading, writing, and other teaching dilemmas.

Rowe, D. (1989). Author/audience interaction in the preschool: The role of social interaction in literacy learning. *Journal of Reading Behavior, 21,* 311–348.

Rowe, D. (1994). *Preschoolers as authors: Literacy learning in the social world.* Cresskill, NJ: Hampton Press.

Rudnick, B. (1995, October). Bridging the chasm between your English-and ESL students. *Teaching Pre-K–8, 28,* 48–49.

Rumelhart, D. (1977). Toward an interactive model of reading. In S. Dornic (Ed.), Attention and performance, VI. Hillsdale, NJ: Erlbaum.

Saddler, B. & Andrade, H. "The Writing Rubric." *Educational Leadership, 62,* 48–52.

Samway, K. (1992). *Writer's Workshop and children acquiring English as a second language.* Washington, DC: National Clearinghouse for Bilingual Education.

Samway, K., & Whang, G. (1995). *Literature study circles in a multicultural classroom.* York, ME: Stenhouse.

Santman, D. (2002). Teaching to the test?: Test preparation in the reading workshop. *Language Arts, 79*(3), 203–211.

Saville-Troike, M. (1988). Private speech: Evidence for second language learning strategies in the "silent period." *Journal of Child Language, 15,* 567–90.

Scarborough, H. S. (2001). Connecting early language and literacy to later reading (dis)abilities: Evidence, theory, and practice. In S. B. Neuman & D. Dickinson (Eds.), *Handbook of Early Literacy Research* (pp. 97–110). New York: Guilford.

Scarborough, H. S. (1998). Early identification of children at risk for reading difficulties: Phonological awareness and some other promising predictors. In B. K. Shapiro, P. J. Accardo, &

A. J. Capute (Eds.), *Specific reading disability: A view of the spectrum* (pp. 75–199). Timonium, MD: York Press.

Scherer, M. (2005). Reclaiming Testing. *Educational Leadership, 63*(3), p. 9.

Schickedanz, J. (1986). *Literacy development in the preschool* (sound filmstrip). Portsmouth, NH: Heinemann.

Schickedanz, J. A. (1998). What is developmentally appropriate practice in early literacy? Consider the alphabet. In S. B. Neuman & K. A. Roskos (Eds.), *Children achieving: Best practices in early literacy* (pp. 20–37). Newark, DE: International Reading Association.

Schickedanz, J., & Casbergue, R. (2004). *Writing in the preschool: Learning to orchestrate meaning and marks.* Newark, DE: International Reading Association.

Schieffelin, B., & Cochran-Smith, M. (1984). Learning to read culturally: Literacy before schooling. In H. Goelman, A. Oberg & F. Smith (Eds.), *Awakening to literacy* (pp. 3–23). Exeter, NH: Heinemann.

Schon, D. (1983). *The reflective practitioner: How professionals think in action.* New York: Basic Books.

Schon, I. (1994). *Tito, tito: rimas, adivinanzas, y juegos infantiles.*   Leon: Editorial Everest.

Schwartz, J. (1983). Language play. In B. Busching & J. Schwartz (Eds.), *Integrating the language arts in the elementary school* (pp. 81–89). Newark, DE: International Reading Association.

Searfoss, L., & Readence, J. (1994). *Helping children learn to read* (3rd ed.). Boston: Allyn & Bacon.

Segal, M., & Adcock, D. (1986). *Your child at play: Three to five years.* New York: Newmarket Press.

Selfe, C. (1999). Technology and literacy: A story about the perils of not paying attention. *College Composition and Communication, 50*(3), 411–436.

Senechal, M. (1997). The differential effect of storybook reading on preschoolers' acquisition of expressive and receptive vocabulary. *Journal of Child Language, 24,* 123–138.

Senechal, M. (1995). Individual Differences in 4-Year-Old Children's Acquisition of Vocabulary during Storybook Reading. *Journal of Educational Psychology, 87,* 218–229.

Serafini, F. (2001a). *The reading workshop: Creating space for readers.* Portsmouth, NH: Heinemann.

Serafini, F. (2001b). Three paradigms of assessment: Measurement, procedure and inquiry. *The Reading Teacher, 54,* 384–393.

Serna, I., & Hudelson, S. (1993). Emergent literacy in a whole language bilingual program. In R. Donmoyer and R. Kos (Eds.), *At-risk students: Portraits, policies and programs.* Albany, NY: SUNY Albany Press.

Shanahan, T. (1988). The reading-writing relationship: Seven instructional principles. *The Reading Teacher, 41,* 636–647.

Shanahan, T. (2000). Research synthesis: Making sense of the accumulation of knowledge in reading. In M. Kamil, P. Mosenthal, P. D. Pearson, & R. Barr (Eds.), *Handbook of reading research* (vol. 3, pp. 209–226). Mahwah, NJ: Erlbaum.

Shannon, P. W. (1988). *Broken promises: Reading instruction in twentieth-century America.* Glenview, IL: Greenwood.

Shonkoff, J. P., & Phillips, D. (Eds.). (2000). *From neurons to neighborhoods.* Washington, DC: National Academy Press.

Shore, R. (1997). *Rethinking the brain: New insights into early development.* New York: Families and Work Institute.

Short, K. G., Schroeder, J., Kauffman, G. Kaser, S. (2002). Thoughts from the editors. *Language Arts, 79*(3), 199.

Sipe, L. (2001). Invention, convention, and intervention: Invented spelling and the teacher's role. *The Reading Teacher, 55,* 264–273.

Sipe, L. (1998). First- and second-grade literary critics: Understanding children's rich response to literature. In T. Raphael & K. Au (Eds.), *Literature-based instruction: Reshaping the curriculum* (pp. 39–69). Norwood, MA: Christopher-Gordon.

Skinner, B. (1957). *Verbal behavior.* East Norwalk, CT: Appleton-Century-Crofts.

Slavin, R. (1989). Students at risk of school failure: The problem and its dimensions. In R. Slavin, N. Karweit, & N. Madden (Eds.), *Effective programs for students at risk.* Boston: Allyn & Bacon.

Slobodkina, E. (1947). *Caps for Sale.* New York: William R. Scott Inc.

Smilansky, S. (1968). *The effects of sociodramatic play on disadvantaged preschool children.* New York: Wiley.

Smith, F. (1988). *Understanding reading* (4th ed.). Hillsdale, NJ: Erlbaum.

Snow, C., Burns, M. S., & Griffin, P. (1998). *Preventing reading difficulties in young children.* Washington, D.C.: National Academy Press.

Snow, C., Chandler, J., Lowry, H., Barnes, W., & Goodman, I. (1991). *Unfulfilled expectations: Home and school influences on literacy.* Cambridge, MA: Harvard University Press.

Snow, C., & Ninio, A. (1986). The contracts of literacy: What children learn from learning to read books. In W. Teale & E. Sulzby (Eds.), *Emergent literacy: Writing and reading* (pp. 116–137). Norwood, NJ: Ablex.

Sochurek, H. (1987, January). Medicine's new vision. *National Geographic, 171*(1), 2–41.

Sowell, T. (1997). Late talking children. New York: NY. Basic Books.

Spandel, V. (2001). *Creating writers through 6-trait writing assessment and instruction.* New York: Addison Wesley Longman.

Spandel, V., & Stiggins, R. J. (1997). *Creating writers: Linking writing assessment and instruction* (2nd ed.). New York: Longman.

Spiegel, D. (1992). Blending whole language and systematic direct instruction. *The Reading Teacher, 46,* 38–44.

Spiegel, D. (1995). A comparison of traditional remedial programs and Reading Recovery: Guidelines for success for all programs. *The Reading Teacher, 49,* 86–97.

Spitzer, M. (1990). Local and global networking: Implications for the future. In D. Holdstein & C. Selfe (Eds.) Computers and writing: Theory, research, and practice (pp. 58–70). New York: Modern Language Association of America

Sprenger, M. (1999). *Learning and memory: The brain in action.* Alexandria, VA: Association for Supervision and Curriculum Development

Stahl, S. (1992). Saying the "p" word: Nine guidelines for exemplary phonics instruction. *The Reading Teacher, 45,* 618–625.

Stahl, S. (1999). Why innovations come and go (and mostly go): The case of whole language. *Educational Researcher, 28*(8), 15–22.

Stahl, S., Duffy-Hester, A., & Stahl, K. (1998). Everything you wanted to know about phonics (but were afraid to ask). *Reading Research Quarterly, 33,* 338–355.

Stahl, S., & Miller, P. (1989). Whole language and language experience approaches for beginning reading: A quantitative research synthesis. *Review of Educational Research, 59,* 87–116.

Stainback, S., & Stainback, W. (1992). *Curriculum considerations in inclusive classrooms.* Baltimore, MD: Brookes.

Stallman, A., & Pearson, P. D. (1990). Formal measures of early literacy. In L. Morrow & J. Smith (Eds.), *Assessment for instruction in early literacy* (pp. 7–44). Englewood Cliffs, NJ: Prentice–Hall.

Stanovich, K. (1986). Matthew effects in reading: Some consequences of individual differences in the acquisition of literacy. *Reading Research Quarterly, 21,* 360–407.

Strickland, D., & Morrow, L. (1990). Family literacy: Sharing good books. *The Reading Teacher, 43,* 518–519.

Strickland, D. S., & Schickedanz, J. A. (2004). *Learning about print in preschool: Working with letters, words, and beginning links with phonemic awareness.* Newark, DE: IRA.

Strickland, D. S., & Shanahan, T. (2004). Laying the groundwork for literacy. *Educational Leadership, 61*(4), 74–77.

Strong, M. (1983). Social styles and the second language acquisition of Spanish-speaking kindergarteners. *TESOL Quarterly, 17,* 241–258.

Strunk, W., & White, E. B. (2005). *The elements of style.* New York: The Penguin Press.

Sullivan, G. (1994). *Slave ship: The story of the Henrietta Marie.* New York: Dutton.

Sulzby, E. (1985a). Children's emergent reading of favorite storybooks: A developmental study. *Reading Research Quarterly, 20,* 458–481.

Sulzby, E. (1985b). Kindergartners as writers and readers. In M. Farr (Ed.), *Advances in writing research, Vol. 1: Children's early writing development* (pp. 127–200). Norwood, NJ: Ablex.

Sulzby, E. (1990). Assessment of emergent writing and children's language while writing. In L. Morrow & J. Smith (Eds.), *Assessment for instruction in early literacy* (pp. 83–109). Englewood Cliffs, NJ: Prentice Hall.

Sulzby, E., & Barnhart, J. (1990). The developing kindergartner: All of our children emerge as writers and readers. In J. McKee (Ed.), *The developing kindergarten: Programs, children, and teachers.* Ann Arbor, MI: Michigan Association for the Education of Young Children.

Sulzby, E., Barnhart, J., Hieshima, J. (1989). Forms of writing and rereading from writing: A preliminary report. In J. Mason (Ed.), *Reading and writing connections* (pp. 31–63). Boston: Allyn & Bacon.

Sulzby, E., & Teale, W. (1991). Emergent literacy. In R. Barr, M. Kamil, P. Mosenthal, & P. D. Pearson (Eds.), *Handbook of reading research* (vol. 2, pp. 727–757). New York: Longman.

Sulzby, E., Teale, W., & Kamberelis, G. (1989). Emergent writing in the classroom: Home and school connection. In D. Strickland & L. Morrow (Eds.), *Emerging literacy: Young children learn to read and write* (pp. 63–79). Newark, DE: International Reading Association.

Swain, M. (1972). *Bilingualism as a native language.* Unpublished doctoral dissertation, University of California at Irvine.

Swanborn, M., & de Glopper, K. (1999). Incidental word learning while reading: A meta-analysis. *Review of Educational Research, 69,* 261–285.

Sweet, A. (1993). *State of the art: Transforming Ideas for teaching and learning to read.* Washington, DC: Office of Research, U.S. Department of Education.

Sweet, A. P., & Snow, C. (2002). Reconceptualizing reading comprehension. In C. C. Block, L. B. Gambrell, & M. Pressley (Eds.), *Improving comprehension instruction* (pp. 17–53). San Francisco: Jossey Bass.

Sylvester, R. (1995). *A celebration of neurons: An educator's guide to the human brain.* Alexandria, Virginia: Association for Supervisio and Curriculum Development.

Tabors, P. (1998). What early childhood educators need to know: Developing effective programs for linguistically and culturally diverse children and families. *Young Children, 53*(6), 20–26.

Tabors, P., & Snow, C. (1994). English as a second language in preschool programs. In F. Genesee (Ed.), *Educating second language children: The whole child, the whole curriculum, the whole community* (pp. 103–126). New York: Cambridge University Press.

Taylor, D. (1983). *Family literacy.* Portsmouth, NH: Heinemann.

Taylor, D. (1986). Creating family story: "Matthew! We're going to have a ride." In W. Teale & E. Sulzby (Eds.), *Emergent literacy: Writing and reading* (pp. 139–155). Norwood, NJ: Ablex.

Taylor, D.,& Dorsey-Gaines, C. (1988). *Growing up literate: Learning from inner-cities families.* Portsmouth, NH: Heinemann.

Taylor, D., & Strickland, D. (1986). *Family storybook reading.* Portsmouth, NH: Heinemann.

Taylor, N., Blum, I., & Logsdon, D. (1986). The development of written language awareness: Environmental aspects and program characteristics. *Reading Research Quarterly, 21,* 132–149.

Teale, W. (1986a). The beginnings of reading and writing: Written language development during the preschool and kindergarten years. In M. Sampson (Ed.), *The pursuit of literacy: Early reading and writing.* Dubuque, IA: Kendall Hunt.

Teale, W. (1986b). Home background and young children's literacy development. In W. Teale & E. Sulzby (Eds.), *Emergent literacy: Writing and reading* (pp. 173–205). Norwood, NJ: Ablex.

Teale, W. (1987). Emergent literacy: Reading and writing development in Early Childhood. In J. Readence and R. Baldwin, (Eds.), *Research in literacy: Merging perspectives* (pp. 45–74). Thirty-sixth yearbook of the National Reading Conference. Rochester, NY: National Reading Conference.

Teale, W. (1989, February/March). Assessing young children's reading and writing. *Reading Today, 6*(4), 24.

Teale, W. (1990). The promise and challenge of informal assessment in early literacy. In L. Morrow & J. Smith (Eds.), *Assessment for instruction in early literacy* (pp. 45–61). Englewood Cliffs, NJ: Prentice-Hall.

Teale, W., & Martinez, M. (1988). Getting on the right road: Bringing books and children together in the classroom. *Young Children, 44*(1), 10–15.

Teale, W., & Sulzby, E. (1986). Emergent literacy as a perspective for examining how young children become writers and readers. In W. Teale & E. Sulzby (Eds.), *Emergent literacy: Writing and reading* (pp. vii–xxv). Norwood, NJ: Ablex.

Teale, W., & Sulzby, E. (1989). Emergent literacy: New perspectives. In D.Strickland, & L. Morrow (Eds.). *Emerging literacy: Young children learn to read and write* (pp. 1–15). Newark, DE: International Reading Association.

Temple, C., Nathan, R., Temple, F., & Burris, N. A. (1993). *The beginnings of writing*. Boston, MA: Allyn & Bacon.

Templeton, S., & Morris, D. (1999). Questions teachers ask about spelling. *Reading Research Quarterly, 34*, 102–112.

TESOL. (1997). *ESL standards for pre-K–12 students*. Alexandria, VA: Author.

Tharp, R., & Gallimore, R. (1988). *Rousing minds to life: Teaching, learning and school in a social context*. Cambridge: Cambridge University Press.

Thompson, R. (2001). Sensitive periods in attachment? In D. B. Bailey Jr., J. T. Bruer, F. J. Symons, & J. W. Lichtman (Eds.), *Critical thinking about critical periods* (pp. 83–106). Baltimore: Paul H. Brookes. Thompson, R. A. & Nelson, C. A. (2001). Developmental science and the media: Early brain development. *American Psychologist, 56*, 5–15.

Thousand, J., & Villa, R. (1990). Sharing expertise and responsibilities through teacher teams. In W. Stainback & S. Stainback (Eds.), *Support networks for inclusive schooling: Interdependent integrated education* (pp. 151–166). Baltimore: Brookes.

Thurber, D. (1993). *D'Nealian handwriting*. Glenview, IL: Scott Foresman.

Tierney, R., & Pearson, P. D. (1983). Toward a composing model of reading. *Language Arts, 60*, 568–580.

Tierney, R., Readence, J., & Dishner, E. (1995). *Reading strategies and practices: A compendium* (3rd ed.). Boston: Allyn & Bacon.

Tincoff, R. & Jusczyk, P. W. (1999). Mama! Dada! Origins of word meaning. *Psychological Science* 10(2) 172–175.

Tompkins, G. (2001). *Literacy for the 21st Century* (2nd ed.). Columbus, OH: Merrill.

Torgesen, J. (1994). *Torgesen test of phonemic awareness*. Shoal Creek, TX: Pro-Ed.

Tough, J. (1977). *The development of meaning: Talking to some purpose with young children*. London: George Allen and Unwin.

Treiman, R., & Kessler, B. (2003). The role of letter names in the acquisition of literacy. In R. Kail (Ed.), *Advances in Child Development and Behavior, 31*, 105–135.

Treiman, R., & Kessler, B., & Pollo, T. C. (in press). Learning about the letter names subset of the vocabulary: Evidence from U.S. and Brazilian preschoolers. *Applied Psycholinguistics*.

Trelease, J. (1989). *The new read-aloud handbook*. New York: Penguin.

Tunmer, W. E., Herriman, M. L., & Nesdale, A. R. (1988). Metalinguistic abilities and beginning reading. *Reading Research Quarterly, 23*, 134–158.

Turner, A. (1987). *Nettie's trip south*. New York: Macmillan.

Turner, E. (1994). *Emerging bilingualism and biliteracy in a primary, multi-age bilingual classroom*. Unpublished Honors Thesis, Arizona State University, Tempe.

Tychsen, L. (2001). Critical periods for development of visual acuity, depth perception, and eye tracking. In D. B. Bailey Jr., J. T. Bruer, F. J. Symons, & J. W. Lichtman (Eds.), *Critical thinking about critical periods* (pp. 67–80). Baltimore: Paul H. Brookes.

United States Dept. of Education. National Commission on Excellence in Education. *A Nation at Risk: The Imperative for Educational Reform*. Washington: GPO, 1983.

United States Dept. of Education. (2002). *Teaching Our Youngest*. Retrieved July 22, 2005, from www.ed.gov/pubs/edpubs.html .

Vacca, R. T., & Vaca, J. L. (2005). *Content area reading: Literacy and learning across the curriculum* (8th ed.). Boston: Pearson Education, Inc.

Valencia, S. (1990). A portfolio approach to classroom reading assessment: The whys, whats, and hows. *The Reading Teacher, 43*, 338–340.

Valencia, S., Hiebert, E., & Afflerbach, P. (1994). *Authentic reading assessment: Practices and possibilities*. Newark, DE: International Reading Association.

van Manen, M. (1995). *On the epistemology of reflective practice: Teachers and teaching: Theory and practice, 1,* 33–50.

Vasquez, O. (1991). Reading the world in a multicultural setting: A Mexicano perspective. *The Quarterly Newsletter of the Laboratory of Comparative Human Cognition, 13,* 13–15.

Veatch, J. (1986). *Whole language in the kindergarten.* Tempe, AZ: Jan V Productions.

Veatch, J., Sawicki, F., Elliot, G., Flake, E., & Blakey, J. (1979). *Key words to reading: The language experience approach begins.* Columbus, OH: Merrill.

Ventriglia, L. (1982). *Conversations of Miguel and Maria.* Reading, MA: Addison–Wesley.

Vernon-Feagans, L. (1996). *Children's talk in communities and classrooms.* Cambridge, MA: Blackwell.

Vernon-Feagans, L., Hammer, C., Miccio, A., & Manlove, E. (2001). Early language and literacy skills in low-income African American and Hispanic children. In S. Neuman & D. Dickinson (Eds.), *Handbook of early literacy research* (pp. 192–210). New York: Guilford.

Virginia Department of Education. Virginia Literacy Foundations Blocks. Retrieved August 9, 2005, from www.pen.k12.va.us/VDOE/Instruction/Elem_M/FoundationBlocks.

Virginia Department of Education. Phonological Awareness Literacy Screening (PALS). www.pals.virginia.edu.

Volk, D. (1997). Continuities and discontinuities: Teaching and learning in the home and school of a Puerto Rican five-year-old. In E. Gregory (Ed.), *One child, many worlds: Early learning in multicultural communities* (pp. 47–61). New York: Teachers College Press.

Vukelich, C., Evans, C., Albertson, B., (2003). Organizing expository tests: A look at possibilities. In *Literacy and Young Children: Research-Based Practices. Solving Problems in the Teaching of Literacy. D. M. Barone & L. M. Morrow (Eds.).* New York, NY: Guildford Press, pp. 261–290.

Vukelich, C. (1992). Play and assessment: Young children's knowledge of the functions of writing. *Childhood Education, 68,* 202–207.

Vukelich, C. (1993). Play: A context for exploring the functions, features, and meaning of writing with peers. *Language Arts, 70,* 386–392.

Vukelich, C. (1994). Effects of play interventions on young children's reading of environmental print. *Early Childhood Research Quarterly, 9,* 153–170.

Vygotsky, L. (1962). *Thought and language.* Cambridge, MA: MIT Press.

Vygotsky, L. (1978). *Mind in society: The development of psychological processes.* Cambridge, MA: Harvard University Press.

Waggoner, D. (1992, October/November). The increasing multiethnic and multilingual diversity of the U.S.: Evidence from the 1990 census. *TESOL Matters, 1,* 1,5.

Wagstaff, J. (1997/1998). Building practical knowledge of letter-sound correspondences: A beginner's word wall and beyond. *The Reading Teacher, 51,* 298–304.

Walker, D., Greenwood, C. Hart, B. & Carta, J. (1994). Prediction of school outcomes based on early language production and socio-economic factors. *Child Development, 65,* 606–621.

Walsh, E. S. (1989). *Mouse paint.* San Diego, CA: Harcourt Brace & Company.

Warner, L., & Morse, P. (2001). Studying pond life with primary-age children. *Childhood Education, 77,* 139–143.

Watson, D. (1983). Bringing together reading and writing. In U. H. Hardt (Ed.), *Teaching reading with the other language arts* (pp. 63–82). Newark, DE: International Reading Association.

Weaver, C. (1994*). Reading process and practice: From sociopsycholinguistics to whole language.* Portsmouth, NH: Heinemann.

Weaver, C. (1995). *Facts on teaching skills in context.* Prepared for the Michigan Language Arts Framework project. Distributed by the Michigan Department of Education Curriculum Development Project.

Weaver, C. (1996). *Teaching grammar in context.* Portsmouth, NH: Boynton/Cook.

Weaver, C., McNally, C., & Moerman, S. (2001). To grammar or not to grammar: That is *not* the question. *Voices from the Middle, 8,* 17–33.

Weigle, S. C. (2002). *Assessing writing.* Cambridge, UK: Oxford University Press.

Wells, D. (1995). Leading grand conversations. In N. Roser, & M. Martinez (Eds.), *Book talk and beyond: Children and teachers respond to literature* (pp. 132–139). Newark, DE: International Reading Association.

Wells, G. (1986). *The meaning makers: Children learning language and using language to learn.* Portsmouth, NH: Heinemann.

Weinstein-Shr, G., & Quintero, E. (1995). *Immigrant learners and their families.* McHenry, IL: Delta Systems.

Weir, R. (1962). *Language in the crib.* The Hague: Mouton.

Weiss, C., Lillywhite, H., & Gordon, M. (1980). *Clinical management of articulation disorders.* St. Louis: Mosby.

White, B. (1985). *The first three years of life.* Englewood Cliffs, NJ: Prentice-Hall.

Whitehurst, G. & Lonigan, C. (1998) Relative efficiency of parent and teacher involvement in a shared-reading intervention for preschool children from low-income backgrounds. *Early Childhood Research Quarterly, 23,* 263–290.

Whitehurst, G., & Lonigan, C. (2001). Emergent literacy: Development from prereaders to readers. In S. Neuman & D. Dickinson (Eds.), *Handbook of early literacy research* (pp. Lonigan, C. 11–29). New York: Guilford.

Wien, C., & Kirby-Smith, S. (1998). Untiming the curriculum: A case study of removing clocks from the program. *Young Children, 53*(5), 8–13.

Wiggins, G. (1993). *Assessing student performance.* San Francisco, CA: Jossey-Bass.

Wilcox, C. (1993). *Portfolios: Finding a focus.* Papers in Literacy Series. Durham, NH: The Writing Lab.

Wilensky, S. (1995). Social studies and literacy in the second grade. In P. Cordeiro (Ed.), *Endless possibilities* (pp. 33–54). Portsmouth, NH: Heinemann.

Wilhelm, J. D. (1997). *"You gotta BE the book."* New York: Teachers College Press.

Willems, M. (2004). *Knuffle bunny.* New York: Hyperion Books.

Willett, J. (1995). Becoming first graders in an L2: An ethnographic study of L2 socialization. *TESOL Quarterly, 29,* 473–503.

Winograd, P. (1989). Introduction: Understanding reading instruction. In P. Winograd, K. Wixson, & M. Lipson (Eds.), *Improving basal reading instruction* (pp. 1–17). New York: Teachers College Press.

Winograd, P., & Arrington, H. (1999). Best practices in literacy assessment. In L. Gambrell, L. Morrow, S. Neuman, & M Pressley (Eds.), *Best practices in literacy instruction* (pp. 210–241). New York: Guilford.

Winship, W. (1993). Writing information books in a first-grade classroom. *Primary Voices K–6, 1,* 7–12.

Winter, J. (1998*). Follow the drinking gourd.* New York, NY: Knopf.

Wixson, K. (1992, May). *Anchoring assessment to curriculum goals.* Paper presented at the International Reading Association Conference, Los Angeles.

Wong-Fillmore, L., & Snow, C. (April, 2000). *What teachers need to know about language.* Educational Resources Information Center, ERIC Clearinghouse on Language and Linguistics. ED-99-CO-0008.

Woodard, C. (1984). Guidelines for facilitating sociodramatic play. *Childhood Education, 60,* 172–177.

The Wright Group. (1998). *Phonemic awareness handbook.* Bothell, WA: Author.

The Wright Group. (1999). *The story box: Reading program assessment guide.* Bothell, WA: Author.

Yaden, D., Rowe, D., & MacGillivary, L. (2000). Emergent literacy: A matter (polyphony) of perspectives. In M. Kamil, P. Mosenthal, P. D. Pearson, & R. Barr (Eds.), *Handbook of Reading Research* (vol. III, pp. 425–454). Mahwah, NJ: Erlbaum.

Yaden, D., Smolkin, L., & Conlon, A. (1989). Preschoolers' questions about pictures, print conventions, and story text during reading aloud at home. *Reading Research Quarterly, 24,* 188–214.

Yaden, D., Smolkin, L., & MacGillivray, L. (1993). A psychogenetic perspective on children's understanding about letter associations during alphabet book readings. *Journal of Reading Behavior, 25,* 43–68.

Yarosz, D. J., & Barnett, W. S. (2001). Who Reads to Young Children?: Identifying Predictors of Family Reading Activities. *Reading Psychology, 22,* 67–81.

Yopp, H. (1992). Developing phonemic awareness in young children. *The Reading Teacher, 45,* 696–703.

Yopp, H., & Yopp, R. (2000). Supporting phonemic awareness in the classroom. *The Reading Teacher, 54,* 130–143.

Zaner-Bloser. (1993). *Handwriting: A way to self-expression.* Columbus, OH: Author.

Zinsser, W. (1998). *Worlds of childhood: The art and craft of writing for children.* Boston, MA: Houghton Mifflin.

AUTHOR INDEX

SUBJECT INDEX